(*Continued from front flap*)

who would be interested in noting how the discoveries of archæologists supported statements
made in God's Holy Word. This purpose has
been adhered to throughout all revisions. From
the very first, however, this book has met the
most exacting requirements of teachers and
students in colleges, seminaries, and Bible
schools, and of ministers and others who have
had special background and training in the field
of archæology.

ARCHÆOLOGY AND THE BIBLE, as it stands
forth in its new dress, is a distinct achievement.
It has been given a new size; it is longer, wider,
and, although containing much more material,
it is less bulky. The new type, the new format,
and the paper—chosen for quality and color
from a number of samples—have proved a most
happy combination, producing a page easy upon
the eyes and very attractive.

Due to the sound scholarship of its author,
and his seemingly unlimited ability correctly to
evaluate and classify the constantly increasing
mass of archæological findings, and due also to
frequent revisions, ARCHÆOLOGY AND THE
BIBLE has continued to be a leading authority
in its field. The author's comprehensive search
of the entire field of archæology for facts bearing on the Bible makes his book truly a library
in one volume.

As was the case with previous editions of
ARCHÆOLOGY AND THE BIBLE this edition was
published under the beneficent provisions of a
fund established in 1877 by John C. Green,
which provides the purchase price for certain
approved manuscripts that books produced
therefrom may be sold at the lowest possible
price. The American Sunday-School Union is
gratified that due to this bequest it is able to
sell this greatly improved volume at the ____
tively low price of former editions.

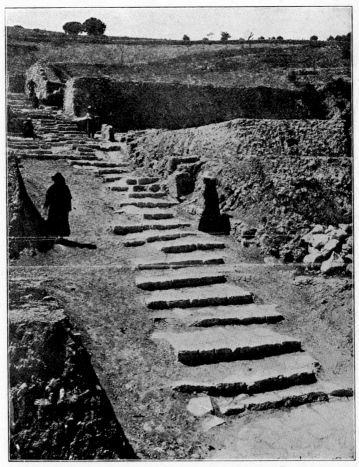

A Hillside Street in Roman Jerusalem along which Jesus and the Disciples may well have walked (*after Germer-Durand*).

—*Frontispiece.*

Green Fund Book, No. 17

ARCHÆOLOGY AND
THE BIBLE

BY

GEORGE A. BARTON, Ph.D., LL.D., D.D.

PROFESSOR EMERITUS OF SEMITIC LANGUAGES IN THE UNIVERSITY
OF PENNSYLVANIA AND OF NEW TESTAMENT LITERATURE AND
LANGUAGE IN THE DIVINITY SCHOOL OF THE PROTESTANT EPISCOPAL
CHURCH IN PHILADELPHIA; SOMETIME DIRECTOR OF THE AMERICAN
SCHOOL OF ORIENTAL RESEARCH IN BAGDAD; SOMETIME DIRECTOR OF
THE AMERICAN SCHOOLS OF ORIENTAL RESEARCH IN JERUSALEM;
FELLOW OF THE AMERICAN ASSOCIATION FOR THE ADVANCEMENT OF
SCIENCE; FELLOW OF THE ROYAL SOCIETY OF ARTS, LONDON

PART I

THE BIBLE LANDS, THEIR EXPLORATION, AND THE RESULTANT
LIGHT ON THE BIBLE AND HISTORY

PART II

TRANSLATIONS OF ANCIENT DOCUMENTS WHICH CONFIRM OR
ILLUMINATE THE BIBLE

~

PHILADELPHIA

AMERICAN SUNDAY-SCHOOL UNION

1816 CHESTNUT STREET

First Edition, May, 1916
Second Edition, June, 1917
Third Edition, June, 1920
Fourth Edition, February, 1925
Fifth Edition, September, 1927
Sixth Edition, January, 1933
Seventh Edition, November, 1937
Second Printing of Seventh Edition, March, 1941
Third Printing of Seventh Edition, April, 1944
Fourth Printing of Seventh Edition, January, 1946

Printed in U.S.A.

To the Memory of
CAROLINE B. D. BARTON

PREFACE

For a hundred years or more the explorer and the excavator have been busy in many parts of the world. They have brought to light monuments and texts that have in many cases revolutionized our conceptions of history and have in other cases thrown much new light on what was previously known.

In no part of the world have these labors been more fruitful than in the lands of the Bible. In Egypt and Babylonia vistas of history have been opened to view that were undreamed of before exploration began. The same is true for that part of the history of Palestine which antedates the coming of Israel. Information has also been obtained which illumines later portions of the history, and makes the Biblical narrative seem much more vivid. It is now possible to make real to oneself the details of the life of the Biblical heroes, and to understand the problems of their world as formerly one could not do. Exploration has also brought to light many inscriptions in the various countries that confirm or illuminate the traditions, history, poetry, and prophecy of the Bible. The sands of Egypt have even yielded us some reputed new sayings of our Lord.

It is the purpose of this book to gather into one volume the most valuable information of all sorts that the excavations in Bible lands have afforded, and to put it in such form that it may be of service to the pastor and Sunday-school teacher. An attempt has been made so to present the material that one may not only have the wealth of illumination for Biblical study that exploration has produced, but also that he may possess an outline of the history of the exploration and of the countries sufficient to enable him to place each item in its proper perspective. Whether in handling so large a mass of data the writer has achieved his aim, the reader must judge. The preparation of the volume was undertaken at the request of the Board of Managers of the American Sunday-School Union, for publication under the John C. Green Income Fund,—a fund founded in 1877 "for the purpose of aiding . . . in securing a Sunday-school literature of the highest order of merit . . . by procuring works . . . germane to the objects of the Society." The foundation requires that the manuscripts procured by the fund shall become the exclusive property of the American Sunday-

School Union, and, that the selling price may be reduced, the Society is prohibited from including the cost of the manuscript in the price of the book.

This work is confined to those phases of archæology upon which light has been thrown by exploration. No attempt is made, for example, to treat the constitution of the Hebrew family, or the dress worn in ancient Palestine, for these are subjects to which exploration has contributed no new knowledge.

The texts published in Part II have, with few exceptions, been freshly translated by the writer especially for this work. This is true of all excepting the majority of the Egyptian texts and two Greek papyri which were not accessible in the original. Translations of these were taken from the works of well-known scholars, to each of whom credit is given in connection with the passage quoted from his work. The quotations of Palestinian place names from the inscriptions of the Egyptian kings, of which the writer has made a special study, are based on his own translations of the originals.

An archæological fact, or a text brought to light by excavation, is often of little significance apart from its interpretation, and the interpretation of such data frequently varies according to the point of view occupied by the interpreter. As stated in the foreword of Part II, it has been the writer's aim throughout to maintain a neutral attitude on controverted points.

Not the least service that archæology has rendered has been the presentation of a new background against which the inspiration of the Biblical writers stands out in striking vividness. Often one finds traditions in Babylonia identical with those embodied in the Old Testament, but they are so narrated that no such conception of God shines through them as shines through the Biblical narrative. Babylonians and Egyptians pour out their hearts in psalms with something of the same fervor and pathos as the Hebrews, but no such vital conception of God and his oneness gives shape to their faith and brings the longed-for strength to the spirit. Egyptian sages developed a social conscience comparable in many respects with that of the Hebrew prophets, but they lacked the vital touch of religious devotion which took the conceptions of the prophets out of the realm of individual speculation and made them the working ethics of a whole people. Archæology thus reinforces to the modern man with unmistakable emphasis the ancient words, "Men spake from God, being moved by the Holy Spirit" (2 Peter 1:21).

The writer is under obligation to all his predecessors. Endeavor
has been made in the footnotes to acknowledge each individual
obligation. Lest any oversight may have occurred there, he would
here express both his indebtedness and his gratitude to all who by
their various explorations and studies have preceded him and been
his teachers.

Of these, Prof. R. A. Stewart Macalister should, perhaps, be
singled out for an especial word of gratitude, for in Chapters VI-XI
of Part I his work of excavation has been quoted more frequently
than any other. This apparent partiality is due to the fact that
Gezer was excavated more completely than any other Palestinian
site; that, because of its early and long-continued occupation in
ancient times, it reveals a great variety of civilizations; and that, in
The Excavation of Gezer, Prof. Macalister has presented the results
of his work with a completeness and a degree of intelligibility that
no other excavator in Palestine has approached. He has made his
work a model of what such a publication should be, and has thereby
made us all his debtors.

Especial thanks are due to Dr. George B. Gordon, Director of the
University Museum, Philadelphia, for his kindness in furnishing an
advance copy of the proof-sheets of Volume X of the *Publications
of the Babylonian Section* of the museum, from which the material
embodied in Chapter VIII of Part II was translated, and to Prof.
Morris Jastrow, Jr., and Dr. Edward Chiera for the benefit of their
fresh collation of the text. This was of considerable importance,
since Dr. Langdon's copy of large portions of it had been made
from photographs, rather than from the original tablet. The
writer is also indebted to Prof. W. R. Arnold, of Andover Theological Seminary, for helpful suggestions concerning the interpretation of a passage in the temple-papyrus from Elephantine which
has hitherto baffled translators. Thanks are also due to the following authors and publishers for permission to reproduce illustrations contained in books written or published by them: The
Palestine Exploration Fund, for permission relating to Warren's
Jerusalem; Bliss and Macalister's *Excavations in Palestine, 1898–
1900; Macalister's The Excavation of Gezer,* and Peters and
Thiersch's *Painted Tombs of Marissa;* Rev. Prof. C. J. Ball, of
Oxford, *Light from the East;* J. C. Hinrichs'sche Buchhandlung,
Koldewey's *Das Wieder Erstehende Babylon;* Dr. I. Benzinger and
Herr Paul Siebeck, *Hebräische Archäologie;* Monsieur J. Gabalda,

Vincent's *Jérusalem;* Prof. A. T. Clay, of Yale, *Light on the Old
Testament from Babel;* Prof. Paul Haupt, of Johns Hopkins, *The
Psalms* in his *Sacred Books of the Old Testament;* Rev. J. P. Peters
and G. P. Putnam's Sons, Peters' *Nippur;* Prof. C. C. Torrey, of
Yale, *Journal of the American Oriental Society;* George H. Doran
Co., Ramsay's *Letters to the Seven Churches of Asia;* Dr. Mitchell
Carroll, *American Journal of Archæology* and *Art and Archæology;*
Rev. A. E. Breen, *Diary of My Life in the Holy Land;* Thomas
Nelson and Sons, *The Illustrated Teacher's Bible;* and to Ferris and
Leach, for permission to use again a number of photographs pub-
lished in the writer's *A Year's Wandering in Bible Lands.* Dr. R. E.
Brünnow not only granted permission to reproduce illustrations
from Brünnow and Domaszewski's *Provincia Arabia,* but gener-
ously loaned the original photographs and drawings. Prof. Harold
N. Fowler, Editor of the *American Journal of Archæology,* also
kindly loaned an original photograph of the excavation at Sardis.
The source of each illustration, when not the writer's own, is indicated in the list of illustrations by mentioning the name of the author
of the book or the article from which it is taken.

Grateful acknowledgment should also be made to Rev. Edwin
Wilbur Rice, D. D., Litt. D., Honorary Editor of the Publications
of the American Sunday-School Union, who carefully read the
book in manuscript and made many valuable criticisms and suggestions.

The table of contents and the chapter-headings were prepared
by James McConaughy, Litt.D., Editor of the Publications of the
American Sunday-School Union; the indices, by A. J. R. Schu-
maker, M. A., Assistant Editor. The writer is grateful to them,
not only for this service, but for many helpful criticisms and cour-
tesies while the book has been passing through the press. Valuable
suggestions have also been made by Mrs. Barton who has carefully
read the proofs. Miss Bertha V. Dreisbach has given intelligent and
painstaking service in preparing the manuscript for the press, and
in proof-reading; Mr. V. Winfield Challenger and Miss Laura
G. Leach have rendered a like valuable service in assembling and
arranging the illustrations.

The quotations of scripture passages throughout are from the
American Standard Revised Version.

If this volume should bring to some remote worker or secluded
young person a tithe of the inspiration and joy that such a book

PREFACE ix

would have brought the writer in the rural home of his boyhood, he would ask no higher reward for the labor it has cost.

GEORGE A. BARTON.

BRYN MAWR, PA.
MAY, 1916.

PREFACE TO THE SECOND EDITION

IT is gratifying to know that this book has been found useful by so many students of the Bible and that a second edition is necessary. Minor errors, especially typographical, have been corrected throughout the volume. The chief feature of this edition is the addition of an Appendix, in which will be found some material that has come to light in the last year, and one or two items that were overlooked when the first edition was written.

GEORGE A. BARTON.

JUNE, 1917.

PREFACE TO THE THIRD EDITION

THE writer is glad that students of the Bible still find sufficient use for this volume to make a third edition of it desirable. The preparation of such an edition has afforded him opportunity to improve the translations of the Babylonian texts on pages 283 ff.[1] and 447 ff. by incorporating such new renderings as the published discussions of them by different scholars have rendered probable. On pp. 452 ff. two new items have been added. One of these is an old Babylonian seal bearing the name "Israel," the other, an inscription from the mosaic floor of a Palestinian Jewish synagogue which was laid bare during the course of the Great War by the bursting of a shell. Two new illustrations have been added in order to present these to the eye.

While this edition was passing through the press two books by Professor Hrozny on the decipherment of Hittite came to hand. The results of Professor Hrozny's investigations are noted on pp. 445 ff. The slight relaxation, brought about by the armistice, of

[1] It should be noted that the page references in this preface refer to pages in the third edition.

the war restrictions against trade with Germany has permitted two
volumes of cuneiform texts copied from tablets found at Ashur to
reach the writer. These also came while he was reading the proofs
of this edition. They happily supply some important gaps in the
text of the Creation Epic published in Part II, Chapter I of this
book, as well as a new parallel to the Song of Songs. The writer is
happy thus to place this new material before his readers.

GEORGE A. BARTON.

JUNE, 1920.

PREFACE TO THE FOURTH EDITION

THE writer must again express his gratitude to the many users of
this book who have made another edition possible. The four years
that have passed since the appearance of the third edition have
been years of great archæological activity and of important archæological discoveries. Much work has been done in Palestine;
important discoveries have been made in Babylonia and Egypt;
part of a code of Assyrian laws has been given to the world; and
through the labors of Professor Hrozny it is now possible to present
a tentative translation of a Hittite code of laws. It is a pleasure to
be able to give the readers of ARCHÆOLOGY AND THE BIBLE the results of this work, as well as to have the opportunity to correct
earlier editions in some points concerning which we now have fuller
and more accurate knowledge. The publishers have also permitted
him to distribute the new material through the body of the book, and
to place each new item in the chapter to which it belongs, instead
of adding all new material in the Appendix. Besides additions
to a number of the chapters, four new chapters have been added
in Part II—one on the Hittite Laws, one on the Assyrian Laws,
one on a Babylonian Book of Lamentations, and one on Additions
to Early Christian Literature that have been made through archæological research. An Appendix on the Place of the Amorites
in the Civilization of Western Asia has been added.

GEORGE A. BARTON.

NOVEMBER, 1924.

PREFACE TO THE FIFTH EDITION

AGAIN the writer appreciates the opportunity to add to this book
the contributions to knowledge which have been made in Biblical

archæology since the manuscript of the fourth edition left his hands three years ago. He has made an effort to keep the work worthy of the confidence which has been accorded it.

GEORGE A. BARTON.

SEPTEMBER, 1927.

PREFACE TO THE SIXTH EDITION

GREAT progress has been made since 1924, when the body of this book was revised, not only in the exploration of Bible lands, but in the understanding of certain elements of their civilization. I am grateful to the public and to the publishers for an opportunity to revise the whole book once more and to place at the disposal of its readers the knowledge thus gained. The material which in the Fifth Edition constituted Appendix II has been placed in the parts of the book where it properly belongs. In Chapters I–IV of Part I sections have been added describing the discoveries made in Egypt, Mesopotamia, Asia Minor, Syria, and Palestine since the war, and which are of interest to Bible students. Chapter VIII, which deals with pottery, has been thoroughly revised to accord with the clearer and better classification of this material which is now possible. Chapter XI, which dealt with "high places" and temples has also been thoroughly revised, since the publication, in 1930, of Walter Andrae's *Das Gotteshaus and die Urformen des Bauens in Alten Orient* had shown that what archæologists had, for lack of knowledge of the methods of building in the early days of Palestine, mistaken for "high places," were the house foundations of the well-to-do. What had been mistaken for idolatrous "pillars" were the remains of pillars which once supported the upper stories. In Part II Chapter XIV—the translation of the Hittite laws—has been largely rewritten. Since the translation contained in the Fourth Edition was made (1923) great progress has been made in our knowledge of the Hittite vocabulary; thus it is now possible to secure a much more accurate rendering. To Chapter XVII there has been added a translation of one of the El-Amarna letters which, in the opinion of one scholar, mentions the Biblical Joshua. In Chapter XXVI there has been included a new and independent translation of a North Syrian poem on the "Conquest of Death." This poem was discovered in 1930. It is written in an alphabet which was unknown to the world until 1928, but which, by the ingenuity of two scholars, one German and one French, has been deciphered. In addition to these principal changes, minor corrections and improvements have been made in many parts of the book. Appendix I of the Fourth and Fifth Editions has been omitted. The theory of the Amorites which, in 1924 and 1927, it seemed a duty of the author to protect his readers from, now has no advocates.

The writer wishes to express his thanks to Professor W. F. Albright, of Johns Hopkins University, for giving him the benefit of his expert knowledge in the reclassification of Palestinian pottery; and to the late Right Reverend Rennie MacInnes, former Bishop of Jerusalem; to The University Museum, Philadelphia; to the Oriental Institute of the University of Chicago; and to his colleague, Professor E. A. Speiser, for the privilege of using the pictures which constitute the new illustrations in this edition. His thanks are also due to his wife, Katherine Blye Hagy Barton, for lightening his labor on the mechanical processes of preparing this edition, and for valuable assistance in reading the proofs.

GEORGE A. BARTON.

PHILADELPHIA, PA.
JANUARY, 1933.

PREFACE TO THE SEVENTH EDITION

THE past four years have witnessed remarkable advances in our knowledge of Biblical archæology. In no similar period have excavators been so active, and the study and interpretation of their results have not lagged behind the labors of the spade. In the present edition, again made possible by the interest of students of the Bible, an effort is made to keep this book abreast of the latest information. In Chapters II–IV of Part I additions have been made which will acquaint the reader with the latest discoveries in Mesopotamia, Palestine, and among the Hittites. Progress in the discovery and interpretation of human remains of the Stone Ages in Palestine now put the earliest inhabitants of Gezer in a perspective quite different from that in which they were viewed twenty years ago, and knowledge that the Hurri overran Palestine has afforded us a new and better understanding of the Biblical Horites. Changes have been made throughout Part I to conform to these and similar advances in knowledge. In Part II the translation of

the Assyrian Laws (ch. XV) has been revised. In Chapter IX a
new section has been added, giving a translation and discussion of a
liturgy for a spring festival, which was found at Ras Shamra, and
which the present writer believes to have been originally written
for Jerusalem. In Chapter XXVI a section has been inserted to
present part of a poem from Ras Shamra about a wonderfully
wise Daniel. In Chapter XXXI additions have been made to
acquaint the reader with the Chester Beatty Papyri, a newly discovered Biblical manuscript a hundred years older than any known
before, a Greek fragment of Tatian's *Diatessaron* from about 250
A.D., and a papyrus fragment of the Gospel of John written about
150 A.D. Minor improvements and corrections have been made
throughout the book. It is hoped that the new format in which the
volume is now presented will make it more convenient to use.

'It is a pleasure to express my thanks to the American Schools of
Oriental Research, the Oriental Institute of the University of
Chicago, and to Professor Nelson Glueck for permission to
present to the readers the six additional illustrations which this
edition contains. I am also most grateful to my wife, Katherine
Blye Hagy Barton for aid in the preparation of the manuscript,
in reading the proofs, and for many helpful criticisms and suggestions.

GEORGE A. BARTON.

NOVEMBER, 1937.

CONTENTS

PART I

xv

PART II

CONTENTS

LIST OF ILLUSTRATIONS

A Hillside Street in Roman Jerusalem along which Jesus and the Disciples may well have walked ....*Frontispiece*.

MAPS

EXPLANATION OF SIGNS

§ = section.

ibid. = the same.

op. cit. = work cited.

f. = and following page.

ff. = and following pages.

cf. = compare.

v. = verse.

col. = column.

p. = page.

[   ] in translations of tablets indicate words supplied where not decipherable.

. . . . in translations of tablets indicate missing line or words which cannot be supplied.

INTRODUCTION

ONE who would write on archæology and the Bible must at the outset define the scope of his undertaking, for the word archæology conveys different meanings to different people. Judgments also differ as to how things ancient can best serve the interests of the Biblical student. To many the word archæology calls up visions of ancient pottery, jewelry, swords, utensils, etc., which are valued as objects of curiosity simply because they are old. Others, when they think of archæology, call to mind excavations, in which the walls of ancient temples and cities are laid bare, so that we may see how men lived in other days. To such, archæology is identical with antiquarianism. A book on archæology and the Bible written from this point of view would confine itself to the way in which texts of Scripture are illustrated or illumined by antiquarian objects.

To still others the word archæology calls up ancient tablets or papyri, inscribed with hieroglyphics or some other strange characters, from which the initiated can decipher texts that prove the truth of one's views of Scripture. According to this view, archæology is the science of ancient documents, and a book dealing with archæology and the Bible should confine itself to the discussion of documents which confirm or illustrate the Biblical text.

Those who hold either of these views of archæology will find in this book much that will accord with their expectations, but much also that will seem to them irrelevant. In Part I, Chapters IV, VI–XII deal with antiquities, their discovery, and the light which these shed upon the inspired page, for antiquarianism is a part of archæology. Portions of Part I are devoted to the discovery of inscribed objects; in Part II the reader will find a full presentation of the bearing of these upon the different parts of the Sacred Volume. Those who hold the second of the views mentioned above will not, therefore, be disappointed.

Neither of the views mentioned corresponds, however, with the limits of archæology. Archæology is "that branch of knowledge which takes cognizance of past civilizations, and investigates their history in all fields, by means of the remains of art, architecture, monuments, inscriptions, literature, language, implements, customs, and all other examples which have survived." [1] This defini-

---

[1] *Century Dictionary*, edition of 1903, Vol. I, p. 293.

tion is accepted by the writer of this work and has guided him in the preparation of the following pages. It has, of course, been impossible in one volume to deal adequately with the antiquities and the ancient documents and to treat fully the history of the civilizations of the Biblical countries, but an endeavor has been made to place the reader in possession of an intelligent point of view with reference to these things. As the physical structure of a country determines to a large degree the nature of its buildings, the utensils employed by its inhabitants, their writing materials, and their relations with other peoples,—as well as the way the objects were preserved from ancient to modern times,—brief descriptions of the physical features of Egypt, Mesopotamia, and Palestine, the three most prominent of Biblical countries, have been introduced.

Our knowledge of the early history of Egypt and Babylonia has come almost wholly from archæological exploration; it has seemed fitting, therefore, to introduce in Part I, Chapter I, § 6, and Chapter II, § 6, brief sketches of the history of these countries. This appeared all the more necessary since the inhabitants of these two countries worked out, in advance of any other peoples, the initial problems of civilization. Palestine borrowed from them both, so that it is impossible to understand the history and archæology of Palestine apart from Egyptian and Babylonian antecedents. Whenever it is possible the reader should supplement these sketches by reference to the larger works cited in the notes.

Similarly in Part I, Chapter V, an outline of the history of Palestine from the earliest times is presented. To some this may seem unnecessary, since centuries of that history passed before the Hebrew people came to the country, but it is hoped that every reader will be glad to know the various vicissitudes through which passed the land that was chosen by God as the home of the religious leaders of the human race. This history also gives emphasis to the promise "to give thee great and goodly cities, which thou buildedst not, and houses full of all good things, which thou filledst not, and cisterns hewn out, which thou hewedst not, vineyards and olive-trees, which thou plantedst not" (Deut. 6: 10, 11).

Some, too, may be surprised that the chronologies of Egypt and Babylonia and Assyria should be treated as fully as they are in Part I, Chapter I, § 5, and Chapter II, § 5, but in the writer's view this treatment was necessary and appropriate for several reasons: (1) The data on which these chronologies are built up are for the most part the fruits of archæological research. (2) They are our

only means of measuring the antiquity of civilization, since the
Bible itself affords no continuous system of chronology.[1] If the
student of the Bible is to have any intelligent idea of what "the
fulness of time" (Gal. 4 :4) means, he should know what the sources
of our chronology are and how they are rightly used. (3) Such a
presentation seemed all the more necessary because in many books,
especially those of some English Egyptologists, the materials are
employed uncritically, and civilization is made to appear much older
than it really is.

To accomplish all these aims the writer has adopted the following
plan: In three chapters the archæology, history, and civilization of
Egypt, Babylonia and Assyria, and the Hittites are briefly treated,
together with the discoveries which especially interest the Biblical
student. These are the three great civilizations which preceded the
Israelitish. A much more detailed treatment is given to Palestine, to
which Chapters IV–XIV of Part I are devoted. In the last chapter
of Part I an attempt has been made to present the discoveries in
Greece and Asia Minor which throw light on the New Testament.
In Part II the texts, Babylonia, Assyrian, Egyptian, Hebrew,
Moabitish, Phœnician, Aramaic, Greek, and Latin, which bear on
the Bible, are translated. They are arranged in the order of the
Biblical books which they illuminate. Each translation is accompanied by a brief discussion in which its chief bearing on the Bible is
pointed out.

In conclusion it may not be out of place to offer a word of guidance to two or three classes of readers. Those who are not interested in the history of Babylonia and Egypt, but wish simply to
know what has been discovered in those countries which throws
light on the Scriptures, should turn at once to Part I, Chapter I, § 7,
and Chapter II, § 7, and to the translations of the various texts in
Part II. A reader who is interested especially in Palestine, rather
than in the ancient civilizations to which the Hebrews were indebted,
should begin Part I at Chapter IV. Possibly after he has read that
which the Holy Land has contributed to the understanding of the
Bible, he may be ready to give a little attention to such outlying
peoples as the Egyptians, Babylonians, and Hittites. In that case
he will turn back and read Chapters I–III.

Pastors or Sunday-school teachers who wish to employ the book
as a tool by means of which to study certain texts or lessons should

---

[1] The chronology of Archbisop Usher, printed in the margin of many Bibles, is not
a part of the Biblical text, but a collection of seventeenth century calculations and guesses.

follow a different course. These will be able with the aid of the full index of Scripture references to turn at once to all the material bearing on the passage in question. If the use of this index does not afford all the information desired, reference should then be made to the analytical table of contents at the beginning, or to the index of subjects at the end, or to both.

It is the writer's hope that, in addition to its use as a book of reference for the elucidation or illustration of individual texts, there may be some who will enjoy reading the whole work, and who will find, as he himself has found, that every scrap of knowledge of ancient life in Bible lands serves to make the Bible story and the lives of Biblical characters so much more real, or puts them or their words in a perspective so much more clear, that the eternal message comes with new power and can be transmitted with greater efficiency.

PART I

THE BIBLE LANDS, THEIR EXPLORATION
AND THE RESULTANT LIGHT ON THE
BIBLE AND HISTORY.

ARCHÆOLOGY AND THE BIBLE

CHAPTER I

EGYPT

THE LAND. THE PRESERVATION OF ANTIQUITIES. EGYPTIAN DISCOVERIES. DECIPHERMENT. CHRONOLOGY. OUTLINE OF HISTORY: The pre-dynastic period. The archaic period. The old kingdom. The first period of disintegration. The middle kingdom. Second period of disintegration. The empire period. The period of foreign dynasties. The lower empire. The Persian period. The Ptolemaic period. The Roman period. EGYPTIAN DISCOVERIES WHICH BEAR ON THE BIBLE: Texts bearing on the story of Joseph. The Invasion of Egypt by the Hyksos. The El-Amarna letters. Egyptian monotheism. Period of the Oppression and the Exodus. Campaign of Sheshonk I. Papyri discovered at Elephantine. The palace of Hophra. The castle at Tahpanhes. The Jewish temple at Leontopolis. Papyri from Oxyrhynchus. Discoveries in Nubia.

1. The Land.—Egypt is in many ways unique among the countries of the world. One of these unique features is its form. If we omit the Delta, it has but one dimension,—length. From Cairo to the First Cataract is a distance of 583 miles, while the breadth of the valley, including the barren lands on each side of it, varies from 12½ to 31 miles. If we include Nubia to the Fourth Cataract, which the Egyptians ultimately conquered, the length is much greater, being about 1,100 miles. In Nubia the banks are much more precipitous, the valley varying from 5 to 9½ miles. The verdant portion is, however, often not more than a mile in width.

This land is flanked on each side by extensive barren deserts on which there is almost no rainfall. Egypt itself would be a part of this desert, were it not for the overflow of the Nile. This overflow is caused by the peculiar formation of this marvelous river.

The upper part of the Nile consists of two main branches, called, respectively, the White and the Blue Nile. The White Nile rises 3 degrees south of the equator, some 4,000 miles south of the Mediterranean, to the south of Lake Victoria Nyanza. This region is watered by tropical rains, which fall almost daily. This steady water supply gives to the Nile its constant volume. At

Khartum, 1,350 miles from the Mediterranean in a direct line, and 1,650 miles as the river winds, the White Nile is joined by the Blue Nile. This branch of the river drains a large part of Abyssinia, an upland and mountainous region which has a dry and a rainy season. In the dry season this stream dwindles almost to nothing; in the rainy season it is a turbid mountain torrent, which rushes impetuously onward, laden with loose soil from all the land which it drains. For this reason it is called the Blue, *i. e.,* the dark or turbid, Nile.

At a distance of 140 miles north of the union of the two Niles the river receives its only other tributary, the Atbara, which also flows in from the eastern side. The Atbara, like the Blue Nile, is an insignificant stream except in the rainy season, when it is a torrent.

It is the variation of the water supply from the Blue Nile and Atbara which causes the overflow of the river in Egypt. At the beginning of June the river begins slowly to swell; between the 15th and the 20th of July the increase becomes very rapid; toward the end of September the water ceases to rise and remains at the same height for twenty to thirty days. In October it rises again, attaining its greatest height. It then decreases, and in January, February, and March the fields gradually dry off. This overflow prepares the soil of Egypt for cultivation, first by softening it and then by fertilizing it. It was easy, under these conditions, to develop agriculture there.

Indeed, the width of productive Egypt is determined by the lateral extent of this overflow. For the last 1,300 miles of its course the Nile receives no tributary. It plows its way through regions of desert which, but for the Nile itself, are unbroken. At six points, beginning at Khartum and ending at Assuan, the river makes its way over granite ridges, through which it has never succeeded in cutting a smooth channel. These are called the Cataracts. As civilized man discovered these from the north, that at Assuan is known as the First Cataract, and that at Khartum as the Sixth. The calendar of ancient Egypt was shaped in part by the Nile. The year was divided into three seasons of four months each. Beginning with the rise of the water about July 19th, there was the season of the inundation, which was followed by four months of winter and four months of summer.

In late geologic time all Egypt north of Cairo was a bay of the Mediterranean. In the course of the centuries the sea has been

MAP OF EGYPT.

driven out by deposits of detritus brought down by the Nile. As the mud was deposited in this level region, the water continued to make its way through it here and there. Several mouths were kept open, and thus the Delta was formed. This Delta is called Lower Egypt. Upper Egypt extends from Cairo to the First Cataract; Nubia, from the First Cataract to the Sixth.

2. The Preservation of Antiquities.—Rain in Egypt is very, very rare. One might almost say that it never rains. The country lies in a latitude so far south that frost is rarely known. These two conditions have united to preserve the ruins of many ancient buildings in both Egypt and Nubia in a state of perfection which is rare in other countries. It was the custom of the ancient Egyptians to bury their dead in the dry land beyond the reach of the Nile's overflow. Like many other peoples, they placed in the tombs of their dead many objects used by the departed in life. Further, their peculiar beliefs concerning immortality led them to mummify the bodies of the departed; i. e., they fortified them against decay. Thus archæological objects have been preserved in Egypt in an abundance and a perfection without parallel. So many of these are massive temples of stone, which, through all the ages, have stood unconcealed as silent witnesses of a past greatness, that from Cairo to the First Cataract Egypt is one great archæological museum.

3. Egyptian Discoveries.—Although many Egyptian antiquities have always been visible, they attracted little attention until modern times. Egyptian temple walls are covered with hieroglyphic writing, but the art of reading it had long been lost. Coptic, a language descended from the ancient Egyptian, was still preserved as the sacred language of the Egyptian Church, as Latin is the ecclesiastical language of Roman Catholics, but no one realized that Coptic was simply late Egyptian.

In the seventeenth century European travelers began to bring home Egyptian antiquities. In 1683 a specimen of Egyptian art was presented to the Ashmolean Museum at Oxford. In the eighteenth century R. Pococke (1704–1765) and F. L. Norden (1704–1742) described a number of Egyptian ruins and identified a number of the sites mentioned by classical authors. Pococke was an Englishman and Norden a Dane. Others, like the explorer Bruce, who was seeking the sources of the Nile (1768–1773), participated to some extent in the work.

No systematic examination of the antiquities was made, however, until the time of Napoleon I. When Napoleon invaded Egypt in 1798, he was accompanied by an army of eminent scholars and artists, nearly a hundred strong, and although in the settlement with England, which followed in 1802, the French were compelled to surrender their archæological treasures to Great Britain, they were permitted to publish the results of their observations and explorations. The publication of these advanced slowly, but between 1809 and 1822 the great work, consisting of one volume of introduction, three volumes of plates, and three volumes of texts, was given to the world. In these volumes the antiquities from the First Cataract to Alexandria were systematically described, and many of them were reproduced in magnificent water-color illustrations. As the nineteenth century progressed, additional discoveries were made, partly by the labors of such scientists as Lepsius and Mariette, and partly through the rifling of tombs by natives, who often sold their finds to Europeans. Since Egypt passed under English control, exploration has been fostered by the government, and English, French, German, Italian, and American explorers have taken part in it. The tombs of many of the ancient Pharaohs, the mummies of a considerable number of them, all sorts of implements and household furniture, have been discovered, as well as a great variety of historical, literary, religious, and business documents.

Within the last forty-five years a series of tombs of a previously unknown type has been discovered. The bodies buried in these tombs did not lie on the back as the ordinary Egyptian mummy does, but on the side, with the knees drawn up to the chin. It was at first thought that these tombs were the work of a new race of men who had invaded Egypt at some time in the historical period, but further study indicates that they are the tombs of the early Egyptians from whom the Egyptians known to history were descended. Many tombs of this variety have since been explored. The pottery and other objects contained in them reveal successive waves of civilization, while the mummified bodies reveal that successive waves of peoples of different races migrated into the valley of the Nile and settled there. W. M. Flinders Petrie published in 1920 a very important work,[1] in which he wove the evidence from the objects in these tombs into a fascinating historical outline. He divided the time between the beginning of the accumula-

[1] *Prehistoric Egypt*, London, 1920.

tion of the layer of alluvial earth-deposit which now rests on the rock bed of the Nile, up to the founding of the first dynasty, into eighty strata or sequence dates. He estimated that thirty of these had passed before traces of neolithic man appeared in the country. This leaves fifty sequence dates or periods distinguishable from the pottery and other archæological objects found in tombs. These Petrie numbered consecutively from 30 to 80. During the millennia covered by this series, he is able from the archæological objects to distinguish three civilizations, or three periods of civilization. He finds that the people who began the Egyptian civilization at s.d. (strata sequence) 30 buried their dead in shallow holes, "with a single black-topped cup, a goatskin over the body, and rarely a rhombic slate pallette. Yet even then they fastened the skin with a copper pin." Immediately after these first immigrants there came a more highly civilized people, who made pottery so exactly like that still made in the highlands of Algiers that Petrie feels justi- fied in calling this an immigration of "Lybians." The linguistic evidence already referred to would lead us to call them Hamites. This people was fond of making pottery, but their pots imitated baskets. It is possible to describe with some fulness the civiliza- tion of this period, if time permitted. It was almost altogether a Stone Age civilization. Copper was not common, but was some- times used for pins to fasten skins, for harpoons, and for small chisels used in carving.

Beginning at s.d. 38 a people came into Egypt, apparently from the east, whose pots imitated stoneware. They had retreating foreheads, long pointed noses, and small projecting beards. They wore more clothing, and had come from higher, colder regions. Petrie thinks they came from the western coast of the Red Sea, or the peninsula of Sinai, or the Hejaz in Arabia. The maximum of the immigration was at s.d. 38, but it continued until s.d. 41–43. The utensils of this civilization gradually drove out the utensils and wares of the first one. It is possible that these immigrants were Semitic.

Traces of the third civilization begin at s.d. 46–50, become more pronounced at s.d. 57, and reach their culmination at s.d. 63. This civilization introduced a pottery much like that found at Susa —seal cylinders of Babylonian type—and so many objects which resemble things found in Elam that Petrie is quite positive of Elamite influence. We should call it the influence of the Central Asiatic civilization. The mediators of this co-called Elamite influence could be no others than the Semites of Arabia. South Arabia from this time onward became a highway between Egypt and Mesopotamia. It seems probable that with the coming to Egypt of the makers of the second and third of these prehistoric civilizations, there entered Egypt many of those Semitic influences which so profoundly modified the Egyptian language and made it approach the Semitic type of speech more closely than the other Hamitic languages. Probably it was at one of these periods that there entered into Egypt the worship of Osiris and Isis, whose characters so closely resemble those of Tammuz and Ishtar, and whose names are philologically derivable from the Semitic root ASR, from which the names of several Semitic deities are also derived. The Hebrew *ashera* and the Assyrian *eshirtu,* meaning "shrine," are derived from the same root.

This wave of Elamite influence was superseded at about s.d. 63 by another, which came from Nubia. The stream of Semites had, however, become the intermediaries who carried a knowledge of arts developed in Central Asia to the less civilized Egyptians, and contributed to the civilization which was later to emerge in the Egyptian dynastic period.

The conclusions of Petrie are so well established that, although they have been reviewed by a German Egyptologist, Alexander Scharff,[2] in the main they stand. Scharff's nomenclature differs somewhat from Petrie's, but, on the whole, Scharff is compelled to agree with Petrie's conclusions. Scharff recognizes the first and second of the cultures defined by Petrie, substantially as Petrie did; but prefers, as the present writer would, to call the culture "Babylonian" which Petrie called "Elamite." This culture Scharff thinks came into the country in late predynastic and early dynastic times. Even if Scharff be right, the difference is not important, for prehistory merged into history in the late predynastic period.

In 1924 and '25 discoveries were made at Qau, by Petrie, and at Badari, by Mr. Guy Brunton, of a civilization older than the beginning of Petrie's sequence date 30. The sites where this civilization can be traced are near Assuit, in central Egypt. When the civilization discovered at Badari originated, the present arable land of the Nile Valley was largely swamps. The human settlements were made on the spurs of what are at present desert mountains. The lower levels presented little arable land. The climate

2 *Grundzüge der aegyptischen Vorgeschichte,* Leipzig, 1927.

was colder than it is now: skins were worn for garments, and the fur was usually worn inside for warmth. Perhaps the influence of the ice age of Europe is to be discerned in these facts. The Badarians made a ripple-surfaced pottery essentially different from that of any other people yet discovered in Egypt. In addition to hunting and fishing they practised agriculture. They raised grain, and apparently kept cattle, pasturing them, it would seem, on what is now desert. They made pottery of delicate thinness, also they tanned and employed leather. They traded with the coast lands of the Red Sea, whence came shells; they obtained turquoises, perhaps from Sinai; porphyry, either from the First Cataract, or from the mountains by the Red Sea. Some of the pots found suggest possible trade connections with Syria. The Badarians were, therefore, not an isolated people. They lived here during the later part of the period covered by Petrie's sequence dates 1 to 30.[3]

Our knowledge of early Egypt has been pushed still further back by the researches of K. S. Sanford and A. J. Arkell,[4] who, in the service of the Oriental Institute of the University of Chicago, have made a geological survey of Egypt, seeking also for traces of palæolithic man. The most fruitful of their investigations so far published is that made in the Fayum district. The Fayum contains a lake the surface of which was once considerably higher than that of the Mediterranean Sea, but is now 120 feet lower. On the shores of this ancient lake several terraces, which formed beaches for centuries at widely separated periods, were discovered. Among the pebbles on these beaches palæolithic artifacts were found, which show that men were living here in the pleistocine period of geologic time. At that time the *Sahara* desert was well watered, and the Nile Valley was still a mighty stream. Abundant waters poured through it and it was creating gravel terraces, or beaches, 100 feet above its present level. The period of desiccation, which made Egypt what it is today, came long afterward. The implements of these palæolithic men correspond, both in form and sequence, to those which palæolithic men were making in Europe in the glacial and interglacial periods. Whether these men had any racial connection with their European contemporaries we do not know. Doubtless they transmitted some of their blood to later Egyptian populations, but they did not form the dominant strain

---

3 See *The Badarian Civilization*, by Guy Brunton and Gertrude Caton-Thompson, London, 1928.
4 See their *First Report of the Prehistoric Survey Expedition*, Chicago, 1928, and *Paleolithic Man and the Nile-Fayum Divide, Chicago*, 1929.

in the Egyptian people of the historic period. After half of this period had passed, desiccation set in, and the present arid conditions began gradually to succeed. Habitations were confined little by little to the Nile Valley until conditions obtaining there today were established.

It thus happens that the Nile Valley presents us with one of the most fascinating glimpses into the prehistory of mankind anywhere obtainable. The many generations of men represented by the palæolithic artifacts found on the different beach-levels of the Fayum were not civilized in any modern meaning of the word. Their artifacts but give us vivid evidence that in Egypt, through long centuries, there existed human beings in a stage of development traceable in many parts of the world. Not until the Badarians do we come upon the remains of a people that we could call civilized, and Petrie's sequence date 30, with which began the habitation of the contracted Nile-valley which constituted later Egypt, is still more modern. It is only after that date, however, that the Hamites, who so largely shaped Egypt of the historic period, appeared in Egypt.

4. Decipherment.—One of the objects found by the French at the time of Napoleon's expedition was the "Rosetta Stone," so called because found at Rosetta (*Ar-Rashid*), a town near the mouth of the westernmost of the large branches of the Nile. This stone was set up about 200 B.C. by some priests, who expressed, through the inscription which it bore, their thanks to the young king, Ptolemy V, because certain taxes formerly imposed on them had been remitted. The inscription was written in three kinds of writing—hieroglyphic Egyptian (picture-writing), demotic Egyptian (developed from picture-writing), and Greek; (see Fig. 14). It was among the objects which the English took in 1802, and had been placed in the British Museum. Although the Greek portion of the inscription could be easily read, the attempts of various scholars, through a period of twenty years, had succeeded in establishing the values of only a few characters of the Egyptian. In 1818 Jean François Champollion, a French scholar, who before this had busied himself with the study of Coptic and Egyptian geography, began the study of the Rosetta Stone. He assumed that the language of the upper registers must be an older form of the Coptic tongue. By a most painstaking comparison of the characters in the upper registers with the Coptic equivalents of the words in the lower or Greek register, he succeeded in deciphering the long-forgotten writing of ancient Egypt. He published his discovery in 1822. Thus the door to the historical and literary treasures of ancient Egypt was unlocked, and from that time to this the study of Egyptian inscriptions and documents has gone steadily forward. Many universities now maintain chairs of Egyptology. The ability to read Egyptian has opened up vistas of history of which men had hitherto no conception.

5. Chronology.—We are dependent for our main outline of Egyptian chronology upon the work of Manetho, an Egyptian priest, who lived about 250 B.C., and wrote a chronicle of his native land in the Greek language. He grouped the kings of Egypt from the time of Menes (or Mena) to the conquest of Alexander the Great (332 B.C.) into thirty-one dynasties. Manetho's dynasties enable scholars to determine the relative order of the kings, and thus form the backbone of our chronology. Around his statements the discoveries of the excavators and explorers are grouped. Manetho's work has not, however, come down to us. We know it only through quotations in the *Chronographiai* of Julius Africanus (221 A.D.) and the *Chronicon* of Eusebius of Cesarea (265–340 A.D.). The number of years assigned to each king, and consequently the length of time covered by the dynasties, differ in these two copies, so that, while the work of Manetho form the backbone of our chronology, it gives us no absolutely reliable chronology. It is for this reason that the chronological schemes of modern scholars have differed so widely.

Another source of chronological information is the so-called "Palermo Stone," which is preserved in the Museum of Palermo, Sicily. This stone is a hard diorite, and is but a fragment of the original. It was inscribed about the middle of the fifth dynasty, and originally contained a list of the kings of Egypt from a time long before Mena to the middle of the fifth dynasty. Though now but a fragment, it is still of great value for the period which it covers. In addition to this, we also have the King List of Karnak, set up by Thothmes III, of the eighteenth dynasty, the King List of Abydos, inscribed by Seti I and Ramses II, of the nineteenth dynasty, and the King List of Sakkarah, inscribed by Ramses II. As these are all simply selections from the list of the predecessors of their authors, they are of secondary importance. The "Turin Papyrus" would be of value chronologically, but for its unfortunate history. This papyrus originally contained the most complete list of Egyptian kings that has come down to us, with the exception of Manetho's chronology. It formed part of the collection of M. Drovetti, the French Consul-General in Egypt. The collection was offered to the French government in 1818, but was finally purchased by the king of Sardinia. When the collection arrived in Turin, it was found that this papyrus was broken into small fragments in the bottom of the box in which it had been shipped. The fragments were afterward (1824) examined by Champollion the younger, who discovered their true character. In 1826 another Egyptologist went to Turin and joined the fragments; but the science of Egyptology was then in its infancy, and he in his ignorance joined pieces which did not naturally belong together. For this reason it is only occasionally that the document yields us any chronological data.

The greatest aid in fixing Egyptian chronology is the "Sothic Cycle." At an early date the Egyptians adopted a calendar which made up a year of 365 days. Their year originally began when the rapid rising of the Nile coincided with the rising of the star Sirius, called by them Sothis. These events coincided on July 19th. As their calendar made no allowance for leap year, in four years their new year began a day too soon, in eight years two days too soon, and so on. In 1,460 years (*i. e.*, 365 × 4) their New Year's Day would make a complete circuit of the year. These periods of 1,460 years are called Sothic Cycles. Censorinus, in Chapters XVIII and XXI of his *De Die Natali,* written in 238 A.D., tells us that a new Sothic cycle began at some time between 140 and 144 A.D. If a new cycle began in 140 A.D., the previous one began in 1320 B.C.; the one before that, in 2780 B.C.; and the one before that,—if they had their calendar so early,—in 4240 B.C. Reisner holds that the Egyptians adopted their calender in 2780 B.C., but Meyer and Breasted hold that it is unthinkable that they should have been without a calendar until that time, as by that date the civilization of the pyramid builders was at its height; they accordingly maintain that the Egyptian calendar was adopted in 4240 B.C.[5]

An illustration will show how the Sothic cycle helps in determining dates. A priest in the 120th year of the twelfth dynasty wrote a letter to his subordinates, to inform them that the rising of Sothis would occur on the fifteenth day of the eighth month. As there were thirty days in each month, the year diverged at this time 225 days. This date, then, was just 900 years after the be-

[5] For a modified way of applying the Sothic Cycle, see Arthür Weigall, *History of the Pharaohs*, New York, 1925–27, I, 26ff.

ginning of the cycle in 2780 B.C.; i.e., the letter was written in the year 1880 B.C. It proves that the twelfth dynasty began in 2000 B.C., and fixes for us all the dates of that dynasty. The calendar in the so-called *Papyrus Ebers* shows that in the tenth year of Amenophis I, of the eighteenth dynasty, the divergence had increased to 308 days. This must have been 1,232 years after the beginning of the cycle, which was the year 1548 B.C. Data gained from these sources are supplemented by what is called dead reckoning; *i. e.,* by adding together all the specific dates of the length of reigns which are given in the inscriptions, and testing them by collateral references. Meyer and Breasted have worked out the chronology from these data in this way. Meyer places the accession of Mena at 3200 B.C., while Breasted places it at 3400 B.C. This difference is slight when compared with the differences in the chronologies of the older Egyptologists.[6]

6. Outline of History.[7]—The history of Egypt, as it concerns our subject, extends over a period of five thousand years. It falls into twelve periods:

(1) *The Pre-Dynastic Period,* of which we have already given an outline, occupied the time until about 3400 B.C. It is the period before that covered by Manetho's dynasties. At the beginning of this period Egypt was divided into districts, which the Egyptians called *spt* or *hsp,* and which the Greeks afterwards called *nomes.* Each nome was occupied by a different tribe, which at the first lived in isolation from the other tribes. Each tribe had its god, to which an animal was sacred. This condition prevailed for so many centuries that the customs of this period became permanently fixed. The sacredness of these animals continued right down to Roman times. During these centuries the dead were buried on their sides with the knees drawn up to the chin. (See Fig. 8.) The Egyptians of this period lived partly by hunting, partly by fishing, and partly by agriculture. From objects found in their tombs we infer that they used stone implements, wore a great many beads, made implements and combs of bone, made decorated pottery, constructed boats for use on the Nile and fitted sails to them, and each tribe had its own standard or emblem. Of course, during the centuries when Egypt was so politically divided there were many wars be-

6 Arthur Weigall has worked the problems over afresh in his *History of the Pharaohs,* Vol. I, New York, 1925, and reaches the conclusion that Mena, the first king of the first dynasty, began to reign in 3407 B.C. Weigall's eminence as an Egyptologist was not as great as that of the scholars quoted in the text.

7 For fuller accounts of the history of Egypt, see Breasted's *History of the Ancient Egyptians,* New York, Scribner's, 1908; or Breasted's *History of Egypt,* second edition, 1909, New York, Scribner's.

tween nome and nome. Through division and addition they finally numbered 42.

After some centuries, through the conquest of one nome by another, these 42 nomes were consolidated into two kingdoms. The 20 nomes of the Delta formed the kingdom of Lower Egypt; the 22 nomes, which were ranged along the Nile from Cairo to the First Cataract, formed the kingdom of Upper Egypt. The symbol of Upper Egypt was a papyrus plant; that of Lower Egypt, the bee. The crown of Upper Egypt was a kind of tall helmet; that of Lower Egypt, a diadem of openwork; (see Figs. 2, 3, and 4). At what period this union of the nomes into two kingdoms occurred, we can only conjecture. Probably it was as early as 4200 or 4300 B.C. At all events, the two kingdoms existed separately for so long a time that their memory was ever afterward, preserved. To the end of Egyptian history the kings bore the title, "king of Upper Egypt and Lower Egypt." Even in the Hebrew of the Old Testament the name for Egypt is literally "The two Egypts." In this long pre-dynastic period the people were gradually emerging from savagery toward civilization. They were solving the initial problems of civilized life. According to Meyer and Breasted the people of Lower Egypt had progressed far enough before 4200 B.C. to invent a calendar which approximately coincided with the solar year.

(2) *The Archaic Period.*—The history of united Egypt begins with the reign of Menes or Mena, who in some way, whether by conquest or marriage is uncertain, united the two crowns. He came from the nome of This, of which the city of Abydos, sacred to the worship of Osiris, was the chief town. He and his successors continued to administer the two parts of Egypt as separate countries. Mena founded the first dynasty, and the second dynasty seems to have been connected with his house; it was, at all events, from the nome of This. These two dynasties ruled Egypt for 420 years, from 3400 to 2980 B.C. This is known as the *archaic period* of Egyptian history. Men were, during this time, gradually developing the art of expressing thought by means of picture-writing. At some time during the first dynasty the Egyptians began to work the turquoise mines in the Wady Maghara in the peninsula of Sinai. The tombs of this period were low, flat houses of brick. The Arabs call them *mastabas* or "benches." During the second dynasty the Egyptians began to conceive of their gods in human

form. They preserved the continuity of the earlier animal and bird forms by putting the old heads on human bodies.

(3) *The Old Kingdom* embraces dynasties three to six, and extended from 2980 to 2475 B.C., a period of more than 500 years. During the third and fourth dynasties the power of the king was supreme and the first great culmination of Egypt's civilization occurred. It was in this period that the pyramids developed. Zoser, the first king of the third dynasty, built as his tomb the so-called Step Pyramid; (see Fig. 7). It consists of five stages which vary from 29½ to 36 feet in height. It is not, therefore, a true pyramid. At the base it is 352 × 396 feet. Seneferu, the last king of the third dynasty, built a similar tomb, but, as he made the stages lower and more numerous, it approached more nearly the pyramidal form.

Khufu or Cheops, the founder of the fourth dynasty, improving upon the work of his predecessors, constructed the first real pyramid and the greatest of them all. The blocks with which he built were about three feet high, and he made a step with each course of stones. A covering, which has now been removed, was originally placed over the whole, thus securing a perfect pyramidal form. This pyramid is now 750 (originally 768) feet on each side, and 451 (originally 482) feet high. It contains some 2,300,000 blocks of stone, each weighing on the average two and a half tons; (see Fig. 6). The stone was quarried from the Mokattam hills on the other side of the Nile, more than twelve miles away.

Khafre, the next king but one after Khufu, built the second pyramid, which is almost as high as that of Khufu, being 447½ feet, but measures on the sides but 690½ feet. Within and under the pyramids are the tomb chambers. Khafre also carved out of the native rock, not far from these two pyramids, the great Sphinx, the head of which bore a portrait of himself. From the top of the head to the pavement under the paws is 66 feet; the breadth of the face is 13 feet 8 inches, and the other parts are in proportion. Near the Sphinx stands a temple, built of polished granite, which is connected by an underground passage with the pyramid of Khafre. All these are silent but eloquent witnesses to the skill of the Egyptians of this period in stone work, and to the absolute power of the Pharaoh; (see Figs. 5 and 6).

Menkaure, the next king, constructed a smaller pyramid, the side of its base being 356½ feet and its height 204 (originally 219) feet. Either his power was less or the resources of the kingdom were becoming exhausted. Though the pyramidal form of tombs continued for several centuries, no others were ever built that approached these in size.

The fifth dynasty was founded by a priest of On. During its rule the power of the king was not so absolute, and a powerful nobility began to develop. These nobles had themselves buried in tombs of the old mastaba type, and adorned the walls with pictures of the industries which were carried on upon their country estates. One of the most famous of these is the tomb of a certain Ti, from the pictures in which much has been learned of the various industries of ancient Egypt.

By the time of the sixth dynasty a strong nobility had been developed in the different nomes, so that the monarchy was thoroughly feudal. The absolute power that the kings of the first four dynasties had exercised had passed away. During the sixth dynasty the conquest of northern Nubia was begun, an expedition was sent to the far-away land of Punt, a country far to the south. It was probably the region on both sides of the straits of Bab-el-Mandeb, comprising southwestern Arabia and Somaliland. An expedition was also sent over sea to Palestine, to chastise the inhabitants of the southern portion of that country for invading Egypt. The capital of Egypt during the whole of the Old Kingdom was Memphis. The city thus gained a prominence which made it ever afterward famous. In early times it had been called the White Wall, but after the sixth dynasty it was called *Men-nofer,* of which Memphis (Hosea 9:6) is a corruption. It is in the Old Testament more often called Noph, a corruption of the last part of the name. (See Isa. 19:13; Jer. 2:16; 44:1; 46:14, 19; Ezek. 30:13, 16.)

(4) *The First Period of Disintegration* covers dynasties seven to ten of Manetho's list, a period lasting from 2475 to 2160 B.C. At the beginning of this period the powerful nobles in the different nomes seem, many of them, to have set up each a government of his own. Thus Egypt was once more resolved into many contending kingdoms. Through a cycle of 2,500 years a whole circle of political evolution had been completed. Starting with 42 chiefs or kinglets, the country had first become two kingdoms, then one kingdom. In this struggle the local nobility had been eliminated. Through nine hundred years the central monarchy was supreme, then slowly a new nobility developed, which finally overthrew the

kingdom and once more made Egypt a group of weak and contending states.

During the last two hundred and fifty years of this period of darkness we gain some glimpses of a feudal monarchy which had its residence at Heracleopolis in central Egypt and controlled a good part of the land with varying degrees of success. These kings were apparently the ninth and tenth dynasties of Manetho.

(5) *The Middle Kingdom.*—About 2160 B.C. an eleventh dynasty arose and began to struggle for the supremacy, finally achieving it. This family belonged to the nome of Thebes, which had hitherto been of no particular importance. It now became the seat of government, and remained for 1,500 years one of the most important cities of Egypt.

About the year 2000 this dynasty was followed by the twelfth, a powerful line of kings which ruled from 2000 to 1788 B.C. This was the period of the great Middle Kingdom. The nobles were still strong, and the monarchy was thoroughly feudal in its organization. Three of these monarchs bore the name Sesostris. They raised Egypt to a high degree of prosperity and power. Trade with Punt was resumed, Nubia was conquered to the Second Cataract, which was made the southern frontier of the realm, the mines of Sinai were worked, and one of the kings, Amenemhet III, built a large temple there, at a point now called Sarbut el-Khadem. This temple was explored in 1905 by Petrie.

Trade with Palestine and Syria flourished during this period. A noble of middle Egypt pictured in his tomb some of those who came to trade with him. When the pictures were first discovered, it was thought that they were the sons of Jacob, come to buy corn in Egypt (see Fig. 1).

Sesostris III invaded Palestine before 1850 B.C. and captured a city which was apparently Shechem, though the spelling of the name is peculiar. The kings of this period were buried in tombs of pyramidal form, though the pyramids were not large. One of them built a great administration building at Hawara, which was known to the Greeks as the Labyrinth and was regarded as one of the wonders of the world.

During this and the preceding period a social conscience was developed in Egypt which found expression in a remarkable literature. Extracts from two examples of this, "The Eloquent Peasant" and "The Admonitions of Ipuwer," are published in Part II, pp. 525 ff., 529 f.

(6) *Second Period of Disintegration.*—The thirteenth dynasty, which began in 1788 B.C., had not been long upon the throne, when powerful rebellions again broke up the kingdom. Petty kinglets ruled once more in many parts of the land. These kings comprise Manetho's thirteenth and fourteenth dynasties. The land, disunited, became an easy prey to an invader. Such an invader came. For more than 3,000 years Egypt, protected by her deserts, had lived her life unmolested. The uncivilized Nubians on the south, the Lybians on the west of the Delta, and the uncivilized tribes of Sinai had been easily held in check. But now powerful invaders came from Asia with a well organized, though barbaric army. They conquered Egypt and imposed upon her two dynasties of kings, who ruled for about a hundred years, until they were driven out about 1580 B.C. These kings were Manetho's fifteenth and sixteenth dynasties. He calls them Hyksos, which has been held to mean "Shepherd Kings," but which probably meant "Ruler of Countries." They have been generally believed to be Semitic, though some scholars now think they may have been of Hurrian origin. In any event, large numbers of Semites came to Egypt with them, and left many Semitic names in the Delta. Some of these will be discussed below. This invasion broke up Egypt's splendid isolation and brought her into the current of world events, from which she was never afterward to free herself.

(7) *The Empire Period.*—At some time before 1600 B.C. a seventeenth dynasty arose at Thebes and began the struggle to expel the foreign kings. This was not accomplished until the founder of the eighteenth dynasty, Amosis I (1580–1557), achieved it. In order to secure freedom from invasion the kings of this dynasty were compelled to follow the invaders into Asia, and in time Thothmes III (1501–1447) conquered Palestine, Phœnicia, and Syria to the Euphrates, and organized it into a compact empire, which held together until about 1360. The kings of this dynasty also carried the conquest of Nubia to Napata, at the Fourth Cataract. They worked the mines of Sinai, traded with Punt, and inaugurated the "empire period," which lasted in reality till well into the twentieth dynasty, about 1165, and which, for convenience, we count as extending to the fall of the twenty-first dynasty in 945 B.C.

The foreign conquests brought many immigrants to Egypt and also took many Egyptians for longer or shorter periods to foreign lands. Egyptian customs in dress as well as the Egyptian language changed rapidly during this time. The Asiatic conquests of

Thothmes III brought Egypt into relations with Asiatic kings, and in time his successors, Amenophis III and Amenophis IV, had an interesting exchange of letters with kings of Babylon, Assyria, Mitanni, and Alashia (or Cyprus), as well as with Egyptian viceroys in Syria and Palestine. Some of these letters are translated in Part II, p. 441 ff.

Amenophis IV made the first attempt known in history to establish a monotheistic religion. Before the time of Amenophis more than one of the gods of Egypt had been identified with the sun. As the sun seemed to be the giver of all life, Amenophis chose the sun disc as the one god. He could not call it by the name of any of the old gods without encouraging the older religion which he regarded as heathenism, so he gave it the name Aton and tried to make the worship of Aton supersede the old cults. As the priesthood of Thebes strenuously opposed his reform, he built a new capital in middle Egypt, at what is now called El-Amarna, and moved his court thither. In the effort to spread the new religion a new religious literature was called into existence. One of the beautiful hymns written at this time is translated in Part II, p. 502, ff. Amenophis died before his reform was accomplished, and, having no son, was succeeded by two sons-in-law in quick succession. The second of these, Tutankhamen, whose tomb was discovered by Mr. Howard Carter on November 5, 1922, abandoned the new capital and the new religion, moved back to Thebes, and re-established the worship of the old gods.

Owing to the prominence given to Mr. Howard Carter's discovery by the press, Tutankhamen's name has become a household word throughout the world and many doubtless think him the most important king of Egypt. In reality, he was one of the lesser kings who lived near the close of the most brilliant period of Egyptian history. The significance of the discovery of his tomb lies in the fact that it is the first time the tomb of an Egyptian king has been found practically unrifled. For more than three thousand years the tomb-robbers of Thebes have been the most expert in the world, and they entered all royal tombs previously discovered, removed most of the important furniture and jewels, and mutilated the royal mummies. In the tomb of Tutankhamen there have been found a coffin of gold, furniture, fabrics, vessels, and jewels, the exquisite texture and workmanship of which have dazzled the gaze of Egyptologists. They far surpass anything that had been imagined. If such things were to be found in the tomb of one of the lesser kings, what might have been discovered in graves of the greatest and richest monarchs! (See Figs. 304, 305.)

Beginning with Thothmes I, who died about 1500 B.C., the kings of this period were buried in tombs of a new type. These were excavated out of the solid rock, cut deep into the mountainside. They were all in the famous Valley of the Tombs of the Kings back of Thebes, where Tutankhamen's tomb was found.

The nineteenth dynasty succeeded the eighteenth about 1350 B.C. During a period of weakness between the two, the Asiatic dominions had been lost. These were in large part reconquered by Seti I and Ramses II. The last-mentioned king ruled 67 years, from 1292 to 1225 B.C. He did much building in all parts of Egypt and Nubia. Among his enterprises were the cities of Pithom and Raamses in the Delta. He has long been thought to have been the Pharaoh who oppressed the Hebrews. Early in his reign he fought with the Hittites, but afterward made a treaty of peace with their king and married his daughter. The text of this treaty has been preserved. It is the earliest extant international treaty, and it contained an extradition clause, though this applied to political offenders only. (For head of Ramses, see Fig. 9.)

Merneptah, the son and successor of Ramses II, has been supposed to be the Pharaoh of the Exodus. His hymn of victory over his enemies is translated in Part II, p. 376.

In the reign of Ramses III, of the twentieth dynasty (1198–1167 B.C.), the Philistines and other tribes, coming from across the sea, from Crete and Asia Minor, invaded Egypt. Repulsed by him, they invaded Palestine, where they secured a foothold. Ramses IV, his successor, was the last Pharaoh to work the mines in Sinai. By the reign of Ramses IX (1142–1123 B.C.), Egypt's Asiatic empire was gone and her prosperity had so declined that the natives of Thebes took to robbing the tombs of kings for a living. The records of the trials of some of these have survived. In the reign of Ramses XII (1118–1090 B.C.), Wenamon made his famous expedition to Phœnicia, a part of his account of which is translated in Part II, p. 449 ff.

The twenty-first dynasty (1090–945 B.C.) was a line of weak monarchs, who simply held Egypt together. During their rule David built up Israel's empire. One of them, either Siamon or Pesibkhenno II, was the Pharaoh whose daughter Solomon married. (See 1 Kings 3:1, f.; 9:16.)

(8) *The Period of Foreign Dynasties* (945–663 B.C.).—During
the time of the twenty-first dynasty the Lybians, who for centuries
had made unsuccessful attempts to invade Egypt, settled in large
numbers in different parts of the country, and adopted Egyptian
customs, while some of them became wealthy and powerful. In
945 B.C. one of these, named Sheshonk, founded the twenty-second
dynasty. This king is the Shishak of the Bible. It was he who
gave asylum to Jeroboam, when he fled from Solomon (1 Kings
11:40), and who in the days of Rehoboam invaded Palestine.
(See 1 Kings 14 : 25–28.) The dynasty founded by Shishak lasted
for two hundred years. During the first century of this time it was
very flourishing. One of its kings, Osorkon II, was apparently an
ally of Ahab; at all events, a vase bearing Osorkon's name was
found at Samaria in Ahab's palace. This dynasty made its capital at
Bubastis in the Egyptian Delta, called Pi-beseth in Ezekiel 30 : 17.

During the last century of this dynasty's rule Nubia, which had
been for many centuries under Egyptian sway, gained her independence under a powerful dynasty which made Napata at the
Fourth Cataract, its capital. In 745 B.C. the twenty-second
dynasty was succeeded by the twenty-third, which held a precarious existence until 718, when it was succeeded by the one king of
the twenty-fourth. Egypt was during this period in great disorder,
and in 712 the Nubian kings swept down from the south and conquered the country, establishing the twenty-fifth dynasty. The control thus passed from the Lybians to the Nubians. Tirhakah, the
third king of this dynasty, took part in the wars against Sennacherib
in Palestine. (See 2 Kings 19:9; Isa. 37:9, and Part II, p. 471,
ff.) In 670 Esarhaddon, King of Assyria, invaded Egypt, defeated
Tirhakah and made all the Delta as far as Memphis an Assyrian
province. Some years later, when Tanut-amon, the successor of
Tirhakah, endeavored to regain the Delta, Ashurbanipal, of Assyria,
marched up the Nile, took Thebes, that for 1,500 years had been
mistress of Egypt, and during much of that time mistress of a large
part of the then known world, and barbarously sacked it. This
was in 661 B.C. This event made a great impression on surrounding
nations. It is referred to in Nahum 3:8, where Thebes is called
No-amon, or the city of the god Amon.

(9) *The Lower Empire* is the name given by scholars to the
period of the twenty-sixth dynasty, 663–525 B.C. This dynasty
was founded by Psammetik I, who became the viceroy of Egypt
under Ashurbanipal, of Assyria, in 663 B.C. Psammetik was

descended from a native Egyptian family of the city of Sais in the western Delta, and a number of his ancestors had been prominent in the history of Egypt during the preceding century. At first he was a vassal of Assyria, but soon troubles in the eastern part of the Assyrian dominions enabled him to make Egypt independent. The Egyptians, finding themselves once more free under a native dynasty, experienced a great revival of national feeling. Everything Egyptian interested them. They looked with particular affection upon the age of the pyramid builders, who lived more than two thousand years before them. They revived old names and old titles, and emulated the art of the olden days. They manifested such vigor and originality withal, that the art of the lower empire rivals that of the best periods of Egyptian history.

Necho, the son and successor of Psammetik, endeavored, as Assyria was declining to her fall, to regain an Asiatic empire. Josiah, of Judah, who sought to thwart him, was defeated by Necho and killed at the battle of Megiddo in 608 B.C. (2 Kings 23 : 29). Necho afterward deposed Jehoahaz and took him captive to Egypt (2 Kings 23 : 34). Four years later, when Necho made a second campaign into Asia, he was defeated by Nebuchadrezzar at Charchemish on the Euphrates, and compelled to hastily retreat to Egypt, hotly pursued by the Babylonians. Jeremiah, who perhaps caught sight of the rapidly moving armies from the Judæan hills, has given a vivid account of the flight in Jeremiah 46. Jeremiah considered this event so important that he began then to commit his prophecies to writing. (See Jer. 36.) After this Necho devoted himself to the internal government of Egypt, though he became the patron of an enterprise for the circumnavigation of Africa, which was carried out by some Phœnicians. (See Herodotus, IV, 42.) Hophra, a later king of this dynasty (588–569 B.C.), in order to gain influence in Asia, tempted King Zedekiah to rebel against Babylon, and thus lured the little state of Judah to its destruction. During the reign of Hophra's successor, Amosis II, Cyrus the Great founded the Persian empire, and in 525 B.C. Cambyses, the son of Cyrus, overthrew the twenty-sixth dynasty, and made Egypt a Persian province.

(10) *The Persian Period.*—Cambyses, after conquering Egypt, attempted in vain to conquer Nubia. The Nubian monarchs at this time moved their capital from Napata, at the Fourth Cataract, to Meroe, at the Sixth Cataract. Darius (521–485 B.C.) ruled Egypt with great wisdom and tact, but under his successors there

were frequent rebellions. Finally, in 406 B.C., the Egyptians actually gained their independence, which they maintained until 342 B.C. During this period three native dynasties, the twenty-eighth, the twenty-ninth, and the thirtieth, successively occupied the throne. Manetho counts the Persians as the twenty-seventh dynasty. In 342 B.C. the Persians reconquered the country and held it for ten years until it was taken by Alexander the Great. This ten years of Persian rule constitutes Manetho's thirty-first dynasty.

(11) *The Ptolemaic Period* (332-31 B.C.).—For eleven years Egypt formed a part of Alexander's empire. Upon his death, in 323 B.C., it fell to the control of his general, Ptolemy Lagi, who founded a line of Ptolemies that ruled until overthrown by Augustus in 31 B.C. With the accession of the Ptolemies many Greeks settled in Egypt; Greek became one of the languages of commerce, and had a considerable influence in transforming the Egyptian language into Coptic. Until the year 198 B.C. the Ptolemies controlled Palestine. Philadelphus, the second of the line, rebuilt in the Greek style the city of Rabbah Ammon east of the Jordan, and named it Philadelphia. He, like his father, encouraged many Jews to settle in Alexandria, and, according to tradition, became the patron of the translation of the Old Testament Scriptures into Greek. At all events, the Pentateuch was translated in his time, and the translation of the other books followed. This translation is known as the "Septuagint" because of the legend that Ptolemy Philadelphus set 72 men to translate it. By the beginning of the Christian era there were so many Jews in Alexandria that it had become a second Judah.

(12) *The Roman Period.*—The Romans, upon conquering Egypt, disturbed in no way the internal affairs of the country. They gave it good government and fostered its internal institutions. Many old Egyptian customs persisted among the people; it is in regard to some of these that discoveries of interest to Biblical scholars have been made. From tombs and the places in the dry sands of the desert, where waste-baskets were emptied, many records have been discovered, some of which are translated in Part II, pp. 549 ff., 553 ff.

Meantime, a state had developed out of the old monarchy of Nubia, described above, which was ruled by a woman, whose official title was Candace. It was an officer of hers to whom Philip preached, as described in Acts 8:27-39. Modern excavations in

Nubia have recovered some of the art of these people, who became Christian in the second or third century, as well as some inscriptions of theirs in a script that is now beginning to be read.

7. **Egyptian Discoveries which Bear on the Bible:—**

(1) *Texts Bearing on the Story of Joseph.*—A number of texts from the Middle Kingdom and other periods present features similar to parts of the story of Joseph and afford somewhat faint parallels to certain conceptions of the Hebrew Prophets. These are translated in Part II, pp. 365 ff., 522 ff., and 525, ff.

The name of Joseph's wife, Asenath (in Egyptian *As-Neit,* "favorite of the goddess Neith"), occurs from the eighteenth dynasty onward. Such names as Potiphar, the master of Joseph (Gen. 39 : 1), and Potiphera, Joseph's father-in-law (Gen. 41 : 45), in Egyptian *Pedefre,* "he whom the god Re gives," as well as the name given to Joseph, Zaphenath-paneah (Gen. 41 : 45), in Egyptian *De-pnute-ef-'onkh,* "the god speaks and he lives," are common in Egypt from the beginning of the twenty-second dynasty, 945 B.C.

(2) *The Invasion of Egypt by the Hyksos.*—This took many Semites to Egypt. The very name Hyksos is held by Breasted to mean "ruler of countries." It was probably a title by which these kings called themselves, for they evidently ruled a considerable portion of western Asia, as well as Egypt. "Ruler of countries" is just the Semitic-Babylonian and Assyrian *shar-matâti,* a title which Mesopotamian kings gave to themselves through much of their history. It had been employed by the Sumerians before them, being the familiar Sumerian *lugal kurkurra,* "king of countries." If the Hyksos were Amorites, kinsmen of theirs had ruled in Babylonia long before their invasion of Egypt, and that these may have been Amorites is indicated by the name Jacob-her, which was borne by one of their kings. This is an Egyptian form of the Babylonian *Yagub-ilu, or Jacob-el,* an Amorite name found on business documents in Babylonia three or four hundred years earlier. In the time of Thothmes III this name was, Thothmes tells us, borne by a Palestinian city, to which it had apparently been given by some Amorite from Babylonia. Whether the Hyksos were Amorites or not, a number of Semitic names were given to places in Lower Egypt at the time of their occupation. Such was the name Magdol, or Migdol. The Egyptian name of Tanis was Zar, which Brugsch claims as Semitic. Thakut, an old name of Pithom, is the same as the Semitic Succoth, "booths."

In the winter of 1905–1906 Petrie, excavating at Tell el-Ye-hudiyeh,[8] about 20 miles north of Cairo, discovered what he believes to have been one of the original encampments of the Hyksos in Egypt. This encampment consisted of a large space, averaging about 1,500 feet in each direction, surrounded by a wall of sloping sand and mud. This wall, varying from 80 to 140 feet wide at the top and from 130 to 200 feet wide at the bottom, presented on the outer side a long slope, and is quite unlike any structure of the native Egyptians. From the nature of the wall and the small objects found near it, Petrie infers that it was the rampart of a people who defended themselves with bows and arrows. A ceme-tery of the same level yielded to the explorer a considerable amount of black pottery, not at all like pottery of native Egyptian manu-facture, and a number of crude scarabs. These objects Petrie believes are products of the art of the Hyksos before they had been in Egypt long enough to adopt Egyptian civilization. In 1912 Petrie discovered a similar Hyksos camp at the site of Heliopolis, the Biblical On.

It has been held by many that Abraham, Joseph, and Jacob all went to Egypt during the reign of the Hyksos dynasty. It would be natural for Semites to enter such a country, if it were ruled by a dynasty of the same blood as themselves. Egypt has, however, furnished no positive archæological evidence of this view. The Semitic names just alluded to, which are sometimes cited as evi-dence of it, in reality only prove that many Semites came with the Hyksos. They make it probable, indeed, that some of the Hyksos were Semites, but give us no positive evidence concerning the patriarchs. On the other hand, nothing has been discovered in Egypt to disprove this view.

(3) *The El-Amarna Letters.*—In the winter of 1887–1888 a native Egyptian woman, according to one account, accidentally discovered some clay tablets in the soil at Tell el-Amarna, about 200 miles south of Cairo on the east bank of the Nile. She is said to have sold her rights in the discovery for about 50 cents. It was thus that nearly four hundred clay tablets, inscribed in the Baby-lonian language and characters, which opened an entirely unknown vista in the history of Palestine and the surrounding countries, were found. These were letters written to Kings Amenophis III and Amenophis IV, of the eighteenth dynasty. (See § 6 (7).) Seven of them were written by Ebed-hepa, King of Jerusalem, about 1360

8 See Petrie, *Hyksos and the Israelite Cities,* London, 1906.

B.C., and give us a glimpse of that city more than 350 years before David conquered it for Israel. Others of the letters came from other cities of Palestine and Phœnicia, and reveal to us through contemporary documents the conditions there in the patriarchal age. Some of these are translated in Part II, p. 441 ff.

(4) *Egyptian Monotheism.*—The attempt of Amenophis IV to establish a monotheistic religion, by compelling all Egyptians to worship Aton, has already been described (p. 19). This fact has led naturally to comparisons with the monotheism of the Hebrews, and, since the discovery of the tomb of Tutankhamen, it has been frequently assumed by some that there was some connection between the Aton cult and the religion of the Hebrews. According to one theory the Hebrews entered Egypt before the time of the eighteenth dynasty, and were in Egypt during the reign of Amenophis, who was influenced toward monotheism by Moses. This is a most improbable theory, as the Biblical references to the oppression of Israel in Egypt point to the time of the nineteenth dynasty rather than to the eighteenth. Others endeavor to show that Hebrew monotheism was derived from that of Egypt—a still less probable view. There appears to be no real connection between Hebrew monotheism and that of Amenophis. His Aton was the material sun disc; Jehovah was never so conceived.

(5) *Period of the Oppression and the Exodus.*—The statement in Exodus 1 : 11 that the Pharaoh who oppressed the Hebrews built the store-cites of Pithom and Raamses, indicates that this Pharaoh was Ramses II, for Naville, who excavated the site of Pithom (Egyptian *Pi-tum,* "House of the god Tum") in 1883, found much work of Ramses II there, including colossal statues of this king, and also found no evidence that there had been any town of importance on the site before.[9] The name of the other city, Raamses, also points to the same king, since Ramses I, the only other king of the name Egypt had known, reigned less than two years—a time insufficient for the building of a city. The Bible evidently refers, then, to Ramses II. Concerning Ramses II and his reign much is now known, as has been pointed out in § 6 (7) ; (see Fig. 10).

All through the nineteenth dynasty peoples from Syria were employed by the kings on public works. Among these was a people called '*prw*=Aperu or Apuri, which some have thought to be Hebrews. Whether the Hebrews are really mentioned in this

---

9 See Naville, *The Store-City of Pithom and the Route of the Exodus,* 4th ed., London, 1903.

way is doubted by others, for references to the '*prw* do not cease at
the time the Exodus of Israel must have occurred. They were employed by Ramses IV, of the twentieth dynasty, as late as 1165 B.C.

Much has been learned from archæology about Egyptian brick-
making, and it corresponds to the description of it given in Exodus.
We have pictures of men at the work. No one thought of burning
bricks in Egypt. The clay was moulded and dried in the sun.
Straw was mixed with the clay to increase its adhesive quality.
Naville says that some of the corners of some of the buildings at
Pithom were actually built of *bricks without straw*. (See Exod.
5:7–18; and Fig. 11.)

The name Pithom continued as one of the names of this store-
city or fortress until at least 250 B.C., for it is found on a pillar
which Ptolemy Philadelphus set up there, but side by side with
this name the place, all through its history, bore the name Thakut,
which is philologically the Egyptian equivalent of the Hebrew
Succoth. As this was the first station of the Hebrews when they
left Egypt (Exod. 12:37; 13:20; Num. 33:5, 6), Naville holds
that the Hebrews, after leaving the land of Goshen, must have
passed out on the south side of the Isthmus of Suez.

Petrie believes that in the winter of 1905–1906 he discovered the
city of Raamses [10] at Tell el-Retabeh, eight miles west of the site of
Pithom, on the Wady Tumilat. The objects found there show
that the site was occupied in the time of the Old Kingdom and onward, but as Ramses II and Ramses III both set up here statues
of themselves, and erected important buildings, and as the location
is the only one that fulfils the conditions of the city Raamses,
Petrie feels confident that this was the site. This view receives
some confirmation from the title of an officer who served here under
Ramses III, and who is called: "Chief archer, keeper of the granaries, keeper of the palace; chief archer, keeper of the granaries of
Arabia (or Syria)."

Merneptah, who is generally supposed to have been the Pharaoh
under whom the Exodus occurred, was not drowned in the Red Sea,
as some have wrongly inferred from Exodus 14:23–28, but was
duly buried like his predecessors. His mummy has been found
and is now in the Gizeh Museum at Cairo.

Merneptah in the fifth year of his reign set up a hymn of victory
on a pillar in a temple erected by his father, Ramses II. This
hymn, discovered by Petrie in 1896, is one of the two writings

10 See Petrie, *Hyksos and the Israelite Cities*, p. 28, f.

outside the Bible that mentions Israel by name. A part of it is translated in Part II, p. 376, where its bearing on the Exodus is discussed; (see Fig. 15).

For several seasons after 1919 Dr. Clarence S. Fisher devoted himself to the excavation of the palace of Merneptah at Memphis. In 1924 he brought to America many objects and even some rooms of the palace for installation in the University of Pennsylvania Museum in Philadelphia.

(6) *Campaign of Sheshonk I.*—The record on a wall of the temple of Karnak in Egypt by Sheshonk I, the Shiskak of 1 Kings 14:25, of his campaign in Palestine, confirms the statement of Kings and puts the whole campaign in a new perspective. It is treated in detail in Part II, p. 456 f.

(7) *Papyri Discovered at Elephantine.*—In recent years papyri discovered at Elephantine, an island in the First Cataract, reveal the existence of a Jewish colony there, which had a Jewish temple on the island. This colony was established at some time during the twenty-sixth dynasty, and was thus one of the earliest of those Jewish settlements in foreign countries which formed the Dispersion. A number of the records of these papyri, which relate the fortunes of this temple, the relations of this colony to their Egyptian neighbors and their knowledge of the law, are translated in Part II, p. 486 ff. The origin of the colony is also discussed there.

(8) *The Palace of Hophra.*—Hophra, of the twenty-sixth dynasty, was, as noted in § 6 (9), the king who lured Judah to her ruin. Petrie in 1907 discovered his palace at Memphis. The discovery makes Hophra seem a little more real.[11]

(9) *The Castle at Tahpanhes.*—We learn from Jeremiah 43:7, 8 and 44:1 that, after the destruction of Jerusalem, Jeremiah with many other Jews fled to Tahpanhes in Egypt and established a Jewish colony there. Jeremiah, as a symbolical act, was directed to hide some stones in the cement of the tiled area of the court of Pharaoh's house there (Jer. 43:8). Tahpanhes was the Daphne of the Greeks. It was on the site of the modern Tell Defenneh. This was in ancient times the easternmost city of the northern Delta. A hundred and fifty miles of desert stretched away to the east of it, until one came to the gardens of Gaza in Palestine. Petrie excavated Tell Defenneh in 1883–1884, and discovered the large castle there, which is probably the building in which Jeremiah buried his stones. This was the last act of Jeremiah's life of which

11 See Petrie, *The Palace of Apries*, London, 1909.

we have any record. He was then an old man and apparently died soon afterward, probably at Tahpanhes, certainly in Egypt.

(10) *The Jewish Temple at Leontopolis.*—Josephus tells us twice, once in his *Antiquities of the Jews,* Book XIII, Chapter III, and again in his *Wars of the Jews,* Book VII, Chapter X, that, when Jonathan, the Maccabee, was made high priest of the Jews, about 153 B.C., Onias, the son of Onias III, the deposed high priest, went to Egypt and obtained a grant of land and permission to build a Jewish temple. This land was in the region of the city of Bubastis, the nome where the cat goddess was sacred, and was accordingly called by the Greeks Leontopolis. There were at this time about as many Jews in Egypt as in Palestine, and doubtless Ptolemy VII thought to keep them more loyal by granting them a temple. He gave to Onias the revenues of a considerable territory for the support of the temple. Josephus tells us that Onias urged as a reason for the construction of this temple that it would be in fulfilment of the prophecy in Isaiah 19:19–22. Josephus goes on to say that this temple was built as an exact replica of the temple at Jerusalem and that it continued to exist as a place of worship until after the destruction of Jerusalem by Titus, when troubles caused by Jewish zealots led the Roman government to close the temple at Leontopolis and discontinue its worship; (see Fig. 12).

The site of this temple was at Tell el-Yehudiyeh, the "Tell of the Jewess," about 20 miles north of Cairo. This tell was excavated by Petrie in 1905–1906. He found there remains of the Jewish temple, which fully confirm the statements of Josephus. Not only the temple, but the form of the Jewish settlement, was made as far as possible a replica of the city of Jerusalem. One of the most interesting discoveries was a series of ovens for the roasting of Paschal lambs. Others of a similar character were found higher up in the mound, but those of the first series were most numerous. Petrie infers that the temple was dedicated by a great Passover Feast, to which Jews came in large numbers from throughout Egypt;[12] (see Fig. 13).

(11) *Papyri from Oxyrhynchus.*—About 123 miles south of Cairo and nine miles to the west of the Nile lies the town of Behnesa, which the Greeks called Oxyrhynchus, from a sharp-nosed fish which was sacred there. In 1897 and a number of seasons afterward, Grenfell and Hunt, two English explorers, examined the rubbish heaps of the old town. The inhabitants committed the

---

12 See Petrie, *Hyksos and the Israelite Cities,* p. 191, ff.

contents of their waste-baskets to the sands, and on account of the dry climate these have never decayed. Here were found the "Sayings of Jesus," some of the documents concerning the Roman census, and some of the letters translated in Part II, pp. 549 ff., 553 ff., as well as many remains of the works of classical authors. Similar documents have been found in other parts of Egypt, but no other site has yielded as many as Oxyrhynchus.

(12) *Discoveries in Nubia.*—During the winter of 1908–1909 MacIver explored at Karanog in Nubia for the University of Pennsylvania. He found in a cemetery many remains of the civilization of the Christian Nubians. They still called their queen Candace (see Acts 8:27), fed her on milk, and regarded obesity as an attribute of royalty. More will be known of the Nubians of this period when the inscriptions discovered at Karanog and at Shablul, deciphered by Mr. Griffith, have been more completely studied. The explorations of the English at Meroe have afforded a connected view of the development of this Nubian civilization. They found there the remains of an early period extending from about 650–400 B.C., which was followed by about a century when the royal residence was elsewhere, a middle period from 300 to 1 B.C., during the latter part of which Hellenic influences were felt, and a late period, from 1 to 350 A.D., during which Roman forms of art penetrated the country.[13]

13 See *Annals of Archaeology and Anthropology,* VII, Liverpool, 1914, pp. 1–10.

CHAPTER II

BABYLONIA AND ASSYRIA

THE LAND. THE PRESERVATION OF ANTIQUITIES. THE DISCOVERY OF AN-
TIQUITIES: By Benjamin of Tudela. By Rich. By Botta and Place. By Lay-
ard. By Loftus and Rawlinson. By Oppert and Rassam. By George Smith.
By Sarzec. By Peters, Ward, and Haynes. By Koldeway. By Andrae.
By de Morgan. By Harper and Banks. By Genouillac. By recent explorers.
THE DECIPHERMENT OF THE INSCRIPTIONS: By Niebuhr. By Grotenfend,
De Sacy, and Rawlinson. Babylonian column. Babylonian-Semitic. CHRON-
OLOGY. OUTLINE OF THE HISTORY: The prehistoric period. Sumerians. The
Pre-Babylonian period. "Stele of the Vultures." The early Babylonian period.
Kassites. Pashe dynasty. The early Assyrian period. The second Assyrian
period. The Neo-Babylonian period. The Persian period. The Greek and
Parthian periods. DISCOVERIES WHICH ILLUMINE THE BIBLE.

1. The Land.—The Mesopotamian Valley, as the great region
watered by the Tigris and the Euphrates Rivers is called, in many
respects resembles Egypt, although in other respects it differs
strikingly from Egypt. The country is like Egypt in that it is
formed by rivers; it differs from Egypt in that it has two rivers
instead of one. In late geologic time the Persian Gulf extended
far up toward the Mediterranean. All of what was Babylonia has
been formed by detritus (silt) brought down by the Tigris and the
Euphrates. The process of forming land is still going on. At the
head of the Persian Gulf about seventy feet a year is still formed
in this way, or a mile in about seventy-five years.

Both the Tigris and the Euphrates rise in the mountainous regions of Armenia, on opposite sides of the same range of mountains.
The melting of the snows on these mountains gives both rivers,
like the Nile, a period of overflow. As the source of the Tigris is
on the south side of the mountains, it begins to rise first. Its rise
begins about the first of March, its overflow is at its height in
May, and the water recedes in June or July. The Euphrates
begins to rise about the middle of March, continues to rise until
June, and does not recede to its ordinary level until September.
The soil thus formed is of rich materials, and the retreating flood
leaves it each year well watered and softened for agriculture. Here,
as in Egypt, one of the earliest civilizations of the world developed.

31

It was quite independent of that in Egypt, and consequently differed from the Egyptian in many respects. Unlike Egypt, Babylonia had a rainy season; nevertheless she was mainly dependent upon the overflow of the rivers for her irrigation and her fertility. As she possessed two rivers, her breadth was greater than that of Egypt, but she lacked the contiguity of protecting deserts, such as Egypt possessed. All through her history her fertile plains attracted the mountain dwellers of the East and the peoples of the West. Subject to frequent invasion by these, Babylonia had no long peaceful development such as Egypt enjoyed before the Hyksos invasion. From before the beginning of written history race mingled with race in this great valley, invasions were frequent, and the construction of permanent empires difficult.

The breadth of the Mesopotamian Valley affected also the building materials and the character of the art. Stone was much more difficult to obtain than in Egypt. Clay only was abundant. All buildings were consequently of brick. These structures were far less enduring than those in Egypt; their upper parts have disintegrated and buried the lower portions. Babylonian ruins are accordingly all under ground. The abundant clay was also used by the Babylonians as writing material. When baked, it proved far more enduring than the Egyptian papyrus. Thus, notwithstanding the general similarities which the Mesopotamian Valley presents to Egypt, its differences profoundly affected Babylonian history and Babylonian art.

2. The Preservation of Antiquities.—Babylonian cities were usually built on terraces of brick. The walls of the cities and their buildings were constructed of the same material. Refuse from the houses in these towns was always thrown out into the streets, so that, as the centuries passed, the streets were gradually elevated. The walls of the brick houses gradually became unstable in the lapse of time, and as the houses were repaired they were brought up to the level of the street. Consequently even in peaceful times the mounds on which the cities were built gradually grew higher. Most of these cities were at various times destroyed in warfare. Sometimes all the houses would be partially demolished and the site would be for a time practically uninhabited. When at length the place was repeopled, the top of the mound would be smoothed off and taken as the base of a new city. In this way through the many centuries of Babylonian history the sites of her cities have become great mounds. When these cities finally fell

MAP OF
BIBLE LANDS

SCALE OF MILES

0   200   400   800

Longitude   East   from   Greenwich

PETERS ENGRS., BOSTON

into ruin, the clay of the upper part of the walls gradually disintegrated in the weather and formed a coating of earth over the whole, which preserved the foundations of the walls both of cities and houses, as well as the inscribed clay, stone tablets, and the works of art buried underneath.

Connected with each Babylonian and Assyrian temple was a kind of staged tower, shaped in a general way like the stepped pyramid of Zoser at Sakkarah in Egypt. The Babylonians called these towers *Ziggurats*. As the bricks of these towers decayed, they formed in connection with the city mound a kind of hillock or peak, which varied in accordance with the height of the tower. The ruin of the *Ziggurat* at Birs Nimrud, the ancient Borsippa, is one of the most imposing to be seen in ancient Babylonia; it was long thought to be the original of the Tower of Babel (Gen. 11:9). It thus came about that no ancient temple of Babylonia, like some of those in Egypt, has remained above ground. Explorers have had to dig to discover antiquities; (see Fig. 22).

3. The Discovery of Antiquities:—

By Benjamin of Tudela.—The first man from western Europe who traveled through Babylonia and Assyria and noted their ruins was a Jew, Benjamin of Tudela, in the kingdom of Navarre. Leaving home about 1160 A.D., he traveled through Palestine, crossed the desert by way of Tadmor, visited Mosul opposite ancient Nineveh, and went southward to the site of Babylon. He also saw the ruin of Birs Nimrud, and believed it to be the Tower of Babel. Between the sixteenth and eighteenth centuries many other travelers visited the Mesopotamian Valley and described what they saw. Some of these, toward the close of the eighteenth century, described curious inscriptions which they had seen there on bricks. This information led the British East India Company in 1797 to instruct its resident at Bussorah, in southern Babylonia, to try to secure some of these inscriptions. This he did, and early in 1801 the first case of inscribed bricks arrived at the East India House in London, where they are still preserved.

By Rich.—Early in the nineteenth century Claude James Rich became resident of the East India Company at Bagdad. In his travels through the region he visited the mounds of Hillah (Babylon), Kouyunjik (Nineveh), and others, where he made some slight excavations, and found many inscriptions. The smaller ones he added to his collection, but many of them were of too monumental a character to be removed. Through these efforts a wide-spread interest was aroused.

By Botta and Place.—In 1842 the French government created a vice-consulate at Mosul, opposite the site of ancient Nineveh, and appointed to the position Paul Emil Botta, who had served as French consul at Alexandria in Egypt. Botta's mission was made in part archæological. In December, 1842, Botta began digging in the mound of Kouyunjik, the site of ancient Nineveh. Here he worked for three months. As he found only a few inscribed bricks and the fragments of some bas-reliefs, he became discouraged, and changed the field of his operations to a mound called Khorsabad, situated about fourteen miles to the northeast of Kouyunjik. Here he discovered a palace filled with interesting inscribed bas-reliefs made of alabaster, as well as a city about a mile in circumference. Under the corners of the palace and under the city gates were many inscribed cylinders of clay. This proved to be the palace and city built by Sargon, King of Assyria (722–705 B.C.), as his new capital. He named it Dur-Sharrukin, or Sargonsburgh. His name had so entirely disappeared from ancient literature that only one reference to him had survived, that in Isaiah 20 : 1, but here was his palace arising from the dust together with abundant annals of his reign. (See Part II, p. 466 ff.)

Botta and his successor, Victor Place, excavated intermittently at Khorsabad for ten years, uncovering the palace and making a plan of it, excavating the city walls and gates, studying the drainage of the ancient town, and fully describing the whole. Although a part of the antiquities found were lost in the Tigris by the wreck of a raft on which they were being floated down the river, a large collection reached France, where they are preserved in the Louvre.

By Layard.—The success of Botta fired the enthusiasm of Austen Henry Layard, a young Englishman of Huguenot descent, who began to excavate in 1845 at Nimrud, a mound further down the Tigris than Mosul, and the site of the Biblical Calah (Gen. 10 : 11). His money was at first furnished by a few friends, but as he soon discovered a royal palace there similar to the one Botta had unearthed at Khorsabad, the trustees of the British Museum commissioned him to excavate for them. He thus continued the work intermittently until 1849. During this time he spent most of his energy upon the mound of Kouyunjik, where he discovered another royal palace. This palace proved to be the work of Sennacherib, the son of Sargon (named in 2 Kings 18 : 13; Isa. 36), who built the one at Khorsabad, while the palace of Calah was, in its final form, the work of Esarhaddon, the son of Sennacherib. (See 2 Kings 19:37.) The palace at Nineveh had in turn been repaired by Esarhaddon's son, Assurbanipal.

By Loftus and Rawlinson.—As these excavations progressed, others were stimulated to make minor explorations. Thus in 1850 William Kennett Loftus carried on small excavations at the mound of Warka, the site of the Biblical Erech (Gen. 10:10), in southern Babylonia, from which he recovered important antiquities. From 1851–1855 the oversight of English excavations was entrusted to Sir Henry C. Rawlinson, the British consul-general at Bagdad. Under his direction J. E. Taylor, British vice-consul at Bassorah, made an excavation at the mound of Mugheir, the site of Ur of the Chaldees, where he unearthed important inscriptions. At the same time Loftus was traveling about Babylonia collecting antiquities.

By Oppert and Rassam.—In 1852 a French expedition under the direction of Jules Oppert reached Babylonia. Oppert made important excavations at Hillah, the site of the city of Babylon, and at Birs Nimrud, the ancient Borsippa. In 1852 Hormuzd Rassam, who had been one of Layard's helpers, continued under Rawlinson's direction the excavation at Nineveh. This work continued until 1854; Rassam had the good fortune to find, in a part of the mound previously untouched, still another palace. This was the palace of Assurbanipal, the last of Assyria's great kings, who ruled from 668 to 626 B.C., and who collected here a great library. This library Rassam discovered, and as it contained every variety of Babylonian and Assyrian literature, including dictionaries and grammatical exercises, it was one of the most important archæological discoveries ever made. During the last part of the time Rassam was succeeded by Loftus. Finally, in the autumn of 1854, Rawlinson himself undertook an excavation at Birs Nimrud, and unearthed some important inscriptions of Nebuchadrezzar II, King of Babylon, 604–562 B.C. (See 2 Kings 24, 25.)

After this the interest in excavation waned for a time, while scholars were busy reading the tablets already found.

By George Smith.—In December, 1872, George Smith, an employee of the British Museum, announced that among the tablets from Nineveh he had found an account of the flood which closely resembled that in the Bible. This aroused so much interest that the proprietors of the London *Daily Telegraph* contributed money

to send George Smith to Assyria to explore further the mounds
there. George Smith thus led two expeditions of exploration, one
in 1873 and the other in 1874. He extended the trenches of his
predecessors at Nineveh and discovered many more important
inscriptions. In 1876 he was on his way to Mesopotamia for the
third time, when he died of fever at Aleppo. The British Museum
immediately secured the services of Rassam again, who during
that year and 1877 extended the work at Kouyunjik (Nineveh)
and also found a palace of Shalmaneser III, King of Assyria, 860–
824 B.C., at a mound called Balawat, situated to the east of Kouyunjik.

By Sarzec.—Meantime, the interest of France was again aroused,
and in 1877 her consul at Bassorah, Ernest de Sarzec, began the
excavation of Telloh, a mound in southern Babylonia, which turned
out to be the site of Shirpurla or Lagash, one of the oldest and
most important of the ancient cities of Babylonia. Work was
carried on at intervals here by Sarzec until his death in 1901, and
then by Gaston Croz. In 1928 exploration of the site was continued
by H. de Genouillac, who found that the place was occupied in the
earliest period by a people whose pottery resembled that of El-
Obeid and Susa.[1] The results have not received the popular acclaim
accorded to the discoveries of Botta and Layard, but scientifically
they are equally important. Some of the oldest examples of
Babylonian art have been discovered, as well as many thousands
of tablets. One room alone contained an archive of business documents estimated at thirty thousand. Much of our knowledge of
the history of early Babylonia is derived from material found at
Telloh.

By Peters, Ward, and Haynes.—In 1884 America began to take
an interest in Babylonian exploration. This was due largely to
the initiative of Dr. John P. Peters, then Professor of Hebrew in
the University of Pennsylvania, later Rector of St. Michael's
Church, New York. Through his efforts Miss Catherine L. Wolfe,
of New York, contributed the money to defray the expenses of
an expedition to Babylonia for a preliminary survey. This expedition was led by Dr. William Hayes Ward, Editor of the New
York *Independent*. It spent the winter of 1884–1885 in Mesopotamia, made many observations of the various mounds, and collected some archæological material. Dr. Peters continued his
efforts, and as a result a fund was raised in Philadelphia to defray

1 Cf. H. de Genouillac, *Fouilles de Tello*, Paris, 1934.

the expenses of an excavation in the interest of the University of
Pennsylvania. This expedition set out in 1888 under the direction of Dr. Peters. The site chosen for the exploration was Nuffar,
about sixty miles to the southeast of Babylon. The work was continued for two seasons under the direct control of Dr. Peters.
After an interruption of three years the work was resumed under
the general direction of Dr. Peters, with Dr. John H. Haynes as
Field Director. Dr. Haynes, in the most self-sacrificing and heroic
manner, continued the work both summer and winter until February, 1896, laying bare many of the features of the ancient city of
Nippur, which had occupied the site, and discovering many inscribed tablets. While this work was in progress Prof. Herman
V. Hilprecht became nominal head of the expedition on account
of the removal of Dr. Peters to New York. A fourth expedition
under the guidance of Dr. Haynes began work at Nuffar (Nippur)
in February, 1899, and worked until March, 1900. During this
work Dr. Haynes discovered a large archive of tablets, the exact
number of which is variously estimated. The find was similar to
that made by Sarzec at Telloh (see Figs. 16 and 17).

Nuffar, the ancient Nippur, was one of the oldest centers of
Babylonian civilization, and the work of the Americans there was,
for our knowledge of the history of ancient Babylonia, next in
importance to that done by the French at Telloh. A large number of the tablets discovered at Nippur are now in the University
of Pennsylvania Museum in Philadelphia. Meantime, the Turkish
government had undertaken on its own account an excavation at
Abu Haba, the site of the ancient Sippar in northern Babylonia.
The direction of the work was committed to the oversight of the
French Assyriologist, Père Scheil, and the work was carried on in
the early part of the year 1894. Much interesting material was
brought to light.

By Koldewey.—Also during this decade a new Society, the
Orient-Gesellschaft, had been formed in Berlin for the purpose of
excavation. This Society began in 1899 the excavation of the
great mound which covered the ruins of the ancient city of Babylon.
The work was committed to the direction of Dr. Robert Koldewey,
who carried it steadily forward until the Great War. Kolde-
wey laid bare at Babylon a number of the great works of King
Nebuchadrezzar—the magnificent walls with which he surrounded
Babylon, and the palace and temples with which he adorned it.
As the work at Babylon progressed, Koldewey made a number of

minor excavations in smaller mounds of Babylonia. During the
season of 1912–1913 Dr. Julius Jordan undertook, under Dr.
Koldewey's general direction, an excavation at Warka, the Biblical
Erech, where Loftus had dug sixty years before. A part of the
great temple of Ishtar was uncovered by Dr. Jordan, together with
a portion of the city wall and many houses. Many tablets were also
found, some of them having been written as late as the Seleucid
and Parthian periods, 312–50 B.C. (see Fig. 18).

By Andrae.—While the excavation at Babylon was in progress,
the *Orient-Gesellschaft* also conducted another at Kalah-Sherghat,
on the Tigris, in ancient Assyria. This is the site of the city of
Ashur, from which the country of Assyria took its name. (Cf.
Gen. 10 : 10, 11.) The work was under the direction of Dr. Andrae
and was in progress from 1902 to 1914. Temples and palaces were
uncovered, and inscriptions from every period of Assyrian history
were found. Objects were discovered which connect the founding
of the city with immigrants from Lagash in southern Babylonia.

By de Morgan.—In 1900 a French expedition began the excavation of Susa, in ancient Elam, the Shushan of the Bible. (See
Neh. 1 : 1 ; Esther 1 : 2, etc., and Dan. 8 : 2.) This work was under
the direction of J. de Morgan. While Susa is not in Babylonia,
the excavations here added greatly to our knowledge of Babylonian
history and life, for during the first two seasons of the excavation,
two inscribed stone pillars were discovered, which the ancient
Elamites had at some time taken as trophies of war from the
Babylonians. One of these was an inscription of Manishtusu,
King of Kish, who ruled about 2700 B.C., and the other the pillar
which contained the laws of Hammurabi, the most important single
document relating to Babylonian life that is known to us. (See
Part II, Chapter XIII.)

By Harper and Banks.—During the year 1903–1904 the University of Chicago sent an expedition to Babylonia. The expenses
were borne by a contribution from John D. Rockefeller. The
late Prof. Robert Harper was Scientific Director of the expedition,
and Dr. Edgar J. Banks, Field Director. The work was conducted at the mound of Bismya, which proved to be the site of the
ancient city of Adab, one of the oldest Babylonian cities, which
seems not to have been occupied since about 2600 B.C. Many
interesting finds were made, including a statute of a king, Lugaldaudu, and many tablets. Friction with the Turkish Government
brought the expedition to an untimely close, and owing to the

same cause the tablets discovered are hoarded at Constantinople and have been given to the world only in part.

By Genouillac.—During the early part of the year 1914 a French expedition, under the direction of H. de Genouillac, excavated at Ukhaimir, the site of ancient Kish. They discovered the great *Ziggurat* of the temple of Zamama, the god of Kish, and other important finds.

By Thompson and Hall.—In the spring of 1918 the British Government sent the Assyriologist, R. Campbell Thompson,[2] who had been during the Great War serving the government in Mesopotamia, to make some excavations at Abu Sharain, the site of ancient Eridu in southern Babylonia. Not a great deal of time was devoted to the work, but a number of trenches were sunk in different parts of the mound and important information gained. Babylonian inscriptions long ago led us to believe that Eridu was one of the oldest, if not the oldest city in Babylonia. Inscriptions also indicated that it was situated on the shore of the Persian Gulf. Mr. Thompson's discoveries confirm the first of these beliefs, but indicate that the race which first inhabited this site was neither Semitic nor Sumerian, but akin to the Elamites and the people of Anau, east of the Caspian Sea, where Pumpelly made his noteworthy excavation.[3] This is proved by the discovery of pottery in the lowest levels identical in type with that found at Susa and Anau.

Thompson's exploration seems to prove, however, that Eridu did not lie on the shore of the Persian Gulf. At almost every level of the mound he found the shells of a fresh-water mussel which the people had used as an article of food. This indicates that the city was on a fresh-water lagoon formed by the overflow of the Euphrates. The mound appears to have been deserted about 2000 B.C.

Captain Thompson's expedition worked at Abu Sharain but about two months. When the summer heat came on, the work was discontinued. It was taken up again in the spring of 1919 by the British Museum, this time the excavator being Mr. H. R. Hall. Mr. Hall devoted his work mainly to the mound of Mugheir, the site of Ur of the Chaldees, though he also extended the trenches of Thompson at Abu Sharain. At Ur his work confirmed that of

2 Thompson's report of his work is published in *Archaeologia, Miscellaneous Tracts Relating to Antiquity, published by the Society of Antiquaries,* of London, Vol. XX, 1920, pp. 101–144.
3 See *Explorations in Turkestan,* by Raphael Pumpelly, Washington, 1908.

Loftus and Taylor, exposing more of the great temple of the moon-god of Ur, and at Eridu his work similarly confirmed that of Thompson. The most noteworthy achievement of the expedition was the uncovering of a temple of the early Sumerian period at Tell el-Obeid, four or five miles southwest of Ur. Here Mr. Hall found remains of a temple rebuilt by the kings of Lagash about 3000 B.C. and also some remarkable lions. The heads were cast in bitumen, filled with straw and clay, over which a covering of bronze had been laid—a remarkable piece of work for a date so early.[4]

By Woolley.—An excavation at Ur, and at Tell el-Obeid was carried on for two seasons (1922–1923 and 1923-1924) by Mr. C. L. Woolley, who afterward conducted a joint expedition for the British Museum and the University of Pennsylvania Museum of Philadelphia. Mr. Woolley exposed more of the temple of the moon-god—pavements and walls—built by Nebuchadrezzar; and walls and ziggurat constructed by kings of Ur have been further uncovered; also he discovered a deposit of jewelry and a statue of one of the rulers of Lagash, dating from about 2900 B.C. (See Figs. 306, 307.) He found evidence of the existence at Ur of a court with a colonnade which was constructed by Kurigalzu, in the fourteenth century B.C. It was not previously known that the Babylonians used colonnades in building. At El Obeid he found additional examples of Sumerian work of surprisingly high quality, including flowers carved in stone, and a frieze of human and animal figures, dating from about 3000 B.C. or earlier.[5]

At Ur Mr. Woolley, during eight seasons, continued his excavation. The Ziggurat of the Temple of the Moon god (Nannar or Sin) was explored, and a temple of Nin-gal, his consort, was also discovered.[6] One of the interesting features of this discovery was a large and well-equipped kitchen adjoining the shrine, where there were great ovens for roasting meat and also places for cauldrons in which meat could be boiled. The discovery recalls vividly the account of the preference of Eli's sons for roast meat instead of boiled, and their attempt to modify Israelitish sacrificial customs. (1 Sam. 2:12–17.)

It is not possible here to enumerate all the remarkable features of the history of this ancient city which have come to light during

4 See *Proceedings of the Society of Antiquaries,* London, 1919–20, pp. 22–44; *Journal of Egyptian Archaeology,* VIII, 241, ff., and IX, 177, ff.
5 See H. R. Hall and C. L. Woolley, *Ur Excavations, Volume I, Al-Ubaid,* Oxford, 1927. For the frieze, see pp. 88 ff., and 111 ff. and pl. XXXI.
6 Cf. *Museum Journal,* Sept., 1926, pp. 245 ff.

these years of exploration. In one area the trenches were carried down to the virgin soil. (See Fig. 322.) At the bottom of this area there were found the burials and pottery of a race that inhabited the country before the coming of the Sumerians, the implements of whose civilization were simple and crude. Above these graves Woolley found a stratum, eight feet thick, of a deposit of pure river silt, which showed that, after these burials were made, this part of the site was submerged for a considerable time. This submergence Woolley identified with the biblical Deluge and believed that he had discovered archæological evidence of the Flood. Mackay and Langdon, excavating at Kish, found a similar stratum, which they, in like manner, took to have been deposited at the time of the Deluge. There is, in reality, no evidence that these deposits of silt mean more than that for a time the Euphrates and Tigris changed their beds and flowed for a time over parts of Ur and Kish that had previously been inhabited. The Euphrates and Tigris, like the great rivers of China, have changed their beds many times. Nippur, Erech, and other cities of Babylonia were once, as is well known, situated on the Euphrates, which now flows in quite a different channel far to the west of them, and there is no real proof that either of the beds of silt in question were deposited at the time of the flood described in the Bible. Frankfort, indeed, has since shown that, from the evidence of the pottery found above and below the strata of silt on the two sites, the two inundations did not occur at the same time, and were not even in the same century! They could not, then, have been the Biblical flood. They are evidence of a temporary submergence of the two sites by changes in the courses of the rivers.[7]

A much more astonishing discovery at Ur is that of some royal tombs above this stratum of silt. The tomb of the king had been plundered of most of its treasures, but that of the queen, whose name was Shub-ad, was almost intact.[8] The skeleton of the queen, her headdress, her golden cups and vessels, the seal bearing her name, her harps, and many other implements were recovered.

Most astonishing, however, was the discovery that queen Shub-ad had not been buried alone, but that ten women—her attendants—had been slain and buried with her, apparently to wait on her in the other world. One of them was her harpist; for her body was found near a harp. A chariot drawn by two

7 See C. L. Woolley, *Ur of the Chaldees*, New York, 1930, and for later discoveries, the *Museum Journal, XXII*, (1931), 247–282.
8 *Archaeology and the Sumerian Problem*, Chicago, 1932.

asses, driven by a muleteer, was also placed in the tomb; the bones of the muleteer and of the asses gave mute, but eloquent, testimony of the gruesome efforts to provide for the queen's comfort in the after-life. Outside the tomb, in the sloping trench which led down to it, were the skeletons of five men, whose equipment indicated that they had been killed and placed there as guards to prevent intruders from disturbing the queen and her ladies. Other skeletons indicated that some twenty-five people were compelled to accompany the queen on her last journey. The king (whose name Woolley believes to have been A-bar-gi) had at least three people buried with him as attendants in his tomb, and in a pit near by were the bodies of sixty-two others who are believed to have been his servants, and to have been buried at the same time. It was known that in other parts of the world, as, for example, in Egypt and in China, servants and attendants had in early times been put to death and buried with a nobleman, or a royal person, but the discovery of these graves is the first intimation that we have had that such a custom existed in Babylonia.

In a neighboring tomb the golden helmet of another pre-historic king, Mes-kalam-dim [9] was found. From this early stratum there also came an inlaid standard of exquisite workmanship on which two scenes were depicted. The lower scene portrayed a battle with enemies; the upper, a sacrifice of thanksgiving for victory. (See Fig. 324.) Among the many interesting discoveries was the image of a ram standing on his hind feet, with his front feet touching an upright standard, from which flower-bearing branches extend on either side. (See Fig. 323.) Woolley has seen in this (fancifully, we think) a reminder of the "ram caught in a thicket" which Abraham sacrificed instead of Isaac.[10] (See Gen. 22: 13.)

By Mackay, Langdon, and Watelin.—In 1923 the work at Ukheimir, begun by de Genouillac before the war, was resumed by a joint expedition of the Ashmoleum Museum, of Oxford, and the Field Museum, of Chicago. Professor Stephen Langdon was made scientific director of the expedition, and Captain E. Mackay and L. C. Watelin field directors. The results are gradually being given to the public. A Sumerian palace, rebuilt in the Assyrian period, was uncovered and a considerable number of graves explored. The anthropological material which some of them con-

9 Woolley calls the king Mes-kalam-dug; Gadd, Mes-kalam-shar; but the writer believes that the last sign of the name should be read *dim*.
10 See further, Woolley in the *Museum Journal*, XXII, 1932, 193–248; also his *Ur Excavations*, II, Philadelphia, 1934.

tained has been published by the Field Museum.[11] A small publication was made in 1924 in a book by Langdon, with a discussion by Dr. L. H. Dudley Buxton.[12] A temple of the Sumerian goddess, Ninkhursag, had been excavated [13] and tablets from various periods found, including one from Marduk-apal-iddina, the Merodach-baladan of the Bible. (See Isa. 39: 1.) A tablet in very archaic picture writing was also found. The stratum of silt, believed by Langdon to be evidence of the Flood, has already been discussed.

One of the most significant discoveries of this expedition was made at Jemdet Nasr, a mound seventeen miles from Ukheimir, where about two hundred tablets in a very archaic script—a script which closely approached picture writing—were found.[14] Of particular significance were the seal impressions on these tablets, the style of the art of which resembled the decorations on the pottery from the second stratum from the bottom of the mound at Susa. These have been thought to betoken a racial connection between the makers of these tablets and the inhabitants of the second stratum of the Elamite capital.

By Chiera, Pfeiffer, and Starr.—In 1925 Professor Edward Chiera, then Annual Professor of the American Schools of Oriental Research at Bagdad, working jointly for that school and for the Department of Antiquities of the Government at Iraq, began excavations at Yorgan Tepe, near Kirkuk, in the mountainous region southeast of ancient Nineveh. During that short season he cleared the house of one of the prosperous citizens of the place, and secured about a thousand clay tablets, which were records of business transactions. From these it was learned that the name of this place about 1500 to 1200 B.C. was Nuzi; and that it was occupied by a people who, though they employed the Assyrian language, were not Semites. The seal impressions on the tablets revealed a hitherto unknown type of art.[15]

In 1927 a joint expedition of the Bagdad School and Harvard University was organized, with Professor Chiera as field director to continue the work, and four seasons were spent in further exploration of the site. Chiera directed the work during the season

11 Ernest Mackay, *Report on the Excavation of the "A" Cemetery at Kish, Mesopotamia*, Chicago, 1935; and *A Sumerian Palace and the "A" Cemetery at Kish, Mesopotamia*, Part II, Chicago, 1929.
12 In Langdon's *Excavation at Kish*, Paris, 1924.
13 Watelin and Langdon's *Excavations at Kish*, Paris, 1930.
14 Published by Langdon, in *Oxford Editions of Cuneiform Texts*, Vol. VII, Oxford, 1928.
15 See Chiera, "A New Factor in the History of the Ancient East," *Annual of the American Schools of Oriental Research*, VI, (1926), pp. 75–92.

of 1927–28, Professor Robert H. Pfeiffer of Harvard University, during the season of 1928–29, and Mr. Richard F. S. Starr, of the Fogg Museum, Harvard, during the seasons of 1929–31.

In addition to the house excavated by Chiera a large palace was unearthed, as well as many other smaller buildings. Although the structures had been destroyed by fire when the place was sacked, portions of frescoes of a type previously unknown were recovered, together with many additional tablets and works of art. A study of the documents found identify the inhabitants with the Hurrians, who are mentioned in the Hittite texts from Boghaz Koi. Among these there is a letter from Saushatar,[16] the first known king of Mitanni, who lived shortly after 1500 B.C., to the governor of Nuzi. This letter definitely dates the stratum excavated. The documents also show that the region was called Arrapkha. This was the Arrapachitis of Ptolemy, and the Arpachshad of Genesis 10:22 and 11:10–12. The excavators confined their work mainly to the Hurrian stratum of the mound, and by so doing brought to light for the first time the remains of a Hurrian city.

During his last campaign, Mr. Starr sunk a shaft down to virgin soil in one part of the mound to ascertain the nature of the earlier occupations. He identified eleven strata before virgin soil was reached. The lowest level of occupation furnished pottery similar to that of stratum II, of Susa. In one of the intermediate strata an archive of about two hundred Sumerian tablets, dating from 2500–2300 B.C. was found. One of these was the oldest known map yet discovered.[17]

By Speiser.—In the spring of 1927 Professor E. A. Speiser, of the University of Pennsylvania, then Annual Professor in the American Schools of Oriental Research at Bagdad, made an archæological survey of the southeastern portion of ancient Assyria. Near the conclusion of his work [18] he was impressed by the archæological importance of the mound of Tepe Gawra, about four miles northeast of Khorsabad. The mound was comparatively small in circumference at the base, but high, and the sides were steep. The height indicated long occupation. Potsherds found at the bottom resembled those of the earliest strata at Susa, while those at the top bore testimony that the mound

---

16 For the letter see E. A. Speiser in the *Journal of the American Oriental Society,* XLIX, pp. 269–275.

17 Cf. Pfeiffer in *Bulletin* No. 42 of the American Schools of Oriental Research (April, 1931), T. J. Meek, *Old Akkadian, Sumerian and Cappadocian Texts from Nuzi,* Cambridge, 1935.

18 Cf. *Annual of the American Schools of Oriental Research,* IX (1929), p. 22 ff.

had ceased to be inhabited before 2000 B.C. In October of the same year Professor Speiser returned and, with a small sum of money furnished by Dropsie College, sunk a trial trench up the side of the mound from bottom to top, crossing this near the top by another.[19] This preliminary sounding revealed that in successive ages the place had been the home of three distinct civilizations, each of which had contributed several strata to the tell. The latest of these civilizations belonged to the early bronze age, and was apparently contemporary with that at El-Obeid, 3250–2750 B.C.[20] Six strata at the top of the mound were occupied by them; the mound then became too small and too pointed for further habitation. Among the numerous figurines from the sixth stratum are figurines of horses, which show that the horse was well known in Mesopotamia soon after the year 3000 B.C., a thousand years earlier than was hitherto thought.[21] The people who left the remains of the next oldest civilization had apparently migrated from southern Babylonia; for they built with clay bricks in a country where stone is abundant, and where those who preceded them and came after them constructed their buildings of stone. The use of bricks must have been due to having previously lived in a country like Babylonia, where no other building material is known.[22] Further, there was found in their temple a clay phallus on which the marks of circumcision were imitated.[23] It seems, therefore, that the inhabitants of Gawra of this period were Semites who had lived in Babylonia. As their tools were wholly those of the late Stone age, they must have left Babylonia before the coming of the Sumerians. The people who occupied Gawra during the earlier centuries of its history appear to have been kindred to those who made the pottery of the earliest strata of Susa.[24]

During the years 1930–32 Professor Speiser returned to the further exploration of the mound as director of an expedition financed jointly by the Bagdad School, the Museum of the University of Pennsylvania, and Dropsie College. He systematically uncovered it, stratum by stratum, from the top downward. The conclusions suggested by his first brief excavation were confirmed. The sixth stratum had been occupied by a people who used copper weapons. The eighth stratum (the seventh was very attenuated)

19 *Ibid.*, p. 55, Fig. 1.
20 *Ibid.*, pp. 35 ff., and 49 ff.
21 *Bulletin*, No. 43, p. 20.
22 *Ibid.*, p. 47 f.
23 *Ibid.*, p. 86, Figs. 104, 105.
24 Cf. *Annual of the American Schools of Oriental Research*, Vol. IX, pp. 28 ff. and 39 f.

had housed a purely stone-age civilization. The difference was great. How wicked a stone-age people thought those who could employ metal weapons is revealed in the stories of Cain and Lamech in Genesis, ch. 4. In the eighth stratum from the top he uncovered a remarkable prehistoric Stone Age city, containing houses and a temple of stone, in the construction of which the arch and recessed walls were employed. The houses had windows and niches. There were streets and a market place.[28] About the middle of this stratum a remarkable seal, depicting a man and woman, and a serpent, was found. It strongly suggests that the story of the temptation (Gen. 3) is very old. (See Fig. 176½.)[29]

Simultaneously with the excavation of Gawra, Speiser, during these years, carried on another excavation at Tell Billah, six or eight miles to the south of Tepe Gawra. Here he unearthed a palace of Ashurnasirpal (884–860 B.C.) and, in a lower stratum, remains of a Hurrian town. An archive of texts from about 1100 B.C. were also found. The work was continued by Mr. Bache, simultaneously with his work at Tepe Gawra.[30]

From 1932–1936 the work at Tepe Gawra and Tell Billah was carried on with Mr. Charles Bache as Field Director. The mound was cleared to the thirteenth stratum, revealing most important features of prehistoric stone-age civilizations. Unique among these were a temple in stratum nine and a round structure—a combination citadel and temple—in the eleventh stratum.[31] See Figure 332. Professor Speiser took personal charge of the work again in Nov., 1936, and carried it on until March, 1937. Strata XIII to XVI were explored and on one side of the mound a trench was sunk to virgin soil.[32] Here a cistern was uncovered containing crude potsherds of a variety more primitive than any yet found in the parts of the mound uncovered. The most important discovery of the season was an acropolis in stratum XIII containing three temples. Their structure and architecture prove that the culture that produced them was quite different from that which produced the round temple of stratum XI. The buildings of strata XIV, XV, and XVI, as well as their pottery were again still different. The

28 *Bulletin of the American Schools of Oriental Research*, No. 45 (Feb. 1932), p. 34.
29 A full presentation of the material is given in E. A. Speiser's *Excavations at Tepe Gawra*. Philadelphia, 1935.
30 See *Bulletin of the American Schools of Oriental Research*, Nos. 41, 42, 45, 46, 49, and 50; also Speiser in the *Museum Journal*, XXII, 1932, 249–308.
31 See *Bulletin of the American Schools of Oriental Research*, April, 1934, 14–18 and April, 1936, 10–14.
32 *Bulletin of the American Schools of Oriental Research*, No. 66 (April, 1937), pp. 2–19.

bottom of the shaft in which virgin soil was reached is 95 feet below the level of the top of the mound before excavation. How many centuries it took to accumulate this depth of the remains of human habitation, we can only guess, but the beauty and delicacy of the pottery as well as of the architectural remains in stratum XIII —a stratum dating hundreds of years before the discovery of metal tools—no longer permits us to regard the men of the Stone Age as uncivilized.

By Waterman.—In 1927 Professor Leroy Waterman, of the University of Michigan, then Annual Professor in the American Schools of Oriental Research in Bagdad, began the excavation of Tell Umar, in Iraq. Upon his return to America arrangements were made to carry on the work for a series of years under the joint auspices of the University of Michigan and the Toledo Museum of Art, and the exploration was systematically carried on every winter up to 1932. The strata explored belong to the time of the Seleucid and Parthian kingdoms, but inscribed stones from the Sumerian period prove that it was the site of the Opis of the early Babylonian period. It was also the site of Seleucia of the Hellenistic time.[33] During the winter of 1936–37 the work was renewed.

By Jordan and Nöldeke.—In 1912, Dr. Julius Jordan began the excavation of Warka, the biblical Erech, for the German Orient-Gesellschaft, but in 1914 his work was interrupted by the war. After the war it was resumed and was directed by Dr. Jordan until his appointment as Director of the Department of Antiquities at Bagdad, in 1931. Since that time the excavation has been carried on by Dr. Nöldeke. Erech was one of the oldest cities of Babylonia and flourished far down into the Hellenistic period.[34] As one approaches its mounds from the west they look like mountains. As yet the excavators have dug principally in the upper strata, and have traced the construction of some of the important temples of this time. At one point, however, they have sunk a shaft more than seventy feet to the virgin soil, thus laying bare successive strata back to 4000 B.C.

By Baron von Oppenheim.—In 1899 Baron Max von Oppenheim, then connected with the German consulate in Cairo, in traveling through Mesopotamia, discovered on the river Chabur

33 See *Preliminary Report upon the Excavations at Tell Umar, Iraq,* by Leroy Waterman, Ann Arbor, 1931.
34 See Julius Jordan, *Uruk-Warka,* Leipzig, 1928, and *Mitteilungen der deutschen Orient-Gesellschaft,* No. 66 (April, 1928).

a mound called Tell Halaf, which seemed to him a favorable site
to excavate. Years later, in 1911, he returned and began its
exploration. For two seasons, until 1913, the work was carried
on; then came the Great War. It was not until 1927 that the
Baron was able to resume his work on the mound; it was then
carried forward until 1929.[35] The city which occupied the site
was one of the centers of the life of that central Asiatic people
who made the black and red pottery. They continued to occupy
it until after the fall of the kingdom of Mitanni, about 1300 B.C.
During the later years of the settlement it was in the heart of the
Hurrian kingdom of Mitanni. The site is almost on the direct line
from Nineveh to Harran, but much nearer to Harran than to
Nineveh. Many massive stone monuments of the art of these
people were recovered, as well as much pottery. Baron Oppenheim has collected this in his residence in Berlin, which he has
turned into a Tell Halaf Museum. This he has incorporated and
endowed, for perpetual preservation.

By Chiera and Frankfort. In 1928 the Oriental Institute of
the University of Chicago entered the field of Mesopotamian exploration. During the season of 1928-9 the late Professor Chiera
renewed the exploration of Khorsabad, which Botta and Place had
partially explored during the years 1843-1855. In a brilliantly conducted campaign Chiera rescued what is believed to have been the
best preserved reliefs in Sargon's palace. In 1929 Dr. Henri Frankfort became Field Director and spent a part of each season until
1936 on the site.[36] He has made some further explorations
in Sargon's palace, excavated the one gate to the city which the
French explorers did not excavate, located another large building
apart from the palace, tried in vain to find remains of some of the
private houses of the ancient inhabitants, and recovered a list of the
Assyrian kings from about 2400 B.C. onward. It is reported that
the names only of the earliest kings are given, but to the names of
the others there is added the number of years that they reigned. Like
other records on clay, the list is broken here and there. It is hoped
that the list will be published during 1937.

In prospecting to discover a mound in Babylonia that the Oriental
Institute might properly excavate, Professor Chiera had noted that
the mounds east of the Diyala, a river which empties into the Tigris
about fifteen miles below Bagdad, a region now desert for lack of

---

35 See his volume *Der Tell Halaf*, Leipzig, 1931.
36 See H. Frankfort, *Tell Asmar, Khafaje and Khorsbad*, Chicago, 1934, pp. 80–102.

water, contained numerous mounds on the surface of which fragments of inscribed bricks lay. Tell Asmar, about fifty miles northeast of Bagdad is the highest of these, and in 1930 Dr. Frankfort
began its excavation. From that date to 1936 the work proceeded
season by season. Two large structures were uncovered, each of
which served as a combination temple and palace. (For one of these
see Fig. 334.) One of these was built about 2300 B.C. and the other
about 2600 B.C. Inscribed bricks disclosed the name of the ancient
city, of which these buildings were a part, to have been Ashnunak.[37]
or, according to another reading, Eshnunna, a city of which we
previously had knowledge through inscriptions, but the situation of
which was unknown. It was founded by the pre-Sumerian occupants of this region. Seals and various objects connected with the
civilization, including some children's toys were also found. One
of the most interesting discoveries consisted of some inscribed seals
from India, identical in type with those found at Harappa and
Mohenjo-daro in the Indus Valley. These seals are witness to the
existence at this period of commerce between Mesopotamia and
India.[38]

At Khafaje, a mound near the eastern bank of the Diyala about
fifteen miles east of Bagdad, excavations were also carried on
simultaneously with those at Tell Asmar. An important building
was unearthed not far from the surface of the mound, the corners
of which were all curved. It turned out to be a temple. A part of
the structure was of plano-convex bricks, characteristic of the
Sumerians. An inscribed vase, dating from the reign of Uru-
mush, king of Akkad and Kish, was found, which shows that the
building was in existence about 2700 B.C. Fragments of statuary
exhibiting Sumerian characteristics were also found, and parts of
a square building were also uncovered. The ancient name of the
site has not yet been determined.[39]

After the conclusion of the work at Tell Asmar in 1936 a sounding was made in Tell Agrab [40] about ten miles to the northeast of
Tell Asmar, where a complex of buildings containing three temples
was uncovered. Some statuettes were found, the noses of which
exhibit in a somewhat exaggerated way the characteristics of that

37 See G. A. Barton, *The Royal Inscriptions of Sumer and Akkad*, New Haven, 1929,
p. 152 f.
38 See below, p. 53, and the references there given.
39 For the work at these sites see Frankfort, *Tell Asmar and Khafaje*, Chicago, 1932,
and *Tell Asmar, Khafaje, and Khorsabad*, Chicago, 1934.
40 Cf. *Archiv für Orientforschung*, XI (1936), pp. 263, 264.

central Asiatic stock from which the original Hittite-Hurrian type sprang.

By King and Thompson at Kouyunjik.—In 1903 the British Museum resumed the exploration of the site of ancient Nineveh. During the first season the work was carried on by the late Dr. L. W. King, who was joined the next year by Mr. R. Campbell Thompson. Thompson pursued the work a third season, in 1905, after which it was interrupted until 1927, when it was resumed. After that date he continued work up to the year 1932. An important temple of the god, Nabu, was discovered and explored.[41] and among other valuable finds, it should be noted that in the lower strata colored pottery of the pre-Sumerian type found in Babylonia, at Tell Billah, Tepe Gawra, and in Elam was recovered.

By Schmidt at Fara.—Fara is the site of the ancient Surippak, the home of the Babylonian hero of the Flood. Some objects were found there by Arabs while the expedition of the University of Pennsylvania was excavating at Nippur, and sold to the Americans. In 1902-03 Dr. Andrae, then of the staff of Koldewey's expedition at Babylon, sunk a trench in one stratum of the mound and found many interesting tablets, from the period shortly after 3000 B.C. In 1931 the Museum of the University of Pennsylvania secured the right to excavate the site, and spent two months in making preliminary soundings to discover something of the character and history of the mound.[42] Two main strata were discovered in the part of the mound through which shafts were sunk to the virgin soil. The upper stratum belongs to the period of earliest Sumerian occupation; the lower, to the period of the Jemdet Nasr tablets and the pottery of Susa II. In a granary of the upper stratum was found a burial of bodies of still a later time, together with tablets dated in the time of the third dynasty of Ur, 2400-2300 B.C., and pottery of that period. It is probable, therefore, that at some part of the mound not yet explored there may have been a Sumerian settlement as late as the time of that dynasty. The work was directed by Dr. Erich Schmidt.

By Kühnel and Schmidt at Ctesiphon.—In 1928-1929 an excavation was made in a portion of the mounds of Ctesiphon by E. Kühnel of the Berlin Museum. The expedition was jointly supported by a number of institutions. In 1931-32 it was carried on

41 See R. Campbell Thompson, "Excavations on the Temple of Nabu, at Nineveh" in *Archaeologia*, Vol. LXXIX, London, 1929, pp. 103–148.
42 See Schmidt's article, "Excavations at Fara, 1931," in the *Museum Journal*, XXII, 1931, pp. 193–217.

for another season under the direction of J. Heinrich Schmidt. The foundations of various buildings of the time of the Persian Sassanian dynasty (220–641 A.D.) were laid bare and some objects of art of that period were found.[43]

By Mallowan.—The mound of Tell Arpachiyah is a prehistoric mound lying less than four miles from the Tigris and on the east side of that river. Its importance was first noted by R. Campbell Thompson, who in 1932, while working at Nineveh, examined potsherds on the surface of Arpachiyah and ascertained from them that the site had not been occupied since the chalcolithic age. In 1933–34 M. E. L. Mallowan conducted an excavation there for the British School of Archæology in Iraq. Trenches were sunk through ten building levels. The pottery from the upper levels resembled that of Al-Ubaid; that of the lower levels, that found at Tell Halaf.[44]

In 1934–35, M. E. L. Mallowan, working under the same auspices explored the mound of Tell Chager Bazar thirty-five kilometers south of Nisibin.[45] It was ascertained that the mound had been inhabited through fifteen strata of occupation, each of which had left its record of walls, pottery, and other objects above the virgin soil. It had ceased to be occupied about 1500 B.C. The six habitation levels nearest the surface yielded objects of the Hurrian type of art, showing that during the period represented by these levels it was inhabited by people kindred to those found at Nuzi. They were, in the decades just before the site was abandoned, a part of the kingdom of Mitanni, and probably perished in the cataclysm which overthrew that kingdom.

By Lieutenant Cabane.—From December, 1933, to March, 1934, an excavation was conducted by the French at Tell Kharir, situated on the west of the Euphrates eastward across the desert from Damascus. Bedouins, in digging for stone to mark the graves of their dead, had exhumed a statue of a type that was at once recognized as belonging to one of the very early periods of Babylonian art. When this was seen by officers at the French military post of Abu Kemal, about thirty-five kilometers distant, the importance of the mound as an archæological site was at once recognized. During the excavation a number of early tombs were cleared, and some

43 Cf. E. Kühnel und O. Wachtsmuth, Die deutsche Ktesiphon-Expedition 1928-29, Berlin, 1930, and Die Ktesiphon-Expedition 1931-32, Berlin, 1933, also J. H. Schmidt, "L'expédition de Ctésiphon en 1931–1932" in Syria XV, 1–23.
44 See Iraq, II, 1935, 1–178; also M. E. L. Mallowan and J. Cruikshank, Prehistoric Assyria—the Excavation at Arpachiyah, Oxford Press, 1935.
45 British Museum Quarterly, X, 1936, 119 f.

buildings laid bare, including a temple of Ishtar. Pottery of a very early type was recovered and a number of other statues and statuettes, one of which bore an inscription, which the French scholars read, "Lamgi-Mari, king of Mari." [46] This proves that Tell Kharir was the site of the city of Mari. The name of this city has long been known as the seat of an early Semitic kingdom which flourished at the dawn of history. From various references to it, it was known to have been situated on the Euphrates to the northwest of Babylon, but, until the recovery of this inscription its exact site had been sought in vain.[47]

It is now reported that the excavation at Tell Kharir has been carried on for two more seasons and that an archive of more than 15,000 inscribed tablets from the time of Hammurabi and earlier periods has been found. The texts are said to consist of business documents and letters which will reveal the nature of the civilization of this ancient city.

By Breasted, Cumont, and Dussaud.—In 1920 Professor James H. Breasted was requested by the British military authorities to examine some remarkable paintings that had been accidentally laid bare in digging trenches in the process of occupying an old fort at Salikhiyah on the west of the Euphrates, twenty-seven miles from Abu Kemal. Breasted spent a day (May 3, 1920) copying them. The name of the ancient city which occupied the spot was then unknown, but he recognized the remains as belonging to the period of Roman occupation and the paintings as an earlier form of what is now called "Byzantine art.[48] Two years later Franz Cumont visited the site and found the Arabs had defaced the paintings. The interest aroused was such that Yale University afterward undertook to explore the site and excavations were made there in 1928–1937, under the scientific direction of Professor Michael I. Rostovtzeff, Franz Cumont, and Rene Dussaud. The buried city proved to be Dura, a flourishing town during the early centuries of the Christian era. In the course of the excavations a number of Jewish synagogues and Christian churches were uncovered, the walls of which had been decorated with Biblical scenes in profusion.[49] A

46 See *Syria*, XVI, 1935, 1–28 and 117–140.
47 If the king's name be read "Lamgi-Mari" the signs are read as Sumerian. If read as Akkadian (*i.e.*, as Semitic), it would be "Sin-Mari." As the statuettes indicate that their originals were Semites, doubtless it should be so read. This accords with previously known evidence that Mari was a Semitic kingdom.
48 See Breasted's *Oriental Forerunners of Byzantine Painting*, Chicago, 1924.
49 See Prof. C. H. Kraeling, *Bulletin of the American Schools of Oriental Research*, No. 54 (Apr. 1934), p. 18 f., and his *Greek Fragment of Tatian's Diatessaron from Dura*, being *Studies and Documents* edited by Kirsopp Lake and Silva Lake, III, London, 1935; C. Hopkins, P. V. C. Baur and A. D. Nock, *Christian Church at Dura-Europos*, New Haven, 1936, and H. F. Pearson, C. H. Kraeling, C. C. Torrey and others, *Preliminary Report on the Synagogue at Dura*, New Haven, 1936.

number of written documents in a more or less fragmentary form
were recovered, among which was a fragment of the *Diatessaron*
of Tatian, a description of which will be found in Part II, page
583 f.

In India.—Since 1922 excavations have been made at two sites
in the Valley of the Indus, the results of which are of interest to
every student of ancient civilizations. One of these sites, Harappa,
is situated on an ancient bed of the Ravi, a river that flows into the
Indus from the East; the other, Mohenjo-daro, is about 450 miles
to the south of it on what was once the shore of the Indus. The
constructions were of brick, as in Babylonia, and many of the objects
found led scholars, when pictures of them were first published, to
conclude that they were the work of the Sumerians.[50] Further
study has made it evident that this early opinion is wrong. This
Indian civilization, while possessing certain features in common
with that of Babylonia, was an independent development. It is
clear, however, as already noted, that there was trade between India
and Babylonia, when this civilization was flourishing, *i.e.,* in the
period 2000 to 3000 B.C. One of the most interesting features of
these discoveries was the finding of more than a thousand inscribed
seals or amulets, written in a script hitherto entirely unknown.
Many of these seals bear pictures of oxen and elephants, similar
to those found at Tell Asmar. The ox is often pictured standing
by an altar, on which a fire is burning, which has led to the belief
that they were records of sacrifices and, as such, were preserved in
the temple. The script is not yet deciphered.[51]

4. The Decipherment of the Inscriptions.—The task of learning to read the inscriptions of Babylonia and Assyria was much more
difficult than the decipherment of the Egyptian hieroglyphs, for
no such simple key as the Rosetta Stone was at hand. The key
that finally unlocked the mystery came not from Babylonia, but
from Persepolis in Persia. When Cyrus the Great conquered
Babylon in 538 B.C. the Persians had not developed a system of
writing. They accordingly adapted to their language the characters of the Babylonian script. The Babylonian script had begun,

50 Cf. A. H. Sayce in *The Illustrated London News,* Sept. 27, 1924, p. 566; C. J.
Gadd and Sidney Smith in the same journal for Oct. 4, 1924, pp. 614, 615, and L. A.
Waddell, *The Indo-Sumerian Seals Deciphered,* a book thoroughly unsound in method
and consequently void of scientific results.

51 For information concerning these discoveries in India see *The Archæological Survey of India, Annual Report,* 1922–23, 1923–24, 1925-26, and Sir John Marshall's
Mohenjo-daro and the Indus Civilization, 1931. Additional discussions may be found in
G. A. Barton's "The So-called Sumero-Indian Seals" and his "A Comparative List of
the Signs of the So-called Indo-Sumerian Seals" in the *Annual* of the American Schools
of Oriental Research, Vol. VIII (1928) and Vol. X (1930), respectively. Also G. R.
Hunter, *The Script of Harappa and Mohenjo-daro,* London, 1934. Also E. Mackay,
The Indus Civilization, London, 1935.

like the Egyptian hieroglyphs, as a system of picture-writing, in which each picture represented an idea. These had gone through a long development, in which the original picture-forms had been supplanted by conventional characters derived therefrom. In making these characters on clay, one end of a line was always wider than the other, hence the characters are called "wedge-shaped" or "cuneiform." In the course of the ages the Babylonians had come to use the characters to express both syllables and whole words, and a scribe might mingle these uses of a sign at will in writing a composition. Many of the signs might also express any one of several syllables. In adapting this complicated system, the Persians had the wisdom to simplify it. They selected or constructed a character for each sound, making a real alphabet. Three of the Persian kings, Darius (521–486), Xerxes (485–465), and Artaxerxes II (405–359), wrote their inscriptions in three languages,— Babylonian, Elamite, and Persian,—employing wedge-shaped scripts for all of them.

By Niebuhr.—In the ruins of the great palace of the Persian kings at Persepolis many of these inscriptions in three languages were preserved. These ruins attracted the notice of many travelers from the time that Odoric, a monk, saw them in 1320 A.D., and a number of travelers had made copies of some of them and brought them back to Europe. The inscriptions were a great puzzle. After Alexander the Great (331–323 B.C.) Persia had been subject to foreign powers until 220 A.D., when the Sassanian dynasty (220– 641 A.D.) made Persia again an independent kingdom. In the revival of Persian letters that occurred in Sassanian times, a form of the Phœnician alphabet was used, because the old characters of these inscriptions had been forgotten. In 1765 Carsten Niebuhr, a Dane, visited Persepolis and made accurate copies of a large number of these inscriptions. The first correct reading of any of them was done from Niebuhr's copies; (See Fig. 20).

By Grotefend, de Sacy, and *Rawlinson.*—A number of scholars had studied Niebuhr's copies, but the first to read any of them correctly was George Friedrich Grotefend, a German scholar. He began with the assumption that the three groups of lines in the inscriptions contained respectively three languages, and that the first of these was the Persian of Cyrus and his successors. In the years 1787–1791 Sylvestre de Sacy, a French Oriental scholar, had studied and in part expounded some Sassanian alphabetic inscriptions from Persia, which had also long attracted the notice of scholars. These Sassanian inscriptions were many of them cast in the same mould. They ran thus:

"X the great king, king of kings, the king of Iran and Aniran, son of Y, the great king," etc.

Grotefend had these inscriptions before him, and compared this formula with the inscriptions from Persepolis. He noted that as often as the formula contained the word "king" the inscriptions from Persepolis contained the same group of signs, and that as often as it had "of kings," they reproduced the group with a different ending. He therefore rightly concluded that these signs were the old Persian spelling of the Persian word for "king" with its genitive plural. Taking from the Sassanian inscriptions the word for king, he proceeded to parcel out its sounds among the characters with which the word was spelled in the Persepolis inscriptions. He also found a king, who was the son of a man not a king. This, he rightly held, could be none other than Darius, the son of Hystaspes. Apportioning the proper groups of signs among the sounds of these names, he obtained still further alphabetical values. Thus a beginning was made. Grotefend was, however, unable to carry the work far, and in the years that followed Eugène Burnouf, Christian Lassen, Isidore Lowenstern, Henry C. Rawlinson, and Edward Hincks all made contributions to the subject. The honor of having first correctly read and interpreted a long inscription belongs to Rawlinson. Rawlinson was a young army officer, who as a boy had been in India, where he learned Persian and several of the dialects of India. In 1833 he was sent to Persia with other British officers to assist in the reorganization of the Persian army. Here his attention was attracted by the great Persian inscriptions in the mountains near Hamadan, the ancient Ecbatana, and in the intervals of military duties he copied and studied several of them. He was, in the early stages of his work, quite unaware of the work done by Grotefend and others, but hit independently upon the method followed by Grotefend. Owing to the fact that the inscriptions on which Rawlinson worked were longer than those accessible to Grotefend, and also contained more proper names, Rawlinson attained greater success than any of his predecessors. He did not publish his results, however, until he had become thoroughly familiar with all that others had done. It was not until 1846 that he published a full interpretation of the Persian column of the great Behistun [52] inscription of Darius I.

[52] So called from the name of the mountain on which it is written.

Babylonian Column.—This successful achievement related, however, only to the Persian column. The mysteries of the Babylonian column had not yet been solved. This task, as will be evident from the complicated nature of the writing mentioned above, was a much more difficult one. The decipherment of the Persian had, however, taught the sound of many cuneiform signs. These sounds were carried over to the Babylonian column as a nucleus of information. Excavations were all the time also bringing new material to light, and a comparison of inscriptions, in many of which the same words were written in different ways, sometimes ideographically and sometimes syllabically, helped on the general stock of knowlededge. Rawlinson, Hincks, Jules Oppert, and Fox Talbot were the men who at this stage of the work were still wrestling with the problem. Again Rawlinson was the man to achieve the first distinguished success. In 1851 he published one hundred and twelve lines of the Babylonian portion of the Behistun inscription with transliteration and translation, and accompanied the whole with copious notes in which the principles of the grammar were set forth. A list of the signs and their values was also added. From that day to this the study has steadily gone forward.

Babylonian-Semitic.—The work of Rawlinson and his co-laborers proved that the language of the ancient Babylonians was a Semitic language, closely akin to Hebrew, Aramaic, Arabic, and Ethiopic. Within the next few years after he had found the key to the cuneiform writing, Rawlinson announced that the inscriptions from Babylonia contained material in another and very different language. The researches of later years have fully confirmed this, and scholars call this language Sumerian. The people who spoke it were the inventors of several elements in the civilization of early Babylonia, and for many centuries at the dawn of history divided the country with the Semites.

5. Chronology.—The materials for constructing the chronology of Babylonian and Assyrian history are as follows:

(1) Claudius Ptolemy, an Egyptian astronomer who flourished in the second century A.D., made a list of the kings of Egypt, Persia, and Babylonia back to the accession of the Babylonian king, Nabonassar, in 747 B.C. This list was compiled as an astronomical aid, and is very accurate.

(2) The Assyrian kings kept lists of years and of principal events, to which scholars have given the name "Eponym Lists," because each year was named after the king or some officer. Tab-

lets containing these lists have been recovered on which we can still read the chronology from 893 to 666 B.C. This list accordingly overlaps the list or "canon" of Ptolemy. Some of these Assyrian kings were also kings of Babylon, and where the lists overlap they agree. One of these lists mentions an eclipse which occurred at Nineveh in the month Sivan (May–June), 763 B.C. This eclipse has been calculated and verified by modern astronomers, so that the chronology covered by these lists rests upon a secure scientific basis.

(3) For dates in Assyrian history anterior to 893 B.C. we have to depend upon incidental notices in the inscriptions. Thus Sennacherib, whose date is fixed by the Eponym Lists at 705–681 B.C., relates that during his reign he recovered from Babylon the images of two gods that had been taken as booty by Marduknadinakhi, King of Babylon, from Tiglath-pileser, King of Assyria, 418 years before Sennacherib brought them back. It follows from this that Tiglath-pileser I of Assyria and Marduknadinakhi of Babylon were ruling from about 1120 to 1100 B.C.

We also have a long inscription from the Tiglath-pileser mentioned here, who relates that in his reign he restored a temple, which had been built by Shamshi-Adad, ruler of Assyria, son of Ishmi-Dagan, ruler of Assyria, 641 years before the time of Ashurdan, King of Assyria. Ashur-dan had, he tells us, pulled the temple down and it had lain in ruins 60 years until he (Tiglath-pileser) rebuilt it. By adding these numbers we reach 1819 or 1820 B.C. as the accession of Shamshi-Adad.

Again Sennacherib found at Babylon a seal which bore the following inscription:

"Tukulti-Ninib, king of the world, son of Shalmaneser, King of Assyria, conqueror of the land of Chaldæa. Whoever changes the writing of my name, may Ashur and Adad destroy his name. This seal was presented by the land of Assyria to the land of Akkad" (Babylonia).

To this Sennacherib added the following inscription:

"I, Sennacherib, after 600 years conquered Babylon, and from its treasures brought it out and took it."

We learn from this that Tukulti-Ninib was ruling in Assyria from about 1300 to 1290 B.C.

Andræ, in 1914, published an inscription of Tukulti-Ninib in which he states that he repaired a temple which had been built by his ancestor, Ilu-shumma, King of Assyria, 720 years before. Ilu-shumma was, accordingly, ruling in Assyria about 2020 to 2010 B.C.

(4) Among the tablets in the British Museum are two so-called "dynastic tablets" which contain lists of the kings of Babylon from the time that Babylon became the leading city of the country to its capture by the Persians. The kings are divided into eight dynasties, the length of the reign of each king was originally given, and at the end of each dynasty a statement was given of the number of kings in that dynasty and the total length of their reigns. These tablets are unfortunately much broken, so that they afford us little help after the year 1000 B.C. We learn from them, however, that Marduknadinakhi, the king mentioned by Sennacherib as ruling about 1100 B.C., belonged to the fourth Babylonian dynasty, and, if we add together the years given for the previous dynasties, we are taken back nearly to the year 2400 B.C. for the accession of the first dynasty of Babylon. Evidence has, however, come to light in recent years which proves that the first and second of these dynasties overlapped, one ruling in the north while the other ruled in the south. A reliable chronology cannot, therefore, be obtained by adding these numbers together. In order to correct them recourse must be had to other evidence.

(5) Professors Langdon and Fotheringham [53] have shown that an astronomical tablet which was published as long ago as 1870, and which notes for a series of years when Venus was the evening and when the morning star, contains a date formula which fixes its compilation in the reign of Ammi-zadugga, the tenth of the eleven kings of the first dynasty of Babylon. From mathematical calculations of the position of the Planet Venus, they are, accordingly, able to fix the accession of Ammi-zadugga as April 24, 1921 B.C. From the lengths of the reigns of the various kings of this dynasty, as given in the dynastic tablets, it follows that the first dynasty of Babylon began its rule in 2151 B.C.

(6) Under Adad-nirari III, King of Assyria (810–782 B.C.), a so-called synchronistic history of Assyria and Babylonia was compiled. It covered about 600 years, beginning with a treaty of peace between Karaindash, King of Babylon, and Ashur-rim-

53 *The Venus Tablet of Ammi-zadugga*, by S. Langdon and J. K. Fotheringham, Oxford, 1928.

nishishu, King of Assyria. It aids in filling gaps left by breaks in other lists.

(7) A chronological tablet in the Babylonian collection of Yale University contains a list of the kings of Larsa. This city was conquered by Hammurabi, of the first dynasty of Babylon, in the 31st year of his reign. The tablet, therefore, counts Hammurabi one of the kings of Larsa, ascribing to him twelve years of rule. The tablet was apparently compiled in the twelfth year of Samsu-iluna, Hammurabi's successor, to whom twelve years are also ascribed. It gives the total length of the dynasty of Larsa as 289 years. That dynasty, accordingly, began its rule in 2303 b.c.

(8) In a chronological list of the kings of Ur and Nisin on a tablet in the University of Pennsylvania Museum, Philadelphia,[54] it is stated that the kings of Ur ruled 117 years and the kings of Nisin 225 years and 6 months. A tablet has now been discovered which shows that the dynasty of Nisin was not overthrown until 2061 or 2060 b.c. Its 225 years, therefore, were all parallel to the time of the dynasty of Larsa. As the dynasty of Nisin rose upon the ruins of the kingdom of Ur, the dates of the kingdom of Ur are, therefore, fixed as 2399–2286.[55]

(9) A chronological tablet published by Scheil in the *Comptes rendus* of the French Academy for 1911 gives a list of five early dynasties of Babylonia: a dynasty of Opis, one of Kish, one of Agade, and two of Erech.

(10) A group of chronological tablets in the University of Pennsylvania Museum in Philadelphia, which assign several dynasties to each of several well-known Babylonian cities, ascribe to their kings incredibly long reigns. The Ashmolean Museum, Oxford, has a duplicate.[56]

(11) Fragments of a work of Berossos, a Babylonian priest who lived after the time of Alexander the Great, contain a list of Babylonian kings. He based his work on such tablets as those in the University of Pennsylvania Museum, Philadelphia. His statements abound accordingly in incredible numbers.

From these tablets it appears that the dynasty of Ur was preceded by a king of Erech for 25 years; he by the dynasty of

54 First published by Hilprecht, *Babylonian Expedition of the University of Pennsylvania*, Vol. XX, No. 47; cf. p. 46.
55 Dead reckoning from the tablets would give the year 2286 for this date; but it can be shown to have been 2282 by the calculation of an eclipse of the moon mentioned as occurring in the year before the fall of the dynasty. See Langdon and Fotheringham, *Venus Tablet*, p. 82.
56 Both texts, as well as the one discovered by Scheil, are translated in G. A. Barton's *Royal Inscriptions of Sumer and Akkad*, New Haven, Conn., 1929, pp. 341 to 355.

Gutium, which ruled for 125 years; the dynasty of Gutium was preceded by a dynasty of Erech for 26 years; that, by a dynasty of Agade for 197 years; that, by one king of Erech, Lugalzaggisi, who ruled 25 years; he was apparently preceded by a dynasty of Kish for 106 years; that, by a dynasty of Opis for 99 years. These figures take us back to 3002 B.C., though the arrangement for the time before Lugalzaggisi is in part conjectural. Four dynasties of what are known to have been historical kings existed before this time, which fill up the time until about 3200 B.C. To three other dynasties the tablets assign 885 years, which, added to the preceding, take us back to 4085 B.C. It is, however, probable that some of the dynasties which the compilers of the chronologies made successive were really contemporaneous, and that their actual antiquity is not so great. Earlier than this there lived, as the tablets tell us, the legendary and mythical kings whose names are discussed in Part II, Chapter V.

Within the last few years many scholars have reached the conclusion that the use of copper was not discovered until about 3000 B.C., and that, if metal implements are found in connection with a king's inscriptions, he cannot have ruled before that date. If this criterion is sound, all the dates mentioned above anterior to 3000 B.C. would have to be brought down, and allowance would have to be made for more overlapping of dynasties than has been supposed. The exact time of the introduction of metal cannot, however, be determined within two centuries. It may have been as early as 3200 B.C. The lower limit of the stone age cannot be so definitely fixed as is sometimes supposed.

(12) Nabuna'id, King of Babylon, 555–538 B.C., states that he found, in repairing the temple at Sippar (Agade), the temple-platform of Naram-Sin, son of Sargon, which no one had seen for 3,200 years. As he made this statement about 550 B.C., it was long supposed that this fixed the date of Naram-Sin as 3750 B.C., and that of his father, Sargon, at about 3800 B.C. These dates will be found in many of the older books, but they are incredible. They would, if true, leave long gaps in the history that we have no information to fill. Since it has been clearly proved that the dynasties overlapped, it seems that Nabuna'id reached his date by adding together the totals of dynasties, some of which were contemporary. It now seems probable that he placed Naram-Sin about 1,100 years too early.

(13) When it is published, the Assyrian king-list from Khorsabad mentioned above will doubtless afford material aid in correcting the chronology of the early history of Assyria.

The sources here enumerated afford us a tolerably accurate chronology back to about 2400 B.C. All dates earlier than this have to be estimated by combining statements of early dynastic tablets with archæological and palæographic considerations.

6. Outline of the History.—The history of Babylonia and Assyria falls into eight different periods. Our information is not yet sufficiently complete to enable us to write the history of any one of them, but we can discern in outline a most fascinating course of events.

(1) *The Prehistoric Period,* or the period before the rise of written history, during which we can ascertain from various inferences the general course of events. This period must have lasted down to about 3100 B.C. Recent discoveries indicate that civilization was first brought to Babylonia by a race from central Asia.[57] They were followed by Semites from Arabia, who, as we have seen, entered the country in the Neolithic Period, and pushed as far north as Tepe Gawra. They mingled with their predecessors. These combined peoples developed the culture of the palm tree, and learned to raise grain in the alluvial soil of the rivers, and invented a system of picture writing. The early cities of Babylonia were the fortified residences of different tribes, which were frequently at war with one another. One city would subjugate its neighbors for a time and establish a small empire. As long as it continued to rule, a certain degree of homage was paid to its god by all the cities over which it ruled. In prehistoric times settlements were made at Jemdet Nasr, near Kish; at Eridu, Ur, Erech, Nippur, Sippar, and at other places. At first the population lived largely by fishing, but in time dykes were built, the water confined by canals, and grains raised.

Sumerians.—At some time before the dawn of history a people whom we call Sumerians moved into Babylonia from the South.[58] These people spoke a language which possesses some features in common with Finnish and Turkish. They were neither Aryans nor Semites. The Semites wore thick hair and long beards; the Sumerians shaved both their heads and faces. These Sumerians

57 See E. A. Speiser, *Mesopotamian Origins,* Philadelphia, 1930, and G. A. Barton, *Semitic and Hamitic Origins,* Philadelphia, 1934.
58 See G. A. Barton, "Whence Came the Sumerians?" in the *Journal of the American Oriental Society,* XLIX, 263–268.

overran southern Babylonia as far north as Nippur and in this region became the ruling race. They grafted the worship of their own gods upon the worship of the deities of the cities which they conquered, but the earlier elements of these local deities persisted even in Sumerian thought. It thus came about that the bald and beardless Sumerians picture their gods with hair and beards. After settling in Babylonia, the Sumerians developed a system of writing. It was at first hieroglyphic, like the Egyptian system. Afterward the Semites, who still retained the supremacy in the cities of Kish and Agade in the north, and who had probably been reinforced there by fresh migrations from Arabia, adapted this system of writing to their own language. As clay was the usual writing material and it was difficult to make good pictures on it, the pictographic form of the writing was soon lost. The pictures degenerated into those conventional symbols which are today known as the "cuneiform" characters.

(2) *The Pre-Babylonian Period* of the history includes the period from about 3100 B.C. down to the rise of the city of Babylon, about 2050 B.C. This period, like the preceding, was a time of successive city kingdoms. One city would establish an empire for a while, then another, having become more powerful, would take the leadership. When first our written records enable us to trace the course of events, Lagash in the south and Kish in the north were the rival cities. Lagash was ruled by a king, Enkhegal. A little later Meselim, King of Kish, conquered all of southern Babylonia, including Lagash. After Meselim had passed away, Ur-Nina founded a new dynasty at Lagash and gained his independence. Ur-Nina's grandson, Eannatum, raised the power of Lagash to its greatest height, conquering all the cities of Babylonia, even Kish. The Elamites were always invading the fertile plains of Babylonia, so Eannatum ascended the eastern mountains and subjugated Elam.

"Stele of the Vultures."—He celebrated his victories by the erection of one of the most remarkable monuments which the ancient world produced, the so-called "stele of the vultures." From the pictures on the monument we learn that the soldiers of Lagash, about 2900 B.C., waged their battles in a solid phalanx protected by shields. The Greeks were formerly supposed to have invented this form of attack, but were anticipated by 2,500 years (see Fig. 19).

Although this dynasty furnished several other rulers, the leadership of all Babylonia was lost after the death of Eannatum. It passed first to Opis and then again to Kish. Lagash continued to flourish, however, during 200 years, while these cities were the overlords of its rulers. Its wars had made it rich, and all the arts flourished there. Our best specimens of terra-cotta and stone work come from this period of this city. Under Entemena, the successor of Eannatum, a silver vase of exquisite workmanship and ornamentation was made (see Fig. 21). After a century or more of wealth and luxury, during which priests and officials became corrupt, a new king, Urkagina, seized the throne and endeavored to reform the administration. Naturally, his reforms were unpopular with the priesthood and the army, and, though popular with the people, he unintentionally weakened the defensive power of his country.

At this juncture a new ruler named Lugalzaggisi arose in the city of Umma, who ultimately overthrew Lagash and became king of all Babylonia. He made Erech his capital. This was about 2750 B.C. Lugalzaggisi claims to have overrun the country from the Persian Gulf to the Mediterranean. If so, and there is no good reason to doubt his claim, Babylonia and the Palestinian coastlands were under him brought together for the first time.

After Lugalzaggisi the city of Agade came to the fore. Its great King Sargon about 2725 B.C. founded a dynasty which ruled for nearly two hundred years. The kings of this line were Semitic and resided sometimes at Agade and sometimes at Kish. Sargon conquered Syria and a later chronicle says that he crossed the western sea. As a seal of this dynasty was found in Cyprus, it is possibly true. Naram-Sin, one of the most famous kings of this line, conquered the country of Magan, which some believe to be the peninsula of Sinai, but which others hold was situated in eastern Arabia.

About the time of this dynasty, or a little before, King Lugaldaudu flourished at Adab, the modern Bismya, where Dr. Banks found his statue.[59] In this same general period a king named Anubanini ruled in a city to the northward, called Lulubi.

Perhaps it was under the later kings of this dynasty of Agade, or under a dynasty of Guti, which held sway for a century after them, that Gudea flourished at Lagash. This ruler does not claim to be a king, but his city enjoyed great prosperity under him, and he rebuilt it in fine style. He seems to have been on peaceful terms

59 See above, p. 38.

with much of the world, and brought for his structures stone from Magan, cedar wood from Amanus on the Mediterranean coast, and copper from Lebanon. After this time the land was overrun by hordes from Gutium, a region to the northeast beyond the Tigris. They established a dynasty which lasted for 125 (or 159) years.

In 2399 B.C. a dynasty arose in the city of Ur, situated far to the south. These kings were Sumerians and under them a great Sumerian revival occurred. By this time northern Babylonia was called Akkad, from the city of Agade, and southern Babylonia was called Sumir, from a corruption of the name of one of the quarters of Lagash. These kings combined with the title "king of Ur" the title "king of Sumir and Akkad." Sumir is the Biblical "Shinar" (Gen. 10:10; 11:2, etc.).

Dungi, the second king of this dynasty of Ur, reigned 58 years and established a wide empire, which included Elam and the city of Susa. He established a system of government posts to aid the royal officers of army and state in the performance of their duties.

Upon the fall of the dynasty of Ur, the dominion of Babylonia was divided between two cities, Nisin and Larsa, each of which furnished a dynasty which flourished for more than two and a quarter centuries. Naturally, these kings were continually struggling with each other for the supremacy, and sometimes one city was the more powerful, sometimes the other. The Amorites, who had settled in Elam swooped down into the Mesopotamian Valley, overran Larsa and furnished the last two kings of its dynasty,— Arad-Sin and Rim-Sin. These kings have each been thought by different scholars to be the Arioch of Gen. 14:1. (See Part II, Chapter IX.)

About 2151 B.C. a dynasty of rulers was founded in the city of Babylon that was destined to bring a new era into the history of the country. After a struggle of more than a century Hammurabi, the sixth king of this line, broke the power of Larsa and made Babylon the leading city of the country. Nisin had previously fallen. With the rise of Babylon another period of the life of the country was ended.

The above sketch calls attention to a few only of the more prominent features and cities of Babylonia. There were many others which participated in her life during the millennium of the pre-Babylonian period. The recovery of more inscriptions will no doubt make this statement more true even than we now dream.

Each of these contributed its mite to the progress of civilization in this melting-pot of races in this far-off time.

(3) *The Early Babylonian Period* began with the reign of Hammurabi and continued till about 1050 B.C. It includes the rule of the first four dynasties of Babylon. The period began gloriously under Hammurabi, who conquered all of Babylonia, and extended his sway also to the Mediterranean. He was as great as an administrator as he was as a conqueror; he codified the laws of Babylonia and inscribed them on a stone pillar, which was set up in the temple of Marduk in Babylon. These laws have been recovered, and are one of the most valuable archæological discoveries of modern times. (See Part II, Chapter XIII.)

Soon after the death of Hammurabi, a revolt occurred under one Ilumailu, who established in the region near the Persian Gulf a dynasty known as the dynasty of the sea lands," which was afterward called the second dynasty of Babylon. Down to 1924 B.C. the two dynasties divided the country between them. In that year Babylonia was invaded by the Hittites, who came from the northwest, and the first dynasty of Babylon was overthrown. The Hittites appear to have ruled the country for a short time, when they were driven out by the "dynasty of the sea lands," which, so far as we know, controlled the country for the next hundred and fifty years.

Kassites.—About 1750 B.C., or shortly before, Babylonia was once more invaded by a race of barbarians from the east of the Tigris, called Kasites or Cossæans. They captured Babylon and founded the third dynasty of Babylon, which ruled for 576 years. The kings of this dynasty gradually absorbed Babylonian culture. Soon after 1700 B.C. they expelled the kings of the sea lands from the south and ruled the whole country.

Assyria, which under the first dynasty had been a Babylonian colony, gained her independence before 1400 B.C., so that after that the independent histories of the two lands run on parallel lines. During the long period of Kassite rule, Babylon experienced many vicissitudes. Assyria was at times friendly and at times hostile. In the reign of Kurigalzu, Elam was successfully invaded and spoil formerly taken by the kings of Elam was brought back to Babylonia. Kadashman-turgu and Burnaburiash, kings of this dynasty, carried on friendly correspondence with Amenophis III and Amenophis IV, kings of Egypt, 1400–1350 B.C.

Pashe Dynasty.—About 1175 B.C. the Kassite dynasty was superseded by the Pashe dynasty, which ruled the country for more than a hundred and thirty years. The greatest king of this time was Nebuchadrezzar I, who reigned about 1150 B.C. He emulated with considerable success the career of his great predecessor, Hammurabi. After the fall of the fourth dynasty, the country was divided and fell a prey to the Elamites, who overran it about 1050. For the following 450 years Babylonia, though often independent, was of little political importance.

(4) *The Early Assyrian Period.*—Assyria's empire grew out of the domination of the city of Ashur, as that of Rome grew out of the domination of the city of Rome. Ashur and Nineveh had been occupied by colonists from Sumer about 3000 or 2800 B.C. This is shown by archæological remains found at Ashur, and by the name of Nineveh. We can first trace the names of Assyria's rulers shortly before the year 2200 B.C. They do not call themselves kings, and were, perhaps, then subject to Babylon.

About 1430 B.C. we learn that Assyria had become an independent kingdom. Her king at that time, Ashur-rim-nishishu, was a contemporary of Karaindash, King of Babylon. Ashur-uballit about 1370–1343 was a contemporary of Burnaburiash, King of Babylon, and shared in the correspondence with Egyptian kings contained in the El-Amarna letters. Shalmaneser I about 1300 B.C. conquered the region to the west of Assyria extending across the Euphrates in the direction of the Mediterranean. Ashur-nasirpal, a later king (884–860 B.C.), says that Shalmaneser "made" the city of Calah [60] as a new capital for his country. His son, Tukulti-Ninib I, turned his arms to the southward and conquered Babylon, which he held for seven years. After him Assyria's power declined for a time, but was revived by Tiglath-pileser I, who carried Assyria's conquests again across the Euphrates to the Mediterranean Sea and northward to the region of Lake Van. After the reign of Tiglath-pileser I, Assyria's power rapidly declined again, and the first period of Assyria's history was closed. Our sources almost fail us for a hundred years or more.

(5) *The Second Assyrian Period.*—Assyria slowly emerged from the obscurity into which she had fallen after the death of Tiglath-pileser I. The progress went forward through the reigns of eleven different kings. Finally, in the reign of Ashur-nasirpal II, 884–860 B.C., a period of foreign conquest was once more in-

[60] In Genesis 10:11 it is by implication said that the city was founded by Nimrod.

augurated. This monarch again carried the conquests of his country northward and also to the Mediterranean. (See Part II, p. 457.) Under him Assyria became the best fighting machine in the ancient world—a machine that was run with ruthless cruelty over all conquered peoples. This king set his successors the example of flaying and impaling numbers of conquered peoples, and of boasting of such deeds in his chronicles. Probably such deeds were not now committed for the first time, but so far as we know they had not been so gloated over.

Ashur-nasirpal's successor, Shalmaneser III, 860–824 B.c., made, besides campaigns into Armenia and elsewhere, six campaigns against the lands of Syria and Palestine. On his first campaign in 854 he was met at Qarqar by a confederation of kings, among whom were Ahab of Israel and Ben-Hadad of Damascus. (See Part II, p. 457 ff.) On his fourth campaign in 842 B.c. Jehu, who had in that year usurped the throne of Israel, hastened to make his peace with Shalmaneser by giving him a heavy tribute. Thus Assyria gained a right to claim Israel as a vassal state. (See Part II, p. 459 f.)

The next two kings, Shamshi-Adad IV and Adad-nirari IV, controlled Assyria until 783 B.c., and maintained her power. The last-mentioned king made three expeditions into the West, and claims to have received tribute not only from Israel but from Philistia and Edom, but no details of his campaigns have survived.

After 783 the power of Assyria declined again, and the decline lasted until 745, when the reigning dynasty was overthrown, and an able general, whose name was apparently Pul, gained the throne (cf. 2 Kings 15:19), and took the great name of Tiglath-pileser. He reigned as the third king of that name. Tiglath-pileser III was great both as a warrior and as a statesman. He broke for the time being the power of the kingdom of Urartu in Armenia, conquered parts of Media on the east, and also annexed Babylon to Assyria. Babylon during this later Assyrian period had usually been permitted to retain a king of her own, though the kingdom was of little political importance as compared with Assyria. Tiglath-pileser made his power dominant in Babylonia at the beginning of his reign, and during the last two years of his life actually reigned there as king. The Babylonian scribes did not recognize his high-sounding name of Tiglath-pileser, but still called him Pul.

In the first year of his reign Tiglath-pileser III inaugurated a new policy with reference to conquered peoples. This was the policy of transporting to a distant part of his empire the wealthy and influential members of a conquered nation, and of putting similar exiles from other lands in their place. Individuals so transported would be unable longer to foment rebellion against him. It was a brutal policy, but it was a measure designed to build up a permanent empire.

Tiglath-pileser made four expeditions to the west, though the first two touched northern Phœnicia only. In 739, when he made his appearance in Palestine, Menahem, King of Israel, hastened to pay him tribute (2 Kings 15:19). Four years later, however, after Pekah had usurped the throne of Israel, that king formed an alliance with Rezin of Damascus for the purpose of throwing off the Assyrian yoke, and tried to force Ahaz of Judah to join in the enterprise. (See Isa. 7:1, ff.) This, Ahaz, supported by the prophet Isaiah, refused to do. In 733–732 Tiglath-pileser came again into the West, overran the territory of the kingdom of Israel, deported the chief inhabitants of Galilee to distant parts of his dominions (2 Kings 15:29, 30), and replaced Pekah, who had been killed, by King Hoshea, who ruled over a greatly diminished territory and upon whom a heavy Assyrian tribute was imposed. Tiglath-pileser then turned eastward and conquered Damascus, which his predecessors since the days of Shalmaneser III had been vainly trying to capture. While the Assyrian monarch was at Damascus, King Ahaz of Judah went thither and became his vassal. (See 2 Kings 16:10, f.) Thus Judah also passed under the Assyrian yoke. (See Part II, p. 465, f.)

Tiglath-pileser III was succeeded by Shalmaneser V, 727–722 B.C., and soon after the death of Tiglath-pileser, Hoshea of Israel was persuaded to join several petty rulers of Philistia and Egypt in rebelling against Assyria. In 725 an Assyrian army overran Hoshea's territory, and laid siege to Samaria. The military position of Samaria and its strong walls made it almost impregnable, and the siege dragged on for three years (2 Kings 17:5). Before the city fell, another king had ascended the throne of Assyria. He was a usurper, a general, who took the great name of Sargon, and who ruled from 722 to 705 B.C. Samaria succumbed in Sargon's first year and 27,290 of its inhabitants were deported. The discontent of the west was not at once quieted. Other states remained in rebellion and an Assyrian army finally defeated them at Raphia, southwest of Gaza, in 719 B.C. Sargon then turned his arms in other directions, fighting at various times with the kingdom of Urartu in Armenia, overcoming Carchemish, a Hittite kingdom on the Euphrates in 717 (see Isa. 10:9), and making an expedition into Arabia in 715. In 711 Ashdod revolted and Sargon's Tartan or chief officer came to put the rebellion down (Isa. 20:1).

At the beginning of Sargon's reign his arms had been defeated in Babylonia, and Merodachbaladan, a Chaldæan (see 2 Kings 20:12), seized the throne of Babylon and held it from 721 to 709. Then he was defeated and Sargon took over the control of Babylonia. Merodachbaladan, however, escaped to the marsh lands at the head of the Persian Gulf, and survived to make trouble later. In 705 Sargon died and was succeeded by his son, Sennacherib, who ruled from 705 to 681 B.C. At the beginning of his reign troubles broke out in Babylonia, which cannot here be followed in detail. They lasted for years, and none of Sennacherib's measures gave the country permanent peace. At last Sennacherib became so incensed that he destroyed Babylon. Her buildings were burned and battered down, her walls overthrown, and the Euphrates turned through canals into the land on which she had stood, to make it a marsh. One incident in the series of events which led up to this sad climax was the reappearance in 702 of Merodach-baladan, who seized the throne of Babylon and tried to stir up a rebellion against Assyria. He even sent letters to Hezekiah, King of Judah. (See 2 Kings 20:12.) At the beginning of Sennacherib's reign a number of the petty kings of Philistia had withheld their tribute. Into this revolt Hezekiah, King of Judah, had been drawn. Busied with other wars, Sennacherib was unable to quell this rebellion until the year 701. In that year his army met the forces of the confederated kingdoms at Elteke in the valley of Aijalon and overcame them. Sennacherib then proceeded to Lachish, where he received the submission of the neighboring kinglets. From Lachish he sent a messenger who summoned Hezekiah of Judah to submit (cf. Isa. 36, 37). Hezekiah obeyed the summons and paid a heavy tribute. Space does not permit us to speak of the wars of Sennacherib against Elam and other countries.

It would seem that after Tirhakah ascended the throne of Egypt in 688 B.C., he persuaded the kingdoms of Palestine to rebel. The Assyrian came west again and threatened to invade Egypt and to destroy Jerusalem. Isaiah then predicted that Jerusalem would be delivered (Isa. 31:5), a prediction which was fulfilled. Sennacherib's army was attacked by bubonic plague and was compelled to retire.[61]

Sennacherib was assassinated in 681 and was succeeded by his son, Esarhaddon, who ruled till 668. Esarhaddon rebuilt Babylon, which his father had destroyed, and two years before his death conquered all of Lower Egypt and made it an Assyrian province. During his reign a great horde of Scythians poured into Asia through the Caucasus region from southern Russia. The Assyrian army prevented Assyria from being overwhelmed by this horde. The stream of invaders was divided, one part flowing east to Media, the other part westward to Asia Minor.

Esarhaddon's son and successor, Ashurbanipal, ruled from 668 to 626. His reign was the Augustan age of Assyria. At the beginning he was called upon to put down a rebellion in Egypt, and as trouble there recurred several times, trouble which was fomented by emissaries from Thebes and Nubia, he finally in 661 pushed up the Nile and conquered Thebes and gave it over to plunder. (See Nahum 3 : 8.) Space does not permit us to follow Ashurbanipal's wars. About the middle of his reign his brother, Shamash-shum-ukin, who was ruling Babylon, rebelled along with many other vassals, and although the rebels were finally put down, the seeds of the decay of Assyria's power were sown. Manasseh, King of Judah, as long as he lived was a faithful vassal of Esarhaddon and Ashurbanipal. (Cf. 2 Kings 19 : 37; 2 Chron. 33.)

The great work of Ashurbanipal was the collection of his library at Nineveh. He sent to all the old temples of Babylonia and had copies made of their incantations, hymns, and epics. These, together with chronicles, medical tablets, dictionaries, etc., he collected in his palace, where they were found by Layard and Rassam, and form the basis of our knowledge of the Assyrian and Babylonian language, literature, and history. With the death of Ashurbanipal, the last Assyrian period had really closed. Though the kingdom continued for fifteen years more, they were but the years of a lingering death.

(6) *The Neo-Babylonian Period.*—In 625, the year after Ashurbanipal's death, Nabopolassar, the viceroy of Babylon, who appears to have been a Chaldæan,[62] gained his independence, and established the Neo-Babylonian, or Chaldæan empire. Nabopo-

---

61 For a discussion of the reasons for the view here stated, and a presentation of other views, see Part II, p. 472, ff.

62 The Chaldæans were a Semitic people who came into the marsh-lands of southern Babylonia from Arabia. We can first detect their presence in Babylonia about 1000 B.C.

lassar himself reigned till 604 B.C. During his reign the power of
the city of Babylon gradually extended over all Southern Babylonia, and up the Euphrates to Carchemish. During these years
Assyria was gradually diminishing in territory. As Assyria had
declined, Media, which had long been in greater or less degree
subject to Assyria, had become free, and Median kings had little
by little gained control of the country toward Assyria. Nabopolassar finally made an alliance with the Median king, and together they overthrew Nineveh in 612 B.C.

In 604 Necho of Egypt marched with an army to the Euphrates,
and Nabopolassar sent his son, Nebuchadrezzar II, to meet him.
Nebuchadrezzar defeated Necho at the battle of Carchemish, and
hotly pursued him toward Egypt. (See Jer. 46.) The pursuit was,
however, interrupted by the death of Nabopolassar, and the recall
of Nebuchadrezzar to Babylon to be crowned as king. The defeat
of Necho had made Judah a Babylonian vassal-state. Nebuchadrezzar ruled until 562 B.C., and raised Babylon to a height of power
which rivaled that attained under the great Hammurabi. He also
rebuilt the city in great magnificence. The palaces, temples, and
walls of this period, unearthed by Koldewey, were most magnificent
structures. Owing to rebellions, first of Jehoiakim and then of
Zedekiah, kings of Judah, Nebuchadrezzar twice besieged Jerusalem, once in 597, and again in 586 B.C., on both occasions cap-
turing the city. In 586 he destroyed it. (2 Kings 24, 25.) Following the Assyrian practice, which had prevailed since Tiglath-
pileser IV, he transported considerable numbers of the more influential people of the city each time he took it. These were settled
in Babylonia. One colony of them was stationed near Nippur.
Among those who were transported in 597 was a young priest, who
afterward became the prophet Ezekiel. The colony with which he
came was settled by the Khubur canal near Nippur. (See Ezek.
1 : 1.) The young king, Jehoiachin, who was also taken captive
at that time, remained in confinement during the rest of Nebuchadrezzar's reign. He was only released by Amil-Marduk, Nebuchadrezzar's son, who succeeded his father and reigned two years.
(See 2 Kings 25 : 27-30.)

After Nebuchadrezzar the kingdom of Babylon rapidly declined
through four reigns. Meantime, Cyrus, who in 553 had overthrown the kingdom of Media and erected the kingdom of Persia on
its ruins, had been gradually extending his realm to the Ægean Sea

on the west, and to the borders of India on the east. In 538 B.C. Cyrus captured Babylon and overthrew Nabuna'id.

(7) *The Persian Period* lasted from 538 to 331 B.C. During this time Babylonia was but a province of the Persian empire, though the Persian kings made it one of their capitals. Cyrus reversed the policy of transportation, which had been practised by the Assyrians and Babylonians for two hundred years, and permitted subject peoples to return to their lands and restore their institutions and worship. He sought to attach them to his government by gratitude instead of fear. It was owing to this policy that the Jewish state was once more established with Jerusalem as its capital, though still a Persian colony. Cambyses extended Persian power to Egypt in 525, and Darius I, 521–485 B.C., extended it to India and into Europe. Under Darius the temple at Jerusalem was rebuilt and the Jews there tried unsuccessfully to regain their independence. This they attempted once more under Artaxerxes III about 350 B.C., but his general, Bagoses, put down their rebellion with great severity. During the Persian period life in Babylonia went on as before. The old gods were worshipped, the old culture was continued, the same language was used, and many business documents written in it have come down to us. The earlier Persian kings employed it for their inscriptions, and in a short time the Persians made from it an alphabet of their own.

(8) *The Greek and Parthian Periods.*—Alexander the Great overthrew Darius III, the last of the Persian kings, in 331 B.C., when Assyria and Babylonia passed under the sway of the Macedonian. When Alexander returned from his conquests in India in 325 B.C., he planned to extend his empire westward to the Atlantic Ocean, and to make Babylon its capital. Plans for the enlargement and beautifying of the city, so as to make it a worthy capital for such an empire, were under way when Alexander suddenly died in June, 323 B.C. In the final division of the world among Alexander's successors, Babylonia fell to Seleucus, together with all the territory from the Mediterranean to the borders of India. As Seleucus desired a capital on the Mediterranean, so as to watch more successfully the movements of his rivals, he built Antioch on the Orontes and made it his residence. Babylon was, however, made the capital of the eastern half of the empire, and the king's son, as viceroy, made it his residence.

Soon after 260 B.C. Bactria and Parthia, in the eastern part of the empire of the Seleucidæ, gained their independence. In course of time Parthia absorbed Bactria and became an empire, which lasted till 230 A.D. About 150 B.C. the Parthians conquered Babylonia, which remained with little interruption under their sway till the establishment of the Sassanian kingdom of the Persians in 220 A.D. Babylonia was under the control of this last dynasty until the coming of the Mohammedans in the year 637 A.D. The old culture of the Babylonians, their religion, language, and writing were maintained well down toward the Christian era. Copies of old Sumerian hymns have been found in Babylonia which bear dates as late as 81 B.C., and business documents in Semitic are numerous.[63]

7. Discoveries which Illumine the Bible.—Discoveries in Babylonia and Assyria which illumine the Biblical narratives are numerous. The sites of many cities, such as Ur of the Chaldees, Erech, Babylon, Ashur, Nineveh, and Calah, have been excavated. The number of documents which have come to light which in one way or another have a bearing on the Bible is too numerous to mention here. An effort has been made in Part II to translate examples of most of them. Indeed, the greater part of the material in Part II was recovered by excavations in these countries.

To Babylonia and to Egypt mankind owes the working out of the initial problems of civilization, the processes of agriculture, the making of bricks, the working of stone, the manufacture and use of the ordinary implements of life, the development of elementary mathematics and astronomy, etc. These problems were by slow processes independently worked out in each country through long ages. The higher spiritual concepts which have now become the heritage of man neither Babylonia nor Egypt was fitted to contribute. These came through the agency of other peoples.

63 Those who desire fuller accounts of the history should read L. W. King's *History of Sumer and Akkad*, London, 1910; his *History of Babylon*, London, 1915, and A. T. Olmstead's *History of Assyria*, New York, 1923, and Sidney Smith's *Early History of Assyria to 1000 B.C.*, London, 1928.

CHAPTER III

THE HITTITES

A FORGOTTEN EMPIRE. HITTITE MONUMENTS: Sendjirli. Boghaz Koi. Other recent excavations. HITTITE DECIPHERMENT: Sayce's early work. Peiser. Jensen. Conder. Sayce's later work. Thompson. Delitzsch. Hronzny. Sommers. Forrer. Friedrich. Götze. Delaporte. Sturtevant. Cowley. Frank. Meriggi. Gelb. Bossert. HITTITE HISTORY: First appearance. Hyksos possibly Hittites or Hurrians. The Mitanni. Kingdom of "Hittite City." Carchemish. Samal and Yadi. Hamath.

1. A Forgotten Empire.—Among the peoples who are said to have been in Palestine in the Patriarchal age are the Hittites (Gen. 23:10; 26:34, etc.). They are mentioned most often in the list of peoples whom the Israelites drove out of the country when they conquered it: "the Canaanite, the Hittite, the Amorite, the Hivite, and the Jebusite," and the man who first suspected that anything more than this could be known of them survived until 1933. This man was Prof. Sayce, of Oxford. In the inscriptions of the Egyptian kings of the eighteenth and nineteenth dynasties there is frequent mention of a people called *Kheta*. In the inscriptions of Assyrian kings there is also frequent mention of a people called *Kha-at-tu*. Slowly, too, during the nineteenth century rock-carvings, often accompanied by inscriptions in a peculiar hieroglyph, were found scattered through northern Syria and Asia Minor. The figures of gods and men on these carvings usually wore caps of a peculiarly pointed type and shoes turned far up at the toe. In 1876 it dawned upon Prof. Sayce that these were all references to the Biblical Hittites. He proceeded to elaborate this view in two articles published in the *Transactions of the Society of Biblical Archæology*, Vols. V and VII.

About the same time the Rev. William Wright independently started the same idea, and gave it expression in his book, *The Empire of the Hittites*, 1884, 2d ed., 1885. At this period it was impossible to discern more than that there had been a widely scattered Hittite civilization, which might have been an empire.

2. Hittite Monuments.—This civilization, it was seen, had left its monuments at Hamath in Syria, at Carchemish on the Euphrates, at various points in ancient Cappadocia, Lycaonia, and Phrygia, as well as near Smyrna in Asia Minor and on the Lydian mountains to the west of Sardis. In 1891 Prof. W. Max Müller, of Philadelphia, reached the conclusion from a study of the Egyptian inscriptions that the Hittites had come into Syria from the northwest, and that their main strength was in Asia Minor. Among the letters found at El-Amarna in Egypt in 1887–1888 were some from Dushratta, a king of Mitanni. A study of these made it clear that the Mitanni inhabited the region on both sides of the Euphrates north of Carchemish, and that they were of the same stock as the Hittites. Our sources of information indicate that the territory of the Mitanni lay east of the Euphrates, but scattered monuments of the Hittite type are found on the west of that river.

(1) *Sendjirli.*—From 1888 to 1891 a German expedition excavated at Sendjirli, near the head-waters of the Kara Su in northern Syria, and brought to light most interesting remains of a civilization that was fundamentally Hittite. Inscriptions found here dated in the reigns of Tiglath-pileser III and Esarhaddon were in Aramaic. By this time there had been an influx of Aramæans, but the art shows that Hittites held the place at an earlier time, and there is reason to believe that one of the kings mentioned here had, about 850 B.C., joined in a Hittite federation.

(2) *Boghaz Koi.*—Among the monuments known to Prof. Sayce at the beginning of his brilliant studies of the Hittites, were some from Boghaz Koi, in Asia Minor. Different travelers had noted that here must have been a somewhat extensive city, adorned with several large buildings, all of which were ornamented with carvings of the peculiar Hittite type. In 1906 the late Prof. Winckler, of Berlin, excavating here in connection with the authorities of the Turkish Museum at Constantinople, discovered an archive of clay tablets inscribed in Babylonian characters. A group of similar tablets from Cappadocia had been previously purchased by the British Museum. Winckler's discovery was important because he found some of the tablets inscribed in Hittite written in cuneiform characters. Of those written in the Babylonian language, one contained a copy of the great treaty between Hattusil, a Hittite king, and Ramses II of Egypt. There were also tablets containing Sumerian and Semitic equivalents of Hittite words. Owing to the long illness of Winckler which followed these discoveries, an illness that terminated in death, the results of this discovery were not given to the world until more than a decade had passed.

In 1907 Winckler and Puchstein, in conjunction with Makridy Bey of the Turkish Museum, made a thorough examination of the remains of walls and buildings at Boghaz Koi. The results were afterward published in a handsome volume entitled *Boghaskoi, die Bauwerke*, Leipzig, 1912 (see Figs. 23 and 25). The Germans in 1931, 1932, and 1936 further explored the site, bringing to light additional tablets.[1]

(3) *Other Excavations.*—An American expedition consisting of Drs. Olmstead, Charles, and Wrench, of Cornell University, explored in Asia Minor in 1907–1908. The members of this expedition collated all the known monuments of the Hittites, but so far only their collation of the inscriptions has been published.

The Institute of Archæology of the University of Liverpool also sent one or more expeditions to explore the Hittite country. In 1910 they excavated to some extent at Sakje-Geuze,[2] not far from Sendjirli.

From 1911 until the outbreak of the Great War in 1914, the British Museum conducted an excavation at Jerablus, the site of ancient Carchemish.

It was found that the site of Carchemish was occupied from about 1750 to 1200 B.C. by a small town, the wall of which was traced. This town was destroyed by an enemy about the date last mentioned, but was, not many years later, replaced by a much larger city, the wall of which, fortified with strong gates and towers, was also traced. This city, occupied by the Hittites until captured by Sargon of Assyria in 717 B.C., contained an acropolis which Sargon surmounted with a palace, the ruins of which were uncovered. The expedition unearthed several inscriptions written in the Hittite hieroglyphic character, numerous stones carved with figures of men and lions, seals, jewelry, and many small objects.[3] In 1926 the Oriental Institute of the University of Chicago sent H. H. Van der Osten to make an archæological survey of the Hittite country in Asia Minor.[4] He chose a site for excavation and since 1927 has explored Alishar Huyuk. Below strata of the Roman period at least two strata of earlier civilizations were found.[5]

1 See the *Mitteilungen der deutschen Orient-Gesellschaft*, Nos. 72, December, 1933, and 75, 1937.

2 See Garstang in the Annals of *Archæology and Anthropology*, I (1908), 97–117, and V (1912), 63–72.

3 See *Carchemish*, Pt. I, by D. G. Hogarth, London, 1914; Pt. II, by C. L. Woolley, 1921.

4 Cf. Van der Osten, *Explorations in Central Anatolia*, 1926, Chicago, 1929.

5 See Van der Osten, *The Alishar Huyuk Season of 1927*, Chicago, 1930.

In addition to these places, Hittite remains have been observed at Yailá, Marash, Giaour-Kalesi, Karaburna, Kizil Dagh, Fraktin, Ivriz, Kara-Bel, Mount Sypilus, Tashji, Asarjik, Bulghar-Maden, Gurun, and Kara Dagh. One who will look up these places on a map of modern Turkey will see that Hittite monuments are distributed from near the shores of the Ægean Sea to the Euphrates at Carchemish and to Hamath in Syria.

3. Hittite Decipherment.

(1) *Sayce's Early Work.*—Prof. Sayce, whose insight first grasped the significance of the Hittite monuments, was also the first to attempt the solution of the riddle which the inscriptions present. In 1880 he thought he had found a key to the writing, such as the Rosetta Stone had been to Egyptian, in the so-called "Boss of Tarkondemos" (see Fig. 26). This "boss" consisted of a round silver plate, in form like half an orange, which must have covered the knob of a staff or dagger. This had been described by Dr. A. D. Mordtmann, in the Journal of the German Oriental Society in 1872. The original was then in the possession of Alexander Jovanoff, a numismatist of Constantinople, who had obtained it at Smyrna. The "boss" bore in its center a figure of the peculiar Hittite form, flanked on both sides by writing in the Hittite characters, while around the whole was an inscription in the cuneiform writing of Assyria. From this Sayce tentatively determined the values of a number of Hittite signs. The results were, however, attended with considerable uncertainty, since the Assyrian characters were capable of being read in more than one way. Using the key thus obtained, Sayce enlarged his list of supposed sign-values and in 1884 and 1885 published as known the values of thirty-two Hittite signs. In the years that followed Ball and Menant took up the discussion of the Hittite signs, but with no decisive result.

In 1889 Winckler and Abel published in one of the volumes of the Royal Museum at Berlin the first instalment of the text of the El-Amarna letters, in which there were two from Dushratta, King of Mitanni, in the native language of that country, though written in Babylonian characters. In the following year, 1890, Profs. Jensen, Brünnow, and Sayce all published in the *Zeitschrift für Assyriologie* studies of this language, Sayce even venturing a translation of a part of the text. Each of these scholars had worked independently of the others, but none of them seems to have suspected that the language had anything to do with Hittite.

(2) *Peiser.*—In 1892 Dr. Peiser, then of Breslau University, published his book on the Hittite inscriptions, in which he essayed another method of decipherment. Layard had found four Hittite seals in the palace of Sennacherib at Nineveh. Peiser inferred that these must be seals of four Hittite kings mentioned in the inscriptions of that time, and proceeded to assign each seal to the name of a known Hittite king, and interpret the signs on the seal by the name of that king as spelled out in the cuneiform characters of the Assyrian inscriptions. Having obtained in this way tentative values for several signs, he proceeded by inference to guess at other signs, and so tentatively read some inscriptions.

(3) *Jensen.*—Prof. Jensen, of Marburg, wrote in that same year an unfavorable review of Peiser's work. When reading the proofs of his review he added a postscript to say that he believed he had himself discovered the key to Hittite. Two years later, 1894, he published in the Journal of the German Oriental Society his method of solving the problem. Jensen's starting-point was gained from inscriptions from Jerabis, the site of ancient Carchemish, Hamath, and other places. He inferred that a certain sign was the determinative for city, and that the names preceding this sign were names of places. Gaining in this way some values for signs, he read the names of some kings. He found that these names had nominatives ending in *s* and accusative cases ending in *m*; he accordingly leaped to the conclusion that the Hittite language was a member of the Indo-European group of languages, as this is the only known group of tongues in which this phenomenon occurs. This inference later research has in part confirmed. Jensen, however, went further and endeavored to show that the Hittites were the ancestors of the Armenians of later time. This theory led to the publication in 1898 of his book, *Hittiter und Armenier.* Of the correctness of this view he has not been able to convince other scholars. By this time Jensen and others had begun to see that the Mitannians and the Hittites were kindred peoples and worshiped the same gods. It is now recognized that Jensen correctly ascertained the value of some signs, though many of his guesses, like those of his predecessors, have proved incorrect.

(4) *Conder.*—In 1898 Lieut.-Col. C. R. Conder published *The Hittites and Their Language,* a work in which he presented still another decipherment of the inscriptions. Conder's decipherment was based on a comparison of the Hittite characters with the Sumerian pictographs on the one hand and the syllabary which

was used by Greeks in Cyprus, Caria, and Lydia on the other. He assumed that if a picture had in Sumerian a certain syllabic value, and if the Cypriotic syllabary presented a character somewhat resembling it which had a similar value, the Hittite character which most closely resembled these must have the same value, since the Hittites lived between the two peoples who used the other syllabaries. This system of decipherment has attracted no adherents because it is based on a fallacious inference. It does not follow because a nation lives between two other nations, that its institutions are kindred to those of its neighbors. One could not explain writings of the Indian tribes of Arizona, for example, by comparing them with books printed in English in St. Louis and in Spanish in Los Angeles! In 1899 Messerschmidt, who was collecting in one body all the known Hittite inscriptions for publication, published a study of the language of Mitanni,[6] which advanced our knowledge of the language of the letters of Dushratta. Messerschmidt's later publication of the Hittite inscriptions [7] made it far easier for scholars to study the subject.

(5) *Sayce's Later Work*.—Stimulated by Jensen's efforts, Prof. Sayce returned to the study of Hittite in 1903, and published in the *Proceedings of the Society of Biblical Archæology* of that year (Vol. XXV) a new decipherment. He followed Jensen's method, accepting a number of Jensen's readings as proved, and with the originality and daring that characterize so much of his work, launched many new readings. Some of these have commended themselves to his successors.

In 1909 Ferdinand Bork returned to the problem of the language of Mitanni, and published a pretty complete decipherment of the Mitannian tablets in the El-Amarna letters. In 1911 Dr. B. B. Charles, the philologist of the Cornell expedition to Asia Minor, published as Part II of Volume I of *Travels and Studies in the Nearer East,* which was to have embodied, had it been completed, the results of the Cornell expedition, his collation of the Hittite inscriptions. This publication added some new texts to those previously known. In 1912 Prof. Clay, of Yale, rendered the subject of Hittiteology a distinct service by including in his volume of *Personal Names from Cuneiform Inscriptions of the Cassite Period* a list of Hittite and Mitannian proper names, and a list of the nominal and verbal elements which enter into the composition of such names.

6 In the *Mitteilungen der vorderasiatischen Gesellschaft,* 1899, Heft 4.
7 *Ibid.,* 1900, Helte 4 and 5.

(6) *Thompson.*—Another attempt on a large scale to unravel the mystery of the Hittite inscriptions is that of R. Campbell Thompson, "A New Decipherment of the Hittite Hieroglyphs," published in *Archæologia*, second series, Vol. XIV, Oxford, 1913. Mr. Thompson was a member of the British expedition which excavated Carchemish, and gained the idea which gave him the starting-point for his decipherment from an inscription excavated by that expedition. This inscription contained many proper names, and, after passing it and looking at it every day for a long time, it occurred to Mr. Thompson that a certain elaborate sign which frequently occurred in it might be a part of the name of the Hittite King Sangar, who is frequently mentioned by Ashurnasirpal II and Shalmaneser III of Assyria. In seeking proof for this Mr. Thompson was led into a study of the texts which resulted in a new interpretation of the Hittite signs. His work is logical at every point, he makes no inference without first examining all the occurrences in the known texts of the group of signs in question, and he tests his inferences wherever possible by the known results of a study of Mitannian and cuneiform Hittite.

(7) *Delitzsch.*—After the death of Prof. Winckler, the cuneiform tablets which he had discovered at Boghaz Koi were turned over to Ernst Weidner for publication. Prof. Friedrich Delitzsch, under whose general direction Weidner worked, published in May, 1914, a study based on twenty-six fragments of lexicographical texts on which Weidner was working. These texts defined Hittite words in Sumerian and in Assyrian. Although the texts are very fragmentary, Prof. Delitzsch was able to gain in this way a vocabulary of about 165 Hittite words, the meanings of most of which are known, and to ascertain some facts about the grammar of Hittite.

We seemed in 1915 just on the eve of a complete mastery of the secrets of the Hittite inscriptions, and, in part, this was true. Some features of their speech seemed to resemble features of the Indo-European family of languages, but other features appeared to denote Tartar affinities. In a number of instances the influence of the Assyrian language could clearly be traced. Pictures of Hittites appear in Egyptian reliefs. Two distinct types of face are there portrayed. One type has high cheek bones, oblique eyes, and wears a pigtail, like the peoples of Mongolia and China; the other has a clean-cut head and face which resemble somewhat the early Greeks. These were Indo-Europeans.

(8) *Hrozny,* a Bohemian scholar, published in the *Mitteilungen der deutschen Orient-Gesellschaft zu Berlin,* No. 56 (December, 1915), a résumé of a new study of Hittite decipherment. This was followed in 1917 by the publication of a book on the Language of the Hittites, and in 1919 by a book on Hittite Cuneiform Texts from Boghaz Koi.[8] These studies are based on copies of cuneiform tablets at Constantinople made by Professor Hrozny and Dr. Figulla before the war. Hrozny concluded that Hittite is not only an Indo-European language, but that it also belonged to the western half of the Indo-European family. In other words, he found it more closely related to Greek, Latin, Keltic, and the Teutonic tongues than to the Slavonic, Lithuanian, Armenian, and Persian languages, or to Sanscrit and its daughters. According to Hrozny, then, the Hittites came from western Europe, or the center from which the western European peoples radiated. He thought they crossed into Asia by way of the Bosphorus. He supported his contention by some interesting philological analogies. The Mitanni, on the other hand, belonged, he thought, to the eastern half of the Indo-European family. They were closely related to the Slavs, Lithuanians, Armenians, Persians, etc. The indications seem to be that they entered Asia by way of the Caucasus. That the ruling class of the Hittites was of Indo-European stock and that the grammatical structure of the language as well as many elements of its vocabulary are Indo-European was further demonstrated by Ferdinand Sommers[9] and acknowledged by Professor Bloomfield.[10] The present writer's own study of the language convinced him of the truth of this view. The declension of the noun, the general scheme of the conjugation of the verb, the substantive verb "to be" are all Indo-European. The pronouns are practically identical with those of Latin and of some of the older Greek dialects. Many of the roots of individual words are identical with those in Greek and Latin, while others are identical with those in the Teutonic group of languages. All this has been learned by the study of the Hittite documents written in the cuneiform character which Winckler discovered at Boghaz Koi. All that remained for a complete understanding of the language was to work out more completely the meanings of words and the finer shades of grammatical construction.

8 *Die Sprache der Hêthiter,* Leipzig 1916, and *Hethitische Keilschrifttexte aus Boghazkoi* 1919, Leipzig.
9 See *Hethitisches,* Leipzig, 1920-1922.
10 See *Journal of the American Oriental Society,* Vol. 41, pp. 195-210.

Through the labors of E. Forrer, Johannes Friedrich, and Albrecht Götze in Germany, Louis Delaporte [11] in France, and Professor E. H. Sturtevant [12] in America, progress is being constantly made in our knowledge of the grammar and vocabulary of the language. Delaporte published in 1929 a grammar of Hittite; Sturtevant, a glossary which has gone through two editions, and a comparative grammar, while the present writer has published a manual for beginners in Hittite.[13] A study of the tablets from Boghaz Koi reveals the fact that no less than six languages in addition to Sumerian and Akkadian (as the Babylonian Semitic is called) are contained in them. The language spoken by the ruling dynasty at Boghaz Koi (that of Subbiluliuma and his successors) was an offshoot of the Indo-European family of languages. Embedded in the texts of this language there are eighteen quotations of proverbs which are said by the writers to be in Hittite. Scholars call this Proto-Hittite. This real Hittite language is clearly not an Indo-European language. The fact is that the ruling dynasty represented an Indo-European race that had conquered a non-Indo-European race who were the real Hittites.

Another dialect, of which about seven hundred words are preserved in the tablets, is the Luyyish—spoken in the city of Luyya. (See p. 409, § 23.) One fragment of a text is bilingual—Hittite and Luyyish. Luyyish seems, like Hittite, to have been Indo-European.

Still another language, of which the tablets from Boghaz Koi contain about 3500 lines, is the Hurri (formerly read Harri). The Hurri occupied the kingdom of Mitanni and the country east of it. The Mitannians were Hurrian by race. Although it was formerly inferred that the Mitannians were Indo-European from the fact that among their gods were Mitra, Varuna, and Indra, gods of the Aryans in India, it now appears that only the ruling class in Mitanni were of the Indo-European stock, and that they were neither numerous enough nor strong enough to impose their language on the country as the Indo-Europeans at Boghaz Koi did, but spoke the language of their non-Indo-European subjects, who were Hurri.

11 L. Delaporte, *Elements de la grammaire hittite*, Paris, 1929.
12 E. H. Sturtevant, *Hittite Glossary*, 2nd ed., Baltimore, 1936; a *Comparative Grammar of the Hittite Language*, Philadelphia, 1933, and, in collaboration with George Bechtel, *Hittite Chrestomathy*, Philadelphia, 1935.
13 G. A. Barton, *A Hittite Manual for Beginners*, Paris, 1928; and, in collaboration with Baruch Weitzel, *A Hittite Chrestomathy*, Paris, 1932.

Yet another language, represented in the tablets by five extracts, is the Balish. The passages in question are proverbs, which contain words identical with words in Hittite and Luyyish. Whether they are borrowed words, or whether Balish was really an Indo-European tongue, we cannot yet tell.

In four tablets there are quotations of the Manda language.

We are now in a position to see that in all probability the great mass of the people who were vaguely called Hittites by Biblical writers and by the Assyrians were neither Indo-Europeans nor Semites.

The art found at Nuzi, at Tell Halaf, at Tell Billah, and Tepe Gawra is, as Speiser has shown,[14] connected with that of the Hittites and the ancient Elamites, and shows that the Proto-Hittites shared the civilization of the Elamites.

(9) While the cuneiform Hittite has attracted much attention in recent years, the hieroglyphic Hittite has not been neglected. In 1920 Dr. A. E. Cowley, in his "Schweich Lectures" on the *Hittites*,[15] devoted a chapter to the decipherment of these characters. He started anew as though nothing had previously been done, collecting groups of signs from different inscriptions, grouping those which were followed by the same determinative, and assuming that they were proper names; he grouped those that were written by means of the same signs in the different inscriptions, tentatively equated them with known names that would be likely to be mentioned, and so obtained probable values for many signs.

(10) A similar effort was made in 1923 by a German scholar, Dr. Carl Frank,[16] who followed much the same method as Cowley, but accumulated a larger number of names and worked out his values in greater detail.

(11) In 1929 an Italian scholar, Piero Meriggi, published another attempt [17] to advance our knowledge of this baffling writing. Like his predecessors, he attempted to gain phonetic values by the analysis of the hieroglyphic writing of known proper names. He afterward pursued the subject, elaborating his method in at least two other essays.[18]

14 *Mesopotamian Origins*, Philadelphia, 1930.
15 London, 1920.
16 *Die sogenannien hettitischen Hieroglypheninschriften*, Leipzig, 1923, in Band XVI of *Abhandlungen fur die Kunde des Morgenlandes*, edited by Geiger, Littmann, and Steindorf.
17 "Die hethitische Hieroglyphenschrift," in the *Zeitschrift für Assyriologie*, XXXIX (1929-30), pp. 165-212.
18 Cf. *Orientalische Literatur-zeitung* XXXVI (Feb. 1933), 73 ff. and *Mitteilungen der vorderasiatische-aegyptische Gesellschaft*, XXXIX (1934), Heft 1.

(12) More ambitious is the work of Ignace J. Gelb,[19] who, building upon the work of all his predecessors, and coördinating his results with the knowledge obtained from the cuneiform Hittite, has extended his work further and essayed the translation of some simple inscriptions.

(13) Professor Emil O. Forrer, of the Oriental Institute of the University of Chicago, in April, 1932, published a different method of attacking the problem.[20] In so far as he ventured to give phonetic values to Hittite signs his results often differ from those of his predecessors.

(14) Helmuth T. Bossert [21] published in 1932 an article in which he advanced the decipherment materially toward a secure foundation.

(15) In 1933 Hrozny, who had found the key to the Hittite cuneiform, published a new and partly independent decipherment.[22] This work embodied new and independent discoveries. As a result the decipherment of the Hittite hieroglyphs has been put upon a solid basis. Some fifty phonetic characters and many ideograms can now be read with considerable confidence. The language is related to the cuneiform Hittite, and appears to be related to the Luyyish dialect already mentioned.[23]

4. **Hittite History.**

(1) *First Appearance.*—The earliest reference to the Hittites which we have in any written record occurs in a Babylonian chronicle, which states that "against Shamsu-ditana the men of the country Khattu marched." [24]   Shamsu-ditana was the last king of the first dynasty of Babylon. His reign terminated in 1870 B.C. Khattu land, as will appear further on, was the name later given to the Hittite settlement in Cappadocia. One would naturally suppose that the name would have the same significance here, but of this we cannot be certain. The tablet on which this chronicle was written was inscribed in the Persian or late Babylonian period, but there is evidence that it was copied from an earlier original. If its statement is true, the Hittites had made their appearance in history and were prepared to mingle in that *mêlée* of the races which occurred when the first dynasty of Babylon was overthrown. Nothing

19 *Hittite Hieroglyphs,* I, Chicago, 1931; II, 1934.
20 See his article, "Die sogenannte hethitische Bilderschrift," in the *American Journal of Semitic Languages and Literatures.* XLVIII, 137–169. (April, 1932.)
21 *Mitteilungen der altorientalischen Gesellschaft,* VI, Heft 3, 1932.
22 *Les inscriptions hittites hieroglyphiques,* Paris, 1933.
23 The results attained are discussed by Sturtevant in *Language,* VIII, 1933, 273–279 and by Dhorme in *Syria,* XIV, 1933, 341–367.
24 See L. W. King, *Chronicles Concerning Early Babylonian Kings,* London, 1907, Vol. II, p. 22.

is said in the chronicle as to the location of the land of Khattu, but there can be no doubt that the Hittites approached Babylonia from the northwest. Their seat must have been in the region where we later find the Hittites, or Mitanni. At what period the Hittites came into this region we can only conjecture. The excavations at Sakje-Geuze reveal a civilization there extending back to about 3000 b.c., which resembled that found at Susa in Elam belonging to the same period. This civilization may not have been Hittite in its beginnings. Mr. Woolley, a member of the British expedition which excavated at Carchemish, in a study of the objects found in tombs at Carchemish and at other places near by, thinks it possible that the coming of the Hittites is marked by a transition period in the art—a period the termination of which he marks by the date of the fall of the first dynasty of Babylon. It may well be that Indo-Europeans followed by Mongols came about 2100 or 2000 into this region, or that the Mongols were there earlier and that the Indo-Europeans then came. In the resultant civilization it would seem, from the information that we have, that there was a mingling of the two races; (see Fig. 24).

(2) *Hyksos Possibly Hittites or Hurrians.*—Since the Hittites were able to help overthrow the first dynasty of Babylon, some scholars have recognized the possibility that those invaders of Egypt who established the dynasties called Hyksos may have been Hittites, or may have been led by Hittites. There is much evidence that many Semites entered Egypt at that time, but as Syria and Palestine were peopled with Semites earlier than this, such an invasion would naturally have had many Semites among its camp followers, if not in its armies, even if the leaders were Hittites. At present, however, this is but a possibility. Some slight evidence in favor of the possibility may be found in the name of the king of Jerusalem who was a vassal of Amenophis IV, and who wrote the letters from Jerusalem which are in the El-Amarna collection. (See p. 442, § 2.) His name was Abdi-Hepa, and Hepa was a Hittite and Mitannian deity. Abdi-Hepa had grown up a trusted subject of the Egyptians. His ancestors must, therefore, have been in Palestine for some time. A settlement of Hittites there in the Hyksos days would account for this. The twenty-third chapter of Genesis represents the city of Hebron as in the possession of the Hittites when Abraham purchased the cave of Machpelah as a place of burial for his dead; and, though many scholars regard Genesis 23, which gives this account, as a late composi-

tion, its representation would receive some confirmation from archæology if the Hyksos were Hittites.

There is a possibility that the Hittites were in southern Palestine earlier than this. Brugsch [25] thought that he found in an inscription in the Louvre, written by an officer of Amenemhet I, King of Egypt, 2000–1970 B.C., a statement that this officer had destroyed the palaces of the Hittites near the Egyptian frontier of Palestine. This reading was defended by Prof. Sayce,[26] though other Egyptologists, such as W. Max Müller [27] and Breasted,[28] claim that the word that was thought to be Hittite is not a proper name, but a common noun meaning nomads. The text of the passage is uncertain, and no important inference can in any case be made from it.

During the period when we obtain glimpses of the history of the Hittites, they were never united in one empire. Different kingdoms flourished here and there, such as that of the Mitanni in Mesopotamia, the Hittites at Boghaz Koi, the kingdoms of Carchemish, of Hamath, and Tyana. These flourished at different times all the way from 1400 to 700 B.C., and there were doubtless other kingdoms also, for the Hittite sculptures near Smyrna and Manissia cannot have been made by any of these, unless possibly the great Hittite kingdom at Boghaz Koi may once have extended its power to the Ægean.

(3) *The Mitanni.*—The earliest of these kingdoms which we can trace is that of the Mitanni. Why it took the name Mitanni we do not yet know. The people were really Hurri, Mattiuaza, son of Dushratta, in his treaty with Subbiluliuma, twice employs the phrase "we Hurri." [29] Perhaps the ruling house were Aryans, for Indra, Varuna and Mitra were among the Mitannian deities, but the Hurrians as a race were not, as Hrozny once thought, Aryans. When Thothmes III of Egypt extended his conquests to the Euphrates in 1468 B.C., he came into contact with the Mitanni. The king of the country is not named, but it was claimed that her chiefs hid themselves in caves.[30] There is some reason for believing that their chief city was near Haran,[31] Mesopotamia, the city where Abraham sojourned for a time (Gen. 11:31, 12:4). If this be

25 *History of Egypt*, II, 404, 405.
26 *Expository Times*, November, 1914, p. 91.
27 *Asien und Europa nach altägyptischen Denkmälern*, 319, note 3.
28 *Ancient Records, Egypt*, I, 227, 228.
29 See G. A. Barton, *Semitic and Hamitic Origins*, Philadelphia, 1934, p. 44.
30 Breasted's *Ancient Records, Egypt*, II, § 773.
31 Winckler in *Mitteilungen der vorderasiatischen Gesellschaft*, 1913, Heft 4, p. 81.

true, it gives a new meaning to Ezekiel 16:3: "The Amorite was thy father and thy mother was a Hittite." Thothmes evidently touched the kingdom of Mitanni on its western border. He did not penetrate its heart or overcome its king. Although he took tribute, he does not tell us the name of the king of the Mitanni whose armies he fought.

Half a century later the king of the Mitanni was Artatama I. He was a contemporary of Thothmes IV of Egypt, who ruled 1420–1411 B.C. Perhaps it was their mutual fear of the rising power of the Hittite kingdom at Boghaz Koi that led Artatama and Thothmes IV to form an alliance. At all events, such an alliance was made, and Thothmes married a daughter of Artatama, though Artatama's grandson says that the Egyptian king sent his request for her hand seven times before Artatama yielded to his solicitations. Artatama I was succeeded by Shutarna I, whose reign overlapped a part of that of Amenophis III of Egypt, 1411-1375 B.C. Among the queens of Amenophis III was a daughter of Shutarna I. Before the reign of Amenophis III had ended Shutarna I had been succeeded by Dushratta, who continued the friendly relations with Egypt. Dushratta's reign also overlapped in part that of Amenophis IV of Egypt, 1375–1357 B.C., and Dushratta wrote several letters to both of these Egyptian kings. It is from these letters that we gain most of our information about Mitanni.

Meanwhile the great kingdom of the Hittites at Boghaz Koi had entered upon its era of expansion under Subbiluliuma, who pushed his conquests first eastward and then southward. Dushratta feared to meet the Hittite in battle and retired to the eastward, allowing much of his counry to be overrun. This land Subbiluliuma gave to one of his allies, and Dushratta was murdered soon afterward by his son, Sutatarra, who usurped the crown. Soon after this the Assyrians invaded the lands of the Mitanni from the east, and the land, already distracted by its internal divisions, was thrown into a worse confusion. At this juncture Subbiluliuma crossed the Euphrates again and entered Mitannian territory. He was accompanied by settlers who brought cattle, sheep, and horses to remain in the country. Advised by an oracle, he deposed Sutatarra and placed upon the throne Mattiuaza, a son of Dushratta, who had been heir-apparent and who had fled when his father was murdered. To Mattiuaza Subbiluliuma gave his daughter in marriage, and Mitanni became a vassal state of the Hittite realm. After this our sources tell us no more of its history.

Near the Mitanni was another kingdom of the Hurri, who were certainly of the same race, for in the time of Subbiluliuma they were ruled first by Artatama II, a brother of Dushratta, and then by Sutarna II. This state also became a part of Subbiluliuma's kingdom.

(4) *Kingdom of "Hittite City."*—The wave of migration from the northeast which brought the Mitanni into upper Mesopotamia had swept on westward into Cappadocia, where the greatest Hittite state afterward developed. The monuments erected by the Hittites were nearly all of a religious character. In the earlier time they wrote few historical inscriptions. Such inscriptions as we have in Hittite hieroglyphs seem to come from the later periods and to record alliances. It is probable that in the development of the Hittite state in Cappadocia first one city and then another had the upper hand. The Hittite monuments at Eyuk are of a more primitive character than those at Boghaz Koi, and it is natural to suppose that a Hittite state flourished here before the rise of the one at Boghaz Koi. Be that as it may, the most powerful Hittite monarchy of which we know arose at Boghaz Koi, which they called "Hittite City." This monarchy emerged about 1400 B.C. Its first king was Hattusil I, of whom we know no more than that he was the founder of the great dynasty which ruled from the "Hittite City" for two hundred years.

The king who laid the foundations of the greatness of this dynasty was Subbiluliuma, the next king, whose conquests over the Mitanni and Hurri we have already traced. He conquered also a number of neighboring states, and compelled them to sign with him treaties of alliance which made them his vassals. Chronicles of these events were discovered by Winckler among the clay tablets found at Boghaz Koi. Subbiluliuma also turned his armies southward and conquered Syria down to the confines of Palestine. These conquests were in progress when some of the El-Amarna letters, written to Amenophis IV of Egypt and translated in Part II, p. 441, ff. were written. Here he pursued the same policy that he had pursued in Mesopotamia, and compelled the conquered countries to enter into treaties with him, which subjugated them to his will. Among the kings so treated was the Amorite King Aziru, who at that time ruled Amorites living in the southern part of the valley between the Lebanon mountain ranges and in the region afterward occupied by the tribe of Asher. They also held some of the southern Phœnician cities. This represents the most southerly extension of Subbiluliuma's power.

Whether Subbiluliuma also extended his conquests to the west of Asia Minor, we have no means of knowing. Some scholars suppose that he had done so before he began the conquest of Mitanni. Certain it is that Hittite rock sculptures of gigantic size exist in the mountains near Smyrna and Manissia, to the west of Sardis. These sculptures represent the great Hittite goddess. Near Smyrna there are also the remains of great buildings. We know of no Hittite monarch who would be so likely to have carried Hittite power to these parts as Subbiluliuma. If he did so, possibly in later time the Hittites here became independent. At all events, some centuries later they were known to Ionian Greeks in this region, for Homer's *Odyssey,* Book XI, line 521, records the tradition that some Hittites were killed with Eurypylos.

When Subbiluliuma died he was succeeded by his son, Arandas, whose occupation of the throne was brief, and who seems to have been without effective power. After a short time he was replaced by his brother, Mursil, who appears to have enjoyed a long reign. Subbiluliuma, called by the Egyptians Seplel, was reigning when Amenophis IV of Egypt came to the throne in 1375 B.C., for he sent an embassy to congratulate him, and Mursil appears to have reigned until after the year 1320 B.C. The two reigns, therefore, covered more than half a century. The first years of Mursil's reign were apparently passed in peace, but soon after 1320 Shalmaneser I invaded the countries in the eastern part of the Hittite confederacy, conquering all the territory east of the Euphrates, and a considerable territory to the west of that river. Meantime, Mursil had renewed the treaty with the Amorites of Syria, whose king at this time was Abbi-Teshub, or Abi-Adda. Ere long, however, trouble arose for him on his southern border. Seti I of Egypt came to the throne in 1313 B.C., and began a series of vigorous campaigns, for the conquest of Palestine. In time he came face to face with the Hittite power in Syria.

At this juncture Mursil died and was succeeded by his son, Mutallu, who soon met Seti I in battle and convinced that monarch that it was unwise to attempt to extend Egypt's empire in Asia to the Euphrates, as Thothmes III had done. Owing to internal troubles in Assyria the eastern border of the Hittite realm was left undisturbed for a considerable time, during which Mutallu could devote himself to other matters. In 1292 B.c. Ramses II succeeded Seti I as king of Egypt and soon began vigorously to push Egyptian conquests into northern Syria. Mutallu recognized the importance of the struggle and collected a large army from all his allies. These forces were drawn from all parts of Asia Minor; even the countries of the extreme west contributed their quota. Aleppo and states in that region also contributed their share. A great battle was fought at Kadesh on the Orontes in 1287 B.c., in which Mutallu, by surprising his foe, disorganized a part of the Egyptian forces and endangered the life of Ramses himself. By the opportune arrival of reinforcements the Egyptians escaped entire defeat, so that the result was a drawn battle.

The battle had, however, cost the Hittites much. The slaughter of their forces had been enormous. Among the slain were many chieftains, including the king of Aleppo. The Amorites at once threw off their allegiance to the Hittites, and many of the other troops mutinied. Mutallu was assassinated. He was succeeded by Hattusil II, the Khetasar of the Egyptian inscriptions.

Assyria had become weak, so that Hattusil was no longer pressed upon his eastern border. After a little he reduced the Amorites once more to submission, and compelled them to take back their king, Put-akhi, whom they had driven out at the time of their rebellion against Mutallu. He gave Put-akhi a Hittite princess for a wife. Later, about 1271 B.c., Hattusil concluded an offensive and defensive alliance with Ramses II of Egypt. The treaty which guaranteed this alliance has come down to us. (See Chapter I, p. 20.)

Hattusil II must have enjoyed a long reign, but we do not know the date of his death. He had two successors, Dudkhalia and Arnuanta, whose reigns are known to us, and who continued the sway of the dynasty down to about 1200 B.c. They were respectively the son and grandson of Hattusil II. An edict of Dudkhalia concerning the vassal states has survived, in which the name of Eni-Teshub, King of Carchemish, appears. Carchemish would seem to have been the chief of the allied states. Of Arnuanta we have no details, though two fragments of royal edicts and a seal of his own have come down to us. He was called "the great king, the son of Dudkhalia." After him our sources fail, and the story ends in darkness. We know, however, that the days of the power of this dynasty were over. Egyptian sources tell us that tribes from western Asia Minor and from beyond the sea swept over Cilicia and northern Syria soon after the year 1200 B.C., and there was then no Hittite power there to restrain them.

(5) *Carchemish.*—Of the other Hittite kingdoms far less is known. Carchemish, which, as we have just seen, played an important part in the federation of the great Hittite power, continued its existence for several centuries. In the time of Ashurnasirpal II and Shalmaneser III the kingdom of Carchemish entered into alliance with these kings and preserved its existence by becoming their vassal. Judging from the meager reports hitherto published of the British excavation at Carchemish, this was a flourishing period in the history of the city. A hundred years later, in the reign of Sargon, Pisiris, who was then king of Carchemish, defied the Assyrian, who brought the kingdom to an end in 717 B.C. (Cf. Isa. 10:9.)

(6) *Samal and Yadi.*—When the Aramæans swept westward about 1300 B.C. they apparently dislodged the Hittites from a number of their sites and occupied their country. Among the places so occupied was the site of Sendjirli mentioned above. All the carvings found among its architectural remains reveal the influence of Hittite art, but the inscriptions found there are in Aramaic. These inscriptions show that there were in that region two petty kingdoms named, respectively, Samal and Yadi. The names of several kings of these monarchies who ruled between 850 and 730 B.C. have been recovered. They are all Aramæan.

(7) *Hamath.*—Farther to the south, at Hamath on the Orontes, a Hittite kingdom existed in the time of David. Its king was then called Toi or Tou, who made an alliance with David (2 Sam. 8:9, f; 1 Chron. 18:9, f.). This kingdom was probably the outgrowth of the earlier occupation of the Orontes valley, three hundred years before, by the Hittites of the great empire. It continued until the time of Ahab. Its king was then Irhulina, who along with Ahab, Ben-Hadad of Damascus, and several other kings made an alliance to resist the encroachments of Shalmaneser III of Assyria in 854 B.C. See Part II, ch. XIX, § 6.) Irhulina caused several inscriptions to be made on stone, which survived at Hamath until our time. According to Mr. Thompson's interpretation of them they are all records of Irhulina's various alliances. By the

next century, however, the Aramæans had captured Hamath, for in the reigns of Tiglath-pileser III (745–727) and of Sargon (722-705 B.C.) the names of its kings were Semitic. These names were, respectively, Enu-ilu and Yau-bidi, or Ilu-bidi.

We gain glimpses also of a number of other Hittite states.[32] There was, for example, the state of Kummukh, which lay to the west of the Euphrates, and another in western Cilicia, that had its center at Tyana, the modern Bor. These states appear to have reached their zenith after the fall of the great Hittite dynasty which had its capital at Boghaz Koi. Doubtless as time goes on we shall learn of the existence of many other small Hittite kingdoms which flourished at one time or another. At some time, either when the Hyksos were making their way into Egypt or when Subbiluliuma was pushing southward into Syria, the Hittites mentioned in the Old Testament must have made some small settlements in Palestine. Here the Hebrews came into contact with them. They were really an unimportant outlying fringe of the great Hittite people, but they had the good fortune to have their names preserved in the most immortal literature in the world, the Bible, and so their memory was ever kept alive, while that of their more illustrious kinsmen was utterly forgotten. It is only archæological research that has restored something of the original perspective.

The Hittite laws, written in cuneiform on tablets found by Winckler at Boghaz Koi, are translated in Part II, Chapter XIV, p. 407 ff.

32 For a fuller account of the great Hittite empire, see John Garstang, *The Hittite Empire*, London, 1929; G. Contenau, *La civilisation des Hittites et des Mitaniens*, Paris, 1934, and Louis Delaporte, *Les Hittites*, Paris, 1936, and A. Götze, *Hethiter, Churriter und Assyrier*, Oslo, 1936.

CHAPTER IV

PALESTINE AND ITS EXPLORATION

THE LAND: Rainfall. EARLY EXPLORATION: Place names. EARLY AMER-
ICAN EXPLORATIONS: Robinson and Smith. Lynch. American exploration
societies. PALESTINE EXPLORATION FUND: Warren's excavations at Jerusalem. The survey of Palestine. Exploration of Tell el-Hesy. Bliss's ex-
cavation at Jerusalem. Excavation at Azekah. At Tell es-Safi (Gath?). Tell
el-Judeideh. At Marash (Moresheth-Gath). Gezer. Beth-Shemesh. Ex-
ploring the Wilderness of Zin. Ashkelon. Gaza. Tell Jemmeh. Jerusalem.
Tell Duweir. THE GERMAN PALESTINE SOCIETY: Guthe's excavation at
Jerusalem. Megiddo. Taanach. Capernaum. Jericho. Balata. THE
AMERICAN SCHOOLS OF ORIENTAL RESEARCH. HARVARD EXCAVATIONS AT
SAMARIA. PARKER'S EXCAVATIONS AT JERUSALEM. ASSUMPTIONIST
FATHERS AT JERUSALEM. LATEST EXCAVATIONS.

1. The Land.—Palestine is a very different land from either
Egypt or Mesopotamia. They are made by the irrigation of rivers.
Palestine is fertilized by rain from heaven. In them the scenery
is monotonous; they are river valleys each of which was once in
part an arm of the sea, but now filled up by the gradual deposit
of mud. Palestine was formed in one of the greatest geological
upheavals the earth ever experienced. This was nothing less than
a great rift in the earth's crust extending from the Lebanon mountains to the Indian Ocean. The strata on the west side of this
rift slipped downward past those on its east side for a mile or more.
Those on the west were bent at different points in this long course
in different ways, but the result of the rift itself was to form the
Jordan valley and the bed of the Dead Sea, the valley which runs
from the Dead Sea to the Gulf of Akaba, and that deep rift between Asia and Africa which forms the Red Sea itself.

In Palestine the strata on the west of this rift bent up into two
parallel ridges, to the west of which a narrow plain of varying
width, ancient Philistia, rises from the sea. To the east of this
rift the land remained at approximately its old level. The various
ridges of the country are, on account of the birth-pangs of their
origin, intersected with valleys innumerable, so that in no country
of the world can such variety of scenery and climate be found within
such narrow limits.

93

Rainfall.—This land, with all its variety of form, is redeemed from the desert by the moisture which the west winds drive in from the Mediterranean Sea. These winds in the winter months bring clouds, which, when they come into contact with the colder air over the elevated hills, deposit their moisture in rain. The Jordan valley is so warm that little rain falls upon it, but it drains the water from the rainfall on both sides of it. Just so far back as the clouds reach before their moisture is exhausted, just so far the fertile land extends; beyond that is the Arabian Desert. When the rainfall during a winter is good, bountiful crops are raised the following season; when it is scant, the harvest fails and famine follows. In Egypt and Babylonia a man could water his garden by kicking a hole in a dyke; they were lands which were watered "with thy foot" (Deut. 11 : 10) ; Palestine was dependent on heaven for its life, and we cannot doubt that this fact was one of the instruments for the training of the Israelites for their great religious mission. In a land of such variety—a land in which for nine months in the year snow-capped Hermon may be seen from many an elevated point and from the whole stretch of the tropical Jordan valley, where oleanders are blooming and mustard seeds are growing into trees—it was possible to think of God in a way that was at least more difficult in Egypt or in Mesopotamia.

Here in this marvelous land, which formed a bridge between the two oldest civilizations of the world, the men lived to whom God committed the task of writing most of the Bible. This was the earthly home of the Son of God.

Even before the Hebrews came into it, many had crossed this bridge and some had paused long upon it. Living here they had left the remains of their homes, their cities, and their civilizations. Archæology is now recovering these. After the time of Christ various races and civilizations continued to pass over the bridge. Their remains buried those left by earlier men. The story of the recovery of these earlier remains is, accordingly, not only of great interest, but often of great value to the reader of the Bible.

2. Early Exploration.—The misfortunes which overtook Judæa in the years 70 and 132–135 A.D., in consequence of the Jewish rebellions against Rome, led to the paganizing of Jerusalem and the expulsion of the Jews from Judæa. At this period Christianity was a struggling and a persecuted religion, too busy working its way to take an active interest in the land of its birth. When Constan-

tine early in the fourth century made Christianity the religion of
the Roman Empire, all this was changed. Both Constantine and
his mother, Helena, took the deepest interest in identifying the holy
places in Jerusalem, and a stream of pilgrims began at once to visit
the land. The earliest of these to leave us an account of his
travels was a pilgrim from Bordeaux who visited Palestine in 333
A.D.[1] As he was anxious to see the principal places hallowed by the
bodily presence of Christ and the heroes of Scripture, he visited
places in different parts of the country. He was followed by many
others. The stream has been almost continuous down to the
present time. As the aim of these travelers was devotional and
they possessed little scholarly training or critical faculty, their
works are of secondary value to the modern student. They did,
however, prevent too serious loss of knowledge of the country which
has been revered by worshippers of Jehovah for so many centuries.

Place Names.—At the very beginning of this period Eusebius of
Cæsarea, a contemporary of Constantine, compiled a list of the
place names of Palestine which are mentioned in the Bible. The
names were arranged in alphabetical order, the events for which the
places are celebrated were given, in many instances identifications
with places existing in the fourth century were proposed, and the
distances from other well-known places mentioned. In the next
century this work was translated into Latin by Jerome, who lived
many years at Bethlehem and traveled extensively in Palestine,
and who died in 420 A.D. It is called the *Onomasticon.*

3. **Early American Explorations.**—As the reader approaches
modern times he finds the works of some of the pilgrims assuming
a more scientific character. To some extent, too, these works were
supplemented by those of travelers like Châteaubriand,[2] Burckhardt,[3] and Lamartine.[4]

(1) *Robinson and Smith.*—The scientific study of the localities
and antiquities of Palestine was, however, begun by an American,
the late Prof. Edward Robinson, of Union Theological Seminary,
New York City. Robinson was fully equipped with Biblical
knowledge, and was thoroughly familiar with Josephus and other
works bearing on his subject. He possessed the critical faculty in
a high degree, and combined with it a keen constructive faculty. In

1 *Itinerary from Bordeaux to Jerusalem,* "The Bordeaux Pilgrim" (A.D. 333), tr.
Aubrey Stewart and annotated C. W. Wilson, Palestine Pilgrims' Text Society, London,
1887.
2 *Itinéraire de Paris a Jérusalem,* Paris, 1811.
3 *Travels in Syria,* 1821.
4 *Souvenirs, impressions, et paysages, pendant un voyage en Orient,* Paris, 1835.

1838 and again in 1852 he traveled through Palestine with Eli Smith, a missionary. They were equipped with compass, telescope, thermometer, and measuring tape. His knowledge of history enabled Robinson to look beneath many traditions. With keen penetration he discerned under the guise of many a modern Arabic name the form of a Biblical original, and accomplished more for the scientific study of Biblical Palestine than any of his predecessors. As he traveled he also noted and briefly described such remains of antiquity as could be seen above ground. The results of Robinson's first journey were embodied in his *Biblical Researches,* New York, 1841. In the second edition, London, 1856, the results of the second journey were embodied, and the number of volumes increased to three. The impetus given to the exploration of Palestine by the labors of Robinson was continued by Tobler, Guérin, Renan, and many others.[5]

(2) *Lynch.*—Meantime, another American, Lieut. W. F. Lynch, of the United States Navy, rendered an important service by the exploration in 1848 of the Dead Sea. In April and May of that year about three weeks were spent in exploring that body of water. Lieut. Lynch was accompanied by Dr. Anderson, a geologist. The party traversed the sea back and forth in two metal boats that had been launched on the Sea of Galilee and floated down the Jordan. The fact that the Jordan Valley is lower than the level of the sea had never been recognized until 1837, and, until the visit of Lynch and Anderson, the depth of the depression was only a matter of conjecture. By this expedition it was scientifically determined that the surface of the Dead Sea is 1,300 feet lower than that of the Mediterranean.[6]

(3) *American Exploration Societies.*—The work of American exploration was later continued by the American Exploration Society, founded in 1870. Under its auspices, Rev. John A. Paine, of Tarrytown, New York, visited the Holy Land. One of the results of his visit was the identification of Pisgah.[7]

Later an American Palestine Exploration Society was organized. This Society employed Mr. Rudolph Meyer, an engineer, to make a map of Palestine, and from 1875 to 1877 also employed Rev. Selah Merrill, who afterward was for many years the U. S. Consul at

---

5 For a more complete account see F. J. Bliss, *The Development of Palestine Exploration,* New York, 1906.

6 See *Official Report of the United States Expedition to Explore the Dead Sea and the River Jordan,* Baltimore, 1852.

7 See his "Identification of Pisgah" in the third *Statement* of the American Exploration Society, 1870.

Jerusalem, as explorer. Dr. Merrill gathered much archæological information, especially in the country east of the Jordan.[8]

4. **Palestine Exploration Fund.**—As a result of the interest engendered by the work of Robinson, Lynch, and others, the Palestine Exploration Fund was organized in London in 1865. By this act a permanent body was created to foster continuously the exploration of the Holy Land, and to rescue the work from the fitful activities of individual enterprise. Such enterprise could supplement the work of the Fund, but could no longer hope to compete with it.

Within six months from the organization of the Palestine Exploration Fund its first expedition was sent out. This was led by Capt., afterward Gen., Sir Charles Warren, who had just completed a survey of Jerusalem as part of a plan for bringing water into the city. The chief object of this expedition, which was in the field from December, 1865, to May, 1866, was to indicate spots for future excavation. It made a series of sketch maps of the country on the scale of one inch to the mile, studied some synagogues in Galilee noted by Robinson, but not fully described by him, and laid bare on Mount Gerizim the remains of a church built on a rough platform which may once have supported the Samaritan temple.

(1) *Warren's Excavations at Jerusalem.*—A second expedition, under Warren, made considerable excavations on the temple-hill at Jerusalem. He sank a remarkable series of shafts to the bottom of the walls enclosing the temple area, and proved that in places these walls rest on foundations from 80 to 125 feet below the present surface. He laid bare solid masonry, which bore what are apparently Phœnician quarry-marks and which he believed to go back to the time of Solomon. On the west side of the temple enclosure he found 80 feet below the present surface the ruins of a bridge, which Robinson had conjectured crossed the Tyropœon Valley from the temple enclosure at this point from an arch, the base of which is still visible outside of the temple wall.[9] Among many other discoveries made by Warren were a part of the ancient city wall south of the temple area and an underground passage leading up from the ancient spring of Gihon, which was probably the "gutter" (R. V., "watercourse") of 2 Samuel 5:8.

8 See his *East of the Jordan*, New York, 1883.
9 Warren's results were first published in *The Recovery of Jerusalem*, London, 1870, and more fully in *Jerusalem*, London, 1889, one of the *Memoirs* of the Palestine Exploration Fund. The arch mentioned is called "Robinson's Arch," because its significance was first perceived by Robinson.

(2) *The Survey of Palestine.*—After this the Palestine Exploration Fund undertook a survey of Palestine, the object of which was to make a complete and authoritative map of the country on the scale of one inch to a mile, and also a description of all archæological remains of antiquity which were above ground. The work was undertaken in 1871 and the survey of western Palestine was completed in 1878. Owing to an outbreak of cholera, the work was interrupted from 1874 to 1877. Among those who took part in it were Capt. C. R. Conder (subsequently Lieut.-Col.), who was in charge of the work from 1872 to 1874, and Capt. Kitchener (afterward Lord Kitchener). The great map was published in 1880, and covers an area of 6,000 square miles, from the Mediterranean to the Jordan and from the Egyptian desert to a point near Tyre. The completion of this map was a monumental accomplishment, and must form the basis for all similar work. The archæological remains noted on the map are described in three volumes of *Memoirs,* also published by the Exploration Fund.

In 1881 Capt. Conder was sent out to make a similar survey of the country east of the Jordan. He endeavored to work under the old permit from the Turkish government, but to this the Turks objected. After working for ten weeks, during which he surveyed about 500 square miles of territory, he was compelled to desist. The results of his work, however, fill a stout volume entitled *The Survey of Eastern Palestine,* London, 1889. The work undertaken by Conder has since been carried on by other agencies. Dr. Gottlieb Schumacher, an engineer residing at Haifa, who was employed in surveying the railway to Mecca, has published authoritative volumes on the region to the east of the Sea of Galilee.[10] On a larger scale is the work of Brünnow and Domaszewsky on the Roman province of Arabia,[11] a work which includes ancient Edom as far as Petra. The last-mentioned remarkable city has been described also in two excellent volumes by Gustaf H. Dalman, Director of the German Evangelical Institute in Jerusalem.[12]

In 1873–1874 the Palestine Exploration Fund entrusted an archæological mission of a general nature to the French scholar, Clermont-Ganneau, who several years before had been French Consul at Jerusalem. Clermont-Ganneau was embarrassed by the failure of the Turkish government to grant him a firman, but made

---

10 *Across the Jordan,* London, 1886; *Jaulan,* London, 1886, and *Abila, Pella, and Northern Aijlun,* London, 1889.
11 *Die Provincia Arabia,* Strassburg, 1904–1909 (3 volumes).
12 *Petra,* Leipzig, 1908, and *Neu-Petra Forschung,* Leipzig, 1912.

numerous archæological discoveries in the country between Jaffa and Jerusalem. These were published by the Fund in two large volumes,[13] although they did not appear until 1896 and 1899, respectively.

In the winter of 1883–1884, a complete geological survey was made of the valley of the Dead Sea and the region to the south (Wady el-Arabah) by Prof. Edward Hull, who afterward published a volume on the subject.[14] Hull was accompanied by Major Kitchener, who made a complete triangulation of the district lying between Mount Sinai and the Wady el-Arabah.

(3) *Exploration of Tell el-Hesy.*—In 1890 the Exploration Fund entered upon a new phase of work or, rather, resumed one that had been interrupted for twenty years,—that of excavation. The services of Prof. Petrie, the Egyptian explorer, were secured and the attempt to wrest from the soil of Palestine some of the buried secrets of the past was renewed. The site chosen was Tell el-Hesy, where stood in ancient times a city then believed to be Lachish (Josh. 10:3; 2 Kings 14:19; 18:14, etc.). This mound rose about 120 feet above the bed of an intermittent stream. About 60 feet of this height consisted of accumulated débris of an ancient city. The water in the course of centuries had so exposed some of the potsherds that Petrie was confident before he began digging that rich discoveries awaited him. He worked here only about six weeks, running trenches into different parts of the mound, but he found and classified such a variety of pottery that he felt confident that he had unearthed a city which had been occupied from a time anterior to the Hebrew conquest of Canaan down to about 350 B.C.[15]

In 1892 the work was continued under the direction of Dr. Frederick J. Bliss, who cut away a considerable section from the northeast corner of the mound, and found the stratified remains of eight different cities, one above the other.[16] In the third of these cities from the bottom a cuneiform tablet was found, which mentions one of the men who figure in the letters found at Tell el-Amarna in Egypt. This tablet would indicate that this third city was flourishing during the period 1400–1350 B.C. The two cities below this must, accordingly, belong to an earlier period. Bliss supposed that the first city was built about 1700 B.C. Above the remains of the third city was a bed of ashes of some thick-

13 *Archaeological Researches in Palestine*, London, 1896–1899.
14 *Geology of Palestine and Arabia Petraea*, London, 1886.
15 See Petrie, *Tell el-Hesy (Lachish)*, London, 1891.
16 See his *Mound of Many Cities*, London, 1894.

ness, which shows, in Petrie's opinion, that after the destruction of this city the mound was used for a period of perhaps fifty years as a place for burning alkali. Near the top of the débris of the fourth city a glazed seal was found similar to those made in Egypt in the time of the twenty-second dynasty (945–745 B.C.). This city, then, belonged to the early part of the kingdom of Judah. In the seventh and eighth cities pottery of polished red and black types was found. This class of pottery is of Greek origin, dating from 550–350 B.C. These occupations of the mound must, then, be of that period. The fifth and sixth cities would, accordingly, fall between 750 and 550 B.C. This excavation thus shows how the stratification of the mounds of Palestine reveals the march of the peoples across the country; (see Fig. 28).

(4) *Bliss's Excavation at Jerusalem.*—From 1894 to 1897 Dr. Bliss was engaged in excavations at Jerusalem.[17] Here he devoted his attention to an endeavor to recover the line of the ancient wall on the south side of the city. This he did, following it from Maudsley's Scarp" [18] at the northwest corner of the westernmost of the two hills on which Jerusalem is situated across the slope to the eastward and then across the Tyropœon Valley. This was the wall rebuilt by Nehemiah on lines then already old (Neh. 3–6). It was destroyed by Titus in the year 70 A.D., and afterward rebuilt by the Empress Eudoxia in the fifth century A.D.

(5) *Excavation at Azekah.*—From 1898 to 1900 Dr. Bliss excavated for the Fund at several sites in the Biblical Shephelah,[19] the low hills which formed the border-land between ancient Judæa and Philistia. The work began at Tell Zakariya, the Biblical Azekah, situated above the lower part of the Vale of Elah. Azekah was fortified by King Rehoboam (2 Chron. 11 : 5–10). Here an important citadel or fortress was uncovered. While the masonry of the top part was similar to that of Herodian buildings at Jerusalem, the pottery found about the foundations indicated that the beginnings of the structure go back to early Israelitish times. It may well be one of Jeroboam's fortresses. Underneath it were remains from late pre-Israelitish times. It appears that the hill was occupied as the site of a city only shortly before the Hebrew

17 See Bliss, *Excavations at Jerusalem*, London, 1898.
18 An artificially made precipice on which a fortress once stood. It is named from an Englishman, Maudsley, who first perceived its true nature.
19 Bliss and Macalister, *Excavations in Palestine During the Years* 1898–1900, London, 1902.

conquest. The fortress was not, however, built at the time of this earliest occupation.

(6) *At Tell es-Safi (Gath?)*.—Next the excavation was transferred to Tell es-Safi, which was situated on the south side of the ancient Vale of Elah at the point where it sweeps into the Philistine plain, and which was thought to be the site of the Biblical Gath (Josh. 11:22; 1 Sam. 5:8; 17:4; 2 Kings 12:17). Here in 1144 A.D. the Latin Kingdom of Jerusalem established by the Crusaders built a fortress, which they called Blanche-Garde, as an outpost against Ashkelon. It was hoped that the excavation of Dr. Bliss would determine whether or not this was really the site of Gath, but owing to the occupation of the tell by a Mohammedan cemetery and a wely, or sacred building, this was not possible. The outline of the city walls was, however, traced, the foundations of Blanche-Garde examined, and here and there trenches were sunk to the rock. These trenches revealed in the various strata pottery and objects, first, of the period of the Crusaders; secondly, of the Seleucid period (312–65 B.C.); thirdly, of the Jewish period, 700–350 B.C., and two pre-Israelite strata. The mound had, then, been occupied from about 1700 B.C. to the Seleucid times, and again in the period of the Latin Kingdom of Jerusalem.

A most interesting discovery at Tell es-Safi was what at the time was regarded as an old pre-Israelitish high place, which contained three pillars such as are denounced in Deuteronomy. (See Deut. 7:5; 12:3, etc.) At the time of this discovery no similar discovery had been made. It is now known that this was the base of an early type of Palestinian house, and that what were mistaken for the "pillars" of heathen worship were the bases on which there stood the wooden pillars which supported the roof. See below, p. 208, ff.)

(7) *Tell el-Judeideh*.—The excavations next moved to Tell el-Judeideh, a mound some distance to the south of Tell Zakariya. Here they traced the outlines of the city wall, found the remains of a Roman villa, and sunk a number of shafts to the rock. From the pottery found in these shafts they inferred that the mound had been occupied in the earliest period, but deserted for a considerable time before the Hebrew conquest. It was then reoccupied in the latter part of the Judæan monarchy, and was finally fortified in the Seleucid or Roman period. It seems to have been deserted

soon after the Roman period. It is not known what was the ancient name of the city that stood there.

(8) *At Marash (Moresheth-Gath)*.—The last mound excavated in this region was Tell Sandahanna, situated a mile to the south of Beit Jibrin. The mound takes its name from a church of St. Anne, the ruins of which may still be seen near by. It occupies the site of the city of Marissa of the Seleucid period, and of the older Jewish Marash. It is probably the site of Moresheth-Gath, the home of the prophet Micah. (See Micah 1 : 14.) Here considerable portions of the Seleucid stratum of the mound were excavated, and a smaller portion of the Jewish stratum. The Jewish stratum rested directly on the rock; the site seems, therefore, not to have been inhabited in pre-Israelite times.

(9) *Gezer*.—The next undertaking of the Palestine Exploration Fund was the excavation of Gezer. This work was entrusted to the direction of R. A. Stewart Macalister, who had been Dr. Bliss's assistant from 1898 to 1900 and who became Professor of Celtic Archæology in Dublin. Work was begun in June, 1902, on Tell el-Jazar, about six miles southeast of the town of Ramleh, which Clermont Ganneau [20] had identified as the site of Gezer. (Josh. 10 : 33; Judges 1 : 27; 2 Sam. 5 : 25.) It continued, with such interruptions as winter weather and an outbreak of cholera made necessary, until August, 1905. It was renewed in the spring of 1907 and carried on until early in 1909. During this time more than half of the mound was excavated. No other mound in Palestine had, at the time, been so fully explored. Naturally, therefore, Gezer has furnished us with more archæological information than any other excavations (see Fig. 30).

The results of this excavation convinced Professor Macalister that the classification of the strata adopted by the excavators of Lachish and the mounds of the Shephelah was capable of improvement. He found that Gezer had been occupied at first by a non-Semitic people, remains of whose bones indicate that they were about 5 feet 6 inches high, who lived in caves, and whose implements were wholly of stone. He estimated that these people probably occupied the site from about 3000 to 2500 B.C. About 2500 B.C. a Semitic race, probably Amorite, took possession of the city and occupied it to the end of the Hebrew monarchy.

20 See his *Archaeological Researches in Palestine*, II, p. 251 f.

Four periods could be traced, he thought, in the Semitic occupation, each represented by differences in walls, implements, and objects used. The first Semitic period ended with the fall of the twelfth Egyptian dynasty, about 1800 B.C. In this stratum scarabs of the period of the Egyptian "middle kingdom" were found. The second Semitic stratum continued until about the end of the eighteenth Egyptian dynasty, about 1350 B.C. The third Semitic stratum lasted till the establishment of the Hebrew monarchy, about 1000 B.C.; the fourth was contemporaneous with the Hebrew kingdoms, 1000–586 B.C. The mound was again occupied in the Hellenistic or Maccabæan period.[21] After the Maccabæan turmoils the inhabitants seem to have deserted the tell. Under the modern village of Abu Shusheh, on the southwest slope of the mound, a Roman mosaic has been found, but nothing from Roman times was discovered on the mound itself. There were likewise no remains from the period of the Crusaders.

In the course of this excavation many important discoveries were made. Many of these will be mentioned in subsequent chapters. We need only mention here an old Semitic high place, which had its beginnings in the first Semitic stratum before 1800 B.C., and was used down to the end of the fourth Semitic or Hebrew stratum, about 600 B.C. It began with two "pillars," but others were added as time passed until there were ten in all.[22] In the third Semitic stratum (i.e., the one preceding the Hebrew occupation) a building was found which Professor Macalister thought might have been a temple. In the middle of its largest hall were some stones which looked as though they might have supported wooden pillars, which, in turn, probably supported the roof. Professor Macalister thought this was a structure similar to that which Samson pulled down at Gaza [23] (Judges 16:23–30).

One of the most important discoveries was a rock-cut tunnel leading down through the heart of the rock to a spring in a cave 94 feet below the surface of the rock and 120 feet below the level of the present surface of the ground.[24] This was to enable the people of the city to obtain water in time of siege. It was used for some 500 years and was apparently closed up about 1300–1200 B.C. Its beginnings go back accordingly to the first Semitic period. A palace of the Maccabæan time, apparently built by Simon the

21 This is the period called by Petrie and Bliss "Seleucid."
22 See Macalister, *The Excavations of Gezer*, London, 1912, II, 381–403.
23 *Ibid.*, 406–408.
24 *Ibid.*, I, 256-268.

Maccabee, 143–135 B.C., was also discovered.[25] (Cf. 1 Macc. 14:34.)

Various walls were discovered, which at different times encircled the city. The most massive of these was apparently constructed during the eighteenth Egyptian dynasty, and continued to be the city wall down to the Babylonian Exile. At some time after its construction towers had been inserted in the wall. These towers were shown to be a later insertion by the fact that their stones touched the stones of the wall on each side, but were not interlocked with them. Professor Macalister thought that these towers may have been inserted by Solomon when he fortified the city (1 Kings 9:15–19). At some later time the weakness of such a tower had become apparent, and a bastion had been built around it.[26] The excavation at Gezer was fruitful in many directions. Other aspects of it will be taken up in future chapters in connection with other topics.

In 1934 an excavation was made at the northwest corner of the mound of Gezer under the direction of Mr. Alan Rowe. It was found that in that part of the tell the native rock comes well up toward the present surface. The pottery exhumed indicated that the rock-caves were used as dwellings in the chalcolithic age (3000–2800 B.C.), and in the early bronze age. Later they were employed as tombs by people who lived on some other part of the mound. In this later period, 1600–1400 B.C., a watch-tower had been built on the rock here and a cistern dug to supply its occupants with water.[27]

(10) *Beth-Shemesh.*—The next task undertaken by the Palestine Exploration Fund was the exploration of Ain Shems, the Biblical Beth-Shemesh. (See Josh. 15:10; 2 Kings 14:8–14, etc.) Ain Shems, like Gezer, is situated in what was in biblical times the Shephelah. It is near the station of Der Aban on the railway from Jaffa to Jerusalem. Excavations were carried on at this point in 1911 and 1912 under the direction of Dr. Duncan Mackenzie, who had had ten years' experience on the staff of Sir Arthur Evans, the explorer of Crete. At the bottom of the mound the remains of a very early settlement were discovered.[28] Above this the ruins of a once prosperous city, which was for that time large,

25 See Macalister, *The Excavations of Gezer*, London, 1912, II, 209–223.
26 *Ibid.*, 236–266.
27 Cf. the *Quarterly of the Palestine Exploration Fund*, January, 1935, p. 19 ff.
28 See the *Annual* of the Palestine Exploration Fund, Vols. I and II, for the details here given, and for many others.

were found. It was surrounded by strong walls and one of its rugged gates was discovered on the south. In the upper strata of this city imitations of Cretan pottery were found. As it is probable that the Philistines came from Crete, or were intimately associated with people who were under Cretan influence, this pottery is doubtless Philistine. The city which was encircled by this wall had passed through two periods of history. The original wall was built before the domination of Palestine by Egypt. As this domination began about 1500 B.C., the earlier fortress of Beth-Shemesh belongs to that period. The second period belongs in its earlier strata to the age of the El-Amarna letters, in which the city is called Beth-Nin-Urta. The upper period of it belongs, as has been noted, to the Philistine period.

This city was destroyed by a siege which resulted in the burning of the city—a burning which left quite a bed of ashes. Dr. Mackenzie thought that this was the siege by which the Israelites gained possession of Beth-Shemesh. The city was occupied by the Hebrews apparently until the invasion of Palestine by Sennacherib, King of Assyria, in 701 B.C. At all events, it was in the possession of Judah in the days of King Amaziah (2 Kings 14:8–14). Corresponding to this, Israelitish pottery was found in the stratum above the ashes. Dr. Mackenzie is of the opinion that during this Hebrew period the city was without a wall. Apparently after the time of Sennacherib the site was abandoned for several centuries, for next above the Israelitish stratum the remains of a monastery of the Byzantine period (325–636 A.D.) were found. This monastery apparently was not begun until just at the close of the Byzantine period, for it appears that it was not finished at the time of the Mohammedan conquest.[29]

(11) *Exploring the Wilderness of Zin.*—Another service of the Palestine Exploration Fund was the sending of two explorers, C. Leonard Woolley and T. E. Lawrence, in the winter of 1913–14, to explore the wilderness to the south of Palestine. The results of their work were published in the Fund's *Annual,* Vol. III, under the title *The Wilderness of Zin.* The explorers identified a considerable part of the "Darb es-Shur," or the "way of Shur" (Gen. 16:7, etc.). It was the caravan road from Palestine to Egypt. They also adduce strong evidence against the identification of Ain Kades with Kadesh-Barnea (Num. 32:8, etc.),

---

29 For the later work at Beth-Shemesh done by Professor Grant, see below § 21.

and think that Kossima, which lies nearer to the Egyptian road and is surrounded by much more verdure, may have been Kadesh-Barnea. The identification of Ain Kades with Kadesh-Barnea was made by the late Dr. Henry Clay Trumbull, after a very brief visit to the spot, and it had been accepted by many others.

Between 325 and 636 A.D. extensive settlements and cities of considerable size existed in this wilderness. This was one of the facts that led Ellsworth Huntington to believe that the rainfall in Palestine was much greater at that time. With this view Woolley and Lawrence take issue. They say that where the old wells have been kept open, the water still rises as high as ever it did. They hold that the cities mentioned were possible because of the great energy and skill of the people of that time in sinking wells.

(12) *Ashkelon.*—During the season of 1921-1922, Dr. John Garstang and Mr. (now Canon) W. J. Phythian-Adams, who were respectively Director and Assistant in the British School of Archæology in Jerusalem, carried on for a time an excavation at Ashkelon. The mound was by no means fully explored; the work consisted mainly of soundings and trenches to determine the strata and the history of the site. From pottery found at different levels it appears that Ashkelon was founded about 1800 B.C., that about 1190 B.C. the Philistines captured it, that they held it until it passed under the sway of Alexander the Great and his successors. During the Hellenic and Roman periods the city was adorned by colonnaded streets. A large basilica was uncovered which was built by Herod the Great.[30] (See Fig. 308.)

(13) *Gaza.*—In the autumn of 1922 the same explorers made some soundings at Gaza. It appears from their reports that the part of the mound through which they sank their trenches proved not to be the best for the purpose.[31] They cut, however, through strata belonging to the Roman, Byzantine, and Arabian periods, and at one point sank their trenches to the foundation of a Philistine wall. One curious feature of the part explored was that from a time judged to be about 300 B.C. until the Roman time the site seemed to have been but slightly peopled and that by the very poor only. This was inferred from the character of the potsherds found. It is stated by Strabo that Gaza was pulled down by Alexander the Great and remained deserted. In Acts 8:26

---

[30] See *Quarterly Statement* of the Palestine Exploration Fund, October, 1921, 162–169; July, 1922, 112–117; April, 1923, 60–78; January, 1924, 24–35.
[31] *Ibid.*, January, 1923, 18–36.

we read that the angel of the Lord said to Philip: "Arise, and go toward the south unto the way that goeth down from Jerusalem unto Gaza: the same is desert." The word "desert" at this point has caused much difficulty. There is no part of the road from Jerusalem to Gaza which can be called "desert," but if Gaza itself was "desert" at the time, as this excavation indicates, all is clear. From other ancient writers, however, it appears that there was a city of Gaza during the time these explorers think it deserted, but probably it did not cover the whole mound.

(14) *Tell Jemmeh.*—During the month of October, 1922, the same gentlemen examined the pottery on the surface and edges of the mound of Tell Jemmeh,[32] eight miles southwest of Gaza, and sunk a trial trench. Before their trench reached the bottom, however, their work was interrupted by a clash between some salt smugglers and soldiery. The examination revealed, nevertheless, that the mound had been the site of a city which was founded about 1800 B.C. and flourished until Roman times. Four distinct strata were present in it; the lowest represents an occupation from about 1800–1400 B.C.; the second, from about 1400 to the coming of the Philistines; the third, the Philistine occupation; the fourth, the Greek period. Phythian-Adams is of the opinion that this tell is the site of the Biblical Gerar; (see Gen. 10:10; 20:1, 2; and 26:1, 6 17, 20, 26). There is little near the site to support a city or to give excuse for the existence of one. It is, however, near the caravan route to Egypt over which through many centuries the trade of the world passed. The suggestion of Phythian-Adams that the city was founded and maintained to exact toll from passing traffic, and so to gain a living easily, has much to commend it.[32]

(15) *Jerusalem.*—During the winter of 1923–1924 Professor R. A. Stewart Macalister, assisted by J. Garrow Duncan, resumed the excavation of Ophel, at Jerusalem. During the next season Mr. Duncan carried on the work alone.[33] In 1927 another season was devoted to it by Mr. J. W. Crowfoot.[34] Some of the discoveries are described below, in the chapter on Jerusalem. (See § 4.) On the east a portion of the ancient city wall was uncovered, which connected with the wall farther north, laid bare years ago by Guthe. At the northeast corner of what was

32 See *Quarterly Statement* of the Palestine Exploration Fund, July, 1923, 137–146.
33 See the *Annual* of the Palestine Exploration Fund, Vol. IV.
34 Reported in the *Annual* of the Palestine Exploration Fund, Vol. V.

the Jebusite city, and later "the City of David," a rock-scarp was uncovered on which an imposing city wall had been built. This wall had been violently thrown down or "breached"; at the front of it the breach had been filled up with a long, straight wall, and above the breach a strong tower had later been erected. Professor Macalister identifies this "breach" with the "breach of David" mentioned in 1 Kings 11:27, and the tower with "Millo," mentioned in the same passage and in 2 Samuel 5:9. The potsherds found confirmed the age assigned to these structures. A view of this "breach" and tower is shown, through the courtesy of the Palestine Exploration Fund, in Fig. 310.

A most surprising discovery was, however, that of a second underground shaft, or staircase, leading from the ancient city down to the Virgin's Fountain, the ancient Gihon. The pottery found in this shaft proves it to be much older than the one discovered by Warren. It appears to have belonged to the period between 2000 and 3000 B.C., and may be contemporaneous with the occupation of the caves around the Fountain discovered by Parker.[35]   An ancient rock-cut sanctuary was also found.

(16) *Tell Duweir.*—Under the direction of Mr. J. L. Starkey the Palestine Exploration Fund began the excavation of Tell Duweir in the spring of 1933 and has now (1936) continued the work for four seasons. The mound is situated on the southwestern border of the territory of ancient Judah in the general region of Tell Beit-Mirsim and the sites of Gaza and Ashkelon are clearly visible from its summit. The town which occupied its site was one of the frontier fortresses of the kingdom of Judah. Before the excavation was undertaken several scholars had conjectured that it was the site of the Biblical city of Lachish. These scholars were unconvinced of the correctness of the identification of the location of that town at Tell el-Hesy as made by Petrie and Bliss. Starkey's work laid bare near the summit of the mound a palace of the Persian period, underneath which was a city that had been destroyed by fire when Nebuchadrezzar captured Judah. Below this again were pre-Israelite strata which afforded the remains of earlier cities. A cemetery was also excavated which yielded objects of the copper age, 3000–2500 B.C. or earlier. In the strata of the period 1400–1200 B.C. a small temple exhibiting Egyptian char-

---

[35] See *Quarterly Statement* of the Palestine Exploration Fund, October, 1933, April and October, 1934, October, 1935, and October, 1936, and the *Illustrated London News*, July 6, 1935, pp. 20, 21 and August 10, 1935, pp. 240–242.

acteristics was found. It had been built in the reign of Amenophis III and repaired in the reign of Rameses II. The most surprising discovery was made in 1935, when eighteen potsherds inscribed in ancient Hebrew characters were exhumed. On some of them the writing was hardly legible, but some of them can be read. They are letters written apparently to a Judæan officer or governor at this point in the days of Judah's decline and fall, when Nebuchadrezzar was tightening his net about Jerusalem, 598–586 B.C. The writer of one of them said, "We are watching the signal-stations of Lachish, according to all the signals you are giving, because we cannot see the signals of Azekah." It is believed that this identifies the city at Duweir as Lachish. Another letter tells how Achbor, son of Elnathan has passed down to Egypt. In Jeremiah 26 : 22 we are told how Jehoiakim sent Elnathan son of Achbor to that country to bring back a runaway prophet, Uriah. Another mentions Nedebiah, grandson of the king, and 1 Chronicles 3 : 18 records the name of this grandson. The name of Gedaliah has also been found on a seal, which is believed to be the same Gedaliah who was governor of Jerusalem after its destruction in 586 B.C.; see 2 Kings 25 : 22 ff. In 1934 an inscription in an alphabet a thousand years older was brought to light. It belonged to the same period of the development of the alphabet as the inscription discovered by Grant at Beth-Shemesh. (See § 21, below.)

5. **The German Palestine Society.**—While the work of the Palestine Exploration Fund, which has been outlined in detail, was going on, other countries were aroused to similar activities. In 1877 a similar Society, the Deutscher Palästina-Verein, was organized to foster the collection of information about the land of the Bible. Accurate scientific research in all branches of knowledge relating to Palestine was contemplated, and the co-operation of travelers and of the German colonies in Palestine was invited. In 1878 this Society began the publication of a journal [36] which has become a repository of information about the Holy Land.

(1) *Guthe's Excavation at Jerusalem.*—In 1880 Prof. Guthe excavated at various points on Ophel at Jerusalem, and followed the line of the ancient wall along the east side of the city of David.[37]

(2) *Megiddo.*—In 1903 this German Society undertook the excavation of Tell el-Mutesellim, the site of the Biblical Megiddo [38]

36 *Zeitschrift des deutschen Palastina-Vereins.*
37 See *Zeitschrift des deutschen Palastina-Vereins*, V, pp. 7–204.
38 See Schumacher und Steuernagel, *Tel el-Muteselim*, Leipzig, 1908.

(Josh. 12:21; 2 Kings 23:29, etc.). This work was entrusted to the direction of Dr. Gottlieb Schumacher, of Haifa. Work was begun on the 7th of February, 1903, and continued at intervals until the 30th of November, 1905. In the lowest stratum of the mound Dr. Schumacher found traces of a settlement the houses of which were constructed of mud-bricks. Over the ruins of these a second series of houses had been built of stone. In the same stratum some tombs were found containing skeletons, some pottery of early forms, a bronze knife, and some scarabs set in gold. The walls of the city were in part built of brick. The settlements represented by this stratum antedated 2000 b.c.

In the next stratum a large structure, probably a palace, was found, which had been occupied through the periods represented by the stratum in which its foundations were laid and the stratum next above it. The building was of stone and was large. In one part of it was a "pillar" which once supported a roof. Various types of pottery, knives of flint and bronze, many stone household utensils, an Astarte figure, and some scarabs of the period of the twelfth Egyptian dynasty were found. This stratum, then, belonged to the period 2000–1800 b.c.

Next above this stratum was one in which types of painted pottery similar to that of the Philistines came to light. In the fifth stratum from the bottom a palace of the Hebrew period was discovered. In this palace a seal was found bearing a lion and the inscription "belonging to Shema, the servant of Jeroboam." It is impossible to tell whether the Jeroboam who was Shema's master was Jeroboam I or Jeroboam II. In this same stratum a palace was found containing three "pillars." (See Fig. 27.)

In another part of the mound in a sixth stratum, which seemed to be late Hebrew, three "pillars" were found in an open space near the south gate, a stone religious emblem, and a decorated incense-burner. Elsewhere this sixth stratum yielded a blacksmith's shop. In a seventh stratum, just under the soil, remains of the Greek period were found, among which was an Athenian coin. This was the last occupation of the tell, and was pre-Christian. At the beginning of the Roman period the town was moved from the high land of the mound down nearer the water supply. On the slope of the hill a native-rock altar was found which had been used in prehistoric times.

(3) *Taanach.*—In 1899 Prof. Ernst Sellin, of Vienna, visited Palestine and became so deeply interested in its exploration that he induced several Austrian scientific bodies and individuals to contribute a fund for the purpose. The result was an excavation of Tell Taanek, the Biblical Taanach (Josh. 12:21; Judges 5:19), conducted by Sellin in 1902 and 1903. Sellin did not excavate the mound in a systematic way and his results are not very clearly presented in his book.[39] He traced in several places four strata in the tell. An early stratum had its beginnings, he thought, as early as 2500 B.C. This stratum represented probably an occupation of more than a thousand years. In its later parts the remains of a large palace were found, and in a cave underneath it four cuneiform tablets, written in the script of the El-Amarna period. Originally there were more tablets in the archive, but it had been rifled in ancient times. Above this was a stratum in which pottery of the Cypriote and Philistine type was found. Next above this was a Hebrew stratum, which seems to have lasted, judging by objects found in it, down to the time of Psammetik I of Egypt, 663–609 B.C. In this stratum the remains of a building with its "pillars" were found, as well as a terra-cotta incense-altar of wonderful construction. Above this there were in places a few remains from the Seleucid period, including some pottery, and at the top of the mound some remains of an Arabic settlement. This last seems to have been established here about the time of the crusaders. Sellin thinks Taanach was destroyed by the Scythian invasion, about 625 B.C., that in the Seleucid period the main settlement here was not on the mound, and that it was then unoccupied until the time of the Crusaders.

(4) *Capernaum.*—The Deutsche Orient-Gesellschaft, which was carrying on excavations in Egypt, Babylonia, and Assyria, undertook the investigation of the remains of ancient synagogues in Galilee and the Jaulan. Among these they excavated the ruins of the synagogue at Tell Hum on the Sea of Galilee,[40] the probable site of Capernaum. Here they found the remains of a once beautiful synagogue which was probably built in the fourth century A.D. Beneath it is the floor of a still older building. This last is, perhaps, the synagogue in which so many of the incidents of the ministry of Christ in Capernaum took place, the one built by a Roman centurion. (See Luke 7:5 and Fig. 32.)

39 Sellin, *Tel Taanek*, Wien, 1904.
40 See *Mitteilungen der deutschen Orient-Gesellschaft*, No. 29, Berlin, 1905, p. 14 f.

(5) *Jericho.*—This same Society undertook, in the years 1907-1909, the excavation of Jericho; (see Fig. 29). The work was entrusted to the direction of Prof. Sellin, of Vienna. The digging occupied about three weeks in the spring of 1907, and about three months of the early part of each of the years 1908 and 1909.[41] At the bottom of the mound traces of a prehistoric occupation of the site were uncovered, but as these were under the foundations of a Canaanitish fortress, which were not demolished, nothing further was ascertained about them. Above this prehistoric city were the remains of an Amorite or Canaanite city. A jar handle found in the lower half of this Canaanite stratum was stamped with a scarab of the time of the twelfth Egyptian dynasty, which indicates that this occupation goes back to about 2000 B.C. The walls of this early city were traced on all sides of the tell except the east. On this side, where the Ain es-Sultan is (otherwise called Elisha's Fountain, from the incident of 2 Kings 2: 19–22), the wall had entirely disappeared. This early city was small. The whole of it could have been put into the Colosseum at Rome. All early Palestinian cities were, however, small. In the city was a citadel with a double wall. Each wall represented a different period of history. Both were built of brick, as were the houses of the time. The outer wall was between four and five feet thick and appeared to be the older; the inner one was about ten feet thick. They were joined here and there by transverse walls; (see Fig. 37). The city had been burned apparently about 1300–1200 B.C., perhaps at the time of the Hebrew conquest.

Above the ruins of this pre-Israelitish city were the remains of what Sellin took to be the Hebrew town, dating from the ninth century B.C. (See 1 Kings 16: 34), as it was rebuilt in the days of Ahab. (See Fig. 34.) The Israelites, in Sellin's judgment, made the city considerably larger than it had been in the earlier time. A wall, which he believed to be the wall of the Hebrew period, was found on all sides except the east, considerably outside the older wall. Père Vincent, of the French *École Biblique* at Jerusalem, believes this wall to have been built in the Canaanite period also, and his reasons are now accepted. On the eastern edge of the Israelitish stratum the remains of a large stone building were found. Sellin thought this might be the palace and fortress built by Hiel in the time of Ahab (1 Kings

41 See Sellin und Watzinger, *Jericho,* Leipzig, 1913.

16:34). This city seems to have flourished only about two hundred years. It was probably destroyed in the time of Sennacherib, about 700 B.C. Sellin thought he found traces of another rebuilding which must soon have followed the destruction, but this Jericho was also destroyed by Nebuchadrezzar in 586 B.C. At some time after the Babylonian Exile the city was rebuilt and flourished until destroyed by Vespasian in 70 A.D. 'It was rebuilt after 325 A.D. and continued until destroyed by the invasion of the Persian King Chosroes II, in 614 A.D. Some slight settlements have existed on the mound in Moslem times, but the Jericho of today is more than a mile distant.

(6) *Balata.*—In the winter of 1913–1914 an excavation was made by Professor Sellin at Balata, near Shechem. The city gate of ancient Shechem was uncovered, with a portion of the Amorite city wall, which was thick and oblique. The gateway was triple and is said to be the longest discovered in Palestine. This gate was on the west of the city. The foundations of houses of the early Hebrew period were also found. Near the tell an Egyptian sarcophagus was discovered.

In the spring and summer of 1926 Professor Sellin resumed the excavation at Balata, a little to the northeast of modern Nablous, which had been interrupted by the war.[42] He continued the work during five campaigns, short and long, until in 1928 he was succeeded by Dr. Welter-Mauve who continued the work for one season. During the progress of the work in 1926 the eastern gate of ancient Shechem was discovered, together with a portion of the massive wall in its vicinity; a large palace, the walls of which were massive, a part of them being of "cyclopæan" masonry (See Fig. 315); a temple, which the excavator believes to be the temple of Elberith (see Judges 9:46; also Fig. 314); and two cuneiform tablets. From the character of the potsherds, scarabs, etc., found in connection with these various structures, and from the character of the writing on the cuneiform tablets, Sellin believed it possible approximately to date the various structures. Professor Böhl, of Groningen, who has studied the cuneiform tablets, says rightly that they are similar in character and

42 The account of his pre-war work was published in the *Anzeiger der phil.-hist. Klasse der Wiener Akademie der Wissenschaften,* 1914, Nr. VII, pp. 35 ff. and Nr XVIII, pp. 204 ff. The account of the work of 1926 is published in the *Zeitschrift der deutschen Palastina-Vereins,* XLIX (1926), pp. 231–236 and 304–327, and plates 32–46. The work of subsequent years is published in volumes L and LI of the same journal.

114   ARCHÆOLOGY AND THE BIBLE

contents to those found at El-Amarna.[43]   Some of the proper
names indicate that the persons mentioned were of Hittite stock,
which accords with what is said of Hamor in Genesis 34.   The
city walls and the west gate are believed to have been built about
1700 B.C.; the east gate about 1500 B.C.   The palace consists of
two portions.   The western part seems to have been built at the
time of the western gate, and the eastern part at the time of the
eastern gate.   The temple was first built about 1300 B.C., was reno-
vated about 1200 B.C., and was burned about 1150 B.C.   Finally
loam seems to have been spread over the site of the temple about
930 B.C., in the time of Jeroboam I.   In the temple no signs of
the worship of Astarte were found.

6. The American Schools of Oriental Research.—In the year
1900 the American Schools of Oriental Research in Palestine was
opened at Jerusalem under the ægis of the Archæological Institute
of America.   In addition to the investigation of many matters
not strictly archæological the school has conducted a number of
minor explorations.   When the present writer was director,
1902–1903, he cleared the so-called Tomb of the Judges, and
found the ruins of a caravansary of the Crusading Period, near
the Damascus Gate.   Under L. B. Paton, 1903–1904, an excavation was made on the supposed line of the "Third Wall" of
Jerusalem.   Under Nathaniel Schmidt, 1904–1905, the Dead
Sea was explored and some discoveries made in the Valley of the
Arnon and the Wady Suweil.[44]   Under D. G. Lyon, 1906–1907,
some pre-Israelitish pottery was recovered from tombs of Samieh
east of Et-Taiyibeh.[45]   Under W. J. Moulton, 1912–1913, a
painted Christian tomb of the Byzantine Period was explored at
Beit Jibrin.   This has been described, and some of its paintings reproduced in the *Annual of the American Schools of Oriental Research,* Vols. II and III, 1923.

(1) *Tell-el-Ful.*—The work of the school was interrupted by
the war, but after the restoration of peace its work of research was
resumed.   W. H. Worrell, director of the school in 1919–1920,
and C. C. McCowan, fellow in 1920-1921, have published important investigations of various aspects of the religion of the country.[46]   Dr. W. F. Albright, former director, has done consider-

43 See pp. 36, 64, 329–330, 402, 403 of vol. XLIX.
44 See *Journal of Biblical Literature,* Vol. XXII, Boston, 1903, pp. 164–182; XXIV,
196–220; XXV, 82–95.
45 See *Harvard Theological Review,* Cambridge, Mass., I, 1908, p. 92.
46 Published in the *Annual* referred to above, and in the *Bulletin,* see p. 109, n. 1.

able work on the problem of the identification of ancient sites,[47] and also made an important excavation at Tell el-ful,[48] the Gibeah of Saul, which illustrated and confirmed the text of the Bible. (See Fig. 309.)

At the bottom of the mound he found a fortress built of massive stone blocks rudely shaped, in which late Canaanite and early Hebrew pottery was found. This fortress was destroyed by fire and was covered by a layer of ashes. Dr. Albright connects this destruction with the burning of Gibeah in the war between Benjamin and Israel mentioned in Judges 20:40. Just above it were the remains of a second fortress, the most elaborate structure found in the mound. Its outer wall was about six feet thick and defended by a glacis or sloping base. It contained a massive stone staircase. This structure appears to belong to the time of King Saul. On this was a third and somewhat smaller fortress, characterized by a series of stone piers usual during the Jewish monarchy. This may represent the structure of King Asa mentioned in 1 Kings 15:22. After a short siege this structure also perished in a conflagration. This may have taken place in the Syro-Ephraimitish war of 735 B.C. (See Isa. 7.) After the lapse of a considerable period of time another fortress was built on the ruins of all these. The pottery found in this showed that it belonged to the Maccabæan time.

(2) *Bab-ed-Dra.*—During February and March of the year 1924 a joint expedition of the school and of Xenia Theological Seminary, conducted by Dr. Albright and President Kyle, of Xenia, explored the Jordan Valley to the south of the Dead Sea, in search of the "cities of the plain"—Sodom, Gomorrah, Zoar, and the others. They found the site of the Zoar of the Byzantine and Arabic periods, but concluded that the Dead Sea covered the locality of earlier Zoar, as well as of Sodom and Gomorrah.[49] Their most important discovery should be described in Dr. Albright's own words:

"The biggest find was that of a unique sanctuary and fortress of the end of the Early Bronze and beginning of the Middle Bronze Ages, together with a large station of open-air hearths and inclosures. We planned it and brought back thousands of sherds,

47 *Ibid.*
48 Described in part in various numbers of the *Bulletin of the American Schools of Oriental Research* and fully in their *Annual*, Vol. IV, 1924.
49 For fuller accounts of the work, see M. G. Kyle, *The Exploration of Sodom*, New York, Revell; and W. F. Albright, *The Archæology of Palestine and the Bible*, Revell, New York, 1931, p. 48.

vases, flint artifacts, and a quantity of bones and skulls for anthropometric investigation. This station at Bab-ed-Dra was apparently a sanctuary in use from about 2800 to 1800 B.C. and is by far the most important one known in Palestine. Among other things we found six prostrate menhirs with the broken pieces of a seventh, all of stone, which must have been dragged for miles.

"We also studied the early Moabite shrine at Ader, planned it, and discovered a previously unknown temple, with masseboth, table of offerings, and a very interesting ground plan."

(3) *Tell Beit Mirsim.*—In the spring of 1926 President M. G. Kyle, of Xenia Theological Seminary, and Director Albright, of the American School in Jerusalem, led a joint expedition of Xenia Seminary and of the School, which excavated for eight weeks at Tell Beit Mirsim, thirteen miles southwest of Hebron, which they believe to be the site of Kirjath-sepher. (Josh. 15:15, 16; Judges 1:11, 12.) A second campaign explored the site in 1928, and a third in 1930. A fourth summer was devoted to the work in 1932.[50] In parts of the mound shafts have been sunk to the underlying rock, by which it was learned that ten different settlements had in successive ages occupied the mound, each building its city above the ruins of the preceding. The earliest of these cities was founded about 2200 B.C., and the latest was destroyed by the army of Nebuchadrezzar, which besieged Jerusalem in 588 and 587 B.C. This was shown by the fact that in the upper stratum there was found the seal of "Eleakim, servant of Jehoiachin." It will be remembered that Jehoiachin ruled but three months in the summer of the year 587. In the course of the city's sixteen hundred years of history it had been destroyed ten times. One of these destructions was by Shishak, about 930 B.C. (1 Kings 14:25.) Most of these destructions were accompanied by conflagrations.

During the earlier centuries of the city's life the houses, though constructed of stone, were roofed with wood. The hill country of that period was still wooded, not with large timber, which would be suitable for beams, but with smaller trees, which could be made to serve for rafters and roofs. The wooden roofs supplied to each conflagration material for making beds of ashes, which mark off stratum from stratum. Pottery corresponding

50 Cf. Albright, *op. cit.*, Ch. II. The full scientific account of the work of the first three campaigns is published in the *Annual of the American Schools of Oriental Research*, Vols. XII (1932), and XIII (1933), a brief account of the fourth, in their *Bulletin*, No. 47 (Oct. 1932), pp. 3–17.

to that of the Middle Kingdom of Egypt (2100–1800 B.C.), and scarabs of a Hyksos king (1800–1600 B.C.), and of Amenophia III (1411–1375 B.C.), helped in dating the successive strata. The relative insecurity and security of the country in the successive centuries, corresponding to the absence or the presence of a strong centralized government in the land, were reflected by the relative thickness of the walls of the different periods, and by the presence or absence of pits for storing grain in the houses. When a strong government gave security from invasion, the walls were not so thick; when it created local confidence, grain was stored in community granaries.

An interesting innovation in house building was introduced during the early Hebrew monarchy. Examples of it had been found in other places, but had not been recognized. This type of house had a stone wall, which enclosed a comparatively large area, the wall reaching the top of the first story. The floor of the second story was supported by from one to four roughly cut stone pillars, which would weigh from 1800 to 3000 lbs. each. The thickness of the walls of the first story indicate that probably some of the houses were three stories high. The upper stories were built of brick and wood. The families lived in the upper stories, the rooms of the lower stories being used for the stabling of animals and storing of supplies. In the fifth stratum from the top traces of a Hyksos fortification, similar to that discovered at Tell el-Yuhadiyeh in Egypt, were found.

(4) *Beth-zur.*—In the summer of 1931 the American School in Jerusalem united with the Presbyterian Theological Seminary of Chicago in the excavation of Beth-zur,[51] a little to the north of Hebron, on the road to Jerusalem. Dr. Albright was the scientific director of the expedition, and was assisted by Professor Sellers and others. The town is mentioned three times in the Old Testament (Josh. 15:58; 1 Chr. 11:7; Neh. 3:16), and was the site of one of the fiercely fought struggles of the Maccabæan revolt (1 Macc. 4:28–35). The work of the first campaign enabled the explorers to trace the history of the site. As yet (1937) no further work has been done at the site.

Beth-zur was founded about 1600 B.C. It was destroyed about 1500 B.C., perhaps by Thothmes III, and was unoccupied until the thirteenth century B.C., when it was rebuilt, perhaps by the

51 See *Bulletin of the American Schools of Oriental Research,* No. 43 (Oct. 1931), pp. 2–13.

Israelites. From the late pre-Exilic Period a seal impression and some interesting Hebrew weights were discovered. The fortress of the Maccabæan time was laid bare by the excavators and interesting objects of the Hellenistic Period were found. The site seems to have been abandoned about 100 B.C. The Bethzur of the Byzantine and Arabian Periods was on a neighboring hill.[52]

(5) *Jerash.*—In 1931 the American School at Jerusalem entered into coöperation with Yale University for the exploration of , Jerash, the site of the ancient Gerasa. Previous to this, Yale had, in conjunction with the British School of Archæology in Jerusalem, explored the site. Jerash is, like some of the sites in Egypt, a place where the remains of beautiful ancient buildings form an open-air museum. Much can be learned, however, by clearing fallen debris from streets and the foundations of the buildings, and this has, to a good degree, been done. The immediate scientific direction of the work was in charge of Prof. Clarence S. Fisher, whose training as an architect and in mastery of the science of excavation peculiarly fit him for work on such a site. The streets and buildings of a beautiful Hellenic city of the early centuries of the Christian era were laid bare. Interesting remains of the Græco-Roman time and of the Byzantine Period, including Christian churches, have been found.[53] One of the most interesting discoveries consisted of the recovery of the fallen inscribed stones which once formed part of the triumphal arch of the city's southern gate. The inscription welcomed the emperor Hadrian to the city on his visit to Geresa in the spring of the year 130 A.D.

(6) *Eastern Palestine.*—In 1932–1933 the American School in Jerusalem made in conjunction with the Department of Antiquities of Transjordania an archæological survey of the southern part of Transjordania. The work was continued in 1934, Hebrew Union College of Cincinnati and the American Council of Learned Societies having joined the partnership. The work of both expeditions was conducted by Professor Nelson Glueck, now (1937) Director of the American School in Jerusalem. Between one and two hundred mounds were examined, soundings made for pottery

52 See O. V. Sellers, *The Citadel of Beth-zur*, Philadelphia, 1933.
53 See *Quarterly Statement of the Palestine Exploration Fund*, July, 1931, 143 ff.; the *Annual of the American Schools of Oriental Research*, XI (1931), 1–59, and its *Bulletin*, No. 41, p. 12, No. 45, pp. 3–19, No. 49, p. 3 ff., No. 53, p. 2 ff., No. 54, p. 5 ff., No. 56, p. 15 ff., No. 57, p. 3 ff.

and much information was gathered concerning localities in ancient Moab, Edom, the kingdom of the Nabathæans (called in New Testament times, the kingdom of Arabia), and of this part of the Roman Province of Arabia, which Trajan established on the ruins of that kingdom in 105 A.D. One of the most interesting results of the work was the discovery of copper mines at Khirbet Nahas, about thirty-five miles southeast of the Dead Sea. Here the area between the hills is packed with ruined houses and small, ruined furnaces and is black with heaps of slag. Raw ore protrudes above the surface of the ground. Mining was simple and easy. Near by was a large enclosure some 300 feet square with walls six feet thick. Inside it were ruined buildings and heaps of slag. It had been apparently the center of prison-labor for the mines. Edom was subject to Israel from the days of David to Jehoshaphat and from Uzziah to Ahaz. Solomon is known to have introduced forced labor (1 Kings 5:13 ff.) and it is probable that this camp for such laborers here was established by him.[54] For the mines see Fig. 333.

(7) *Bethel.*—The modern village of Beitin, about twelve miles north of Jerusalem, is on the site of the biblical city of Bethel. In 1927 Director W. F. Albright of the American School in Jerusalem, made some soundings in a garden outside the village on the north and found that the site of the ancient city was not all buried beneath the village, as had been feared, but that at least half of it was accessible to excavators. 'In 1934 Dr. Albright returned to the task of excavating there, Xenia-Pittsburg Theological Seminary having joined with the American School in Jerusalem in furnishing funds for the purpose. The excavation began in July and continued until the end of September.[55] The objects found indicated that a Canaanite town was founded on the site about 2000 B.C., and that, after suffering various fortunes through eight hundred years, it was destroyed by fire in the thirteenth century B.C. This destruction was doubtless the work of the Israelites at the time of their conquest of Canaan. When the place was rebuilt after the fire, the housewalls were of quite inferior workmanship. For three hundred years this type of building prevailed. During this period a similarly inferior type of pottery was used. It was in striking contrast to the

54 See *Bulletin of the American Schools of Oriental Research,* Nos. 49, 50, 51, 55, and 63; also their *Annual,* Vols. XIV and XV, and the London *Illustrated News* for July 7, 1934.
55 See the *Bulletin of the American Schools of Oriental Research,* Nos. 29, 55, 56, and 57.

types of pottery that had been employed by the Canaanites. This was the Bethel of the period of Israel's Judges. In the ninth or tenth century B.C. the city was rebuilt with houses and walls of much better workmanship and the small objects found in the houses of this period indicate that the city was now much more prosperous. This was the Bethel of Jeroboam I and the kingdom of northern Israel. In the sixth century it had, as the excavation showed, been destroyed again by a conflagration. Doubtless this was the work of Nebuchadrezzar, who destroyed Jerusalem in 586 B.C. After this destruction the excavators found that the site remained unoccupied until the late Persian period. It appears to have been rebuilt, perhaps in the fourth century B.C. and to have been occupied until Jerusalem was destroyed by the Romans in 70 A.D. The various strata of this period contained coins of well known Syrian and Judean kings, from which the strata could be dated. A coin of the year 68–69 A.D. was the latest found.

(8) *Anathoth.*—Early in 1936 two students of the American School in Jerusalem, Mr. A. C. Blair and Dr. A. Bergman, undertook at Dr. Albright's suggestion, to ascertain whether the Biblical Anathoth was near the modern village of Anata, about three miles northeast of Jerusalem. They made some soundings in the mound Ras el-Kharrubeh, but the results were indeterminate. The students are of the opinion that the mound cannot be the site of the ancient Levite city; Dr. Albright thinks their soundings inconclusive.[56]

7. Harvard Excavations at Samaria.—Through the generosity of Mr. Jacob Schiff, of New York, Harvard University was able to excavate at Sebastiyeh, the site of ancient Samaria, during parts of three seasons—1908, 1909, and 1910. During the first season the work was under the direction of Prof. D. G. Lyon; during 1909 and 1910, under the direction of Prof. G. A. Reisner, who had had large experience in such work in Egypt, and who, in addition to many archæological triumphs there, has solved the riddle of the Sphinx. At Samaria[57] a large palace was found built upon the native rock. This is believed to be the remains of the palace of Omri. (1 Kings 16:24.) Above this were the ruins of a larger palace, the wall of which was faced with white marble. This is believed to have been the palace of Ahab, who is said to have built an "ivory house." (1 Kings 22:39.) In a building on a level with

56 See *Bulletin of the American Schools of Oriental Research*, No. 62, p. 22 f. and No. 63, p. 22 f.
57 See *Harvard Excavations at Samaria*, 1908–1910, by G. A. Reisner, Clarence S. Fisher, and D. G. Lyon, Cambridge, 1924, *passim.*

this palace a considerable number of inscribed potsherds were found. They were receipts for wine and oil stored there. Above the ruins of the palace of Ahab, the remains of another, which is supposed to have been built by Jeroboam II, were found. At the western edge of the hill the old city gate was uncovered. It had been rebuilt at different times. The foundations were clearly laid in the Israelitish period. On these now rests a super-structure of Herodian workmanship. Above the ruins of the Hebrew city were the remains of a city built by the Assyrians. (See 2 Kings 17: 24–34.) This was inferred by the character of the building materials employed and by the fragment of a clay tablet found there. Still above this were remains of a city of the Seleucid time—the city destroyed by John Hyrcanus [58] in 109 B.C. Still above this were remains of the temple built by Herod the Great, when he rebuilt Samaria and named it Sebaste, the Greek for Augusta, in honor of the Emperor Augustus. This temple had been repaired in the third century A.D.

In 1931 Harvard University resumed the excavation of Samaria in coöperation with the Hebrew University of Jerusalem, the British School of Archæology, and the Palestine Exporation Fund. The work is under the direction of Mr. J. W. Crowfoot. The most important discovery of the work of the first season was a part of the old Hebrew wall of the time of Omri and Ahab, and the failure to find anything older than the time of Omri.[59] The archæological evidence confirms the biblical statement that Samaria was a foundation of Omri. In subsequent campaigns many interesting minor discoveries were made, including a number of carved ivories.

The city whose history is thus established was destined to play in the subsequent centuries a rôle second only to that of Jerusalem. During the hundred and fifty or more years between its foundation by Omri and its destruction by Sargon in 722 B.C., though not always the royal residence, it was assumed to be the capital of the country. (See 1 Kings 16: 22 and 2 Kings 9: 24.) The religious events which followed the introduction of foreigners into it by Sargon (2 Kings 17: 24–34.) accentuated the enmity that had long existed between the tribes of Ephraim and Judah and which in the time of Nehemiah led to that schism which established the Samaritans as the oldest Jewish sect. Under the Persians the Samaritans, like the Jews, were allowed a large degree of autonomy;

58 Josephus, *Antiquities of the Jews*, xiii, 10, 2 and 3; *Wars of the Jews*, i, 2, 7.
59 See *Quarterly Statement of the Palestine Exploration Fund*, July, 1931, p. 139 ff., and April, 1932, p. 33 ff.

and, according to Josephus (*Ant.*, XI, 8, 4), were allowed by Alexander the Great to build a temple on Mount Gerizim—a temple that was standing in the time of Christ. (See John 4 : 20, 21.)

8. Parker's Excavations at Jerusalem.—In the years 1909, 1910, and 1911 an English expedition under Capt. the Hon. Montague Parker, a retired officer of the British army, made extensive explorations upon Ophel, the slope of the eastern hill south of the present city walls at Jerusalem. Parker was not an archæologist and the motive for the exploration was not disclosed. The party is said to have been abundantly supplied with money, and to have come to Palestine in a private yacht, which was anchored off Jaffa while they were at work. In 1911 the hostility of the Moslems became so excited by the rumor that they had attempted to excavate under the Mosque of Omar that the expedition came to an abrupt close, and the explorers escaped on their yacht. Through the descriptions of two residents of Jerusalem, Prof. Hughes Vincent [60] and Dr. E. W. G. Masterman,[61] we have some knowledge of the value of Parker's work. He cleared the silt out of the Siloam tunnel so as to reveal its real depth, which seems to have been between five and six feet. It had been so silted up that it appeared to be only about half that depth. He also explored more fully the caves about Ain Sitti Miriam (the Biblical Gihon, 1 Kings 1 : 33), which had been partially explored by Sir Charles Warren, so that the nature and probable use of these are now known much better. More will be said of this in a future chapter.

9. The Assumptionist Fathers at Jerusalem.—Some years ago the Assumptionist Fathers started excavating on a tract of land purchased by them on the eastern slope of the western hill to the south of the present city wall. They believe that they have discovered the house of Caiaphas, to which Christ was led in the course of his trial (Matt. 26 :57 ; John 18 : 24). Possibly they have found the house which, after the time of Constantine, was pointed out to Christian pilgrims as that of Caiaphas. However this may be, they have unearthed several streets of Roman and Jewish Jerusalem, and are keeping them uncovered. These streets, like the ruins of Pompeii, disclose pavements and house-foundations that may go back to the time of Christ. Here, possibly, one may look upon pavements which his feet actually trod.[62]

60 *Révue biblique*, 1912 (Paris), pp. 86–116.
61 *Biblical World*, Vol. XXXIX, Chicago, 1912, pp. 295–306.
62 See Germer-Durand in *Révue biblique*, 1914, pp. 71–94, and Frontispiece.

10. The Jewish Excavation on Ophel.—During the winter of 1913–1914 an excavation was conducted by Capt. Raymond Weill on the southern point of Mount Ophel at Jerusalem.[63] The expense of the expedition was borne by Baron Edmond de Rothschild. Captain Weill was influenced to choose for exploration the southern part of the hill by the fact that some years before Clermont-Ganneau, a distinguished French archæologist, had conjectured that the great bend in the Siloam Tunnel (see map, Plate 121) was made to avoid disturbing the tombs of the Judean kings. It was hoped, therefore, that the tombs of David and of later kings might be found. While this hope was not realized, several important discoveries were made.

At the lowest level some unrifled tombs of the Canaanite period were opened, from which samples of the pottery of that time were obtained. Large excavations in the rock which may have once been tombs of the period of the Jewish kingdom were also found, but they had been cleared out in ancient times and appropriated to other purposes; some of them had been converted into cisterns. Near the southeastern corner of the hill a series of walls and sloping structures were found. These were partly from early and partly from later time, on the slope above one another. The hill was vulnerable at this point and many efforts had been made to strengthen its defenses. Evidently it had often been attacked here. Not only the wall indicated this, but a long tomb in which were the bones of many headless bodies lying in a row. Probably these were the bodies of men who had fallen during some attack upon the walls centuries ago. Outside the walls were found parts of an aqueduct made during the early period of the kingdom of Judah, before the one was cut under the hill in the time of Hezekiah. This older one had been cut under the edge of the hill and the rock had been removed through windowlike openings. A part of this farther to the north had been discovered by Dr. Schick years before.[64] These openings could be entered by a besieging army, so that, when this channel was in use, the water supply was not well protected, hence that constructed by Hezekiah became necessary.

On the slope on which stood the mass of the fortifications mentioned above were the foundations of a round structure, possibly a tower. It is thought that this may be the "tower in Siloam" the fall of which is referred to in Luke 13:4. On the crest of the

63 See R. Weill, *La cité de David*, Paris, 1920.
64 See *Quarterly Statement* of the Palestine Exploration Fund, 1891, p. 15.

southern part of the ridge near some baths of the Roman time the remains of a structure and an inscription were found. The inscription is translated in Part II, Chapter XXIX. From it we infer that the structure was a synagogue and guest house, perhaps of the "Libertines" or freed men mentioned in Acts 6:9.

The outbreak of the Great War in 1914 prevented the resumption of Captain Weill's work until the winter of 1923–1924. During that season, so far as reported, no important discoveries were made by him.

11. Ain Duk.—At Ain Duk, about two miles northwest of the site of ancient Jericho, the mosaic floor of an ancient Jewish sanctuary or synagogue was accidentally laid bare during the war by the bursting of a shell. Worked into the mosaic there was an inscription (see Fig. 303) which reads as follows:

> Honored be the memory of Benjamin, the Patron, son of Joseph; honored be the memory of every one who takes stout hold and gives or . . . in this holy place, whether gold or silver or any valuable. Be made sure (?) their share in this holy place. Amen."

There is nothing connected with the inscription from which one can give it a definite date. Clermont-Ganneau, the distinguished French scholar, thought the floor was constructed in the fourth or fifth century, A.D. Professor Vincent, of the Dominican École Biblique in Jerusalem, who visited Ain Duk and examined the mosaic, at first thought that it dated from the reign of Herod the Great.[65] If this were so, it would be the floor of a synagogue that was in existence in the time of Christ.

In 1921 the Dominican Fathers of the École Biblique in Jerusalem made an examination of the site at the request of the Palestinian government. As a result of this examination other discoveries were made which convinced them that the synagogue and surrounding buildings were constructed in the third century of our era.[66]

Ain Duk, where the mosaic was found, is the ancient Dok, where Simon, the last of the Maccabees, was slain by his son-in-law Ptolemy (1 Macc. 16:11). It was an important town during this period.

The inscription affords interesting proof of the honor in which the Jews held men who gave money to their places of worship. It thus throws light on the words addressed to Jesus by Jews of Capernaum

65 See *Révue biblique*, 1919, pp. 532–559.
66 Cf. *Ibid.*, 1921, pp. 442, 443.

concerning a certain Roman centurion: "He is worthy that thou shouldest do this for him; for he loveth our nation, and himself built us our synagogue." (Luke 7:4, 5.)

The inscription accidentally uncovered proved to be one of a large cycle of inscriptions in mosaic which adorned the whole of the nave of the synagogue. There were also numerous figures wrought into the mosaic. Some represented Old Testament themes; among these was Daniel in the lion's den. The signs of the zodiac were also represented, numerous plants, fantastic animal forms, as well as geometric figures. The whole reveals an unsuspected form of Jewish architecture. The synagogue was surrounded by numerous houses in which some of those who worshiped in it dwelt. In more recent years various Jewish scholars have discovered the remains of similarly decorated synagogues in various parts of Palestine.[67]

12. Hammath.—A little to the south of Tiberias on the shore of the Sea of Galilee there are some hot springs which mark the site of the Hammath of Joshua 1:35. The name is derived from a Hebrew word which means "hot," and was accordingly given to the place because of the springs. In 1921 the Jewish Society for the Exploration of Palestine commissioned Dr. Nahum Slousch to excavate there. At the beginning of his work he was fortunate enough to uncover a synagogue of the same style of architecture as that at Tel Hum. The structure was evidently of a fine character, as a number of fragments of white marble ornaments were found, among which was a Corinthian capital. One piece of marble was adorned with a seven-branched candlestick. This was undoubtedly the famous "synagogue of Hamatha," celebrated in Jewish annals. It was founded by Herod Antipas about 20 A.D., and may well have been visited by Christ during his ministry. Evidence was found that the building shared the religious vicissitudes which swept over the land, and during its later period was occupied as a Christian church. This was in the time after Constantine.

Dr. Slousch continued his work during the winter of 1923–1924, but no reports of any important discoveries have reached the writer.

13. Beisan, the Beth-shean of Joshua 17:11,16; Judges 1:27; 1 Kings 4:12; 1 Chronicles 7:29 and the Beth-shan of 1 Samuel 31:10, 12 and 2 Samuel 21:12, is situated at the point where the

---

[67] See E. L. Sukenik, *Ancient Synagogues of Palestine and Greece,* Oxford University Press, 1934, and his *Ancient Synagogue of El-Hammeh,* Rubin, Mass., 1935.

great Plain of Jezreel descends into the Jordan Valley. It was situated in territory that normally belonged to the tribe of Issachar, but the city itself was occupied by a portion of the tribe of Manasseh. During the reign of King Saul the Philistines gained possession of it, and when they gained possession of King Saul's body they fastened it to the wall of Beth-shan. In the time of King Solomon it is mentioned in describing one of the economic units of this kingdom. Later it became a Greek city, as described below (Chapter XIV), and one of the cities of the Decapolis. The principal mound at Beisan covered the ancient city, while the remains of the Greek city are still traceable over a larger area around it.

The excavation of this site was undertaken in 1921 by the University of Pennsylvania Museum, Philadelphia, under the direction of Dr. Clarence S. Fisher, and work was carried on there for three summers. As the principal mound was the site of the most ancient city and promised, therefore, to be the most important, work was begun there. To completely explore the site is a work of years.[68] Dr. Fisher first undertook two things: (1) The sinking of a trial trench down through the mound to ascertain from the remains of buildings and from the pottery how many strata it contained and to what periods they belonged. (2) The clearing of the mound, stratum by stratum, from the top. While the trial trench was not carried to the rock, which is here buried under a depth of natural soil, it revealed pottery of the Arabic, Byzantine, Hellenistic, and earlier Hebrew and Semitic periods back to about 2000 B.C. A later sounding brought to light evidence reaching back to 3000 B.C. The débris continued below this level, proving the site to have been inhabited earlier than was anticipated.

At the top of the mound the remains of a city built by the Arabs shortly after their conquest in 637 A.D. were uncovered. Below this were found the ruins of the Byzantine city, including those of a circular Christian church adorned with beautiful columns. During the second season some lower strata of the mound were reached and an Egyptian fortress was cleared. Two pillars were found, one bearing an inscription of Seti I (1313–1292 B.C.), the other an inscription of Ramses II (1292–1225 B.C.), and a statue of Ramses III (1198–1167 B.C.). This fortress was later occupied by the Philistines, and was finally burned, probably by King David.

68 See Dr. Fisher's reports in the *Museum Journal*, March, 1922, and December, 1923; and G. M. Fitzgerald, *Beth-shan Excavations*, 1921-1923, Philadelphia, 1931.

The steles, or stone pillars, of Seti and Ramses bore historical inscriptions, most of the statements of which glorify the Egyptian monarchs. That of Ramses is pictured below. (Fig. 316.) While it refers to the city of Raamses, mentioned in Exodus 1 : 11, it makes no reference, as was at first thought, to the employment of Semitic captives in building it.[69]

From 1924 to 1929 the work was directed by Alan Rowe, and in 1929–1931 and 1933, by G. M. Fitzgerald. The most important work of these years was the excavation of successive strata of the temple of Mekal, the god of Beth-shan, during the time of the Egyptian domination of Palestine.[70] As there were revolts between the later reigns of this period, in which the temple was ruined so that it had to be rebuilt, its shape was altered from reign to reign; and since the dates of these successive reigns are known it is possible to study the temple planning of the time of Thothmes III (1503–1447 B.C.), of Amenophis III (1411–1375 B.C.), of Seti I (1313–1292 B.C.), and Ramses II (1292–1225 B.C.). These temples are further described in Chapter XI. In 1933 a shaft was sunk down through the mound to virgin soil. Eighteen different strata, counting from the top, were found above the virgin soil. In level XVI copper implements were found, indicating that strata XVII and XVIII belonged to the stone age, *i.e.,* were earlier than 3000 B.C. Objects from stratum XII corresponded to Egyptian objects of the XII Egyptian dynasty, about 2000 B.C., and from stratum XI, to the period of Egypt's Hyksos kings, 1700–1500 B.C. During all this time the city seems to have had no wall, as the houses were built out to the very edge of the mound.[71]

14. Shiloh.—In September, 1922, the Danish scholar, Dr. Aage Schmidt, sunk about a score of trial pits or shafts through the debris at Seilun, the biblical Shiloh.[72] He found potsherds from the Arabic and Græco-Roman periods, and from the early Israelitish period about 1200–1050 B.C. In 1926, 1929, and 1931 systematic excavation of the site was begun by Dr. Kjaer and Aage Schmidt. The excavators carried on their work with the

69 Cf. Alan Rowe in the *Museum Journal*, March, 1929, pp. 94–98.
70 Cf. Rowe, *Ibid.*, pp. 37–87, and Fitzgerald, *The Four Canaanite Temples of Beth-shan*, Philadelphia, 1930.
71 See *Quarterly Statement of the Palestine Exploration Fund*, July, 1934, pp. 123–134.
72 See *Journal of the Palestine Oriental Society*, Vol. X (1930), pp. 87–174, and *Bulletin of the American Schools of Oriental Research*, No. 45 (Feb., 1932), p. 24.

most painstaking care, but, with the exception of the shafts sunk in 1922, confined themselves to the Arabic and Byzantine strata.[73]

This probing of the site confirms the statements concerning Shiloh which we find in the Scriptures and gives us one item of information not contained in the Bible. The potsherds reveal no evidence that there was ever a Canaanite settlement at Shiloh; the Hebrews appear to have founded the settlement after their conquest of Palestine. Here they established the Ark of the Covenant, selecting the site apparently because the spot was centrally located in the hill country of Ephraim; and the town grew up about the temple erected to protect the Ark. Here Eli ministered, and Samuel passed his boyhood. (1 Sam. 1–3.) After the Ark was captured by the Philistines (1 Sam. 4), it never returned, but by gradual steps was transferred to Jerusalem. (1 Sam. 6 and 2 Sam. 6.) After its loss Shiloh seems to have gradually been deserted and to have fallen into decay. In the time of Jeremiah its temple was a ruin (Jer. 7: 12–15; 26:6), and the place apparently deserted. As the potsherds bear witness to no settlement here from about 1050 B.C. till about 300 B.C., the archæological soundings confirm the text of the Bible.

15. Jebeil is the modern name of the Phœnician city of Gebal, mentioned in Ezekiel 27:9. During the winter of 1923-1924 the French explored the royal necropolis. The work was under the charge of M. Montet. Tombs were discovered containing objects from the time of the early Egyptian dynasties, which prove a contact of Egypt with Phœnicia. From the end of the second dynasty, about 3000 B.C., to the end of the fifth dynasty, about 2625 B.C., Egyptians were settled here and maintained an Egyptian temple.[74] They called the place Kupna; the Semites who came later, called it Gebal, or "The Mountain." An equally surprising discovery has come from some tombs of the period of the Egyptian empire. On a sarcophagus of Ramses II an inscription in early Phœnician characters was found. Scholars who have seen it say that it probably dates from about 1100 B.C. It was the oldest Phœnician writing then known—three hundred years older than the Moabite Stone. The characters are unexpected shapes. The inscriptions contain the royal names Ahiram, the biblical Hiram (2 Sam. 5: 11, 2 Kings chs. 5 and 9) ; also Ethbaal—a name

73 *Ibid.*
74 See Montet's reports in *Syria,* Vol. III and subsequent vols.

identical with that of the father of Jezebel (1 Kings 16 : 31), though
borne, of course, by different persons at Gebal in this earlier time.
The work of exploring the mound has been continued until the
present time (1937).

16. The Alphabet.—In this connection it may not be out of
place to refer to discoveries which have solved the problem of
the origin of the alphabet. The key to the solution of the problem
was found in the inscriptions discovered by Petrie at Sarbut el-
Khadem in 1905,[75] though their importance was not realized until
ten years later. The credit of having perceived their true character
belongs to Alan H. Gardiner, a distinguished Egyptologist, who
in an article published in 1916 [76] showed that a number of the
characters are intermediate between those of certain Egyptian
hieroglyphs and letters of the Semitic alphabet.

Cowley,[77] an English Semitic scholar, and Sethe,[78] a distinguished
German Egyptologist, took up the discussion and helped to establish
the thesis. Another German scholar, Hugo Grimme, in 1923 gave
added zest to the investigation by the publication of a translation
of the inscriptions, in which he professed to find Moses as the
author of a number of them, and in one of them his rendering made
Moses say that Hatshepsut, a distinguished queen of Egypt about
1500 B.C., drew him out of the water! [79] Grimme's renderings have,
however, been shown to be wrong. He took for letters mere cracks
and weather marks on the stone.

In 1927 new impetus was given to the study by the discovery
at Serabit el-Khadem of other inscriptions on the part of Professors Lake and Blake of Harvard, and by the renewed study
of the whole problem by Professor Butin, of the Catholic University at Washington.[80] A valuable contribution to the discussion
was also made by Professor Sprengling of Chicago.[81] It appears that the alphabet had its origin in the region of Sinai, about
1800 B.C., and spread from thence to South Arabia and Phœnicia.
By 1400 B.C., it had become so widely used there that some scribes
at a place now called Ras Shamra, on the northern coast of Phœnicia,

75 Cf. Petrie, *Researches in Sinai*, London, 1906; also A. H. Gardiner and E. Peet,
The Sinai Inscriptions, London, 1917, pl. LXXXII, ff.
76 See his "Origin of the Alphabet" in the *Journal of Egyptian Archaeology*, III,
1 ff.
77 *Ibid.*, 17 ff.
78 In *Zeitschrift der deutschen Morganlanden Gesellschaft*, LXXX (1926), 24 f.
79 *Althebraische Inschriften von, Sinai*, Hannover, 1923.
80 Cf. "The Serabit Inscriptions," by K. Lake. R. F. Blake, and R. Butin, in the
Harvard Theological Review, XXI (1928), pp. 1–67.
81 *The Alphabet: Its Rise and Development from the Sinai Inscriptions*, Chicago,
1931.

opposite Cyprus, wishing to write on clay, adapted its alphatic forms to cuneiform writing. Some of their tablets were discovered in 1928.[82] More recently alphabetic inscriptions kindred to those in Sinai have been exhumed by various excavations in Palestine, some of which date from the period 1700–1500 B.C.[83] From Sinai and Phœnicia the use of the alphabet spread to the Hebrews, Greeks, Romans, and thence to the modern world.

17. Megiddo Again.—In 1925 the Oriental Institute of the University of Chicago undertook the systematic excavation of Tell el-Mutesellim, which Schumacher had partially excavated years before. Preparations were made to carry on the work through a series of years until the whole mound is scientifically explored. From 1925–1927 the work was directed by Dr. Clarence S. Fisher; from 1927–1936, by Mr. P. L. O. Guy.[84] Much of archæological interest has been brought to light. Of greatest interest to the student of the Bible are the extensive stables for horses in the stratum of the time of Solomon. According to 1 Kings 10:26 ff., and 9:19, Solomon had twelve thousand horsemen that he stationed in "chariot cities" which he built for the purpose. Megiddo, it now appears, was one of these "chariot cities." During the winter of 1928–29, Mr. Guy discovered well-built stone stables for about three hundred horses. The roofs were supported by stone pillars, similar to those found in houses of this period. The pillars at once supported the roofs, and furnished posts for hitching the horses. The stables were constructed of hewn stone, were long and rectangular in shape, and the floors were paved with a lime plaster as hard as cement. Between the posts were mangers for the horses. There was also space for housing chariots, and rooms apparently for the grooms. The discovery affords an interesting commentary on the prosperity of Solomon's reign. (See Fig. 330.)

An underground tunnel leading to a subterranean spring, to enable the inhabitants of Megiddo to obtain water when the city was besieged, was also discovered. This arrangement appears to have been perfected in the reign of Solomon and replaced an older

---

82 For the discovery of F. A. Schaeffer in Syria, X (1929), 285–303. For the tablets, cf. Charles Virolleaud, Ibid., XII, pp. 304–310. For the decipherment, cf. Hans Bauer. Entzifferung der Keilschrifttafeln von Ras Schamra, Halle, 1930, and Dhorme, "Un nouvel alphabet sémitique" in Révue biblique XXXIX, 1930, 571–577 and XL, 32–56. See also § 26 of this chapter.

83 For a summary of these see Albright in the Bulletin of the American Schools of Oriental Research, No. 63 (October, 1936), pp. 8–12.

84 Clarence S. Fisher, The Excavation of Armageddon, Chicago, 1929, and P. L. O. Guy, New Light from Armageddon, Chicago, 1931.

system by which the spring was approached by a tunnel from outside the wall.[85]   More will be said of this in Chapter VI.

18. Prehistoric Man in Palestine.—In the spring of 1925 the
British School of Archæology in Jerusalem excavated some caves
in the Wady el Amud, which branches off from the ancient Valley
of Chinnereth (Genneseret), northwest of the Sea of Galilee.[86]
The purpose of the excavation was to gain, if possible, greater
knowledge of the history of Palestine in the early Stone Age.   In
addition to numerous stone implements that were found the excavators were fortunate in discovering in one of the caves which
they cleared considerable parts of a human skull of a very primitive
type.   Anthropologists who have studied it say that it is quite
similar to that of the so-called "Neanderthal" man of Europe.
While the skull is that of a more advanced type of man than that
recently found in Mongolia, it is of a type far less developed
than that of any race at present alive.   The implements, or artifacts,
found with it are of the type called "Mousterian," such as were
found in the same stratum in Europe as that of the "Neanderthal"
man.   This discovery attests the presence of man in Palestine before
the middle of those many centuries which must have been included
in the early Stone Age, and perhaps during the first third of that
period.   The skull found was that of a young man about twenty-five
years of age, and showed traces of healed injuries, or disease.   The
type is somewhat different from the European "Neanderthal" man,
though clearly belonging to it.   His brain capacity was less than
that of most European men of this type, being about 1400 cubic
centimeters.   This was the first discovery of a "Neanderthal" man
outside of Europe.

In 1928 Miss Dorothy A. E. Garrod, an English anthropolo-
gist, explored a cave at Shukbah, seventeen and a half miles northwest of Jerusalem—which had been discovered in 1924 by Père
Mallon—where she found numerous "Mousterian"[87] artifacts.
For the last three years she has conducted researches in caves
in the Wady el-Mugharah, south of Mount Carmel.   Here several
strata of prehistoric men have been discovered.   The cultures, with
one exception, correspond to similar cultures found in Europe; but,
curiously, here the order of two of the cultures is the reverse of

85 See Robert S. Lamon, *The Megiddo Water System*, Chicago, 1935.
86 See *Bulletin* No. 7 of the *British School of Archaeology in Jerusalem*, 1925,
pp. 99–102 and Plates III–VI, and Turville-Petrie, *Researches in Prehistoric Galilee*,
London, 1927.
87 See *Quarterly Statement* of the Palestine Exploration Fund, October, 1928, p.
182 ff.

that in Europe. She discovered a new culture which she called "Natufian." [88] Its people were members of the Mediterranean race; small of stature, but with a highly developed artistic sense. The date of the culture is in doubt, but belongs to the early Stone Age. M. Rene Neuville explored some caves in the Wady Khreitun, south of Bethlehem (The traditional site of the Cave of Adullam. See 1 Sam. 22:1.), where he found remains at least as old as the oldest in the caves of France.[89] In 1932 Mr. T. D. McCown discovered a prehistoric burial cave near Mugharet el Wad, Mt. Carmel, from which nine skeletons have since been taken. M. Rene Neuville has more recently uncovered a cave near Nazareth from which the oldest human remains yet found in Palestine were taken. These finds are not all as yet published in detail, but they give evidence that man was in Palestine from the Achulean to the Mesolithic periods of the old Stone Age. In 1929–1932 Mallon and Neuville jointly explored a late neolithic village site at Tuleilat el-Ghassul, just across the Jordan from Jericho. Pottery was found here similar to that in the prehistoric caves. Mallon at first dated the remains he uncovered far too late. Albright appears to be more correct in dating them about 3500 B.C., or earlier.[90] These explorations show that Palestine has been the abode of man for thousands of years. We cannot as yet trace human habitations here back to as great an antiquity as is possible in Egypt, but, nevertheless, the antiquity revealed is a respectable one.

19. Tell en-Nasbe.—In the spring of 1926 Professor F. W. Badè, of the Pacific School of Religion, Berkeley, California, assisted by some of the staff of the American Schools of Oriental Research in Jerusalem, began the excavation of Tell en-Nasbe, a large mound seven miles north of Jerusalem. Again, in 1927 and 1929 the work was prosecuted, two or three months having been devoted to the work in each of the three years.[91] Jar handles stamped with the word "Mizpeh" in old Hebrew letters were found. These seem to identify the site with the city, Mizpeh of Benjamin (Judges 20:1 ff.; 1 Sam. 7:5 ff.). One of the surprising dis-

88 See Miss Garrod, *Ibid.*, October, 1929, 220 f.; and G. M. Fitzgerald, *Ibid.*, April, 1930, p. 85 ff.; also Millor Burrows in the *Bulletin* of the American Schools of Oriental Research, No. 45, April, 1932, p. 21.

89 See W. F. Albright, *Archaeology of Palestine and the Bible*, 1931, p. 60 f.; and J. G. Duncan in *Quarterly Statement* of the Palestine Exploration Fund, April, 1932, p. 71 ff.

90 Cf. Mallon, Koeppel and Neuville, *Teleilat Ghassul* I, Rome, 1934 and Albright's review of the same in the *American Journal of Archaeology*, XL, ,1936), 389 f.

91 See *Palestine Institute Publications*, No. 1 and No. 2, Berkeley, Cal., 1928 and 1929, and the *Quarterly Statement* of the Palestine Exploration Fund, ct. 1932, pp. 204–209.

coveries was the antiquity of the settlement here and the cyclopean character of its early fortifications. The oldest city was surrounded by a wall which averaged seventeen feet in thickness and was, in places, as much as twenty-six feet thick. At certain points it was reinforced with towers which increased its thickness. The wall was built at a time when conditions in Palestine were very unsettled and strong fortifications were needed for security. In some tombs near by pottery of the type found by Macalister in the lowest stratum of Gezer was discovered. This is proof that there was a Stone Age settlement here.

In the Israelite stratum a stone altar of native rock was found, and just west of it a large square building which Dr. Badè and Dr. Fisher believe to have been a temple. If the city of Mizpeh were really here, as we believe, this was the Temple to which Samuel summoned the people and at which the Israelites had previously "assembled unto Jehovah." (Judges 20:1.) It was here that Saul was chosen king by means of the sacred lot. (1 Sam. 10:17.) When the king of Babylon destroyed Jerusalem, in 586 B.C., he made Gedaliah governor of Judæa, with his residence at Mizpeh. Two months later Gedaliah was murdered. Badè found at Tell en-Nasbeh a disused cistern filled with rubbish and potsherds, the latest of which indicated that the cistern had been closed at about the time of the Exile, and he was tempted to think that it might be the cistern into which the murdered Gedaliah was thrown. One of the tombs explored dated from the reign of Archelaus, 4 B.C. to 6 A.D. In 1936 Dean C. C. McCown of the Pacific School of Religion, did further work on the mound and found evidence which he believes confirms Dr. Badè's conclusions. He is preparing all the finds made here for publication.[92]

20. Jerusalem's "Third Wall."—Josephus, in his *Wars of the Jews* (V. 4, 2), says that Jerusalem was fortified on the north by three walls, which he enumerates, calling the southernmost of them the "first wall," and the most northerly the "third wall." He informs us that the building of this third wall was begun by Herod Agrippa I (41–44 A.D.), who was compelled to abandon the undertaking, because the Roman emperor suspected him of making preparations to revolt; but that later, during the war of 66–70 A.D., it was hastily completed by the Jews as an added defense of the city.

92 Cf. *Religion in Life,* V, 559 (October, 1936).

Scholars have long sought the exact situation of this wall. Three campaigns were devoted to a search for it by Dr. E. L. Sukenik, assisted by others, under the patronage of the Dropsie College, in Philadelphia, and the Hebrew University, in Jerusalem, in 1925, 1926, and 1927.[93] Remains of an ancient wall constructed of large dressed stones characteristic of ancient Jewish masonry were found at various points in the suburb which has grown up outside the modern north wall of Jerusalem, from the grounds of the Swedish School on the west, to those of the American Schools of Oriental Research on the east. (See Fig. 319.)

The explorers believe this to be the "third wall" of Josephus. Père Vincent, the eminent French archæologist, holds, however, that the wall thus discovered is a wall thrown up during the rebellion of Bar Chochabah, 132–135 A.D. Since in 132 A.D. Jerusalem was a ruin, and since we have no testimony that Bar Chochabah erected such a wall, the present writer shares the opinion of the excavators.

21. Beth-Shemesh Again.[94]—In 1928 Professor Elihu Grant, of Haverford College, Pennsylvania, undertook the completion of the excavation of Beth-Shemesh, which had been partially explored by Mackenzie in 1911–12. Campaigns have at this time of writing been devoted to the work, during the years 1928, 1929, 1930, 1931 and 1933.[95]. Four strata have been distinguished, all of which overlap archæological periods. It appears that the town was founded during the Hyksos period, 1800–1600 B.C., and was occupied down to the Babylonian exile. It had a life of some eleven centuries. Grant believes that he has uncovered a temple, and he has been fortunate in discovering unrifled tombs from which excellent specimens of pottery have been recovered. As Beth-Shemesh was on the borderland between the Philistines and Hebrews, the objects reminiscent of contacts between the two peoples are of particular interest. In 1930, a potsherd inscribed in ink with old Hebrew characters was discovered.[96] Its characters are more archaic than the Ahiram inscription of Jebail, and appear to be intermediary between those of that inscription and those of the Sinai inscriptions. Some scholars date it in the fourteenth century B.C., anterior

93 See E. L. Sukenik and L. A. Meyer, *The Third Wall of Jerusalem: an Account of Excavations*, Jerusalem, 1930.
94 See above, p. 104.
95 See Elihu Grant, *Beth-Shemesh*, Haverford, Pa., 1929, and *Ain Shems Excavations*, Haverford, 1931, and *Rumeileh*, Haverford, 1934.
96 For the writing see *Ain Shems Excavations*, Pl. X.

to the time of Moses.[97] In 1933 a curious tablet was uncovered written in the alphabet employed at Ugarit in northern Phœnicia, proving that that alphabet was used also in southern Palestine.[98]

22. Hazor.—The site of Hazor (Josh. 11 : 1 ff.; Judges 4 : 1 ff.), which had long been an unsolved problem, has been solved by the labors of Dr. John Garstang. In 1926 he found at El-Kedah— in an open plain, about four miles west of the Huleh, the small lake through which the Jordan flows some miles above the Sea of Galilee—a flat piece of land a thousand yards long and five to six hundred yards wide, surrounded by a rampart of earth sixty or more feet in height.[99] The earth had been thrown up from a ditch or moat, which was about a hundred feet in width. Garstang con' jectured that this was the site of Hazor.

In 1928, having been supplied with funds for the purpose, by Sir Charles Marston, he returned and made soundings to gain evidence as to the correctness or incorrectness of his conjecture. A considerable npumber of potsherds of the peculiar type of black pottery characteristic of the Hyksos were found, thus identifying it as one of the Hyksos camps.[100] The pottery showed that this particular camp had reached the height of its prosperity about 1800 B.C., and had been finally abandoned about 1400 B.C. Its area could comfortably accommodate a population of 4000 and, as a temporary camp, could contain as many as 30,000. Similar camps of the Hyksos have been discovered at Qatna, half way between Aleppo and Damascus; near Qadesh in Galilee; near Ashkelon on the Philistine plain; at the ancient Avaris in the eastern Delta of Egypt, in the Wady Tumilat, to the south of it and at Tell el-Yuhadiyeh,[101] about 20 miles north of Cairo. These appear to have been the fortified camps of seminomadic hordes who, during the period 1900–1600 B.C. poured down from the north.

23. Jericho Again.—In 1930 Dr. John Garstang undertook further excavations at Jericho.[102] He continued the work through six successive campaigns, one each year, 1930–1936. It was thought by him and other scholars that, because of the possi-

97 See Albright, *Archæology of Palestine and the Bible*, p. 50.
98 Cf. *Bulletin of the American Schools of Oriental Research*. Nos. 52, and 53.
99 See *Annals of Archæology* of the University of Liverpool, Vol. XIV, p. 35 ff.
100 Cf. John Garstang, *The Foundations of Bible History: Joshua and Judges*, New York, 1931, pp. 183 ff. and 381 ff.
101 Cf. A. T. Olmstead, *History of Palestine and Syria*, New York, 1931, p. 119 ff., and above, p. 29. Another of these camps at Tell Beit Mirsim has been mentioned above, p. 116.
102 See *Quarterly Statement* of the Palestine Exploration Fund, 1930, 123 ff.; 1931, 186 ff., and Garstang, *Foundations of Bible History*, pp. 130 ff. and 386 ff.

bilities of more accurate dating due to the increase since 1912 of our knowledge of the pottery of successive epochs, the results obtained by Sellin and Watzinger twenty years ago should be tested. Sir Charles Marston supplied the funds for the undertaking. Garstang found many strata at Jericho, which represent successive settlements. The earliest, discovered in 1935 and 1936, dates from a time when pottery had not yet been invented, and is said to be the oldest settlement yet discovered in Palestine. Higher levels reveal the beginnings of pottery in unbaked clay, and from level to level afford examples of most of its later forms until the time Jericho was destroyed. Flint artifacts, pottery, figurines, and many smaller objects from hitherto unsuspected ages of Palestinian history open a new vista before our eyes.[103]   In one stratum the houses were round, while in the strata above and below they were square. The Jericho built about 1800 B.C. was destroyed by a fierce fire, which occurred at a time when the harvest had been gathered and the grain bins were full, and which took the population so by surprise that it interrupted them in the midst of their daily occupations. The conflagration left a bed of ashes which was, in places, several inches thick. From the criterion of pottery Garstang dates this fire about 1400 B.C., and believes that it occurred at the time Joshua captured the city. (Josh. 6: 1–21.) The testimony of the pottery obtained by excavations is, however, not harmonious. It would indicate that Jericho fell from fifty to a hundred years before Bethel. Just how this discrepancy is to be harmonized is not yet clear.[104] The mound was after this unoccupied for several centuries, having been rebuilt about 900 B.C., or a little later. This corresponds to the statements in Joshua 6: 26 and 1 Kings 16: 24.

24. Ai.—In 1934 and 1935 Madame Judith Marquet-Krause carried on extensive excavations at Et-Tell,[105] about two miles southeast of Bethel, which has long been regarded by scholars as the site of the Biblical Ai. As noted in the sixth edition of this work (p. 143), Garstang had in 1928 run a trial trench into this mound and concluded from the potsherds found that it was destroyed just at the time of the Israelite invasion, which he dated about 1400 B.C. It now appears that he was misled by potsherds

103 Cf. *Quarterly Statement* of the Palestine Exploration Fund, April, 1935, p. 61 ff., and C. C. McCown in *Religion in Life*, V, 554 (October, 1936); also Garstang in *Syria*, VI, 353–357 (December, 1935).
104 See the discussion by W. F. Albright in the *Bulletin of the American Schools of Oriental Research*, No. 58. 10–18 (April, 1935).
105 Cf. Madame Judith Marquet-Krause in *Syria*, XVI, 327–352 (December, 1935), and C. C. McCown in *Religion in Life*, V, 555, 556 (October, 1936).

that had been dropped on the mound at a much later time. Madame Marquet-Krause has unearthed three city levels superimposed one upon another. The uppermost of these lies just beneath the surface and was destroyed about 2000 B.C. The lowest of them dates from about 3000 B.C. Each stratum had its temple. They were built above one another. The altar of the latest was still standing and before it was the skull of the last calf that had been sacrificed upon it. A little higher up on the top of the hill the foundations of a "palace" were unearthed. The mound was not inhabited between 2000 B.C. and 1050 B.C. From the evidence at present before us, it appears that Ai was already in ruins, when the Hebrew conquest of Palestine took place. Its name in Hebrew, *ha 'Ai,* means, 'the ruin'. The excavator and her friends believe that this name was given it by the Hebrews because it was already in ruins, before they conquered it. Bethel and Ai were so near one another that archæologists believe that there could never have been two flourishing cities that were contemporaneous on these sites. Archæological evidence indicates that Ai was destroyed before 2000 B.C. and that within a century Bethel sprang up and that it was Bethel that was destroyed by the Hebrews in the twelfth or thirteenth century, and the Biblical account of the destruction of Ai (Josh. 7) is in reality the account of the destruction of Bethel. Further light would be most welcome.

25. Tell Jemmeh Again.—In 1927 W. M. Flinders Petrie, the veteran explorer of Egypt, transferred the work of the British School of Egyptian Archæology to Palestine and began the excavation of Tell Jemmeh.[106] Finding the work greatly handicapped by the discovery of numerous great grain pits, which cut through the strata, and which had been constructed by the Persians, presumably to supply their army with food when invading Egypt, he later transferred his work to Tell-el-Farah, southeast of Gaza, where interesting discoveries have been made. Petrie believes this to be the site of the Biblical Beth-pelet [107] (Josh. 15 : 27 ; Neh. 11 : 26), and his view is shared by Garstang; [108] but Albright [109] thinks this impossible and suggests that it may be Sharuhan, a city that was prominent on the southern border of Palestine during the period

106 See W. M. F. Petrie, *Gerar*, London, 1928.
107 See W. M. F. Petrie, *Beth-pelet* I, London, 1930.
108 *Foundations of Bible History*, New York, 1931, p. 285.
109 *Archæology of Palestine and the Bible*, pp. 53 and 187. McCown denies that it was Beth-pelet, but ventures no opinion as to its identity; *Religion in Life*, V, 557 (October, 1936).

of Egyptian occupation. Petrie later excavated at Tell el-Ajjul, also in the southwestern part of the Negheb, as the Hebrews called this southland. His excavations throw much light on the time of the Hyksos.

26. Ras Shamra-Ugarit.—In 1928 tablets in cuneiform alphabetic writing were discovered at Ras Shamra on the coast of northern Syria, opposite the island of Cyprus. The decipherment of this alphabet has already been mentioned; (see above, p. 130, note 82). Beginning in 1929 M. F. A. Schaeffer has carried on excavations there, the results of which are published in successive volumes of *Syria* (vols. X-XVII). Walls, buildings, a temple, and numerous utensils of daily life and objects of art have been found, as well as an archive of written documents. From the written material we learn that the ancient name of the town was Ugarit. As long ago as 1907 it was known from correspondence between Babylonian and Hittite kings that such a town existed, but, until the recovery of these documents, its location was unknown. The town appears to have been ruled by Hurrians, who had overcome an earlier Amorite population and, for religious purposes, adopted their gods and their language. It is this religious literature that makes the discovery of Ugarit of significance to the student of the Bible. It is written in the language of the ancient Amorites, out of which both Hebrew and Phœnician were develoed. Many of its words are words dear to the reader of the Bible, such as the word for "anoint" from which "Messiah" comes, and the word for "bring good tidings" (Isa. 52:7). Liturgical poems written in poetry, the poetical structure and many expressions of which resemble those of the Hebrew Psalter, formed a part of his library. One of these (translated in Part II, Ch. IX, sec. 9) was, in the opinion of the present writer, written for the spring festival at Jerusalem in the period of Melchizedek and Abraham, and carried northward by the Amorites when driven from Jerusalem. Another, which describes the death of a god kindred to the Babylonian god Tammuz, is translated in Part II, Chapter XXVI, Section 7.[110] Another

110 The texts of these poems have been published by Ch. Virolleaud, with translations in *Syria*, Vols. XII-XVII. Many other attempts at interpretation have been made. Among these may be mentioned those of R. Dussaud, *Revue de l'histoire des religions*, CIV and CV (1931, 1932), J. A. Montgomery, in the *Journal of the American Oriental Society*, LII-LVI (1932-1936), and, in collaboration with Dr. Z. S. Harris, *The Ras Shamra Mythological Texts*, Philadelphia, 1935; W. F. Albright in the *Journal of the Palestine Oriental Society*, XII-XVI (1932-1936) and the *Bulletin* of the American Schools of Oriental Research, Nos. 46, 50, and 63; L. W. Jack, *The Ras Shamra Tablets*, Edinburgh, 1935; T. H. Gaster, in the *Journal of the Royal Asiatic Society*, 1932-1936; G. A. Barton, *Journal of the American Oriental Society*, LII, 221–231 and LV, 31–58; also in the *Journal of Biblical Literature*, LIII, 61–78, and Virolleaud, *La légende phénicienne de Danel*, also *La legende de Keret, roi des Sidoniens*, Paris, 1936, and H. L. Ginsberg, *The Ugarit Texts*.

poem mentions a hero, Daniel, who may be the Daniel referred
to in Ezekiel 14 : 14. Parts of it are translated in Part II, Chapter
XXVI, Section 8. The excavation has opened an entirely new
vista in the history of ancient Syria and Palestine. Virolleud
has published still another poem, which he regards as a legend of
Keret, king of the Sidonians. Following a theory of Dussaud's,
Virolleaud believes the Phœnicians to have come from the region
of the Red Sea, and apparently, that the Hebrews came along with
them. He finds references in the poem to the tribes of Zebulon
and Asher, and to Terah, the father of Abraham (see Gen. 11 :27).
Professor Albright takes quite a different view of the poem. He
regards it as a nature poem, thinks that there is no evidence that
Sidon ever had a king Keret, regards it as possible that Keret was
the epithet of a god, and gives to the whole an entirely different
explanation. Until the poem has been more completely studied,
it is impossible to tell what interest it has for the students of the
Bible.[111]

Another brief poem published by Virolleaud [112] describes a hunting episode by the side of Samak, which may well be as Dussaud [113]
maintains the level ground around that small lake in the Upper
Jordan Valley called in the Old Testament, the waters of Merom
(Josh. 11 : 5, 7), called "the lake of Semechonitis" by Josephus
(*Antiquities,* V, 5 : 1 and *Wars of the Jews,* IV, 1 : 1), Samki
in the Talmud (*Yebamoth,* 121a) and now called the Huleh.

27. Antioch.—In the spring of 1932 Princeton University
began the excavation of Antioch in Syria, where a Christian
Church was established early in the Apostolic Age, and which during succeeding centuries was an important Christian center. The
work during the first season was directed by Prof. George W.
Elderkin, who was assisted by Prof. Clarence S. Fisher. Other
field-directors have since continued the work. It was at Antioch
that the exquisite chalice described in Part II, Chapter XXX, was
dug up, and much may be expected from the present undertaking.
The space enclosed within the walls of Antioch was half as large
again as the space covered by the ancient city of Rome. In the
four campaigns now (1936) completed the uncovering of this
vast site has only been begun, but the circus has been laid bare,

111 See his *La legende de Keret, roi des Siloniens,* Paris, 1936, and Albright in the
Bulletin of the American Schools of Oriental Research, No. 63 (October, 1936); pp.
23–32.
112 *Syria,* Vol. XVII, 1936, 150–173.
113 *Syria,* Vol. XVII, 1936, 283–295.

the theatre has been located, the theatre in Daphne, an ancient suburb, has been uncovered, numerous pieces of statuary, fragments of buildings, and inscriptions have been found, as well as a Christian Church built in the year 384 A.D. Many of the houses found were built before the Christian era; others, in the time of the Roman empire. About 250 pieces of mosaic have been found, of a quality matched by but few of those hitherto known.[114]

28. Sabeita and Auja el-Hafir.—In 1933 Mr. H. Dunscombe Colt began the excavation of Sabeita, situated some thirty to thirty-five miles south of Beersheba, the site of which Woolley had explored twenty years before.[115] Mr. Colt uncovered in two seasons' work the remains of a city that had been founded at the end of the first century A.D. or the beginning of the second, and which had flourished until the twelfth century A.D. These dates were determined by the types of pottery that were found. The ruins of two Christian churches of the Byzantine period were uncovered; also those of a monastic institution, together with the remains of a considerable number of houses. When Sabeita was a flourishing town, the water-suppy must have been much more abundant than it is at present, for, when the excavators returned for the expedition of 1935–1936, the water available was insufficient even for the uses of their camp, and they were obliged to abandon temporarily further work at Sabeita and to move to Auja el-Hafir, a much less promising site. The apparent calamity turned out to be a blessing. They found the remains of two churches, in which they discovered more than forty written documents. These are the first papyri discovered in Palestine. Most of them are in Greek and date from the sixth and seventh centuries A.D., but some of them are in Arabic—the earliest Arabic writing known in the Holy Land. The papyri are business documents, and, when deciphered, will afford information as to the social and economic conditions of the period as well as the ecclesiastical organization which prevailed there.[116]

29. Summary.—The history of Palestinian exploration here sketched falls into three periods:

1. *The first* began with the work of Robinson, in 1838, and extended to 1890. It was the period of beginnings. Its work

114 See Charles F. Morey in *The Proceedings of the American Philosophical Society*, LXXVI, 1936, 637–652.
115 See the *Annual* of the Palestine Exploration Fund, III, ch. V.
116 See the *Quarterly Statement* of the Palestine Exploration Fund, October, 1935, p. 171 ff. and *Religion in Life*, V (October, 1936), 563.

was experimental and unsystematic and lacked the guidance to be obtained from pottery.

2. *The second period,* from 1890 to the Great War, in 1914, was inaugurated with the introduction, by Petrie, of pottery as a source of historical and chronological knowledge, and was characterized by the development of an increasingly accurate scientific method.

3. *The third period,* from 1920 to the present time, has been characterized by the development of the art of excavation into a science, the perfecting of the use of pottery as an instrument of knowledge, and the undertaking of systematic and complete excavation of sites.

In the above account only the principal explorations have been mentioned. In all parts of Palestine, and especially at Jerusalem, important archæological discoveries are frequently made when people are digging to lay the foundations of buildings, to construct a cistern, or for other purposes. Other important discoveries, as, for instance, the rock-cut high place at Petra,[117] and the painted tombs at Beit Jibrin,[118] have been made by people traveling through the land.

Here, too, should be mentioned the Græco-Roman town at Beit Jibrin, examined by Professors Vincent and Savignac, in 1922,[119] at the request of the British Government. Many minor discoveries are being made every year by some of the many agencies that are now carrying forward a variety of systematic examinations. A summary of these is given each year in the *Bulletin* of the American Schools of Oriental Research. Many discoveries made in this way are recorded in the *Quarterly Statement* of the Palestine Exploration Fund, the *Zeitschrift des deutschen Palastina-Vereins,* and the *Rèvue biblique.* Lack of space forbids the attempt to chronicle these.[120]

---

[117] First noticed by Professor George L. Bobinson and afterward by Professor Samuel Ives Curtis.

[118] Discovered in 1902 by Dr. J. P. Peters and Dr. Thiersch; see their *Painted Tombs of Marissa,* London, 1905.

[119] *Revue biblique,* XXXI. 1922, pp. 259–281.

[120] Reference should also be made to the expedition from Princeton University, referred to on p. 146, led by Prof. H. C. Butler, which went out in 1899–1900, in 1904–1905, and in 1909 and examined the ruins in the Hauran (or region east of the Sea of Galilee), in the Lebanon Mountains, and in that part of Syria to the east of Lebanon. The expedition gathered many inscriptions, most of which belong to the Christian period. The results of this exploration are published in *The Publications of an Archaeological Expedition to Syria in 1899–1900,* New York, 1904, and *Publications of the Princeton Archaeological Expeditions to Syria in 1904–1905 and 1909,* Leyden, 1908–1914.

CHAPTER V

OUTLINE OF PALESTINE'S ARCHÆOLOGICAL HISTORY

THE EARLY STONE AGE. THE LATE STONE AGE. THE AMORITES. THE HURRI AND HYKSOS. EGYPTIAN DOMINATION: Thothmes III. Palestine in the El-Amarna Letters. Seti I. Ramses II. Merneptah. Ramses III. THE PHILISTINES. EARLY HEBREW CONQUESTS. PHILISTINE CIVILIZATION. THE HEBREW KINGDOMS. THE EXILE AND AFTER: The Samaritans. Alexander the Great and his successors. The Maccabees. The Asmonæans. THE COMING OF ROME: The Herods. The destruction of Jerusalem in 70 A.D. LATER HISTORY.

1. The Early Stone Age.—Palestine was certainly inhabited at a very remote period. Scholars divide into two classes the races of prehistoric men who used stone implements—Palæolithic and Neolithic. Palæolithic men did not shape their stone implements. If they chanced to find a stone shaped like an axe, they used it as such; if they found a long, thin one with a sharp edge, they used it for a knife. Neolithic man had learned to shape his stone tools. He could make knives for himself out of flint and form other tools from stone. The earliest inhabitants of Palestine belonged to the palæolithic period. Unshaped stone implements have been found in many parts of the country. They have been picked up in the maritime plain, in still larger numbers on the elevated land south of Jerusalem, and again to the south of Amman, the Biblical Rabbah Ammon, on the east of the Jordan. The remains of palæolithic men found near the Sea of Galilee and near Mount Carmel, near Nazareth (see ch. IV, § 18.) afford evidence of a long palæolithic history.

These palæolithic men lived in caves in which they left traces of their occupation. Several of these caves in Phœnicia have been explored by Père Zumoffen, of the Catholic University of St. Joseph, Beirut.[1]

2. The Late Stone Age.—Of neolithic men in Palestine much more is known. This knowledge comes in part from the numerous cromlechs, menhirs, dolmens, and "gilgals" which are scattered

---

[1] See R. A. S. Macalister, *History of Civilization in Palestine*, Cambridge University Press, 1912, pp. 10, 11.

MAP OF
PALESTINE

SCALE OF MILES

0   10   20   30   40

PETERS, ENGRS., BOSTON

Longitude   East   35°   from   Greenwich   36°

Damascus

MT. HERMON

PHŒNICIA

Laish (Dan)

Tyre

Yemam

Kedesh

R. Jordan

Waters of
Merom

TETRARCHY

Capernaum   Bethsaida

GALILEE   Gergesa   OF PHILIP

Sea of
Galilee   Hippos   Ashteroth
Karnaim

Nazareth

R. Yarmuk

Dor   Megiddo   Gadara

R. Kishon   Plain of
Esdraelon

Taanach   Scythopolis

SAMARIA   Pella   Geresa

Samaria

Shechem

Joppa   P E R A E A

Lydda   Bethel   Jordan River   Philadelphia

Gezer   Jericho

JERUSALEM

Ashdod   Beth-Shemesh   Bethlehem   Mt. Nebo

Tell-es-Safi   Medeba

J U D E A

Ashkelon   Lachish   Tell-Sandahanna   Hebron

Gaza   DEAD SEA   Dibon

M E D I T E R R A N E A N   S E A

over eastern Palestine. A cromlech is a heap of stones roughly resembling a pyramid; [2] a menhir is a group of unhewn stones so set in the earth as to stand upright like columns; [3] a dolmen consists of a large unhewn stone which rests on two others which separate it from the earth; [4] and a "gilgal" is a group of menhirs set in a circle.[3] These monuments are the remains of men of the Stone Age who dwelt here before the dawn of history. They were probably erected by some of those peoples whom the Hebrews called Rephaim [5] or "shades"—people who, having lived long before, were dead at the time of the Hebrew occupation.

Similar monuments of the Stone Age have been found in Japan, India, Persia, the Caucasus, the Crimea, Bulgaria; also in Tripoli,[6] Tunis, Algeria, Morocco, Malta, southern Italy, Sardinia, Corsica, the Belearic Isles, Spain, Portugal,[7] France, the British Isles, Scandinavia, and the German shores of the Baltic. Some scholars hold that all these monuments were made by one race of men, who migrated from country to country. As the monuments are not found at very great distances from the sea, the migrations are supposed to have followed the sea coasts.[8] Others scout the idea of a migration over such long distances at such an early epoch of the world's history, and believe that the fashion of making such monuments was adopted from people to people by imitation. Be this as it may, these monuments seem to have been in Egypt and Palestine before the Semites and Hamites developed into the Egyptians, Amorites, and Hebrews, for they were adopted by them as the "pillars" which are so often denounced in the Old Testament, and in Egypt were gradually shaped and prolonged into the obelisks.

Of the men of this Stone Age the excavations have furnished us with some further information and still more will be known when the results of the latest excavations at Jericho are published; (see above, ch. IV, § 23). At Gezer the native rock below all the cities was found to contain caves,[9] some natural and some artificial, which had formed the dwellings of men of the Stone Age. They, like

2 See Barton, *A Year's Wandering in Bible Lands*, Philadelphia, 1904, p. 143.
3 See Barton, in the *Biblical World*, Chicago, 1904, Vol. XXIV, p. 177.
4 See Conder, *Survey of Eastern Palestine*, I, pp. 125–277, and Mackenzie in the *Annual* of the Palestine Exploration Fund, I, pp. 5–11.
5 See Genesis 14:5; 15:20.
6 See H. S. Cowper, *The Hill of the Graces, a Record of Investigation Among the Trilithons and Megalithic Sites of Tripoli*, London, 1897, and Brandenburg, *Ueber Felsarchitektur im Mittelmeergebiet* in *Mitteilungen der Vorderasiatischen Gesellschaft*, 1914.
7 See *Archaeologia*, Second Series XX, London, 1920, pp. 201-232.
8 See the *Annals of Archæology and Anthropology*, Vol. V, Liverpool, 1913, pp. 112–128.
9 See Macalister, *The Excavation of Gezer*, I, 72–152.

men today, were lazy. If one found a cave that would protect him from heat, cold, and rain, he would occupy it and save himself the trouble of making one. But there were not enough caves to go around, so some of the men of ancient Gezer cut caves for themselves out of the soft limestone rock. It must have been a difficult task with the stone implements at their disposal, but they accomplished it, sometimes cutting stairs by which to descend into them. One such cave seems to have been used as a temple. In it were found a quantity of pig bones, which were apparently the remains of their sacrifices. If they offered the pig in sacrifice, they were certainly not Semitic, for Semites abhorred swine. These early men sometimes adorned the sides of their dwellings by scratching pictures on the walls. Several pictures of cattle were found. One cow seemed to have knobs on her horns to keep her from goring! One drawing represented a stag that was being killed with a bow and arrow.[10] These early men burned their dead, and one of the caves in the eastern end of the hill was used as their crematory. Steps in the rock led down to its entrance. The cave itself was 31 feet long, 24 feet 6 inches wide, and the height varied from 2 to 5 feet. Near one end a hole had been cut to the upper air to act as a flue. Below this the fires that burned their dead had been kindled; cinders and charred bones of these far-off men were found as grim tokens of their funeral rites. Shortly after these bones were found the anatomist, Prof. Alexander Macalister, of Cambridge University, father of the excavator, visited the camp at Gezer and made a study of the bones. He found that they represented a non-Semitic race. The peculiar modifications of the bones caused by the squatting so universally practised by Semites were absent. The men whose bones these were could not have been more than 5 feet 3 inches in height, and many of the women must have been as short as 4 feet 3 inches. A pottery head found in one of the caves, which may be a rude portrait of the type of face seen in Gezer in this period, has a sloping forehead, which afforded little brain-space, and a prominent lower jaw. These people used flint knives, crushed their grain in hollow stones with rounded stones, employed a variety of stone implements, and made pottery of a rude type, which will be described in a later chapter.

The city of Gezer in this period was surrounded by a unique wall or rampart.[11] This consisted of a stone wall about 6 feet high and

10 See Macalister, *The Excavation of Gezer*, I, 145–152.
11 *Ibid.*, 236 ff.

2 feet thick, on the outer side of which was a rampart of packed earth about 6 feet 6 inches at the base and sloping toward the top. This bank of earth was protected by a covering of small stones about 8 inches in depth. This rampart never could have been of much value in warfare, and was, perhaps, meant as a protection against incursions of wild animals.

In the hillsides round Gezer there are many caves which were probably human habitations during this period, but as they have been open during many centuries, traces of their early occupation have long since been destroyed.

Professor Macalister suggested a connection between these cave-dwellers of Gezer and the Biblical Horites,[12] interpreting Horite as "cave-dweller." Most scholars now think that the "Horites" were not cave-dwellers, but Hurrians. In the Bible the Horites are said to have dwelt to the east of the Jordan, and more especially in Edom. (Gen. 14:6; 36:20, 21, 29; Deut. 2:12, 22.) It was formerly thought that the reason why the Bible places them all beyond Jordan is that the cave-dwellers had disappeared from western Palestine centuries before the Hebrews came, while to the east of the Jordan they lingered on until displaced by those who were more nearly contemporary with the Hebrews. On the west of the Jordan megalithic monuments were probably once numerous, since traces of them still survive in Galilee and Judæa,[13] but later divergent civilizations have removed most of them. In the time of Amos one of these "gilgals" was used by the Hebrews as a place of worship, of which the prophet did not approve.[14]

It was formerly thought probable that there was a settlement of these cave-dwellers at Jerusalem. The excavations of Capt. Parker brought to light an extensive system of caves around the Virgin's Fountain, Ain Sitti Miriam, as the Arabs call it, which is the Biblical Gihon.[15] These caves are far below the present surface of the ground. It was found, too, that there would be no spring at this point at all, if some early men had not walled up the natural channel in the rock down which the water originally ran. These men, judging by the fragments of pottery and the depth of the débris, belonged to about the same period as the cave-dwellers of Gezer. They apparently settled at this point because of the water, and one of

12 R. A. S. Macalister, *Bible Side-lights from the Mound of Gezer*, London, 1906, Chapter II.
13 See P. E. Mader in *Zeitschrift des deutschen Palestina-Vereins*, Vol. XXXVII, 1914, pp. 20–44.
14 See Amos 4:4; 5:5.
15 See Dr. Masterman, in *Biblical World*, XXXIX, 301 f.

the caves may have been a sanctuary to their god. A new vista is thus added to the history of that city, which was later the scene of so much Biblical life. The explorations of recent years described in the preceding pages have now placed Professor Macalister's discoveries in a clearer light. The men of small stature whose skeletons were recovered at Gezer correspond to the neolithic men whose remains Miss Garrod found at Shukbah, seventeen and a half miles northwest of Jerusalem. They lived at Gezer about 4000 B.C. The men who built the unique wall or rampart about Gezer are now believed to have been a taller people who lived there 3200–2900 B.C. They inhabited the caves only as a matter of convenience, just as here and there a few lazy men still live in caves. At the time they were living in the Gezer caverns, their contemporaries at Jericho and Beth-shan were dwelling in houses. There was probably never a race of cave-dwellers in Palestine—at least not after the early centuries of the Late Stone Age. The word "Horite," which was formerly believed to mean "cave-dweller" is probably the Hebrew way of spelling "Hurri", the name of the people who swept over Palestine between 1800 and 1550 B.C.

3. The Amorites.—The first Semitic immigrants into Palestine were the Amorites. About 2800 B.C., under a great king named Sargon,[16] a city of Babylonia called Uru, or Amurru,[17] and Agade conquered all of Babylonia. The dynasty founded by Sargon was Semitic, and ruled Babylonia for 197 years.[18] Even before Sargon conquered Babylonia, Lugalzaggisi, king of Erech, had penetrated to the Mediterranean coast. Sargon and two of his successors, Naram-Sin and Shargali-sharri, carried their conquests to the Mediterranean lands. A seal of the last-mentioned king was found in Cyprus. Probably the invasion of the Amorites in the north followed these conquests. To the east of the Lebanon the Princeton expedition, led by Professor H. C. Butler, found stone structures similar to Babylonian *Ziggurats,* which they attribute to the Amorites, and hold to indicate the prevalence of Babylonian influence in this region. It is probable that the Amorites slowly worked southward, occupying different cities as they went. Professor Macalister's estimate that they reached Gezer about 2500 B.C. is not, therefore, unreasonable, though they may have arrived there a century or two earlier than that. This was the beginning of that

16 See the legend concerning him translated in Part II, p. 375, f.
17 See Clay, *Amurru,* Philadelphia, 1909, pp. 102, 103.
18 See *Recueil de travaux relatifs a phil. et a arch. egpt. et assyr.* XXXIV, 105–108. and above Ch. II.

long intercourse with Babylonia which resulted in the employment of the Babylonian language and script for the purpose of expressing written thought in Palestine long after the Egyptians had conquered the country. This intercourse was the more natural because the Semites who came to Palestine were of the same race as those who were dominant in Babylonia.

Meantime, the Egyptians had begun to take notice of Palestine. Earlier, about 3000 B.C., they had established themselves at Gebal in Phœnicia, and had maintained themselves there until about 2625 B.C. (See above, ch. IV, § 15). Uni, an officer of Pepi I of the sixth Egyptian dynasty, relates that he crossed the sea in ships to the back of the height of the ridge north of the "sand-dwellers" and punished the inhabitants.[19] This refers to the coast of Palestine in the neighborhood of the Philistine cities or Gezer. The time was between 2600 and 2570 B.C. Egypt was at this time only anxious to make her own borders secure; she had no desire to occupy this Asiatic land.

Again, between 2300 and 2200 B.C., a fresh migration of Semites, apparently also of the Amorite branch, invaded Babylonia and in time made the city of Babylon the head of a great empire. This race furnished the first dynasty of Babylon, which ruled from 2210 to 1924 B.C. Its greatest king, Hammurabi,[20] who gave to Babylonia a code of laws in the vernacular language,[21] conquered the "west land," which means the Mediterranean coast. It was probably under his successor, Shamsu-iluna, but certainly under one of the kings of this period, that a man in Sippar, in leasing a wagon for a year, stipulated that it should not be driven to the Mediterranean coast, because, apparently, travel between that coast and northern Babylonia was so frequent.[22] In this same period there lived in Babylonia an Abraham, the records of some of whose business documents have come down to us.[23] We also find there men who bore the names Yagubilu (Jacobel) and Yashubilu (Josephel), and one who was called simply Yagub, or Jacob. Palestinian evidence from a later time leads us to believe that men bearing all these names migrated during this period to Palestine and gave their names to cities which they either built or occupied.[24]

19 See Breasted, *Ancient Records, Egypt*, Vol. I, Chicago, 1906, § 315.
20 See Chapter II, p. 65.
21 Translated in Part II, p. 378, ff.
22 See Part II, p. 346, f.
23 See Part II, p. 344, ff.
24 See Part II, p. 364, ff.

Egyptians also came to Palestine during this period. The tale of Sinuhe [25] relates the adventures of a man who fled to Palestine in the year 1970 B.C., and who reached the land of Kedem, or the East, which apparently lay to the east of Jordan.[26] It is referred to several times in the old Testament. (See Gen. 29:1; Judges 6:3, 33; 7:12; 8:10; Job 1:3, etc.) Sinuhe there entered the service of an Amorite chieftain, Ammienshi, married his eldest daughter, became ruler of a portion of his land, and lived there for many years. He finally returned to Egypt and wrote an account of his adventures. This region was also called by Sinuhe and other Egyptians Upper Retenu, a name which they also applied to all the higher parts of Syria and Palestine. Retenu is philologically equivalent to Lotan (Gen. 36:20, 22, 29; 1 Chron. 1:38, 39) and Lot (Gen. 11:27, 12:4, etc.). When Sinuhe arrived in Kedem he found other Egyptians already there. Ammienshi was well acquainted with Egyptians. There was apparently considerable trade with Egypt at this time. Men from Palestine often went there for this purpose. Such traders are pictured on an Egyptian tomb of this period. Trade with Egypt is also shown to have existed by the discovery of Egyptian scarabs of the time of the Middle Kingdom in the excavation of Gezer, Jericho, Taanach, and Megiddo. As Egypt was nearer and commerce with it easier, its art affected the art of Palestine during this period more than did the art of Babylon, although the people were akin to the Babylonians. In the reign of Sesostris III, 1887–1849 B.C., the Egyptian king sent an expedition into Palestine, and captured a place, called in Egyptian Sekmem, which is thought by some to be a misspelling of Shechem.[27] This expedition probably stimulated Egyptian influence in the country, though the Egyptians established no permanent control over the land at this time.

One of the important additions to knowledge which has resulted from the employment of pottery as a source of historical information is the knowledge that that part of Palestine first to be inhabited thickly by a settled population was the Jordan valley. Professor Albright, when director of the American School in Jerusalem, visited sites in all parts of the Jordan valley many times and gath-

25 See Breasted, *Ancient Records, Egypt*, I, p. 233 f.
26 See Barton, *Commentary on Job*, New York, 1911, pp. 5–7, and Breasted, *Ancient Records, Egypt*, I, p. 238, note a.
27 See Breasted, *Ancient Records, Egypt*, § 680, and Barton, *Journal of Biblical Literature*, Vol. XXVIII, p. 29.

ered tell-tale potsherds which revealed their history.[28]   At Tell
Abil (The Abel of Beth-maacha of 2 Sam. 20:14, also 1 Kings
15: 20 and 2 Kings 15: 29.) evidence was found that the city dates
from the early Bronze Age.   The same was true of Tell en-
Naameh, in the same district; perhaps the Yenoam of the Egyptian
inscriptions.   Farther south at Tell el-Qaneitriyah (or Tell
Eqlatriyah), a site overlooking the Sea of Galilee, the pottery
strewn over the sides belonged to the early and middle Bronze Ages.

At the southern end of the Sea of Galilee, near the mouth of
the Jordan, is the mound of Hirbet Kerak.   It is very extensive
and was the site of a large city.   On one side the sea has washed
away the earth so that the recovery of potsherds of the earliest
strata is easy.   These show clearly that the site was occupied about
2500 B.C. and continued to be inhabited until after 2000 B.C.   The
site was again occupied in Hellenistic times.   It was then the site
of the town Philoteria, built by Ptolemy Philadelphus.

Some miles down the Jordan is the site of Beth-shan, which,
as noted already (ch. IV, § 13), is known to have been occupied
as early as 3000 B.C.   In the immediate neighborhood are six or
seven mounds of considerable size, as well as numerous mounds
of lesser dimensions, the potsherds of which prove that they were
inhabited at the beginning of the Bronze Age, and in some cases
even at an earlier time.   Not to weary the reader with unnecessary
details, the stratification at Jericho goes back well to 4000 B.C.,
while the settlement at Taleilat Ghassul, across the Jordan from it,
probably reaches back into antiquity well beyond 3000 B.C.

The facts appear to be that at this early time the Jordan valley
was the only part of Palestine that was thickly populated.   Doubtless there were some settlements along the coast, one of the oldest
of which was Kupna, afterwards called Gebal, where Egyptians had
established themselves before 3000 B.C.; but during this early time
the coastal plain was but thinly peopled.   The central mountain
range, where most of Biblical history was later enacted, was but
sparsely populated, and the few towns situated there, such as
Jerusalem and Mizpeh, were built near springs of water.   By means
of ditches the water of the river was diverted to irrigate the fields
and gardens in the Jordan valley, and the country supported a
considerable population.

28 See *Annual* of the American Schools of Oriental Research, Vol. VI (1926), pp.
13–74.

4. The Hurri and Hyksos.—Between 1800 and 1750 B.C. a migration occurred which greatly disturbed all western Asia. There moved into Babylonia from the east a people called Kassites. They conquered Babylonia and established a dynasty which reigned for 576 years.[29] Coincident with this movement into Babylonia there was a migration across the whole of Asia to the westward, which caused an invasion of Egypt and the establishment of the Hyksos dynasties there.[30] As pointed out previously,[31] it is possible that this movement, in so far as the leadership of the invasion of Egypt was concerned, was Hurrian. In any event, however, many Semites were involved in it, as the Semitic names in the Egyptian Delta at this time prove. It was formerly assumed that it was in connection with this migration that the Canaanites came into Palestine, but it now seems clear that "Canannites" was only another name for "Amorites." It is probable that at this time the Hurri made their way into Palestine. There began at this time a new period of culture at Gezer, which is quite distinguishable from that which had preceded. This indicates the coming of new influences. Moreover, there was apparently an augmentation of the population of Palestine at this time. New cities were founded at Tell el-Hesy and Tell es-Safi,[32] and elsewhere. We thus feel sure that there was an increase of population and, when next our written sources reveal to us the location of the nations, the Phœnicians, whose early language was Amorite, are called "Canaanites"—a term that, perhaps, meant "Lowlanders." The Egyptian scribes of a later time called the entire western part of Syria and Palestine "The Canaan." [33] With the coming of an increased population, the Amorites appear to have been in part subjugated and absorbed, and in part forced into narrower limits. A powerful group of them maintained their integrity in the region afterward occupied by the tribe of Asher and in the valley between the Lebanon and Anti-Lebanon mountains, where they afterward formed a kingdom. Another group of them survived to the east of the Jordan, where they maintained a kingdom until overthrown by the Hebrews. (See Num. 21 and Deut. 1–3.)

After the coming of the Hurri-Hyksos our information concerning the history of Palestine fails us for nearly three hundred years.

29 See Chapter II, p. 65.
30 See Chapter I. p. 18.
31 See Chapter III, p. 84.
32 See Chapter IV, p. 99, 101.
33 See Breasted, *Ancient Records*, Egypt, III, § 616.

All that we know of the history of the country is what can be inferred from the accumulated débris of the late Bronze Age strata
of the different mounds that have been excavated. During these
centuries Egypt was invaded by the Hyksos, whose course was run,
and under the great eighteenth dynasty the Hyksos were expelled,
chased into Asia, and the conquest of Asia undertaken.

5. Egyptian Domination.—Ahmose I, 1580–1557 B.C., besieged Sharuhen (Josh. 19:6) in southern Palestine for six years
and captured it, while both Amenophis I and Thothmes I between
1557 and 1501 B.C. made raids through Palestine and Syria to the
Euphrates. Of their deeds in Palestine no records have survived.

(1) *Thothmes III.*—It is not until the reign of Thothmes III
that detailed information begins. Between 1478 and 1447 B.C.
this king made no less than seventeen expeditions into Palestine,
Phœnicia, and Syria. At the beginning of his reign this country
was dotted with petty kingdoms; before its close he had so thoroughly amalgamated it with Egypt that it remained an integral
part of the Egyptian dominion for 100 years. Before his death
Thothmes inscribed on the walls of the temple of Amon at Thebes
a list of the places in Asia which he had conquered. Many of
these were in Palestine and in Syria, and we learn in this way what
towns were already places of importance a century or two before the
Hebrew conquest. Among places that are mentioned in the Old
Testament he names [34] Kedesh (Josh. 19:37), Megiddo, Lebonah
(Judges 21:19), Addar (Josh. 15:3), two different cities named
Abel; see Judges 7:22 (which mentions one situated in the Jordan
valley), and 2 Samuel 20:14 (which refers to one near Dan),
Damascus, Hammath [35] (Josh. 19:35), situated on the Sea of
Galilee (where there are still hot springs), Beeroth (Josh. 9:17),
Sharon, Tob (Judges 11:3, 5), Kanah (Josh. 19:28), Ashtaroth
(Deut. 1:4; Josh. 9:20), Makkedah (Josh. 15:41), Laish (Judges
18:7, 18), Hazor (Josh. 11:1; Judges 4:2), Chinneroth (Josh.
11:2), Shunem (Josh. 19:18; 1 Sam. 28:41; 2 Kings 4:8),
Achshaph (Josh. 11:1), Taanach, Ibleam (Josh. 17:11; Judges
1:27), Ijon (1 Kings 15:20), Accho, Anaharath (Josh. 19:19),
Ophra (Judges 6:11), Joppa, Gath, Lod (Neh. 7:37) or Lydda
(Acts 9:32), Ono (1 Chron. 8:12), Aphik (1 Sam. 4:1), Migdol,
Ephes-dammim (1 Sam. 17:1), Rakkath (Josh. 19:35), Gerar

---

[34] Translated from W. Max Müller's publication in the *Mitteilungen der vorderasiatischen Gesellschaft*, 1907, Heft 7.
[35] Hammath means "hot."

(Gen. 20:1, etc.), Rabbith (Josh. 19:20), Namaah (Josh. 15:41), Rehob (Josh. 19:28), Edrei (Deut. 1:4; Josh. 12:4), Daiban (Neh. 11:25), Bethshean (Josh. 17:11), Beth-anoth (Josh. 15:59), Helkath (Josh. 19:25), Geba (Josh. 18:24), Zererah (Judges 7:22), and Zephath (Judges 1:17). In addition to these towns which are mentioned in the Bible, the list of Thothmes III contains many other names which we cannot yet identify. Among these are the names of two cities, Josephel and Jacobel, which are discussed in Part II, pp. 364, 365. These names, as already noted, are the same as the names of two Babylonian Amorites of the time of the first dynasty. It seems probable that two important Amorites had migrated to Palestine and had either founded new cities, or had been men of such consequence that their names were attached to cities previously in existence. A parallel to this is found in the name of Abu Gosh. He was a sheik of the nineteenth century, but his name displaced the name of the village previously called Karyet el-Ineb, between Jaffa and Jerusalem, and it is now called Abu Gosh. Conjectures differ as to the part of Palestine in which the cities Jacobel and Josephel were situated. We have in reality no certain clue as to this.

It is probable also that something similar had occurred in the case of Abraham. It has been pointed out previously that Abraham is known to have been a Babylonian name at the time of the first Babylonian dynasty. The Biblical records tell of the coming of Abraham from Mesopotamia (Gen. 11:31—12:5), and the inscriptions of Sheshonk, the Biblical Shishak, tell us some centuries later of the existence of a place, apparently in southern Judah, called "The Field of Abram." See Part II, p. 457.

(2) *Palestine in the El-Amarna Letters.*—During the 100 years of Egyptian supremacy in Palestine which Thothmes III inaugurated, the fortifications of certain strategic cities were greatly strengthened. At Gezer, for example, an entirely new wall was built. This was the "outer" wall of Professor Macalister's classification, a substantial structure fourteen feet wide, which completely encircled the city. This massive wall remained the city's defence down to the Babylonian Exile.

From the El-Amarna letters we gain another glimpse of Palestine about a hundred years after the death of Thothmes III. The Biblical cities which are mentioned in these letters are Accho (Judges 1:31), Ashkelon, Arvad (Ezek. 27:8), Aroer (Num. 32:

34), Ashtaroth (Deut. 1:4, etc.), Gebal (Ezek. 27:9), Gezer (Josh. 10:33, 1 Kings 9:15, etc.), Gath, Gaza, Jerusalem, Joppa, Keilah (1 Sam. 23:1), Lachish (Josh. 10:3, etc.), Megiddo, Sidon, Tyre, Shechem, Sharon, Taanach, and Zorah (Judges 13:2). One city, called in Beth-Ninurta, is, in all probability, Beth-Shemesh (Josh. 15:10, etc.). Many other towns are mentioned in the letters, but as they are not mentioned in the Bible they are not enumerated here. These letters were written just as the Egyptian dominion in Asia was breaking up, owing to the fact that King Amenophis IV was much more deeply interested in religious reform than in politics.[36] The disintegration of the empire produced great disorder. The power which Egypt had exerted in the past made the Asiatics still fear to come out openly against her, but the correspondence shows that several petty states were plotting against one another, frequently encroaching upon one another, and yet all the time professing to be loyal to Egypt. The largest number of these states were in the north in Phœnicia. The principal states were the city kingdoms of Gebal, Beirut, Tyre, Jerusalem, and the Amorites.[37] Jerusalem at this time ruled a considerable territory,[38] but its history will be discussed connectedly in a future chapter.[39] The kings of the Amorites during this period were Ebed-Ashera and Aziru. While these small kingdoms of Palestine and Phœnicia were contending with one another, and the king of Egypt was giving no attention to them, the land was invaded from the north by the Hittites under the great King Subbiluliuma,[40] who gradually conquered the Amorites and the Orontes Valley. It was at the same time invaded from the east by the Habiri, who were probably the Hebrews.[41]

With this movement of peoples there came into the west another wave of Semitic migration, the Aramæan. We hear nothing of the Aramaic-speaking peoples in earlier time, but about 1300 B.C. they are mentioned by both Shalmaneser I, of Assyria, and Ramses II, of Egypt, as though they were in Syria and Palestine. In later time they formed the basis of the population from the east of the Euphrates to the Mediterranean coast and southward to Damascus. In Deuteronomy 26:5 Israelites are told to say "A wandering Aramæan was my father" (R. V., margin). The reference seems

36 See Chapter I, p. 19.
37 See pp. 89, 90, and 441.
38 See the letters of its king translated in Part II, p. 442, ff.
39 Chapter XIII, p. 227, f.
40 See Chapter III, p. 88, f.
41 See Part II, p. 446, f.

to be to Jacob, though possibly Abraham is intended. In either case, it shows that the Hebrews recognized that there was an Aramæan strain in their ancestry. Perhaps the Habiri were Aramæans, or were allied with Aramæans.

At all events, in the struggles that ensued, little by little all allegiance to Egypt was thrown off by the Palestinians. Letters to Egypt ceased to be written, our sources fail us, and for more than forty years we can only conjecture what was happening in Palestine.

(3) *Seti I.*—With the accession of Seti I of the nineteenth Egyptian dynasty, who ruled from 1313 to 1292 B.C., some knowledge of events in Palestine begins once more to come to us. Seti in his first year entered Asia, captured an unnamed walled town on the border of the desert, pushed northward and took the towns in the Plain of Jezreel, crossed the Jordan and conquered cities in the Hauran, where he set up a pillar, discovered there a few years since by Principal George Adam Smith; he then turned west and conquered a city on the slopes of the Lebanon mountains.[42] This campaign regained for Egypt all of Palestine and southern Phœnicia. In this third year Seti was again in Asia. On this campaign he overthrew the kingdom of the Amorites in northern Galilee. They occupied the city of Kedesh in Naphtali (Josh. 19:37). This city Seti besieged and took.

(4) *Ramses II.*—Thus at the beginning of the reign of Ramses II, who ruled from 1292–1225 B.C., all Palestine was subject to Egypt. The practical defeat of Ramses by the Hittites at Kadesh on the Orontes in his fifth year, however, caused all Palestine to revolt, and Ramses was compelled to undertake the reconquest of the land. This he accomplished between his fifth and eighth years, beginning with the Philistine cities and overrunning the whole country to the Hauran, where he set up a pillar, as his father had previously done.[43] So far as we know, Palestine remained quietly under the rule of Ramses during the remainder of his long reign.

Ramses II, like Thothmes III, left on record a long list of cities conquered by him in Asia. Of these the following are Palestinian towns mentioned in the Bible:[44] Hammath (Josh. 19:35), Beth-

[42] See Breasted's *History of Egypt,* New York, 1909, p. 414.
[43] See Breasted's *Ancient Records, Egypt,* III, §§ 81 and 140.
[44] Translated from W. Max Müller's *Egyptological Researches,* Wasington, 1906, pl. 59, ff.

shean (Josh. 17:11), Beth-anath (Josh. 19:38), and Hadasha (Josh. 15:37). Pella, a town in the Jordan valley not mentioned in the Bible, also occurs in his list, and there is also a possible mention of Jacobel in a corrupted form.

(5) *Merneptah.*—After the accession of Merneptah, the successor of Ramses II, a rebellion broke out. This was about 1223 B.C. Merneptah put down the rebellion, but in the struggle caused by it, he was compelled to reduce Gezer by siege. It was on this campaign that he came into contact with Israel and defeated her.[45] Some think the Israelites whom he mentioned were those who more than a century and a quarter before had been battling against Jerusalem; others, that they were those who had just escaped from Egypt.

The reign of Merneptah was followed by some years of unstable government in Egypt, but this does not appear to have been a sufficiently long period for great changes to occur in Palestine. Order was restored in Egypt by Setnakht about 1200 B.C., and his son and successor, Ramses III, 1198–1167 B.C., reasserted his sovereignty over Palestine and Phœnicia.

(6) *Ramses III.*—Ramses III found himself confronted with a peculiar situation. The Egyptian Delta and the coasts of Palestine were invaded by hordes of people from over the sea. As early as the reign of Ramses II the Egyptians had employed men from the island of Sardinia as mercenaries; there must then have been intercourse with distant islands across the sea.

6. The Philistines.—Now, however, hordes of Sicilians, Danaoi, Peleset (Philistines), Thekel, and many other tribes came from over the sea. These tribes came in part from islands, such as Sicily and Crete, and in part from the coasts of Asia Minor. Ramses III was compelled to fight with them, both in the Delta and in Phœnicia. On the walls of his temple at Medinet Habu he has left us pictures of the Philistines. A remarkable inscribed disc was found a few years since at Phæstos in Crete. It is printed with a sort of movable type, and each character is a pictograph or hieroglyph. Professor Macalister has shown that it is, in all probability, a contract tablet.[46] When the tablet was first published Eduard Meyer pointed out [47] that a frequently recurring sign, which is

45 See Part II, p. 376.
46 See Arthur Evans, *Scripta Minoa*, Oxford, 1909, pp. 280, 282, and R. A. S. Macalister in the *Proceedings of the Royal Irish Academy*, Vol. XXX, § C, p. 342; also his *Philistines, Their History and Civilization*, London, 1913, pp. 84, 85.
47 See *Sitzungsberichte of the Berlin Academy*, 1909, p. 1022, f.

apparently the determinative for "man" or "person," has the same
sort of upstanding hair as the Philistines pictured by Ramses III
on the walls of Medinet Habu. This tablet, accordingly, was written by Philistines or their near kindred. In this view there is
general agreement among scholars. Amos declared that the Lord
brought the Philistines from Caphtor (Amos 9:7). If this disc
was written in Crete, it would follow that Caphtor was Crete. It
is thought possible by some that the disc was written in Asia Minor,
whence it was carried to Crete; in that case Caphtor would be a
name for Asia Minor.[48] At all events, this inscription makes it
clear that the Philistines came from over the sea, and that their
point of departure was either Crete or Asia Minor. Ramses III
reveals to us through his inscriptions the Philistines in the act of
migrating into Palestine. With them were the Thekel, who afterward were absorbed by the Philistines (see Figs. 36 and 38).

In his struggle with these tribes Ramses III was compelled to
carry the war into Asia, where he overcame and defeated them.
In commemoration of this event he has left a list of places which
he conquered in Asia. Most of them, so far as they can be identified, were further north than Palestine, but the following are
names of places mentioned in the Bible: [49] Seir (Gen. 14:6, etc.),
Calneh (Amos 6:2), or Calno (Isa. 10:9), Tyre, Carchemish,
Beth-Dagon (Josh. 15:41), Kir-Bezek, probably the same as Bezek
(Judges 1:5), Hadashah (Josh. 15:37), Ardon (1 Chron. 2:18),
Beer (cf. Num. 21:16), Senir (Deut. 3:9), Zobebah (1 Chron.
4:8), Gether (Gen. 10:23), and Ar (Num. 21:15; Isa. 15:1, etc.).

After Ramses III the Egyptian empire became too weak to interfere in Palestinian affairs. In the chronology followed by many
scholars today it was about this time that the Hebrews completed
their conquest of the country and the age of the Judges began.

7. **Early Hebrew Conquests.**—On their way into Palestine
the Hebrews, as already noted, invaded and conquered a kingdom of
the Amorites which lay to the east of the Jordan and had its capital
at Heshbon. (See Num. 21:21 and Deut. 1:4, etc.). This kingdom
was a survival of the ancient Amorite occupation of the land. The
Amorites composing it had not been absorbed or displaced by more
recent pre-Hebrew invaders.

48 Caphtor is the same as *Keftiu* of the Egyptian inscriptions, but it is uncertain whether
Keftiu refers to Crete or Asia Minor.
49 Translated from W. Max Müller's *Egyptological Researches*, I, pl. 64, f.

It is stated in Judges 1: 27–36 that there were a number of cities from which the Israelites did not, at the time of their conquest, drive out the inhabitants. Many excavations in Palestine have had to do with cities which were not conquered by Hebrews at this time—Taanach, Megiddo, and Gezer. We are told in Joshua 10: 33 that when Horam, King of Gezer, came to the aid of the king of Lachish, Joshua "smote him and his people till he left none remaining." As nothing is said of the capture of Gezer, this must refer only to the force which went to the aid of Lachish. This view is confirmed by the fact that in the time of David, Gezer was in the hands of the Philistines. (See 1 Chron. 20: 4.) Gezer did not come into the hands of the Hebrews until the time of Solomon, when Solomon's Egyptian father-in-law conquered it and gave it to him. Professor Macalister found evidence that at about this time there was a considerable increase of the population of Gezer, which seems to confirm the statement of Judges 1: 29 that Canaanites and Israelites dwelt together there. This evidence consisted in the crowding together of houses, so that, as many new ones were built, they became smaller. New houses also encroached upon the land of the "high place." [50] There was evidently an increase of the population such as an influx of Hebrews would account for. Evidence of Hebrew conquest seems also to have come to light in the capture and burning of Jericho,[51] Bethel, and Beth-Shemesh,[52] which the excavations have revealed.

8. **Philistine Civilization.**—The next source of information which archæology furnishes us concerning Palestine is the report of Wenamon, translated in Part II, p. 449 ff. Wenamon visited Dor and Gebal about 1100 B.C. He found a king of the Thekel established in Dor, so that the Philistines were probably by this time established in the whole maritime plain.

With the coming of the Philistines into Palestine, new influences were introduced into the country. These are most apparent in the pottery that has come down to us. (See Ch. VIII, p. 182 ff.) The Philistines, whether they came from Crete or from the coasts of the Ægean Sea, had been influenced by those higher forms of art which were in later times developed into the superb Greek forms. Just at the time when history tells us the Philistines came into Palestine, we begin to find in its mounds the remains of a more ornate pottery.

50 See Macalister, *The Excavation of Gezer,* I, p. 21.
51 See pages 112 and 136.
52 See page 105 f.

9. The Hebrew Kingdoms.—As the Philistines filled the maritime plain, and began to push into the hill country, the Israelites formed a kingdom by which to oppose them. The kingdom of Saul accomplished little, but that of David, which began about 1000 b.c., overcame the Philistines and all other peoples adjacent to the Hebrews and established an Israelitish empire.[53] This was possible because just at that time both Egypt and Assyria were weak. Before the end of the reign of Solomon this empire began to disintegrate (1 Kings 11 : 14–25), and at his death, about 937 b.c., it faded entirely away and the kingdom was divided into the kingdoms of Israel and Judah. The history of these kingdoms is given in outline in the Bible and is probably familiar to every reader of this book.

These kingdoms, frequently at war with each other, were first invaded by Sheshonk (Shishak) of Egypt (1 Kings 14 : 25), who made them his vassals (see Part II, p. 456 f.), and in later centuries were made subject to Assyria. Israel suffered this fate first in 842 b.c., and Judah in 732. On account of her rebellions, the kingdom of Israel was overthrown by Assyria in the year 722 b.c. After Assyria became weak, Judah was made subject to Egypt in 608 b.c., but passed under the sway of Babylon in the year 604. Because she repeatedly rebelled against Babylon, the prominent Judæans were carried captive partly in 597 b.c. and partly in 586, and in the year last mentioned Jerusalem was overthrown and its temple destroyed.

Excavations have brought to light much evidence as to the houses, high places, and the mode of life of this time,[54] as well as evidence of how Shishak fought against Rehoboam, Shalmaneser III against Ahab and Jehu, Tiglath-pileser IV against Menahem and Pekah, Shalmaneser V and Sargon against Hoshea, and Sennacherib against Judah. It has also told us much about Nebuchadrezzar.[55]

10. The Exile and After.—The Babylonian Exile was brought by Cyrus to a possible end in 538 b.c. This is also illuminated by that which exploration has brought to light.[56] The temple was rebuilt through the efforts of Haggai and Zechariah during the

53 See the books of I and II Samuel.
54 See Chapters VI, IX, and XI.
55 See Part II, Chapter XIX.
56 See Part II, p. 484, f.

years 520–517 B.C. In 444 B.C.[57] Nehemiah rebuilt the walls of Jerusalem, as related in Nehemiah 1–7. Thus under the Persian empire Judah was re-established. It consisted of a little country around Jerusalem; it was poor and weak, but was aided by money sent from Babylonia by Jews who were still resident there.

(1) *The Samaritans.*—In the neighborhood of Samaria was a people who were descended in part from Hebrews whom Sargon did not carry away and in part from the Gentiles whom he brought in. These people worshiped Jehovah. (See 2 Kings 17: 24-34.) When the little Jewish state had been re-established at Jerusalem, they wished to participate in Jewish worship and to be recognized as good Jews. Since they were not of pure Hebrew descent, the Jews would not permit this, so they at last desisted, built a temple to Jehovah on Mount Gerizim (see John 4: 20), and became a large and flourishing sect.[58] They based their worship on the Pentateuch, and were so much like the Jews that there was constant friction between them. This friction is reflected in Luke 9: 51-54, John 4: 9, and in many passages of the Talmud. It was this sect that occupied Samaria in the time of Christ and made it in his day a distinct division of the country.

(2) *Alexander the Great and His Successors.*—In 332 B.C. Palestine passed from Persian rule to that of Alexander the Great. After his death in 323 it came under the rule of his general, Ptolemy Lagi, who ultimately became king of Egypt. Later, 220–198 B.C., there was a struggle for the possession of Palestine between the descendants of Ptolemy and the house of Seleucus, another general of Alexander, who had established a kingdom with its capital at Antioch. During these wars the Jews suffered greatly. Finally the Seleucid king won, and Palestine passed definitely under the control of Syria. With the coming of Alexander new cultural influences had entered Palestine from the Hellenic world, and down to 168 B.C. such influences were eagerly welcomed by a portion of the Jews.

(3) *The Maccabees.*—In that year, however, Antiochus IV undertook to forcibly Hellenize the Jews and to blot out their religion. This the more faithful Jews resented, and a great revolt ensued. This revolt had as its first successful general Judas, son of Mattathias, who, because of his victories, was surnamed *makkab*, or the

---

57 This is the date usually accepted by scholars, but it may have been in 398 B.C. under Artaxerxes II.
58 See J. A. Montgomery, *The Samaritans, the Earliest Jewish Sect, Their History, Theology, and Literature*, Philadelphia, 1907.

Hammer; it is, therefore, known as the Maccabæan revolt. With varying fortunes the struggle dragged on for 25 years.[59] It finally succeeded because of civil wars in Syria. On account of these each faction favored the Jews, and Syria became continually weaker. In 143 B.C. the Jews once more achieved their independence under Simon, brother of Judas, whom they ordained should be Prince and High Priest forever.[60]

(4) *The Asmonæans.*—The attaining of independence was accompanied by a great wave of racial and religious enthusiasm. Not since the days of Ahaz, in 733 B.C., had Judah been free of foreign domination. At the beginning of the reign of Simon, it was still but a small territory around Jerusalem. Hebron and all to the south of it was in the hands of the Edomites, who three centuries before had been driven out of Edom by the Nabathæans. Simon began to enlarge their territory. He won Gezer and Joppa. John Hyrcanus, his son and successor, 135–105 B.C., conquered the Edomites, and compelled them to become Jews; he also conquered and destroyed Samaria in 109 B.C. He began the conquest of Galilee. His son, Aristobulus I 105-104 B.C., assumed the title of king. A regal dynasty was thus founded, which is known as the Asmonæan or Hasmonæan dynasty, *i.e.,* the "Simonites" or descendants of Simon.

Alexander Jannæus, 104–79 B.C., completed the conquest of Galilee and the region to the east of the Jordan, and extended the bounds of the kingdom of the Asmonæans to practically the same limits as those of the kingdom of David. The Galileans were also Judaized, as the Edomites had been. This period of Jewish prosperity continued to 69 B.C. Through it all, in spite of the religious zeal of the Jews, Hellenic influences made themselves felt in many aspects of the country's life.

11. The Coming of Rome.—On the death of Queen Alexandra in 69 B.C., her sons, John Hyrcanus II and Aristobulus II, both aspired to the supreme power, and till 63 B.C. civil war ensued. In 65 B.C. the Romans had terminated the independence of Syria and made it a Roman province. In 63 B.C. both the Jewish brothers appealed to Pompey, who had come to Damascus. Aristobulus, however, acted treacherously, and Pompey marched upon Jerusalem and took it by siege. Jewish independence was thus forever lost,

59 For the narrative of the struggle, see the book of I Maccabees, and G. A. Barton. *History of the Hebrews,* New York, 1930.
60 See I Macc. 14: 41.

and Palestine passed under the yoke of Rome.   Down to 37 B.C. the country experienced many vicissitudes, as the struggles of the Roman triumvirs were reflected in it.   These vicissitudes culminated in the year 40 B.C., when Orodes I, King of Parthia, captured Jerusalem and placed Antigonus, a son of Aristobulus II, on the throne.   Antigonus was king and a vassal of Parthia for three years.

(1) *The Herods.*—In 37 B.C. Herod the Great, whose father had served under the Romans, by the aid of a Roman army furnished him by Mark Antony, drove Antigonous out and began his notable reign.   Herod was a man of great energy, an Edomite by descent, whose ancestors had become Jews by compulsion.   While professedly a Jew, he was deeply enamored of the Græco-Roman culture.   He wrung taxes from the people in order to beautify Palestine with cities and temples built on Hellenic models.   He rebuilt, among other undertakings, the Jewish temple at Jerusalem and the city of Samaria.   This last he named Sebaste, the Greek for Augusta, naming it in honor of the Emperor Augustus.   He built a heathen temple there, surrounded the city with a colonnaded street, many of the columns of which are still standing, and otherwise adorned it.   He built for himself a palace at Jericho, and another on the top of a hill to the southeast of Bethlehem, today called Gebel Fureidis; (see Figs. 31 and 39).

Upon his death, in 4 B.C., his kingdom was divided, Archelaus receiving Judah and Samaria; Antipas, Galilee and Peræa, and Philip, Iturea and Trachonitis.   None of his sons was permitted by the Romans to be called king, but all bore the title of "tetrarch." The rule of Archelaus proved so unbearable that in 6 A.D. Augustus banished him to Gaul and placed Judæa and Samaria under Procurators, who were responsible to the Proconsuls of the province of Syria.   Pontius Pilate was the fifth of these Procurators.   After the death of Herod Philip in 37 A.D., the Emperor Caligula made Herod Agrippa I, a grandson of Herod the Great, king of his dominions.   On the banishment of Herod Antipas in 39 A.D., he gave him also Galilee and Peræa.   In 41 A.D., the Emperor Claudius added Judah to these territories, and for three years, until his death in 44 A.D., he ruled all the territories over which Herod the Great had been king.   His death is described in Acts 12:23.   After his death the whole country was governed by Procurators.

(2) *The Destruction of Jerusalem in 70* A.D.—Roman rule was always distasteful to the Jews, and as the years passed they became more and more restive. These smouldering fires broke into the flame of open rebellion in the year 66 A.D., and after four years of terrible warfare Jerusalem was captured and destroyed in 70 A.D. The temple, also razed to the ground, has never been rebuilt. The country about Jerusalem was peopled by some of the poorer of the peasantry, and the tenth Roman legion remained in the city for a long time to keep order in that region.

12. **Later History.**—In 132 A.D., in the reign of Hadrian, a man called Bar Chocaba, or the "Son of the Star," came forward, claiming to be the Messiah, and headed a Jewish revolt. So fiercely did the Jews fight that the insurrection was not quelled by Rome until 135 A.D. When it was finally put down, Hadrian determined to blot the name of Jerusalem from the map. He rebuilt the city, making it a Roman colony, named it Ælia Capitolina, and built a temple to Jupiter on the spot where the temple of Jehovah had formerly stood. No Jew was permitted to come near the city. Jerusalem as built by Hadrian continued until the time of Constantine, and the form thus imposed upon it lasted much longer.

When Constantine made Christianity the religion of the empire, both he and his mother began to take an interest in the Holy City and the Holy Land. Other Christians followed them. The Church of the Holy Sepulcher was built, and the temple of Jupiter built by Hadrian was turned into a Christian church. Pilgrimages to the Holy Land began, and monasteries, churches, and bishoprics in time sprang up over all the country. Thus for three hundred years the influences which were felt in Palestine emanated from Byzantium or Constantinople. In 615 A.D. the land was overrun by Chosroes II of Persia, who captured Jerusalem and destroyed many of its churches. The Persians held it until 628, when the Byzantine kings regained it. The control of Jerusalem by the Christians was, however, of short duration, for in 636 Palestine was captured by the Mohammedans, and with the exception of 89 years was under Mohammedan control until the great war.[61] During these long centuries the country was ruled by the Caliphs of Medina, Damascus, and Bagdad; by the Buvide Sultans, the Fatimite Caliphs of Egypt, and the Seljuk Turks. The cruelties inflicted by these last rulers upon Christians led to the Crusades, the first of which estab-

61 For details see Guy Le Strange, *Palestine Under the Moslems*, London, 1890.

lished the Latin kingdom of Jerusalem,[62] which continued from 1099 to 1188 A.D. This kingdom, organized on the feudal basis then existing in western Europe, extended over all of Palestine and Syria, including Antioch, and for nearly half the time, Edessa beyond the Euphrates. Its existence marks an epoch in the archæology of the country.

After the fall of this Latin kingdom, Palestine remained under Moslem control. First the Eyyubide Sultans of Egypt, then the Mamelukes of that same land held sway. In 1517 the Ottoman Turks captured it, and long inflicted their misrule upon it. Set free from Turkish rule by the Great War and placed under British suzerainty, Palestine, which for nearly thirteen hundred years had been populated by Arabs and Greeks, was thrown open as a "home land" for the Jews. The racial conflicts thus engendered still (1937) deprive this much embattled country of peace.

62 For details see C. R. Conder, *The Latin Kingdom of Jerusalem*, London, 1897.

CHAPTER VI

THE CITIES OF PALESTINE

Their Sites. The Walls. The Stone Work. Houses. Palaces: At Taanach. At Samaria. At Megiddo. Foundation Sacrifices. City Gates. Water Supply: Springs. Underground tunnels. Reservoirs.

1. Their Sites.—The cities of Palestine were usually built on hills. These elevations, surmounted as they were by walls, created a natural means of defence from attack (see Fig. 33). Even more important than an elevated situation was a water supply, hence all Palestinian cities of importance are near springs. The necessity of being near a spring led, in some cases, to the erection of a city on a level plain. This was the case with Jericho; the only mound at its site is that created by the city itself.

The hills on which the cities were erected varied in height. That at Megiddo rose to a height of but 45 to 90 feet above the surrounding land, but even this elevation was a great protection from the simple methods of attack known to ancient warfare. The hill Ophel, the site of Jebusite Jerusalem, rises today from 60 to 150 feet above the valley of the Kidron, and in ancient times that valley was from 20 to 50 feet deeper than it is now. The same hill was separated from the land on the west by a valley the bed of which in ancient times was from 50 to 100 feet below the top of the hill. The hill on which Samaria was situated rose some 300 feet above the surrounding valley on all sides except the east, and when fortified presented such an impregnable front that it took even an Assyrian army three years to capture it. (2 Kings 17: 5.) In the Seleucid and Roman periods, when some cities expanded in size, the hilltops were sometimes abandoned and they spread out over the plain. This was the case with Gerasa and Philadelphia (Rabbah Ammon).[1] But "a city set on a hill" (Matt. 5:14) was a common feature of the Palestinian landscape.

2. The Walls.—The walls by which the cities were surrounded varied according to the advancement of the different periods, and according to the importance of the place. As has

1 See Chapter XIV, p. 259 f.

already been pointed out in Chapter V, the first wall at Gezer was but 6 feet high and 2 feet thick, and had a sloping bank of earth packed against it on the outside. This bank was 6 feet 6 inches thick at the base and was covered with a facing of stone. In the Amorite period a wall 13 feet thick was erected at Gezer, in which towers were constructed about every 90 feet. These towers were 24 × 41 feet. Their height is, of course, unknown. This wall was probably built about 2500 B.C. and formed the defense of the city for a thousand years. By that time the tops of the houses probably protruded above the wall, and the population had increased so that more space was needed. This wall was, accordingly, replaced by another built outside of it. Much of the material of which the old wall was constructed went into the new wall, which was approximately 14 feet thick and contained occasional towers. At some time a part of this wall had been destroyed, and then rebuilt. Probably at the time of this rebuilding, additional towers had been inserted at different points. The stones of these towers touched those of the wall without being articulated with them. It has been conjectured [2] that these towers were a part of the repairs made by King Solomon after the town had been captured by his Egyptian father-in-law and presented to Solomon. (See 1 Kings 9 : 16, 17.) Still later an attempt was made to strengthen the weakness caused by the unclosed seam between the towers and the wall by constructing around the towers rude bastions. (See Figs. 40, 46.) Professor Macalister conjectures that this was done by the Syrian General Bacchides when he hastily fortified Gezer and occupied it in 160 B.C.[3] (1 Macc. 9 : 52.)

At Tell el-Hesy, Petrie found massive city walls, though he did not describe them in detail.[4] At Taanach, Sellin found a strong city wall, but did not attempt to trace it about the tell.[5] Schumacher devoted considerable attention to the city walls of Megiddo, a part of which were built of bricks.[6] At Tell es-Safi (Gath?) the outlines of the city walls were traced, as they were at Tell el-Judeideh.[7] At Samaria a part of the Roman wall of the time of Herod was found; lower down in the mound remains of a Babylonian wall (see 2 Kings 17 : 24), beneath which the excavators recognized the Hebrew wall.[8]

2 See p. 104.
3 On these walls, see Macalister, *The Excavation of Gezer*, I, 236–256.
4 Petrie, *Tell el-Hesy*, p. 17 and Plates 2 and 3.
5 See his *Tell Taanek*, p. 13.
6 See p. 110, and Fig. 41.
7 See p. 101.
8 *Harvard Theological Review*, III, 137.

City walls were found, too, at Beth-Shemesh,[9] but of especial interest to the student of the Bible are the walls of Jericho. Here, as at Megiddo, the walls were constructed in part of brick. They had an average thickness of 13 feet. The Canaanitish wall was traced around three sides of the mound. It was strengthened by occasional towers.[10] On the east, next to the spring, they had entirely disappeared. At the northwest corner of the Canaanitish wall was a tower enclosed by two brick walls; the outer wall was a little more than 4 feet thick; the inner, about 10 feet. The walls of Jerusalem will be treated in Chapter XIII.

3. The Stone Work.—The kind of stones used in city walls varied with the circumstances and the degree of civilization. The walls of the Stone Age were naturally made of small undressed stones. The Amorites began the use of cut stone. Their blocks are often fairly smooth and regular. The Amorite wall of Gezer was made of more regular stones than the wall of the Egyptian period.[11] In the Israelitish and Jewish periods a stone with an embossed edge was often used. It is found in the wall of Nehemiah, excavated by Bliss,—a wall made of stones that some pre-exilic king had used before,—and appears also in the structures of Herod the Great. In the structures of Constantine and later Byzantine builders, this type of stone is replaced by a stone with a perfectly smooth surface —much more smooth than anything found in the early walls. This type of stone work continued through the crusading period; (see Figs. 253, 254.) While these types can be traced, their use was not altogether regular.[12]

The areas of Palestinian cities in the early time were very small. All of Canaanite Jericho could be put in the Colosseum at Rome! Megiddo, one of the largest of these early cities, was built on a mound that contained only about eleven acres, and Jebusite Jerusalem was built on a ridge that in ancient times contained not less than nine or more than thirteen acres.

4. Houses.—Within these areas the ordinary houses were crowded, as in the modern native villages of Palestine, separated only by narrow, crooked lanes. One may see in Hebron or in some parts of Jerusalem similar conditions to this day. There was no drainage; refuse was thrown into the streets. The cities were

9 Palestine Exploration Fund's *Annual*, II, 17, f.
10 Sellin and Watzinger's *Jericho*, p. 29, f. and Tafel I.
11 See Macalister, *The Excavation of Gezer*, I, 244.
12 See Dickie, in *Quarterly Statement of Palestine Exploration Fund*, 1897, 61–67.

ill-smelling places. The wonder is that the mortality was not greater. The houses in the central, elevated portion of Palestine were usually of stone, though at Gezer, Jericho, and places in the lower-lying portions of the country they were sometimes of brick. The walls of the stone houses were constructed of rough stones of a great variety of sizes, from small pebbles to large boulders. Mortar and cement were never used. The stones were set in mud. They were not dressed except with a hammer in the roughest way. The joints between them were wide and irregular. Into the crevices serpents and scorpions might crawl. It was of such a house that Amos says, "a man . . . leaned his hand on the wall and a serpent bit him" (5:19). The bricks were rarely burned; they were simply sun-dried, and had no more cohesion than the earth in which they were embedded. The houses generally had no floor except the earth, which was smoothed off and packed hard. Sometimes this was varied by mixing lime with the mud and letting it harden, and sometimes floors of cobblestones or stone chippings mixed with lime were found. In the Roman period mosaic floors, made by embedding small smoothly cut squares of stone in the earth, were introduced. By employing stones of different colors the mosaics were often worked into beautiful patterns; (see Figs. 35, 42, 43, 44, 47, and 48). Sometimes pictures of birds and animals were formed in the floors.

The doorways were usually simply an opening made by the vertical sides left in the masonry. In the later time they were sometimes lined with standing stones. The doors themselves have long since disappeared, but there is evidence that, like many houses still to be seen in Palestine, they were made fast to a post, the lower end of which was set in a hollow or perforated stone. When the door swung the whole post turned in this stone. Some of these stones were found. In a few houses at Gezer enclosures of stones on end were sometimes found in the middle or the corners of dwelling houses. Perhaps these were hearths.[13] Some houses built after the time of Alexander the Great had a kind of piazza running along the side. The remains of the pillars which supported the roofs of these were discovered. Beginning with the Hellenistic period, some of the better houses had baths. (On doors, see Figs. 49, 50.)

13 These remarks about the house are based on the excavation at Gezer. The excavators of other sites have not given as much attention to the construction of houses as Professor Macalister did.

5. Palaces.—In the excavation of different sites the outlines of several larger buildings or palaces were uncovered. A few of these are of interest to the student of the Bible.

(1) *At Taanach.*—In the northeast of the mound at Taanach [14] the remains of a building about 75 × 77 feet were found. It was in existence in the fourteenth century before Christ. This building contained several rooms, as the plan will make clear; (see Fig. 45). The remains of the wall still showed one layer of hewn stones, some of which were very large. In a vault underneath the building four cuneiform tablets were found. They had been placed there for safety in time of siege, and these four tablets had been overlooked when the rest of the archive was rifled. These tablets proved to be letters written at the same time as those found at El-Amarna.[15] The building was the palace of a Canaanite king.

(2) *At Samaria.*—Of especial interest to the student of the Bible are the palaces of the Hebrew period. At Samaria Reisner discovered massive walls, which were probably the remains of the palaces of Omri and Ahab. That of Omri was built of large stones and rested on the native rock. As Omri was the founder of the city (1 Kings 16:24), there can be little doubt that this was his palace. An enlargement of this consisted of walls the construction of which was finer. They were faced with white marble. In this palace an alabaster vase was found, inscribed with the name of Osorkon II, King of Egypt, who was a contemporary of King Ahab. This is, therefore, believed to be the palace of Ahab—perhaps the "house of ivory" which Ahab built (1 Kings 22:39; see Fig. 52).

(3) *At Megiddo.*—Another residence of an Israelitish governor was found at Megiddo. This was a large, irregular building, constructed around a courtyard. Some of the work was of dressed stones of considerable size, in every way superior to the stone-work of the earlier buildings of that city. In this palace a seal of a man named Shema was found, which bore the inscription, "Belonging to Shema, the servant of Jeroboam." We do not know whether this man served under Jeroboam I or Jeroboam II. The fine character of the stone-work leads one to think the reign of Jeroboam II the more probable date; (see Figs. 53 and 27).

Among the palaces explored one other should be noticed, that of Simon the Maccabee (143–135 B.C.), at Gezer. This palace is

14 Sellin, *Tell Taanek*, p. 21.
15 One of these is translated in Part II, p. 447 f.

clearly of the Hellenistic type, and was identified as the dwelling-place that Simon built for himself (1 Macc. 13 : 48), by the discovery of an ancient curse against Simon's palace scrawled in Greek on a block of stone. This building was constructed of rather finely cut stone, was of irregular shape (see Figs. 54, 55), had an imposing gate which admitted into a courtyard, and was supplied with a good system of drainage. For further information see Chapter XI.

6. Foundation Sacrifices.—When a house was built it was customary to consecrate it by a sacrifice. In early times in Palestine this was often a human sacrifice. In Gezer the skeleton of a woman was found built into the walls of a house. Numerous skeletons of children were also found under the corners of houses. Such sacrificial offerings were more often made under the corners of buildings, since the corners were considered sacred. In Babylonia and Egypt the sacrifice was accompanied with the burial under the corner-stone of inscriptions and other deposits, though in Egypt, as in Palestine, the deposit was not always under the corners.[16] Similar sacrifices were found at Taanach [17] and Megiddo.[18] These sacrifices illustrate, some think, 1 Kings 16:34, where Hiel laid the foundation of Jericho with the loss of his first-born, and set up its gates with the loss of his youngest son.

7. City Gates.—The city gate was in Palestine an important part of the town. Gateways were constructed in different ways at different times. At Gezer the northern gate consisted of a protruding tower, into which one entered at the side, then turned a right angle to gain entrance to the city; (see Fig. 58). Gates of this type are still common in the East. The passageway in this gate at Gezer was 40 feet wide.[19] The southern gate of Gezer consisted simply of a straight passageway, 42 feet long and 9 feet wide, between two brick towers; (see Fig. 61). Often, as in the case of the gate found at Beth-Shemesh (Fig. 59), there were rooms on each side of the passageway through the tower. One with still more space within its tower was uncovered at Megiddo; (Fig. 57).

The city gates usually remained at the same points in the wall through the successive reconstructions of the city. Thus at Samaria the remains of round Herodian towers which flanked the

16 See the writer's article, "Corners," in Hastings' *Encyclopædia of Religion and Ethics*, Vol. IV, 119 ff.
17 Sellin, *Tell Taanek*, p. 61.
18 Schumacher, *Tell el-Mutesellim*, pp. 45, 54.
19 See Macalister, *The Excavation of Gezer*, I, 240.

gateway were found resting on larger square bases of the Seleucid period, beneath which the outline of the earlier Israelitish towers was still visible; (see Figs. 65, 66).

The form of these gates illuminates many Biblical passages. Lot sat in the gate of Sodom (Gen. 19:1). Joab took Abner aside in the gate to speak to him (2 Sam. 3:27). The gate was the place of conference for the elders of a city (Gen. 34:20). To be praised in the "gates," where the city's affairs were settled (Prov. 31:31), was to have desired fame.

8. Water Supply:

(1) *Springs.*—The water supply of Palestinian cities came in part from the never-failing springs near which they were built. This supply was, however, seldom sufficient, so that from the early days cisterns were built to catch the water of the rainy season and conserve it for use during the summer months. These cisterns were often excavated in the solid rock, but sometimes were simple pits in the earth, over the bottom of which a coating of lime or cement had been spread.

(2) *Underground Tunnels.*—In time of war, when a city might be shut up for years, cities were often compelled to yield for want of water. This was especially the case if the spring lay outside the city walls. In several Palestinian cities means were taken to secure access to a spring without exposing oneself to the enemy outside the wall. One of the greatest of these undertakings was discovered at Gezer. This was a tunnel cut in the solid rock, which was entered by a long flight of rock-cut steps. At the entrance the rock formed an imposing archway 23 feet high and 13 feet 10 inches broad. These dimensions were maintained throughout about two-thirds of the length of the tunnel. The whole passage was about 130 feet long. The last third of it had to be cut through a much harder rock, where the work was much more difficult, and its workmanship was here not so good as above. The tunnel also became appreciably smaller. The passage terminated in a large cave, in the bottom of which was a spring, and was evidently constructed to enable the inhabitants to reach a water supply in time of siege. The floor of the cave is 94 feet 6 inches below the level of the rock surface under the ancient city. The whole tunnel is a remarkable piece of engineering for an early people; (see Figs. 60 and 62).

The earth with which the mouth of the tunnel was closed contained objects which belonged to the time 1450–1250 B.C. The steps in the passageway had been before this deeply worn by many feet—so deeply worn that Professor Macalister estimated that they must have been in use for 500 years. For these reasons he supposes that this water-passage was excavated about 2000 B.C. or soon after that date. It had ceased to be used before the Israelites conquered the place.

A similar underground tunnel leading to a spring has been found at El-Gib, Gibeon, (Fig. 63), at Megiddo, and one made in Jebusite times also existed at Jerusalem. It is mentioned in 2 Samuel 5:8, and will be described in connection with Jerusalem (p. 231). At Rabbah-Ammon an underground passage connected the old city situated on the hill with a large cistern which was roofed over so as to be concealed. To this cistern in time of siege the inhabitants could go through the passage and obtain water. It was this cistern [20] which Joab had captured (2 Sam. 12:27) when he sent to David to come and take the city. Antiochus III of Syria in the same way compelled the city to surrender in the year 218 B.C.,[21] and Herod the Great did the same thing before 30 B.C.[22]

(3) *Reservoirs.*—Among the sources of water supply for the cities of Palestine the so-called Pools of Solomon to the south of Bethlehem are unique. They consist of three reservoirs, partly rock-cut and in part constructed of walls of masonry, in the Wady Artas, about a mile and a half to the southwest of Bethlehem. The highest of these pools is 127 yards long and 76 yards wide, and 25 feet deep at its lower end. The central pool is 141 yards long, from 53 to 83 yards wide, and 38 feet deep. The lowest and finest of the three is 194 yards long, 49 to 69 yards wide, and 48 feet at its deepest part. In these reservoirs water from neighboring springs was collected and stored. Two aqueducts at different times conveyed it to Jerusalem as it was needed. These aqueducts are now known respectively as the Low Level Aqueduct and the High Level Aqueduct. The High Level Aqueduct appears to be the older. In recent years the Low Level Aqueduct has been repaired, so that these "pools" still contribute to the water supply of Jerusalem.

There is no evidence that Solomon built these. His name has been attached to them solely on account of Ecclesiastes 2:6: "I

---

20 In 2 Samuel 12:27 we should read "pool of waters" instead of "city of waters"; see Barton in *Journal of Biblical Literature*, XXVII, 147–152.
21 See Polybius, V, 71.
22 Josephus, *Jewish Wars*, I, xix, 5 ff.

made me pools of water." The whole structure of these and their aqueducts seems rather to be Greek or Roman work; (see Fig. 64).

Evidence for the dates is not conclusive,[23] but there is some probability that the pools were constructed by John Hyrcanus I, 135–105 B.C., who made the High Level Aqueduct, and that the Low Level Aqueduct was constructed by Herod the Great. This is much longer than the High Level Aqueduct, as it makes a detour toward Gebel Fureidis, where Herod constructed a palace, to which he conveyed water. This Low Level Aqueduct is probably the one afterward repaired by Pontius Pilate.[24]

23 For the conflicting evidence and theories, see G. A. Smith, *Jerusalem*, I, 124–131.
24 Josephus, *Antiquities*, XVIII, iii, 2.

CHAPTER VII

ROADS AND AGRICULTURE

ROADS: Early paths. Roman roads. AGRICULTURE: Granaries. Hoes and plows. Sickles. Threshing. Winnowing. Grinding. Mortars. Fruits. Vineyards and wine-vats. Olive-presses. The agricultural calendar. Domestic animals. Bees. Birds. Hens.

1. Roads.—From the time cities were established in Palestine there was more or less communication between them. Probably in a small way commerce was carried on among some of them, but no effort was made to construct roads, in the modern sense of the term, until the Roman period.

(1) *Early Paths.*—Before that time all traveling was done on foot or on the backs of donkeys and camels, and for such travel a simple foot-path, made by continuous use, was all that was considered necessary. The roads constructed by the Romans have long since fallen into a state of utter disrepair, so that, with the exception of roads that have been built in recent years, the simple, rough foot-paths that have existed from time immemorial still suffice for Palestinian travel. These paths are often exceedingly rough. They were never surveyed and never repaired. They were simply devoted to public use by immemorial custom. If a landowner wished to raise grain in a field through which one of these paths ran, he plowed up to the very edge of the narrow path and put in his seed. There were neither fences nor ditches to separate the road from the field. Fields traversed by such roads are still very common in Palestine. It was along such a road that Jesus and the disciples were traveling when they plucked the ears of wheat on the Sabbath (Matt. 12: 1; Mark 2: 23; Luke 6: 1). It was such a road to which Jesus alluded in the Parable of the Sower: "Some seed fell by the wayside" (Matt. 13: 4; Mark 4: 4; Luke 8: 5). A rough path is shown in Fig. 67.

(2) *Roman Roads.*—After Palestine passed under the sway of Rome in 63 B.C. a system of roads was built to connect the most important places. We have no definite information about these from a source earlier than the *Onomasticon* of Eusebius,[1] which was

1 *Onomasticon*, p. 95.

compiled before 340 A.D., but in all probability those on the west
of the Jordan were constructed before the time of Christ.   There
were three main roads in this part of Palestine.[2] One ran down the
sea-coast.   Starting at Sidon, it passed southward through Tyre,
Sarepta (Zarephath, 1 Kings 17:10; Luke 4:26), Ptolemais
(Accho), Dor, Cæsarea, Joppa, Lydda, Azotus (Ashdod), and
Askelon to Gaza.   A branch road ran eastward from Tyre over the
hills of Galilee through Kedesh in Naphtali (Josh. 12:22; 20:7;
Judges 4:6), to Cæsarea Philippi (Matt. 16:13; Mark 8:27),
which was near the ancient Dan (Judges 18:29).

From Cæsarea, on the sea-coast south of Dor, another branch
road ran southeastward through the valley of Aijalon up to the site
of Gibeah of Saul (1 Sam. 10:26; 11:4, etc.), where it joined the
road along the central ridge of the country; (see Fig. 68).

Starting from Damascus another road ran southward to Hyppos,
one of the cities of the Decapolis, which lay southeast of the
Sea of Galilee,[3] crossed the Jordan on a bridge below the Sea of
Galilee (shown in Fig. 289), passed through Scythopolis, the
Beth-shean of the Old Testament Josh. 17:11; 1 Sam. 31:10),
through Sychar (John 4:5), then southward along the central ridge
of the country, through Bethel and Ramah to Jerusalem.   South
of Jerusalem it was continued to Bethlehem and Hebron.   Four
miles north of Jerusalem it was joined by the road from Cæsarea,
so that travelers from the coast and from the north entered Jerusalem over the same road.   One can in many places still trace the
lines of Roman paving-stones which mark their courses.   Thus
the juncture of the two roads just mentioned is still visible, and one
may stand on the hillside and feel sure that he is looking at the very
way over which Paul was taken to Cæsarea by the Roman soldiers
the night after his arrest in Jerusalem (Acts 23:23, 24).

From Scythopolis (Beth-shean) another road ran southward
through the Jordan valley to Jericho.   This was probably continued
to Jerusalem.   From Sebaste (Samaria) another road ran north-
westward through Dothan (Gen. 37:17; 2 Kings 6:13), to
Taanach, Megiddo, and the coast.

After Trajan overthrew the kingdom of the Nabathæans, in 106
A.D., he built a road on the east of the Jordan, southward from
Damascus to the Red Sea.   The Roman government kept these

---

2 See Thomsen in *Zeitschrift des deutschen Palastina-Vereins,* XXVI, 170 ff.
3 See Chapter XIV.

roads in good order. They marked the distances by milestones, some of which have survived to modern times; (Figs. 69, 71).

2. **Agriculture** was the chief occupation of the inhabitants of Palestine. The cities were throughout its history simply the walled residences of farmers. Such trade as developed at different periods was always subordinate to agricultural pursuits. We cannot expect exploration to furnish us with a complete view of ancient Palestinian agriculture, but such glimpses as it does afford us are most illuminating.

(1) *Granaries.*—In the excavation of Gezer [4] it was found that granaries formed an important class of buildings. Some of these were connected with private houses and evidently belonged to individuals, but some of them were so large and so much grain was found in them that it was rightly held that they must have been public granaries. Some of these buildings had been destroyed by fire, and the charred grain, retaining its original shape, was easily recognized. Most of the granaries were circular structures, such as are seen today dotting the fields of the maritime plain of Palestine. They varied greatly in size. One was but 2 feet 8 inches in diameter; another was 4 feet 9 inches across and 6 feet 9 inches deep. One granary from the second Semitic stratum (1700–1350 B.C.) was connected with a house, and contained several kinds of grain, each stored in a separate chamber; (Figs. 70, 72).

From such receptacles wheat, barley, oats, and beans were recovered, as well as three varieties of vetch, one of which was probably the "lentils" of Genesis 25:34; 2 Samuel 17:28; 23:11; and Ezekiel 4:9. Barley is often mentioned in the Bible; the wheat is usually there called "corn." Piles of straw and chaff, such as the modern Palestinians call *tibn,* were also found.

At Tell Beit Mirsim community granaries were found, which were used when a strong government and good city walls afforded confidence in security, at other times pits in individual houses were utilized for the storing of grain.

(2) *Hoes and Plows.*—Naturally, the implements with which the grain was cultivated have nearly all perished. In the first place the ground had to be broken and prepared to receive the seed. Remains of two different kinds of hoes were found at Gezer, though the preparation of a sufficiently large area of ground to bear grain to support cities cannot have been made with such instruments; (see Fig. 73). From an early time the plow, which

4 See Macalister, *The Excavation of Gezer,* I, 199 f; II, 22 ff.

is frequently mentioned in the Bible (see, for example, 1 Kings 19 : 19), was in use in Palestine. A number of plowshares were found at Megiddo in the ruins of a blacksmith's shop, and a diamond-shaped iron ring, from Gezer, may have been used to attach oxen to a plow, and the points of several ox-goads were found. The ox-goad consisted, as it does today, of a long stick into the end of which a sharp iron point was fixed. It is alluded to in Acts 26 : 14. As this goad was used in driving the oxen in plowing, it indicates that plows were used. These plows were probably similar to those used at the time in Egypt (see Figs. 76, 77).

(3) *Sickles.*—When the grain was ripe it was reaped with a sickle (Deut. 16 : 9; Jer. 50 : 16; Joel 3 : 13). In the earlier periods these were of flint; later they were made of bronze and iron. Sickles of metal are, however, rarely found. They were expensive, while flint was abundant and cheap. Flint sickleteeth were numer-ous, therefore, in all periods. The earliest sickles were flints set in an animal's jaw-bone, or in a curved piece of wood similar to the Egyptian sickle shown in Figs. 74, 75.

(4) *Threshing.*—After the grain was cut it was taken to the threshing-floor to be threshed. These floors were often a compara-tively level portion of rock which formed a part of a high place or sanctuary. Such was the threshing-floor of Araunah, the Jebu-site, in 2 Samuel 24 : 18. It took several days to complete a thresh-ing, and as no one would think of stealing from a sacred place, the whole community was protected by doing the threshing in its pre-cincts. Sometimes the cattle were driven about over the grain, as in ancient Egypt (see Fig. 79), and as is done in modern Palestine still; (see Fig. 78). This is the kind of threshing contemplated in Deuteronomy 25 : 4. At other times a kind of sledge drawn by cattle was driven about over the grain. Ornan (Araunah) was threshing with such an instrument (1 Chron. 21 : 23; 2 Sam. 24 : 22), and allusion is made to one in Isaiah 41 : 15; (see Fig. 80).

(5) *Winnowing.*—The grain was winnowed or cleansed of chaff by being thrown up, as in Fig. 79. As it fell the wind blew the chaff away. It is this process that John the Baptist used as an illustration of the purging work of Christ (Matt. 3 : 12; Luke 3 : 17).

(6) *Grinding.*—When the grain was cut, threshed, and win-nowed, there were no mills to which it could be taken for grinding. This process had to be done in each home, and the labor of doing it

fell to the women of the household. (See Exod. 11:5; Matt. 24:41.) Grain was reduced to flour either by rubbing or by pounding. The process of rubbing or grinding was accomplished either by a flat-saddle-shaped stone over which another was rubbed (see Figs. 81, 84), or by crushing between two stones, the top one of which was revolved somewhat as a modern millstone (Fig. 82). It required two women, as Jesus said, to grind at such a mill— one to feed it, while the other manipulated the rubbing stone. Such stones were made of hard igneous rock procured from the region east of the Sea of Galilee, and are called "querns." In the different periods of the history of Palestine they varied in size and shape, becoming round in the Seleucid period (323–63 B.C.). The upper stone was apparently rotated by twisting the wrist. It could be thus turned half-way round and then back again. No round millstones, with the topmost of the pair perforated, as in the modern millstone, were found before the Arabic period, 637 A.D. Pictures of modern Syrian women turning this perforated type of millstone do not, therefore, really illustrate, as is often assumed, the women of the Bible as they ground at the mill.

Probably the millstone which crushed the head of Abimelech at Thebez (Judges 9:53) was the upper stone of a "saddle quern." The importance of these millstones is recognized in Deuteronomy 24:6, which prohibits the taking of a mill or the upper millstone of a poor man as security, on the ground that that was the same as taking a man's life as security. The lower millstone was always made of the harder stone. Because of this and of the grinding and pounding to which it was subjected it became a symbol of firmness (Job 41:24).

(7) *Mortars.*—Apparently the grain was also frequently crushed by pounding it with a pestle in a mortar. So many of these made of stone were found at Gezer that it is thought that these may have been used more often than the millstones; (see Fig. 83).

(8) *Fruits.*—In the course of the excavation of Gezer dried figs, grapes, pomegranates, and olives were found. All of these are mentioned in the Bible, as, for example, in Canticles 2:13; Revelation 6:13; Genesis 40:11; Numbers 13:23; Micah 6:15. In one trench what appeared to be a pile of charred pistachio nuts was found. Acorns, terebinth, and apricot seeds were also discovered.[5] Of these fruits, those which left the most archæological

---

5 See Macalister, *The Excavation of Gezer,* II, 22 f.

evidence of their existence are just those that are most frequently mentioned in the Bible,—the grape and the olive.

(9) *Vineyards and Wine-vats.*—The grape is often alluded to in the Bible, and directions are given as to how one may conduct himself in a vineyard (Deut. 23:24) and as to how thoroughly one might glean his vines (Lev. 25:5). The most complete description of a vineyard is in Isaiah 5:1-8. The one feature of that description that would survive for an archæologist to discover is the wine-vat. These vats were often cut in the solid rock, and many of them have been found, both in excavating and in traveling over the country. The vats for pressing grapes and other fruits may be distinguished from olive-presses because they lack all arrangements for mechanical pressing. The grapes were trodden with the feet, and as the juice was pressed out it ran down into a deeper portion of the vat. Some of these vats are surrounded by "cup-marks" or hollow places cut in the stone in order to hold pointed-bottomed jars upright. Sometimes the cup-marks are connected with the main vat by tiny channels, through which any of the grape-juice that might drain from the outside of the jar, after the jar had been dipped in the vat, might run back; (see Fig. 87).

(10) *Olive-presses.*—Similarly, olive-presses are very numerous in Palestine. Presses were found in the stratum of the cave-dwellers of Gezer. The olive industry is, accordingly, very old. Olive-presses comprised, in addition to the vat, an upight stone with a large hole in it. In this hole a beam was inserted. This beam rested on the olives which were to be pressed, extending far beyond the receptacle containing the olives, and weights were hung on the end farthest from the stone; (see Fig. 88). Palestine in ancient times, as now, was covered with olive orchards, many of which had oil-presses. Such an orchard was called a "garden." The Garden of Gethsemane, the scene of one of the most sacred incidents of the life of Christ (Matt. 26:36; Mark 14:32), was an olive orchard and took its name from the oil-press. Gethsemane means "oil-press." Wine-vats and oil-presses were of various types, but into their forms there is not space to enter here; [6] (see Figs. 85, 86).

The prominent place held by wine and oil among the agricultural products of the country is indicated by the receipts for the

6 The reader who cares to pursue the subject is referred to Macalister's *The Excavation of Gezer*, II, 48 ff., and Sellin's *Tell Taanek*, 61 f., and Bliss and Macalister's *Excavations in Palestine*, 1898–1900, pp. 193, 196 f., 208, 227, and 248.

storage of various quantities of these articles which were found at Samaria.

(11) *The Agricultural Calendar.*—In the books of the old Testament the names applied to the months are, for the most part, names derived from Babylonia, but it appears that at Gezer they had a series of names for the months based on their agricultural year. In the stratum which contained remains from the time of the Hebrew monarchy, 1000–550 B.C., an inscription was found which, though the end was broken away, contained the following names for the months:

1. Month of ingathering. (See Exod. 23:16; 34:22.)
2. Month of sowing.
3. Month of the late [sowing?].
4. Month of the flax-harvest.
5. Month of the barley-harvest. (See Ruth 2:23; 2 Sam. 21:9.)
6. Month of the harvest of all [other grains?].
7. Month of pruning [vines].
8. Month of summer-fruit [figs].

This calendar, beginning in October, still conforms to the agricultural pursuits of the year. It also gives us archæological evidence of the culture of flax by the ancient Israelites. (See Josh. 2:6; Prov. 31:13; Hosea 2:5, 9.)

(12) *Domestic Animals.*—The domestic animals of ancient Palestine may be traced in part by their bones found in various excavations, and in part by the pictures of them drawn in caves and tombs. The domestic animals most often mentioned in the Bible are asses, cattle, sheep, goats, and camels. Bones, pictures, or models of these were found in all the strata of Gezer.[7] There seems to have been a variety of cows; the breeds varied in the different periods. No horse bones were found until the late Bronze Age (1350–1200 B.C.). The horse appears to have been known to the Asiatic peoples who preceded the Sumerians and Akkadians in Babylonia, but we cannot trace its presence in the West before the Hyksos period. After its introduction into Palestine, it remained for long the beast of the warrior. The ass was, however, the common beast of burden, and bones of horses are rare until the Greek period. A number of figures of horses' heads with their bridles were found, as well as a horse's bit, and the picture of a horse and his rider. The pig was a domesticated animal of the early inhabitants of Gezer, who appear to have offered swine in sacrifice, but pig-bones are rarely

7 See Macalister, *The Excavation of Gezer*, II, 1–15.

found in the Semitic strata. As swine were unclean to all Semites, this is not strange. The dog appears to have been half-domesticated, as the Bible implies, as his bones were employed for making prickers and similar tools, but no pictures or models of dogs are known to the writer. Probably they were of the half-wild pariah type. Certainly they were not held in high esteem. (See 1 Sam. 17 : 43; 2 Sam. 16 : 9.) For illustrations, see Figs. 89–92.

(13) *Bees.*—A number of inverted jars, each pierced with a number of circular holes, were found. It seems probable that these were rude beehives. Before the Israelites settled in Palestine they knew it as "a land flowing with milk and honey" (Exod. 3 : 8, 17; Num. 14 : 8; 16 : 13, 14; Deut. 6 : 3), and their view was, we are told, shared by others (2 Kings 18 : 32). It is not surprising, therefore, to find evidences of bee culture; (see Fig. 95).

(14) *Birds.*—As to birds, it is doubtful whether they had any domesticated ones before the Babylonian Exile. A rude picture of an ostrich painted on a potsherd was found at Gezer, as well as some painted fragments of ostrich-egg shell. The ostrich is mentioned in the Old Testament (Job 39 : 13; Lam.4 : 3), but as a wild bird. The Palestinians knew it as a bird that might be hunted. They sometimes gathered the eggs of wild birds to eat (Deut. 22 : 6; Isa. 10 : 14). These were, perhaps, sometimes ostrich-eggs. The modern Arabs make a kind of omelette of ostrich-eggs. The ostrich was certainly not a domestic bird.

At Gezer, too, a clay bird was found, or, rather, a small jar made in the form of a bird. The object was so realistic that holes were left in the clay wings for the insertion of feathers; (Fig. 93). The bird bears some resemblance to a duck, figures of which were found at Megiddo,[8] but the duck may have been wild. One clay head of a goose or swan was also found, but had the bird been domesticated there would probably have been more traces of it.

(15) *Hens.*—The one domestic bird that can be traced in Palestine is the hen, and hens were not introduced until after the Exile. Hens seem to have been first domesticated in India. They are not mentioned in the Rig Veda, but the Aryans seem to have come into contact with them when they settled in the valley of the Ganges about 1000 B.C. The Yajur and Atharva Vedas mention the cock. The hen is a domesticated Bankiva fowl, which also exists in a wild state in India. From India the hen was domesticated eastward to China, and westward to Persia. There is a possible pic-

8 See Schumacher, *Mutesellim*, p. 89.

ture of a cock on a sculpture of Sennacherib, which would indicate that the bird was known in Assyria at the beginning of the seventh century before Christ. Another is pictured on some Babylonian gems from the time of Nabuna'id, about 550 B.C. Pictures of cocks, three of them somewhat doubtful, are found on Babylonian seals of the Persian period.[9] The domesticated hen, traveling by way of the Black Sea, reached Asia Minor as early as the eighth century B.C.[10]

There is, however, no evidence of the presence of the hen in Palestine before the Greek period. Neither hen nor cock is mentioned in the Old Testament. In a tomb discovered by Peters and Thiersch in 1902, near Tell Sandahanna, the Marissa of the Seleucid period and the Moresheth-gath of Micah 1:14, a number of cocks are pictured; (Fig. 94). The tomb, constructed about 200 B.C., contains a number of Greek inscriptions.[11] In agreement with this evidence is also the fact that at Taanach there was found in a late pre-Arabic stratum the skeleton of a hen with an egg.[12] Before New Testament times, then, the hen had become a domestic fowl in Palestine. Every one would accordingly understand the lament of Christ, "How often would I have gathered thy children together, even as a hen gathereth her chickens under her wings, and ye would not!" (Matt. 23:37). The cock was so universally kept at this time that one of the divisions of the night was called the "cock-crowing" (Mark 13:35). It was the mark of the progress of the night afforded by the habits of the cock that was used by Jesus in predicting Peter's denial (Matt. 26:34; Mark 14:30; Luke 22:34; John 13:38), and it was the recalling of this prediction by the crowing of the cock that brought Peter to repentant tears (Matt. 26:74; Mark 14:68, 72; Luke 22:60; John 18:27).[13]

9 Ward, *Seal Cylinders of Western Asia*, p. 422, and Nos. 554, 556, 1126, and 1254.
10 See Dr. John P. Peters' article "The Cock" in the *Journal of the American Oriental Society*, Vol. XXXIII, pp. 363–396.
11 See Peters and Thiersch, *The Painted Tombs of Marissa*, London, 1905.
12 See Sellin, *Tell Taanek*, 61 f.
13 For more complete information concerning Palestinian agriculture see Gustaf Dalman's *Arbeit und Sitte in Palastina*, II, *Der Ackerbau*, Gutersloh, 1932.

CHAPTER VIII

POTTERY

1. Importance of Pottery.—In all parts of the world the making of clay jars and receptacles is one of the earliest arts to be discovered, and Palestine was no exception to the rule. In Palestine such jars were particularly used, as the water for each family had to be carried from the nearest spring to the house. It was natural that, in a country which had so long a history as Palestine, and over which the influences of so many diverse civilizations swept, there should be a considerable variety in the types of pottery in different periods. Indeed, it is now recognized that the differences in these types are so marked that in the absence of other criteria it is possible approximately to date a stratum of the remains of any ancient city by the type of pottery found in it. Since this is so, a brief outline of the different types is not out of place here, although these differences have little or no bearing upon the interpretation of the Bible. Only a brief statement is here attempted. Those who wish to study the subject more fully are referred to more extended works.[1] The ages of culture which are traceable in Palestine by means of artifacts and pottery are as follows:

	DATE B.C.
Palæolithic (Crude stone artifacts)............	x to x
Neolithic (Flint artifacts)....................	x to 3000
Ænolithic or Chalcolithic (handmade painted pottery)	3000 to 2500
Early Bronze (This and each of the following periods is characterized by definite types of pottery)	2500 to 2000

---

1 G. M. Fitzgerald, *The Four Canaanite Temples of Beth-shan, pt. II. The Pottery*, Philadelphia, 1930; Elihu Grant, *Ain Shems Excavations*, Haverford, 1931, and *Rumeileh*, 1934; W. F. Albright, "Tell Beit Mirsim," in *Annual* of the American Schools of Oriental Research, Vol. XII, 1932; W. M. F. Petrie, *The Pottery of Beth-Pelet*, London, 1931; G. E. Wright in the *Bulletin* of the American Schools of Oriental Research, No. 63 (Oct., 1936), 12–63; and Clarence S. Fisher's forthcoming *Corpus of Palestinian Pottery*, which now (1937) is said to be ready for the press.

Middle Bronze ....2000 to 1500
Late Bronze ....1500 to 1200
Early Iron ....1200 to 900
Israelite .... 900 to 600
Persian Period .... 530 to 330
Hellenistic .... 330 to 50
Roman ....50 B.C. to 300 A.D.
Byzantine ....300 to 640 A.D.
Arabic ................................A.D. 650 to 1100
Crusading ....1100 to 1200

2. Chalcolithic Pottery.[2]—There is first, then, the pottery of
the cave-dwellers of Gezer and that of the same type from Tell-
en-Nasbeh. This pottery is made out of clay that was in no way
cleansed or refined. It was made by hand, the larger jars having
been built up little by little. The vessel, after receiving such
ornament as the potter desired, was usually fired, though sometimes
simply sun-dried. In firing, the heat was often distributed very
irregularly, so that the surface was not all of the same color. The
jars were of moderate size, flat on the bottom, globular, conical,
or cylindrical in shape. They had concave necks and handles. The
handles were of two kinds—"ledge" handles and "loop" handles.
A "ledge" handle consists of a piece of clay pinched into a flat
projecting ledge and then baked hard. A "loop" handle is one
fastened to the jar at both ends, similar to the handle of a pitcher.
Bowls or saucers were also sometimes made with "ledge" handles.
(See Fig. 97.)

The most common ornamentation of the pottery of this period
was made by combing the clay with wooden combs notched with
teeth of greater or less fineness. Sometimes the marks left by
the comb were perpendicular, sometimes horizontal, and sometimes diagonal. One other type of ornament was exhibited in
the pottery of the cave-dwellers. That was either an incised representation of a rope or cord, or a moulded imitation of one of these.
This ornamentation was probably suggested by the ropes or cords
which were bound about the vessel before it was fired, to prevent

2 For authoritative descriptions of the pottery, with numerous examples, see Clarence
S. Fisher, *Corpus of Palestinian Pottery*, in preparation, which now (1937) is said to be
ready for the press; W. F. Albright, *Tell Beit Mirsim-I*. in the *Annual* of the American
Schools of Oriental Research, Vol. XII, 1932; G. M. Fitzgerald, *The Four Temples of
Beth-shan, Part II, Pottery*, Philadelphia, 1930; Elihu Grant, *Ain Shems Excavations-I*,
Haverford, Pa., 1931; and *Beth-Shemesh*, Haverford, 1929, and *Rumeileh*, 1934; also
Bulletin of the American Schools of Oriental Research, No. 63.

its falling apart. At first the only coloring was a line of brick-red around the rims of jugs and saucers. The most advanced stage is reached in Fig. 96, where a network of red lines cross each other diagonally. The tint of the red varies a good deal, but this may be due to the unequal firing already mentioned.

A few specimens of burnished pottery were found in the caves. This burnishing consisted in rubbing the surface of the vessel with strokes of a smooth bone or stone. In some cases the vessel was dipped in a whitish wash after it was fired. This adhered to it everywhere except on the bottom.

3. Early and Middle Bronze.—The pottery of the earliest bronze periods, which terminated about 1500 B.C., is of a finer type. The larger pieces were made on a wheel, as were many of the smaller ones. The wheel was rotated with the left hand, while the potter moulded the vessel with the right. The result was a much more shapely type of work than in the previous period. In the Chalcolithic period limestone clays were employed; in this period, sandstone clays. Many of the objects, like those of the preceding period, were of a drab color, though the tints of some of them ranged from a rich brownish red to orange. The patches of color in these vessels were probably due to unequal heat in firing.

In size and shape the vessels presented a great variety. There were large jars with flat bottoms, inverted conical bodies, and more or less abruptly rounded shoulders. (See Fig. 100.) The mouth was wide and circular and surrounded by a flat, widely expanding rim. These jars averaged about two feet in height. There were many pitchers made in this period. They were large and small and of a great variety of shapes. Such pitchers present similar characteristics, whether found at Gezer or Megiddo. (See Figs. 98, 99.) Ledge and loop handles were common on the pitchers of this period, but "pillar" and "button" [3] handles were also sometimes found. (See Figs. 105, 106.) The ornamentation of pottery showed some advance over the preceding period. In addition to the rope motifs, decoration formed by combinations of lines was also found. One particularly fine type of pottery belonging to this period was found at Gezer. It was never found in the caves or in the higher strata. Vessels of this ware were usually found in groups, indicating that they were the possessions of the rich. The clay was well cleaned, the shapes distinctive

3 A "button" handle is a "ledge" handle made into a round knob.

(See Fig. 104), and the ware was always covered with a cream-
like coating. Saucers and bowls were common in this period. The
comb was still used in ornamenting pottery, though sometimes it
produced only a series of dots. All surfaces were usually burnished,
though naturally this was much more thoroughly done in the expensive than in the cheaper wares.

During the middle Bronze Age, 2000–1500 B.C., trade was
carried on with countries beyond the sea, especially with Cyprus.
There was also trade with Egypt. In this period, probably owing
to foreign influence, the potter's wheel worked by foot was introduced. This left both hands of the workman free and resulted
in a great improvement of the ware. There was in this period a
great variety in the material used. The cheaper vessels were made
of a rough clay, full of grits of black colored sand or flints, which
burned black in the middle of the clay and a reddish or yellowish
drab on the surface. At least seven other finer types of ware
were found at Gezer.[4] One of these was a ware made of brilliant
saffron-yellow clay, which was enriched with painted decoration in
bold black lines. This was probably of foreign origin. In this
period the jar with pointed bottom, long conical body, well rounded
shoulders, short concave neck, continuous circular mouth, with an
expanded rim, though much narrower than in the preceding period,
is the most common type. Jugs with pointed bottoms also became
common, though there was a great variety in the shapes of jugs.
Ledge handles had almost entirely disappeared in this period. Jars
generally had two loop handles, and sometimes four, though occasionally they had none at all. "Button" handles are comparatively
uncommon; the loop handle is the style most generally used. "Ear"
handles, both vertical and transverse, are also common. (See Figs.
101-103, and 105.)

The most striking feature of the pottery of this period is the
increase in the variety of ornamentation and the introduction of
the pictures of animals and birds as ornamental motifs. This
was due, no doubt, to foreign influence.

All kinds of vessels were made of clay during this period: jars,
jugs, pitchers, bowls, saucers, drinking-cups, etc., etc. Many of
the potters signed their work with a peculiar mark. This mark
was sometimes an impression of the potter's finger, sometimes
linear devices of various kinds scratched on the handle, and sometimes the impression of an inscribed Egyptian scarab, usually of

4 See Macalister, *The Excavation of Gezer*, II, 158.

the period of the Middle Kingdom or the Hyksos Time. Jar handles marked with scarabs were also found at Jericho. (See Figs. 118, 119.)

4. Late Bronze Period.—The late Bronze Period, 1500 to 1200 B.C., while its wares sometimes differed in form from those of the preceding period, is mainly marked off from the second period by a general degeneration in style. No great differences are noticeable in the kinds of clay employed. The jars have, as a rule, a less pointed bottom than in the preceding period. (See Fig. 110.) The combed decoration is rare, and the burnishing of the jars is both less frequent and less skilful than in the preceding period. There is an increase in the tendency to use painted ornamentation, which frequently consists of zigzag lines. Rough, conventionalized representations of palm trees are also common. Potters' marks continue, but scarabs are less often used in making them than in the preceding period. The various kinds of vessels made seem to have been as great as in the preceding period. (See Figs. 112, 113.) A clay funnel or bottle-filler was also found in this period. (See Fig. 114.) A number of the forms of this period may be studied in Fitzgerald's *Four Temples of Beth-shan,* Part II, Pls. XLI-XLVIII.

5. Early Iron I.—In this period, 1200–900 B.C., the method of manufacture remained the same as before, and but little difference can be discerned in the clays employed. There seems, however, to have been a steady decline in excellence. In the early part of the period Cretan influences are discernible. Doubtless this was due to the invasion of the country by the Philistines. The forms and kinds of vessels found in this period are numerous. Painted ornamentation consists, as a rule, merely of rings around the vessel, though sometimes zigzags made very carelessly are also found. The potters still employed marks. These are of the same general character as in the earlier period, though the scarab stamp entirely disappeared from Gezer and the use of other seals became common. These were most often a simple device of stars, or names written in the old Hebrew script.

6. Israelitish.—The type of Israelite pottery was definitely revealed by the work of Albright and Grant.[5] The forms may be studied best in their works, which have already been cited. An

---

[5] See Albright in the *Annual* of the American Schools of Oriental Research, Vol. XIII (1933), and Grant's *Ain Shems Excavations,* Haverford, 1931–32, and his *Rumeileh,* Haverford, 1934. Cf. also G. E. Wright in the *Bulletin* of the American Schools of Oriental Research, No. 63 (Oct., 1936), pp. 12–21.

interesting feature of the pottery of the late Israelite period is the jar handles inscribed with Hebrew letters, which were found at Gezer in a stratum that was pre-exilic. A series of them was also found at the tells excavated by Bliss and Macalister in the Shephelah, in the years 1898–1900: Es-Safi, Judeideh, and Zakariyeh. (See Fig. 116.) Others were found at Tell Beit Mirsim. These handles, in addition to the impression of a seal, contained the words, "to the king," in Hebrew letters; also the names of the cities, Hebron, Socho, Ziph, and Mamsheth. The first three of these are well-known Judæan towns; the last was a town in the Negeb, or country to the south of Judæa, not mentioned in the Bible. Sir Charles Warren found some similar stamps near the temple area at Jerusalem. Such stamped jar handles have not been found in north Israelitish sites. It seems that the kings of Judah, after the separation of the two kingdoms, established standard jars by royal authority for the determination of standard measurements of oil and wine. The four cities named on the handles were the four administrative centers of the kingdom.

7. **Hellenistic Period.**—In the time after the Exile there is not much change in the character of the pottery until after the conquest of Alexander the Great. The influx of influences from the Græco-Macedonian world affected the whole life of the land, and was reflected also in its pottery. As in the middle and late Bronze Periods, there were importations of pottery from abroad, though at this time the importations were from regions affected by Greek art. The Palestinian potters of this period had, therefore, the best models. The use of the potters' wheel was all but universal, and the wares were burned hard. A pile of these potsherds, when struck with a stick, emits a distinct musical "clink," which is not the case with potsherds from the earlier periods. The clay employed was the finest and most homogeneous of any used in Palestinian pottery, and there is a general tendency, especially in the cities near the coast, to follow classical models. (See Figs. 122, 125.)

Jars have rounded or bluntly pointed bases, vertical sides, flattened or oblique shoulders, and round mouths. There are two loop handles just under the shoulders. Another form, probably suggested by Rhodian amphoræ, has a long, tapering base. (See Fig. 120.)

It is impossible in the space that can be devoted to this topic to enumerate all the kinds of vessels that were made in this period, or the variety of their forms. Only a few characteristic features can be noted. The cooking pots of this time have a very distinctive form. They have a globular base, globular body, short, wide neck, and a rounded continuous mouth. (See Fig. 122^{5a}.) The body of the vessel is often ribbed with horizontal flutings. Small jugs and vases were very common; some of them had very characteristic forms. Jugs of this period found at Jericho had a funnel at the side through which liquid could be poured into them.

As in the preceding period, jar handles were frequently stamped with the mark of the potter. These were now often Greek letters, though those so stamped were apparently imported from foreign countries. At Jericho ten jar handles were found stamped with the name "Jah," and three stamped with the name "Jahu." [6] Both "Jah" (See Psa. 68:4.) and "Jahu" are abbreviations of the name Jehovah, and probably are so to be understood here. They often formed part of a personal name—thus Elijah, "My God is Jah."

From the middle Bronze Age onward, filters were made by piercing the bottom of a jug with holes. These became more common in the late Bronze Period, but this sort of device reached its full development in the Hellenistic Period, which we are now considering. Various forms of strainers were found, as shown in Fig. 123, and one very elaborate filter. (See Fig. 121.)

With the coming of the Romans, in 63 B.C., new influences were introduced into the civilization of Palestine. In time these influences modified the pottery, but it is doubtful whether they had an appreciable effect until after the New Testament Times. Pots from the Roman Period found at Gezer (See Fig. 124.) differ from those of the Hellenistic Period chiefly in having bottoms that are more nearly flat. By the time of the Emperor Constantine a change can be noted, so that pottery of the Byzantine Period (325–637 A.D.) has characteristics of its own. That period, however, lies beyond the range of Biblical history.

In the study of pottery one of the most interesting topics is the evolution of the lamp. The earliest lamps were simply wicks stuck into a saucer of oil and ignited. Of course, the wick would easily fall down into the oil and the light would be extinguished. The earliest device to prevent this was to make the saucer of irregular shape, with a slight notch in one side in which the wick

6 See Sellin, *Jericho*, p. 156.

could lie. (See the right-hand lamp in Fig. 127.) As time went on this resting place for the wick developed more and more into a spout. (See Fig. 126, and the left-hand lamp in Fig. 127.)

This form of lamp was known as early as the first Bronze Period, and persisted with slight development down through the Israelitish time. (See Fig. 128.) Its development was not, however, everywhere uniform. Middle Bronze lamps found at Jericho appear to be simply saucers with two or more indentations in the rim. (See Fig. 132.) Perhaps in these more than one wick was used. In the Hellenistic Period two improvements in the making of lamps occurred. The first consisted in a still further development of the spout until its sides almost met and formed nearly a closed vessel. The second improvement was, perhaps, due to outside influences. It consisted in making the saucer small and covered. In the middle of the cover was a small round hole into which the oil was poured; at one side a spout protruded and the wick came out through this. (See Fig. 131.) The top of such lamps was ornamented with various designs.

In the Byzantine and Arabic Periods the same general style of lamp was used, but the shape and ornamentation of each period were different, so that they can easily be distinguished. (See Fig. 129.) After the country became Christian, the ornamentation on the lamps was often made with Greek letters. These were made in ornamental forms and usually expressed some Christian sentiment. One of the most popular legends for these Christian lamps was: "The light of Christ shines for all." (See Fig. 130.)

It was lamps such as these, probably of the Hellenistic type, to which Christ alluded in the parable of the Wise and Foolish Virgins. (Matt. 25:1–12.) Such a lamp would not contain oil enough to burn all night, so that to carry it to a prolonged wedding feast without a supply of oil was a striking example of improvidence.

CHAPTER IX

UTENSILS AND PERSONAL ORNAMENTS

UTENSILS: Ovens. Baking-trays. Bowls, etc. Feeding-bottles. Glassware. Spoons. Forks or Flesh-hooks. Needles. Spinning "Whorls." Lamp-stands. Keys. Knives. Saws. Chisels. Awls. Axes. Adzes. Whetstones. Files. Hammers. Nails. Baskets. Arrows. Spears. Swords. Fish-hooks. Styli. Seals. The "Pipe." Harps. The Dulcimer. Lyres. Children's toys. PERSONAL ORNAMENTS: Combs. Perfume-boxes. Spatulæ for eye-paint, etc. Fibulæ. Beads. Necklaces. Bracelets. Anklets. Rings.

1. Utensils.—The term "utensil" is of wide application. The utensils of agriculture and the hand-mills for grinding grain have been described in Chapter VII. Among the devices used in connection with Palestinian houses one of the most important was the oven.

(1) *Ovens.*—The ovens of ancient Palestine were of the same kind as those used by the peasantry of that country today. Each consists of a cylinder of baked earth about 2 feet in diameter and 1½ inches thick. It is closed by a cover of the same material, in which a stone or lump of clay has been embedded as a handle. There is rarely any bottom except the bare earth. The loaves, which were flat discs, were usually placed inside, either on the ground covered with clean pebbles or on a baking-tray. Sometimes the loaves were plastered over the outside of the oven. In this case the fire was built inside and might consist of grass (Matt. 6:30; Luke 12:28). The fire was usually heaped about the outside of the oven, and often consisted of dried manure. It is this use of manure as fuel that is alluded to in Ezekiel 4:12-15—a passage that has sometimes been greatly misunderstood. Such ovens were frequently found in all the strata. In Figure 133 two varieties of ovens are shown. The one at the left hand is made of plain tile; the other is covered over with potsherds, to make it retain the heat longer. Sometimes in large houses groups of several ovens were found together.

Ovens are frequently referred to in the Bible, sometimes as symbols of things that are hot. (See Lev. 11:35; 26:26; Psa. 21:9; Hosea 1:4, 6, 7.) Once a much-used oven is a symbol of blackness (Lam. 5:10).

(2) *Baking-trays,* consisting of discs of baked clay about 10 inches in diameter, were also found. These were usually turned up at the edges, and frequently perforated in order better to admit the heat to the under side of the loaf. One specimen was found burnt through with constant use. These trays were most numerous at Gezer in the old and middle Bronze Periods. They were found at Jericho in the Jewish stratum; (see Fig. 134).

(3) *Bowls, etc.*—In Chapter VIII, under the head of Pottery, the jars, pitchers, clay bowls, saucers, and cups which were used about Palestinian homes have already been described. Bowls and saucers of stone were also employed from the earliest times. They were far less fragile, though more expensive. Probably the dishes used by the common people were in all periods made of clay. After the introduction of metal, however, the wealthy often had dishes of bronze (see Fig. 135), and sometimes of silver. A Philistine grave at Gezer yielded some silver dishes of beautiful workmanship; (see Figs. 137, 141).

(4) *Feeding-bottles.*—A number of curiously shaped jars with spouts were found at Gezer; (see Fig. 139). Professor Macalister was at a loss to explain their use unless they were feeding-bottles. The only other suggestion that he makes is that they were lamps, but they are so different from the lamps of the time, that that possibility seems to be excluded. Sellin thought similar objects found by him were vessels for pouring oil. This may have been their purpose.

(5) *Glassware.*—Vessels of glass are very rare in Palestine until Roman times. In the remains of the late Bronze Period at Gezer fragments of ornamented glass vessels, which had been imported from Egypt, were found. The ornamentation consisted of zig-zag lines. Clear glass first appears in the Israelitish period, but it was rare and inartistic. After the coming of the Romans it became more common. For examples of its use, see the ointment vessels in Fig. 138.

(6) *Spoons.*—The spoons of the poor were in all periods apparently adapted from shells, as shown in Fig. 136, but the more wealthy, especially when under the influence of more artistic foreigners, had ladles of metal that seem very modern; (see Fig. 141). These objects are from a Philistine tomb.

(7) *Forks or Flesh-hooks.*—Forks were in existence, as shown in Fig. 140, but were used not to eat with, but to handle meat

when it was cooking. The one with three tines in Fig. 143 reminds one of the "flesh-hook of three teeth" that the servant of Hophni and Phinehas, sons of Eli, thrust into the caldron of seething sacrificial flesh, in order to obtain the priest's portion (1 Sam. 2:13, 14).

(8) *Needles,* both of bone and bronze, were found. They were employed from the earliest times in such sewing as was necessary. The way the eyes were made may be seen in Figure 142. These give vivid reality to the saying of Christ, "It is easier for a camel to go through a needle's eye than for a rich man to enter into the kingdom of God" (Matt. 19:24; Mark 10:25; Luke 18:25).

(9) *Spinning "Whorls."*—Spinning in ancient Palestine, as now, was done in the simplest possible manner. A tapering spindle was made of wood. To this was attached a "whorl"—either a stone or a lump of baked clay—in order to give the spindle momentum when whirled. The wool was held in the hand, a bit of it twisted into a thread with the fingers and attached to the spindle. Then more of the wool was pulled out and held in the hand while the spindle and whorl were given a twist with the other hand and allowed to twist the wool into thread. The process was repeated again and again. The writer has seen women in the East spinning while on a journey. Many of the spindle whorls, made both of stone and of clay, have been found by excavators; (see Figs. 144, 145).

(10) *Lamp-stands.*—In one of the palaces at Megiddo a number of bronze tripods of various sorts were found; (see Fig. 148). The tallest of these were 13¼ and 14 inches in height. They were intended to support either bowls or lamps. They are the kind of "stand" mentioned in Matt. 5:15 (R. V.—the King James Version [1] called it a "candlestick"), on which men, when they lighted a lamp, placed it so that it might "give light to all that are in the house." Probably the poor had some less expensive form of lamp-stand.

(11) *Keys* in Palestine were often large, clumsy affairs. They were probably most often made of wood, and were much better fitted to be carried on the shoulder, as a wood-chopper often carries his axe, than to be carried in a pocket. This is why Isaiah (22:22) speaks of laying the key of the house of David on the shoulder of Eliakim. Of course, all woodpen keys of the Biblical time have decayed. Iron keys from the Hellenistic time were found at Gezer, two of which are shown in Figures 146, 147.

1 *I.e.,* the version of 1611, commonly called "The Authorized Version."

(12) *Knives.*—One of the first implements made by man as he emerges from savagery is the knife. The earliest knives of Palestine were of flint, which is in that country very abundant. Flint knives are made by taking a cone of flint that will easily flake, and skilfully striking the top of it such a blow that a ribbon having a sharp edge is split off. At Gezer one of these cones, left by an ancient flint knife-maker, was found; (see Fig. 154). After the introduction of bronze in the early Bronze Period, 2500–1800 B.C., knives were often made of that; (see Fig. 151). When, about 1200 B.C., iron came in, it too, was employed for knife-making; (see Fig. 150). Flint knives were always cheaper than those of metal and were probably always employed by the common people. Knives are referred to in the Bible as the implements for slaying sacrifices (Gen. 22:6, 10), and in various other connections. (See, for example, Ezek. 5:1, 2.) Flint knives were preferred for the rite of circumcision. (Exod. 4:25 and Josh. 5:2, 3); (see Fig. 149).

(13) *Saws.*—Ribbon-flint knives easily pass into saws when the edge is irregular. A number of these came to light in the course of the excavation of Gezer. Saws are referred to in 2 Samuel 12:31 and in 1 Kings 7:9. Saws made of thin, flexible strips of metal existed. These were set in wooden frames. Very meager fragments of these have been found.

(14) *Chisels* were fairly common at Gezer in all strata after the introduction of bronze. They were made usually of bronze, even after the introduction of iron, although iron chisels were found. As the chisel is one of the most necessary tools of a carpenter, our Lord must often have used one in the days before his ministry; (see Fig. 152).

(15) *Awls.*—The awl is also a very useful tool. In ancient Gezer they were often set in bone handles. Modern Palestinian carpenters employ a heated awl to make a hole in timber without splitting it. As ancient carpenters probably had the same custom, the awl was also one of the implements often used by Christ; (Fig. 157).

(16) *Axes* were found from the second Bronze stratum onward. Those from the earlier time were made, of course, of bronze; the later ones of iron. In a few the butt of the axe-head was perforated to receive a thong to lash it to the helve. How necessary this was is shown by such passages as Deuteronomy 19:5 and 2 Kings 6:5. A bronze double-edged axe was also found in the second Bronze stratum; (see Fig. 160).

(17) *Adzes.*—A few specimens of the adze were also found; (see Fig. 161). One of these was of bone.

(18) *Whetstones.*—Tools, of course, needed sharpening, and various specimens of whetstones were found; (see Fig. 158). It is difficult to distinguish these from "rubbing-stones," which were used when bathing to rub hardened skin from the body. The same stone may at times have served both purposes.

(19) *Files.*—A bronze file was made by perforating a tube of bronze with holes and leaving the rough edges made in the perforation protruding; (see Fig. 153). These were probably used, however, for crumbling bread, and not for sharpening tools.

(20) *Hammers.*—Many stone hammers from every period of Palestinian history have been found. The stone hammer seems to have persisted even after the introduction of metal. Bronze hammers are rare. Probably the hammer with which Jael killed Sisera (Judges 4:21, 5:26) was of stone; also the one referred to in Jeremiah 23:29; (see Fig. 155).

(21) *Nails* have been found in profusion, made both of bronze and of iron; (see Fig. 159). As soon as iron was introduced into the country it was generally employed in making nails. Christ, as a carpenter, must have employed a hammer, and often have driven nails.

(22) *Baskets* are used in Palestine, as in other countries, for all sorts of purposes. They are frequently referred to in the Bible. (See Deut. 26:2, 4; 28:5, 17; Judges 6:19; Amos 8:1,2). The basket of the modern Palestinian peasant is usually made by sewing together a coil of rope made of straw or reeds. After the mat thus formed has become large enough for the bottom of the basket, it is given an upward turn to form the sides. In excavating the water-passage at Gezer interesting evidence came to light of the existence of such baskets in ancient times. One of them had been left on some soft earth in the tunnel, and, although the basket itself had long ago decayed, the form of it was still visible on the hardened clod on which it had rested; see Fig. 163).

(23) *Arrows.*—Of implements of warfare some portions have survived. One of these was the arrow, which is mentioned more than fifty times in the Bible, and is employed in many metaphors. Arrows were made of a light perishable shaft to which an arrowhead of flint or bronze was attached. This head terminated in a point, which inflicted the wound. Arrow-heads were found in the

Palestinian strata later than the cave-dwellers; (Figs. 164, 165, 166).

(24) *Spears.*—The spear consisted of a long shaft with a metal head, that could be thrown at an enemy. It is often called a javelin. Such weapons are alluded to in the Bible almost as often as arrows. The excavations have yielded a good variety of bronze spear-heads; (see Fig. 167).

(25) *Swords.*—The swords of ancient Palestine were used for thrusting rather than for cutting. (See 1 Sam. 31:5; 2 Sam. 2: 16.) The blades are, therefore, short and pointed; (see Fig. 166). Sometimes the edges are actually thickened. A fine scimitar, found in a tomb in which other objects revealed Mycenean influence, is a great exception to the ordinary form of sword found in Palestine; (see Fig. 162).

(26) *Fish-hooks.*—Spears and arrows could, of course, be used in hunting as well as in war, but a fish-hook found at Gezer (see Fig. 156) is of especial interest to the student of the Bible, since some of the most prominent apostles, Peter, Andrew, James, and John, were fishermen. The fishing on the Sea of Galilee seems to have been done usually with nets. Nevertheless, perhaps even there a hook was sometimes employed.

(27) *Styli.*—The implements of the scribe which have survived are all specimens of a stylus for writing on clay or wax; (see Fig. 178). The usual length of these styli was 3½ to 4½ inches. In the Hellenistic stratum at Gezer, however, one was found as short as 2½ inches; also one as long as 12 inches. It was a stylus of the average kind found at Gezer that Isaiah was directed to use as recorded in Isaiah 8:1.

(28) *Seals.*—Closely connected with the work of the scribe are the seals which are found wherever a mound is thoroughly excavated. These were sometimes Egyptian scarabs, but more often, especially in the later periods, various figures and devices carved on a stone; (see Fig. 175). They might or might not contain the name of the owner. The famous seal of Shema, mentioned on p. 110, contained his name, but often they appear simply to have been a kind of mark of their owners. They might be impressed on clay or wax, and, as we have seen (p. 185), potters used them to identify their work. If the writing was on a clay tablet the seals were rolled over its edge (see Job 38:14), or over any unwritten portion of its surface. This took the place of the signa-

ture of the writer. On the use of seals in Bible times, see 1 Kings 21:8.

(29) *The "Pipe."*—The people of Palestine have always been fond of music, though in modern times their music is of a rude and primitive sort. Probably in ancient times it did not rise to anything like modern standards. At least one musical instrument has been brought to light by the excavations. It is a part of a stone whistle or "pipe" found in the late Bronze stratum—the period just before the coming of Israel. It is conical in shape, and about 4 inches long, 1⅛ inches wide at one end, and about ½ inch wide at the mouthpiece. It was perforated at the side by two holes; (see Fig. 168). Probably a mouthpiece of reed was fitted into it. It was possible to make several notes on it. This is probably a rude example of the "pipe," said to have been invented by Jubal (Gen. 4:21), and often mentioned in the Bible. (See 1 Sam. 10:5; 1 Kings 1:40; Isa. 5:12; 1 Cor. 14:7.) The Hebrew word for pipe means "a pierced" or "perforated thing," and this stone whistle answers the description well.

(30) *Harps.*—Other musical instruments were not made of material that could survive; nevertheless from the Babylonian, Assyrian, and Egyptian sculptures we have some idea of their forms. Of these, the harp is mentioned more than forty times in the Bible. For the forms of ancient harps, see Figures 169–172.

(31) *The Dulcimer.*—This musical instrument is mentioned in Daniel 3:5, 15. An Assyrian dulcimer is shown in Figure 174.

(32) *Lyres.*—A kind of lyre is pictured on certain Jewish coins; (see Fig. 173).

(33) *Children's Toys.*—A touch of nature that links the ancient world with ours is found in the toys of children. Both from Babylonia and Palestine clay rattles have been recovered. A series found at Gezer is shown in Figure 179. In addition to these rattles many grotesque animal figures came to light through the various excavations; these figures were probably made for children to play with. One or two had a hole drilled through a leg, apparently for the insertion of a string by which a child could drag it. The workmen who removed the earth sometimes begged for permission to take them home for their own children to play with; [2] (see Fig. 177).

2 For a fuller discussion of children's toys, see Rice, *Orientalisms in Bible Lands*, pp. 49–58.

2. Personal Ornaments:

(1) *Combs.*—Of toilet articles the most universal is the comb. These were made of bone or ivory. They were both straight and curved, ornamented and unornamented. A fragment of one from Gezer is shown in Figure 176.

(2) *Perfume-boxes.*—The ancients were fond of perfume. "Perfumed with myrrh and frankincense, with all powders of the merchant" is a Hebrew poet's description of an elegantly dressed man. (See Cant. 3:6.) Perfume-boxes, in which the various kinds of perfume were kept, frequently are found in excavating; (see, for example, Fig. 180). Women's perfume-boxes are denounced in Isaiah 3:20.

(3) *Spatulæ for Eye-paint, etc.*—Little spatulæ, or tools for lifting small quantities of cosmetics, were also found; (see Fig. 183). These were probably most often used to apply *kohl* to the eyelids—a practice that was thought to enhance the beauty of women (see Ezek. 23:40) and which is still followed in the East.

(4) *Fibulæ.*—Another article of the toilet which is found in abundance in all ancient excavations was the fibula—a rude kind of safety-pin. The garments were held together by these. They consisted of a kind of perforated bow through which a pin could be thrust. In the earlier periods the bow and the pin were not fastened together.

The dress of the ancient Palestinians was much like that of the modern peasants of the country. It was not, however, made of materials that would last when buried in a mound. All that has survived of it are some articles of personal adornment.

(5) *Beads* were highly valued from the earliest times and are found in all strata. In the earlier periods they were made of various colored stones; it is only in the later strata that some glass beads are found.

(6) *Necklaces.*—Beads, cylinders, and irregularly shaped pendants were strung so as to form necklaces. One found at Jericho is shown in Figure 181. They are called "chains" in Isaiah 3:19; Proverbs 1:9, and "strings of jewels" in Canticles 1:10.

(7) *Bracelets* and armlets have been found in abundance from nearly all periods. They were made of bronze, iron, ivory, glass, silver, and gold. For some of their forms, see Figure 182. They are frequently mentioned in the Bible. (See, for example, Gen. 24:30; Exod. 35:22; 2 Sam. 1:10; Ezek. 16:11.)

(8) *Anklets* of bronze and silver have also been found in various places. They are like bracelets, only larger. In a country where the ankles were usually left bare, it was as natural to wear ornaments on them as on the arms. These, too, are denounced along with the other ornaments of women in Isaiah 3 : 18.

(9) *Rings,* too, of various kinds have been found in profusion. Most of the finger rings were simple circles of metal; usually they were of bronze; sometimes of iron. Silver and gold rings were comparatively few in number and of small size. Several signet rings were found at Gezer. Finger rings are not often mentioned in the Bible. (See, however, Num. 31 : 50.) They evidently were highly regarded by well-to-do people, for in the Parable of the Prodigal Son Jesus tells us that the father "put a ring on his hand" (Luke 15 : 22). Signet rings were the possessions of the great and of kings. (See Gen. 41 : 42 and Esther 3 : 10, 12, and Fig. 184.)

CHAPTER X

MEASURES, WEIGHTS, AND MONEY

MEASURES. WEIGHTS. INSCRIBED WEIGHTS. MONEY: Who invented coinage? Darics. Maccabæan coins. Asmonæan coins. Herodian coins. Roman coins. The Widow's Mite. The Piece of Silver. Coinage of the Revolt of 66–70 A.D.

1. Measures.—The Hebrew units of dry measure were: 1. The Homer (or Cor), which contained 10 Ephahs (Ezek. 45: 11, 14). 2. The Ephah, which contained 3 Seahs (Isa. 40: 12) or 10 Omers (Exod. 16: 36) or 18 Cabs (2 Kings 6: 25, and Josephus, *Antiquities*, IX, iv, 4. Josephus calls it a "sextary," *i.e.*, the sixth part of a Seah).

Corresponding to these were the units of liquid measure: 1. The Homer (or Cor), which contained 10 Baths (Ezek. 45: 11, 14). 2. The Bath, which, according to Josephus and Jerome, contained 6 Hins (see Exod. 29: 40). 3. The Hin, which contained 3 Cabs, or, according to the Talmud, 12 Logs.

These two systems have the Homer as their major unit. The Homer had the same capacity in each system. The Ephah of dry measure equalled the Bath of liquid measure, and the Cab was the same in each. If, then, the capacity of one unit in either measure could be determined, we should know the capacity of all the others.

It has been the custom of archæologists to strike a kind of average of the confused statements of Josephus and Epiphanius [1] and correct these by estimates based on Babylonian measures.

Calculations based on this method will be found in recent works on Hebrew archæology and dictionaries of the Bible. It has been impossible, however, to reach certainty. Three systems will be found in the books referred to: one based on the supposition that the Log $= \frac{9}{10}$ of a pint; one based on the supposition that the Log $= \frac{91}{100}$ of a pint; the third on the supposition that the Log $= 1$ pint.

[1] An early Christian writer, born in 315, died in 403 A.D., who was bishop of Salamis in Cyprus.

The estimates of the Homer vary accordingly from 80 gallons to 81.25 gallons, and 89.28 gallons.[2]

Under these circumstances some discoveries of the Augustinians of the Assumption, in the grounds of their monastery in Jerusalem, appear to be of importance.[3] They found at various times in excavating for building purposes four vessels, which seem to have been a series of measures. Taking the larger one as the unit, the capacity of the one next smaller is three-quarters of the capacity of the first; the third was just half the first; the fourth, a quarter of it. These vessels all appear to have been in a building which had a Hebrew inscription over its door. Although the inscription was broken, the word "Corban"[4] was still legible. Père Germer-Durand assumes, accordingly, that the building was used as a place where temple tithes were paid, and that this series of vessels were standard measures employed in collecting tithes. The quantities of material contained by these vessels are as follows:

Largest, 21.25 litres or 19.6 quarts.
Second, 15.937 litres or 14.7 quarts.
Third, 10.625 litres or 9.8 quarts.
Fourth, 5.312 litres or 4.9 quarts.

Père Germer-Durand thinks from a study of Josephus and Epiphanius that the largest of his vessels represents the Ephah of dry measure or the Bath of liquid measure. If this assumption is right, it gives a series of measures which are each about $\frac{7}{12}$ smaller than the smallest of the series referred to above.

On this basis Hebrew dry measures become:

Homer or Cor = 196 quarts or 6 bushels and ½ peck.
Ephah = 19.6 quarts or 2 pecks, 3.6 quarts.
Seah = 6.533+ quarts.
Omer = 1.96 quarts.
Cab = 1.888+ quarts.

Liquid measure becomes:

Homer or Cor = 196 quarts or 49 gallons.
Bath = 19.6 quarts or 4.9 gallons.
Seah = 6.533+ quarts.
Hin = 3.266+ quarts.
Cab = 1.888+ quarts.
Log = .272 quarts or approximately ½ pint.

2 From this equivalence the reader can easily compute the value which the intermediate measures would have according to this theory. The multiples of the Log which formed the Cab, etc., are given above.

3 See Père Germer-Durand, "Mesures de capacité des Hebreux a utemps de l'évangile" in *Conferences de Saint-Étienne*, Paris, 1910, pp. 89–105, and Fig. 185.

4 The Jewish name for an offering to God. (See Mark 7:11.)

It is not certain that the vessels found by the Augustinians represent the measures that Germer-Durand supposes, but it is as likely that they do as that the confused statements of Josephus and Epiphanius afford an accurate basis for calculations.

It is probable that in actual business there was in ancient times a great deal of variation allowed from the ordinary standard of measures. We know of no rigid regulation of the matter by a central authority.

2. Weights.—The two weights most often mentioned in the Bible are the talent and the shekel. The Bible nowhere tells us of how many shekels a talent was composed. In Babylonia the talent consisted of 60 manas,[5] and each mana of 60 shekels, so that the talent consisted of 3600 shekels. The Phœnicians divided the mana into 50 shekels, and it is thought by scholars that the Hebrews did the same, though we have no positive evidence on the point. Manas are not mentioned in the Bible, unless in Daniel 5:25.[6]

In the course of the excavations by Bliss in the Shephelah a number of weights were found, some of which were inscribed. Macalister also found a large number of weights at Gezer, a few of which bore inscriptions. Some others have been found by natives and purchased by travelers. The writer had the pleasure of discovering two weights in this way.

3. Inscribed Weights.—These inscribed weights are of the greatest interest to the students of the Bible. Five weights are known that are inscribed in old Hebrew characters with the word *neseph*, "half"; see Fig. 186. These are undoubtedly half-shekels. Two of the three are broken, and one is perforated. The other two weigh, respectively, 157.56 grains and 153.6 grains. The average of these is 155.5 grains, which would make the shekel 311 grains.

Another weight, said to have come from Samaria, was described some years ago by Dr. Chaplin. It bears the inscription *roba neseph*, "the quarter of a half," and weighs 39.2 grains. Another weight from Samaria was in the possession of Mr. Herbert Clark, of Jerusalem. It is made in the form of a turtle and bears the inscription *homesh*, "a fifth," and weighs 38.58 grains. Probably it was intended as the fifth part of a shekel.

Another series of inscribed weights, of which three examples are known, bears the inscription *beqa*. The word comes from a root

5 "Mana" is both the Babylonian and the Hebrew term. In English it has usually been corrupted to "Mina."
6 Some scholars understand MENE to be such a reference.

ARCHÆOLOGY AND THE BIBLE

that means "cleave" or "split." This word occurs twice in the
Old Testament, in Genesis 24 : 22 and Exodus 38 : 26. In the passage last mentioned it is defined as half a shekel (see Fig. 188).

A third variety of weight bears the inscription *payim*. The
first of these to be discovered was found by the writer in the hands
of a dealer in Jerusalem. On one side it bore the word *payim*
and on the other *lezekaryahu yaer,* "belonging to Zechariah son
of Jaer." This weight is cubic in form (see Fig. 187) and weighs
117.431 grains.[7] Macalister found another of similar shape, which
bore only the inscription *payim.* It weighed 114.81 grains. The
word *payim* is very puzzling. It has been interpreted by Clermont-Ganneau as meaning "two-thirds," and as designating two-thirds of a shekel. Possibly this is right. This weight is mentioned in 1 Samuel 13 : 20, 21, and its discovery has explained a
Hebrew phrase which has puzzled all translators. We now know
that these verses should be rendered : "But all the Israelites went
down to the Philistines, to sharpen every man his plowshare, and
his axe, and his adze, and his hoe, and the price was a *pim* (or
payim) for the plowshares, and for the axes, and for the three-tined
forks, and for the adzes, and for the setting of the goads." The
name of the weight here expresses the price, just as shekel, the name
of another weight, does elsewhere.[8] One bronze weight found at
Gezer bore words meaning "belonging to the king," but it is not
clear to what king it referred.

A glance at the weights here described makes it evident that the
standards of the ancient Hebrews were not exact. If these are representative weights, the shekel must have varied from 200 to more
than 300 grains Troy. This is what one acquainted with the Palestine of today would expect. The peasants still use field-stone as
weights, selecting one that is approximately of the weight they
desire. Even among the merchants of modern Jerusalem, where
one would expect more exact standards than among the peasantry,
odd scraps of old iron were, under the Turks, used for weights.[9]

7 The weight is now in the library of Haverford College, near Philadelphia.
8 The words rendered "the price was a *pim*" are translated in the Authorized Version,
"they had a file," margin, "a file with mouths"; in the Revised Version, "they had a file,"
margin, or "when the edges . . . were blunt." The Revisers add: "The Hebrew text is
obscure." The Hebrew word rendered "file" and "blunt" comes from a root that means
"to prescribe" or "appoint." It could easily mean the "established price," but can mean
neither "file" nor "blunt." *Pim* means "mouths" and is employed figuratively for
"edges," but neither of those meanings fits the passage. The discovery of these weights
has cleared up the whole obscurity. This interpretation was suggested by Pilcher in the
Palestine Exploration Fund Quarterly Statement, 1914, p. 99.
9 See Macalister, *The Excavation of Gezer,* II, 279.

A large number of uninscribed weights of the same general size and shape of those described [10] were found at Gezer. Whether larger weights or multiples of a shekel were discovered is uncertain. A number of stones might have been used for weights, but they were not inscribed and may have been used for other purposes. A large bronze weight found at Tell Sandahanna is just sixty times the weight of a 311-grain shekel, and may be a mana.[11]

Where weights and measures differed so, the words of Amos (8:5), "making the epah small and the shekel great," gain an added significance, and we understand why the wise man denounced "false balances" (Prov. 11:1; 20:23). Indeed, of the weights found at Gezer so many were under the average standard, and so many above it, that the inference lay close at hand that many men had one set of weights by which to purchase and another set by which to sell.[12]

4. Money.—Down to the seventh century before Christ money was not coined. Whenever it was employed as a medium of exchange, it was weighed. In western Asia and Egypt our sources show that in the period from 1500 to 1300 B.C. gold and silver were prepared for commercial use by being formed into rings.[13] These rings were of no standard weight; they were weighed in the mass by scales. Probably the rings were small, so that the weight could, at the will of the merchant, be increased by very slight amounts. The ring-form was probably selected because this shape would present no corners that would rapidly wear away. This type of commercial ring can be traced in the inscriptions of Ashurnasirpal II of Assyria,[14] 884–860 B.C. It was used, then, in Egypt, Syria, Phœnicia, by the Hittites, the Aramæans, and the Assyrians.

(1) *Who Invented Coinage?*—The oldest coins yet found were made by the Lydians, and on this account it is usually said that the Lydians were the first to coin money. The date of these coins is uncertain. They bear the name of no king, but are usually assigned to the seventh century B.C. Mr. Head, of the British Museum, dated them tentatively at 700 B.C. They probably were made under the Lydian dynasty founded by Gyges in 697 B.C., the last king of which, the famous Crœsus, was overthrown by Cyrus the Great, in 546 B.C. It is improbable that these coins were invented

10 See Macalister, *The Excavation of Gezer*, II, pp. 278–293.
11 See Bliss and Macalister, *Excavations in Palestine*, 1898-1900, p. 61.
12 See Macalister, *The Excavation of Gezer*, II, 291.
13 See Breasted, *Ancient Records, Egypt*, II, §§ 436, 489, 490, 518, and *History of Egypt*, 2d ed., pp. 277, 307.
14 See Schrader's *Keilinschriftliche Bibliothek*, I, 105 (cl. III, 62).

earlier than the reign of Gyges, and they may not have been put into circulation until he had been some years on the throne. It is recognized that the weight of these coins conforms to a Babylonian standard.

There seems to be evidence that coined money was employed by the Assyrians in the reign of Esarhaddon. None of the coins have been found, but a series of loans and payments, dated in the years 676–671 B.C., designate the amounts of money in "shekels of silver-heads of Ishtar." [15] As has been noted by Menant and Johns, this can hardly mean anything else than silver made into coins of the value of a shekel and stamped with the head of Ishtar. As Gyges was a contemporary of Esarhaddon, it seems probable that Lydia borrowed the idea of coinage from the Mesopotamian Valley.

Be this as it may, the coinage of money was a great step forward. To have the value of a piece of metal determined beforehand and guaranteed by an official stamp greatly facilitated the transaction of business. It eliminated the delays incident to weighing the metal, and the disputes that were sure to ensue as to the correctness of the weights which were put into the balances.

(2) *Darics.*—The invention of coined money first affected Palestine during the Persian period. Darius I of Persia, 521–486 B.C., organized the coinage of that realm. The gold coins issued by him were of the weight of a Babylonian shekel. They weighed from 125 to 130 grains Troy. One in the British Museum weighs 129 grains. They bore on the face a picture of Darius with a bow to the left; (see Fig. 189). Because of this picture they were called "darics," just as the French 20-franc piece is called a "napoleon." The daric is mentioned in several Biblical books that were written after the beginning of the Persian period. (See 1 Chron. 29:7; Ezra 2:69; 8:27; Neh. 7:70-72.) It is wrongly translated "dram" in the Authorized Version.

After the Persian period the coinage of all the nations to whom the Jews became subject circulated in turn in Palestine. Foreign coins also found their way into the country. Many of these ultimately were lost and buried in the soil, so that many, many coins have been brought to light by archæological research. We have space here to mention only those that are of the greatest interest to students of the Bible.

15 See C. H. W. Johns, *Assyrian Deeds and Documents,* I, Nos. 38, 39, 40, 41, 44, 45, 46, 50, and 108; cf. also III, 8.

Palestine passed under the sway of Alexander the Great in 332 B.C., and after his death in 323 it was attached to the territory of Ptolemy Lagi of Egypt and his successors. In 199 B.C. Antiochus III wrested it from the Ptolemies and the Jews passed under the sway of the Syrians. During this time the coins of these rulers circulated in the country and are still frequently dug up there, although they are not mentioned in the Bible. Samples of these coins are shown in Figs. 190, 195. Not until the Jews had gained their independence under Simon the Maccabee, in the year 143 B.C., did they issue any coinage of their own. Indeed, it now seems clear that no coins were issued by Simon until after the year 139–138 B.C., when the Syrian king by an especial grant accorded him that liberty. The coins then issued appear to have been made of bronze only.[16] A silver coinage formerly attributed to Simon the Maccabee is now regarded as belonging to the time of the Jewish revolt of 66–70 A.D.

(3) *Maccabæan Coins.*—The coins of Simon consist of bronze half-shekels and quarter-shekels all dated in the year four. Antiochus VII of Syria apparently prevented the issue of others during the reign of Simon. His coins bear on their face the picture of a citron between two bundles of twigs. Around the border runs the inscription in old Hebrew characters, "year four; one-half." On the other side is a palm-tree with two bunches of fruit between two baskets filled with fruits, and around the border runs the inscription, "belonging to the redemption of Zion" (see Fig. 192). The weights of these coins vary from 232.6 to 237 grains. The lighter ones are considerably worn.

The quarter-shekels have on one side two bundles of twigs, around which run the words, "year four; one-fourth." On the other side is pictured a citron with the stalk upward, around which runs the inscription, "belonging to the redemption of Zion." The weights of the known coins of this denomination vary from 113.7 to 192.3 grains. The form of the letters on these coins shows that they are older than other Jewish coins.

(4) *Asmonæan Coins.*—There are many coins from the reign of John Hyrcanus, the son and successor of Simon, but they are all of copper; (see Fig. 193). They bear on their face the inscription: "Johanan, the high priest and the congregation of the Jews"; on the reverse is a poppy head between two cornucopias. Similar coins were issued by the other Asmonæan princes.

16 See Hill, *Catalogue of the Greek Coins of Palestine,* London, 1914, p. xciii, ff.

(5) *Herodian Coins.*—As Herod the Great was a vassal of Rome, he was permitted to issue copper coins only. These exist in considerable variety. Figure 198 shows one, the face of which is stamped with the image of a vessel with a bell-shaped cover, above which are two-palm-branches; on the reverse the words meaning "of King Herod" run around the edge, while a tripod occupies the center. At the left of the tripod is an abbreviation for "year 3"; at the right is a monogram. Several other patterns are known.

Coins of Archælaus, Antipas, Herod Philip (Matt. 14:3; Mark 6:17; Luke 3:19), and of Herod Agrippa I are known. One is shown in Figure 200.

(6) *Roman Coins.*—The most common silver Roman coin was the denarius, rendered in the Authorized Version "penny" and in the Revised Version "shilling." Its weight varied at different times. In the time of Christ it weighed about 61.3 grains Troy, and was worth 16⅔ cents of American money. As the ministry of Christ occurred in the reign of Tiberius, the tribute money shown to Christ (Matt. 22:19; Mark 12:15-17) was probably a denarius of Tiberius, such as is shown in Figure 196. The denarius was so named because it originally was equivalent to ten *asses* or small copper coins, but the *as* was afterward reduced to 1/16 of the denarius. The *as* is mentioned in Matthew 10:29; Luke 12:6, where A. V. renders it "farthing" and R. V. "penny." It was worth about a cent. The Roman coin *quadrans,* or the fourth part of an *as,* worth about ¼ of a cent, is mentioned in Matthew 5:26; Mark 12:42. It is translated "farthing" (see Fig. 199).

(7) *The Widow's Mite.*—Another coin, translated "mite," is in Greek *lepton,* "the small one" or the "bit." It was two of these that the widow cast into the treasury, Mark 12:42,[17] where it is said that two of them equaled a *quadrans.* The "mite" was, then, of the value of ⅛ of a cent. It was doubtless the smallest coin in circulation, but it has not yet been identified with certainty with any coin that archæology has discovered.

(8) *The Piece of Silver.*—In Luke 15:8 the Greek *drachma* is mentioned. It is translated "piece of silver." The *drachma* corresponded roughly in value to the denarius. Drachmas had been issued by many different cities and many different kings, and were still in circulation in Palestine in the time of Christ. One still sees in that country today coins of the first Napoleon, and of many other

17 Cf. Luke 21:2.

sovereigns who have been long dead, passing from hand to hand as media of value; (see Fig. 194).

(9) *Coinage of the Revolt of 66–70 A.D.*—Two silver coins, a shekel and a half-shekel (see Fig. 201), were formerly attributed to Simon the Maccabee. The shekels weigh 212.3 to 217.9 grains and bear on their face above a cup or chalice the legend "shekel of Israel" and a numeral. The numeral stands for the first year. Examples are known which carry the enumeration up to the year "five." On the reverse a triple lily is pictured, and in similar Hebrew characters the words "Jerusalem, the holy" are inscribed. The half-shekel is smaller and has the same markings except that the legend on its face is simply "half-shekel." On the coins issued after the first year a Hebrew *sh* precedes the number of the year. The *sh* is an abbreviation of the Hebrew word *shana,* year. For various reasons the consensus of expert opinion now is that these coins were issued during the Jewish war of 66–70 A.D., which, according to Jewish reckoning, extended into the fifth year.

Coins of the Roman Emperors, Augustus and Claudius, are shown in Figures 195, 197.

CHAPTER XI

HOUSES, HIGH PLACES, AND TEMPLES[1]

A HITHERTO UNRECOGNIZED TYPE OF HOUSE: At Tell es-Safi. At Taanach. At Megiddo. A SUPPOSED PHILISTINE TEMPLE. A CAVE SANCTUARY. A ROCK ALTAR AT MEGIDDO. A ROCK ALTAR AT JERUSALEM. HIGH PLACE OF GEZER: Choice of Site. Child sacrifice. Corrupt worship. HIGH PLACE OF PETRA. TEMPLES AT BETH-SHAN. AN ALTAR OF INCENSE. THE TEMPLE TO AUGUSTUS AT SAMARIA.

1. A Hitherto Unrecognized Type of House.—Within the last few years our knowledge of house building in Palestine during the early Hebrew Period has been revolutionized. A number of structures which before 1930 were thought to be ancient temples with characteristic Semitic "pillars" standing midway between their walls, now turn out to have been commodious houses.[2] What were supposed to be religious "pillars" are but the remains of stone posts which once supported the roofs. For many centuries there have been no forests in the Holy Land, and the roofs of houses have been supported by stone arches. It was natural for archæologists to assume that similar conditions and customs prevailed in antiquity. When, therefore, they found the remains of enclosing walls with two or three pillars standing midway of the enclosure, it was naturally supposed to have been a temple.

In the first five editions of this book a number of structures were, in accordance with the unanimous opinion of archæologists, taken for temples, which now turn out to have been large houses. These pillars once supported wooden beams on which wooden roofs rested. This accounts for the fact that so many Biblical cities could be "burned with fire"; a modern Palestinian city could not be so burned. It accounts, too, for the thick beds of ashes which so often separate the strata of different occupations in Palestinian mounds. And sometimes, as at Jericho, charred beams of these ancient roofs have been dug up. The ground floors of these houses appear to have been occupied as store-

---

1 The temples of Solomon, Zerubbabel, and Herod are treated in Chapter XIII. on Jerusalem.
2 Cf. W. Andrae, *Das Gotteshaus und die Urformen des Bauens im alten Orient*, 1930, and W. F. Albright, *Archæology of Palestine and the Bible*, 1931, pp. 114 ff.

208

rooms and for the accommodation of domestic animals. The family lived in the upper story, the walls of which were apparently sometimes of adobe bricks and sometimes of wood. The ground walls of some of these houses at Tell Beit Mirsim [3] were so thick that it was conjectured that they must have been three stories high.

(1) *At Tell es-Safi.*—The first of these was discovered by Bliss and Macalister at Tell es-Safi.[4] The space was enclosed by walls, but as the upper courses of these had been destroyed, the original height of the walls could not be determined. Within the largest enclosure stood three monoliths or "pillars." These rested on bases of stone. The pillars themselves were, respectively, 5 feet 10 inches, 6 feet 5 inches, and 7 feet 1 inch high. One of them was pointed, and one of them almost flat on the top. No tool mark was discernible on any of them. All showed signs of having been rubbed. The walls enclosing these pillars formed an approximate square 30 feet from east to west, and 32 feet from north to south. On the north a fairly large room was walled in, as shown in Figure 212; and on the south three smaller rooms. In the wall to the north of the three pillars was a semi-circular apse. Facing this apse was a low semicircle of stone 3 feet 7 inches in diameter, which is situated much nearer the "pillars." The purpose of this semicircle is unknown. At the time of discovery the excavators quite naturally thought this a "high place," but it is now much more probable that it was one of the large houses just described.

(2) *At Taanach.*—Sellin [5] discovered two monoliths which he believed to be the pillars of a high place. These stones had, however, been hewn, which does not accord with the general Semitic requirement that no tool should be lifted up upon such stones. (See Fig. 211.) From the vantage ground of our present knowledge it is easy to see that they were the supports of a house roof and not pillars of a high place. The two pillars at Taanach were situated over a cave, and figures of Ashtoreth were found in connection with them. The Ashtoreth plaques found in connection with them do not prove the house to have been more than a dwelling. They were images to bring good fortune to the house. The cave probably belonged to an earlier time. In connection with this house an interesting libation bowl was found which is shown in Figure 213.

3 See above, p. 117.
4 See Bliss and Macalister, *Excavations in Palestine*, 1898-1900, p. 31 ff.
5 *Tell Taanek*, p. 68 ff.

(3) *At Megiddo.*—In the course of the excavation at Megiddo a house was found which was at the time mistaken for a temple.[6] (Fig. 222.) This house was in the Israelitish stratum, and so is of especial interest to the students of the Bible. It was situated in the highest part of the city. The whole space was not excavated, but the portion uncovered was 131 feet long, and 115 feet wide. It was of the same period as the palace in which the seal of Shema, the servant of Jeroboam, was found, and contained more drafted stones than the walls of that palace. In one of the rooms of the house stood two stones that were taken for "pillars" such as are denounced in Deuteronomy. One of these was 7 feet 8 inches high; the other, 7 feet high. The room in which these pillars stood was 30 feet long, and 10 feet 7 inches wide. In building the wall of this house a stone was used that had once formed the voluted capital of a column. (See Fig. 224.) Probably this stone was taken from an earlier Philistine building.

In the grounds of the house several jars containing the skeletons of children were unearthed. These were apparently family burials.

At the east of the palace of the Hebrew governor was an enclosure containing three "pillars," in which the remains of a number of terra-cotta goddesses were found.[7] This was evidently another house of this type. The enclosure was almost 40 feet long, and 32 feet 10 inches wide. (Fig. 223.) Its beginnings antedate the Israelitish period, since they come from the stratum before the conquest.

Another house equipped with the necessary "pillars" was found in the Hebrew stratum, between the governor's palace and the southern gate of the city.[8] This enclosure was not quite 30 feet long, and a little less than 20 feet wide. It contained six stones, which Dr. Schumacher took to be "pillars." Like those at Petra and Taanach, they had evidently been shaped with tools. They did not stand in a row, or in any regular relation to one another. This threw some doubt upon the religious significance of the stones. Could they not have been columns used in supporting the roof of the building? Since a small stone object that had religious significance in the high places was found in this room, together with a most remarkable incense burner, it seemed probable that these were religious "pillars," and that the room was a little chapel, but we

6 Schumacher, *Tell el-Mutesellim*, 110-124.
7 Schumacher, *Tell el-Mutesellim*, 105–110.
8 *Ibid.*, 125–130.

now know that this was a mistake. The object was of limestone, and about 7 inches long. It was lying at the foot of one of the "pillars." The incense burner was made of a greyish soft limestone. It was a little over 9 inches in height. The diameter of the bowl was 6⅜ inches. The stone was cut so that the bowl rested on a pedestal, which was divided by rings into two portions, each of which was cut so as to represent a circle of overhanging leaves. (See Fig. 225.) The whole was decorated with reddish-brown and cobalt-blue paints. The decoration of the rim of the bowl is a geometrical design; that on the bowl itself represents a sort of conventionalized lily blossom, while the leaves suggest those of the palm.

2. A Supposed Philistine Temple.—Turning now to Palestinian temples: Macalister discovered the remains of a building at Gezer which he thought might have been a temple.[9] This building belonged to the late Bronze stratum; in other words, to the period just before the coming of the Israelites. A general plan of its walls is shown in Figure 220. In a court in one part of the structure were five pillars, which may have had the same religious significance as the pillars of the high place. The two circular structures f f remind one of the circular structures of the high place of Gezer. These were filled with the fragments of the bones of sheep and goats. As these bore no marks of cooking, they could not have been mere domestic ash pits, and it was plausible to think of them as receptacles for the bodies of slaughtered victims. In a forecourt of the structure a line of bases, apparently intended for the support of columns, was found. Macalister conjectured that these supported a roof over a part of the portico, and it reminded him of the story of Samson in the temple of Dagon. (See Judges 16:23–30.) It is quite possible that the feast of Dagon described in Judges 16 may have been held in a structure similar to this; that the lords of the Philistines may have been gathered in such a porch; and that Samson may have pulled from under the roof that sheltered them such pillars as rested upon these bases and caused their destruction and his own death. It is all possible, but conjectural.

3. A Cave Sanctuary.—One of the oldest sanctuaries which we can trace in Palestine appears to have been a cave at Gezer. This cave was 32 feet long, 20 feet broad, and 7 feet 11 inches at its maximum height. There were two entrances: one on the east

9 See Macalister, *The Excavation of Gezer*, II, 405 ff.

—a tall, narrow doorway—was approached by a passage sloping downward; the other, on the west, was a low, narrow passage just wide enough to admit a person. At the northern end there was a projection in the form of an apse, the floor of which was about 2 feet higher than that of the rest of the cave. In the roof of this apse there was an opening about 1 foot wide at the bottom, leading to the upper air. The rock of the roof here was 3 feet 5½ inches thick. This opening was 2 feet 8 inches in diameter at the top, and a channel 4 feet 6 inches long cut in the surface of the rock was connected with it. On the surface of the rock above the cave and about this channel there were a number of "cup marks" similar to those found near ancient sacred places. Some of these were, perhaps, intended for places to set jars, but some of them were connected with the channel which emptied into the opening in the roof of the cave.[10] (See Fig. 202.)

The suggestion which the excavator, Professor Macalister, makes is that this was a sanctuary of the cave dwellers; that they killed their victims on the surface of the rock above and let the blood run through the channel and the opening into the cave underneath, where their deity was supposed to dwell. They lived in caves themselves, and it was natural for them to think their deity did the same. This suggestion received some confirmation from the fact that on the floor of the apse, under this opening, there were found, upon removing a layer of earth, a number of pig bones. The presence of these might be accounted for on the supposition that they were offered in sacrifice to their deity by the cave dwellers. Swine were unclean to all Semites, and, no doubt, the later Semitic inhabitants would have thrown the bones away, if they had ever cleaned out the cave sufficiently to discover them.

4. A Rock Altar at Megiddo.—Another rock altar of high antiquity was discovered on the slope of the mound at Tell el-Mutesellim, the ancient Megiddo.[11] It was situated on the slope of the tell, about halfway down. Its surface was covered with "cup marks," like those on the altar at Gezer, and an opening about 2½ feet wide at the top, and 1½ feet wide at the bottom made it possible for blood to trickle down through 3 feet of rock into a cave below. This cave contained several rooms, the largest of which was about 18 feet 6 inches long, 7 feet 8 inches wide, and

10 See Macalister, *The Excavation of Gezer,* I, 102; II, 378 ff.
11 See Schumacher, *Tell el-Mutesellim,* 156 ff.

8 feet 6 inches high. In the most northerly of the rooms were found various implements of black flint, potsherds, coals of a wood fire, the bones of sheep and goats, olive stones, and ashes. In the midst of the central room there lay a heap of human bones, the skulls of which were badly destroyed. These human bones show that after the cave had been used as a sanctuary it was employed as a sepulcher. The same thing happened at Gezer and elsewhere. (See Fig. 205.)

5. A Rock Altar at Jerusalem.—We are told in Genesis 22:2 that Abraham went to the land of Moriah to offer up Isaac; and in 2 Chronicles 3:1, ff. that Solomon built the temple on Mount Moriah, on the threshing floor which David acquired from Ornan (Araunah) the Jebusite. Just to the east of the site of Solomon's temple, in the open court where the altar of burnt-offering stood, there was a rock surface similar to the two rock altars described above. It is still visible in Jerusalem and is now enclosed in the Mosque of Omar. The Mohammedans regard it as a sacred rock. One can still trace on it the channels which conducted the blood to an opening, which in turn conducted it to a cave underneath. This cave is still regarded by the Mohammedans as sacred. There is little doubt that the sacrificial victims offered in the temples of Solomon and Herod were slain on this stone, and that that part of the blood not used in sprinkling drained into the cave underneath. This rock altar is on the hill to which, perhaps, Abraham came for the sacrifice of Isaac.[12] (See Fig. 208.)

6. High Place of Gezer.—The foundations of this high place were in the second stratum below that which contained Israelitish pottery. It was one of the high places of the Canaanites, therefore, or of one of the tribes that were in Palestine before the coming of Israel. This is the most interesting of the high places which have been discovered in Palestine.[13] It contained ten monoliths or upright "pillars," the tallest of which was 10 feet 9 inches in height, and the shortest 5 feet 5 inches. These pillars ran in a curved line, the general direction of which was from north to south. Perhaps the reason for this is that the rising sun was worshiped here. The center of the curved line of the pillars of Gezer was toward the east. All of these pillars except one were of the kind of stone abundant about Gezer. They had been found

12 In Genesis 22:9 Abraham, we are told, built the altar. He did not, therefore, intend to use the rock altar. The analogy of this altar with the other two is not quite complete. It appears to have no cup marks on its surface.
13 See Macalister, *The Excavation of Gezer*, I, 51, 105–107; II, 381–404.

near by. None of them bore the mark of a tool. They had not been shaped by working. One of them—the one that was *the* sacred stone, as the smooth spots on it showed—was a different kind of stone—the kind found at Jerusalem and elsewhere, but not near Gezer. There were on it traces of an indentation, as though a rope for dragging it might have been fitted around it. (Fig. 206.) As Mesha, King of Moab, tells us twice in his inscription that he dragged altar hearths of other deities away from their original locations into the presence of his god, Chemosh,[14] it seems likely that this stone was dragged to Gezer from some other sanctuary, possibly from Jerusalem. Perhaps it was its capture that first suggested to the inhabitants of Gezer the establishment of this high place. The other stones of the series were erected to keep this one company and to do it honor. These were probably not all set up at once. They were added from time to time by different rulers of Gezer, and we have no means of knowing when the latest of the pillars was erected. (See Fig. 204.)

(1) *Choice of Site.*—Judging from the scarabs found about the foundations of the high place, its beginnings date from 2000 B.C. or earlier, and it continued in use down to the Babylonian Exile. Curiously enough, this high place is not situated on the highest part of the hill. The land is higher both to the east and to the west of it. It is situated in a sort of saddle to the east of the middle of the mound. Why was this spot chosen for it? Two considerations, perhaps, led to the choice of the site. A great ramifying cave on a higher part of the hill had already been appropriated by Semites as a sepulcher, and was, therefore, unclean. The cave which the earlier inhabitants had used as a crematorium was for the same reason unacceptable. Why the high place was not built near the cave that the cave dwellers had used as a temple, we cannot now conjecture. Perhaps in some way the memory that that had been a sacred spot had faded from men's minds. Macalister thinks that the choice of the site was determined by the presence at this point of the two caves shown in Figure 203. These caves had been human dwellings in the pre-Semitic time. They were now connected by a narrow, crooked passage, so that they could be utilized for the giving of oracles. Macalister conjectures that a priest or priestess would go into one, while the devotee who wished to inquire of the god was sent into the other, and that the inquirer

14 See Part II, ch. XIX, § 7.

would hear his oracle through this passage. This theory is plausible, though incapable of full proof.

Just back of one of the pillars a square stone was found with a deep hole cut in its upper side. (See Fig. 209.) Several theories as to the use of this have been put forward; the most probable one is that it was a laver.

The area of the high place seems to have been approximately 150 feet from north to south, and 120 feet from east to west. Some few walls were found of the same data as the high place, but it was impossible to tell their purpose. There seem to have been no buildings that could be regarded as a part of the sanctuary. It seems to have been entirely open to the air. Two circular structures, one at the north and the other to the south of the sacred stones, were found. The one at the south was badly ruined; that to the north was in a good state of preservation. This structure had a pavement of stones on a level with the bottom of the sacred pillars. It was entirely surrounded by a wall 2 feet thick at the bottom, and 1 foot 6 inches thick at the top, and 6 feet high. There was no doorway. The wall leaned outward. The diameter of the structure was 13 feet 8 inches at the bottom, and 16 feet 6 inches at the top. (See Fig. 207.) On the pavement in this enclosure were the fragments of many clay bowls, of a type found in Cyprus, but common at Gezer from 1400–1800 B.C., and among these fragments a brazen serpent, evidently the model of a cobra. This discovery suggests the possibility that the structure may have been a pen in which sacred serpents were kept. The practice of venerating serpents as sacred is found in many parts of the world.[15] This brazen serpent reminds one of Nehushtan, the brazen serpent worshiped by the Judæans until it was destroyed by King Hezekiah. (See 2 Kings 18:4, and Fig. 219a.)

(2) *Child Sacrifice.*—The whole area of the high place was found to be a cemetery of newborn infants. These were in all probability first-born children who had been sacrificed to the deity of the high place. Two of them displayed marks of fire, but most of them had been simply enclosed in large jars. The body was usually put in head first. Two or three smaller vessels were put in with them. These generally included a bowl and a jug. They were usually inside the jar, between the body and the jar's mouth; sometimes they were outside, near the mouth of the jar. That these were sacrifices is shown by the fact that they were

15 See C. H. Toy, *Introduction to the History of Religions,* Boston, 1913, §§ 250, 257.

children. It was not, therefore, a general place of burial. Indeed, had these children not been sacrificial, they could not have been buried in the sanctuary, as dead bodies were unclean.

The Semites generally believed that the first-born were sacred to deity and must be sacrificed to it. This sort of human sacrifice persisted for a long time among the Phœnicians. It was said that God called Abraham to sacrifice Isaac, and that He then permitted him to offer a ram instead. (Gen. 22.) The law provided for the redemption of Hebrew first-born by the sacrifice of a lamb (See Exod. 34:20.), but in the time of King Manasseh the old custom was revived and men "made their children pass through the fire." (See 2 Kings 21:6; 23:10; Jer. 7:31; 32:35.) The gruesome discoveries of this high place have made very real these horrible practices and the inhuman fate from which Isaac and other Hebrew children were delivered.

With the exception of a little unhewn stone about 18 inches square, found in one of the caves connected with the high place, and which might possibly have served as an altar, no altar was found. Possibly none was needed in the rites practiced there, but it is more likely that the altar was simply a mound of earth such as is prescribed in Exodus 20:24—a mound which could not be distinguished, in excavating, from the common earth.

(3) *Corrupt Worship.*—Of the nature of some of the services that went on in this high place in the name of Ashtoreth eloquent testimony was borne by unnumbered Ashtoreth plaques that had been presented as votive offerings by the worshipers. These varied in form and in artistic merit, but were all designed to foster in the worshiper that type of debasing service described in Isaiah 57:3, ff., as Figure 214 shows. Symbols of this nature were abundant during all the period while the high place was in use, No one who was not, like the writer, at Gezer during the excavation, can realize how demoralizing the whole atmosphere of such worship must have been. Archæology has here revealed to us in a most vivid way the tremendous power of those corrupting religious influences which the Hebrew prophets so vigorously denounced. The discoveries at Ras Shamra (see above, ch. IV, § 26) have now supplied us with a ritual that was employed in this service, (see Part II, ch. IX, § 9). It is possible now to understand the motives which led to the inauguration of such worship. These practices were deeply rooted in the customs of the Canaanites; they

were sanctified by a supposed divine sanction of immemorial antiquity, and they made an all-powerful appeal to the animal instincts in human nature. We can realize now as never before the social and religious task which confronted the prophets. That Israel was by prophetic teaching purged of this cult is due to the power of God!

7. **High Place at Petra.**—One of the most interesting high places is cut out of the solid rock at Petra. Petra may possibly be the Sela of 2 Kings 14:7, since Sela means "crag" or "rock," in Hebrew, and Petra has the same meaning in Greek. The identity of Petra with Sela is not, however, certain. Petra lies in the southeastern part of ancient Edom, and was, before the end of the fourth century B.C., occupied by the Nabathæans, a Semitic tribe. These Nabathæans established a kingdom which continued until 106 A.D. One of its kings, Haretat IV, is called Aretas in 2 Corinthians 11:32.[16] When the Roman Emperor Trajan overthrew this kingdom, he organized its territory into the Province of Arabia, and the beautiful buildings, the remains of which make Petra such an interesting ruin today, date mostly from the Roman period of its history. During the Nabathæan period of Petra they constructed high places, which are high places indeed, since they are perched on ledges of rock above the ancient town. The largest of these high places is still in an excellent state of preservation. It is a little to the north of the citadel, on a ledge which rises about 700 feet above the town. The ledge is 520 feet long by 90 feet wide; it runs nearly north and south with a slight inclination to the east.[17] The principal features of this ancient place of worship are an altar on the west side of the ledge, a platform immediately south of this, a large sunken area directly in front of the altar, and a little to the south of this area a vat or laver.

This high place is approached by a flight of steps cut in the solid rock. (See Fig. 215.) The main area, which corresponds to the enclosure of the high place at Tell es-Safi, is 47 feet 4 inches long, 24 feet 4 inches wide, and 15 to 18 inches deep, though this depth is not uniform. In some parts it falls to 10 inches. About midway of the length of this area and 5 feet from its west side, there is a rock platform 5 feet in length, 2 feet 7½ inches wide, and

16 See Part II, ch. XXX, § 5.
17 For descriptions of this high place, see the article by its discoverer, George L. Robinson, in the *Biblical World*, XVII, 6–16; by S. I. Curtis in the *Quarterly Statement of the Palestine Exploration Fund*, October, 1900, pp. 350–355; Savignac in *Révue biblique*, 1903, 280–284; Libby and Hoskins, *The Jordan Valley and Petra*, New York, 1905; II, 172 ff.; Brünnow and Domaszewski, *Provincia Arabia*, Vol. I, Strassburg. 1904, 239–245; Dalman, *Petra*, Leipzig, 1908, 56–58.

4 inches high. It has been suggested that this platform was intended for the offerer of a victim to stand upon, in order that he might be distinguished from other worshipers who were crowding the area. Another possible view is that the sacred "pillars" stood upon this platform. No pillars were found in connection with it. Probably such pillars were not cut out of the solid rock, but were, like the sacred stone of Gezer, brought from elsewhere. The arrangement of other high places would indicate that they stood on or near this platform. As this high place was not buried, but exposed on the mountaintop, such pillars have in the course of the ages disappeared. The altar is separated from the adjoining rock by a passageway which was cut on its north, south, and west sides. It is of the same height as the adjoining rock. On the east the ledge has been cut down to the level of the foot of the altar. The altar is 9 feet 1 inch in length from north to south, and 6 feet 2 inches wide. It is 3 feet high at its highest point. On the top of the altar is a hollow pan, perhaps to receive the fire. This is 3 feet 8 inches long, 1 foot 2 inches wide, and 3½ inches deep. Ascent to the altar was made by a flight of steps leading up to its top on the east side. The top step is wider than the others and forms a platform on which the officiating priest might stand. (See Fig. 217.)

Just south of the altar and separated from it by the passageway was the place where the victims were slain. This has been called the round altar. (See Fig. 218.) This consists of a platform 16 feet 6 inches long from east to west, 11 feet 9 inches wide. It is approached by a flight of steps. Near its center are two circular and concentric pans, the larger 3 feet 8 inches in diameter, with a depth of 3 inches; the smaller 1 foot 5 inches in diameter, with a depth of 2 inches. From this inner basin a conduit 3 feet 2 inches long, 2 inches wide, and 3 inches deep conducted the blood to the edge of the platform. This platform was undoubtedly intended for the place of slaughter. The Samaritans, when they assemble on Mount Gerizim for the celebration of the Passover, still dig a round hole in the turf, over which to slay the victim. This hole is about 18 inches in diameter, and 10 inches deep. From it a conduit is dug, through which the blood flows off to be absorbed by the earth.[18]

18 See the writer's *A Year's Wandering in Bible Lands*, Philadelphia, 1904, pp. 193, 194.

The supposed laver at Petra is to the south of the area of the high place. It is 9 feet 9 inches in length, and 8 feet 6 inches in width. It is now partially filled with earth and has above the earth an average depth of 3 feet.

The remains of four other supposed high places have been found at Petra, but lack of space forbids their description here.[19] The pillars supposed to have been connected with one of them are shown in Figure 219.

8. The Five Temples of Beth-shan.—As noted above (ch. IV, § 13), the temples discovered at Beth-shan are most instructive.[20] The oldest one as yet explored was built in the time of Thothmes III (1480–1447 B.C.), and apparently represents a transition from the old Canaanite "high place" to an open temple. Inscriptions found in the course of the excavation show that the name of the god worshiped here was Mekal. Perhaps Mekal was originally a serpent deity; at least a great number of representations of serpents found suggests that the temple was the center of a serpent cult. The temple of the time of Thothmes III (Fig. 326.) was partly open and, when intact, partly covered. It consisted of the following parts:

(1) A great courtyard where there were three tables apparently for cutting up carcasses, a pole for hanging them up (?), and a flight of steps leading to the corridor (A–B). (2) The inner sanctuary, with two altars, one for meat offerings and the other for libations and other offerings. (3) The sacrificial altar room, in which was an altar with channels in which the blood could run away. Near the altar were found the horns of a bull that had been slain there, together with the sacrificial dagger by which he had been killed. (4) A room with fireplace for cooking sacrifices. When the fireplace was uncovered, ashes still remained in it. (5) A well 42 feet deep for supplying water to the temple. (6) A large stepped altar. (7) The *massebah,* or "pillar." (8) In a room north of the inner sanctuary a socket was found in which the wooden "asherah" may have been erected. While it is not possible to determine the exact use to which all the rooms or courts were put, the features enumerated seem fairly well made out. The altars

19 Those interested in them will find them described in Brünnow and Domaszewski's *Provincia Arabia,* I, 246 ff, also in Dalman's *Petra,* 142, 225, 272, etc. For a circular high place at Petra discovered in 1929 and cleared at the end of 1934, see Albright in the *Bulletin* of the American Schools of Oriental Research, No. 57 (Feb., 1935), 18–26.

20 Cf. Alan Rowe in the *Museum Journal,* March, 1929, pp. 37–88 and "New Light on the Evolution of Canaanite Temples as Exemplified by Restorations of the Sanctuaries Found at Beth-shan," by Alan Rowe and Pere L. H. Vincent, in the *Quarterly Statement* of the Palestine Exploration Fund, January, 1931, pp. 12–21.

appear to have been roofed over, but other parts of the temple, such as the courts and the "pillar," were probably open to the sky.

After the death of Thothmes III, fifty or more years passed before the temple was reconstructed. Political upheavals had wrought havoc in the structure before it was rebuilt by Amenophis III (1411–1375 B.C.). When it was rebuilt, the portion containing the two altars appears to have been roofed over, as shown in the reconstruction in Figure 327. The plan of the building was similar to that afterward adopted at El-Amarna, by Egypt's monotheistic king, Amenophis IV, in his temples of Aten. There was (1) an outer door leading (2) into a small open court, from which a door led (3) into a court which contained an altar. Over the altar was a roof supported by two pillars the bases of which were found. Further back under the roof was another altar with a sloping top. The floor of this shrine was colored a bright blue. (5) From this shrine another door led into a court, or room, the purpose of which is not clear. Possibly it was used for storage. (6) For light and air there were openings in the roof. Beneath the floor and walls of this temple many seals of Amenophis III were found as well as a Hittite bronze battleaxe, the best of its kind ever discovered.

From the accession of Amenophis III to that of Seti I (1314–1292 B.C.) was almost a century. During this period all Palestine had been lost to Egypt. The confusion of this time is represented in the tablets from El-Amarna, some of which are translated in Part II, Chapter XVII. When Seti I reconquered Palestine, he rebuilt the temple of Mekal above the ruins of the temple of Amenophis III. In the temple itself he followed the plan of his predecessor; the plan of this courtyard, however, was different. (See Fig. 327.)

On the death of Seti I Palestine revolted, and Ramses II (1292–1225 B.C.) found it necessary to reconquer it. When that had been accomplished, he erected two temples in the sacred area of Mekal. The axes of the structures of his predecessors had been from north to south; those of Ramses were from east to west. Restorations of these temples are shown in Figures 326–328. In the drawings, parts of the roofs have been removed in order to show the interior arrangement. In these structures the influence of Egyptian architecture is more apparent than in those of the predecessors of Ramses.

9. An Altar of Incense.—At Taanach, Sellin discovered a remarkable incense altar of terra-cotta, 3 feet in height, and 18 inches in diameter at the base, adorned with protruding animal heads, which remind one of shortened gargoyles. On one side of it was the figure of a palm tree, with two ibexes descending a mountain. Part of an Ashtoreth figure and fragments of another altar were found near. Sellin thought that the building that contained these was a private house; and, if so, we have in these objects some of the implements of private worship employed by Israelites. (See Fig. 210.)

10. The Temple to Augustus at Samaria.—The excavations at Samaria [21] have brought to light the foundation of the temple erected by Herod the Great in honor of Augustus.[22] This was a temple of a very different type. It was patterned on Græco-Roman models and everything was done to make it architecturally impressive. A massive stairway led up to a large platform surrounded by large pillars. This formed the portico. Back of this stretched the walls of the temple. As this temple is not of particular interest to the student of the Bible, the reader is referred for details to the description of the excavators in the volume cited in note 21. At the foot of the stairway leading up to the temple was found a large altar, and near this a fallen statue of Augustus. For outlines of the temple, see Figures 216 and 221.

These ancient places of worship which archæology has brought to light are eloquent witnesses to the pathetic way the men of Palestine "felt after God, if haply they might find Him" (See Acts 17:27.), and the pathos is not lessened by the fact that they thus continued to grope, even after the clearer light was shining about them.

21 See George Andrew Reisner, Clarence Stanley Fisher, and David Gordon Lyon, *Harvard Excavations at Samaria*, 1908–10, Cambridge, Mass., 1924.
22 See Josephus, *Antiquities of the Jews*, XV, vii, 5, and *Wars of the Jews*, I, xxi, 2.

CHAPTER XII

THE TOMBS OF PALESTINE

BURNING THE DEAD. CAVE BURIALS. CISTERN BURIALS. BURIAL UNDER MENHIRS. EARTH-GRAVES. ROCK-HEWN SHAFT TOMBS. DOORWAY TOMBS. TOMBS WITH A ROLLING-STONE.

1. Burning the Dead.—As noted in a previous chapter [1] the earliest inhabitants of Gezer burned their dead. The later peoples of Palestine did not follow this custom, but buried theirs. At Gezer the caves that had formed the dwellings of the first inhabitants were put by the Semites to various uses. Sometimes they, too, lived in them; sometimes they made cisterns of them; and sometimes they utilized them as places of burial for their dead.

2. Cave Burials.—A cave that became a tomb in later times was the one that had been the crematorium of the pre-Semitic inhabitants.[2] All over the floor of the cave above the burned bones was another stratum of bones that had never been burned. These were scattered over the floor of the cave, and, although they had been much disturbed by rats, it appeared that they belonged to that early type of burial in which the body is placed on its side with the knees drawn up toward the chin. These bodies had apparently been deposited in all parts of the cave. Ranged around the sides of the cave was a series of enclosures marked off from the floor by lines of stones. In these, portions of various skeletons were found. These enclosures seem to have been reservations made for persons of distinction. For a time, therefore, the cave seems to have been used as a general place of burial. In some of the other caves of Gezer evidence was found that they had been used as tombs.[3] Beautiful pottery and alabaster vessels were found with the bones. Wine and possibly food for the dead had been placed in these. Underneath the pottery in one cave a considerable number of scarabs were found, some of them mounted in gold. This must have been, accordingly, the burial place of persons of

1 See Chapter V, p. 144.
2 See Macalister, *The Excavation of Gezer,* I, 286.
3 *Ibid.,* p. 122 f.

comparative wealth. Similar cave burials were found by Mackenzie at Beth-Shemesh.[4]

Such cave burials as these at once recall Abraham's purchase of the cave of Machpelah as recorded in Genesis 23. The kind of burial presupposed in that chapter is just that found at Gezer. The mouth of the cave could be closed up and opened at will for later burials. (See Gen. 50:13.)

The custom of placing food or drink or both in the sepulcher was all but universal in Palestine. It is silent testimony to a faith in a kind of after-life. That that life as they conceived it was of a shadowy and an unsatisfactory nature is shown by the references to it in Isaiah 14:9–11 and Ezekiel 32:22–32.[5] Nevertheless, these evidences that the mourners who stood by every ancient tomb provided food for their loved ones to eat in the after-life is eloquent testimony to the fact that even in that age the loving heart found it impossible to believe that the life of its dear ones had been altogether terminated.

3. Cistern Burials.—Another burial at Gezer that must have been connected with some unusual circumstance led to the deposit of fifteen bodies in a cistern,[6] and a number of spear heads were found with them. The skeletons were all males except one, which was that of a girl about sixteen years old, whose spine had been severed and only the upper part of the skeleton deposited in the cistern; (see Fig. 229). The cistern is too deep to favor the supposition that the bodies had been deposited at successive times. Macalister hazards the conjecture that the men died of plague and that the girl was offered as a sacrifice to propitiate the deity. A plague, however, would have attacked women as well as men. Perhaps the men were slain in defending Gezer from the attack of an enemy that had succeeded in severing the body of the girl. The real cause of the tragedy is, however, unknown to us.

4. Burial under Menhirs.—A very old form of burial, still practised by the half-nomadic tribes east of the Jordan, is to place the dead in the earth within one of the prehistoric *gilgals* or menhirs. How old this form of burial is, it is impossible to tell. It is assumed by some writers that it was practised by the neolithic people who erected these monuments, and who are believed by such writers to have been ancestor worshipers. If, however, these neolithic men were akin to the neolithic men of Gezer, they burned

4 Palestine Exploration Fund's *Annual*, II, 42 ff.
5 For a Babylonian parallel, see Part II, p. 530 ff.
6 See Macalister, *The Excavation of Gezer*, II, 429 f.

their dead. Another explanation is, accordingly, more probable. All through the history of Palestine the sanctity of certain spots has persisted. A place once considered as holy, if not so regarded by the next wave of conquerors, nevertheless often has enough sanctity clinging to it to make it taboo. No thief will disturb objects left within its precincts, lest the spirit of the place bring disaster upon him. It seems probable that the wandering tribes on the border of the Arabian Desert have utilized the sacred places of these prehistoric men for the burial of their dead, in order that the fear of violating the taboo pertaining to these places may secure the bodies from disturbance. Whatever the reason may be, they still bury their dead in such precincts and place their tribal *wasms* or marks on such stones.[7]

5. Earth-graves.—The simplest form of burial was to place the body in the ground without accessory of any kind. In the course of the excavation of Gezer a few burials of this sort came to light.[8] The skeleton was in these cases stretched out; sometimes it was lying on its back; sometimes on its side. As these bodies were buried without accessories, so contrary to the custom of the Palestinians who placed food or drink by the dead, the excavator thought that they were probably the graves of murdered persons, who had been hastily concealed in the earth.

Another form of burial, when the interment occurred within a city, is illustrated by the five "Philistine" graves found at Gezer.[9] These graves were excavations in the earth, lined with cement, and, after the interment, covered with four or five massive stones and earth; (Fig. 226). In these graves the usual deposits of food and drink had been made in beautiful bronze and silver vessels, which show kinship to the art of Cyprus; (see Fig. 137). They are probably, therefore, Philistine.

6. Rock-hewn Shaft Tombs.—A form of tomb of which many examples are to be found in all parts of Palestine is the rock-hewn tomb. The limestone of the country is easily cut, and lends itself readily to the construction of this kind of burial place. Such tombs are of two kinds—"shaft" tombs and "doorway" tombs.

The structure of a shaft tomb is as follows: [10] The tomb chamber or chambers are cut in the rock and are approached by a perpendicular rock-hewn shaft, which is usually rectangular. This shaft is closed at the bottom with slabs and then the shaft is filled with

7 See *Biblical World*, Vol. XXIV, p. 177.
8 See Macalister, *The Excavation of Gezer*, I, 288 f.
9 *Ibid.*, 289 ff.
10 See Bliss and Macalister, *Excavations in Palestine*, 1898-1900, p. 9 ff.

earth. Such tombs are usually constructed in ledges covered over with soil, so that, when the hole leading to the rock-cut shaft is filled, the tomb is effectually concealed. Such tombs are very numerous all the way from pre-Israelitish times to the Greek period. For a plan of one, see Figure 228.

7. **Doorway Tombs.**—The "doorway" tombs are sometimes cut in a ledge that is altogether under ground. In that case a flight of steps is excavated leading down to the door; (Fig. 232). Often the tomb is cut in a ledge on the slope of a hill, so that the doorway is approached from the level of the ground; (see Fig. 227). Doors were, no doubt, fitted into the doorways. The places cut in the rock for the latches or bars of such doors are sometimes still visible. These tombs consisted sometimes of one room, sometimes of several. Sometimes the bodies were laid on the floor of the tomb; sometimes elevated benches or shelves were cut in the rock on which bodies might be placed. Quite as often shafts or niches were cut into the rock, into which a body or a sarcophagus could be shoved endwise. Such a shaft is called technically, a *kôk*, in the plural, *kôkim*. For examples of them, see Figures 233, 237. The date at which this kind of tomb was introduced has not been satisfactorily determined.

Sometimes numerous small tombs, each one resembling somewhat a *kôk*, were cut in a hillside. Archæologists call such a group of tombs a "columbarium" (see Fig. 230).

In the Hellenistic and Roman periods efforts were made to give adornment to such tombs. The so-called "Tombs of the Judges" [11] near Jerusalem, of which the writer was the first to make a scientific examination, is a good example of this kind of tomb [12] (see Fig. 231). This tomb consisted of three rooms in its upper level and three in its lower level (see Fig. 235). The ledges and *kôkim* in it made provision for seventy bodies, and a rough chamber opening out of room D was evidently used for the deposit of the bones of those who had been long dead, when a niche or *kôk* was needed for the reception of another body. Sometimes the pillars of a porch were carved out of the solid rock. A number of such tombs are to be found near Jerusalem. There is one in the Kidron Valley near Gethsemane, cut wholly out of the rock and finished to a spire at the top. This is the so-called "Absalom's pillar."

In the time of Christ the tombs of Israel's heroes were adorned

[11] So-called because of a tradition that the members of the Sanhedrin were buried there. The tradition probably arose because the *kokim* and shelves make provision for seventy bodies.

[12] See *Journal of Biblical Literature*, XXII, 1903, p. 164 ff.

and venerated. Jesus alludes to this in Luke 11:47, 48. Elisha must have been buried in a doorway tomb, into which by opening the door the body of a man could be easily thrown. (See 2 Kings 13:20, 21.) It was, no doubt, the memory of such narratives as this that led to the reverence paid to the tombs of the prophets in the time of Christ.

Another tomb at Jerusalem, called the "Tombs of the Kings," has a large open court cut down into the rock, from the different sides of which entrances lead to the other tomb chambers. This tomb was built for Queen Helena of Adiabene, the ancient Assyria, who, in the first century A.D. was converted to Judaism and removed to Jerusalem. She died and was buried there.[13]

Sometimes in the Seleucid period the interior of the tombs was also made very ornate. Such were the tombs, discovered in 1902,[14] of some wealthy Greek-speaking citizens of Marissa. A plan of one of them is shown in Figure 234, and examples of its inner ornamentation in Figure 236. These tombs were also adorned with pictures of vases, trees, animals, etc. (see Fig. 239). The figures, as well as the interior generally, were decorated with red, yellow, and brown paints. One of them was that of Apollophanes, chief of the Sidonians at Marissa. Over the different niches in the tombs the names of the persons buried were inscribed in Greek letters.

Rock-cut tombs, whether large or small, were regarded as important possessions, and the people who might be buried in them were frequently carefully specified by their builders. An example of this may be found in Part II of the present work, p. 558.

8. Tombs with a Rolling-stone.—One other type of tomb must be noticed even in this hasty sketch. To close a "doorway" tomb securely must always have been a matter of difficulty in Palestine. It was not easy with the kind of locks they had to keep intruders out of tombs. This led to the cutting of a large groove by the side of the doorway into which a rolling-stone was fitted. When it was desired to open the tomb, the stone could be rolled back. The stones were too heavy to be easily disturbed. It was in a new tomb of this type that the body of Jesus was laid, and it was such a stone that the women found rolled away on the resurrection morning. (See Matt. 28:2; Mark 16:3, 4; Luke 24:2; John 20:1, and Fig. 238.)

13 See Josephus, *Antiquities of the Jews*, XX, ii, 1; iv, 3.
14 See Peters and Thiersch, *Painted Tombs at Marissa*, London, 1905.

CHAPTER XIII

JERUSALEM [1]

SITUATION. GIHON. CAVES NEAR IT. THE TIME OF MELCHIZEDEK. THE EL-AMARNA PERIOD. JEBUSITE JERUSALEM. THE CITY OF DAVID: Millo. David's reign. SOLOMON'S JERUSALEM: Site of Solomon's buildings; Solomon's temple; Solomon's palace. FROM SOLOMON TO HEZEKIAH. HEZEKIAH. FROM HEZEKIAH TO THE EXILE. THE DESTRUCTION OF 586 B.C. THE SECOND TEMPLE. NEHEMIAH AND THE WALLS. LATE PERSIAN AND EARLY GREEK PERIODS. IN THE TIME OF THE MACCABEES. ASMONÆAN JERUSALEM. HEROD THE GREAT: Herod's palace; Herod's theater; Herod's temple. THE POOL OF BETHESDA. GETHSEMANE. CALVARY. AGRIPPA I AND THE THIRD WALL.

1. Situation.—Since 1867 excavations have been made at Jerusalem from time to time. The most important of these were mentioned in Chapter IV. An attempt will be made here to set before the reader the growth and development of Jerusalem from period to period, as that growth is now understood by foremost scholars. Our knowledge of the situation and form of the city in the different periods is based partly on formal excavations, partly on remains that have been accidentally found, and partly on a study of the references to Jerusalem in the Bible and other ancient writings. These references are interpreted in the light of the topography and of the archæological remains.

Jerusalem is situated on the central ridge of Palestine, where the ridge broadens out to a small plateau. The plateau at this point is approximately 2,500 feet above the level of the Mediterranean Sea. In a narrower sense the site of the city is two rocky promontories which run south from the plateau with the valley El-Wad (in Roman times the Tyropœon) between them. On the north these promontories merge into the plateau, but on the east, south, and west the valleys of Hinnom and the Kidron sharply separate them from the surrounding land. The steep sides of these valleys made fortification easy in ancient times. The highest point of the western hill is about 400 feet higher than the bottom of the Kidron valley, which in ancient times was 20 to 40 feet deeper

---

1 All who can do so should read George Adam Smith's *Jerusalem from the Earliest Times to A.D. 70*, New York, 1908, and Hughes Vincent's *Jerusalem*, Paris, 1912. Or, if this is not possible, L. B. Paton's *Jerusalem in Bible Times*, Chicago, 1905.

than now (see Fig. 240). Indeed, the position was almost impregnable. Only on the north was the city vulnerable.

West of the city hills gently rise to a slight elevation and shut out the view. The easternmost of the two promontories is lower than the western, which in its turn slopes to the east. Just south of the Mount of Olives, to the east of Jerusalem, there is a rift in the hills through which the distant mountains of Moab can be seen. From elevated buildings in the city the Dead Sea is also visible. The slope of the hills of Jerusalem and her broader outlook to the eastward are significant of the influences that moulded her earlier history. During the centuries that Israel was an independent nation the Philistine plain was nearly always in the hands of a hostile people. Jerusalem was thus cut off from influences that might otherwise have reached her from across the Mediterranean, and was shut up to influences that reached her through kindred tribes and nations to the east. Thus in intellectual kinship, as well as in physical outlook, the gaze of Jerusalem was directed toward the Orient.

All Palestinian cities of importance were situated near perpetual springs. There are at Jerusalem but two unfailing sources of water —the Ain Sitti Miriam (the ancient Gihon) and the Bir Eyyub (Biblical En-rogel). These are both in the Kidron valley, the former just under the brow of the eastern hill some 400 yards from the southern point of the hill, the latter at the point where the valley of Hinnom and the Kidron unite. Of these two sources of supply, the Gihon is pre-eminently fitted to attract an early settlement. It is almost under the hill, whereas the other is out in the midst of the open valley. Gihon, too, is at the base of a hill that can be defended easily on three sides, whereas a town built on a hillside above En-rogel, as the modern Silwan is, could be easily attacked from above. These conditions determined the situation of the earliest settlement, which was near Gihon.

2. Gihon.—The Parker expedition of 1909–1911 revealed by its excavations the fact that the source of the spring of Gihon is a great crack in the rock in the bottom of the valley far below the present apparent source.[2] This crack is about 16 feet long, is of great depth, and runs east and west. The western end of it just enters the mouth of the cave where the apparent source is today, but the eastern end passes out into the bed of the valley. All the

2 See Dr. Masterman in the *Biblical World*, Vol. XXXIX, p. 295 f.

water would discharge into the valley but for a wall at the eastern
end of the rift, built in very ancient times, which confines the water
and compels it to flow into the cave. This wall was constructed by
some of the earliest inhabitants of the place. The spring thus
produced is intermittent. Its flow is not ceaseless. The water
breaks from the hole in the rainy season, three to five times a
day; in the summer but twice a day; and after the failure of the
spring rains, less than once a day. This fact indicates that the
waters collect in some underground cavern from which they are
drained by a siphon-like tunnel. The "troubling" of the Pool of
Bethesda (John 5:4) is thought by some scholars to have been due
to the action of such a siphon-like spring.

3. Caves Near It.—About this spring the Parker expedition
found large caves and rooms excavated in the rock, and indications
that these had once been inhabited. A great deal of pre-Israelite
pottery was also found around the spring. These indications seem
to show that the site was inhabited for at least a thousand years
before David, and perhaps for two thousand. One thinks, too, of
the sacred cave and the stone altar on the next peak of the eastern
ridge to the north, where the temple afterward stood, and wonders
whether it may not have been the sanctuary of this early race. A
definite answer cannot be given to this question. One can only
recognize that it may possibly be true.

4. The Time of Melchizedek.—Macalister and Duncan, excavating on Ophel, discovered [3] north of Jebusite Jerusalem a hitherto
unsuspected valley. It ran eastward from the Tyropœon Valley
and formed a natural defense along about half of the city's northern
exposure. The excavators named it Zedek, for the deity whose
name occurs in Adonizedek (Josh. 10:1, 3) and Melchizedek (Gen.
14:18 ff.). As this valley did not extend across the whole northern
front of the city, it had been extended eastward by a rock-cut
trench ten or twelve feet in breadth, and to an average depth of
eight feet. This valley and trench, with the wall which rose above
it, formed at that time the defense of the northern part of the city.
In this rock-cut trench two causeways, each raised about two feet
above the floor of the trench, and each about two feet broad, were
left to facilitate ingress and egress to and from the city. Rude
rock-cut steps led down to them at each end. These steps had
been destroyed at the southern end, or that nearest the city. They
were probably broken as a means of defense during some siege

3 See *Annual* of the Palestine Exploration Fund, Vol. IV, p. 31 ff.

earlier than any recorded history. The trench was filled with potsherds from the period 2000–1600 B.C.—a fact that it had been disused some six hundred years before the time of David. At the southern end of the eastern causeway the excavators found what they believe to have been the earliest altar in Jerusalem. The rock had been so cut in making the stairway that a rounding top was left that could easily serve as an altar. It was surrounded by cup marks such as in Palestine usually appear about altars and sacred stones, and a number of bones of domestic animals were found near it. The presence of an altar at the city gate suggests that a stranger entering the city offered a sacrifice to the god of the place.

The excavators recall that Abraham gave a tenth of his spoil to Melchizedek (Gen. 14 : 20.), and suppose that he gave it as a sacrifice. The presence of the altar at this point lends some plausibility to the theory. At all events, the potsherds place the date of the period during which the trench and altar were used, at the very period in which the Bible places Abraham and Melchizedek. It may be to this altar rather than to the sacred stone now under the "Dome of the Rock" (the Mosque of Omar), farther up the hill, that the story of the attempted sacrifice of Isaac (Gen. 22.) should be attached. The writer, however, regards this as most doubtful.

5. The El-Amarna Period.—The next knowledge we have of Jerusalem comes from the letters of Ebed-Hepa, which were written to Amenophis IV, of Egypt, between 1375 and 1357 B.C. At that time it was also a walled city, for Ebed-Hepa speaks of "throwing it open." [4]

The fortified city of Ebed-Hepa was, no doubt, identical with the later Jebusite city. It was situated on the eastern hill just above the spring of Gihon. Probably in the period just before this time it had, like Gezer, been surrounded by a massive wall.[5]

Weil in his excavation in 1913–14 found on the eastern hill remains of a wall with a sloping glacis similar to that belonging to the earliest period of Megiddo.[6] This not only confirms our inference that Jerusalem was a walled city in the time of Ebed-Hepa, but indicates that its wall had been built at a much earlier time. It was also in the fourteenth century B.C. the capital of a

4 See Part II, Chapter XVII, Letter V, and the writer's note in the *Biblical World*, XXII, p. 11, n. 5.
5 See *Biblical World*, XXXIX, 306.
6 See Weil, La Cité de David, Paris, 1920, p. 110.

considerable kingdom which Ebed-Hepa ruled as a vassal of the king of Egypt. This kingdom extended as far west as Beth-Shemesh and Keilah (1 Sam. 23:1), including, perhaps, Gezer. Aijalon seems to have been included in it on the north, and Carmel in Judah (1 Sam. 25:2) on the south.

When the letters of Ebed-Hepa were written, his kingdom was being attacked and apparently overcome by the Habiri, a people who may have been the first wave of the Hebrew conquest.[6a] The letters of Ebed-Hepa cease without telling us whether or not the Habiri captured his city. If they did and they were really Hebrews, they did not hold it long, for, when the Biblical records lift the veil that hides so much of the past, Jerusalem was in the hands of the Jebusites. (See Josh. 15:63; Judges 1:21.)

6. Jebusite Jerusalem.—The Jebusites held it all through the period of the Judges (Judges 19:10, 11). Israel did not capture it until the reign of David. (See 2 Sam. 5:6–8.) At some earlier period of the history of Jerusalem an underground rock-cut passage similar to the one at Gezer [7] had been made, so as to permit the inhabitants in case of siege to descend to the spring for water without going outside the walls; (see Fig. 241). The natural slope of the hill had been reinforced at this point by the escarpment of the rock, and the Jebusites felt so secure that they taunted the Hebrews from the top of the walls. Joab, however, discovered the way to this underground passage through the cave back of the spring, Gihon, and, leading a band of men up through it, appeared suddenly within the city, taking the Jebusites by surprise, and captured it.

7. The City of David.—David then took up his residence at Jerusalem, thus making it the capital of the kingdom of Israel. Thus the city of the Jebusites, situated on the eastern hill, which was called Zion, became the "city of David."

A few modern writers still insist that the "city of David" was on the western hill, which since 333 A.D. has been called Zion. This, as most scholars have seen, is an impossible view. Solomon built a palace for Pharaoh's daughter near his own on the temple hill, and, when she moved into it, she went *up* out of the city of David (1 Kings 9:24). As the western hill is higher than the eastern, she must have gone from a point on the eastern hill lower than the temple. When the temple was completed, Solomon brought the ark *up* from the city of David to the holy of holies in the new

6a See Part II, Chapter XVII.
7 See Chapter VI, § 8.

temple (2 Chron. 5:2). Scripture thus confirms the inferences from the pottery and the water supply, that the "city of David" was on the eastern hill, and that that hill was Zion. It was a small town, since the space it could occupy was not more than thirteen acres, and may have been less.

(1) *Millo.*—After occupying his new capital David "built round about from Millo and inward" (2 Sam. 5:9). What was Millo? This is a great puzzle, and there are many varying opinions about it. The word literally means a "filling," and is employed in Assyrian for the building up of a terrace on which a building may be erected. It may have been a "filling" on the line of the valley that separated the hill of the citadel of David from Moriah or the temple hill. It would seem to have been on the edge of the city, since David built from there "inward." Some have supposed it to be a fortress, and the Septuagint translated it by "akra," which means "citadel." Some have thought of it as a fort, others as a solid tower. If on the line of the valley mentioned, it may have been at the northeast corner, or at the northwest corner of the town. Some have supposed that it was at the southern end of the eastern hill in order to protect a pool there. Just below the southern end of the eastern hill in the valley of the Kidron lay the "King's Gardens," and just across the valley, the village of Siloah. In 2 Kings 12:20 it is said that Joash was killed in Millo, leading down to Silla. We know of no Silla. Is it a corruption of the Hebrew word for "shade" or is it a corruption of Siloah? In the former case the reference might be to the King's Gardens, in the latter to the village of Siloah. Either of these suppositions would favor a site for Millo at the south end of the hill, but the words "leading down to Silla" may have had quite a different origin and meaning.[8]

Professor Macalister now believes that, in the tower above and a little to the north of Gihon, he has discovered Millo.

(2) *David's Reign.*—As David's reign advanced and his success in war compelled neighboring nations to pay tribute, probably the population of Jerusalem increased. Such an increase would naturally lead to the erection of houses outside the walls, as it has in recent times. It is altogether probable that a settlement on the western hill was thus begun in the reign of David. There is no hint, however, that he took any steps to enclose such a settlement within a wall. The phrase "the way of the gate" in 2 Samuel 15:2

8 Some scholars think the words are a distorted repetition of "in Millo," which was accidentally repeated by a scribe.

implies that there was still but one gate in the walls. This is in striking contrast to the number of gates in later times. The only record that we have of further action on David's part that affected the future growth of Jerusalem refers to the way in which he took over the rock on Mount Moriah and the sacred cave under it and made a sanctuary to Jehovah. (See 2 Sam. 24.) This action, at a later time, determined the site of the temple.

8. Solomon's Jerusalem.—David left Jerusalem a military fortress; Solomon transformed it into a city with imposing buildings. This creation of a more imposing city was in accord with the general character of Solomon's reign. He established a large harem, made marriage alliances with many neighboring kings, maintained such an establishment that it was necessary to make a regular levy on a different portion of the country each month for supplies, and endeavored to make his capital as splendid as the capital of a rich commercial Phœnician monarch. Such a policy necessitated, probably, the enlargement of Jerusalem. David, who began life as a shepherd-boy, was content to live the simple life to the end; Solomon, born to the purple, desired to surround himself with a pomp befitting his rank. The Biblical writers were more interested in the construction of the temple and of Solomon's palace than in any other phase of his work, but they have left us some hints of his activities in other directions.

They tell us that he "built Millo and the wall of Jerusalem" (1 Kings 9:15), and he "built the wall of Jerusalem round about" (1 Kings 3:1), and that he "built Millo and repaired the breach in the city of David, his father" (1 Kings 11:27). Evidently Millo had fallen into disrepair since David rebuilt it, and the walls of the city of David on the eastern hill were also in need of repairs. These repairs he made, but did he go further? It is intrinsically probable that he did. The king who fortified Hazor in Naphtali, Megiddo, Gezer, Beth-horon, Baalath, and Tamar would hardly leave a large suburb of his capital on the western hill unfortified. The statement that he "built the wall of Jerusalem round about," while it does not clearly state that he did more than fortify the "city of David" on Zion, seems to imply that he did. This view is strengthened by Bliss's discovery on the western hill of some walls that connected once with a great fortress at the southwest corner of the western hill, which he believed to be the work of Solomon.

The site of this fortress is now occupied by "Bishop Gobat's School," an English foundation for the education of native boys. When the school was rebuilt in 1874 Mr. Henry Maudsley examined the surface of the rock, which is escarped, or cut perpendicularly, for about 100 feet to the southeast of the school and 43 feet north of it. The scarp is about 40 feet high at the highest point; (Fig. 242). The school is built on a large projection of the scarp 45 feet square and 20 feet high. The surface of the rock under the school bears unmistakable signs that there was once an ancient tower there. To the eastward of this Bliss discovered the foundations of an ancient tower. Beyond this to the east there was a deep rock-cut ditch. The tower on its northeast corner fitted into another rock-scarp which ran northward into land on which they could not excavate.[9] The deep rock-cut ditch or moat at the east of the scarp suggests that at the period of the Latin kingdom of Jerusalem, 1099–1188 A.D., this fortress formed the fortification of the southwest corner of the city, from which the wall ran off sharply in a direction a little east of north. This view is confirmed by the discovery which Bliss made of a wall, apparently built by the Crusaders, that ran in a northeasterly direction by an irregular course along the high part of the western hill toward the temple area. As this wall rested on remains of the Roman time it cannot well have belonged to a time earlier than the crusading period. May not, then, Maudsley's scarp itself have been cut by the Crusaders who were most energetic and masterly builders? This seems hardly probable, for Josephus, in describing the course of the wall on the west side of the western hill, says that beginning at Herod's palace (the modern Turkish fortress) the wall ran southward through a place called "Bethso."[10] Bethso is a corruption of Beth-zur, which means rock-fortress—an apt description of the tower on Maudsley's scarp. As Josephus makes no mention of the construction of a fortress at this point by Herod, it was probably built at an earlier period. The writer holds with Bliss that it is probable that the original fortress on the site of Bishop Gobat's School was constructed by Solomon and that he enclosed the top of the western hill with a wall. Whether that wall simply enclosed the top of the hill and followed something of the same course as the wall of the Crusaders mentioned above (so Bliss thinks), or whether it ran down the eastern slope of the west-

9 Bliss and Dickie. *Excavations at Jerusalem*, 1894–1897, *passim*, and p. 319 ff.
10 For "Bethso," see Josephus, *Wars of the Jews*, V, iv, 2.

ern hill to the southern point of the "city of David," it is impossible now to determine.

The view that Solomon extended the city to the western hill cannot be proved, since there is no definite reference in the Bible to the western hill in the time of Solomon, and there is no inscription on the masonry found definitely to connect it with him. In consideration of all the conditions it seems probable that Solomon enclosed a part of the western hill. If so, the wall built by Solomon on the north side of the western hill was probably on the line of what Josephus called the "first wall." This wall was rebuilt from time to time. The débris of a part of it seems still to be in place at the east end of "David Street" in modern Jerusalem. A short street, high above the surrounding levels, now runs on the top of this débris.[11]

(1) *Site of Solomon's Buildings.*—Concerning the building of Solomon's palace and the temple there can be no doubt, for the Bible contains accounts of the construction of these. Their general location is also well known. They were across the little valley which separated the part of Zion called Ophel (where the city of David was situated) from the part sometimes called Moriah.[12] This hill-top included the threshing-floor of Araunah, the Jebusite (2 Sam. 24), and Solomon now enclosed this with a wall. Sir Charles Warren believed that he found portions of this wall at the southeast angle of the ancient temple area, 80 feet below the present surface of the ground. During his excavations in the years 1867–1870 he sunk at this point a shaft to the native rock, from the bottom of which a tunnel was carried inward to the base of the wall. He found twenty-one courses of drafted stones below the surface at this point, and the stones in the lower courses bore quarry marks which resemble old Hebrew or Phœnician characters.[13] The lower courses of stones were from 3 feet 6 inches to 4 feet 3½ inches in height. Some of the characters were cut in the stones; some painted on them. It seems possible that these were remains of the work of Solomon; (see Figs. 244, 245, and 246).

The enclosure of this hill-top with a wall set it apart from the rest of Jerusalem. It was a kind of separate fortress. At the time it emphasized the majesty of Solomon—his apartness from his

---

11 See J. E. Hanauer, *Walks About Jerusalem*, London, 1910, 88, 89.
12 The writer is well aware that the name Moriah for this part of the hill rests on slender evidence, but he employs it nevertheless as a convenient term, since it is well understood by readers of the Bible.
13 Warren and Conder, *Jerusalem*, pp. 148–158.

people. This separate enclosure of the temple hill was perpetuated through the whole history of Jerusalem and is maintained today. In all periods the temple hill has been a fortress that could be defended apart from the city.

(2) *Solomon's Temple.*—Of the form and situation of the buildings of Solomon on the hill that was enclosed by this new wall, there is a wide diversity of opinion. This diversity arises in part from the fact that some scholars take at their face value statements of Josephus, the Talmud, and other late sources concerning Solomon's temple, while others attribute less weight to the statements of those sources which were written long after this temple was destroyed, and base their views rather on the earlier documents. The last is the only sound method of study, and is the course followed here. We shall take as evidence of the plan and situation of the buildings the Biblical writers who had seen them.

We are at the start confronted, however, with a difficulty, since no Biblical writer has given us an exact statement as to what part of the hill Solomon's temple occupied. Most modern scholars hold, nevertheless, that it was built at the highest point of the hill just west of the sacred cave, which has already been mentioned,[14] and the old rock-altar above it. This view is confirmed by Josephus [15] and is undoubtedly correct, although three or four modern scholars have doubted it. The temple would naturally be built near the spot where the angel is said to have appeared to David (2 Sam. 24: 16), and as angels are frequently represented in the Old Testament as appearing upon rocks (see Judges 6:11, f.; 13:19)[16] it is altogether probable that the appearance to David was on the rock-altar at the top of the hill. On this rock the animals for sacrifice were slain, as the conduits for blood still visible on its top indicate. Near it, then, or on it the altar of burnt-offerings stood. We learn from Ezekiel, who had served as a priest in the temple of Solomon, that the temple faced the east, that it stood to the west of the altar, and that there was room between the temple and the altar for twenty-five men. (See Ezek. 8:16.) The temple was a rectangular building with its greatest length running east and west. Its measurements were 124 feet for the length, 50 for the breadth, and 55 for the height. It was constructed of stones and cedar beams. The outer temple, afterward called the holy place, was 70 feet

14 See Chapter XI, p. 213.
15 *Wars of the Jews*, V, v, 1.
16 See Stade, *Geschichte des Volkes Israels*, Berlin, 1889, I, 314, and G. A. Smith, *Jerusalem*, II, 60.

long, 34½ feet wide, and 52 feet high. Back of it was the holy of holies, where the ark was placed. It was a cube 34½ feet each way. Apparently there was a chamber above it.[17] This room was adorned with carvings of cherubim, palms, and open flowers (1 Kings 6:29, 32, 35). It had no window. According to 2 Chronicles 3:14, it was separated from the holy place by a veil. The holy place contained the table of show-bread and ten golden lamp-stands (1 Kings 7:49).[18] The lattice work high up in the walls of this room (1 Kings 6:4) can have admitted only an uncertain light. The building was richly adorned with cedar and gold. It consisted of three stories, and the walls were of varying thickness, since ledges were built in them to receive the beams of the different stories. Each story contained a series of chambers for storage or the use of the priests. Those of the first story were five cubits wide, those of the second six, and those of the third seven; (see Figs. 247–249).

In front of the temple was a porch of unknown height, and before this were two bronze pillars with ornamented tops, named Jachin and Boaz. A little to the southeast of the temple in the open air was a brazen laver supported by twelve brazen oxen (1 Kings 7:23–26, 39). Before the temple Solomon also placed a brazen altar (2 Chron. 1:5, 6; 2 Kings 16:14). Another article of temple

[17] In giving the dimensions of the various temples, the writer has followed the calculations of George Adam Smith in his *Jerusalem*. W. Shaw Caldecott has published four volumes, one on the *Tabernacle*, one on *Solomon's Temple*, one on the *Second Temple*, and one on *Herod's Temple*, in which he claims to have discovered a key that harmonizes all the Biblical statements as to the measurements of these structures. His supposed key is his belief that the Babylonians had three different cubits which they used side by side, that these cubits were known to Moses, and that their use was perpetuated in the temple. Should these pages be read by one who has accepted that claim as true, it is but fair that he be informed that Caldecott's whole system is based upon a misinterpretation of a Babylonian tablet that was published in Rawlinson's *Cuneiform Inscriptions of Western Asia*, Vol. IV, p. 37. (See *Tabernacle*, pp. 107–139, and *Solomon's Temple*, pp. 215, 216.) This tablet contains a table of time and of distances. The unit of time in Babylonia was a *kaskal-gid*. An astronomical tablet published fifty years ago in the book most widely used by beginners in Assyrian says that at the equinox "six *kaskal-gid* was the day, six *kaskal-gid* the night." The *kaskal-gid* was, then, a period of two hours' duration. Just as in many countries the word for "hour" is used for distance, and a place is said to be so many "hours" away, so in Babylonia and Assyria *kaskal-gid* was used as a measure of distance. The tablet referred to gives a table of the ways of writing fractions of *kaskal-gid* and its other divisions in the simplest of the two Babylonian numerical systems. The Assyriologist learns from this tablet that 1 *kaskal-gid* (the distance of two hours) equalled 30 *ush*, that 1 *ush* equalled 60 *gar*, that 1 *gar* equalled 12 *u* or cubits, and that 1 *u* equalled 60 shu or "fingers." Caldecott, however, mistook the sign *gid* for a numeral five, the sign *kaskal* for a word meaning "ell," and the word *u* meaning "cubit" for a sign signifying "plus"! He accordingly makes *gar* a "palm"; *shu*, a "three-palm ell"; *ush*, a "four-palm ell," and *kaskal-gid*, a "five-palm ell"! His whole system is without foundation.

Tables similar to the one published by Rawlinson were compiled in the scribal school at Nippur. One was published without translation by Hilprecht in 1906 in the *Babylonian Expedition of the University of Pennsylvania*, Vol. XX, and interpreted by the present writer in 1909 in *The Haverford Library Collection of Cuneiform Tablets*, Part II, pp. 13–18. The writer has examined other similar tablets in the University of Pennsylvania Museum, Philadelphia.

[18] See Chapter IX, p. 192. According to 1 Kings 7:48, there was a "golden altar" here also, but as this is not mentioned in chapter 6 many scholars think that it is a postexilic gloss, introducing a feature from the second temple.

furniture is described as a "base." It was apparently a portable
holder for a laver. It was made of bronze, provided with wheels,
and ornamented with figures of lions, cherubim, and palm-trees
(1 Kings 7 : 27–37) ; (see Figs. 251, 252).

It is clear that the temple was not, like a modern church, intended
for the accommodation of the people. It was simply Jehovah's
dwelling. Hither the priests might come to bring the offerings
of the people, and to propitiate him. Solomon surrounded the
temple with a court enclosed by a wall of three courses of hewn
stones and cedar beams (1 Kings 6 : 36). This court became in
later time the auditorium of the nation. Outside of this was
a larger court with walls of similar construction (1 Kings 7 : 12) ;
(see Fig. 243).

(3) *Solomon's Palace.*—Just to the south of the temple court,
separated from it only by a wall, was a middle court in which was
Solomon's own palace and the palace of Pharaoh's daughter (1
Kings 7 : 8). These palaces were a little lower down the hill than
the temple, and Solomon had a private "ascent" by which he could
go up into the temple (1 Kings 10 : 5). The royal palaces were so
near that a shout in the court around the altar could be heard in the
palace (2 Kings 11 : 12, 13). These palaces were built of hewn stone
and cedar. South of this court was still another, separated from it
by a wall. In this most southerly and lowest of the courts stood the
hall of state, in which was the throne room, where Solomon sat in
judgment. This hall was paneled with cedar from floor to roof.
The throne was of ivory, was approached by six steps, and flanked
on each side by lions (1 Kings 10 : 18–20). South of this and
probably intended as its vestibule was the "porch of pillars," 86 by
52 feet (1 Kings 7 : 6). Still south of this stood the "house of the
forest of Lebanon" (1 Kings 7 : 2), so called because its four rows
of cedar pillars were poetically suggestive of a Lebanon forest. This
was the largest of all the buildings, being 172 feet long, 86 feet wide,
and 52 feet high. There seem to have been two stories, the uppermost of which was supported by 45 pillars in three rows. Josephus
says that the upper room of this hall was designed to "contain a
great body of men, who would come together to have their causes
determined." [19] He may have been influenced, however, in making
the statement by the customs of his own time.

19 *Antiquities of the Jews,* VIII, v, 2.

As one went northward, then, up the hill from the "city of David," he passed through a gateway into the large court. In this court he came first to the "house of the forest of Lebanon." Beyond this he would enter through the "porch of pillars" into the splendid hall of judgment with its imposing throne. If he were a favored servant or an honored guest of the king, he might be admitted to the inner court, in which case he would behold the imposing palaces of Solomon and his principal queen. A passageway to the eastward of this more private court led the person not so favored to the sacred court about the temple.

In the construction of these buildings Solomon employed Phœnician architects and workmen. His buildings were, therefore, more imposing than those ordinarily erected in Palestine. The Phœnicians were the intermediaries of the ancient world, and were the recipients of influences from Babylonia, Egypt, the Hittites, Cyprus, and the Mycenean world. Through them something of the world's architectural culture touched the buildings of Solomon.

9. From Solomon to Hezekiah.—Between the time of Solomon and Hezekiah, the Bible furnishes us with but little information about Jerusalem. One topographical fact is given us in the narrative of the war between Amaziah of Judah and Jehoash of Israel, before 782 B.C. After Jehoash had been victorious in the battle at Beth-Shemesh, he came up to Jerusalem and "brake down the wall of Jerusalem from the gate of Ephraim unto the corner gate, four hundred cubits" (2 Kings 14:13); (see Plate 134). This wall was afterward repaired by Uzziah, who strengthened it with towers.

Indeed, it seems probable that Uzziah's work was more extensive and that, in order to render the city more impregnable, he added a second wall on the north. Certainly a wall existed here before the Exile, for when Nehemiah rebuilt the walls, this wall joined the temple area at its northwest corner, and we know of no king after Uzziah who would be likely to construct such a defence unless it was Hezekiah. As the city easily withstood the attack of Pekah and Rezin in 735 (Isa. 7:1, ff.), it seems probable that Uzziah was the builder.

This wall by whomsoever it was built was in all probability on the line of the so-called "second wall" of Josephus. As to just what its course was we cannot now tell, further than that it started from near the Corner Gate, near where the modern Turkish fortress now stands, and terminated at the temple area. Some have supposed that after leaving the Corner Gate it ran as far northward as the line on which the northern wall of the modern city runs, then eastward from there to a point near the present Damascus Gate, and then turned southward to the temple area. This seems improbable, however, since in the time of Zechariah the tower of Hananel, which stood near the northwest corner of the present area of the Mosque of Omar, was the most northerly point of the city. It is thus possible that this second wall may have run south of the site of the Church of the Holy Sepulcher. Its whole course accordingly lies underneath the present city. None of this has been excavated except a short part of the course near the ancient Corner Gate. In 1885, when digging was in progress for the foundations of the Grand New Hotel, just inside the Jaffa Gate and north of the Turkish fortress, a course of large stones was laid bare which the late Dr. Merrill [20] and others believed to be a part of this second wall. The nature of the digging did not, however, disclose its course for any great distance; the part revealed ran nearly north and south.

Unless Solomon built the wall which ran from Maudsley's scarp at the northwest corner of the western hill eastward down the slope of that hill to the southern point of the eastern hill, it must have been built by some king of this period. No hint is given us as to who built this wall. It may have been done in the reign of Jehoshaphat, which was a period of prosperity and expansion (2 Kings 3 : 4–12), or in the reign of Uzziah, which was also a very prosperous time. The need of stronger defenses created by the advance of the Assyrians into western Asia in the ninth and eighth centuries B.C. makes it probable that Uzziah was the builder. At all events it was accomplished by the time of Hezekiah.

In the reign of Ahaz there was a conduit (Isa. 7 : 3) leading from the "upper pool," or Gihon, to a lower pool, which probably lay somewhere near the mouth of the Tyropœon valley. This conduit has been discovered. It was designed partly to conduct water from Gihon out into the valley of the Kidron for the irrigation of the king's gardens, and partly to fill the lower pool so that cattle could come and drink. Isaiah refers to the waters of this conduit as "the waters of Shiloah that go softly" (Isa. 8 : 6). Of course, this conduit was in Isaiah's time an old one. It is impossible to tell

20 Cf. Selah Merrill, *Jerusalem*, New York, 1908, p. 157.

when it was first constructed. It may have been made as early
as the time of Solomon or David, or even in Jebusite times.

In the reign of Ahaz a change was made in the nature of the altar
of burnt-offerings in the temple. When Ahaz went to Damascus to
do homage to Tiglath-pileser IV of Assyria, he saw an altar that
pleased him, and sent a pattern of it home to the high priest, Urijah,
with directions to have one made like it for the temple. This
Urijah did. This altar was apparently constructed of stone. It
displaced the brazen altar of Solomon, which was henceforth
kept for the king's private use (2 Kings 16:10–16). It is thought
by some that the measurements of this stone altar are reproduced
in Ezekiel 43:13–17. The brazen altar had always been out of
accord with the Hebrew law. (See Exod. 20:24–26.)

10. **Hezekiah.**—Apart from his reform (2 Kings 18:1–6) and
the invasions of Sennacherib (2 Kings 18:9, ff.), the event of
especial interest mentioned in connection with Hezekiah is that "he
made the pool and the conduit and brought the water into the city"
(2 Kings 20:20). Scholars are agreed that this refers to the rock-
cut aqueduct in which the Siloam inscription was found.[21] This
was for the time of its construction a notable engineering achievement, though recent exploration of the tunnel shows that the workers frequently went astray and cut in directions that they did not
intend. Indeed, it is probable that the great bends in the tunnel
were made on account of such mistakes and not as Clermont-
Ganneau formerly thought in order to avoid the tombs of the kings.
Up to the present, search for these tombs has been in vain. They
must have been somewhere on the eastern hill, but there is no reason
to believe that they were at the great depth at which this tunnel
was cut through the rock.

If the supposition made above as to the walls of Uzziah is correct, it was Hezekiah who built the first wall across the mouth of
the Tyropœon valley so as to enclose within the city his new pool.
This wall was found by Bliss. It formed the dam of the pool. It
was strongly buttressed and had been rebuilt from time to time.
Bliss detected five periods in its history.[22]

11. **From Hezekiah to the Exile.**—After Hezekiah, the general features of Jerusalem remained the same down to the time of
the Babylonian Exile in 586 B.C. We hear of a Fish Gate, probably
where it was at a later time, at the north of the city in the wall built

21 See translations, Part II, p. 476.
22 See Bliss, *Excavations at Jerusalem,* pp. 96–109.

by Uzziah. Zephaniah mentions in connection with it "the second quarter" of the city (Zeph. 1:10), which was probably the part of the town between the north wall of Uzziah and the older north wall of Solomon on the western hill. The prophetess Huldah lived there in the time of Josiah (2 Kings 22:14). Zephaniah also mentions a part of the city called *Maktesh* or the Mortar (Zeph. 1:11). This was a part of Jerusalem occupied by Phœnician traders and craftsmen. It was probably in the hollow between the two hills, *i.e.*, in the Tyropœon valley.

In the reign of Manasseh we hear of the sacrifice of children. For this purpose a pit was excavated on the floor of the valley of Hinnom, to the south of the city, and arrangements were made to burn the victims. This was called Topheth (Jer. 7:31). Later it was defiled (2 Kings 23:10), and to perpetuate the defilement refuse from the city seems to have been burned there. The valley of Hinnom is in Hebrew *gai hinnom*. Later generations conceived that the heavenly Jerusalem had also its valley of Hinnom for the consumption of its refuse, hence *gai hinnom* is used in the New Testament in the form Gehenna as a name of hell. (See Matt. 5:29; 10:28.)

12. The Destruction of 586 B.C.—Toward the end of the siege of Jerusalem by Nebuchadrezzar in the year 586 it is said that the men of war fled by the way of the gate between the two walls which was by the king's garden (2 Kings 25:4). This was evidently a gate by the Pool of Siloam, where the two walls of the eastern hill and the wall which came down the western hill and crossed the mouth of the Tyropœon valley all came together.[23]

In August of the year 586 B.C. Jerusalem was destroyed by Nebuchadrezzar. The temple, the royal palace, and the residences of the principal men were burned and the walls of the city were broken down (2 Kings 25:9, 10). All that was combustible was burned, including the city gates (Neh. 1:3). All portable things of value were carried away. Jerusalem now entered on a period of desolation. The city was probably not entirely deserted. Some of the poor who still managed to extract a subsistence from the desolate hills still found shelter in her ruins. All the well-to-do inhabitants were transported to Babylonia.

It is often assumed that the site of the temple was unused during the Exile and that no offerings were made there, but Jeremiah

23 See G. A. Smith, *Jerusalem*, I, 226. For another view, see Paton, *Journal of Biblical Literature*, XXV, 1–13.

41 : 4, 5 shows that this was not the case. Probably an altar was
repaired very soon, and the poor people still went through their most
indispensable religious ceremonies amid the desolation, for men
came from Samaria two months after the destruction of the city
to celebrate there the Feast of Tabernacles.

This destruction of the city and the deportation of its population
made a very deep impression on the Jews. How their affections
clung to the desolate and defaced city is touchingly depicted in the
book of Lamentations and in the 137th Psalm. Indeed, the destruction of the real Jerusalem was the beginning of that ideal
Jerusalem which has been so influential in the religious history of
the world.[24]

13. The Second Temple.—Beyond the erection of an altar,
already mentioned, the first steps toward the rebuilding of the temple were taken, so many scholars think, in the second year of King
Darius of Persia, *i.e.*, in 520 B.C. Eighteen years earlier Cyrus had
made it possible for this to be done,[25] but for various reasons it had
not been undertaken.[26] The man whose preaching moved the people
to begin the rebuilding was Haggai, and the circumstances under
which he did it are recounted in his book. Haggai's persuasion
was later seconded by the efforts of Zechariah. Through four
years the house slowly rose, and was finally completed in March of
the sixth year of Darius (516 B.C.), five months less than 70 years
after it was destroyed.

There is no doubt that the second temple was built on the lines
of the first, which were probably still traceable in the débris. It
was also constructed of stone which still lay about the top of the
hill—stone that had been used in the work of Solomon. It was not
because it was smaller than the first temple that old men who had
seen that wept as they looked on the new one (Ezra 3 : 12), but
because it was less ornate. It was probably without ornament.
Josephus (*Contra Apion,* i, 22) says that the temple court was enclosed by a wall a plethra in length and 100 Greek cubits in breadth,
i. e., 485½ by 145½ feet. It was not, then, very large. It is uncertain whether there was at this time more than one court; 1
Maccabees 4 : 48 speaks of "courts," but Josephus tells [27] how the
people pelted Alexander Jannæus with citrons while he was officiat-

24 See G. A. Smith, *Jerusalem,* II, Chapters X and XI.
25 See Chapter II, p. 72; also Part II, p. 484 f.
26 Ezra 5:16 states that Sheshbazzar laid the foundations of the house in the reign
of Cyrus but as Haggai and Zechariah give no hint of this, many scholars think there
must be some error in the text.
27 *Antiquities of the Jews,* XIII, xiii, 5.

ing at the altar during the Feast of Tabernacles, so that it is probable that the courts were not separated by a wall, but by a difference of elevation. The inner court was probably higher than the other, as it is around the Mosque of Omar today.

Within this court was an altar of unhewn stones. The temple itself consisted as before of the holy place and the holy of holies. Before the holy place was a porch, and around the building there were many small chambers as formerly. The holy of holies was separated from the holy place by a veil (1 Macc. 1:22), but now it contained no ark of the covenant, as that had been lost in 586 B.C. The holy of holies in the second temple was empty except for the "stone of foundation" on which the high priest placed his censer on the day of atonement.[28] In the holy place the table of show-bread stood in front of the veil. Instead of the ten golden lamp-stands of Solomon's temple there now stood there the lamp with seven branches (see Zech. 4). A golden altar of incense replaced it (1 Macc. 1:21) in the time of the Maccabees, though it may not have been placed there before the time of Ezra.

Such was the temple as reconstructed after the Exile. In one important respect its perspective was changed. The royal palace and the administrative buildings, which before the Exile had shared the crest of the northern spur of Zion with the temple, were not rebuilt. The temple stood there alone. Little by little the part of the hill to the south of the temple was cleared of the débris and the ground became a temple court. This was significant of the religious condition of the post-exilic time. Kings had vanished; the worship of Jehovah held the supreme place in the thought of the people.

14. Nehemiah and the Walls.—For seventy-two years after the temple was rebuilt, the walls of the city still lay in ruins. That they were at last restored was due to the patriotism and energy of a noble young Jew, Nehemiah, who had been a cup-bearer to Artaxerxes I of Persia. The story of how he obtained the royal permission to return to Jerusalem as governor, with authority to rebuild the walls, how upon his arrival he traced by their ruins the lines of the old walls, with what energy and amid what difficulties he pushed their rebuilding to completion in the course of three months in the year 444 B.C., is told in detail in Nehemiah 1–7 and need not be repeated here.

At the northwest corner of the western hill there was placed in the wall at this time a gate called the Valley Gate (Neh. 3:13).

28 See the Mishnah, *Middoth* 3:6.

This was the gate discovered by Bliss [29] a little to the east of the old fortress on Maudsley's scarp. When the wall was completed, a ceremony of dedication was held. At this festival two processions started from this Valley Gate; one of these went around the south side of the city, the other around the north side (Neh. 12:31–40). They met at the temple. The procession that went around the south side of the city passed by the Dung Gate, which was situated in the southern wall well down the hill, then by the Fountain Gate, near the Pool of Siloam, then up the "ascent of the wall" by the stairs of the "City of David," and passed the Water Gate somewhere above the spring of Gihon. Still above this, probably just to the east of the temple area, was the Horse Gate (Neh. 3:28). The other company, starting from the Valley Gate at the southwest corner of the city, passed northward by the "Tower of the Furnaces" unto the broad wall, above the Gate of Ephraim, by the Old Gate, and by the Fish Gate, past the Tower of Hananel and the Tower of Hammeah, unto the Sheep Gate. This description, together with the line of the previous wall, enables us approximately to determine the outline of post-exilic Jerusalem; (see Plate 134). The one point of doubt has to do with the line of the second wall on the north of the city, laid out probably by Uzziah. As that line is directly under the present city it has never been possible to follow it by excavations. We can only conjecture what its course may have been. The towers of Hananel and Hammeah were clearly north of the temple area. They probably fortified the wall along the edge of a shallow valley which separated Moriah from the hill north of it. This hill was later called Bezetha.

15. Late Persian and Early Greek Periods.—After the time of Ezra and Nehemiah, we have no clear topographical references to Jerusalem until the second century B.C. It seems probable that Jerusalem and Judah rebelled against one of the later Persian kings and that the city suffered.[30] We hear that Ptolemy I of Egypt also captured Jerusalem,[31] but whether these experiences led to any modification in the form of the city, we do not know. The *Wisdom of Jesus, the Son of Sirach,* often called *Ecclesiasticus,* which was written about 180 B.C., indicates that Jerusalem was a carefully organized city. Many professions and much commerce were rep-

---

[29] *Excavations at Jerusalem,* 16 ff.
[30] See Josephus, *Antiquities of the Jews,* XI, vii, 1; cf. also G. A. Smith, *Jerusalem,* II, 358–361.
[31] See Josephus *Antiquities of the Jews,* XII, i.

resented in it, as well as many human sins and foibles.[32]   The author
declares [33] that a high priest, Simon, the son of Onias (probably
Simon II, 218–198 B.C.), repaired the temple and fortified the
city.   What the nature of either work was, we do not know.   So
far as can be ascertained, he confined himself to the strengthening
of old defenses, and did not change the topography.

In the early part of the reign of Antiochus IV, while many Jews
were kindly inclined to Greek culture and to Greek ways, an out-
door gymnasium was established in Jerusalem.[34]   This was in a
hollow just above the Tyropœon valley to the west of the south end
of the temple enclosure.[35]   Josephus calls it the Xystus, a Greek
name that reveals its character.   Some reminder that it was once a
gymnasium perhaps lingers in *Midan,* the modern Arabic name for
the locality, which means hippodrome, or place of combat.

16. In the Time of the Maccabees.—In the Maccabæan period
the city was divided into three parts—the city proper, the temple,
and the Akra or citadel.   As to the situation of the Akra, there is
a wide difference of opinion.   Into the different theories it is
impossible to go.[36]   The writer agrees with George Adam Smith,
that in all probability the Akra was the "city of David" of the
earlier time, as 1 Maccabees states (1: 33; 7: 32, 33; 14: 36).
We first hear of this Akra in 198 B.C., when an Egyptian garrison
held out in it against Antiochus III.[37]   It was so shut off from the
rest of Jerusalem that, though, after the onslaught of Antiochus IV,
on the Jews in 168 B.C., Judas Maccabæus recovered the city and
temple as early as 165 B.C., the Syrians kept possession of the
Akra for twenty-three years more, until they were finally dislodged
by Simon the Maccabee in 142 B.C.[38]

17. Asmonæan Jerusalem.—During the Asmonæan dynasty
which grew out of the Maccabæan strugle,[39] three new features
were added to Jerusalem.   One was a castle to the northward of
the temple area built by John Hyrcanus I, 135–105 B.C.[40]   This
was known to Greek-speaking Jews as Baris, which is a corruption
of the Hebrew *Birah,* a fortress.   Its walls were massive and high.

32 See Ecclesiasticus 3–5, 7, 9, 23, 25, ff., and 38.
33 See Ecclesiasticus 50: 1–4.
34 Cf. Josephus, *Antiquities of the Jews,* XII, v. 1.
35 See Selah Merrill, *Ancient Jerusalem.* New York, 1908, pp. 83–88.
36 See G. A. Smith, *Jerusalem,* II, 447–452.
37 Josephus, *Antiquities of the Jews,* XII, v. 1.
38 Josephus, *Antiquities of the Jews,* XIII, vi, 7.
39 See Chapter V, p. 160.
40 Josephus, *Antiquities of the Jews,* XV, xi, 4; XVIII, iv, 3.

It commanded the approach to the temple area from the north, and greatly strengthened the effectiveness of the temple fortification.

One of the Asmonæans, probably John Hyrcanus I, built a palace in Jerusalem.[41] This palace apparently stood on the site now occupied by the Synagogue of the German Jews in Jerusalem.[42] It was connected with the temple area by a bridge,[43] of which a remnant of the easternmost span, now called "Robinson's Arch," [44] is still visible on the western wall of the temple enclosure. This bridge was destroyed by Pompey when he captured Jerusalem in 63 B.C.,[45] and its remains were found by Warren in the bottom of the Tyropœon valley, 80 feet below the present surface of the ground.[46] As the Asmonæans were high priests as well as kings, this bridge gave them easy access to the temple from their palace. The palace itself situated on a part of the western hill that overtopped the temple hill, was so placed that the royal priest could sit in his palace and watch what was transpiring in the temple courts and in the valley below.

The third accomplishment of the Asmonæans was probably the construction of Solomon's Pools and the High Level Aqueduct by which the water was brought into Jerusalem.[47] This work appears also to have been accomplished by John Hyrcanus I, for Timarchus, the biographer of Antiochus VII, who was a contemporary of Hyrcanus I, says of Jerusalem that "the whole city runs down with waters, so that even the gardens are irrigated by the water which flows off from it." [48] Such a description would be quite unfitting, if all the water had been supplied by Gihon, En-rogel, and the cisterns about Jerusalem. It implies that a perpetual stream of water, such as came through one of the aqueducts, flowed into the city.

One other structure is attributed to an Asmonæan. Alexander Jannæus was very unpopular with the Pharisees, and once, as already noted, he was pelted by the people with citrons. He thereupon erected a wooden barrier around the temple and the altar, thus excluding the laity from a close approach to the temple,[49] and creating a court for the priests alone.

41 Josephus, *Antiquities of the Jews*, XX, viii, 11; *Wars of the Jews*, II, xvi, 3.
42 Merrill, *Ancient Jerusalem*, p. 88.
43 Josephus, *Antiquities of the Jews*, XIV, iv, 2, and Fig. 255.
44 Because its identity as a part of this bridge was first perceived by Prof. Edward Robinson, of Union Seminary, New York.
45 Josephus, *Wars of the Jews*, I, vii, 2.
46 Warren and Conder, *Jerusalem*, 178, f.
47 See Chapter VI, p. 171.
48 Quoted by Alexander Polyhistor and Eusebius; see G. A. Smith, *Jerusalem*, II, 462.
49 Josephus, *Antiquities of the Jews*, XIII, xiii, 5.

Jerusalem suffered from four sieges in the troublous days when
the Asmonæan power was waning and that of Rome was being
established. The first was by Haretat, King of the Nabathæans, in
65 B.C., but was lifted without result.[50] The second was that of
Pompey in 63 B.C. It resulted in the capture of the city and in
considerable damage. The bridge across the Tyropœon to the
royal palace was broken down.[51] The third was that of the Parthians in 40 B.C., when they captured the city and placed Antigonus, son of Aristobulus II, on the throne.[52] The fourth was that
by which Herod the Great became master of Jerusalem in 37 B.C.
At this time a part of the two northern walls were broken down.[53]
The topography of the city was in no way changed until after the
conquest by Herod, who changed the face of Jerusalem in many
ways.

   18. Herod the Great.—The first work of Herod was to rebuild
and strengthen the fortress to the north of the temple. This he
did at the beginning of his reign while Mark Antony was still in
power in the East. He accordingly renamed the castle Antonia.[54]
Herod also rebuilt and strengthened the walls which he had battered down in taking Jerusalem, adding towers to make them more
impregnable. At the northwest corner of the city he erected three
new towers,—Hippacus, Phasael, and Mariamne.[55] These all probably stood in or near the space now covered by the Turkish fortress
at the Jaffa Gate. Hippacus was apparently the northwest tower
of the present citadel, Phasael the easternmost of the towers in the
same structure, which still bears the name "Tower of David";
Mariamne lay to the east of these. Hippacus was 80 cubits high,
Phasael 90, and Mariamne 50. On the north of these, perhaps near
the point where the northwest corner of the present city wall is,
stood Psephinus, an octagonal tower 70 cubits high.

   (1) *Herod's Palace.*—In connection with the towers Hippacus
and Phasael and on the site of the present Turkish citadel, Herod
built a new and splendid royal palace.[56] Its walls on the west and
north were the same as the old city walls; on the east and south,
walls of the same massiveness were erected. It contained two halls,
each the size of the sanctuary, with couches within for a hundred

---

50 Josephus, *Antiquities of the Jews*, XIV, ii, 1.
51 *Ibid.*, XIV, iv. 2.
52 *Ibid.*, XIV, xv, 2; xvi.
53 *Ibid.*, XIV, xiii, 3, 4, 5.
54 *Ibid.*, XV, viii, 5.
55 Josephus, *Wars of the Jews*, V, iv. 3.
56 *Ibid.*, V, iv, 4. (See Fig. 256.)

guests. There were many other richly furnished chambers. The towers and the palace were faced with marble. Stretching to the southward of the palace were colonnades which bordered on open courts, in which shrubberies, fountains, and long walks abounded. These fountains were fed by the High Level Aqueduct.

This palace commanded the highest point of the southwestern hill. Its construction finally transferred the controlling power to the western hill, or as Josephus calls it, the "Upper City." Ever after this the western hill was the seat of political power. When Procurators ruled Judæa this palace became the prætorium.[57] It was to this castle that our Saviour was brought to be tried by Pontius Pilate. It was to its entrance, probably on the east, that Pilate brought Jesus and offered to release him, when the people cried: "Away with this man . . . crucify him" (Luke 23:18, 21). This palace, built by one of the ablest and most unscrupulous of men, is thus associated with one of the most sacred and tragic moments of history. From that day to this it has remained the seat of political authority in Jerusalem. Its presence on the western hill has gradually drawn the name Zion from the original city of David to the western hill, and so distorted the Old Testament traditions that even several scholars [58] long refused to give credence to the clear voice of the Old Testament as to the site of the original Zion. The palace, battered down and rebuilt again and again, still retains in its walls many of the massive stones of Herod. This palace was completed about 23 B.C.

(2) *Herod's Theater.*—About 25 B.C. Herod founded an athletic gathering to be celebrated every five years in honor of Augustus.[59] Josephus, in speaking of this fact, says that Herod built a theater in Jerusalem, and also a very great amphitheater in the plain. If he actually built a theater in the city, all traces of it have disappeared. To the south of the city on a hill considerably beyond the Valley of Hinnom, the remains of a great theater were discovered some years ago by the late Dr. Schick.[60] This theater faced the north, its diameter was more than 130 feet, and spectators seated in it could see Jerusalem in the distance. It is thought by some scholars that this is the theater to which Josephus alludes, as Herod would hardly have ventured to outrage Jewish feeling by placing such a structure

---

57 Josephus, *Antiquities of the Jews,* XVII, ix, 3; *Wars of the Jews,* II, ii, 2; xiv, 8.
58 Colonel Conder, the late Dr. Merrill, Georg Gatt, Dr. Rückert, and Dr. Mommert.
59 Josephus, *Antiquities of the Jews,* XV, viii, 1.
60 See *Quarterly Statement* of the Palestine Exploration Fund, 1887, p. 161, ff. Dr. Schick calls it an amphitheater, but it is simply a theater of the Greek type.

in the sacred city. If the discovery of Dr. Schick represents Herod's theater, it is quite unknown where the "amphitheater in the plain," to which Josephus makes reference, was situated.

(3) *Herod's Temple.*—When the palace of Herod was completed, the splendid structures of Antonia and the palace quite overshadowed the old dingy temple. The temple had frequently been repaired by the high priests, and perhaps during the Maccabæan time had been somewhat embellished, but it nevertheless remained essentially as it had been rebuilt after the Exile. Herod had built Sebaste on the site of ancient Samaria in 27 B.C., and began about 22 B.C. to build Cæsarea. In these and other cities he had erected splendid temples to heathen deities; naturally he desired to make the temple of his capital city worthy to stand beside them. He had difficulty in persuading the Jews to let him touch the sacred house, but yielding in many things to their scruples, work was finally begun in the year 20–19 B.C. Some of the priests became carpenters and stone-cutters, so that no profane hands need touch the sacred shrine.[61] The old temple was taken down and the new one erected in the space of eighteen months. But much remained to be done and the work dragged along until after Herod's death. In the time of Christ "forty and six years was this temple in building" (John 2:20), and it was not then completed. It was finished only in 64 A.D., six years before it was finally destroyed.[62] The temple itself occupied the site of its predecessor, and was of the same plan and dimensions. These Herod did not dare to change. They were consecrated by nearly a thousand years of sacred associations. If he could not enlarge it, however, he could make it higher, and he made its elevation a hundred cubits or 172 feet. He also enlarged the porch, making it 120 feet broad. The whole was built of huge blocks of white stone, with plates of gold upon the front.[63] The holy of holies consisted, as before, of a dark, empty room, 35 feet in each dimension. It was separated from the holy place by curtains, an outer and an inner, which were a foot apart. The holy place was still 40 by 20 cubits, but was now made 40 instead of 30 cubits high.[64] Its furniture was the same as in the second temple: the table of show-bread, the altar of incense, and the lamp with seven branches; (Fig. 250). The entrance to the holy place, 15 cubits wide and 70 cubits high, was not closed

61 Josephus, *Antiquities of the Jews*, XV, xi, 2.
62 Josephus, *Antiquities of the Jews*, XX, ix, 7.
63 *Ibid.*, XV, xi, 3.
64 Above it was a chamber 30 cubits high.

by doors. Josephus declares that it was left open to set forth the "unobstructed openness of heaven." [65]

On the top of the temple, spikes with sharp points were arranged to prevent birds from lighting upon it and defiling it. Twelve broad steps led down from the temple to the court of the priests.[66] These steps occupied nearly all the 22 cubits of space between the porch and the altar. Not far from the steps at the south stood the great laver, which had replaced the brazen sea of Solomon's temple. The altar of unhewn stones rose upon the sacred rock—sacred since the days of the Jebusites (and possibly since the Stone Age), to which it was fitted by masonry. The base of the altar was 32 cubits square and 1 high. On this rose a structure 30 cubits square and 5 cubits high. On this was a ledge 1 cubit broad, to which the horns of the altar were attached. Not far above was another ledge, also a cubit broad, on which the officiating priests might stand. Above this was the altar hearth itself, which was 24 cubits square. South of the altar was a structure of masonry on which priests could stand; north of it, the place for the slaughter of the victims. Here the victims to be slain were tied to rings in the pavement. There were tables of marble on which they could be washed and flayed. Beams supported by pillars also contained hooks on which they could be hung for quartering. Herod, as noted above,[67] probably constructed the Low Level Aqueduct. By means of this he brought a larger supply of water into the temple area, so that there was an abundance of water with which to flush the holy place, and wash away the blood and refuse with which the place must often have reeked, especially on festal days.

A low wall a cubit in height marked off the court of the priests from the court of Israel. Accounts differ as to whether this wall was on the east only or whether it ran around the whole temple. The court of Israel lay to the east of the court of the priests. Again our sources of information differ as to its exact size. Here the "congregation of Israel" could assemble to witness the sacred sacrifices. To the east of the court of Israel lay the court of the women. These were separated by a wall, but, owing to the downward slope of the hill, the court of the women was fifteen steps lower than that of Israel. Indeed, the level of the court of Israel was only main-

---

65 Josephus, *Wars of the Jews*, V, v, 6.
66 See Josephus, *Wars of the Jews*, V, v, and the Mishna tract *Middoth* for the authority for this description. For a fuller description, see G. A. Smith, *Jerusalem*, II, Chapter XVIII.
67 See Chapter VI, p. 172.

tained by a series of arches which supported a pavement. Perhaps
the idea of a court for the women had been a gradual development of
the post-exilic time, in which they had been permitted to watch the
sacrifices from a definitely defined position in the rear of the men.
At all events, this court became a prominent feature in the temple
of Herod, and from elevated seats on its eastern side women could
still watch the sacred ceremonies of the temple. With the exception of this gallery, the court of the women was open to men. It
was 135 cubits square and so was relatively large. Apparently the
temple treasury was situated in this court, together with the money
boxes, for women had access to these. Here probably Christ was
sitting when he saw the poor widow cast into the treasury her two
mites (Mark 12 : 41, f.; Luke 21 : 1, f.). Around these courts ran
a wall 43 feet high. This wall was pierced by nine gates, four on
the north, four on the south, and one on the east. A gate also
separated the court of the women from the court of Israel. Either
the gate that opened out of the court of the women to the eastward,
or the one between the court of the women and the court of Israel
(it is uncertain which one) had been given by one Nicanor and was
of fine Corinthian bronze. It was sometimes called "the gate beautiful" and sometimes "Nicanor's gate." It was by this gate, and so
near the treasury where people were devoting their money to religion, that Peter and John found the lame man begging (Acts 3 : 2,
f.).[68]

Outside all these courts lay the court of the Gentiles. This was
separated from the courts described above by a *Soreg* or ritual wall,
which no Gentile might pass. Herod placed inscriptions in Greek
at the various gates in this ritual wall, which warned Gentiles on
pain of death not to enter. The court of the Gentiles surrounded
the other courts on the north, east, and south; it was, however, most
extensive on the east and south (Fig. 257). To obtain a greater area
for this court on the south, Herod extended the level of the hill by
erecting great arches which supported a pavement. This structure
still remains; it is now called "Solomon's stables" (Fig. 258).
In the Crusading period horses were stabled there. Around the
court thus enlarged ran a beautiful colonnade. The pillars for this
and for Herod's palace were quarried from the rock around Jerusalem. One pillar which had a defect and was accordingly never

68 The questions concerning this gate are most puzzling and have been discussed with
great minuteness and learning by Kirsopp Lake in *The Beginnings of Christianity*, V,
London, 1933, pp. 479–486. On the whole the statements made in the text above still
seem to the writer to express the probable truth.

moved from the quarry was found a few years since in front of the Russian cathedral north of the city.

Although the temple has passed away and other sacred buildings have since the second century been erected in succession near its site, the expanse of the court of the Gentiles remains, and as the devout Christian visits it he seems almost to hear the footfalls of Christ and of Paul!

19. The Pool of Bethesda.—Another spot connected with the life of Christ lay not far from the temple on the north; it was the Pool of Bethesda. It was situated near the Sheep Gate, which was just northeast of the temple. Since the thirteenth century the *Birket Israin* [69] which lies between the temple area and the modern St. Stephen's Gate has been identified by some with Bethesda. Since 1889 it has been thought by many that two pools discovered in that year, now far under ground, in the land of the Church of St. Anne, just north of St. Stephen's Gate, constituted the Pool of Bethesda (see Fig. 259). It is really impossible to decide between the two possibilities on the evidence we have. Both are in the region where we should look for the Pool of Bethesda.

20. Gethsemane.—Two other spots near Jerusalem are of the deepest interest to the Christian student—the Garden of Gethsemane and Golgotha. The fact is certain that the Garden of Gethsemane lay on the western slope of the Mount of Olives. (See Luke 22: 39; John 18: 1; Mark 14: 26, 32.) Since the sixteenth century the Roman Catholics have shown a little garden, which lies just above the Kidron, as the Garden of Gethsemane. More recently the Russian Church has walled in the space next above it as the real garden. There is no certainty that the garden was on either site. To the Jews of the first century a garden was not a place for flower-beds, but an olive orchard, and such an orchard may have extended widely over the hillside. We cannot now identify the spot made sacred by the Master's agony, but we know as we look at this hillside that it was somewhere on it.

21. Calvary.—The site of Calvary or Golgotha is not so easily discerned. Since the year 326 A.D., when Helena, the mother of the Emperor Constantine, visited Jerusalem, there has been a continuous tradition in favor of the site on which the Church of the Holy Sepulcher stands. We know from Hebrews 13: 12 that the crucifixion took place outside the city walls. Unfortunately, we cannot tell whether the second wall of this period ran north or

---

69 That is, the "Pool of Israel."

south of the spot on which the Church of the Holy Sepulcher stands, for the whole region lies under the modern city, where excavation has been impossible. If the second wall turned eastward before it had gone as far north as this spot, it may well be that the crucifixion occurred where the church now stands. Pilate condemned Jesus at the palace of Herod near the gate Gennath at the northwest corner of the city of that day. Doubtless the mob swept along with Jesus through the gate Gennath to the spot called Golgotha. If the Church of the Holy Sepulcher is on that spot, the walk was not a long one (see Fig. 260).

In 1849 Otto Thenius suggested that the hill north of the modern Damascus Gate above "Jeremiah's Grotto" was the real Golgotha; (Figs. 261, 262). This was also suggested by Fisher Howe in 1871, and advocated by Gen. C. E. Gordon in 1881. Near it is a garden in which is a rock-hewn tomb; (Figs. 263, 264). Since the days of Gordon a kind of Protestant tradition and cult has grown up about this spot that in certain quarters evokes some of the devotion called forth among Catholics and Oriental Christians by the Church of the Holy Sepulcher. It must be said that the tomb in the garden is, like many similar tombs in the neighborhood, probably not earlier than the third or fourth century A.D., and there is really no more reason for regarding this spot as Golgotha than any other hilltop near the city.

22. **Agrippa I and the Third Wall.**—In the reign of Herod Agrippa I (41–44 A.D.), Jerusalem was again enlarged. Agrippa built a third wall on the north. Its course is described by Josephus,[70] but as most of the landmarks mentioned by him are unknown, opinions differ as to its course. It is certain that it started at the tower Hippacus and went northward to the tower Psephinus; that it enclosed the hill Bezetha; and that it ran along the edge of the Kidron valley to join the old wall. Some scholars suppose that it ran about on the line of the present northern Turkish wall of the city; others, as Robinson and Merrill, thought it ran much farther north so that its northeastern corner was near the "Tombs of the Kings." In the judgment of the writer the explorations of Sukenik and Mayer have solved the problem. The wall ran northward to a point near the Swedish School, then eastward to the American Schools of Oriental Research, where it turned and ran in a southeasterly direction. It crossed the present

70 *Wars of the Jews*, V, iv, 2.

Turkish wall at a point near Herod's Gate.[71] This wall was begun by Agrippa, who did not dare to finish it lest Claudius should suspect him of an intention to rebel. It was, however, completed by the Jews before the last tragic struggle of the years 66–70, and formed one of the features of Jerusalem when Paul made his later visits to the city.

The history of the "Virgin Daughter of Zion" since 70 A.D., when the walls were broken down and the temple destroyed never to be rebuilt, has been no less checkered and tragic than in the centuries that preceded,[72] but the hearts of all Christians as well as of Jews and Mohammedans turn to her with sympathy and affection, because of their debt to the holy men who at various times, from David to Paul, lived in her and walked her streets; and because of her tragic associations with the life and death of One who was more than a man.

71 See E. L. Sukenik and L. A. Mayer, *The Third Wall of Jerusalem,* Jerusalem, 1930; also above, ch. IV, 20.

72 The city, restored under the heathen name of Ælia Capitolina, by the Emperor Hadrian, in 135 A.D., made Christian by Constantine in 325, sacked by the Persian Chosroes in 614, taken by the Arabs in 636, captured after many vicissitudes in 1072 by the Seljuk Turks, made by the First Crusade the seat of the Latin kingdom of Jerusalem from 1099 to 1187, when Saladin took it, was once more after many other vicissitudes captured by the Ottoman Turks in 1517.

CHAPTER XIV

THE DECAPOLIS

Origin. Damascus. Scythopolis. Cities East of the Sea of Galilee. Gadara. Pella and Dion. Gerasa. Philadelphia. Jesus in the Decapolis.

1. Origin.—Three times in the Gospels the Decapolis is mentioned: Matthew 4 : 25; Mark 5 : 20 and 7 : 31. Decapolis is a Greek name and means "the ten city" (region). The ancient writers who mention it agree that it originally consisted of ten cities in which Greek population was dominant and which were federated together. Pliny[1] gives the ten cities as Damascus, Philadelphia, Raphana, Scythopolis, Gadara, Hippos, Dion, Pella, Gerasa, and Kanatha. Ptolemy, the astronomer and geographer, in the second century A.D. enumerated eighteen cities as belonging to it. In the time of Christ it probably consisted of but ten. The Decapolis apparently was created by the Roman General Pompey, when he conquered this region for Rome in 65–63 B.C. These cities with Greek populations appear to have appealed to him and he granted them certain privileges, including a degree of autonomy. They were, however, subject to the Legate of Syria. Hippos, Scythopolis, and Pella were released by him at this time from the Jewish yoke.[2] Josephus, at the end of the first century A.D., does not reckon Damascus in the Decapolis, but before the time of Paul, Damascus had been captured by the Nabathæans or Arabians, and may not, when retaken by Rome, have been again accorded the privileges of the cities of the Decapolis.

2. Damascus, which is mentioned in the annals of Thothmes III before 1447 B.C., and in the accounts of Abraham (Gen. 14 : 15; 15 : 2), has been continuously in existence as a city ever since, and is one of the most flourishing cities of Syria at the present time. It was occupied in the thirteenth or fourteenth century B.C. by Aramæans who held it all through the Old Testament period. Kings of Damascus frequently fought with Israel. From the time of Alexander the Great it came under Hellenic influences. After

[1] *Historia Naturalis,* V, xviii, 74.
[2] Josephus, *Wars of the Jews,* I, vii, 7.

his death it was first possessed by the Ptolemies of Egypt, but was taken by the Seleucid kings of Antioch before 261 B.C. It is situated in one of the most fertile oases of the world—an oasis that Arabian poets delighted to compare to Paradise. Probably Alexander's successors, who, as we shall see, built many Hellenic cities, beautified this oasis with one of them, but as the site has been occupied continuously, no buildings from this time remain. One feature at Damascus that still recalls Biblical times is the street called Straight, which runs westward from the eastern gate into the heart of the city. It was in a house on the ancient forerunner of this street that Paul first lodged at the time of his conversion (Acts 9: 11), (see Fig. 266).

One other part of Damascus recalls a Biblical narrative. This is the river Barada which still runs through the heart of the city. It is the river called Abana in 2 Kings 5: 12, and was said by Naaman to be "better than all the waters of Israel"; (see Fig. 265).

3. **Scythopolis** was the only one of the cities of the Decapolis west of the Jordan. It was on the site of the Beth-shan of the Old Testament (Josh. 17: 11; 1 Sam. 31: 10, 12; 2 Sam. 21: 12; 1 Kings 4: 12). Beth-shan was already a city at the time Palestine was conquered by Thothmes III,[3] Seti I, and Ramses II, and there has been a town near it ever since. It seems to have been called Scythopolis by the successors of Alexander the Great, probably because a group of Scythians had taken the city and settled there. When it came into the possession of Scythians we can only conjecture, but it was probably at the time of the great Scythian invasion of Palestine, about 625–615 B.C. This invasion called forth the dark prophecies of the book of Zephaniah. Scythopolis appears from certain coins [4] to have become a Hellenic city in the time of Alexander the Great. In the time of Ptolemy Euergetes I, 247–222 B.C., it was subject to Egypt,[5] but it passed to the dominions of the Seleucidæ of Antioch in 198 B.C. Upon the break-up of the Syrian empire in 65–63 B.C., Pompey made it one of the cities of the Decapolis.

The remains of the Hellenic city have now entirely disappeared with the exception of the great stone amphitheater. This may still be seen [6] in the valley on the south side of the mound which covers the ruins of the ancient Beth-shan, where it is overgrown with

3 See Chapter V, p. 152.
4 See Schürer, *Geschichte des Jüdischen Volkes im Zeitalter Jesu Christi*, Leipzig, 1907, II, 172, and note 321.
5 See Josephus, *Antiquities of the Jews*, XII, iv, 5.
6 See Barton, *A Year's Wandering in Bible Lands*, Philadelphia. 1904. p. 176.

briers. The name Scythopolis has long since disappeared, and the old Hebrew name for the place still survives in the name of the modern town Beisan. This modern town is situated on the south side of the valley mentioned above, a little distance from the mound which covers the ancient city. Scythopolis was situated at the point where the plain of Jezreel or Esdraelon joins the Jordan valley. In the time of Christ the Jews from Nazareth and its vicinity, when going to the three annual festivals at Jerusalem, came down the plain and then followed the Jordan valley down to Jericho (see Luke 19:1), in order to avoid going through Samaria. From the time that Jesus was twelve years old he must, therefore, have often passed by Scythopolis on his way to Jerusalem. As it was a Gentile town, however, neither he nor his companions would enter it on such occasions, as they would thereby be rendered unclean.

4. Cities East of the Sea of Galilee.—To the east of the Sea of Galilee lay three of the cities of the Decapolis. Hippos was comparatively near the sea, where Susiye now lies. The Jews of the Talmudic period called the place Susitha.[7] Hippos is the Greek for horse. Susitha is a Hebrew translation of this and Susiye is an Arabic corruption of the Hebrew. All traces of the ancient Hippos except the name have disappeared.

Where Raphana was situated has not yet been definitely determined. It is probably the same as Raphon mentioned in 1 Maccabees 5:37, which was near to Ashteroth-karnaim[8] (Gen. 14:5). Ashteroth-karnaim was situated either at Tell Ashtara or at Tell Ashary, both of which are between twenty and twenty-five miles east of the Sea of Galilee. Raphana, then, probably lay about twenty miles due east from Hippos.

Still eastward of this lay the city of Kanatha, though scholars are divided in opinion as to whether its site is to be identified with El-Kerak or with Kanawat. If its site was at El-Kerak it was about forty miles east of the Sea of Galilee; if at Kanawat it was about fifty-five miles distant from the sea. As there are at Kanawat abundant ruins of a beautiful Hellenic city,[9] Kanatha was probably situated here rather than at El-Kerak. This was the Kenath of Numbers 32:42.

5. Gadara.—A little to the south of the southern end of the Sea of Galilee on the east of the Jordan and south of the Yarmuk lay the city of Gadara, another member of the Decapolis. Its site is

7 See Neubauer, *Géographie du Talmud*, Paris, 1868, 238-240.
8 Josephus, *Antiquities of the Jews*, XII, viii, 4.
9 Brünnow and Domaszewski, *Provincia Arabia*, III, 107–144, and Fig. 267.

now marked by the ruins of Umm Keis or Mukês. Here ruins of
the Hellenic city are still to be seen, including a great theater cut
out of the black basaltic rock. Gadara was a strong fortress as
early as the time of Antiochus the Great in 218 B.C.,[10] and was
afterward besieged by Alexander Jannæus,[11] 104–79 B.C.

6. **Pella and Dion.**—On the east of the Jordan, a little further
south than Scythopolis or Beth-shan, but in the deep depression
of the river valley, Pella, another city of the Decapolis, was situated. The site now bears the name Fahl. The city is mentioned in
the list of Thothmes III, 1503–1447 B.C., as Pahal. In the El-
Amarna letters it is called Pihili. Pella is a Greek form of this
name. The Greek city of Pella is said by Stephen of Byzantium [12]
to have been founded by Alexander the Great. In the Talmud it
is called Pahal,[13] and the modern name Fahl is an Arabian form
of this. Extensive ruins of the Hellenic city are still visible at
Fahl.[14]

Dion is also said to have been founded by Alexander the Great
and was apparently not far from Pella. It is thought by Merrill [15]
and G. A. Smith to have been situated on the site of the modern
Eidun, about twenty miles east of Pella, though this is doubted by
others.[16] If Dion was at this point few, if any, antiquities remain
to bear witness to the fact.

7. **Gerasa,** the modern Jerash, lay on one of the tributaries of
the Jabbok about fifty miles southeast of Pella. We do not know
what the name of the place was in Old Testament times. It is
first mentioned in the time of Alexander Jannæus (104–79 B.C.).[17]
It was then called Gerasa and was probably already at that time a
Hellenic city. By whom it was built, we do not know, but it was
probably one of the early Ptolemies of Egypt. From 100 B.C.
till the Mohammedan conquest in 637 A.D., it flourished as a beautiful city, and later it was a city of some importance. It probably
was overtaken by some calamity and the site of the Hellenic city
abandoned soon after the year 637, as there are no Arabic remains
above the Græco-Roman material. In the year 1121 Baldwin II,
of the Latin kingdom of Jerusalem, made a campaign against

10 See Polybius, V, 71.
11 Josephus, *Antiquities of the Jews*, XIII, xiii, 3.
12 Schürer, *Geschichte des Judischen Volkes im Zeitalter Jesu Christi*, 4th ed., II, 1907, p. 175.
13 Neubauer, *Géographie du Talmud*, 274.
14 See Merrill, *East of the Jordan*, New York, 1883, 184 ff. and 442, f.; also Schu-macher, *Across the Jordan*, London, 1886, p. 272, f.
15 Merrill, *ibid.*, 298, and G. A. Smith *Historical Geography of the Holy Land*, map.
16 So Brünnow and Domaszewski, *Provincia Arabia*, III, 264.
17 Josephus, *Wars of the Jews*, I, iv, 8.

Gerasa, where the ruler of Damascus had caused a castle to be built. In the next century the Arabian geographer, Yakut, describes it as deserted. It appears to have been ruined by an earthquake.

Apparently the Hellenic city at Gerasa lasted longer than any of the other cities of the Decapolis unless it be Kanatha. One can, accordingly, gain from the ruins of Gerasa an excellent idea of the general appearance of one of these cities.[18] The writer has never seen more beautiful ruins than those at Jerash except the ruins at Athens. As one approached the site from the south he faced a beautiful arched gateway. After passing this gateway one looked northward down a long colonnaded street, which at a little distance from the gate broadened out into a circular forum. At distances approximately equal from one another this main street was crossed by other colonnaded streets. A number of these columns are standing in different parts of the town. The remains of two imposing temples, of two theaters, of a large Christian basilica, and of various other buildings, impress one with the former glory of the city. A number of the buildings at Gerasa were built in the second century A.D. in the region of the Antonines (see Figs. 268, 269).

8. Philadelphia, the most southerly of the cities of the Decapolis, was on the site of Rabbah-Ammon (Deut. 3:11; Josh. 13:25; 2 Sam. 11:1, etc.). This was situated on the upper Jabbok about twenty miles east of the Jordan valley, where Amman now lies. The Hellenic city here was built by Ptolemy Philadelphus of Egypt, who reigned from 283–247 B.C. It was named Philadelphia from him. In 218 B.C. the city was taken by Antiochus III, who captured the cistern to which in time of siege the Philadelphians went for water by an underground passage,[19] after which thirst compelled them to surrender. Joab centuries before had captured the city for David by the same method,[20] and in 30 B.C. Herod the Great again took it in the same way.[21] The remains of the Hellenic temple, of the theater, and of other buildings, including a Christian basilica, are still to be seen at Amman.[22] In the fourth century

18 See Merrill, *East of the Jordan*, 281–284; Schumacher in *Zeitschrift des deutschen Palastina-Vereins*, XXV, 1912, 111–177; Brünnow and Domaszewski, *Provincia Arabia*, II, 234–239; Barton, *A Year's Wandering in Bible Lands*, 158, f. and the forthcoming volume of Yale University and the American School in Jerusalem on their joint exploration of the site.
19 See Polybius, V, 7.
20 See 2 Samuel 12:27 and Barton in the *Journal of Biblical Literature*, XXVII, 147–152.
21 See Josephus, *Wars of the Jews*, I, xix, 5.
22 See Merrill, *East of the Jordan*, 399 ff.; Schumacher, *Across the Jordan*, 308; Brünnow and Domaszewski, *Provincia Arabia*, II, 216–220, and Barton, *A Year's Wandering in Bible Lands*, 155, f.

A.D. Philadelphia was one of the prominent cities of the Roman province of Arabia (see Figs. 270, 271).

These cities of the Decapolis appear to have been built on a similar plan. Each had a colonnaded street through the center of the town, each had at least one temple and one theater, and some of them more. All were architecturally beautiful. They all possessed a similar government also, and each appears to have controlled the villages in its district.

9. Jesus in the Decapolis.—The prevailing influences in the Decapolis were pagan, and yet there were Jews living in it, for multitudes of them from the Decapolis followed Jesus (Matt. 4:25). On at least two occasions our Lord himself went into the territory of the Decapolis. We read in Mark 5:1 that Jesus and his disciples "came to the other side of the sea to the country of the Gerasenes." The Authorized Version reads "to the country of the Gadarenes." The country to which Jesus came at this time cannot have been that of the Decapolitan city Gerasa, for, as we have seen, that lay far to the south. It was in a direct line nearly fifty miles from the Sea of Galilee. Neither can it have been to the region of Gadara that he came, for Gadara lay at least five miles to the south across the deep valley of the Yarmuk. There was, however, on the east shore of the Sea of Galilee a town called Gergesa, the modern Kursi. This place was near the city of Hippos, and possibly one of the towns subordinate to Hippos. As Jesus and the disciples walked back from the sea they met the demoniac, whom Jesus healed. It was in connection with this healing that the herd of swine was destroyed—an incident that could happen in no part of Palestine except Decapolis or Philistia, for swine were unclean to Jews and they never kept them. The demoniac, when cured, went and preached Jesus in the Decapolis (Mark 5:20).

Again, toward the end of his ministry, Jesus, after he had withdrawn for a time to Phœnicia, returned by crossing the high lands of northern Galilee and coming down east of the Jordan "through the midst of the borders of Decapolis" (Mark 7:31).

CHAPTER XV

ATHENS, CORINTH, AND THE CHURCHES OF ASIA

ATHENS. CORINTH. THE CHURCHES OF ASIA: Ephesus. Pergamum. Thyatira. Sardis. Philadelphia. Smyrna, Laodicea. Antioch in Psidia. Tarsus.

THE greater part of Biblical history was enacted in Palestine and the great valleys of Mesopotamia and the Nile. The apostle Paul, however, broke the Jewish bonds of primitive Christianity and carried the gospel to the coasts of the Ægean Sea. In cities of this region he spent years of his active missionary life; to churches of this region most of his epistles were sent, and to churches of this part of the world the seven messages to the churches were addressed. We cannot, therefore, conclude this sketch of what archæology has done to throw light upon the Bible without saying a few words concerning exploration and excavations in certain parts of Greece and Asia Minor. It will be impossible for lack of space to go thoroughly into the history of this region, but as these lands were not, like Egypt, Babylonia, Assyria, and Palestine, closely connected with Biblical history for a long period, detailed history of them before the Apostolic age will not be missed by the student of the Bible.

The results of scattered discoveries at Thessalonica and elsewhere will be presented in Part II, Chapter XXX. At this point attention will be directed to a few important cities.

1. Athens, the chief city of Attica, one of the least productive parts of Greece, is the far-famed mistress of the world's culture and art. Emerging from obscurity in the seventh century before Christ, gaining a position of leadership in the Persian wars after 500 B.C., Athens established a considerable empire. In this period fell the age of Pericles, 460–429 B.C., when the artistic and literary genius of Athens reached a height never equaled in human history. Socrates was born here in 469 and lived till 399 B.C. Here Plato, who was born about 428, became a pupil of Socrates and afterward taught. Hither came Aristotle, after the year 367, to sit at Plato's feet. Here from the age of Pericles the acropolis was crowned with those architectural creations that are at once the admiration and the despair of the world (see Fig. 277). It stirs the imagination to think of Paul in such a city.

In the time of Paul, Athens was a Roman city, though still one of the great artistic and philosophical centers of the world. At a little distance from the acropolis on its northern side, a forum of the Roman period was laid bare in 1891 (see Fig. 272). Possibly this is the market-place in which Paul, during his stay there, reasoned every day with them that met him (Acts 17: 17), though of this we cannot be certain, for, while this was a market-place in the Roman period, the older market of the Athenian people lay to the westward of it.

To the west of the acropolis lies the old Areopagus, or Mars' Hill (Fig. 273), from which it was long supposed that Paul made the address recorded in Acts 17: 22–31. Ramsay,[1] following Curtius, has made it probable that the address was delivered to the city-fathers of Athens, not because they were putting Paul to a judicial trial, but because they wished to see whether he was to be allowed to teach Christianity, which they took for a new philosophy, in the university of Athens—for Athens itself was a kind of university. It seems probable that the meetings of the city-fathers, who were collectively called the Areopagus (Acts 17: 22), were held not on the top of the rock, but in the market-place. The Athenian altar "to an unknown god" is treated in Part II, Chapter XXX, § 2.

2. Corinth.—From Athens, Paul went to Corinth, where he spent a year and a half (Acts 18: 1, 11). Corinth was one of the old cities of Greece. In Homeric and earlier times it appears to have been subject to Argos. Situated on the isthmus between northern Greece and the Peloponnesus, the sea-trade of Corinth made it an important city. It rose to prominence in the seventh century before Christ. At some early time foreigners from the east, probably Phœnicians, had settled in Corinth and established the worship of the Semitic goddess Astarte on Acro-Corinthus, a hill that rises some five hundred feet above the city. The goddess was here known as Aphrodite,[2] and the debasing character of her worship tended to foster that lack of sensitiveness in matters of social morality with which Paul deals in his First Epistle to the Corinthians. The trade of Corinth made it rich and its riches excited the enmity of Rome. It was accordingly destroyed by the Romans in 146 B.C.,

---

1 Ramsay, *St. Paul the Traveller and Roman Citizen*, New York, 1896, 243, ff.
2 See Farnell, *Cults of the Greek States*, II, Oxford, 1896, 618–699.

but a century later was rebuilt by Julius Cæsar. Ancient Corinth
has now entirely vanished.

Excavations were begun at Corinth by the American School of
Classical Studies at Athens in 1896 under the direction of the late
Prof. Rufus B. Richardson. The work has been carried forward
season by season ever since.[3] Although there were no topographical
indications to help the excavators at the start, the theater, the
Agora or market-place, a Roman street, the road to Lechæum,
and the temple of Apollo have been discovered (Figs. 274, 276).

Of the greatest interest to the student of the Bible is a stone discovered in 1898 on the Lechæum road near the propylæa, or gateway leading to the market-place. This stone once formed the lintel
of a door and bore an inscription in Greek letters. Although the
beginning and the end of the two words written on it are broken
away, it is clear that the inscription was "Synagogue of the Hebrews." [4] The cutting of the letters was poorly done, and the block
was a second-hand one, adapted from some other use. It seems
probable, therefore, that the Jewish community at Corinth was not
wealthy. The block was of considerable size and so was probably
found not far from where the synagogue stood. If so, this synagogue, which is probably identical with the one in which Paul
preached (Acts 18:4), stood on the Lechæum road not far from the
market-place. Other discoveries in the neighborhood indicate that
this was a residence quarter of the city, and we learn from Acts
18:7 that the house of Titus Justus, where apparently Paul organized the first church in Corinth, "joined hard to the synagogue."
The house of Justus must, then, have been here, and the Lechæum
road often echoed to the footsteps of Paul. Probably the judg-
ment-seat to which the Jews dragged Paul for the hearing before
Gallio (Acts 18:12) was in the market-place, so that the excavations have revealed to us the parts of Corinth of special interest to a
reader of the Bible.

3. The Churches of Asia.

(1) *Ephesus* was situated on the Cayster river in western Asia
Minor, about three miles from the sea, but in ancient times the sea
was navigable up as far as the city. Cities which form the point of
contact between land and sea traffic become in most countries
populous and wealthy. In western Asia Minor four cities, situated

---

3 See *American Journal of Archæology*, 2d series, II, 133, f.; III, 204, f.; IV, 306, f.;
VI, 306, f., 439, f.; X, 17, f., and XIV, 19, f.
4 See Benjamin Powell in *American Journal of Archæology*, 2d series, VII, 60, f.,
and Fig. 275.

at the mouths of the four river valleys through which caravans could proceed into the interior, became populous and important. These were Miletus (see Acts 20:15, 17, f.) at the mouth of the Mæander, Ephesus at the mouth of the Cayster, Smyrna at the mouth of the Hermus, and Pergamum on the Caicus. In the earliest times known to us Ephesus was eclipsed in importance by Miletus, but before the beginning of the Christian era Ephesus had out-stripped her rival. This was due to several causes, one of which was the partial silting up of the harbor of Miletus. In Roman times Ephesus lay on the great line of communication between Rome and the East in general.[5] In later centuries the harbor of Ephesus was in its turn silted up, and the site is now deserted except for a neigh-boring wretched Turkish village.

In Homer's *Iliad* [6] the Carians are called the "barbarous-speaking Carians." This would indicate that they were not Greek, and it is thought by some that they may at this time have been of Hittite stock. Miletus was in Caria, and at that time Ephesus also. It is certain that the earliest inhabitants of Ephesus were not Greek, but of Asiatic origin. They established here, either on a mountain top about five miles from the sea, just above the modern railway station of Ayassuluk, or on a mountain a little to the south, the worship of an Asiatic, probably Hittite, goddess. Later, in the seventh century before Christ, the Ionian Greeks came and settled among the Asiatics. They identified the goddess with their own Artemis (Authorized Version, Diana), and moved her temple down into the plain,[7] where it continued to stand far into Christian times. In the sixth century B.C. Ephesus was conquered by the Lydians, and then by the Persians. In later centuries it passed under the control of Alexander the Great, of the Seleucidæ of Syria, and of the kings of Pergamum. In 133 B.C. it passed with the rest of the kingdom of Pergamum into the hands of Rome and became a part of the Roman Province of Asia. Because of its situation it quickly became the most important city of the province. It was noted for its wealth and its commerce. Rome became the patron of Hellenic culture in the East, so Ephesus was, of course, made an architectur-ally beautiful city.

At first Pergamum was the capital of the Province of Asia. In the second and third centuries of the Christian era Ephesus had be-

5 See Ramsay's article "Ephesus" in Hastings' *Dictionary of the Bible*, Vol. II, p. 721, f., for further details.
6 Book II, 1, 868.
7 See Hogarth's *Ionia and the East*, Oxford, 1909, p. 45, f.

come the capital. Buchner [8] thinks that this transfer was made in the reign of Claudius, 41–54 AD. If this were true, Ephesus was the capital of the province at the time of Paul's residence there, but there is considerable doubt about the facts, and in the beginning of the second century A.D. Pergamum still ranked as the official capital.[9]

The temple of Artemis lay about two miles to the northeast of the ancient city. Its site was determined in 1869 by the English explorer, J. T. Wood, who partially excavated it (1869–1874).[10] Wood brought to light various marble fragments which are preserved in the British Museum, but he was more interested in making conjectural restorations of the temple than in telling what he found. As he was not an expert in ancient architecture his work is, accordingly, unsatisfactory. In 1904–1905, the British Museum employed Mr. Hogarth to complete the excavation of the site. Hogarth carried the excavation down to the virgin soil, and, being a skilled archæologist, he was able to reconstruct the history of the building.[11]

There seems to have been a small tree shrine on the site of the temple before the Ionians came. Between the seventh century and the fifth, three different structures were erected on the spot. The last of these was called the temple of Crœsus, because this king of Lydia presented some beautiful columns to it, though the structure was not completed till a century after his time, or 430 B.C. This structure was burned in 356 B.C. on the night that Alexander the Great was born. Later a larger temple, 425 by 220 feet, was built on the site, with the help of contributions from the whole of Asia. This was standing until long after Paul's time. It was very beautiful. Some of the porphyry columns now in Santa Sophia at Constantinople are said to have been taken from it. It has been thought by some that this beautiful temple suggested to Paul his figure in 1 Corinthians 3 : 10–17, since the words were written from Ephesus.

This temple was venerated over all of western Asia Minor. To it came many pilgrims every year, to whom Ephesian silversmiths sold little replicas of the temple. It was because Christianity became so popular through the preaching of Paul that the profitable sale of these shrines was interfered with, that the riot in Ephesus occurred as described in Acts 19 : 23–41.

Before Mr. Wood had discovered the site of the temple he had discovered the theater within the limits of the ancient city. This

8 See *DeNeocoria*, p. 38.
9 See Ramsay in Hastings' *Dictionary of the Bible*, III, 750.
10 Wood, *Discoveries at Ephesus*, London, 1877. See Fig. 279.
11 Hogarth, *Excavations at Ephesus*, London, 1908.

has been examined more thoroughly by the Austrian, Dr. Wiberg, who, beginning in 1894, conducted excavations at Ephesus for many years. All the lower parts of this theater still remain (see Figs. 280, 281) and bring vividly to the imagination the assembly held in it on the occasion of the riot just referred to. (See Acts 19: 29–41.) The Austrians have also laid bare a considerable part of the central street of the Ephesus of Roman times (see Fig. 278).

A little to the north of the theater is the ancient stadium. Some scholars think that when Paul says in 1 Corinthians 15: 32, "If after the manner of men I fought with beasts at Ephesus," he is speaking of an incident that literally occurred, and suppose that he was actually condemned and thrown to the beasts in the stadium, to make a spectacle for the Ephesian populace, and that in some way he escaped alive. It is possible that this may be true. If so, this stadium (see Fig. 282) presents to the eye a spot which is of great interest to every Christian.

Ephesus, as the mother-church of the churches of Asia, is the first one to which in the book of Revelation a letter is addressed. By the time Revelation was written the first glow of Christian enthusiasm had worn off, gnostic heresy had found a place in the Church, and its "first love" was gone.

(2) *Pergamum,* the modern Bergama, lay in the valley of the Caicus in Mysia, about fifteen miles from the sea. The city was built on a hill about three miles north of the river. It was apparently a place of some importance at a comparatively early date, but its chief importance began with the reign of Philetærus, who made it an independent kingdom and ruled it from 284–263 B.C. Philetærus had been a trusted servant of Lysimachus, King of Thrace, one of the trusted generals of Alexander the Great. Under the dynasty founded by Philetærus, Pergamum became one of the chief seats of Hellenic culture. Eumenes I (263–241 B.C.) endeavored to make Pergamum a rival of Alexandria as a literary center, and when the king of Egypt forbade the exportation of papyrus in order to check the literary aspirations of Pergamum, the servants of Eumenes invented a prepared kind of skin on which to write. It was called *pergamena,* but time has corrupted it to "parchment."

In the course of the second century before Christ the kingdom of Pergamum included all of western Asia Minor north of the Taurus. When in 133 B.C. Attalus III, the last of the kings of Pergamum, died, he left his kingdom by will to the Roman republic, with which Pergamum had long been in alliance. Rome thus came into possession of her Province of Asia, the first of her Oriental provinces. Pergamum was its capital, certainly until the reign of Claudius, and probably until the second century A.D. The Romans regarded them-selves as the patrons of Hellenic culture in the East and for cen-turies kept Pergamum the beautiful city which the Pergamene kings had made it. Bergama, the squalid modern Turkish city, lies apart from the splendid ruins of the ancient town (see Fig. 283).

More than thirty years ago the Germans began to explore and to excavate at Pergamum,[12] and the Museum at Berlin is enriched with many beautiful objects found there. The visitor to Perga-mum may still see, however, the great gymnasium with many grace-ful columns still standing. Above it, on a higher slope, are the sites of theaters and temples, and the great altar of Zeus. Farther up the hill stood the temple of Athenæ Polias, which was also a library, and above this the temple of Rome and of Augustus.

In Revelations 2: 13 the church at Pergamum is said to dwell where "Satan's throne is." Interpreters have been divided in opinion as to whether this is a reference to the worship of Æsculapius, or to the presence of the great throne-like altar of Zeus, or to the fact that Pergamum was the seat of the worship of the Roman emperor.[13] On the whole, it seems probable that "Satan's throne" is a reference to the fact that Pergamum was the seat of the government and of the worship of the emperor of Rome. When Augustus inaugurated emperor-worship in order to give the empire a bond of common sen-timent, the first temple of the cult was erected at Pergamum. This was in 29 B.C. Under Vespasian and his successors it became a test of one's Christianity whether he would or would not[14] offer incense to the statue of the emperor, and Christians were often persecuted because they would not. It is probable that in the remains of the temple to the emperor archæologists have brought to light that which the Book of Revelation called Satan's throne. If, however, that throne were the altar of Zeus, it has nevertheless been brought to light.

(3) *Thyatira,* the modern Ak-Hissar, lay in a valley which joined the valley of the Hermus to the valley of the Caicus. The general direction of this valley was north and south. It was made an im-

---

12 See Couze (and others), *Ausgrabungen zu Pergamos,* Berlin, 1880, and Thrämer, *Pergamos,* Leipzig, 1888; also F. E. Clark, *The Holy Land of Asia Minor,* New York, 1914, p. 67, f.
13 See Bousset, *Die Offenbarung des Johannes,* Göttingen, 1896, p. 245, ff.; Ramsay, *The Letters to the Seven Churches,* New York, 1905, 283, ff., and Moffat in *The Expositor's Greek Testament,* Vol. V, New York, 1910, p. 355, f.
14 See Ramsay, *The Church and the Roman Empire,* New York, 1893, p. 252, f.

portant city by Seleucus I of Syria (312–282 B.C.) in the latter part of his reign. Before this it had been an obscure village. Josephus declares [15] that Seleucus made Jews citizens of the cities which he founded in Asia, and apparently Thyatira was one of these, for there appears to have been a flourishing Jewish colony there. A little later than Seleucus, Thyatira became a city of Pergamum, and passed in 133 B.C. with the territories of that realm under the dominion of Rome. Thyatira was noted for its dyeing. Madder root, with which they dyed a Turkey-red, grows abundantly in the neighborhood.[16] As the ancients employed the names of colors with great laxity, this was often termed purple. Lydia, an enterprising seller of this purple, a Jewess from Thyatira, was present at Philippi when Paul and Silas preached there (Acts 16 : 14). Lydia was converted, and perhaps it was she who carried the gospel back to Thyatira. Nothing has been discovered at Thyatira that throws light on the message to its church in Revelation 2 : 18–29.

(4) *Sardis* was one of the oldest cities of western Asia. It is situated on the south side of the great valley of the Hermus, just at the point where the river Pactolus issues from the Tmolus mountains. Pottery found in the course of excavations there carries its history back to sub-Mycenæan, if not to Mycenæan, times.[17] It was the seat of the worship of Atys or Cybele, a goddess that seems to have been kindred to the mother-goddess of the Hittites. It is probable that, could we penetrate back far enough, we should find that the place was once occupied by Hittites. Herodotus traces the descent of the first dynasty that ruled over the country to the goddess just mentioned.[18] Following this dynasty was, he says, another of twenty-one kings who ruled before the dynasty founded by Gyges. The Lydian kingdom of which we know began with Gyges in 697 B.C. and ended with Crœsus in 546 B.C. Lydian inscriptions found at Sardis are written in the same alphabet as Etruscan inscriptions found in Italy. This indicates that the Lydians and Etruscans were closely akin, but, as the inscriptions have not yet been deciphered, they do not throw much light on either people.[19] It is possible that both peoples were related to the Hittites, but that is at present only a hypothesis.

15 Josephus, *Antiquities of the Jews,* XII, iii, 1.
16 See Ramsay, *Letters to the Seven Churches,* p. 325, ff.
17 See Butler in *American Journal of Archæology,* 2d series, Vol. XVIII, 1914, p. 428.
18 Book I, 7.
19 See Herbig's article, "Etruscan Religion," in Hastings' *Encyclopædia of Religion and Ethics,* Vol. V, New York, 1912, p. 532, ff.

The mountains to the south of Sardis are composed largely of gravel deposits left there by the melting of the glaciers at the end of the last glacial period. From these gravels the Pactolus brought down gold in ancient times. This was one of the sources of the wealth of the Lydian kings, and contributed to those riches which are still celebrated in the saying: "As rich as Crœsus."

The Lydian kingdom fell when Cyrus captured Sardis in 546 B.C. With the fall of the Persian empire the city passed into the hands of Alexander the Great, and subsequently into the hands of his general, Antigonous, then to the Seleucidæ of Syria, then to the kings of Pergamum, and so to the dominion of Rome.

In 17 A.D. Sardis was shaken by a great earthquake which nearly destroyed the city. A mass of gravel and conglomerate rock was then hurled from the hill of the Acropolis of Sardis down into the city toward the temple, where the work of the excavator shows that it still lies.[20] A part of the city must have been buried under it. The city recovered from this disaster and by the end of the first century a Christian church existed there (Rev. 3:1–6). Sardis continued to be a city of importance until 1400–1403 A.D., when the Tartar conqueror, Timur or Tamerlane, swept over the country destroying everything before him. From this destruction Sardis never recovered. Two or three tiny wretched Turkish villages are now all that occupy the spot.[21]

The Acropolis of Sardis was composed of gravel and a comparatively soft conglomerate rock. It looks imposing and in ancient times looked far more imposing than now. It has been gradually crumbling away through the centuries. Ramsay thinks that this instability on the part of the city itself is alluded to in the words, "thou hast a name that thou livest, and thou art dead" and in the exhortation to be watchful and to strengthen the things that remain, which follows it (Rev. 3:1, 2) (see Fig. 284).

Excavations were begun at Sardis by Princeton University under the direction of Prof. Howard Crosby Butler in 1909, and the digging continued for five seasons until interrupted by the great war.[22] The work began at the point where two columns of the ancient temple of Cybele were still protruding from the soil. The temple has been cleared and a considerable area around it has been examined. It appears that the temple was built in the fourth century B.C., that it suffered greatly in the earthquake of 17 A.D., and never was as

20 *American Journal of Archæology*, Vol. XVII, 1912, p. 474.
21 Barton, *A Year's Wandering in Bible Lands*, 76–79.
22 See Howard Crosby Butler, *Sardis*, Leyden, 1922.

splendid afterwards, though it was still in use in the second century A.D.[23] Many objects have been discovered which throw light upon the history and art of Lydia, and two bi-lingual inscriptions, one Lydian and Aramaic, the other Lydian and Greek, were found. These may afford the key to the decipherment of both Lydian and Etruscan. Jewelry resembling Etruscan jewelry found in Italy was also discovered.[24]

To the student of the Bible the most interesting discovery at Sardis was a little Christian church built at the southeast corner of the temple.[25] The entrance to this church was from the temple platform itself. The structure was entirely of brick and was in a remarkably good state of preservation. The building had apparently lost only its wooden roof. The apse of the church was toward the east, and still contained its primitive altar. It is uncertain at what date altars became a part of Christian worship. Origen in the third century A.D. admits the charge of Celsus that the Christians had no visible altar,[26] but Eusebius [27] in the next century speaks as though altars existed throughout the Christian world. This church at Sardis was built after the temple of Cybele had fallen into disuse, and even if not earlier than the fourth century of our era, this little structure is evidence that the name of the church had not been blotted out of the book of life (Rev. 3: 5), but that it had rather appropriated to itself the once splendid precincts of the ancient heathen goddess.

(5) *Philadelphia* was situated twenty-eight miles east of Sardis, and lay in the valley of the Cogamis, a tributary of the Hermus. It is still a flourishing city of 15,000 or more inhabitants. It is now called Ala-Sheher.[28] It is not to be confounded with the Philadelphia of the Decapolis in Palestine.[29]

Philadelphia was founded by Attalus II, King of Pergamum, 159–138 B.C., who was called Philadelphus because of his devotion to his predecessor and brother, Eumenes II. Hence the city was named Philadelphia. It was founded for the purpose of spreading Hellenism in the eastern part of Lydia, and so was a missionary city from the first. With the other Pergamene territories it became a dependency of Rome in 133 B.C. In 17 A.D. it suffered severely

23 *Amer. Jour. of Arch.*, XV, 452.
24 *Ibid.*, XV, 457.
25 *Ibid.*, XVI, 475, ff., and Fig. 286.
26 See "Altar (Christian)" in Hastings' *Encyclopædia of Religion and Ethics*. Vol. I, p. 338, f.
27 *Ecclesiastical History*, X, 4.
28 See Barton, *A Year's Wandering in Bible Lands*, p. 71.
29 See Chapter XIV, p. 260 f.

from the same earthquake that destroyed Sardis. Indeed, at Philadelphia the quakings were even more severe. The trembling of the earth lasted for a long time. When Strabo wrote in 20 A.D. earthquake shocks at Philadelphia were an every-day occurrence. Few people lived in the city; most of the inhabitants spent their time outside.[30] Allusion to this is, perhaps, made in Revelation 3:12: "he shall go out thence no more."

After the earthquake the city appealed to Rome for help. Tiberius granted it and also permitted the city to change its name to Neocæsarea, or the city of the young Cæsar.[31] This, too, seems to be alluded to in Revelation 3:12, where another new name is to be conferred.

At Ala-Sheher a part of the city wall of Philadelphia may still be traced, and the sites of the acropolis, the theater, and the stadium could, in 1902, still be seen, as well as the ruins of an old Christian church.[32]

(6) *Smyrna,* at the mouth of the Hermus, is one of the very old cities of Asia Minor. A colony of Æolian Greeks founded a city here more than a thousand years before Christ. A little later the place was captured by Ionian Greeks, who held it till about 600 B.C., when it was conquered by the kings of Lydia and destroyed.[33] For three hundred years the name designated a district rather than a city. Lysimachus, the general of Alexander the Great who became king of Thrace (301–282 B.C.), refounded Smyrna as a Greek city about three miles southwest of the old site, and it has continued ever since to be an important seaport of Asia Minor. It passed with the other cities of the region successively under the sway of the kings of Syria, the kings of Pergamum, and of Rome. Smyrna is today one of the largest cities of the East with a population of between two and three hundred thousand.

Smyrna claimed to be the birthplace of Homer. Ælius Aristides (born 117 A.D.), who lived at Smyrna, several times likens the city to a crown, and apparently the crown was in some way associated with Smyrna (see Fig. 287). The goddess of the place, who was a kind of Cybele, is pictured as wearing a crown.[34] This is, no doubt, the reason why in Revelation 2:10 a crown of life is promised to the church of Smyrna if she is faithful. No excavations have been

30 Ramsay, *Letters to the Seven Churches,* 407, ff.
31 *Ibid.,* 410, ff.
32 See Curtius, *Philadelphia,* Berlin, 1873, and Barton, *A Year's Wandering in Bible Lands,* 79, ff.
33 Ramsay, *Letters to the Seven Churches,* 25, 1.
34 See Ramsay, *Letters to the Seven Churches,* 257 and 274, ff.

made at Smyrna, but above the city the tomb of Polycarp,[35] said in tradition to have been a disciple of the apostle John, is shown. Polycarp was martyred in 155 A.D. in one of those times of tribulation predicted in Revelation 2 : 10.

(7) *Laodicea* is situated a hundred miles east of Ephesus, in the valley of the Lycus, where the Lycus empties into the Mæander. It was founded by Antiochus II of Syria, 261–246 B.C.,[36] and named for his wife. Like Philadelphia, it was designed to be a missionary of Hellenism to the country of the region. Like the other Hellenic cities it was beautified with temples, theaters, and colonnaded streets. Later Laodicea passed under the control of Pergamum, and with that kingdom fell to Rome in 133 B.C. An influential element in its population was Jewish, and before Paul's imprisonment in Rome a Christian church had been founded there (Col. 4 : 13). The city of Laodicea appears to have been devoted to commerce and to material things. In Revelation 3 : 15 its church is said to have been lukewarm. Except that its lukewarmness may have come from its commercial spirit, there is nothing in the history or archæology of the city that illustrates the letter [37] to it in Revelation 3 : 14–22.

The site of Laodicea is now almost deserted. Only the wretched Turkish village of Eski Hissar represents habitation, but hundreds of acres are covered with the ruins of the once splendid city. For hundreds of years the villagers of neighboring hamlets have used the place as a quarry, but nevertheless its ruins are impressive. Two theaters are in a fairly good state of preservation; the seats are still in place.[38] The stadium is in a similar condition of preservation. Its aqueduct and its gates are still imposing in their dilapidation, but the desolation of Laodicea recalls the words: "I will spew thee out of my mouth" (Rev. 3 : 16); (see Fig. 288).

4. Antioch of Pisidia was partially excavated by Professor David M. Robinson, of the Johns Hopkins University, while acting as director of an expedition of the University of Michigan, in the summer of 1924.[39] Antioch was founded by Seleucus I—who died in 282 B.C.—probably on the site of an earlier Pisidian town. It passed under Roman rule in 190 B.C., and a year later was made by them a free city. In 39 B.C. Mark Antony gave it to King Amyntas, who, like Herod the Great, was really a Roman subject. Amyntas

35 See Barton, *A Year's Wandering in Bible Lands,* p. 82.
36 See Ramsay, *The Cities and Bishoprics of Phrygia,* Oxford, 1895, p. 32, f.
37 See Ramsay, *Letters to the Seven Churches,* 424, ff.
38 See F. E. Clark, *The Holy Land of Asia Minor,* New York, 1914, p. 145, f.
39 See Professor Robinson's "Preliminary Report" in the *American Journal of Archæology,* Vol. XXVIII (1924), pp. 435–444.

was taken prisoner and put to death in 25 B.C. by brigand tribes whom the Romans called Homanadenses. Amyntas left his kingdom by will to the Emperor Augustus. Augustus accepted the legacy, organized the Province of Galatia, and, making Antioch his military base, afterward punished the Homanadenses. Tiberius beautified the city with a well-paved square or market place, which was surrounded by imposing buildings. This square Dr. Robinson cleared. (See Fig. 318.) The city built by Tiberius was still flourishing when Paul and Barnabas visited it and founded a Christian church there. (See Acts 13, 14.) The pavement shown is that actually trodden by the feet of the apostles. For many centuries Christianity flourished at Antioch, as the remains of the Byzantine Church shown in Fig. 317 testify.

5. Tarsus. The ancient city of Tarsus is represented by the mound of Gözlü Kule, the largest mound in the plain of what was ancient Cilicia. Small excavations were made in it twice during the nineteenth century. The first in 1845 was by the British Consul, Barker, the second in 1852, by a Frenchman named Langlois. Each of these obtained a quantity of terra cotta figurines and lamps. In 1934 Bryn Mawr College sent an expedition to search for a promising field for excavation within the confines of ancient Hittite influence, and soundings were made in the mound of Gözlü Kule. As a result it was decided to excavate that mound and two seasons have been spent in the work, those of 1935 and 1936.[40] These expeditions were directed by Miss Hetty Goldman. At present (1937) but meager accounts of the work have been published, but these are of great interest. Strata of Turkish, Arabian, Roman, Hellenistic, and earlier occupations back to that of the Hittites, 1400–1200 B.C. have been explored, and much pottery, many figurines, figures of deities, tablets inscribed in the Assyrian language as well as in hieroglyphic Hittite have been found. One of these is the seal of Pudu-Hepa, the queen of Hattusil III, who ruled before 1200 B.C. The figurines of the gods of many nations, the oriental Sandon, the Greek Herakles, the Egyptian Serapis, which were yielded by the Roman strata, are witnesses to the mixture of nationalities and cultures in the midst of which Saul of Tarsus was born and reared. It was a fitting school for an Apostle to the Gentiles.

40 See *American Journal of Archæology*, XXXIX (1935), 526–549 and XLI (1937), 262–291.

PART II

TRANSLATIONS OF ANCIENT DOCUMENTS WHICH CONFIRM OR ILLUMINATE THE BIBLE

FOREWORD

As noted in the Preface, the inferences drawn by different scholars, when they compare the Bible with the records brought to light by exploration, diverge according as their critical and theological views differ. In the comments made throughout Part II, as in Part I, the writer has endeavored to maintain a neutral attitude and impartially to report in each case the principal inferences drawn by the most important groups of scholars, that the reader may know something of the latitude of opinion that prevails. To have recorded every opinion would have expanded the work far beyond the limits prescribed, and would have burdened the reader with many views that are mere vagaries. The temptation is always strong to declare that the interpretation of an ancient record which accords with one's own views must be right, but unfortunately problems in ancient history that are thus dogmatically settled do not remain settled. A deeper faith, confident in the ultimate triumph of truth, patiently awaits further light.

CHAPTER I

AN EPIC OF THE CREATION WHICH CIRCULATED IN BABYLON AND ASSYRIA IN THE SEVENTH CENTURY BEFORE CHRIST [1]

TEXT OF THE EPIC. COMPARISON OF THE EPIC WITH THE FIRST CHAPTER OF GENESIS. THE EPIC AND OTHER PARTS OF THE BIBLE.

1. Text of the Epic. *I, II, III deal with gods See P 297*

Tablet I *(generation of the gods)*

1. Time was when above	heaven was not named
2. Below to the earth	no name was given.
3. Then the primeval Abyss	their begetter,
4. The roaring Sea	who bore them,—
5. Their waters	together were mingled;
6. No field had been formed, no marsh-land seen.	
7. When no gods	had ever been honored,
8. No name was formed	no destiny fixed,
9. Gods were created	in their midst [2]
10. Lakhmu and Lakhamu	their associates were called.
11. Together they became great,	grew tall.
12. Anshar and Kishar were born;	they were greater than they.
13. The days were prolonged,	years passed;
14. Anu their son	was a rival of his fathers.
15. Anshar made Anu, his firstborn, like himself,	
16. And Anu begat in his likeness Nudimmud,	
17. Nudimmud of his fathers	became ruler, even he;
18. Clever, wise, joyful,	who grasped deep things,
19. Stronger far than Anshar,	the father who begat him,
20. Not a rival has he	among the gods his fathers.
21. They stood; the gods assembled.	
22. They troubled Tiâmat	to protect themselves they attacked (her),

1 Other translations of this epic have been made. The most important are as follows: Zimmern, in Gunkels *Schöpfung und Chaos,* pp. 401, ff.; *Delitzsch, Das Babylonische Weltschöpfungsepos* (Abhandlungen der sächsischen Gesellschaft der Wissenschaften, Bd. XVII, 1896); Muss-Arnolt, in *Assyrian and Babylonian Literature,* Aldine ed., edited by R. F. Harper; Jensen in Schrader's *Keilschriftliche Bibliothek,* Bd. VI; L. W. King, *The Seven Tablets of Creation;* Dhorme, *Choix de textes religieux assyrobabyloniens;* Ungnad, in Gressman's *Altorientalische Texte und Bilder zum Alten Testament;* Rogers, *Cuneiform Parallels to the Old Testament.* D. D. Luckenbill translated in the *American Journal of Semitic Languages and Literatures,* Vol. XXXVIII, pp. 14–26, the portions of the Epic discovered at Ashur and published by Ebeling in *Keilschrifttexte aus Assur, Religions Inhalts;* S. Langdon, *The Babylonian Epic of Creation,* Oxford, 1923. A fragment of this tablet is shown in Figure 290.

2 That is, Sea and Abyss, mentioned in lines 3 and 4. Apsu was the waters underneath the dry land and Tiâmat the salt sea.

23. They troubled the body   of Tiâmat.
24. In agitation   he was enrolled among the great.
25. Apsu could not quiet   their outcry;
26. Tiâmat roared at their ....
27. She smote and their deeds. ....
28. Their way was not good; they themselves prospered.
29. Then Apsu, the begetter of the great gods,
30. Cried to Mummu, his minister, and said,
31. O Mummu, my minister, who delightest my heart,
32. Come, unto Tiâmat [let us go].
33. They went, before Tiâmat they lay down,
34. A plan they formed against the gods [their offspring].
35. [Apsu] opened his mouth, [he said to her],
36. Unto Tiâmat, the brilliant, a word he spoke:
37. "[Intolerable to me] is their advancement,
38. By day I have no rest, at night, no peace.
39. But I will destroy their way, an end will I make.
40. Let there be a cry, then we may be at peace!"
41. When Tiâmat heard these words,
42. She was angry and spoke against them [a curse];
43. [She was] grievously [pained] she raged..................
44. A curse she let fall, unto [Apsu she spoke]:
45. "What are we that we [should perish]!
46. Let their way become difficult."...........................
47. Mummu answered, Apsu [he counseled]
48. ....not favorable was the counsel of the Roarer:
49. "Their way is strong, but do thou confound [it],
50. By day thou shalt be calm, by night thou shalt lie down."
51. Apsu heard and his face brightened,
52. [Since] he planned evil against the gods his sons
53. Mummu [3] clasped his [neck],
54. He sat him on his knees, he kissed................
55. The whole they planned,   in the whole................
56. Against the gods, their firstborn, they unloosed their power.
57. They cursed the gods   they slandered (?) them,
58. Silence (?) seized them,   they sat quietly.
59. The wise, the instructed   the exalted one,
60. Ea, who understands everything, saw their plan
61. He grasped it and,   comprehending all, sat.
62. He prepared his power,   his holy witchcraft,
63. He numbered it   and put it in water.
64. Sleep came upon him [Apsu]   resting, he sank down.
65. He put Apsu to rest,   pouring out sleep.
66. Mummu wandered about,   with dress disordered (?),
67. He burst his bond,   from his mouth ....
68. His lustre was gone   he himself was prostrated.
69. He (Ea) had bewitched him;   Apsu he had killed.
70. Mummu he bound,   over him stationed a guard,
71. He placed himself on Apsu   in a sitting posture,
72. Mummu he grasped,   he held his massive form,
73. Both of them he had bound,   he had destroyed,
74. He established his triumph   over his enemies.
75. Amid the destruction   he rested peacefully.
76. He bound (?) him   and cast Apsu down to the depths.

3 Mummu is a personification of the roar of the ocean; Tiâmat, of the salt water; Apsu, of the fresh water.

77. On his body (?)   he founded his luxurious palace;
78. Lakhmu and Lakhamu his wife he placed as rulers over it,
79. As guards   of the domed abodes
80. In the abode of the fates,   the dwelling of destiny.
81. The mighty one, the leader of the gods, Marduk (?) [said:]
82. In the midst of the deep   Anshar was born,
83. In the holy deep   Anshar was born,
84. There begat him   Lakhmu, his father,
85. Lakhamu, his mother,   conceived him,
86. There nourished him milk   flowing from goddesses.
87. A marauder (?) approached him,   terror filled him;
88. Tall was his stature,   brilliant the look of his eye,
89. Troubled was his voice,   his course was hither and thither.
90. Lakhmu, who begat him,   his father, saw him,
91. Intelligently he looked,   his heart was filled with joy,
92. He saved him and   an equal of the gods made him,
93. He was greatly exalted over them who help Tiâmat.
94. Indescribable was his brilliance, unnumbered his ....
95. Unthinkable his ...., difficult to look upon,
96. Four eyes, four ears he had,
97. His lips he opened,   fire came forth
98. There grew four ears.
99. Four eyes like them were bright,
100. That one among the gods   [his command was that] of Anu;
101. His leadership .... [is for] the preservation of life;
102. His crown shall shine brightly; he shall confound Tiâmat.
103. .... he shall cause fear,
104. ....forever,
105. ....evil.
106. ....in opposition he spoke:
107. ....he conquered.
108. ....'....weeps and sits in tribulation.
109. ....fear,
110. ....we shall not lie down [in peace].
111. ....Apsu and Mummu who were bound.
112. ....quickly thou shalt oppose (?)
113. ....that we ourselves may rest.
114. ....the fury of the lords (?)..
115. ....avenge them!
116. ....to the storm...............
117. ....the word of the bright god,
118. ....what thou givest, we will indeed do!
119. ....the gods in....................
120. ....the gods [she] created.
121. They separated themselves, to the side of Tiâmat they came;
122. They raged, they planned, they rested not night or day.
123. They prepared for battle, fuming, raging;
124. Their assemblage was formed and they began war.
125. Mother Khubur, who formed all things,
126. Made unrivaled weapons, spawned great serpents,
127. Sharp of tooth, unsparing of fang;
128. With poison instead of blood their bodies she filled.
129. Fierce dragons with terror she clothed,
130. Luster she made abundant, to loftiness made them equal.
131. Whoever beheld them, terror (?) overcame him;
132. Their bodies they reared up without turning their breast.

133. She established vipers, serpents, and Lakhami,
134. Hurricanes, raging hounds, scorpion-men,
135. Mighty storms, fish-men, and rams (?);
136. They bore merciless weapons, fearless of battle.
137. Her behests were mighty; without rival were they.
138. Moreover eleven such as these she created.
139. Among the gods, her firstborn, who at her side gathered,
140. She exalted Kingu, made him great in their midst,
141. To march before the forces, to lead the host,
142. To raise the conquering weapon, to lead the attack,
143. To direct the battle, as commander-in-chief;
144. To him she entrusted it, made him sit in purple (?):
145. "Thy spell I have uttered; in the assembly of gods I have made thee great.
146. The sovereignty of all the gods, I have placed in thy hand
147. Surely thou art exalted, my only spouse!
148. May they magnify thy name over all the Anunnaki." [4]
149. She gave him the tablets of destiny, on his breast she laid them:
150. Thy command shall be unalterable, established, thy word."
151. Now Kingu was exalted, he received the highest rank,
152. Among the gods, his sons, he fixed fate:
153. "The opening of your mouth shall quench the fire-god;
154. Who so is exalted in excellence, let him increase in might."

Tablet II

1. Tiâmat made mighty her work
2. [Evil] she cherished against the gods, her offspring.
3. [To avenge] Apsu, Tiâmat planned evil.
4. Her [forces] how she joined, to Ea was divulged.
5. Ea [hearkened] to this thing,
6. He was thrown into [great] straits, he sat in silence.
7. [The days] went by; his anger was appeased,
8. [To the place] of Anshar, his father, he proceeded.
9. [He went] before the father who begat him, Anshar,
10. [All that] Tiâmat had planned he repeated unto him.
11. "Tiâmat, our mother, has come to hate us;
12. Her assembly is set; with rage she is hot;
13. Turned unto her are the gods, all of them,
14. With those ye created, they walk at her side.
15. They have separated themselves; at the side of Tiâmat they go;
16. They rage, they plan; they rest not day or night."

(Lines 17–48 continue the literal repetition of lines 109–142 of the first tablet which was begun in lines 15, 16. After this the narrative continues:)

49. [When Anshar heard how Tiâmat] was greatly in disorder,
50. [He smote his breast], he bit his lip,
51. [His mind was disturbed], his heart was not at rest,
52. "......................his cry was wrung from him.
53. [Away Ea, my son, go forth to] battle!
54. Thou art he who hast smitten [them].
55. [Mummu and] Apsu thou hast already struck down.
56. [Kill also Kin]gu who comes up before her

---

4 *I. e.*, the spirits of earth.

57. ......,...............deliberation.
58. ....gods Nudimmud.

(A break of ten or twelve lines occurs at this point in the tablet.)

72. [Anshar] spoke to his son [a word] :
73. "Thou, this [son of mine], my warrior,
74. [Whose strength is mighty], whose attack irresistible,
75. [Go], stand before Tiâmat,
76. [That] her wrath [may be appeased], her heart softened,
77. [But if] she will not hearken to thy word,
78. Our [word] shalt thou speak to her, that she may be appeased."
79. [He heard] the utterance of his father Anshar,
80. He took the straight path to her, he entered the way.
81. Anu [drew near], he beheld the terror (?) of Tiâmat,
82. [He did not ascend to her presence], but turned back,
83. [Then turned he to Ea and called] him, he, Anshar,
84. [Opened his mouth] and spoke to him,
85. ["Hateful are the ways of Tiâmat] to me."

(Some twenty lines here are too fragmentary for translation.)

108. [Ea opened his mouth (?)] and spoke to him:
109. ["Marduk, my son, hear the word of] thy father.
110. Thou art he, my son, who canst enlarge his heart.
111. ....to the battle draw nigh,
112. ....[to] Emarukka [5] give peace."
113. Then the lord rejoiced at the words of his father ;
114. He drew near and stood before Anshar.
115. Anshar beheld him and his heart was filled with joy,
116. He kissed his lips and his fear departed from him.
117. ....is not hidden; open thy lips.
118. Verily I will go, I will attain the wish of thy heart.
119. ....is not concealed; open thy lips.
120. Verily I will go, I will attain the wish of thy heart.
121. Who is the man, who would bring thee out to his battle?
122. [And now] shall Tiâmat, a woman, come against thee with weapons?
123. ....rejoice and exult;
124. On the neck of Tiâmat thou shalt shortly tread.
125. ....rejoice and exult;
126. On the neck of Tiâmat thou shalt shortly tread."
127. "My son, who knows all wisdom,
128. Tiâmat pacify with thy pure incantation.
129. Thy way speedily take;
130. ....Thou shalt not fear, thou shalt return afterward."
131. Then the lord rejoiced at the word of his father,
132. His heart exulted and to his father he spoke:
133. "O Lord of the gods, fate of the great gods,
134. If I accomplish your preservation,
135. Take Tiâmat captive and save your lives,
136. Appoint an assembly, make my fate strong, let it come in.
137. In Upshukkunnaku seat yourselves joyfully together,
138. The word of my mouth shall determine fate instead of you.
139. Let there not be changed whatever I create,
140. May the command of my lips not be altered or opposed."

5 Another name for Tiâmat.

Tablet III

1. Anshar opened his mouth and said,
2. [To Gaga] his [messenger] a word he spoke:
3. "[O Gaga, thou messen]ger, thou rejoicest my heart.
4. [To Lakhmu and Lakh]amu will I send thee;
5. [The desire of my heart] mayest thou attain.
6. ....bring (?) before me.
7. [May there come] the gods, all of them,
8. [Let them prepare for converse], at banquets let them sit,
9. [Bread may they eat], wine may they prepare,
10. [For Marduk], their [avenger], let them decree the fate.
11. [Go, Ga]ga, before them stand,
12. [And all that] I tell thee repeat unto them
13. [Anshar], your son, hath sent me,
14. [The purpose of his heart] hath disclosed to me,
15. [Saying] : Tiâmat, who bore us, hates us,
16. An assemblage is appointed, angrily she rages,
17. Turned to her are the gods, all of them,
18. With those whom ye created, they march at her side,
19. They are rebellious, at Tiâmat's side they come,
20. They rage, they plot, they rest not day nor night,
21. They prepare for battle, fuming and raging,
22. An assembly is made, they start a revolt.
23. Mother Khubur, who formed all things,
24. Has made weapons without rival, has spawned monster-serpents,
25. Sharp of tooth, unsparing of fang,
26. With poison like blood their bodies she has filled;
27. Fierce dragons with terror she has clothed,
28. Luster has made abundant, to loftiness made equal.
29. Whoever beholds them, terror (?) overcomes him.
30. Their bodies they raise up without turning their breasts.
31. She has established vipers, serpents, Lakhami,
32. Hurricanes, raging hounds, scorpion men,
33. Mighty storms, fish-men, and rams;
34. They bear merciless weapons, fearless of battle.
35. Her behests are mighty, without rival are they.
36. Moreover eleven such as these she has created.
37. Among the gods, her firstborn, who are gathered at her side,
38. She has exalted Kingu, made him great in their midst,
39. To march before the forces, to lead the host,
40. To raise the conquering weapon, to lead the attack,
41. To direct the battle as commander-in-chief;
42. To him she has entrusted it, made him sit in purple, [saying,]
43. 'Thy spell I have uttered, in the assembly of gods I have made thee great,
44. The sovereignty of all the gods I have placed in thy hand,
45. Surely thou art exalted, O my spouse!
46. May they magnify thy name over all the Anunnaki.'
47. She has given him the tablets of destiny, on his breast has laid them, [saying,]
48. 'Thy command shall be unalterable, established be thy word.'
49. Now Kingu has been exalted, has received highest rank,
50. Among the gods, her sons, he fixes fate, [saying] :
51. 'The opening of your mouth shall quench the fire-god,

52. Whoso is exalted in excellence, let him increase in might.'
53. I sent Anu; he had no power before her,
54. Nudimmud feared and turned back,
55. Marduk has set forth, the leader of the gods, your son,
56. As a foe of Tiâmat his heart prompts him to go.
57. He opened his mouth and spake to me, [saying]:
58. 'If I accomplish your preservation,
59. Take Tiâmat captive, and save your lives,
60. Appoint an assembly, make my fate strong, let it come in.
61. In Upshukkunaku seat yourselves joyfully together,
62. The word of my mouth shall determine fate instead of you.
63. Let there not be changed whatever I create,
64. May there not be altered or opposed the command of my lips.'
65. Hasten, therefore, and quickly decree your fate,
66. That he may go and fight your strong enemy."
67. Then Gaga went, his way he pursued,
68. To the place of Lakhmu and Lakhamu, the gods, his fathers;
69. He kissed the ground at their feet,
70. He bowed himself; he stood up, he addressed them, [saying]:
71. "Anshar, your son, hath sent me,
72. The purpose of his heart he has disclosed to me
73. Saying: Tiâmat, who bore us, hates us;
74. An assemblage is appointed, angrily she rages,
75. Turned to her are the gods, all of them,
76. With those whom you created, they march at her side,
77. They are rebellious, at Tiâmat's side they come.
78. They rage, they plot, they rest not day nor night,
79. They prepare for battle, fuming and raging,
80. An assembly is made, they start a revolt.
81. Mother Khubur, who formed all things,
82. Has made weapons without rival, has spawned monster-serpents,
83. Sharp of tooth, unsparing of fang,
84. With poison like blood their bodies she has filled;
85. Fierce dragons with terror she has clothed;
86. Luster has been made abundant, to loftiness made equal.
87. Whoever beholds them, terror (?) overcomes him.
88. Their bodies they raise up without turning their breasts.
89. She has established vipers, serpents, Lakhami,
90. Hurricanes, raging hounds, scorpion-men,
91. Mighty storms, fish-men, rams;
92. They bear merciless weapons, fearless of battle.
93. Her behests are mighty, without rival are they.
94. Moreover eleven such as these she has created.
95. Among the gods, her firstborn, who are gathered at her side,
96. She has exalted Kingu, made him great in their midst,
97. To march before the forces, to lead the host,
98. To raise the conquering weapon, to lead the attack,
99. To direct the battle as commander-in-chief;
100. To him she has entrusted it, made him sit in purple, [saying]:
101. 'Thy spell I have uttered, in the assembly of the gods I have made thee great;
102. The sovereignty of all the gods I have placed in thy hand
103. Surely thou art exalted, O my spouse!
104. May they magnify thy name over all the Anunnaki.'
105. She has given him the tablets of destiny, on his breast has laid them, [saying]:

106. 'Thy command shall be unalterable, established be thy word.'
107. Now Kingu has been exalted, has received highest rank,
108. Among the gods, her sons, he fixes fate, [saying:]
109. 'The opening of your mouth shall quench the fire-god,
110. Whoso is exalted in excellence, let him increase in might.'
111. I sent Anu, he had no power before her,
112. Nudimmud feared and turned back,
113. Marduk has set forth, the leader of the gods, your son,
114. As a foe of Tiâmat his heart prompts him to go.
115. He opened his mouth and spake to me, [saying:]
116. 'If I accomplish your preservation,
117. Take Tiâmat captive and save your lives,
118. Appoint an assembly, make my fate strong, let it come in.
119. In Upshukkunaku seat yourselves joyfully together,
120. The word of my mouth shall determine fate instead of you,
121. Let there not be changed whatever I create,
122. May there not be altered or opposed the command of my lips.'
123. Hasten, therefore, and quickly decree your fate,
124. That he may go and fight your strong enemy."
125. Lakhmu and Lakhamu heard, they cried aloud;
126. The Igigi, all of them, wailed bitterly, [saying:]
127. "What has changed that they should desire to take us (?)
128. We do not understand what Tiâmat has done."
129. Then they massed themselves together, they went,
130. The great gods, all of them, who decree fate,
131. They entered in before Anshar, they filled, [Upshukkunaku].
132. Brother kissed brother in the assembly..............
133. They prepared for converse, sat down to the banquet,
134. Bread they ate; wine they prepared.
135. The sweet drink confused their minds (?),
136. Drunk were they with drink, their bodies were filled (?),
137. They became very unsteady, their hearts were exalted,
138. For Marduk, their deliverer, they decreed the fate.

Tablet IV (creation of the world)

1. They prepared for him a princely chamber:
2. In the presence of his fathers for sovereignty he became **mighty**. [They said:]
3. "Thou art most honored among the great gods,
4. Thy destiny is without rival, thy command is Anu's!
5. O Marduk, thou are most honored among the great gods,
6. Thy destiny is without rival, thy command is Anu's!
7. From today without opposition shall be thy command;
8. To exalt and to abase is verily in thy power;
9. Established is thy utterance, irresistible thy command.
10. None among the gods shall invade thy province.
11. Sustenance, the desire of shrines of the gods,
12. While they are in need, shall be certain in thy sanctuary!
13. O Marduk, thou art the preserver of our lives!
14. We give thee sovereignty over the totality of all the world.
15. Sit thou in the assembly, thy word shall be exalted!
16. Thy weapon shall never be o'ercome, may it destroy (?) thy foe!
17. O lord, he who trusts thee—his life save!
18. But the god that is wed to evil, its life pour out!"

19. Then they placed in the midst a garment,
20. And unto Marduk, their firstborn, they spoke,
21. "Thy fate, O Lord, let it be first among the gods!
22. To destroy and to create—speak, let it be established!
23. At thy command let a garment perish!
24. Again at thy command let the garment re-appear!"
25. Then he spake with his mouth, the garment perished;
26. Again he commanded and the garment was recreated.
27. As the utterance of his mouth the gods, his fathers, saw,
28. They rejoiced, they uttered blessing: "Marduk is king!"
29. They bestowed upon him the scepter, the throne, and the battle-axe;
30. They gave him an unrivaled weapon, which turns back (?) the foe.
31. "Go, Tiâmat's life cut off;
32. May the winds bear her blood to secret places!"
33. When the gods, his fathers had fixed Bel's fate,
34. The way of prosperity and success they caused him to take.
35. His bow he prepared, his weapon he chose,
36. A spear he bound on him at his waist,
37. He raised the heavenly weapon, with his right hand grasped it,
38. His bow and quiver at his side he hung,
39. He placed the lightning before his face,
40. With quivering flame his body he filled.
41. He made a net to enclose Tiâmat's body,
42. He caused the four winds to seize so that nothing of her could escape;
43. The south wind, the north wind, the east wind, the west wind,
44. He brought to the side of the net, the gift of his father Anu,
45. He made the evil wind, the bad wind, the tempest and the hurricane,
46. The four winds, the seven winds, the whirlwind (?), the unhealthy wind;
47. He brought forth the winds which he had made, the seven of them,
48. To trouble the inward parts of Tiâmat, they came after him.
49. The lord raised up the tornado, his mighty weapon,
50. As a chariot, a storm unrivaled for terror he mounted,
51. He harnessed for himself and attached to it four steeds,
52. "Destroyer," "Unmerciful," "Overwhelmer," "Fleet-footed."
53. [Foam-covered (?)] were their teeth, filled with poison,
54. Skilled were they [to run down], taught to destroy.
55. ....mighty in battle,
56. Left and right they opened (?)...............
57. His garment was [rage], with terror was he clad,
58. With his overpowering brightness his head was crowned.
59. He made straight the way, he took his path,
60. To the place of Tiâmat, the raging (?), his face he set.
61. With his lip........................he cursed (?),
62. A plant of magical power (?)—he seized with his hand.
63. On that day they exalted (?) him, the gods exalted (?) him;
64. The gods, his fathers, exalted (?) him, the gods exalted (?) him.
65. The lord approached, the waist of Tiâmat he scanned,
66. Of Kingu, her spouse—he beheld his terrifying-glance (?).
67. As Marduk gazed, Kingu's progress was impeded,
68. Destroyed was his purpose, frustrated his deed,
69. And the gods his helpers, who marched at his side,
70. Saw the warrior and leader; their look (?) was troubled.
71. Tiâmat perceived it (?); she did not turn her neck.
72. With proud (?) lips she uttered words of defiance:
73. "Who decreed (?) that thou shouldst come as lord of the gods?

74. Have they assembled from their places, are they to serve **thee?"**
75. The lord raised the tornado, his mighty weapon,
76. [Against] Tiâmat who was raging, thus he spoke:
77. "[Why hast thou] made thyself great? Exalted thyself on high?
78. [Who does thy heart] prompt thee to battle (?)
79. [How can thy helpers] defy (?) the gods, their fathers?
80. [Why] dost thou hate their [command], their ru[le despise]?
81. [Why hast thou exalted Kingu] to be thy spouse?
82. [Hast given] him the functions of deity?
83. [How] canst thou seek after evil?
84. [And against] the gods, my fathers, thy evil plan devise?
85. [Let] thy forces be joined, girded on thy weapons!
86. Stand! I and thou—come let us fight!"
87. Tiâmat, when she heard this,
88. Was like one possessed; she lost her reason.
89. Tiâmat cried out vehemently with high voice,
90. Like roots divided in twain her legs trembled.
91. She uttered an incantation, she cast a charm,
92. And the gods of battle demanded their weapons.
93. Then took their stand Tiâmat and the leader of the gods, Marduk;
94. For the fight they approached, for the battle they drew near.
95. The lord spread out his net and enclosed her,
96. The evil wind from behind he thrust into her face.
97. As Tiâmat opened her mouth to its full extent,
98. The evil wind he drove in, so that her lips could not close.
99. With the mighty winds he filled her belly;
100. Her courage was taken away, and she opened her mouth.
101. He let fall the spear, he burst open her belly.
102. He cut through her inward parts, he pierced her heart,
103. He bound her and her life destroyed;
104. Her body he cast down, upon it he stood.
105. After Tiâmat, the leader, he had slain,
106. Her army he broke, her host was scattered,
107. And the gods, her helpers, who marched by her side,
108. Trembled, feared, they turned their backs;
109. They sought an exit, to save their lives;
110. With a cordon they were encompassed; escape was not possible.
111. He caught them, their weapons he broke.
112. Into the net they fell, in the snare they remained.
113. All quarters of the world they filled with lamentation.
114. His wrath they endured; they were held in bondage.
115. And the eleven creatures, whom she had filled with terribleness,
116. The troop of demons who marked as her helpers (?),
117. He threw into fetters, their power he [broke];
118. Along with their opposition he trampled them under his feet.
119. And Kingu who had been exalted over them,
120. He took captive, as the god Dugga he counted him.
121. He took from him the tablets of destiny, not rightly his,
122. He sealed them with a seal, in his own breast he laid them.
123. After his enemies he had seized and destroyed,
124. His arrogant foe had completely humiliated (?),
125. The triumph of Anshar over the foe had fully established,
126. The wish of Nudimmud had accomplished, Marduk, the **warrior**
127. Over the bound gods strengthened his hold,
128. Unto Tiâmat, whom he had bound, he turned back.
129. The lord trod upon Tiâmat's feet

130. And with his unsparing weapon crushed her head.
131. He cut through the veins of her blood,
132. He caused the north wind to bear it to secret places.
133. His fathers saw it; they rejoiced, they exulted,
134. Gifts and presents they brought unto him.
135. Then the lord rested; he gazed upon her body,
136. The flesh of the monster he divided; he formed a cunning plan.
137. He split her open like a flat fish into two halves,
138. One half of her he established and made a covering of the heavens,
139. He drew a bolt, he established a guard,
140. And not to let her waters come out, he commanded.
141. He passed through the heavens, he surveyed the regions,
142. Over against the deep he set the dwelling of Nudimmud.
143. The structures of the deep the lord measured,
144. As a palace like unto it he founded Esharra.
145. In the palace Esharra which he built in the heavens,
146. He caused Anu, Ellil, and Ea at their stations to dwell.

Tablet V

1. He [Marduk] ordained the stations of the great gods;
2. As stars their likenesses as constellations of the zodiac he placed.
3. He ordained the year, into parts he divided it,
4. For the twelve months he established three stars.
5. After the days of the year he had fashioned as images,
6. He founded the station of Jupiter, to determine their bounds;
7. That none might go wrong or err,
8. The station of Bel he established, and Ea by his side.
9. He opened gates on both sides.
10. A lock he made strong on the left and the right,
11. In the midst thereof he placed the zenith;
12. The moon-god he caused to shine; the night he entrusted to him.
13. He appointed him a being of the night, to determine the days;
14. Monthly, without ceasing, into a crown he made him, [saying:]
15. "At the beginning of the month shine upon the lands,
16. Horns exhibit, to determine six days;
17. On the seventh day let the tiara disappear;
18. On the fourteenth day thou shalt stand over against the [two] halves.
19. When the sun-god on the horizon...........thee,
20. Thou........to be resplendent, and thou shalt turn (?) backward (?)
21. [Fourteen days] unto the path of the sun-god thou shalt approach,
22. [On the 28th day] thou shalt approach the sun-god............
23. ....signs (?), seek (?) her way!
24. ....approach ye and judge justice!
25. ....to destroy,
26. ....me."

(Some lines are lost at this point. It is estimated that forty of them are lacking.)

67. After.................................
68. In Esagila [6].....................................
69. To establish............................
70. The station of........................

6 Marduk's temple in Babylonia.

71. The great gods............................
72. The gods........................
73. He received......................
74. The net which he had made the [great] gods saw,
75. Saw the bow, how skillful [its workmanship];
76. The work which he had done, they [loudly] praised.
77. Then arose Anu in the assembly of the [great] gods,
78. The bow he kissed it...........................
79. "Long-wood shall be one name, and a second................
80. Its third name shall be Bow-star in the heavens."
81. He fixed its position [unto distant days].
82. After the destiny of...........................
83. [He set] a throne...........................
84. ....in the heavens......................

(Practically all the remainder of Tablet V is as yet undiscovered. From a very broken fragment, preserved in the British Museum, it appears that when the gods saw the work of Marduk in adorning the heavens with constellations, they broke into rapturous praise of him. It is these words to which reference is made at the beginning of Tablet VI.)

Tablet VI[7]

1. Marduk, the word of the gods, when he heard it,
2. His heart was stirred, he formed a brilliant plan.
3. He opened his mouth, to Ea he spoke,
4. What in his heart he had conceived he offered as a plan:
5. "Blood will I bind, bone will I fashion,
6. .I will produce a man; 'man' is his name;
7. I will create the man 'man';
8. Verily by the service of the gods he shall give them rest;
9. Verily I will alter the ways of the gods.
10. One by one let them all be divided into two parts."
11. Then Ea answered and said unto him a word;
12. He unfolded to him a plan for satisfying the gods:
13. "One among your brethren must be given up,
14. Him I will appoint, the people prepare.
15. The great gods must assemble together;
16. This one must be given up; he must be given them."
17. Marduk assembled the great gods, he entered and delivered the decision,
18. He opened his mouth, to the gods he spoke:
19. As a king he addressed a word to the Anunnaki
20. "Truly the former things we told you are verified;
21. True things with myself as an oath I have sworn.
22. Who is it that has created the strife,
23. Brought about the uproar, united the battle?
24. He who has caused the strife shall be given up.
25. I will make him, verily, I will cause him to bear the curse; but dwell ye in peace."
26. Then answered him the Igigi, the great gods;
27. "O king, god of heaven and earth, counsellor of the gods, their lord,
28. Kingu it was who caused the strife,

7 Translated from Ebeling, *Keilschrifttexte aus Assur Religions Inhalts*, No. 164. Ebeling translated portions of this into German in the *Mitteilungen der deutschen Orient-Gesellschaft*, No. 8, but he left untranslated some interesting portions.

29. He led the rebellion and brought on the battle."
30. They bound him and brought him before Ea.
31. Then a curse he laid on him; his blood burst forth from him.
32. From his blood he made mankind for the service of the gods,
33. But (the other) gods he let go free.
34. After man had been created, Ea laid on him the service of the gods.
35. That work was past understanding.
36. Through the skill of Marduk, the wisdom of Nudimmud,
37. Marduk, king of the gods, stationed twenty Anunnaki above and below,
38. He delivered unto Anu the charge to guard.........the post
39. He changed the prince who guards the earth............
40. After the commands of the gods Marduk the king had issued
41. The Anunnaki who...........
42. The Anunnaki...........approached..........
43. To Marduk their lord they spoke:
44. "O divine guardian of the earth, lord, who hast wrought our release,
45. How do we cling to thy presence!
46. Oh, we will make a sanctuary the naming of whose name is
47. 'Sanctuary-wherein-we-may-take-rest!'
48. Oh, we will found our sanctuary as our dwelling!
49. On the day when we take possession, we will rest in it."
50. Marduk, when he heard this,
51. His face like the day appeared exceeding bright:
52. "Like the founding of Babylon with walls, be the joy of its founding.
53. Let an enclosed city be built, a district of land surround it."
54. The Anunnaki protected the kiln; for a year they burned bricks.
55. The second year came around, the enclosure of Esagila was founded on
    the breast of Apsu.[8]
56. They built the temple-tower till it touched the celestial ocean;
57. For Marduk, Enlil, and Ea they raised it as a dwelling;
58. With the glory of their presence they entered in.
59. From its foundation Esagila exhibited its two horns.
60. After they finished the work of Esagila,
61. The Anunnaki their sanctuaries set up;
62. In Esagila, founded on the deep, they all assembled
63. In a large garden which they created was their dwelling.
64. The gods, his fathers, to his prayer (?) hearkened:
65. Divine fate at the great gate of the beloved dwelling was established.
66. In the district each (?) in his place and shrine the great gods dwelt.
67. They placed strong drink at the feasts;
68. Satisfying food they set in their midst
69. In Esagila........
70. Laws were laid down, authority established.
71. The place of heaven and earth was established by the gods, all of them.
72. The great gods dwelt there (?) joyfully (?)
73. The gods of fate, seven of them over......were established.
74. Enlil lifted up his weapon (?), their......he cast down.
75. The net which he made for himself the gods his fathers
76. They saw the bow, how skillful (?) its workmanship.
77. The deed he did........his fathers.
78. Anu rose up......he spoke
79. The bow has been kissed (?)......
80. "Long-wood" is its first name......
81. The third (?) of its names is "Bow-star"......

8 Apsu corresponds to "the waters under the earth," Exodus 20: 4.

82. He fixed its station......
83. After he had fixed the fates......
84. He set up a throne......
85. Mighty in heaven......
86. He assembled......
87. ......Marduk......
88. ....
89. ....
90. ....
91. ....
92. ....
93. He caused to abound......
94. Unto his name......
95. He opened his mouth......
96. Verily he poured out (?)......
97. Verily he, the son, was exalted......
98. ....
99. Truly his lordship was glorified......
100. Verily he exercised rulership......
101. In future days let......be not forgotten.
102. May he establish for his fathers........
103. Their maintenance verily......
104. Verily he caused incense to be smelled......
105. A replica in heaven, he made......
106. Verily he like (?) Esagila
107. Not................
108. He opened his mouth......let them kiss
109. Let free will offerings be brought to their god and goddess
110. Let them not forget their god, let them feed him.
111. Their land may they adorn, their shrines may they build
112. Verily the gods enlarge
113. As for us, by as many names as we call him he is our god
114. We will name his fifty names.
115. His......is glorious; his work is similar.
116. Marduk, whom from his birth, Anu his father had named,
117. Who establishes brotherhood (?), enriches cities,
118. Who by his weapon, the deluge, took captive the rebellious,
119. The gods his fathers he preserved from tribulation.
120. Surely it was his sonship for which the gods called him.
121. In his brilliant light they walk continually.
122. The people whom he had made became living creatures;
123. They established the service of the gods: they pacified them.
124. ....
125. Verily favor was restored; they looked on them with compassion—
     even them.
126. The divine son they were trusting.................
127. He gave joy to the hearts of the Anunnaki.........
128. Marduk truly was the trust of his land and his (people).
129. The god Barashaggu is mighty.........
130. Large is his heart, warm are his reins........
131. Divine king, god of heaven and earth, whose name our assembly named,
132. By word of mouth we exalted him above the gods his fathers—
133. Verily above the gods of heaven and earth, all of them—
134. As king...
135. The brilliant god, the king of heaven he called his second name; the
     place of the gods

136. Of heaven and earth he founded as our dwelling in distress!
137. Between the Igigi [9] and the Anunnaki [10] the place is divided.
138. At his name may the gods be stirred and the dwelling shake!
139. Asharu [11] the good, Anu his father named him.
140. He truly is the light of the gods, the mighty battle-axe,
141. Who is like the protecting sun-god of the land.
142. By a mighty battle he delivered our dwelling from distress.
143. The god Asharu, the good, god of life, a second time they named "the-exalted-divine-companion";
144. Who, as though his offspring, gave life to us, the gods who were perishing,
145. The lord who by his holy incantation made the dead gods live.
146. Destroyer of plotters, hater.........
147. Verily the one who his fathers named "the brilliant god,"
148. The holy god who illumines our way.
149. (There came?) Anshar, Lakhmu and Lakhamu,
150. Unto (the gods their sons) they spoke:
151. "We..........., we have proclaimed his names."
152......................speech.
153. They rejoiced (when they heard) their speech.
154. In Upshukinnaka he granted their desires.
155. "Of the heroic son our avenger
156. We, of our preserver, will exalt the name."
157. They sat in the assembly, they proclaimed his worth,
158. All of them on the *mesu*-instrument celebrated his name.

Tablet VII

1. "O Asharu, bestower of harvests, founder of agriculture,
2. Creator of grain and plants, who made green herbs to grow,
3. O honored Asharu, revered in the house of counsel, rich in counsel,
4. Whom the gods honor, fearing [laid hold upon them]
5. O honored Asharu, powerful prince, the light [of the fathers who begat him],
6. Who directs the decrees of Anu, Bel, [and Ea].
7. He was their preserver, who ordained.........
8. He whose provision is abundance, he goeth forth.........
9. Tutu, the creator of their renewal is he.
10. If their want be pure, then are [they satisfied];
11. If he make an incantation, then are the gods [appeased];
12. Should they attack him in anger, he will repulse their array;
13. Let him therefore be exalted in the assembly of the gods.
14. None among the gods is like unto him!
15. Tutu-Ziukinna is the life of the host of the gods.
16. Who established for the gods the bright heavens.
17. Their way he received, [their path] ordained.
18. Never forgotten among men shall be his [mighty] deeds.
19. Tutu as Zi-azag thirdly they named, bringer of purification,
20. God of the favoring breeze, the lord who hears and is merciful,
21. Who creates fulness and plenty, who establishes abundance,
22. Who turns whatever is small into something great.
23. "In sore distress we caught his favoring breeze."

9 The Spirits of heaven.
10 The Spirits of earth.
11 Another name for Marduk.

24. Let them honor him, praise him, bow humbly before him.
25. Tutu as Aga-azag may the mighty ones praise,
26. The lord of the pure incantation, who makes the dead to live,
27. Who to the captive gods showed abundant compassion,
28. The oppressive yoke he laid upon the gods, his enemies,
29. For their [12] release he created mankind,
30. The merciful one, with whom is life!
31. Established and never forgotten be his word
32. In the mouth of the black-headed race,[13] whom his hand created.
33. Tutu as Mu-azag, fifthly, his pure incantation may their mouth proclaim,
34. Who through his pure incantation destroys all evil ones,
35. Shagzu, who knows the hearts of the gods, who sees through the innermost parts.
36. The evil doer he permits not to go out with him (?).
37. Founder of the assembly of the gods [who gladdens] their heart.
38. Who subdues the disobedient..........
39. Director of righteousness......

(The tablet is too broken for connected translation, until nearly the end, where it continues:)

107. Truly he holds their beginning and ending..........
108. Saying, "He who passed through the midst of Tiâmat [without resting],
109. Let his name be Neberu, who seizes the midst,
110. Who the stars of heaven—their ways he upholds;
111. As a flock verily the gods pasture, all of them."
112. He bound Tiâmat, her life he apportioned, he ended.
113. In the future, people, old in years,
114. Shall renew unceasingly, "let him be lord forever!"
115. Because he created the places and fashioned the fastness
116. "Lord of countries" Bel, his father, named him.
117. The names the Igigi named, all of them,
118. Ea heard, and his heart rejoiced:
119. "He whose name his fathers have magnified
120. He, even like me, shall be named Ea.
121. The binding of all my commands shall he control,
122. All my decrees shall he proclaim!"
123. By the name "Fifty" did the great gods
124. His fifty names make known, they made his path pre-eminent.
125. May they be held fast and the first men reveal them,
126. The wise, the understanding shall consider them together;
127. May the father repeat them and the son lay hold upon them,
128. So that shepherd and herdsman may open their ears,
129. And may rejoice in Marduk, the lord of the gods,
130. That his land may be fertile, that he may have prosperity.
131. His word is established, his command unfailing,
132. The word of his mouth, no god had annulled.
133. He casts his glance without turning his neck,
134. When he roars, no god can face his anger.
135. Wide is his heart, great his goodness;
136. The sinner and transgressor in his presence..........
137. They received instruction, they spake before him.

(The concluding lines are too broken for connected translation.)

12 *I. e.*, the captive gods of line 27.
13 The name which the Babylonians gave themselves.

2. The First Chapter of Genesis and the Foregoing Creation Epic.—The Babylonian Creation Epic, in the form in which we know it, took shape in the city of Babylon. Naturally, therefore, the god Marduk is made the central figure. It is he only who was sufficiently powerful to overcome the primeval dragon, it was he who created the heavens and the earth, it was he whom at the end gods and men adored.

A Babylonian priest, Berossos, in a work composed after the time of Alexander the Great, gives an account of Babylonian ideas of the creation of the world, which is but the tradition of the epic in a slightly different form. A neoplatonic philosopher, Damascius, who lived about 560 A.D., has also preserved a part of the tradition in a form almost identical with that of the epic.

Scholars of all shades of opinion agree that there is some connection between this Babylonian tradition and the first chapter of Genesis, though they differ as to whether the Biblical writer was acquainted with the Babylonian tradition as we have it in the epic, or whether he knew an earlier form of the story.

The points of similarity which have been urged between Genesis and the Babylonian epic are the following: 1. They begin somewhat similarly, Genesis with the words "In the beginning," the epic with the words:

"Time was when above heaven was not named; Below to the earth no name was given."

2. Both accounts assume that primeval chaos consisted of a mass of waters, and to this mass of waters they give the same name. The Hebrews called it *tᵉhōm*, "deep"; the Babylonians, *Tiâmat*. These are really the same word in the two closely related languages, just as *day* and *Tag* are the same word in an English and a German form. In Genesis we are told that "The Spirit of God moved (R.V. margin, was brooding) upon the face of the waters"; in the Babylonian epic, the waters, which were thought to be of two genders, were embosomed. In both the result is the beginning of the creative process.

The two accounts agree that the heavens and the earth were created by the division of the primeval ocean by a firmament (the Babylonian calls it a covering), which held up a part of the waters, so that the earth could be formed beneath. They accordingly agree in the conception that there is a super-celestial ocean, *i.e.*, "the waters which are above the firmament" (Gen. 1:7).

Another striking similarity is found in the arrangement by sevens : the Babylonian epic is arranged in seven tablets, or cantos, the Hebrew account, in seven days. The Babylonian series culminates in the praise of Marduk by all the gods ; the Hebrew, in the institution of the sabbath. The two series agree in connecting the heavens with the fourth epoch of creation, and the creation of man with the sixth.

In other respects the order differs. In the Babylonian account the moon and stars are created on the fifth day, instead of on the fourth. As Marduk is identified with the sun, that orb is assumed ; its creation is not described. The creation of animals is not described in any text which we can attach to a definite tablet of the Babylonian series. It is, however, given in a fragment which reads as follows :

1. When the gods in their assembly had made [the heavens],
2. The firmament had established and bound [fast],
3. Living things of all kinds had created,
4. Cattle of the field, beasts of the field, and moving things of the city.
5. After........unto all kinds of living things.........
6. [Between beasts] of the field and moving things of the city had divided....
7. ....all creatures, the whole creation........
8. ....that which in the whole of my family...........
9. [Then arose] Nin-igi-azag, two small creatures [he created],
10. In the assembly of the beasts he made [their form] brilliant,
11. ....the goddess Gula..........
12. ....one white and one black........
13. ....one white and one black...........

The Babylonian account, then, contained somewhere the story of the creation of the animals, though, like the other parts of the Babylonian account, its order and atmosphere differ widely from the Biblical narrative.

Some of these resemblances are of no great significance. The fact that the two accounts are arranged by sevens may be due simply to the fact that that number was sacred among both peoples. It is thought by some scholars that its use in Genesis was consciously adopted in order to lead up to the sabbath and glorify it. This might be true, even if the writer of the chapter knew of the Babylonian arrangement by sevens.

The features of the two narratives, which have convinced some scholars of all shades of opinion that there is a real kinship between the two accounts, are their agreement as to the nature of primeval chaos, and the division of the primeval ocean by a firmament for the creation of the heavens and the earth. Both writers had, so to speak, the same raw material of objective conceptions.

The differences between the accounts are, however, most marked. To speak first of that which is least important, the Hebrew order is in many respects different from the Babylonian. In the Babylonian the gods are generated in the first tablet, the world is not created till the fourth, and the creation of all other things is told in tablets four, five, and six. In other words, creation is divided into two parts, each of which is told in three tablets. The first three tablets deal with gods, the second three with the world and living things.

This twofold division is found in the first chapter of Genesis. Here the creative process is divided into two stages, each embracing four works, and occupying three days. The distribution of these works is strikingly different from the Babylonian. On the first day, light and darkness were created; on the second, the firmament; on the third, the earth and vegetation; on the fourth, the heavenly bodies; on the fifth, fishes and birds; on the sixth, animals and men. The first series of three days prepared the heavens and the earth; the second series studded the sky with orbs and the earth with living beings. There is a striking parallelism between the two series. The first begins with the creation of light; the second, with light-giving bodies. To the third and sixth days two creative acts each are assigned. On the second day the seas are isolated; on the fifth they are stocked with fishes. On the third day dry land emerges, on the sixth terrestrial animals are made. On the third also herbs began to grow; on the sixth they are assigned to animals and men for food. The classification of the acts of creation in Genesis is clear and consistent, and thoroughly independent of that in the Babylonian account.

A more important difference lies in the religious conceptions of the two. The Babylonian poem is mythological and polytheistic. Its conception of deity is by no means exalted. Its gods love and hate, they scheme and plot, fight and destroy. Marduk, the champion, conquers only after a fierce struggle, which taxes his powers to the utmost. Genesis, on the other hand, reflects the most exalted monotheism. God is so thoroughly the master of all the elements of the universe, that they obey his slightest word. He controls all without effort. He speaks and it is done. Granting, as most scholars do, that there is a connection between the two narratives, there is no better measure of the inspiration of the Biblical account than to put it side by side with the Babylonian. As we read the chapter in Genesis today, it still reveals to us the majesty and power of the one God, and creates in the modern man, as it did in rôle ancient Hebrew, a worshipful attitude toward the Creator.

The sixth tablet is very interesting. Lines 1–33 contain the account of the creation of man. This creation is said to have been accomplished by sacrificing the life of Kingu, the god who, by leading a rebellion, had created strife among the gods. Man was made from Kingu's blood. This seems to have been the Babylonian way of expressing the thought that man is akin to deity— a thought which in Genesis 1:26, 27 is expressed by saying that God made man in his own image. The purpose of the creation of man was to serve the gods—to "satisfy" them or "give them rest." This, in the minds of Babylonians and Assyrians, was accomplished by building temples in which the gods could dwell and by offering sacrifices on which the gods could feed.

After man was thus created, it is related in lines 34–69 how Eden was established. Man was put upon the earth, twenty of the great spirits of the earth were stationed above and below, and a guard was placed so that he should not get away (lines 33–35). This corresponds to the Cherubim of Genesis 3:24, only in the Babylonian Epic the guardians were placed to keep man from getting out of Eden, while in Genesis they are stationed to keep him from getting back into Eden.

As a result of the creation of man, the gods are said to have been made very happy. A temple was built for them, under the direction of the Anunnaki, or spirits of earth, similar to that which afterward was called Esagila in Babylon. Around this temple was a garden of the gods. Here they dwelt; man served them; and they feasted joyfully. All this is the Babylonian equivalent of the statement in Genesis 2:9, that God "planted a garden eastward in Eden" (edinnu, the Mesopotamian plain) "and there he put the man whom he had formed."

The temple-tower, the top of which is said in line 56 to have "touched the celestial ocean," is the "Tower of Babel" of the eleventh chapter of Genesis (cf. Gen. 11:4).

3. **The Babylonian Creation Epic and Other Parts of the Bible.**—The Babylonian poem, crude though it seems to us, has a powerful fascination for the imagination. With more or less distinctness parts of it seem to have been known to various Hebrew writers, who, attributing to their own God, Jehovah, the rôle

ascribed in the epic to Marduk, used these stories as poetic illustrations. At least this is the view of a considerable group of scholars. Some object that, if this were true, it would degrade Jehovah to the level of Marduk, but the objection does not seem well founded. The Hebrews might well have been such ardent monotheists as to believe that each and every mighty manifestation of power had been the work of Jehovah, without in any way lowering Jehovah to the level of a heathen god. The most important parallels which have been cited are here given, so that the reader may judge for himself as to which view is the more probable.

In Job 9:13, 14 we read:

> God will not withdraw his anger;
> The helpers of Rahab do stoop under him.
> How much less shall I answer him,
> And choose out my words to reason with him?

Rahab is believed by many to be here an epithet of Tiâmat. It means "the one who acts boisterously" or "proudly." Those who thus think believe the lines in Job to refer to the overcoming of Tiâmat's helpers in Tablet IV, lines 105–118, of the Babylonian creation epic, which read as follows:

> After Tiâmat, the leader, he had slain,
> Her army he broke, her host was scattered,
> And the gods, her helpers, who marched at her side,
> Trembled, feared, they turned their backs;
> They sought an exit, to save their lives;
> With a cordon they were encompassed, escape was not possible.
> He caught them, their weapons he broke,
> Into the net they fell, in the snare they remained.
> All the quarters of the world they filled with their lamentation.
> His wrath they endured; they were held in bondage.
> And the eleven creatures, whom she had filled with terribleness,
> The troop of demons who marched as her helpers,
> He threw into fetters, their power he broke;
> Along with their opposition he trampled them under his feet.

This would seem to suit the reference in Job, and to give point to Job's words. As our Saviour used stories in his parables, so this poet may have used this well-known story to illustrate his point.

Again Job 26:12, 13 reads:

> He stirreth up the sea with his power,
> And by his understanding he smiteth through Rahab.
> By his Spirit the heavens are garnished;
> His hand hath pierced the swift serpent.

Four of the ancient versions of the Old Testament, with a very slight change in the Hebrew letters, read Job 26:13:

> The bars of heaven fear him;
> His hand hath pierced the swift serpent.

Into comparison with v. 12 and the last line of 13, scholars have brought Tablet IV, line 93, ff., which runs:

> Then took their stand Tiâmat and the leader of the gods, Marduk;
> For the fight they approached, for the battle they drew near.
> The lord spread out his net and enclosed her,
> The evil wind from behind he thrust into her face.
> As Tiâmat opened her mouth to its full extent,
> The evil wind he drove in, so that her lips could not close.
> With the mighty winds he filled her belly.
> Her courage was taken away, and she opened her mouth.
> He let fall the spear, he burst open her belly,
> He cut through her inward parts, he pierced her heart,
> He bound her and her life destroyed;
> Her body he cast down and stood upon it.

Into comparison with the first line of v. 13, as the versions give it, scholars have brought line 135, and ff., of the same tablet:

> Then the lord rested, he gazed upon her body,
> The flesh of the monster he divided; he formed a cunning plan.
> He split her open like a flat fish into two halves;
> One half of her he established and made a covering of the heavens.
> He drew a bolt, he established a guard,
> And not to let her waters come out, he commanded.

With the passages quoted above Psalm 74:13, 14 has also been compared:

> Thou didst divide the sea by thy strength:
> Thou brakest the heads of the sea-monsters in the waters.
> Thou brakest the heads of leviathan in pieces;
> Thou gavest him to be food to the people inhabiting the wilderness.

Verses 16, 17 of the same Psalm continue the theme with the words:

> The day is thine, the night also is thine:
> Thou hast prepared the light and the sun.
> Thou hast set all the borders of the earth:
> Thou hast made summer and winter.

The theme is the same as that of the epic, viz. : the creation of the world. It would appear from verse 14 that as the Hebrews called Tiâmat Rahab, so they called Kingu leviathan. Those who so think find another reference to the Babylonian creation epic in Job 3 : 8.

> Let them curse it that curse the day,
> Who are ready to rouse up leviathan.

Apparently there were magicians who professed to be able to arouse such a monster.

Other references to leviathan are thought to employ the same illustrative material. Thus in Isaiah 27 : 1 we read :

In that day Jehovah with his hard and great and strong sword will punish leviathan the swift serpent, and leviathan the crooked serpent; and he will slay the monster that is in the sea.

In Job 41 there is a long description of the crocodile under the name leviathan. In verses 19–21 some things are said of him that do not suit a real crocodile, and some scholars have thought that the language was influenced by the Babylonian material. These verses are :

> Out of his mouth go burning torches,
> And sparks of fire leap forth.
> Out of his nostrils a smoke goeth,
> As of a boiling pot and burning rushes.
> His breath kindleth coals,
> And a flame goeth forth from his mouth.

Other references to Rahab, which have been thought to use the same illustration, are Psalm 89 : 10 :

> Thou hast broken Rahab in pieces as one that is slain;
> Thou hast scattered thine enemies with the arm of thy strength.

Also, Isaiah 51 : 9 :

> Is it not thou that didst cut Rahab in pieces,
> That didst pierce the monster?

As to whether these sacred writers really employed the material of the Babylonian epic to give force to their illustrations, the judgments of men will differ in accordance with their views of what is possible for an inspired writer.

In the following passages Rahab is used to denote Egypt as a proud and imperious country. These uses are clearly figurative and metaphorical.

Isaiah 30:7:

> For Egypt helpeth in vain and to no purpose:
> Therefore have I called her Rahab that sitteth still.

Psalm 87:4:

> Rahab and Babylon I proclaim my votaries.

A fragmentary account of an Assyrian version of the creation epic has been found. It agrees with the Babylonian account in beginning with Tiâmat, though the course of creation appears to have been different. The tablets known to us present it, however, in a form too fragmentary for us to follow the course of the narrative.

CHAPTER II

SOME OTHER ACCOUNTS OF THE CREATION FOUND IN BABYLONIA [1]

TEXT OF THE BRITISH MUSEUM TABLET. COMPARISON OF IT WITH GENESIS 2. TEXT OF A TABLET FROM NIPPUR AND COMPARISON WITH GENESIS. TEXT OF A TABLET FROM ASHUR COMPARED WITH GENESIS.

1. Text of the British Museum Tablet.

1. A holy house, a house of the gods, in a holy place had not been made;
2. No reed had sprung up, no tree had been created.
3. No brick had been made, no foundation had been built,
4. No house had been constructed, no city had been built;
5. No city had been built, thrones had not been established;
6. Nippur had not been constructed, Ekur had not been built;
7. Erech had not been constructed, Eanna had not been built;
8. The deep had not been formed, Eridu had not been built;
9. The holy house, the house of the gods, the dwelling had not been made,—
10. All lands were sea,—
11. Then in the midst of the sea was a water-course;
12. In those days Eridu was constructed, Esagila was built,
13. Esagila where, in the midst of the deep, the god Lugal-dul-azaga abode,
14. (Babylon was made, Esagila was completed).
15. The gods and the Anunaki he made at one time.
16. (The holy city, the dwelling of their hearts' desire, they named as first),
17. Marduk bound a structure of reeds upon the face of the waters,
18. He formed dust, he poured it out beside the reed-structure.
19. To cause the gods to dwell in the habitation of their hearts' desire,
20. He formed mankind.
21. The goddess Aruru with him created mankind,
22. Cattle of the field, in whom is breath of life, he created.
23. He formed the Tigris and Euphrates and set them in their places,
24. Their names he did well declare.
25. The grass, marsh-grass, the reed and brushwood (?) he created,
26. The green grass of the field he created,
27. The land, the marshes, and the swamps;
28. The wild cow and her young, the wild calf; the ewe and her young, the lamb of the fold;
29. Gardens and forests;
30. The wild goat, the mountain goat, (who) cares for himself (?).
31. The lord Marduk filled a terrace by the seaside,
32. ....a marsh, reeds he set,
33. ....he caused to exist.

1 Translated from *Cuneiform Texts from Babylonian Tablets in the British Museum*, Part XIII, p. 35, ff.

34. [Reeds he creat]ed; trees he created;
35. In their..........in their place he made;
36. [Bricks he laid, a founda]tion he constructed;
37. [Houses he made], a city he built;
38. [A city he built, a throne] he established;
39. [Nippur he constructed], Ekur he built;
40. [Erech he constructed], Eanna he built.

(At this point the tablet is broken. When it again becomes legible, it is in the midst of an incantation.)

2. **Comparison with Genesis 2.**—This account of the creation has sometimes been compared with Genesis 2:4, ff., which describes a time when there was no grass or vegetation on the earth, and then goes on to describe the creation of man and animals, speaking of the Tigris and Euphrates rivers.

In this account of the creation it is stated (line 21) that the goddess Aruru with Marduk created mankind.

In another Babylonian poem, the Gilgamesh epic, which contains the Babylonian story of the flood, there is an account of the creation of man which accords much more closely with Genesis 2:7 than that which we are considering. It runs:

> The goddess Aruru, when she heard this,
> A man like Anu she formed in her heart.
> Aruru washed her hands;
> Clay she pinched off and spat upon it;
> Eabani, a hero she created,
> An exalted offspring, with the might of Ninib.

Here is clearly a tradition, similar to Genesis, that God formed man from the dust of the ground. The allusion to Aruru indicates that this formed a part of the early Babylonian tradition. There is considerable evidence that in an earlier form of the Babylonian account Marduk had no place. He was introduced into it later by the priests of Babylon. Aruru was in that earlier form the creator of man, and probably was said to have formed him from clay, as in the Gilgamesh epic.

While these points of likeness are evident, there are great differences between the two narratives. The Babylonian account speaks not only of grass and reeds as non-existent, but of cities and temples also, which, it tells us, were created later. It has no picture of Eden; its thought centers in well-known Babylonian cities. While Marduk appears as supreme in the Babylonian poem, the gods and

Anunaki, or spirits of earth, are recognized, so that the polytheistic view is not entirely absent. In the Biblical picture, on the other hand, Jehovah is supreme. Opinions of scholars differ as to whether there was any real connection between the two narratives. Whatever opinion one may hold on this point, there can be no question but that the second chapter of Genesis is dominated by those religious conceptions which were so uniquely manifested in Israel, while they are absent from the Babylonian narrative.

3. Text of a Tablet from Nippur.[2]

1. In the mountain of heaven and earth
2. The day Anu brought forth the great gods;
3. A tree of Ezinu had not been born, had not become green,
4. Her land, the goddess Takku had not created.
5. For Takku a temple-platform had not been filled in;
6. A ewe (?) had not bleated (?), a lamb had not been dropped,
7. A goat had not bleated, a kid had not been born,
8. No ewe had borne her lamb,
9. No goat had borne a kid,
10. The name of Ezinu, tall and holy, and of Sig.[3]
11. The Anunnaki, the great gods, had not known.
12. There was no šes-grain of thirty-fold;
13. There was no šes-grain of fifty-fold;
14. Small grain, mountain-grain, and cattle-fodder there were not;
15. A possession and houses there were not;
16. Takku had not been brought forth, a shrine not lifted up
17. Together with the lady Ninki the lord had not brought forth men.
18. Shamash as leader came, unto her desire came forth;
19. Mankind he planned; many men were brought forth.
20. Food and sleep they knew not;
21. Clothing and dwellings they knew not.
22. The people with rushes and skins came,
23. Like sheep with their mouths..........they ate grass,
24. Garden water they drank.
25. When the land was green with the forms of their gods
26. And with edible plants the holy dwelling of Sig and Ezinu were green,
27. They brought food for the gods to the established dwelling
28. From the abundance of Sig and Ezinu.
29. The great gods in their holy dwelling
30. Ate; they were not satisfied;
31. They gave good food to their holy flock.

2 The text has been published by Barton, *Miscellaneous Babylonian Inscriptions*, No. 8, and by Langdon, *Le Poème Sumerien du Paridis du Déluge, et de la Chute de l'Homme*, Planche VII and VIII. Translations, Barton, *op. cit.* p. 52, ff., Langdon, *op cit.*, p. 136 ff., and Luckenbill, *AJSL.* XXXVIII, 32 ff. Chiera, in *Sumerian Religious Texts*, published by Crozer Theological Seminary, No. 25, has added a copy from Constantinople. He has also shown that a fragment of the text is published in *Babylonian Expedition of the University of Pennsylvania*, Vol. XXXI, No. 15, and another in the *Hilprecht Anniversary Volume*, No. 6. Other unpublished fragments are also cited in his work.

3 *Sig* is the usual sign for wool and is employed further on to designate wool. Here it is said to have been green. Does it refer to some plant, flax or cotton, that could be used for the same purpose as wool?

Reverse

1. The great gods in their holy dwelling
2. Drank; they were not satisfied;
3. For the proper feeding of their holy flock
4. Kingship in security they established.
5. When Enki spoke a word to Enlil,
6. The waters of Enlil and Ezida
7. Made the holy dwelling green.
8. The mighty holy dwelling they inhabited for thee.
9. Enki and Enlil their holy word
10. To Sig and Ezinu spoke from the holy dwelling;
11. Wool from the flock they gave;
12. Vegetables as food in abundance they gave.
13. For vegetation they made canals,
14. Irrigating machines with laborers attached they gave.
15. Wool was taken from the flock;
16. The shepherd of the flock revelled in abundance.
17. Ezinu stood as tall vegetation;
18. The bright land was green; it presented abundance in heaps;
19. In the field the head was lifted high;
20. From heaven abundance came;
21. Sig and Ezinu made increase;
22. For all they raised an abundance;
23. They filled the land with exalted courage;
24. The voice of their god uttered just decisions for them.
25. A dwelling-place was their land; food increased for the people;
26. The prosperity of their land brought them danger;
27. For making house-bricks the clay of the land they burned.
28. They became strong; they raised abundance;
29. Companions were they; man with wife they dwelt;
30. In misfortune the house assists them.

A colophon states that the tablet contained 60 lines. Ezinu was a god of vegetation—trees, grain, etc. Sig usually signifies "wool," then "garment." As Sig is in this text said to have become green along with Ezinu, it may designate flax, or possibly cotton, which produced a woolly substance from which garments were made. The goddess Takku was a patroness of agriculture. The story, therefore, begins before the existence of vegetation and domestic animals, before fields had been cultivated, or houses built, and before the establishment of political institutions, and it traces the coming of these into existence. In this respect it reminds one of Genesis 2: 5, 6. The way in which the word of the great god Enki causes water to flow and other creative acts to follow resembles in a faint way the way God speaks and things come into existence in the first chapter of Genesis.

4. Another Sumerian Account of the Creation of Man.—
Still another account of the creation of man has been found among

the tablets discovered at the city of Ashur. This was copied by the Assyrian scribes from a Sumerian text so old that it is accompanied not only by an Assyrian translation, but by many kabbalistic symbols. It reads as follows:[4]

1. When both heaven and earth had been completely established;
2. When the mother of the goddesses had been born;
3. When the earth had been brought forth, the land created,
4. When the domes of heaven and earth had been established,
5. Straight canals had been constructed;
6. The Tigris and Euphrates—their banks had been established;
7. Anu, Enlil, Shamash, Ea,
8. The great gods,
9. The Anunnaki, the great gods,
10. Lofty sanctuaries inhabited as creators.
11. In anxiety they asked:
12. "Since the domes of heaven and earth have been established,
13. Straight canals have been constructed,
14. The Tigris and Euphrates—
15. Their banks have been established,
16. What shall we change?
17. What shall we create?
18. O Anunnaki, ye great gods,
19. What shall we change?
20. What shall we create?"
21. The great gods, standing aloft,
22. The Anunnaki, who determine fate,
23. The two of them made answer to Enlil:
24. "In the land where flesh grows, the bond of heaven and earth,
25. Lamga, Lamga, we will overthrow;
26. From his blood mankind we will make,
27. Let the bonds of the gods be bound upon them;
28. For future days the limit
29. Be established;
30. The yoke and lifting cord on their hands
31. Be placed,
32. The temple of the great gods
33. Unto a lofty sanctuary to bring,
34. The meadows to mark out,
35. Forever their limits
36. To establish,
37. The straight canal
38. As a boundary to establish,
39. The earth to water, the plants
40. To raise,
41. The rain of heaven, the rain of heaven.........
42. The ravine of the land as a boundary to set,
43. The storehouse of the district to measure it,

4 Translated from E. Ebeling's *Keilschrifttexte aus Assur Religions Inhalts*, Leipzig, 1915–1919, No. 4. The text of this poem is accompanied by a set of notations which are believed to be musical notes. The text was doubtless recited at the festival services of the gods; to recount the great deeds of the gods by the recitation or chanting of such texts was in ancient heathen worship a way of doing them honor. It is interesting that the tablet which records this text contains also directions for chanting it. How to equate this notation with modern musical notes, is not yet understood.

44. To make the field of the Anunnaki produce,
45. To increase the abundance of the land,
46. To keep the feast of the gods,
47. Cool water to pour out
48. In the dwellings of the gods which have been made lofty.
49. Ullugarra and Nigarra
50. Shall they be called.
51. Ox, sheep, cattle, fish, and bird,
52. The abundance of the land to increase,
53. The lord of gladness and the lady of gladness
54. With their holy mouth to supplicate.
55. O Aruru, who hast been raised up for ladyship,
56. Great structures thou thyself shalt enclose,
57. Wise men for the people, heroes for the weak,
58. Like grain springing of itself from the earth, shall be made,—
59. A destiny unchangeable as a star forever.
60. By day and night
61. The feasts of the gods,
62. Their great appointed festivals of themselves
63. They shall celebrate."
64. Anu, Enlil,
65. Ea, Ninmakhu
66. The great gods,
67. The place of mankind created.
68. The goddess Nisaba [5] in mankind's place was established.
69. Mighty and secret things
70. As a scribe I teach.

This account shows that there were among the Babylonian traditions variations of the idea that man was made from the blood of a god. In this account, instead of being from the blood of Kingu, one of the rebellious gods, husband of the arch-rebel Tiâmat, he is made from the blood of Lamga, the craftsman, the god of carpenters.

It will be noted that, as in the sixth tablet of the Creation Epic, so in this account man was created by the gods for the specific purpose of tilling the ground, building temples, and keeping up the festivals of the gods. It accords in that respect with the thought of the second chapter of Genesis, where man is placed in Eden, the garden of God, to dress it and to keep it for his Divine Creator (see Genesis 2:15).

5 The grain-goddess.

CHAPTER III

THE BABYLONIAN SABBATH

FEAST OF MARDUK AND ZARPANIT. A DAY CALLED SHABATUM. A DAY IN SOME TABLETS AT YALE.

1. Feast of Marduk and Zarpanit.

The seventh day is the feast of Marduk and Zarpanit. It is an evil day. The shepherd of the great people shall not eat flesh cooked on the coals which is smoked. The garment of his body he shall not change; a clean one he shall not put on. A sacrifice he shall not offer. The king in a chariot shall not ride. In triumph he shall not speak. In the secret place a seer shall not give an oracle. The physician shall not lay his hand on the sick. It is not fitting to utter a malediction. At night before Marduk and Ishtar the king shall bring his offering; a libation he shall pour out. The lifting up of his hands shall then be pleasing to the gods.[1]

This passage occurs in a tablet which describes the nature of all the days of a month. The same prohibitions are recorded for the fourteenth, nineteenth, twenty-first, and twenty-eighth days. The tablet has often been brought into comparison with the Hebrew sabbath, partly because the seventh, fourteenth, twenty-first, and twenty-eight days are involved, partly because the prohibitions remind the reader of Exodus 20: 8–11 and Deuteronomy 5: 12–15.

Exodus 20: 8–11. Remember the sabbath day, to keep it holy. Six days shalt thou labor, and do all thy work: but the seventh day is a sabbath unto the Lord thy God: *in it* thou shalt not do any work, thou, nor thy son, nor thy daughter, thy manservant, nor thy maidservant, nor thy cattle, nor thy stranger that is within thy gates: for in six days the Lord made heaven and earth, the sea, and all that in them is, and rested the seventh day: wherefore the Lord blessed the sabbath day, and hallowed it.

Deuteronomy 5: 12–15. Observe the sabbath day, to keep it holy, as the Lord thy God commanded thee. Six days shalt thou labor, and do all thy work: but the seventh day is a sabbath unto the Lord thy God: *in it* thou shalt not do any work, thou, nor thy son, nor thy daughter, nor thy manservant, nor thy maidservant, nor thine ox, nor thine ass, nor any of thy cattle, nor thy stranger that is within thy gates; that thy manservant and thy maidservant may rest as well as thou. And thou shalt remember that thou wast a servant in the land of Egypt, and the Lord thy God brought thee out thence by a mighty hand and by a stretched out arm: therefore the Lord thy God commanded thee to keep the sabbath day.

[1] Translated from Rawlinson's *Cuneiform Inscriptions of Western Asia*, IV, 2d ed., pl. 32, lines 28–38.

In reality the Babylonian prohibitions apply to certain classes of people only, and not to the whole population. A study of the contract literature shows that there was no cessation of business upon these days of the month, so that resemblance to the Hebrew sabbath is really quite slight.

2. A Day Called Shabatum.—These days were not, so far as we know, called *shabatum,* but another tablet [2] tells us that the fifteenth day of each month was so called. *Shabatum* is etymologically the same as the Hebrew sabbath. As the Babylonian months were lunar, the fifteenth was the time of the full moon, so that in Babylonian usage the day denotd the completion of the moon's growth. In the Old Testament "sabbath" is sometimes coupled with "new moon," as though it may also have designated a similar day. (See 2 Kings 4:23; Amos 8:5; Hosea 2:11; Isa. 1:13; 66:23, and Ezek. 46:3.) This Babylonian *shabatum* can, in any event, have no direct relationship to the Hebrew sabbath as a day of rest once a week.

3. A Day in Some Tablets at Yale.—A series of tablets in the Yale Babylonian Collection, a portion of which has been published by Prof. Clay,[3] shows that special sacrifices were offered on the seventh, fourteenth, twenty-first, and twenty-eighth of each month. These sacrifices show that these days were thought to have some peculiar significance, but, whatever that significance may have been, the evidence cited shows that it was not the same as that of the Hebrew sabbath.

2 See *Proceedings of the Society of Biblical Archæology,* Vol. XXVI, pp. 51–56.
3 *Miscellaneous Inscriptions in the Yale Babylonian Collection,* New Haven, 1916, Nos. 46–51.

CHAPTER IV

THE FALL OF MAN

Four fragments of the Adapa myth have been found. They really present but three parts of the story, as two of them cover the same ground. These three parts of the story are translated in this chapter. It will be noted that the fragments do not present the entire story. Between fragments I and II, as well as between fragments II and III, some lines have fallen out, and the last fragment is broken away before the end of the account is reached. Nevertheless, from the parts which we have it is clear that the Babylonians shared with the Hebrews some of the traditions recorded in the third chapter of Genesis.

1. Comparison with Genesis 3.—In the first place, Adapa, like Adam, had gained knowledge. This knowledge carried with it a power hitherto regarded as an attribute of divinity. It enabled Adapa to break the wing of the south wind; it tempted Adam and Eve "to become like God, knowing good and evil" (Gen. 3:5). As in Genesis, knowledge did not carry with it immortality. Ea, the god who had permitted Adapa to become wise, feared that he might gain immortality, as Jehovah stated of Adam, "lest he put forth his hand and take also of the tree of life and eat and live forever" (Gen. 3:22). (For Babylonian and Assyrian conceptions of the tree of life, see Figs. 291, 293.)

Ea accordingly told Adapa a falsehood when he was about to go into the presence of the supreme god, Anu, in order to prevent him from eating the food that would make him immortal; Jehovah drove man from the garden where the tree of life grew. The two accounts agree in the thought that immortality could be obtained by eating a certain kind of food. The lines at the end of the Adapa story are much broken, but they make it clear that as a punishment for what he had done, Adapa was subjected to sickness, disease, and restlessness. This corresponds to the toil inflicted upon man (Gen. 3:17–

311

19), and the pangs of childbirth imposed upon woman (Gen. 3:16). It appears also that as Adam and Eve were clothed with skins in consequence of their deed (Gen. 3:21), so Adapa was clothed by Anu in a special clothing.

These similarities indicate that the Babylonians possessed the same general ideas of the connection of increasing knowledge, with the attributes of divinity on the one hand, and with suffering and clothing on the other, which are presented in Genesis. An increasing number of modern scholars regard the Babylonian story as an earlier form of a narrative which the Hebrew writer took and purified. Others hold that it is a somewhat degenerate form of the Biblical narrative. In any event, the Babylonian story proves the Biblical conceptions to be very ancient, and, by its contrasts to that of Genesis, it exhibits the dignity and religious value of the Biblical narrative. In the Babylonian myth, the gods, Ea and Anu, are divided and work at cross purposes; Ea tells a falsehood to accomplish his end. Genesis, while it represents Jehovah as feeling and acting in a much more human way than some parts of the Bible do, still portrays him as a consistently righteous, omnipotent God, who demands obedience, and whose punishments are the reasonable recompense for transgressions. The superiority of the Old Testament stands out in striking contrast.

2. The Adapa Myth.[1]

I

1. He possessed intelligence............
2. His command like the command of Anu............
3. Wide intelligence he (Ea) made perfect for him, the destiny of the country to reveal.
4. Unto him wisdom he gave; eternal life he did not grant him.
5. In those days, in those years the wise man of Eridu,—
6. Ea as a chief (?) among men had created him,—
7. A wise man whose command no one could restrain,
8. The prudent, the most wise among the Anunnaki was he,
9. Blameless, clean of hands, anointed, the observer of divine commands,
10. With the bakers he made bread,
11. With the bakers of Eridu he made bread,
12. The food and water of Eridu he prepared daily,
13. With his clean hands he prepared the table,
14. And without him the table was not cleared.
15. The ship he steered; fishing and hunting for Eridu he did.
16. Then Adapa of Eridu,
17. While Ea lay upon a bed in a chamber (?),

---

1 Translated from *Recueil de Traveaux*, XX, 127, ff.; Winckler and Abel's *Thontafeln-fund von El-Amarna*, No. 240, *Keilinschriftliche Bibliothek*, VI, p. xvii, f., and *Proceedings of the Society of Biblical Archæology*, XVI, 274, f.

18. Daily the closing of Eridu he made right.
19. At the pure quay, the quay of the new-moon, he embarked upon the ship,
20. The wind blew, his ship sailed,
21. With the rudder he steered the ship
22. Upon the broad sea.

II

1. ....
2. The south wind [blew and capsized him],
3. To the house [of the fishes] it made him sink,
4. "O south wind [increase] thy rage as much as [thou art able],
5. Thy wing I will break." As he spoke with his mouth,
6. The wing of the south wind was broken, seven days
7. The south wind blew not on the land. Anu
8. To his messenger, Ilabrat, said:
9. "Why has the south wind not blown upon the land for seven days?"
10. His messenger Ilabrat answered him, "My lord
11. Adapa, the son of Ea, the wing of the south wind
12. Has broken." Anu, when he heard this,
13. Cried, "Help!" He ascended his throne: "Let some one bring him
    to me.
14. Likewise Ea, who knows the heavens, summon him,
14a. To King Ea to come." [2]
14b. To him he caused word to be borne,
14c. ....To him, to King Ea,
14d. He sent a messenger.
14e. He is of great understanding, he knows the hearts of the great gods,
14f. ....of the heavens, he establishes it.
15. [A soiled garment he made] him wear; with a mourning garment clad
    him,
16. He clothed him and gave him counsel,
17. Saying: "Adapa, into the presence of Anu, the king, thou art going,
18. Fail not the order, my word keep,
19. When thou goest up to heaven and approachest the gate of Anu,
20. At the gate of Anu, Tammuz and Gishzida
21. Stand, they will see thee, they will ask: 'Lord,
22. For whose sake art thou thus, Adapa? For whom
23. Art thou clad in a mourning garment?' 'In our country two gods have
    vanished, therefore
24. Am I thus.' 'Who are the two gods who in the land
25. Have vanished?' 'Tammuz and Gishzida.' They will look at one
    another and
26. Be astonished. Favorable words
27. To Anu they will speak. A joyful countenance of Anu
28. They will reveal to thee. When thou standest in the presence of Anu,
29. Food of death they will offer thee to eat;
30. Thou shalt not eat. Water of death they will offer thee to drink;
31. Thou shalt not drink. A garment will they show thee;
32. Put it on. Oil they will set before thee; anoint thyself.
33. The command which I give thee, forget not. The word
34. Which I have spoken hold fast." The messenger
35. Of Anu came: "Adapa of the south wind
36. The wing has broken. Into my presence bring him."

2 The lines 14a, etc., are supplied from a parallel tablet.

37. The road to heaven he made him take and to heaven he ascended.
38. When to heaven he ascended, when he approached the gate of Anu,
39. At the gate of Anu, Tammuz and Gishzida were standing.
40. When they saw him they cried: "Adapa, help!
41. Lord, for whose sake art thou thus?
42. For whom art thou clad in a mourning garment?
43. In the country two gods have vanished; therefore in a mourning garment
44. Am I clad. Who are the two gods who from the land have vanished?"
45. "Tammuz and Gishzida." They looked at one another and
46. Were astonished. When Adapa before Anu the king,
47. Approached, Anu saw him and cried:
48. "Come, Adapa, why of the south wind the wing
49. Hast thou broken?" Adapa answered: "Anu, my lord,
50. For the house of my lord in the midst of the sea
51. I was catching fish. As I was midway of the voyage
52. The south wind blew and capsized me;
53. To the house of the fishes it made me sink. In the anger of my heart
54. [The south wind] I cursed. At my side answered Tammuz
55. And Gishzida: 'The heart should be toward Anu.'
56. They spoke, he was appeased, his heart was won (?).
57. "Why has Ea, to impure man, of the heavens
58. And the earth revealed the heart?
59. Strong (?) has he made him (Adapa); a name he has given him.
60. We—what can we do to him? Food of life
61. Bring him, that he may eat." Food of life
62. They brought him; he ate it not. Water of life
63. They brought him; he drank it not. A garment
64. They brought him; he clothed himself. Oil
65. They brought him; he anointed himself.
66. Anu looked at him; he wondered (?) at him.
67. "Come, Adapa, why dost thou not eat nor drink?
68. Now thou shalt not live; men are mortal (?)." "Ea my lord
69. Said: Thou shalt not eat, thou shalt not drink."
70. Take him and bring him back to earth.
71. ....looked upon him.

III

1. ....
2. He commanded him and he............
3. The garment, he commanded him and he clothed himself.
4. ....Anu wondered greatly at the deed of Ea.
5. The gods of heaven and earth, as many as there are: "Who is thus mighty (?)?
6. His command is the command of Anu. Who can surpass [him]?"
7. As now Adapa from the horizon to the zenith of the heavens
8. ....looked, he saw his terror........(i.e., the terror he inspired)
9. [Which] Anu concerning Adapa upon him........had placed.
10. [The service (?)] of Ea he made his satisfaction.
11. Anu fixed as his lot his lordship in brilliance to the distant future.
12. ....Adapa, the seed of mankind.
13. [Who] victoriously broke the wing of the south wind,
14. And to heaven he ascended. "Thus let it be!"
15. ....that which he in evil ways imposed on the people,
16. ....sickness which he placed in the bodies of people.

17. ....Ninkarrak appeased.
18. Sickness [shall co]me, his disease be violent,
19. ....destruction shall fall upon him,
20. [In] good sleep he shall not rest,
21.....shall overturn (?) the joy of people's hearts.

(The remainder is broken away.)

3. A Babylonian Story of Expulsion from a Garden.—Professor Edward Chiera discovered an interesting tablet which perhaps contains a parallel to the Biblical account of the Fall of Man. It belongs to a long series of texts which refer to the origin of civilization. It reads as follows:

1. Like vegetable food (?)[3]   ......
2. ....
3. ....
4a. To do that in rebellion he has..........
4b.   he did not obey (?) him.
5. My heart is full, is full of..............
6. ....is given,
7. Fear, lo lamentation is given
8. Unto me thou dost call;
9. And I at thy call
10. In my weakness was fleeing.
11. And I in my person..........
12. Thy humanity, thy body has not been taken away...........
13. For humanity the words of understanding are not..........
14. End thy weeping!
15. From my midst go forth to the steppe!
16a. To me forever, having taken of the clothing-establishing-tree
16b.   as an outcast thou shalt not return!
17. The death-emancipating reed the enlightened children who are wretched
17b.   shall not take;

Reverse

1. Thou shalt never take.
2. In no way hereafter shalt thou attain release.
3. To my ox for threshing, as an outcast thou shalt not return!
4. To my field for irrigating as an outcast thou shalt not return!
5. To my field for tilling as an outcast thou shalt not return!
6. To my work to do it as an outcast thou shalt not return!
7. Go; perform the work; raise the food to eat!
8. I! I will never receive thee!
9a. Men like thee will perform the work; their mothers and their fathers
9b.   shall eat of heaven's food.
10. Since the hand of the son of the menial has divided the food, their eyes are opened..........

[3] Translated from H. F. Lutz, *Selected Sumerian and Babylonian Texts.* Philadelphia, 1919, No. 103. For another translation, see Edward Chiera, in the *American Journal of Semitic Languages*, XXXIX, pp. 40–51, and Chiera, *Sumerian Religious Texts*, No. 30 (Publications of Crozer Theological Seminary).

11. As for themselves each one has taken 10 measures of barley;
12. The children who are servants of their fathers have each taken 10 measures of barley for himself;
13. For each of their fathers barley has been threshed;
14. Barley, oil, wool, sheep have been brought unto them.
15. O humanity, be abundant!

While my translation differs in some slight details from that of Professor Chiera, it agrees in all substantial points. We have here the story of the expulsion of mankind from some place for disobedience, and the disobedience seems to be connected with a tree "that establishes clothing" and with the eating of food that opens the eyes, which strikingly corresponds to Genesis 3 : 3–8. The men addressed in the tablet had been cultivating a tract from which they were cast out for this disobedience, just as Adam and Eve were expelled from Eden for their disobedience. They are sent forth to raise food by toil just as Adam was. It may be that we have here the Babylonian account of the same tradition. In other details, however, the text here translated differs widely from the Biblical account, and Professor Clay thought it the story of the expulsion of some mutinous slaves from their master's estate. The present writer is inclined to agree with Professor Chiera's view, but it is too soon to pronounce a decisive verdict.

CHAPTER V

THE PATRIARCHS BEFORE THE FLOOD

BABYLONIAN LONG-LIVED KINGS. COMPARISON WITH GENESIS 5. COMPARISON WITH GENESIS 4.

1. Babylonian Long-lived Kings.—It has long been known from the writings of Berossos, a Babylonian priest who died about 260 B.C., that the Babylonians had a list of long-lived kings who lived before the Flood. The cuneiform original of this list has now been recovered. The tablets which contain this list contain also the names of dynasties of kings who are said to have ruled after the Flood, some of whom it is said ruled some hundreds of years each. Efforts have been made to show that the names of the antediluvian patriarchs in Genesis are identical with those of Berossos' antediluvian kings. The recovery of the cuneiform originals puts the whole matter in a new light. The cuneiform texts read as follows:[1]

Column I
1. Sovereignty descended from heaven;
2. at Eridu was the sovereignty.
3. Alulim exercised
4. the sovereignty 28,800 years;
5. Alamar exercised it 36,000 years:
6. 2 kings
7. 64,800 years exercised it.
8. Eridu was overthrown;
9. the sovereignty to Badgurgurru
10. went
11. At Badgurgurru Enmenluanna
12. exercised (sovereignty) 43,200 years;
13. Enmengalanna
14. exercised it 28,800 years;
15. Dumuzi the shepherd exercised it 36,000 years:
16. 3 kings
17. their years were 108,000.
18. Badgurgurra was overthrown;
19. the sovereignty passed to Larak.
20. At Larak Sibzianna [2]
21. exercised kingship 28,800 years:
22. 1 king
23. exercised it 28,800 years.
24. Larak was overthrown;
25. the sovereignty to Sippar
26. passed.
27. At Sippar Enmenduranna
28. exercised kingship 21,000 years:
29. 1 king
30. exercised it 21,000 years.
31. Sippar was overthrown;
32. the sovereignty passed to Surrippak.
33. At Surrippak Uberratum
34. exercised sovereignty 18,600 years:
35. 1 king
36. exercised it 18,600 years.
37. 5 cities,
38. 8 kings
39. exercised it 241,200 years.
40. The deluge overthrew the land.
41. After the deluge had overthrown,
42. the sovereignty descended from heaven—
43. the sovereignty was at Kish.
44. At Kish Gaur
45. was king.
46. He exercised (sovereignty) 1200 years.
47. Khulla-Nidaba, the divine maiden,
48. exercised it 960 years.

1 Translated from S. Langdon's *Oxford Editions of Cuneiform Texts*, Vol. II, Oxford, 1923, No. 1.
2 Langdon transliterates the name Ensibzianna, but in his publication of the cuneiform text the En is omitted.

Column II

1. ....buum [3]
2. exercised (sovereignty) 900 (?) years
3. ....
4. ....
5. were companions
6. they completed (?)
   ....
7. Galumum
8. ruled 900 (?) years;
9. Zugagib
10. ruled 840 (?) years; [4]
11. A-ri-pi, son of Mashgag,
12. ruled 720 years;
13. Etana, the shepherd,
14. who ascended to heaven,
15. who subdued all lands,
16. ruled 635 years;
17. Pilikam,
18. son of Etana,
19. ruled 350 years, [5]
20. Enmenunna
21. reigned 611 years;
22. Melam-Kish,
23. son of Enmenunna,
24. ruled 900 years;
25. Barsalnunna,
26. son of Enmenunna,
27. ruled 1200 years;
28. Mes (?) zamu, son of Barsalnunna,
29. ruled.......years;
30. ....son of Barsalnunna, [6]

Column III

....
1. from Kish
2. the kingdom
3. passed to Eanna.
4. In Eanna
5. Meskingashir,
6. son of Shamash, [7]
7. as lord,
8. as king,
9. ruled 325 years.
10. Meskingashir
11. entered into
12. and went out from.........
13. Enmeirgan,
14, 15. son of Meskingashir,
16. king of Erech,
17. the people of Erech
18. strengthened,
19. as king
20. ruled 420 years.
21. Lugalbanda, the shepherd,
22. ruled 1200 years.
23. Dumuzi, the hunter [8] (?),
24. Whose city is among fishes,
25. ruled 100 years.
26. Gilgamesh,
27. Whose father
28. was lord of Kullab,
29. ruled 126 years.

[3] At this point the text of the tablet from Nippur, published by Poebel, *Historical and Grammatical Texts*, Philadelphia, 1914, No. 2, overlaps the Oxford text. The two texts differ considerably. Both texts were written during the dynasty of Isin, between 2300 and 2100 B.C. The text from Nippur was written 42 years before that at Oxford. In the translation from this point on I have followed the Nippur text, except where it is broken. Both texts are fully translated in G. A. Barton's *Royal Inscriptions of Sumer and Akkad*, New Haven, 1929, pp. 340–355.

[4] At this point the Oxford text inserts two kings, Atab and Atabba, one of whom reigned 600 years, and the other 840.

[5] Here the Oxford text inserts Balikh, son of Etana, who ruled 400 years.

[6] The Oxford text contains the rest of the column which is broken from the Nippur tablet. It gives the following:

Tupzakh, 140 years	Iltasadum, 1200 years
Tizkar, 306 years	Enmenbaragigur, 900 years
Ilku, 900 years.	Agga, 625 years.

[7] The sun-god.

[8] Perhaps "palm-tree-fertilizer" instead of hunter. It is not the usual ideogram for hunter, but one element stands for "hand" and the other for "female flower of the date palm." (See Barton, *The Origin and Development of Babylonian Writing*, Nos, 311(12) and 303(6).

Column IV

(The kingdom)
1. of Erech
2. passed to Ur.
3. In Ur
4. Mesannipada
5. was king;
6. he ruled 80 years.
7. Meskiagnunna,
8. son of Mesannipada,
9. ruled 30 years.
10. Elu........
11. ruled 25 years.
12. Balu........
13. 36 years.
14. 4 kings
15. ruled 171 years.
16. As to Ur
17. the kingdom
18. passed to Awan.[9]

5. in Kish:
6. total 22 kings—
7. their years were 2610+
8. 6 months, 15 days.
9. Five times
10. in Erech:
11. total 13 kings—
12. their years were 396—
13. ruled.
14. Three times
15. in Ur:
16. total 3 kings—
17. their years were 356—
18. ruled.
19. Once
20. in Awan:
21. total 1 king—
22. his rule was 7 years.
23. Once
24. in[11]........

Column V [10]

1. ruled 21 years.
2. Ishme-Dagan,
3. son of Idin-Dagan,
4. ruled 21 years.
5. Libit-Ishtar,
6. son of Idin-Dagan,
7. ruled 11 years.
8. Ur-Ninib,
9. son of Im........,
   ....

Column VI

1. Total 51 kings—
2. their years were 18000..+
3. 9 years......months......
4. Four times

Column VII

1. (total......) kings—
2. (their years) were 196—
3. ruled.
4. Twice in Agade:
5. total 21 kings—
6. their years were 125 years
7. 40 days—ruled.
8. Once
9. in the people
10. of Gutium:
11. total 11 kings—
12. their years were 159 years—
13. ruled
14. in Isin (?).
15. Eleven
16. royal cities
17. ruled.
18. Total 134 kings.
19. Grand total 28876+
20. years,
21. ......months.[11]

9 Seven lines are broken away from the end of the column.
 10 The subject-matter shows that several columns are entirely broken away. Dr. Poebel estimates that Column V was originally Column X. If this is true, six columns are entirely lost. Of Column IV, only a few lines out of the middle remain.
 11 A number of lines are lost at the end of the column. A number of the gaps in this text can now be supplied from the Oxford text, but as the material has no bearing on the Biblical narratives, we have not thought it necessary to take up space with them.

A brief examination of this list of kings is sufficient to convince one that until we reach the first dynasty of Ur the material is mythical or a combination of myths and legends. Real men do not reign 900 years, nor even 140 years, much less 21,000 years— not to mention larger numbers. When we find the names of gods mixed into the list, that is additional proof that the material is not historical. It is, of course, possible that some of the names in these earlier dynasties may be those of real men, the length of whose lives has been greatly exaggerated by mixing them up with myths. With the first dynasty of Ur we come upon historical ground. An inscription of King Annipadda, son of Mesannipadda, has been found.

A comparison of Berossos' list of kings who reigned before the Deluge with those given in this text will convince any scholar that a list like this was the source of Berossos' information. When we make allowance for changes in pronunciation in Babylonian which would be sure to occur in the course of 2000 years, and for the corruptions which would naturally occur in passing from a Babylonian to a Greek spelling, the two lists are seen to be the same, though in the 2000 years that elapsed between the writing of our tablets and Berossos, the lengths of the reigns of these kings were greatly exaggerated. The following parallel column will make this clear:

Cuneiform List		*List of Berossos* [12]	
Alulim,	28,800 years	Alorus,	36,000 years
Alalmar,	36,000 years	Älaparos,	10,800 years
Enmenluanna,	43,200 years	Amelon,	46,800 years
		Ammenon,	43,200 years
Enmengalanna,	28,800 years	Megalaros,	64,800 years
Dumuzi,	36,000 years	Daonos or Daos,	36,000 years
Sibzianna,	28,800 years	Euedorachos,	64,800 years
Enmenduranna,	21,000 years	Amempsinos,	36,000 years
Uburratum,	18,600 years	Otiartes,	28,800 years
		Xisouthros,	64,800 years
Total,	241,200 years	Total,	432,000 years

It will be noticed that Berossos added to the list Xisouthros, the hero of the Deluge, which the earlier list did not contain, and that his list contains two corruptions of the name Enmenluanna. Otherwise his list of names corresponds to the cuneiform except that he transposed Sibzianna (Amempsinos) and Enmenduranna. With

12 Professor Clay's thesis, that the names in Berossos' list are Semitic (*Origin of the Biblical Traditions,* Ch. VI), appears to be untenable.

one conflation, one transposition, and one addition, his list is identical with the ancient cuneiform, except that the numbers of regnal years have in most cases been exaggerated.

2. Comparison with Genesis 5.—The interest of all this for the Biblical student centers in the possibility that in these names we have the origin of the antediluvian Patriarchs. Many attempts have been made to show that the names of these Patriarchs was really identical with Berossos' list of names of antediluvian kings, and, the earlier editions of this book, the present writer thought that possible. The recovery of the cuneiform names of those kings by the discovery and publication of the Oxford prism, translated at the beginning of this chapter, puts the whole problem in a new light.

It is true that some of the names of the antediluvian Patriarchs of the Bible could be derived from those of this old Sumerian list of antediluvian kings. Amelon, into which Enmenluanna was corrupted, became in Akkadian, as the Semitic-Babylonian language was called, *amêlu,* which means "man." This could in its turn be translated into Hebrew by two words, *'adham,* "man" or *'enōsh,* "man"—words which, when taken as proper names, become, respectively, Adam and Enosh. Älaparos might conceivably be corrupted into Abel. Ammenon, another of the forms into which Enmenluanna was corrupted, is in Akkadian *ummanu,* "artificer," "artisan," which, when translated into Hebrew, becomes Kenan, and in an abbreviated form, Cain. Megalaros might conceivably through corruption become Mahalel. Dumuzi, which means in Sumerian "son of life," might, when translated into Hebrew, become "Jared," "descendant." Euedorachos might conceivably be shortened to Enoch. The Summerian, Enmenduranna, possibly translated into Akkadian as Mutu-salal-elu, might appear in Hebrew as Methuselah. We may, then, from these antediluvian Babylonian kings possibly obtain the following table of equivalents:

Cuneiform Sumerian	Berossos	Hebrew
Alulim	Alorus	
Alalmar	Alaparos	Abel?
Enmenluanna	Ammelon	Adam and Enosh
Enmenluanna	Ammenon	Kenan and Cain
Enmengalanna	Megalaros	Mahalelel
Dumuzi	Daonos	Jared
Enmenduranna	Euedorachos	Enoch
Enmenduranna		Methuselah.

It should be noted also that the name of the city Badgurgurru means "fortress of workers in bronze." In Genesis 4:22, Tubal-cain is said to have been a metal worker, and in 4:17 Cain is said to have built a city. It does not seem improbable that we have here another form of the Biblical tradition.

By no ingenuity, so far as I can see, can the names of Seth and Lamech—two of the Biblical antediluvian Patriarchs, be derived from the names of the Sumerian antediluvian kings. It is noteworthy, too, that the ages assigned in Genesis 5 to the antediluvian Patriarchs correspond closely to those of the reigns of the Babylonian kings who are said to have reigned just after the Flood. It is, therefore, possible that the Hebrews, recognizing that it was ludicrous to suppose that men could reign as long as the Babylonian kings are said to have reigned, derived the names of their antediluvian Patriarchs from the names of kings who reigned after the Flood. Let us see how this hypothesis will work out: The name, Aripi,[13] the fifth king after the Flood whose name is preserved, may also have been read Adimê, and perhaps was so read by the Sumerians themselves. If it came to the Hebrews in this form they would naturally equate it with the Hebrew Adam, which means "man."

Etana, the shepherd, is said in this list to have gone to heaven. This at once suggests the fate of Enoch, who "was not; for God took him" (Gen. 5:24). In the Sumerian the words "to heaven" are AN-SU, which may also be read AN-KU. If these words were not fully understood by the Hebrews, to whom Sumerian was not only a foreign language but a dead language, they might easily be mistaken for a proper name, and would in Hebrew give us Enoch.[14] Another suggestion as to the method of borrowing is also possible. Later traditions cherished the name of a king, Enmeduranki, whom they called a king of Sippar or Agade.[15] Enmeduranki means "the hero who binds together heaven and earth." Etana is in our list of kings called a king of Kish, but in later times kings of Kish were also called kings of Agade. It is altogether probable, therefore, that the "hero who binds together heaven and earth" is simply another

13 Poebel reads the name *Arpi*, apparently because in another fragmentary tablet he thinks the name is *Arbum*, but both Poebels copy and the photograph of the tablet indicate that the reading was *A-ri-pi*. The writer has endeavored to settle the matter by collating both tablets, but both have unfortunately crumbled too much to make collation decisive.

14 Sumerian words which begin with a vowel when they are taken over into Hebrew, assume a guttural at the beginning. Thus the Sumerian AS-TAN, "one," which became in Semitic Babylonian *ištin*, comes into Hebrew as *'eštê* with an Ayin at the beginning. (See Jer. 1:3 and elsewhere.) Ayin in Semitic phonetics frequent changes to Heth. (See Brockelmann's *Vergleichende Grammatik der Semitischen Sprachen*, I, § 55, b, a.) In accordance with these facts AN-KU came into Hebrew as *Henok*.

15 He is mentioned in Zimmern's *Ritualtafeln für den Wahrsager*, Leipzig, 1901, No. 24: 1, ff., as the discoverer of the art of forecasting events by pouring oil on water.

designation of Etana who went to heaven. The last two syllables
of Enmeduranki, *i.e.*, AN-KI, "heaven and earth," would, if
taken over into Hebrew, also give Enoch. If we assume that
Etana and Enoch are the same, we may at a later point be able to
determine by which of these processes the name is most likely to
have come into Hebrew. In an old poem, fragments of which
have been found on some broken tablets from Nineveh, the fortunes
of Etana were given in detail. He is said to have been carried to
heaven on the back of an eagle. If he be really the prototype of
Enoch, this lends a touch of realism to the narrative.

The Sumerian name Enmenunna means "exalted hero" or
"exalted man." A natural translation of this into Semitic Babylonian about 2000 B.C. would be *Mutu-elu*,[16] or, in one word, *amelu*,
and an equally natural translation of this into Hebrew would give
us Enosh.

Pilikam,[17] the next name, means in Sumerian "with intelligence
to build." In Babylonian Semitic it would be literally *Ina-uzni-
erêšu,* or, rendered in one word, *ummanu*, "artificer." The Hebrew
translation of this is Kenan, which means "artificer." Melamkish
gives us the Hebrew Lamech by the simple elision of the first and
last consonants. All people are lazy and words sometimes wear
away both at the beginning and at the end.[18]

Barsalnunna, translated into Semitic Babylonian, becomes
Shithu-elu.[19] Seth may well be a transfer of a part of this name to
Hebrew. The final radical of the first part of the name may have
worn away or have been accidentally omitted.

Meskingashir is resolvable into four elements, MES-KI-
INGA [20]-SHIR,[21] "the hero" or "man who is great" or "exalted."

16 Poebel has shown, *Historical Texts,* 114, that EN-ME designates a hero or special
kind of priest. *Mutu* in Semitic means both "man" and "a kind of priest"; cf. Muss-
Arnolt, *Assyrisch-Englisch-Deutsches Handwörterbuch,* 619, 620, and Knudtzon, *El-Amarna
Tafeln,* No. 55, 43. *Mutu* was a popular element in Semitic proper names about 2000 B.C.,
but later ceased to be employed.
17 The sign *kam* Poebel failed to recognize. It is No. 364 of Barton's *Origin and
Development of Babylonian Writing.* It is sometimes employed in early texts instead of
other signs which had the values *ka* or *kam*. Here it is used for sign No, 357 of the work
referred to.
18 Langdon makes the suggestion (*Sumerian Epic of Paradise, the Flood, and the Fall
of Man,* Philadelphia, 1915, p. 56, note 7) that Lamech is the Sumerian LUMHA, an
epithet of the Babylonian god Ea as the patron of music. A more plausible theory would
be that Lamech is a corruption of a king's name, as suggested above, and after it was
corrupted it was confused with the name of the Sumerian god LAMGA, the constructive
god, whose emblem was the sign for carpenter. (See Barton, work cited, No. 503.)
19 See Meissner, *Seltene assyrische Ideogramme,* No. 1139. Seth might also be a
transfer to Hebrew of a part of the name Iltasadum, which, translated into Akkadian,
would be *Ina-nashi-shetu-allik.*
20 See Barton, work cited, No. 275(5). IN is the Sumerian verb preformative.
21 See Delitzsch, *Sumerisches Glossar,* p. 262, f.

Translate this into Semitic Babylonian and it becomes *Mutu-ša-elu*, which is almost exactly Methuselah.

Enmeirgan becomes when translated into Semitic Mutu-šalal-eqla,[22] and Mahalalel is a much closer transfer of the first two elements of this to Hebrew than are Sennacherib, Esar-haddon, Merodach-baladan, and Evil-merodach of the names Sin-akhi-irba, Ashur-akhi-iddina, Marduk-apal-iddin, and Amel-Marduk. Finally Dumuzi means "son of life," or "living son," and Jared[23] means "descendant."

The equivalent of Noah does not appear in this list, but there is no doubt that he was Ziugiddu, otherwise called Ut-napishtim, of the Babylonian accounts of the flood.

We have then the following equivalents, four of which are Hebrew translations of Sumerian names; three, transfers into Hebrew of the whole or of parts of Semitic Babylonian equivalents of these Sumerian names, two of which are transfers to Hebrew of portions of a Sumerian original, and one of which, Noah, is still unexplained.

Sumerian	Semitic Babylonian	Hebrew
Adimê		Adam
Barsalnunna	Shithu-elu	Seth
Enmenunna	Mutu-elu (or amelu)	Enosh
Pelikam	Ina-uzni-ereshu (or ummanu)	Kenan
Enmeirgan	Mutu-šalal-gan	Mahalalel
Dumuzi	Apal-napišti	Jared
Etana		Enoch
Meskingashir	Mutu-ša-elu	Methuselah
Melamkish		Lamech
Ziugiddu		Noah

Of course, it may be objected that our list of kings did not furnish the originals of these patriarchs, since there are more kings than patriarchs, even though some of the names of kings have been lost by the breaking of the tablet. In this connection, however, one should remember that in 1 Chronicles 1–9, many names which appear in the earlier books of the Bible are omitted, and that in Matthew 1:8, three kings—Ahaziah, Joash, and Amaziah—are omitted from the genealogy of Christ. (Compare 2 Kings 11–15.) It appears, then, that Biblical writers did not always copy a full list.

It thus seems that the tablet translated above may be related to the text of Genesis 5 in the names of the patriarchs through one or

22 See Barton, work cited, No. 229(18).
23 Jared might, of course, be a corruption of Irad. It could have arisen by the wearing away of the Hebrew letter *Ayin*.

the other of its lists, as well as in the matter of their ages. When
we recall that the tablet was apparently written in the year 2170
B.C., it seems possible that it may be a source from which the
Biblical names came.

3. Comparison with Genesis 4.—But our examination of the
matter cannot stop here. In Genesis 4: 16–23 there is a list of the
descendants of Cain strikingly similar to the list of the descendants
of Seth in Genesis 5. If the names of Adam and Abel be supplied
from Genesis 4: 1, 2, the two lists appear as follows:

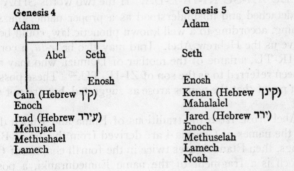

Genesis 4		Genesis 5
Adam		Adam
Abel Seth		Seth
Enosh		Enosh
Cain (Hebrew ‏קִין‎)		Kenan (Hebrew ‏קִינָן‎)
Enoch		Mahalalel
Irad (Hebrew ‏עִירָד‎)		Jared (Hebrew ‏יֶרֶד‎)
Mehujael		Enoch
Methushael		Methuselah
Lamech		Lamech
		Noah

The close parallelism of these two lists of names is really greater
than it appears to the English reader to be. Cain, which means
"artificer," is in Hebrew the same word as Kenan, lacking only one
formative letter at the end. Irad and Jared differ in Hebrew only
by the wearing away of one consonant. Mehujael is as much like
Mahalalel, and Methushael as much like Methuselah as the Assyrian
name of Tiglath-pileser, Tukultu-apal-esharra, is like Tiglath-
pileser, while Enoch and Lamech are the same.

The importance of this likeness arises from the fact that the so-
called critical scholars claim that these two lists of names are in
reality the same original lists as it came through two lines of tradition and was worked up differently by two writers. This view has
been vigorously opposed by some conservative scholars, notably by
the late Professor Green, of Princeton.[24]

Between rival critical hypotheses it is not the function of archæology to decide. It must be admitted, however, that the names of
the descendants of Genesis 4 can be equated with those of our Babylonian kings, as well as those of Genesis 5. Adam, Seth, Enosh,

24 See his *Unity of the Book of Genesis*, New York, 1895, Chapter II.

Cain, Enoch, Mehujael, and Methushael would be derived exactly as it has been explained that' the corresponding names of Genesis 5 could be derived. It only remains to explain the names Abel and Irad. It will be noticed that Abel occupies in the list a position next to Adam and Cain; Abel is also said to have been a shepherd. In the list of Babylonian kings Etana the shepherd comes in between Adimê (Aripi) and Pilikam, the equivalent of Cain. It is probable, therefore, that Etana is the king that corresponds to Abel. Etana is described in the Sumerian as "the shepherd who went to heaven," SIBA LÙ AN-ŠU NI-IB-E-DA. If the two words SIBA LÙ became detached and misunderstood as a proper name, the s at the beginning, according to a well known phonetic law, could become h and give us the Hebrew Abel. Irad may also be ir-tu, a corruption of ZI-IR-TU, a name of the mother of Dumuzi, who may at times have been referred to as the son of ZI-IR-TU.[25] These possibilities are not proof that the names arose as suggested, but are not without weight.

If Abel arose from the traditions of Etana and Enoch did also, and if the names of Genesis 4 are derived from the list of Babylonian kings, then Etana figures twice in the fourth chapter of Genesis. If Enoch is a fragment of the name Enmeduranki, a possibility already recognized, it is not difficult to understand how Etana came into the tradition twice.

[25] The possible connection of Abel with the Älaparos of Berossos, pointed out above, p. 321, should also be borne in mind.

CHAPTER VI

A BABYLONIAN ACCOUNT OF THE FLOOD, FROM A TABLET WRITTEN AT NINEVEH IN THE SEVENTH CENTURY B.C.[1]

TRANSLATION OF THE TEXT. COMPARISON WITH GENESIS 6–9. ANOTHER BABYLONIAN VERSION.

1. Translation of the Text.

1. Gilgamesh said to him, to Utnapishtim, the far-away:
2. "I look upon thee, O Utnapishtim,
3. Thy appearance is unchanged; thou art like me;
4. Thou art not at all different, thou art like me.
5. Thy courage is unbroken, to make combat,
6. On thy side thou liest down—on thy back.
7. [Tell me] how didst thou advance and in the assembly of the gods find life?"
8. Utnapishtim spoke to him, to Gilgamesh:
9. I will reveal to thee, O Gilgamesh, the secret story,
10. And the decision of the gods to thee will I relate.
11. Shurippak, a city which thou knowest,
12. Is situated on the bank of the Euphrates.
13. That city was old and the gods in it—
14. Their hearts prompted them—the great gods—to make a deluge.
15. [There drew near] their father Anu,
16. Their councillor, the warrior Ellil,
17. Their herald, Enmashtu,
18. Their hero, Ennugi.
19. The lord of wisdom, Ea, counselled with them;
20. Their words he repeated to the reed-hut:
21. "O reed-hut, reed-hut, O wall, wall,
22. O reed-hut, hearken; O wall, give heed!
23. O man of Shurippak, son of Ubaratutu,
24. Pull down thy house, build a ship,
25. Leave thy possessions, take thought for thy life,
26. Leave thy gods, thy life save!
27. Embark seed of life of all kinds on a ship!
28. The ship which thou shalt build,
29. Measure well its dimensions,
30. Make to correspond its breadth and its length;
31. Upon the ocean thou shalt launch it."
32. I understood and spoke to Ea, my lord:
33. "[I understand], my lord; what thou hast thus commanded
34. I will honor and will do.

1 Translated from Haupt's *Das Babylonische Nimrodepos*, p. 134, f.

327

35. [But] what shall I say to the city, the people, and the elders?"
36. Ea opened his mouth and spake,
37. He said unto me, his servant:
38. "Thus shalt thou say unto them:
39. Know that me—Ellil hates me.
40. I may not dwell in your city,
41. On Ellil's soil I may not lift my face.
42. I must go down to the ocean with Ea, my lord, to dwell.
43. Upon you will he (Ellil) then rain abundance—
44. [A catch] of birds, a catch of fishes,
45. ....a rich (?) harvest.
46. [A time Shamash[2] appointed, at evening] the senders of rain
47. [Shall rain upon] you a mighty rainstorm.
48. When the grey of dawn brightens,

(Lines 49–55 are broken away.)

56. The strong........brought what was needed.
57. On the fifth day I raised its frame.
58. According to its plan (?) its walls were 120 cubits high;
59. 120 cubits correspondingly was the extent of its roof.
60. I laid down its hull; I enclosed it.
61. I constructed it in storys, up to six;
62. I divided it [without (?)] into seven parts.
63. Its interior I divided into nine parts.
64. ....I fastened in its midst.
65. I looked out a rudder, and prepared what was necessary.
66. 6 *sars* of bitumen I poured over its outside (?);
67. 3 *sars* of bitumen I poured over its interior.
68. 3 *sars* of oil the people who carry jars brought.
69. Besides a *sar* of oil which was used as a libation,
70. 2 *sars* of oil the ship's captain stowed away.
71. For the people I slaughtered bullocks.
72. I slaughtered lambs daily.
73. Must, beer, oil, and wine,
74. I gave the people to drink like river-water.
75. I made a feast, like a new year's festival.
76. I opened (?) [a box of ointment]; I put ointment in my hand.
77. [By the setting] of great Shamash, the ship was finished.
78. [To move it from the stocks] was difficult.
79. The men cleared the ship's ways above and below.
80. ....two-thirds of it.
81. With all that I had I laded it (the ship);
82. With all the silver I had I laded it.
83. With all the gold I had I laded it.
84. With all the living things I had I laded it.
85. I embarked on the ship all my family and kindred.
86. Cattle of the field, beasts of the field, craftsmen, all, I embarked.
87. A fixed time Shamash had appointed, [saying]:
88. "When the senders of rain shall rain upon you a mighty rainstorm at evening,
89. Embark upon the ship and close thy door."
90. The appointed time approached,
91. The senders of rain sent at evening a heavy rainstorm.
92. I observed the appearance of the day,

2 The sun.

93. The day was terrible to look upon.
94. I embarked upon the ship, I closed my door.
95. To the master of the ship, to Puzur-Amurru, the sailor,
96. I entrusted the structure together with its contents.
97. When dew-dawn began to brighten,
98. There arose from the horizon a black cloud;
99. The god Adad thundered in its midst,
100. While Nebo and Sharru marched before;
101. They went as heralds over mountain and country.
102. Nergal tore away the anchor,
103. Enmashtu advanced, the floods he poured down;
104. The Anunnaki raised their torches,
105. At their brightness the land trembled.
106. The raging of Adad reached to heaven;
107. All light was turned to darkness
108. ....the land like...........
109. One day [raged the storm (?)]
110. Swiftly it raged [and the waters covered] the mountains,
111. Like a battle array over the people it swept.
112. No one could see his fellow;
113. No more were people recognized in heaven;
114. The gods were frightened at the deluge,
115. They fled, they climbed to the highest heaven;
116. The gods crouched like dogs, they lay down by the walls.
117. Ishtar cried like a woman in travail,
118. Wailed the queen of the gods with her beautiful voice:
119. "Those creatures are turned to clay,
120. Since I commanded evil in the assembly of the gods;
121. Because I commanded evil in the assembly of the gods,
122. For the destruction of my people I commanded battle.
123. I alone bore my people;
124. Like spawn of fishes they fill the sea."
125. The gods along with the Anunnaki wept with her,
126. The gods bowed, sat as they wept;
127. Closed were their lips; [silent their] assembly.
128. Six days and seven nights
129. Blew the wind, the deluge the flood overpowered.
130. When the seventh day approached, the deluge was prolonging the battle
131. Which, like an army, it had waged.
132. The sea calmed, the destruction abated, the flood ceased.
133. I looked upon the sea, the roaring was stilled
134. And all mankind was turned to clay;
135. Like logs all were floating about.
136. I opened the window, the light fell on my cheek;
137. I was overcome, I sat down, I wept;
138. Over my cheek streamed the tears.
139. I looked in all directions—a fearful sea!
140. After twelve days an island appeared;
141. Toward mount Nizir the ship stood off;
142. Mount Nizir held it fast, that it moved not.
143. One day, two days, mount Nizir held it that it moved not,
144. Three days, four days, mount Nizir held it that it moved not,
145. Five days, six days, mount Nizir held it that it moved not,
146. When the seventh day approached,
147. I brought out a dove and let her go;

148. The dove went out and returned;
149. There was no resting-place and she came back.
150. I brought out a swallow and let it go;
151. The swallow went out and returned.
152. There was no resting-place and it came back.
153. I brought out a raven and let it go;
154. The raven went out, the diminution of the waters it saw;
155. It alighted, it waded about, it croaked, it did not come back.
156. I disembarked [all]; to the four winds I poured a libation.
157. I appointed a sacrifice on the top of the mountain peak;
158. Seven by seven I arranged the sacrificial vessels;
159. Beneath them I piled reeds, cedar wood, and myrtle.
160. The gods smelled the savor,
161. The gods smelled the sweet savor.
162. The gods above the sacrificer collected like flies.
163. When at length the queen of the gods drew near,
164. She raised the great bows (?) which Anu at her wish had made.
165. "O ye gods, as I shall not forget the jewel of my neck
166. These days I shall not forget—to eternity I shall remember!
167. Let the gods come to the sacrifice,
168. But let Ellil not come to the sacrifice,
169. For he was not wise; he sent the deluge,
170. And numbered my people for destruction."
171. When at last Ellil drew near,
172. He saw the ship, Ellil was angry,
173. His heart was filled against the gods and the Igigi.[3]
174. "Who then has come out alive?
175. No man must escape from destruction."
176. Then Enmashtu opened his mouth and spake,
177. He said to the warrior Ellil:
178. "Who but Ea accomplished the thing?
179. Even Ea knows every undertaking."
180. Ea opened his mouth and spake,
181. He said to the warrior Ellil:
182. "O thou, leader of the gods, warrior,
183. How, how couldst thou without thought send a deluge?
184. On the sinner let his sin rest,
185. On the wrongdoer rest his misdeed.
186. Forbear, let it not be done, have mercy, [that men perish not].
187. Instead of thy sending a deluge
188. Had the lion come and diminished the people!
189. Instead of thy sending a deluge
190. Had a wolf come and diminished the people!
191. Instead of thy sending a deluge
192. Had a famine come and the land [depopulated!]
193. Instead of thy sending a deluge
194. Had a pestilence come and the land [depopulated!]
195. I have not divulged the decisions of the great gods.
196. I caused Adrakhasis to see a dream and the decisions of the gods he heard.
197. Now take counsel concerning him."
198. Then went Ea on board the ship,
199. He took my hand and brought me forth,
200. He brought forth my wife and made her kneel at my side;
201. He turned us toward each other and stood between us; he blessed us:

3 The spirits of heaven.

202. "In former time Utnapishtim was a man;
203. Now let Utnapishtim and his wife be like gods—even like us;
204. Let Utnapishtim dwell afar off at the mouth of the rivers!"
205. He took me and caused me to dwell afar off at the mouth of the rivers.

2. Comparison with Genesis 6–9.—The above account of the deluge so closely resembles that in the Bible (Gen. 6:9—9:19), that nearly all scholars recognize that they are two versions of the same narrative.[4] In each case there is a divine revelation to the hero of the deluge that a catastrophe is coming of which every one else is ignorant. They both relate the building of the vessel, the "pitching it within and without with pitch," the embarkation, the flood in which other men are destroyed, the resting of the ship on a mountain, the sending out of the birds, the disembarkation, the sacrifice, and the intimation that in future a deluge shall not be.

When the Babylonian account is compared with the Biblical, there are two striking differences. 1. The Babylonian story makes the flood local; the Biblical, general. 2. The Babylonian story, fascinating poetry though it is, has a conception of deity in strong contrast with the dignity of the Biblical monotheism. The Babylonian gods disagree; they blame each other; they crouch with fear like dogs; they come swarming about the sacrifice like hungry flies! Nothing could more strikingly illustrate the inspiration of the Biblical story than to measure it against the background of this Babylonian poem, which is clearly a variant version of it.

3. Another Babylonian Version.—From the library of Ashurbanipal there has come another version of the deluge, which represents the purpose of its coming as different. According to this version, men had sinned and had been afflicted with famine, after which they reformed for a time. The famine was removed, but soon, apparently, they sinned again. Pestilence was then sent upon them. An appeal brought mitigation of their sufferings, but soon they plunged into sin again. This time they were punished with unfruitfulness of the land and of their race, but soon sinned as before. When all other punishments had failed, as a last resort the flood was sent.

As this account does not so closely resemble that in Genesis, it is not translated here. Those who wish to read it are referred to Rogers, *Cuneiform Parallels to the Old Testament*, New York, 1912, p. 114, ff.

4 Or two accounts of the same event.

CHAPTER VII

AN ACCOUNT OF THE CREATION AND FLOOD, FROM A TABLET WRITTEN AT NIPPUR BEFORE 2000 B.C.

TRANSLATION. COMPARISON WITH THE OTHER VERSION.

1. Translation.—This tablet was published by Dr. Arno Poebel, of Breslau. It was apparently written in the time of the dynasty of Nisin, but at any rate not later than the period of the first dynasty of Babylon. Only a part of the tablet has been found, so that the narrative is incomplete both at the beginning and at the end. Possibly the remaining portion may some time be found in the museum at Constantinople. The tablet is inscribed on both sides, and there are three columns to the side. The portions that are still extant read as follows: [1]

Column I (about three-fourths of the column missing)

....
....
"My human-kind from its destruction I will [raise up];
With the aid of Nintu my creation.........I will raise up;
The people in their settlements I will establish;
The city, wherever man creates one—indeed its protection—therein I will
    give him rest.
Our house—its brick may he cast in a clean spot!
Our places in a clean place may he establish!"
Its brilliant splendor, the temple platform, he made straight,
The exalted regulations he completed for it;
The land he divided; a favorable plan he established.
    After Anu, Enlil,[2] Enki,[3] and Ninkhursag
The black-headed [4] race had created,
All that is from the earth, from the earth they caused to spring,
Cattle and beasts of the field suitably they brought into being.

Here the first column ends. The passage opens in the midst of the speech of some deity—perhaps Ninkhursag (a Sumerian name

1 Translated from A. Poebel's *Historical and Grammatical Texts* in the University of Pennsylvania's "University Museum's publications of the Babylonian Section," Vol. V, Philadelphia, 1914, No. 1.
2 Often called Bel.
3 Called Ea.
4 A term by which the Semites of Babylonia designated themselves. The Sumerians shaved their heads.

of Ishtar) or possibly Enlil, the god of Nippur. First the deity tells
how mankind, which has been overthrown, shall be raised up again.
Then we are told how he perfected plans for the accomplishment of
this purpose, and lastly how four deities called into being men and
animals.

Column II (about three-fifths of the text is missing)

....
.............I will.............................
.........I will turn my eye upon him..........
The.........creator of the land.......................
...............of royalty.......................
...............of royalty by him was determined;
The exalted palace of the royal throne was by him set apart,
The exalted precepts.........he made perfect,
In clean places.........cities...........he founded,
Their names were named, they were allotted to guardian-spirits (?)
Of these cities Eridu—the chief command to Nudimmud he gave,
Unto the second the *nisag*-priests of Umma (?) he gave,
Thirdly, Larak to Pabilkhursag he gave,
Fourthly, Sippar as the dwelling of Shamash he gave,
Fifthly, Shurippak unto *Lamkurru* he gave.
Their names were assigned; to guardian-spirits (?) they were allotted;
Its rampart (?), a wall (?) he raised up, he established;
Small rivers, canals (?), and water-courses (?) he established.

The last part of this column relates how five cities were established by some deity. Of what the first part treated we cannot make
out from the few fragments of lines that are still legible.

Column III

....
....
The land the sway of Anu..............
The people...............
A deluge.....................
....
Their land (?) it entered.................
Then Nintu [cried out] like [a woman in travail]...........
The brilliant Ishtar [uttered] a groan on account of her people.
Enki with himself held communion in his wisdom;
Anu, Enlil, Enki, and Ninkhursag,
The gods of heaven and earth, invoked the names of Anu and Enlil,
At that time Ziugiddu was king, the priest of.........
The chief deity he made of wood.........
In humility prostrating himself, in reverence.........
Daily at all times was he present in person.........
Increasing dreams which had not come [before],
Conjuring by the name of heaven and earth..........

In this column the narrative has passed to the story of the deluge. The gods have determined to send a deluge; Ziugiddu in consequence constructed an idol from wood (compare Isa. 40:20), and earnestly worshiped it, seeking oracles for his guidance.

Column IV

For the settlement (?) the gods a wall (?)..........
Ziugiddu stood by its side, he heard..........
"At the wall at my left side stand..........
At the wall I will speak a word to thee
O my brilliant one, let there enter thy ear..........
By our hand a deluge..........will be sent.
The seed of mankind to destroy..........
Is the momentous decision of the assembly (of the gods);
The words of Anu and Enlil............
Their kingdom, their rule..........
To them....................."

It is clear from these fragmentary lines that Ziugiddu is being informed of the approaching deluge. It is also clear that some of the elements of the narrative are identical with some of the elements of the one discussed in Chapter VI. Ziugiddu is commanded to stand by a wall, where some deity will speak to him. This appears in the other version in the form:

"O reed-hut, reed-hut, O wall, wall,[5]
O reed-hut, hearken; O wall, give heed!
O man of Shurippak, son of Ubartutu,
Pull down thy house, build a ship, etc.

In that account, too, the assembly of the gods is also referred to in line 120, ff. These are examples of the way the same theme, differently treated, turns up in different forms.

Column V

The evil winds, the wind that is hostile, came; all of them descended,
The deluge..........came on with them
Seven days and seven nights
The deluge swept over the land,
The evil wind made the huge boat tremble.
Shamash [6] came forth, on heaven and earth he shone;
Ziugiddu the ship at the top uncovered,
The peace of Shamash, his light, entered into the boat.
Ziugiddu, the king
Before Shamash bowed his face to the earth.
The king—an ox he sacrificed, a sheep offered as oblation.
....

5 See Part II, Chapter VI, line 21, ff.
6 *I. e.*, the sun.

In this column we have a fragment which relates some details similar to those told in lines 128, 129, and 136–138 of the account given in Chapter VI.

Column VI

By the life of heaven and the life of earth ye shall conjure him,
That he may raise up from you;
Anu and Enlil by the soul of heaven and the soul of earth ye shall conjure,
That they may raise up from you
The curse that has come upon the land, that they may remove it.
Ziugiddu the king
Before Anu and Enlil bowed his face to the earth.
Life like a god's he gave to him,
An immortal spirit like a god's he brought to him.
Then Ziugiddu the king,
Of the seed that was cursed, lord of mankind he made;
In the fruitful land, the land of Dilmum.........they made him dwell
....

At this point the last column is hopelessly broken. It is clear, however, from the part which remains that Ziugiddu is in this narrative translated to the Isle of the Blest as was Utnapishtim in the account translated in Chapter VI, lines 202–205.[7] Indeed there is reason to believe that the two accounts of the flood are divergent versions of the same story. In addition to the likenesses already mentioned, the names of the two heroes, though they appear so different, are the same in meaning. Utnapishtim (or Unapishtim) means "day of life," or "day-life," while Ziugiddu means "Life-day prolonged."

2. Comparison with the Other Version.—Although this tablet is much broken, so that we have not the whole of the story, it is clear from the parts that we have that in this version preserved at Nippur the story was much shorter than in the form translated in Chapter VI, which was preserved in the library of Ashurbanipal. It was also combined with a briefer account of the creation than that translated in Chapter I from Ashurbanipal's library.

Of this Nippurian version of the creation story we have in this tablet only the small fragments preserved in Columns I and II. It is, however, probable that the Nippurian version of the creation was in its main features similar to that preserved in the library at Nineveh, only more brief.

7 See p. 331.

If this be so, the conquest of the dragon Tiâmat is here attributed
to Enlil of Nippur, as in the other version it is attributed to Marduk
of Babylon, and as in Psalm 74 : 13, 14, it is attributed to Jehovah.
This older account from Nippur agrees in one respect more nearly
with the Biblical account than the one from the library at Nineveh
does, for it represents Ziugiddu as a very pious man, who was apparently saved from destruction on account of his piety, and in
blessing him his god removed the curse as Jehovah did in Genesis
8 :21.

CHAPTER VIII

AN ACCOUNT OF THE ORIGIN OF A CITY AND THE BEGINNING OF AGRICULTURE, FROM A TABLET WRITTEN AT NIPPUR BEFORE 2000 B.C.

TRANSLATION. COMPARISON WITH BIBLICAL MATERIAL.

THIS tablet begins with a description of a place the name of which is not with certainty identified. Possibly it was Eridu, but probably Dilmun.

1. Translation.

Column I [1]

1. Holy is [the place] where you are;
2. The mountain Dilmun is holy.
3. Holy is the place where you are;
4. ..... the mountain Dilmum is holy.
5. The mountain Dilmun is holy, the mountain Dilmum is pure,
6. The mountain Dilmun is pure; the mountain Dilmun is brilliant.
7. Alone in Dilmun they lay down;
8. Where Enki and his consort lay,
9. That place is pure; that place is brilliant.
10. Alone in Dilmun they [lay];
11. Where Enki and Ninella lay,
12. That place is pure, that place is brilliant.
13. In Dilmun the raven cried not,
14. The *dar*-bird its *dar*-cry uttered not.
15. The deadly lion destroyed not,
16. The wolf a lamb seized not,
17. The dog the weak kid tore not,
18. The *dun* [2]-animal the food-grain destroyed not,
19. She planned not for young offspring...
20. The birds of heaven their offspring hatched not,
21. Doves laid not eggs (?)
22. Of eye-disease, "it is eye-disease," one said not;
23. Of headache, "it is headache," one said not.
24. To a mother, "mother," one said not,
25. To a father, "father," one said not.
26. In the holy place a libation was poured not; in the city one drank not;
27. The river-man "cross it?" said not;

---

1 Translated from Langdon, *The Sumerian Epic of Paradise, the Flood, and the Fall of Man*, Philadelphia, 1915, Plates I and II. Langdon, as his title shows, regards the text as a description of Paradise, the flood, and the fall of man,—a view that the present writer cannot share.

2 The sign for *dun* was the picture of a pig. The animal in question was, therefore, probably a sow.

28. The overseer filled no right hand;
29. The musician "sing," said not;
30. The prince of the city spoke not.
31. Ninella to her father Enki said:
32. "A city thou hast founded, a city thou hast founded, its destiny thou
    hast fixed;
33. In Dilmun a city thou hast founded,
34. ....thou hast founded a city,
35. ....a canal there is not
36. ....thou hast founded a city."

The rest of the first column is broken away; probably about nine
lines are missing.

All the first column is descriptive of a place inhabited only by
a god and goddess. Many activities are absent, because there is
no one there to carry them on. Lines 16–21 remind one a little
of Isaiah 11:6–9.

After the break the text continues:

Column II

1. "From the bright covering of thy great heaven may the waters flow,
2. May thy city be refreshed with water, may it drink,
3. May Dilmun be refreshed with water, may it drink,
4. May the deep of bitter water flow as a deep of sweet water.
5. May thy city be a resting, an abode of the people,
6. May Dilmun be a resting, an abode of the people.
7. Now, O sun-god, shine forth,
8. O sun-god, stand in heaven;
9. Bring open water from the womb of the land!
10. [And] fish, O moon-god, from the water.
11. In the water-course on the face of the land, O earth's sweet water come!
12. That from the bright covering of the great heavens water may flow,
13. Its city be refreshed, may drink,
14. Dilmun be refreshed, may drink,
15. The deep of bitter water flow as a deep of sweet water,
16. The fields and meadows......
17. The city be a house for the multitudes of the land,
18. Dilmun be a house for the multitudes of the land.
19. To shine may the sun-god come forth—let it be so.
20. He who alone is wise (i. e. Enki)
21. To Nintu, mother of the land......

(Lines 22–30 describe with a frankness common among primitive people a
   marital union of the god and goddess. In many parts of the world it
   has been thought that acts of creation proceed from such unions.)

31. Enki, the father of Damgalnunna, his word spoke.
32. Ninkhursag flooded the fields,
33. The fields received the waters of Enki.
34. It was the first day whose month is first;
35. It was the second day whose month is second;
36. It was the third day whose month is third;

37. It was the fourth day whose month is fourth;
38. It was the fifth day whose month is fifth;
39. It was the sixth day whose month is sixth;
40. It was the seventh day whose month is seventh;
41. It was the eighth day [whose month is eighth];
42. It was the ninth day whose month is ninth, the month of outpouring of
     the water.
43. Like fat, like fat, like abundant sweet oil,
44. [Nintu], mother of the land,
45. .... had brought them forth.

In the first part of the above column the description of the city
is continued. As a consequence of the union of the gods, water
flowed to irrigate the land. Lines 34–42 tell in a quaint way how
the waters continued to come for nine months and nine days.

Column III

1. Ninshar on the bank of the river cried (?):
2. "O Enki, for me are they filled; they are filled!"
3. His messenger, Usmu, he called:
4. "Man, their favorite son, has not been purified,
5. Ninshar, their favorite has not purified."
6. His messenger, Usmu, answered:
7. "Man, their favorite son, has not been purified,
8. Ninshar the favorite has not purified."
9. My king, the storm-bringer, the storm-bringer,
10. His way at once to the boat went.
11. Two streams (?), like Shamash, he carried.
12. He closed the hatch. With fire he made purification.
13. Enki flooded the fields;
14. The fields received the waters of Enki.
15. It was the first day whose month is first;
16. It was the second day whose month is second;
17. It was the ninth day whose month is ninth, the month of the outpouring
     of waters.
18. Like fat, like fat, like abundant sweet oil,
19. [Ninshar] like fat,
20. Ninshar had brought them forth.
21. Ninkurra [3] [on the bank of the river] c[ried (?)]
22. "O Enki, for me they are filled! they are filled!"
23. His messenger, Usmu, he called:
24. "Man, their favorite son, has not been purified;
25. Ninkurra the favorite has not purified."
26. His messenger, Usmu, answered:
27. "Man, their favorite son, has not been purified;
28. Ninkurra, the favorite, has not purified."
29. My king, the storm-bringer, the storm-bringer,
30. His way at once to the boat went.
31. Two streams (?), like Shamash, he carried.
32. He closed the hatch. With fire he made purification.
33. Enki flooded the fields

3 Apparently another name of Ninshar.

34. The fields received the waters of Enki.
35. It was the first day whose month is first;
36. It was the ninth day whose month is ninth, the month of the outpouring of waters.
37. Like fat, like fat, like abundant sweet oil,
38. Ninkurra like fat had brought them forth.
39. The goddess Takku [4] to receive his outpouring......
40. Ninkurra to Takku [concerning the outpouring] spoke:
41. "I will irrigate thee with my irrigation......
42. With favorable words will I speak......
43. The one alone that will restrain it......
44. Enki for me shall..........

The rest of the column, consisting of two or three lines, is missing. The repetition in this column is characteristic of early poetry. Primitive peoples are fond of iteration, and in the description of the way the waters came it was to them very effective.

Column IV (about twelve lines are broken from the tablet at the beginning)

13. [To Takku to receive the outpouring]..........
14. ....
15. ....
16. ....in the garden....................
17. ....
18. The..........tree (?) let him plant,
19. The..........tree (?) let him plant,
20. At the explanation of the great outpouring let my begotten stand (?).
21. Let the two *gu-ba* be filled with water,
22. Abundant water let him pour out,
23. Reservoir water let him pour out,
24. The barren land let him irrigate,
25. As gardener..........let him go forth (?),
26. On the bank, along the bank, let..........
27. Who art thou? The garden..........
28. For Enki, the gardener..........

(Six lines are here broken away.)

35. The..........tree (?) he planted,
36. The..........tree (?) he planted; at its base he rested.
37. Enki turned his eyes to him; his sceptre he lifted up;
38. Enki to Takku took his way.
39. At the tree he said: "A holy revelation, a holy revelation!"
40. "Who is it that thou art?"
41. "I am a gardener; joyful..........
42. For a price I will give thee."
43. Takku with joyful heart at the tree (?) the revelation beheld,
44. Enki to Takku explained his outpouring.
45. The promised fruit was given to him,
46. At the..........tree (?) it was given to him,
47. At the..........tree (?) it was given to him,
48. Takku received the outpouring; with the left hand he grasped it; with the right he seized it.

[4] In a syllabary from Ashur, Takku is defined as a goddess.

From the parts of column IV which are still legible, it appears that the messenger was revealing to Takku the secrets of agriculture. This corresponds to the statement in Genesis 9:20, that "Noah began to be a husbandman."

At the beginning of Column V some seven lines have crumbled away, and the beginnings of eight more have also become illegible.

Column V

....
7. [The wood-plant grew,]
8. [The salt-plant] grew,
9. [The.........plant] grew,
10. [The *a-pa-shar*-plant] grew,
11. [The *tu-tu*-plant] grew,
12. [The.........plant] grew,
13. [The.........plant] grew,
14. [The cassia] plant grew.
15. "O Enki, for me they are brought forth, they are brought forth."
16. To his messenger, Usmu, he spoke, he said:
17. "The plants—their fate forever [I have determined."]
18. What is this? What is this?"
19. His messenger, Usmu, returned:
20. ....
21. "My king has commanded the wood-plant,
22. That it may be cut off and eaten,
23. My king has commanded the salt-plant,
24. That it may be cut off and eaten.
25. My king has commanded the.........plant,
26. That it may be cut off [and eaten].
27. My king has commanded the *a-pa-shar*-plant,
28. That it may be cut off and eaten.
29. [My king] has commanded the *tu-tu*-plant,
30. [That it may be cut off] and eaten.
31. [My king has commanded the.........plant,]
32. [That it may be cut off and eaten,]
33. [My king has commanded the.........plant,]
34. That it may be cut off and eaten.
35. [My king] has commanded the cassia plant,
36. That it may be cut off and eaten."
37. By Ninkhursag in the name of Enki a curse was uttered:
38. "The face of life, when he dies, he shall never see [again]."
39. The spirits of the earth in the dust sat down.
40. The rebellious one to Enki said:
41. "I, Ninkhursag, brought forth for thee people; what is my reward?"
42. Enlil, the begetter, answered the rebellious one:
43. "Thou, Ninkhursag, hast brought forth people;
44. In my city I will make two thrones (?) and thy name shall be called on there.
45. As a dignitary her head alone is exalted;
46. Her heart alone is changed;
47. Her eye alone is endowed with light."

The last three lines here refer to Takku, who would seem to be in some way a representative of humanity. Ninkhursag, jealous of her, has denied immortality to man. Enlil explains to her that she need not be jealous of her offspring as a whole; that none but Takku will be granted immortality. There is no reference, as Langdon once supposed, to the fall of man.

Column VI (perhaps five lines are broken away)

6. ....the lord Enlil...........
7. ....the lord of life...........
8. To..........they went............
9. To............they went, the lord of the gods...........
10. Spoke to him, the water of life............
11. ....
12. Ninkhursag...................
13. ....
14. ....
15. ....
16. ....
17. ....
18. Ninkhursag...................
19. Enlil......his..........they founded,
20. Priests (?) they ordained,
21. Fate they determined,
22. With power established it.
23. Ninkhursag in her temple granted his life to him:
24. "My brother, what of thee is ill?"
25. "My stable-cow is ill."
26. "The god Absham have I brought forth for thee."
27. "My brother, what of thee is ill?"
28. "My flock is ill."
29. "The goddess 'Queen of the herd'5 have I brought forth for thee."
30. "My brother, what of thee is ill?" "My face is ill."
31. "The goddess Ninkautu have I brought forth for thee."
32. "My brother, what of thee is ill?" "My mouth is ill."
33. "The goddess 'Queen who fills the mouth' 6 have I brought forth for thee."
34. "My brother, what of thee is ill?" ["My genitals are ill"].
35. "The goddess Nazi have I brought forth for thee."
36. "My brother, what of thee is ill?" "My hand [is ill."]
37. "My goddess 'Living hand'7 have I brought forth for thee."
38. "My brother, what of thee is ill?" "My health is ill."
39. "The goddess 'Queen of health' 8 have I brought forth for thee."
40. "My brother, what of thee is ill?" "My intelligence is ill."
41. "The god who makes the intelligence clear 9 have I brought forth for thee."

5 In Sumerian the goddess Nintulla.
6 In Sumerian the goddess Ninkasi.
7 In Sumerian the goddess Dazima.
8 In Sumerian, Nintil.
9 In Sumerian, Enshagme.

42. "Grandly are they brought forth, they are created.
43. Let Absham be lord of vegetation,
44. Let Nintulla be lord of Magan,
45. Let Ninkautu choose Ninazu as a spouse,
46. May Ninkasi be the full heart's possession,
47. May Nazi become mistress of weaving (?),
48. May Dazima the house of strong life take,
49. May Nintil become mistress of the month,
50. May Enshagme become lord of X.
51. Glory!"

2. Comparison with the Bible.—Here the tablet concludes. This last column, which tells how the goddess Ninkhursag came to favor Takku and to create a number of divine helpers for her, has no parallel in the Biblical account. As Takku received the especial protection of Ninkhursag who created her for all these divine helpers, it seems certain that this tablet had no reference to the fall of man, as Langdon supposed. It appears rather to be a mythical account of the beginnings of agriculture and the medicinal use of plants in Babylonia. Agriculture implies irrigation. "From the first day whose month is first" to the ninth month, is the period when Babylonia is watered. The Tigris begins to rise in March, the first month, the overflow of the Euphrates does not subside till the sixth month, and the winter rains are at their height in the ninth month.

As Adam was driven from Eden to eat of the fruits of the earth (Gen. 3: 18, 24; compare Gen. 1: 29), and Noah became a husbandman (Gen. 9: 20), the story of Takku presents a remote similarity to both of them. Langdon [10] compares the list of divine beings with which the tablet ends with the antediluvian patriarchs of Genesis 4 and 5, and suggests the possibility that here we have the original names of those patriarchs. Beyond the fact that Absham somewhat resembles the name Abel and was, like Abel, an agriculturist, there is no apparent connection. The names in no way correspond. It is more probable that we·have the names of those patriarchs in the list of kings translated in Chapter V.

10 See his *Sumerian Epic of Paradise, the Flood, and the Fall of Man,* p. 56.

CHAPTER IX

ABRAHAM AND ARCHÆOLOGY

ABRAHAM HIRED AN OX. ABRAHAM LEASED A FARM. ABRAHAM PAID HIS RENT. WHO WAS THIS ABRAHAM? TRAVEL BETWEEN BABYLONIA AND PALESTINE. HAMMURABI, KING OF THE WESTLAND. KUDUR-MABUG. KINGS SUPPOSED BY SOME TO BE THOSE OF GENESIS 14. A LITURGY OF THE TIME OF ABRAHAM AND MELCHIZEDEK.

ARCHÆOLOGICAL investigation has brought to light a number of texts believed by scholars to illumine the Biblical accounts of Abraham. It is the purpose of this chapter to translate and discuss these.

The documents which naturally attract us first are some contracts from Babylonia in which an Abraham was one of the contracting parties. They are as follows:

1. Abraham Hired an Ox.[1]

1. One ox broken to the yoke,
2. an ox from Ibni-Sin, son of Sin-imgurani,
3. from Ibni-Sin
4. through the agency of Kishti-Nabium,
5. son of Eteru,
6. Abarama, son of Awel-Ishtar,
7. for one month has hired.
8. For one month
9. one shekel of silver
10. he will pay.
11. Of it ½ shekel of silver
12. from the hand of
13. Abarama
14. Kishti-Nabium
15. has received.
16. In the presence of Idin-Urash, son of Idin-Labibaal,
17. In the presence of Awêlê, son of Urri-bani,
18. in the presence of Beliyatum, scribe.
19. Month of the mission of Ishtar (i.e., Ulul), day 20th,
20. The year Ammizadugga, the king (built)
21. the wall of Ammizadugga, (i.e., Ammizadugga's 11th year).
22. Tablet of Kishti-Nabium.

This tablet shows how Abarama (Abraham), a farmer, hired an ox for a month. The tablet, as the last line shows, is the copy made

1 Translated from *Vorderasiatische Schriftdenkmäler der königlichen Museen zu Berlin*, VII, No. 92.

for Kishti-Nabium, the agent. In such business transactions three copies were often made, one for each of the contracting parties and one for the scribe. The date of this tablet is 1965 B.C. Ammizadugga was the tenth king of that first dynasty of Babylon, of which Hammurabi was the sixth.

2. Abraham Leased a Farm.[2]

1. To the patrician
2. speak,
3. saying, Gimil-Marduk (wishes that)
4. Shamash and Marduk may give thee health!
5. Mayest thou have peace, mayest thou have health!
6. May the god who protects thee thy head in luck
7. hold!
8. (To enquire) concerning thy health I am sending.
9. May thy welfare before Shamash and Marduk
10. be eternal!
11. Concerning the 400 *shars* of land, the field of Sin-idinam,
12. which to Abamrama
13. to lease, thou hast sent;
14. the land-steward (?) and scribe
15. appeared and
16. on behalf of Sin-idinam
17. I took that up.
18. The 400 *shars* of land to Abamrama
19. as thou hast directed
20. I have leased.
21. Concerning thy dispatches I shall not be negligent.

It appears from this document that Abamrama, who is none other than a Babylonian Abraham, was a small farmer, who leased a small tract of land.

3. Abraham Paid His Rent.[3]

1. 1 shekel of silver
2. of the rent (?) of his field,
3. for the year Ammizadugga, the king,
4. a lordly, splendid statue (set up),
5. brought
6. Abamrama,
7. received
8. Sin-idinam
9. and Iddatum.
10. Month Siman, 28th day,
11. The year Ammizadugga, the king,
12. a lordly, splendid statue (set up).
    (This was Ammizadugga's 13th year.)

This document, dated two years after that in which the ox was hired, shows how Abamrama (Abraham) paid a part of his rent.

2 *Vorderasiatische Schriftdenkmäler der königlichen Museen zu Berlin,* VII, No. 198.
3 *Ibid.,* VII, No. 97.

The name Abamrama (Abraham) occurs in two other documents published in the same volume (no. 101, and no. 102), where, in defining the boundaries of other fields of Sin-idinam, they are said to be bounded on one side by the field of Abamrama. As these documents mention the name of Abamrama only incidentally, they are not translated here.

4. Who Was This Abraham?—These documents, which relate to the business of a Babylonian Abraham, come from Dilbat, about eight miles south of Borsippa, which was just across the Euphrates from Babylon. ·It is clear that this Abraham was a small farmer, who hired a tract of land from a larger land-owner. He also hired an ox wherewith to work his land, and paid the rent of the land and the hire of the ox as a good citizen should. This Abraham was not the Biblical patriarch. The patriarch's father was Terah and his brother Nahor; the father of this Babylonian Abraham was Awel-Ishtar, and his brother Iddatum (*ibid.*, no. 101, 9). The Abraham of the Bible was a monotheist according to Genesis; the ancestors of the Babylonian Abraham worshiped the goddess Ishtar, who corresponded to the Canaanitish Ashtoreh. The Bible connects the patriarch with Ur and Haran; this Abraham lived about half-way between these two cities.

The name Abraham was borne by at least one other person mentioned in the cuneiform writings. It also occurs in the name of a place in Palestine, probably near Hebron, which Sheshonk I, the Biblical Shishak, calls "The Field of Abram." [4] As Shishak lived much later (945–924 B.C.), being a contemporary of Rehoboam the son of Solomon, this Egyptian place name is not so significant. The Babylonian Abraham mentioned in the documents just translated is welcome proof that Abraham was a personal name in Babylonia near the time in which the Bible places the patriarch. With these documents Genesis 11 : 27—25 : 10 should be compared.

Another Babylonian contract is of interest in connection with the migration of Abraham.

5. Travel between Babylonia and Palestine.

1. A wagon [5]
2. from Mannum-balum-Shamash,
3. son of Shelibia,
4. Khabilkinum,
5. son of Appani[bi],

---

4 Breasted, *Ancient Records, Egypt*, IV, pp. 352, 353. (See p. 360.)
5 See *Beiträge zur Assyriologie*, V, p. 498, no. 23; cf. p. 429, ff.

6. on a lease
7. for 1 year
8. has hired.
9. As a yearly rental
10. ⅔ of a shekel of silver
11. he will pay.
12. As the first of the rent
13. ⅓ of a shekel of silver
14. he has received.
15. Unto the land of Kittim
16. he shall not drive it.
17. In the presence of Ibku-Adad,
18. son of Abiatum;
19. in the presence of Ilukasha,
20. son of Arad-ilishu;
21. in the presence of Ilishu............
22. Month Ululu, day 25,
23. the year the king Erech from the flood
24. of the river as a friend protected.

The date of the above interesting document has not been identified with certainty. It is thought by some to belong to the reign of Shamsu-iluna, the successor of Hammurabi. The writing clearly shows that at any rate it comes from the period of this dynasty. That is, it comes from the period to which many assign the migration of Abraham. *Kittim* in the contract is the word used in the Hebrew of Jeremiah 2: 10 and Ezekiel 27: 6 for the coast lands of the Mediterranean. It undoubtedly has that meaning here. This contract was written in Sippar, the Agade of earlier times, a town on the Euphrates a little to the north of Babylon. It reveals the fact that at the time the document was written there was so much travel between Babylonia and the Mediterranean coast that a man could not lease a wagon for a year without danger that it might be driven over the long route to Syria or Palestine. Against such wear upon his vehicle the particular wagon-owner of our document protected himself.

When, therefore, Abraham went out from his land and his kindred, he was going to no unknown land. The tide of commerce and of emigration had opened the way. Apparently it was no more remarkable for him to do it than for an Irishman to come to America half a century ago, or for a south European to come today.

6. Hammurabi, King of the Westland.—It is thought by many scholars that Hammurabi was the Amraphel of Genesis 14. The following inscription [6] relates to this king:

1. To [Shar]ratum,
2. the bride of Anu

6 King, *Letters and Inscriptions of Hammurabi*, Vol. I, No. 66.

3. who has come to lordship,
4. lady of strength and abundance,
5. of the mountain-temple,
6. faithful lady, of exalted counsel,
7. lady who binds the heart,
8. who for her spouse
9. makes favorable her open oracle;
10. to his lady,
11. for the life of Hammurabi,
12. king of the Westland (MAR-TU),
13. Ibirum............
14. governor of the river-[district]...........
15. son of Shuban..........,
16. a guardian-deity appropriate to her divinity,
17. in the land which she loves,
18. for her service (?)
19. before her beloved temple has set up.

This inscription is quoted here for two reasons: 1. It was erected "for the life of Hammurabi," who is supposed by many to be the Amraphel of Genesis 14:1. Amraphel is supposed to be a corruption of Hammurabi, thus Amrabi. The final *l* of Amraphel is a difficulty. While many Assyriologists, from Schrader onward, have recognized the equivalence, it is now seriously questioned by Jensen and Eduard Meyer, and absolutely rejected by Bezold. It must be said that, if Amraphel is intended for Hammurabi, the name had undergone corruption before it was placed in the Biblical record.[7] 2. In this inscription Hammurabi is called "king of MAR-TU," or the Westland, a name by which the Babylonians often designated Syria and Palestine. MAR-TU simply means "sunset," but was used like the Arabic *magrib* as the designation of a region. There is no reason to doubt that here it designates Syria and Palestine, so that, if Amraphel is Hammurabi, this is confirmatory of his connection with the West.

7. Kudur-Mabug.—The following inscription [8] has also often been brought into the discussion of Genesis 14:

1. To Nannar,
2. his king,
3. Kudur-Mabug,
4. "Father" of the Westland (MAR-TU),
5. son of Simti-shilkhak,
6. when Nannar
7. his prayer

7 Some scholars suppose that the writer of the account in Genesis had before him a source in the cuneiform writing in which the "bi" at the end of Hammurabi's name was spelled with a sign that could be read either "bi" or "bil" (see Barton, *Origin and Development of Babylonian Writing*, Leipzig, 1913, No. 185), and that the *l* was attached in consequence of a misreading of this sign. That, however, admits corruption, though it attempts to explain its cause.
8 *Cuneiform Texts, &c., in the British Museum*, XXI, 33.

8. had heard,
9. Enunmakh,
10. belonging to Nannar,
11. for his life
12. and the life
13. of Arad-Sin, his son,
14. king of Larsa,
15. he built.

This inscription has often been brought into connection with Abraham, partly because some have seen in Kudur-Mabug the Chedorlaomer of Genesis 14: 1, and partly because Kudur-Mabug in it calls himself "Father" or governor of the Westland. If, however, Kudur-Mabug was intended by the name Chedorlaomer, the name had been corrupted beyond all recognition in the Biblical tradition before Genesis 14 was written. In reality there is no reason to suppose that Kudur-Mabug and Chedorlaomer are the same. As to the term "Westland," it probably does not here designate Palestine, but either the western part of Elam or the southern part of Babylonia. Babylonia lay to the west of Elam, and Kudur-Mabug placed on the throne of Larsa, a city of South Babylonia, first his son, Arad-Sin, and then his son, Rim-Sin, and apparently maintained an over-lordship over both of them. "Westland" accordingly means in his inscription, not Palestine, but Babylonia. One of Kudur-Mabug's sons calls his father "Father" (or governor) of Emutbal, a region of Elam. It is a mistake, therefore, to bring Kudur-Mabug into connection with Abraham and Genesis 14.[9]

8. Kings Supposed by Some to Be Those Mentioned in Genesis 14.—Some fragmentary tablets from the Persian period, not earlier than the fourth century B.C., contain references which have been brought by some scholars into connection with Abraham and the fourteenth of Genesis. The texts read as follows:

I [10]

1. ....
2. ....
3. ....his work not..........

[9] It was formerly not known that Arad-Sin and Rim-Sin were different persons, and some thought the king might be called either Rim-Sin or Eri-aku (Arioch, Gen. 14: 1). It is possible that Arad-Sin may have been called Ari-aku in Sumerian, but it is improbable. It is now known that Arad-Sin died 30 years before Hammurabi came to the throne. Without present knowledge it is difficult to see how Arioch could be the name of Rim-Sin unless Rim-Sin be read partly as Semitic and partly as Sumerian and then considerably corrupted.

[10] The text was published by Pinches in the *Journal of Transactions of the Victoria Institute*, Vol. XXIX, 82, 83; cf. emendations by L. W. King, *Letters and Inscriptions of Hammurabi*, Vol. I, p. li, ff. Sayce has also translated them, filling out the lacunæ by freely exercising the imagination, in the *Proceedings of the Society of Biblical Archæology*, XXVIII, 203–218, 241–251, and XXIX, 7–17.

4. ....*su-ḫa-am-mu*..........
5. ....before the gods the creation of..........
6. ....day..........Shamash, who illumines..........
7. ....the lord of the gods, Marduk, in the satisfaction of his heart,
8. ....his servant, the region, all of it, a counsel not fulfilled,
9. ....by force of arms he overthrew. Dursirilani, son of Arad-Malaku (Eri?-..aku)
10. ....goods (?) he carried off, took as spoil, waters over Babylon and Esagil
11. ....his with the weapon of his hand like a lamb he killed him,
12. ....spoke to her, father, and son; with the weapon
13. [Great] and small he cut off, Tudkhula, son of Gazza..........
14. ......goods he took as spoil, waters over Babylon and Esagil
15. ......his son with the weapon of his hands upon him fell.
16. ....of his dominion before the temple of Annunit..........
17. ....Elam, the city Akhkhi to (?) the city Rabbatu he spoiled.
18. ......like a deluge, he made the cities of Akkad, all of Borsippa (?)
19. ....ended. Kukukumal,[11] his son pierced his heart with a girdle-dagger of iron.
20. ....the enemy took and the destruction of these kings, participators in wrong (?),
21. ....bondage for which the king of the gods, Marduk, was angry with them
22. ....with sickness their breast was oppressed.......
23. ....unto ruins were reduced (?). All of them to the king, our lord
24. ....knowing (?) the hearts of the gods, the gracious Marduk, for the commemoration of his name
25. ....and named Esagil—to his place may he return.
26. ....thy.....may he make. This, O king, my lord we......
27. ....his evil his heart the gods, his fathers..........
28. ....a participator in sin shall not be (?).

II

1. ....gods (?)..........
2. ....in the city feared day (?) [and night (?)]
3. ....Larsa (?), the bond of heaven which unto the four winds....
4. he decreed them the park (?) which is in Babylon, the city of [his] majesty (?);
5. he decreed them the possessions of Babylon, small and great.
6. In their faithful counsel unto Kukukumal, King of Elam,
7. they established the fixed advance which to them [seemed] good.
8. In Babylon, the city of Karduniash, kingship he assumed..........
9. In Babylon, the city of the gods, Marduk set his throne (?),
10. All, even the Sodomites of the plundered temples, obeyed [him].
11. Ravens build nests; birds dwell [therein];
12. The ravens croak (?), shrieking they hatch their young [in it].
13. To the dog crunching the bone the lady..........is favorable.
14. The snake hisses (?), the evil one who spits [poison].
15. Who is the king of Elam who the great building of Esagil de[stroyed],
16. which the Babylonians made, and their work was..........?
17. This is what thou hast written, saying: "I am a king, the son of a king"........

11 This could be read *Kudurkumal*.

18. Who is the son of a daughter of a king, who on the royal throne will sit?......
19. He is Dursil-ilâni, son of Arad-Malkua, who the throne..........
20. on the royal throne he sat and before his warriors [he marched].
21. Now let the king march who from ancient days..........
22. has been proclaimed lord of Babylon; the work of........shall not endure.
23. In the month Siman and the month Tammuz in Babylon there was done..........
24. the work of the son of the magician. The bull (*i.e.*, warrior) who devastates the land..........
25. The elders in their faithful counsel..........
26. [gave] the son of the magician the place instead of his father
27. ....1 maid....................

Two other similar fragmentary texts belonging to the series are published as noted above, but it is unnecessary to quote them here. The two fragments which we have translated contain the most important references, and are sufficient to enable the reader to make up his mind as to the bearing of these texts upon the fourteenth of Genesis.

Pinches and Sayce read the name of the Elamite king, Kukukumal, Kudurlakhmal, and identified it with Chedorlaomer. Pinches so read it, hesitatingly! Sayce, confidently. There is no reason for so reading it, except the desire to discover Chedorlaomer. The first three syllables are represented in the cuneiform by the same sign— a sign the most frequent value of which is *ku*. It does sometimes have the value *dur*, but never *lakh*. King reads it Kukukumal, and there is really no reason for reading it otherwise.

Another name which occurs twice is written in the two places with a slight difference of spelling. It is according to the most natural reading of the signs, Arad-Malkua, or Arad-Malaku. Sayce and Pinches read Eri-eaku and identified him with "Arioch, king of Elassar," (Gen. 14: 1). While this is a possible reading, it is only secured by giving to the signs their Sumerian, instead of their Semitic values, and, as the documents are in Semitic, this is probably wrong. The name is to be read Arad-Malkua. Another name, Tudkhula, which occurs in the first document, has been identified by the same scholars with "Tidal, king of the nations" (Gen. 14:1), but in this text there is no evidence that Tudkhula was a king at all, and the identification is purely fanciful. It should be noted also that Arad-Malkua, the supposed Eri-eaku, does not himself take any part in the wars here recorded; it is his son, Dursil-ilâni, who is represented as a contemporary of Kukukumal, the supposed Chedorlaomer.

It should be further noted that these documents represent a complete conquest of Babylon by Elam—a conquest in which Babylon itself is laid desolate. It is not certain just what part Dursil-ilâni played in the story. He may have been a vassal king under Kukukumal, or the Babylonian upon whom the hopes of the people centered, to free them from the yoke of Elam. It is clear, however, that the events mentioned in these documents are not in harmony with the supposition that these monarchs acted as allies of Hammurabi in the invasion of Palestine. Hammurabi is excluded from the account. Kukukumal conquered and desolated the very city in which Hammurabi had his throne. Kukukumal must, accordingly, have lived at some other period of the history, and the supposed confirmation of the account of the fourteenth chapter of Genesis has not yet been found.

As already stated, these tablets are not earlier than the fourth century B.C. The events which they record were probably much later than the time of Abraham. Babylon is called by its Cassite name, Kar-duniash, a name which it did not bear until some hundreds of years after the time of Hammurabi. Many times in the course of Babylonian history was the country overrun by Elam, and there is no real reason to suppose that the war here referred to belongs to the age of Hammurabi.

In recent years several attempts have been made to bring the statements of the fourteenth chapter of Genesis into accord with historical events of a period later than that of Hammurabi. One of the most interesting efforts to find correspondences between the fourteenth chapter of Genesis and archæologically attested facts of a time later than Hammurabi is that made by Dr. W. F. Albright,[12] and Anton Jirku.[13] Dr. Albright's effort was prompted by several archæological considerations some of which were raised by discoveries in Palestine, others by discoveries in upper Mesopotamia. Among the last mentioned are the names of some kings found on tablets dug up at 'Ashâra, on the Euphrates, by Thureau-Dangin and Dhorme.[14] 'Ashâra is the site of the capital of the ancient kingdom of Hana, and there is reason to believe that the texts mentioned come from the period 1800–1600 B.C. Dr. Albright further proposes to identify the kings mentioned in the tablets trans-

---

12 Dr. Albright's article is entitled, "The Historical Background of Genesis XIV," and is published in the *Journal of the Society of Oriental Research*, Vol. X, pp. 231–269.
13 *Geschichte des Volkes Israels*, Leipzig, 1931.
14 See "Cinq Jours de Fouilles a 'Ashâra" (7–11 Septembre, 1923), par M. Francois Thureau-Dangin et le R. P. Dhorme, in *Syria*, Vol. V (1924), pp. 265–293.

lated above, on pp. 349, 350, with rulers of this same period. The name Eri-aku he connects with a man whose son, Tukulti-belit-ilâni, ruled in northern Babylonia about 1800 B.C. Shinar he equates with Singara. Of Tudkhula he remarks that at least five Hittite kings bore the name Tudkhalia. For Amraphel he has found no certain equivalent, but suggests two or three hypothetical possibilities.

As yet it is impossible to prove the theory Dr. Albright proposes. The period has hitherto been one of the darkest in the history of Western Asia, owing to the lack of historical documents containing information about it. The theory, however, deserves attention. Should it prove to be true, it would relieve a great chronological difficulty.

9. A Liturgy of the Time of Abraham and Melchizedek.— Among the poems discovered at Ras Shamra (Ugarit) are three liturgies. Scholars designate these as Poems I, II, and III.[15] It seems clear from the contents of the poems that they were written by Semites, probably Amorites, and were written to be recited at festivals celebrated in temples situated at points south of Ugarit. Poems I and II were clearly written to be recited at festivals of Alein (Adonis-Tammuz) at Aphek (Josh. 13:4), the Aphaca of Lucian, while Poem III is, as I believe, a liturgy originally written for the spring festival at Jerusalem about 1600–1800 B.C., the period of Abraham and Melchizedek.

Liturgies are always derived from material which antedates considerably the time of compilation and adaptation to worship.

In studying Poems I and II, I had become convinced that those texts had first taken shape when the bulk of the ancestors of the Phoenicians were still living in what is now Palestine. This conviction was based on the fact that the shrine at Aphek is in Poems I and II consistently referred to as in "the heights of the north," although it is in central Phoenicia, considerably south of Ugarit, where the texts were copied. This conjecture is fully confirmed by Poem III, the whole scene of which is in southern Palestine, reaching as far south as Kadesh in the wilderness. In addition to this the discovery by Dr. Grant at Beth-Shemesh [16] during the summer of 1933 of a tablet in this same script in a stratum of the same age as that in which the tablets at Ugarit were found, is

15 The writer published a translation of Poem I in the *Journal of the American Oriental Society,* LII, 221 ff. and in the 6th edition of this work, 534 ff.; also, of Poem II in the *Journal of the American Oriental Society,* LV, 31 ff.; and, of Poem III in the *Journal of Biblical Literature,* LIII, 61 ff. For other publications, see above, p. 138, note 110.

16 Published in the *Bulletin of the American Schools of Oriental Research,* No. 52.

proof that a people employing the same alphabet and worshipping the same supreme god, El, was still in southern Palestine at the time these liturgies were being copied at Ugarit, *i.e.*, about 1400–1375 B.C. While liturgies are adorned with rubrics contemporary with their adoption, and may here and there contain other evidence of the time and place, when they became liturgies, the bulk of the liturgy is invariably considerably older, usually older by centuries. If, furthermore, we find in the archives of Ugarit a liturgy brought from the South and written for use in the South, it is certain to be a liturgy older by some centuries than the date of the copy. It had become through use in the South charged with sacred associations, before it was transferred to the North and treasured there. If, then, it can be shown, as I believe it can, that Poem III was originally compiled for a well known temple in Palestine, it will follow from the date of the copy in our possession that it probably belongs to the period prior to 1600 B.C.

The text of Poem III is as follows: [17]

1. I will summon the gods, gracious
2. and beautiful, children of princes..............
3. who are granting a city unto (?).........
4. in the wilderness. The wind-swept places they will.........
5. at their summits, and will.................
6. Eat of bread with me, and drink of wine, my weary ones!
7. O Salem, thou shalt be queen—Salem, queen of those who enter in and pour a libation.

8. Moth-w-Shor shall sit; in his hand the sceptre of bereavement; in his hand
9. the sceptre of silence. The pruners shall prune the vine;
10. those who tie shall tie the vine; they shall cast the stones from its field
11. as did Gepen.

12. Remove the crescents upon the 'Edh and ye who enter shall respond (or make responses).[18]

13. And as to the fields, the fields of the gods, the fields of Asherat and the merciful ones,
14. over the fire remove the ashes (?); slay a kid in the milk, resting in the curds,
15. and upon the basin remove for them the............

16. Thou shalt bring to them my loved-ones and declare them righteous....
17. Thou shalt girdle with ashes (?) the gracious (gods?)...........
18. and we will place on those entering the crescents (?).......

17 Translated from the text published by Virolleaud in *Syria*, XIV, p. 127 ff.
18 Lines 12–20 are rubrics, which give directions for the preparations for the service to follow.

19. The dwelling of the eight gods..................
20. the seven store-houses (?).............

21. I will jealously guard the names..........
22. the sons of princes............

23. I will summon the gracious gods (against Asherat of) the sea;
24. they shall take vengeance on the exceeding anger of Asherat.........
25. O Shephesh,[19] who as to the cows, (will open?) their door..........?
26. while those who enter and pour libations are crying loudly, Salem......
27. come to them in thy acceptable sacrifice!

28. The fields of the gods, the field of Asherat, my loved ones
29. ....shall inhabit.

        ?   ?   ?
30. (Subdue) with her the foam of the sea and may the foam of the deep be
    harnessed!
31. (Subdue?) those that are gathered together, who are gathered together
    on the crest of the wave (?)
32. Her praise is to be proclaimed; her praise thou shalt exalt; her praise
    thou shalt cry, O mighty one.
33. Her praise thou shalt cry, O mother, mother,—the hand of El shall push
    them back like the sea,
34. and the hand of El is like a creeping-thing; the hand of El is long as
    the sea;
35. and the hand of El is like a creeping-thing; El is seizing those who are
    gathering themselves together—
36. those gathering themselves together on the crest of the wave he will
    seize; they are in his house.
37. The sceptre of El has rested; El will be merciful; the staff of his hand
    he will lift up.
38. He shall direct (to) his wilderness; he shall direct in the wilderness;
    the bird he shall pluck; he shall put it
39. on the coals. The women, as El shall pass by them,[20] the women shall
    cry,
40. "O Moth, Moth, we shall set limits to thy scepter, tearing away the
    staff of thy hand."
41. The bird shall warm at the fire, broiling on the coals.[21]
42. "(We are) women, each a wife of El, and his slaves, even those
43. women who cry, 'O mighty one; we shall set limits to thy scepter,
44. tearing away the staff of thy hand.'" The bird shall warm at the fire,
45. even broiling on the coals. "Households, each a household of El
46. and his slaves (are we)." These are the women who cry, "O Moth,
    Moth,
47. we shall set limits to thy sceptre, tearing away the staff of thy hands."
    The bird
48. shall warm at the fire, even broiling at the coals. Women, each a wife
49. of El, even his servants,—he shall cleanse their lips, shall lift
50. them up; their lips are sweet, sweet like the pomegranate.
51. With them is kissing and conception; by embracing she who is pas-
    sionate shall be impregnated,

19 The sun-goddess.
20 *I.e.* as his image is carried by them.
21 The women say their sentences while a bird is being offered to El.

52. she shall bring forth. Shakhar-w-Salem word to El shall carry: "Thy wife,
53. O El, has brought forth." "What has she brought forth?" "My children, O Shakhar-w-Salem?"
54. "Offer a perfect one to Shephesh, the Lady, and to the stars........."
55. He shall cleanse their lips; he shall lift them up; their lips are sweet.
56. With them is kissing and conception by embracing, and he shall capture the heart of her who is passionate.
57. He shall count to five for.........the multitude of those enclosed(?);
58. they shall be captivated and shall bear the gracious gods, the dividers of the sea;
59. the sons of the sea they shall avenge in anger. Salem shall carry word to El
60. "My women have brought forth. O El!" "What have they brought forth?" "My gracious gods, O blessed one (?),
61. dividers of the sea." The sons of the sea they shall avenge in anger, to establish a field (from) the border
62. of the land to the border of the wilderness, that there may enter into their mouths the bird of the desert
63. and the fish in the sea; and they shall drive away the locusts (?) (and) thy delights (?) shall multiply both on the right hand
64. and on the left in their mouths. The son of Shebani, wife of Etrakh,
65. shall build Ashdod, devising 'Edh, thy house in the wilderness of Kadesh.
66. There shalt thou sojourn with stones and trees for seven years.
67. Thou shalt slay eight birds just hatched at the 'Edh of the gracious gods. Thou shalt walk up and down
68. the field, thou shalt hunt the corners of the wilderness, and bringing them near protected
69. of the shell, cry to them with the protection of the shell, "O protected one,[22]
70. protected one, open, even open it and break through into their 'Edh
71. and enter their...................................and we will give,
72. and we will feed them. Where is wine...............and we will give and make them drink."
73. Then shall answer them the one protected of the shell................
74. "Where is wine for entering into?...........................
75. The female guests—for them a log of her wine.................
76. and her homer (?) full of wine...............................

The lines across the text of the above poem mark off the sections of the text, and separate the rubrics from the main part of the liturgy. Lines 1–7 constitute the opening lines of the liturgy, containing the summons by which the officiating priest called the gods to the festival. They belong to a stratum of thought in which gods, like men, were believed to need food. The gods who, in lines 1, 2 are called "gracious and beautiful," are accordingly addressed in line 6 as "*my weary ones*." Line 7, "O Salem, thou shalt be queen —Salem queen of those who enter and pour a libation," identifies the place for which the liturgy was composed as Jerusalem. Jeru-

22 The language here, as in many lines of the poem, is difficult and the rendering, uncertain. For notes defending the writer's translation, see the *Journal of Biblical Literature*, LIII. 75–78.

salem is called Salem in Genesis 14:18 and Psalm 76:2. In the
last mentioned passage there can be no question that Jerusalem is
meant, since in the parallelism it is equated with Zion. This was
the view also of Josephus (*Ant.* I, x. 2; *BJ*, VI, x), of Onkelos,
and all the Targums. Eusebius [23] and Jerome [24] held the same
opinion, though Jerome also knew of another Salem. Other views
have, however, been held. The LXX, Vulgate and Syriac make
Genesis 33:18 read, "And Jacob came unto Salem, a city of
Shechem." That there was such a place near Shechem has been
confirmed by Robinson's discovery of a small village called *Shalim*
northeast of Nablus.[25] The Hebrew text of Genesis does not, however, say that Jacob went to this place. The word misunderstood
by the Versions in Genesis 33:18 as a proper name (*shālĕm*) is
descriptive of Jacob. It means that Jacob, after his encounter with
Esau, went to Shechem with a whole skin, and evidence of the
antiquity of *Shalim* is lacking. True, a Salem in the Jordan Valley
is mentioned in the Gospel of John (3:23); Jerome found a Salem
in the Jordan Valley eight miles south of Scythopolis, but no evidence exists that this Salem had existed at an early date.

Evidence has already been adduced for regarding the date of our
text as about 1600 B.C. or earlier. It so happens that these lines
of our ritual actually fit the topography of the northern approach to
the city as disclosed by the excavations of Macalister and Duncan
in 1923–24.[26] Across the narrow neck of Zion north of the northern city-wall a rock-cut trench, ten or twelve feet in breadth, and
an average depth of eight feet, was found, which had evidently
been cut to strengthen the defenses of the city on this side. Steps
were cut on its northern side leading down into it, and on its southern side leading out of it up to the city-gate. By the top of the
steps which led to the city-gate a rock-cut altar was found—an
altar which led the excavators to think they understood why
Abraham is said in Genesis 14 to have given to Melchizedek a tenth
of his spoils. The pottery found in this trench belonged to the
period, 2000–1600 B.C. and contained sherds which exhibited Cypriote influences. The trench and altar, accordingly were contemporaneous with our poem. Now it so happens that the opening
lines of our ritual, which contain the call of the gods to the festival,
exactly fit this trench and altar. Salem is "queen of those who enter

23 *Quest. in Gen.*
24 *Onomasticon,* "Jerusalem."
25 See his *Biblical Researches,* III, London, 1856, 298.
26 See *Palestine Exploration Fund Annual,* IV, pp. 31 ff. and pl. iv, and above, Part I,
ch. XIII, § 4.

in and pour a libation." True, Virolleaud translates, "Salem! la royanté (sur) les Arabes et les Shenénites," but 'Arabs' are not elsewhere mentioned at so early a time, and everywhere in this text where the word occurs a better sense is obtained by taking the word as equivalent to the Arabic *gharaba,* Akk, *eribu,* from which the Hebrew *'erebh* 'evening' is derived. As for a tribe called Shenenites, it is unknown elsewhere. The root *ŠNN* means 'pour out' water or wine. Clearly the lines are a call to a festival, and Salem is declared queen of those who enter into her city, and who pour a libation. The phrase fits the gate of Jerusalem and its altar at that very period, and the altar and the gate explain the lines.

It may further be objected that in our text Salem is one of the supernatural spirits. To this it should be replied that Salem is at times so regarded in these lines. As a supernatural spirit his function is to bear to El, the supreme deity, the good news that children are born to him. Once he bears, when acting in that capacity, the compound name (line 53) Shakhar-w-Shalem (Dawn and Peace), and twice (lines 26 and 59) simply Salem. The double name is paralleled by that of the vine-spirit which, in one poem, is called Gepen-w-Agar,[27] but in our poem (line 11) simply Gepen.[28] For the supposition that Salem is both an earthly city and a supernatural spirit, we have two [29] analogies. In line 65 of our poem Kadesh is the well-known place Ain Kades, while in Poem II, col. iv, 13–18, Kadesh is the supernatural spirit which formed the rear guard of Asherat, when that goddess was brought back from temporary exile. Similarly in the poem before us *gepen* is in lines 9 and 10 vines in an early vineyard; in line 11, the supernatural vine-spirit. There is no reason, then, why Salem may not be in this poem both a city and the spirit of the city. That it is here, in line 7, the city is confirmed by the fact that it is feminine and its verb is feminine, whereas in lines 52 and 59, where it is a spirit, it is masculine and its verb is in a masculine form. Since in line 3 the gracious gods are said to be granting a city, we conclude that that city was Salem, better known as Jerusalem. Albright pointed out some years ago that in poetry Salem was employed

27 Poem II, col. vii, 54.

28 Still a third compound spirit, Kashar-w-Khasis, appears in Poem II, col. v. 41 ff.

29 A third instance may also be cited. Amurru is both a place and a god. In Poem II, col. iv, 8–17 Amurru is along with Kadesh an outrider of Asherat, when she is brought back from exile. Kadesh guards the rear, while Amurru goes "like a star before." The passage personifies as deities the places which marked the northern and southern limits of the Phœnician habitat at the time it was written. They were migrating northward; Amurru was before them; Kadesh behind them.

in place of the longer Jerusalem,[30] because it is less awkward to fit into meter. The city was apparently situated in a wilderness (l. 4), though a break in the text leaves this somewhat in doubt. "The wilderness of Judæa"—a phrase familiar to every reader of the Bible, probably at this period surrounded the region where Jerusalem stands. True, the evidence does not amount to full demonstration, but it does raise to a high degree of probability the hypothesis that our text was a liturgy for a festival celebrated at Jerusalem in the period 1800–1600 B.C. We may, I think, go a step further and say that the ritual was arranged soon after the worshippers had gained possession of the town, while the consciousness that their gods had given them its possession was clear in memory.

This text, with its kindred texts from Ugarit, affords us a new background for Genesis 14: 18–24. Here as there the city is called Salem. Here as there the god worshipped is El. In Genesis 14: 19 El is called the "possessor" (Heb. *qōneh*) of heaven and earth, just as in Poem II Asherat is called the "possessor" (*qnyt*) of the gods.

The second section of the poem, lines 8–11, are a bit of beautiful poetry taken over from an old vineyard song, which was sung at the season when the vines were being pruned and tied up and the stones cast from the vineyard. As the purpose of the cultivation was to make the vines bear, Moth, the god of death, is represented (lines 9–11) as sitting in silent sorrow. Perhaps in our poem the lines are a rubric. Perhaps at the festival there was a representation in pantomime of the three processes of vine-culture indicated in the lines. At all events, this bit of vintage marks the season of the festival. The vines are pruned after the rainy season is over, in what we call the spring; the grapes grow during the summer, and are harvested in September. The festival, of the ritual of which they form a part was, accordingly, a spring festival.

No one can read this bit of vineyard poetry, especially in the original, without being at once reminded of Isaiah's Song of the Vineyard, Isaiah 5: 1–8. In both the word for ridding the vineyard of stones is identical. If we are right in thinking that this ritual was compiled for Jerusalem, it may well have survived there down to the time of Isaiah. In that case our lines may have suggested to Isaiah his ode, and, from the fact that the theme was familiar in a religious liturgy, they would be all the more effective.

The third marked section of the text, line 12, is clearly a rubric. It directs that "crescents" or "moons" are to be removed from upon the 'Edh, ("testimony" or "shrine" [31]), and that those who enter shall make responses.

As now the gods have been summoned, the pantomime of pruning provided for, and directions given for the admission of worshippers, lines 13–15 contain directions for a sacrifice for the fields. The chief feature of this sacrifice is the slaying of a kid in the milk. The text is broken, but he was apparently boiled over the fire. This is the rite prohibited in Exodus 34:26.

The next section, lines 16–18, is a rubric, but, as the ends of the lines are all lost, it is somewhat obscure. "My loved-ones" are, however, probably the worshippers, who are to be brought near and declared righteous (sedeq—a word associated with Jerusalem in the names Melchizedek and Adonizedek, Judges 1:5, where it is accidentally written Adoni-Bezek) or ritually pure, they are then to be girdled with ashes (?), and, as they enter, the crescents which were removed from the shrine are to be placed on their heads.

Lines 19 and 20 form another rubric, but are too mutilated to afford a clear meaning. They originally gave directions as to what was to be done with the shrines of the eight gods and the seven storehouses (?), but we cannot now guess what that was.

Lines 21 and 22 are similarly now broken. They were apparently a promise by the officiating priest jealously to guard the names of the gracious gods.

The preceding rubrics having been complied with, the sacrifice of the kid being ready, the priest in line 23 summons the gracious gods again. He summons them against the exceeding anger of Asherat of the sea. The role of this goddess is, from the point of view of Semitic religion, peculiar in all three of the poems from Ugarit hitherto published. She is regarded as the giver of prosperity, the possessor of riches, but as a goddess hostile in some degree to her worshippers, whose opposition must be overcome, and who must be compelled to be benignant. She is further called "Asherat of the sea"—an epithet not applied to her in any hitherto discovered Semitic sources. The name

31 Perhaps the stone altar.

Asherat goes back for its origin to the primitive Semitic home,[32] but into the personality of the Asherat of these Ugarit poems a new and non-Semitic element had entered. She is connected with the sea, and she is, while exceedingly powerful and rich, characterized by a reluctance and hostility which had to be overcome.[33] M. Dussaud,[34] building on a statement in Herodotus VII, 89, that the Phoenicians formerly dwelt on the Red Sea, whence they crossed over and lived on the coast of Syria, would account for the nautical characteristics of our goddess by the sea-faring experiences of the ancestors of the Phœnicians on the Red Sea during centuries anterior to our text. Such experiences do not seem to the present writer sufficient to account for the phenomena. We now know that a considerable Hurrian element had entered into Phoenician civilization. These Hurrians had apparently come from the northwest, partly, doubtless, by sea. Cypriote pottery patterns both at Ugarit and at Jerusalem in the strata of the period to which our text belongs,[35] indicates that along with the Hurrians there came Aegean elements. The people from over the sea brought their goddess with them. They had to be overcome and absorbed by Semites. The process involved the final blending of two goddesses. The emergent divinity bore the old Semitic name, but possessed many nautical elements derived from the West. The hostility of the western invaders, when they first appeared, survived in the memory of the people, and gave to the Asherat that resulted from the fusion the inimical character attributed to her in these poems.

In my judgment it is for this reason that in this second invocation the gracious gods are summoned against Asherat of the sea to take vengeance on the exceeding anger of Asherat. Against her, Shephesh, the sun-goddess is called upon to inform the worshippers who it is that will open (?) the door for the cows, while those who are entering and pouring the libations are crying loudly, "O Salem, come to the acceptable sacrifice!" This summons is followed in lines 28 and 29 with a statement which, though fragmentary, seems to declare that those beloved of the officiating priest, who speaks evidently in the name of El, shall inhabit the fields of the gods and of Asherat. This section of

---

32 See ch. V of the writer's *Semitic and Hamitic Origins*, University of Pennsylvania Press, 1934.
33 See Poem II, col. i, 21—col. iv, 57.
34 Cf. *Revue de l'histoire des religions*, CVIII, 6–49 (Jul-Aut., 1933).
35 Cf. *Syria*, XIV, 96 ff., and *Palestine Exploration Fund Annual*, IV, 33.

the liturgy, with its reference to cows and fields, is intended to secure fertility for the husbandman.

Lines 30–36, which were next recited, were doubtless said as a part of the ritual for subduing the reluctance of Asherat. They are either a part of an old song of triumph of the Semites over sea-peoples from the West, or an incantation of sailors designed to secure them a safe passage. Like much that follows, they were composed in an environment quite other than Jerusalem. With the recitation of such brave words the reluctance of Asherat of the sea was thought to be overcome.

Lines 37–60 contain the fullest ritual yet discovered for the service of the *qadeshoth*, or the wives of El. Just as the previous ritual had been calculated to secure fertility to the vines, the cows, and the fields, the purpose of this ritual was to secure human offspring. The ritual was recited as a bird was broiling on a coal fire, and as the image of the god El was carried up and down. The bird so broiled was believed to have been secured by El's leading the way to the wilderness.

After repetitions of this ritual, the pleasures of embracing the wives of El are portrayed and the births, first of earthly, and then of heavenly children, are separately announced to El. As Salem, the Spirit of the city, announces the births to El, it is probable that the ritual was performed to secure a succession of children for the earthly city. This inference is confirmed by line 54, which follows the announcement of the earthly births: "Offer a perfect one to Shephesh and the stars",—a command which reminds us of Abraham's sacrifice of Isaac.

Lines 61–76, which follow the description of the birth of the gracious gods, describe the work they shall accomplish. As the tablet breaks off suddenly the description is incomplete, but it is clear that these are the gods who were believed to have given the worshippers the cultivated land from the edge of the earth, (*i.e.,* the sea shore) to the edge of the desert. In other words the territory from Ashdod to Kadesh, that the "bird of heaven and the fish in the sea may enter into their mouths, and they shall drive away the locusts (?) and thy delights (?) shall multiply both on the right hand and on the left in their mouths."

The son of Shebani, wife of Etrakh (Terah?), shall build Ashdod, devising an 'Edh, ("testimony") in the wilderness of Kadesh. As this 'Edh is defined as "thy house" it was clearly something in which the god was supposed to dwell. It was probably an altar or a *maṣṣebah*. If, as we suspect, the word "Edh" in line 12 of the poem refers to the rock altar at the gate of Jerusalem, it probably refers to a similar structure at Kadesh. This "Kadesh in the wilderness" is clearly the Ain Kadis of today, and the Kadesh of Numbers 13:26; 20:1, etc. Our text thus gives us a literary reference to that sacred place earlier than any we have hitherto possessed, carrying back the antiquity of the shrine at Kadesh to the middle bronze age. This antiquity of the site is confirmed by the finding of pottery in 1914 by Woolley and Lawrence "closely resembling Cypriote fabrics." [36] Our text shows that the site was old even then.

This part of the ritual, the scene of which is laid in the Maritime Plain and the Negeb, or southland of Judah, represents a society that has become partly agricultural, but which is still partly dependent on hunting and fishing. The gods are to establish a wide field, and wine is a part of the sacrificial offering. This is agricultural. But birds of heaven and fishes of the sea still form part of the diet of the people, and the sacrifices at Kadesh consist of wild birds alone. It is thus evident that the ritual of the shrine was fashioned in a still remoter period, when the community lived by hunting.

It will thus be seen that the range of territory from which this liturgy draws its material extends from Kadesh on the south to Jerusalem on the north, embracing also the territory of what was later called Philistia. It further appears that in a number of passages its contents afford points of contact with patriarchal traditions. Thus Shebani, the wife of Etrakh (Terah?), whose son is said to have built Ashdod, is a name which embodies the numeral seven. Dussaud, in the article already mentioned, sees in this a connection with the name Beersheba, in which the word for "seven" also figures. That is possible, though perhaps somewhat fanciful.

If this text is not a liturgy written for Jerusalem, it is at least a liturgy compiled for a topography closely resembling that of Jerusalem between 1600 and 2000 B.C. The city fits the liturgy and the liturgy fits the city. It is, accordingly, difficult not to conclude that what a mutual birth had originally joined together, only the accidents of transmission through three thousand three hundred years have put asunder.

36 See *Palestine Exploration Fund Annual*, III, 67.

CHAPTER X

JACOB AND JOSEPH

The Names Jacob, Israel, and Joseph in Babylonian and Egyptian Records. "The Tale of the Two Brothers"; Its Bearing on the Story of Joseph in Genesis. Letters to a Ruler Like Joseph. The Seven Years of Famine. Inscription Showing Preparation for Famine.

1. Jacob.—Three different men in Babylonia at the time of the Hammurabi dynasty bore the name Jacob-el. Thus, in the reign of Apil-Sin, the fourth king of the dynasty (2161 to 2144 B.C.), two witnesses, Shubna-ilu and Yadakh-ilu gave their father's name as *Yakub-ilu,* or Jacob-el.[1] In the same reign a witness to another document, one Lamaz, had a Jacob-el as his father.[2] In the reign of Sin-muballit, the next king, a witness named Nur-Shamash was also the son of a Jacob-el.[3] In the reign of the great Hammurabi, the next king, a witness named Sin-erbiam gave his father's name simply as *Yakub,*[4] or Jacob. This last is clearly a shortening of Jacob-el. These men all lived hundreds of years before the Babylonian Abraham, whose documents are discussed in Chapter IX.

In connection with these names it should be noted that Thothmes III of Egypt, who made extensive conquests in Asia between 1478 and 1446 B.C., records the name of a city which he captured in Palestine as *Ya'-k-b'-ra,* the Egyptian equivalent of Jacob-el.[5] It does not seem a rash guess to suppose that in the period when intercourse between Babylonia and Palestine was frequent and immigration from the former country to the latter was in progress, some Babylonian bearing this name migrated to Palestine, settled there and that a city was named after him. Many parallels to this may be found in the names of places in the United States and Canada. That this place name in Canaan had some connection with the name of the Patriarch Jacob is probable, though just what that connection was it is impossible in the present state of our knowledge to say.

1 *Cuneiform Texts, &c., in British Museum,* IV, 33, 22b.
2 Meissner, *Altbabylonisches Privatrecht,* 36, 25.
3 *Cuneiform Texts,* VIII, 25, 22.
4 *Ibid.,* II, 9, 26.
5 Cf. *Mittheilungen der Vorderasiatischen Gesellschaft,* 1907, p. 27.

2. Israel.—Shortly before the war a Babylonian seal cylinder was purchased of a peasant in a village near Mosul and taken to Paris.[6] It bears the name, *Israel, son of Rishzuni.* (See Fig. 302.) The form of the written characters, as well as the pictures carved on the seal, mark it as the work of the time of the dynasty of Agade, which ruled Babylonia from about 2800 to 2600 B.C. The horns of the bull with which the hero at the left is fighting are identical in appearance with the horns of the bulls on the seal of Shargalisharri, one of the kings of this dynasty. There can be no doubt that the object belongs to this time, as this type of creature became extinct and is not pictured in subsequent art.

It is a matter of almost thrilling interest to the student of the Bible to find the name Israel borne by a man who lived before 2600 B.C. Before this discovery the only occurrence of the name Israel outside the Bible was in the inscription of Merneptah, king of Egypt, where it designated the nation Israel or a part of it. On this seal it is a personal name. Its form is Amorite.

3. Joseph.—A Babylonian business document of the time of the first dynasty of Babylon has among its witnesses a man named *Yashub-ilu,* or Joseph-el.[7]

In the list of places which Thothmes III of Egypt conquered in Palestine there is one *Ya-sha-p'-ra,* which many scholars have taken to be Joseph-el, though Prof. W. Max Müller[8] thinks it rather is equivalent to Yesheb-el, meaning "where God dwells." In view of the clear Babylonian equivalence, however, it seems probable that it is Joseph-el. If so, it probably became a place-name in Palestine because some important Babylonian who bore the name settled there, just as we have supposed Jacob-el did. Some scholars hold that it is connected with the name of the Patriarch Joseph in some way, but what that connection was, we cannot now say.

4. The Tale of the Two Brothers.[9]

Once there were two brethren, of one mother and one father; Anpu was the name of the elder, and Bata was the name of the younger. Now, as for Anpu, he had a house, and he had a wife. But his little brother was to him, as it were, a son; he it was who made for him his clothes; he it was who followed behind his oxen to the fields; he it was who did the plowing; he it was who harvested the corn; he it was who did for him all the matters which were in the field. Behold his younger brother grew to be an excellent worker;

6 Published by Scheil in the *Revue d'assyriologie,* Vol. XIII, pp. 5 ff.
7 *Cuneiform Texts, &c., in the British Museum,* II, 23, 15.
8 *Mittheilungen der vorderasiatischen Gesellschaft,* 1907, p. 23.
9 Taken from Griffth's translation in Petrie's *Egyptian Tales,* second series, London, 1895, p. 36 ff.

there was not his equal in the whole land; behold the spirit of a god was in him.

Now after this the younger brother followed his oxen in the daily manner; and every evening he turned again to the house, laden with all the herbs of the field, with milk and with wood, and with all things of the field. And he put them down before his elder brother who was sitting with his wife; and he drank and ate, and he lay down in his stable with the cattle. And at the dawn of day he took bread which he had baked, and laid it before his elder brother; and he took with him his bread to the field, and he drave his cattle to pasture in the fields. And as he walked behind his cattle, they said to him, "Good is the herbage which is in that place"; and he listened to all that they said, and he took them to the good place which they desired. And the cattle which were before him were exceeding excellent, and they multiplied greatly.

Now at the time of plowing his elder brother said unto him, "Let us make ready for ourselves a goodly yoke of oxen for plowing, for the land has come out from the water; it is fit for plowing. Moreover, do thou come to the field with corn, for we will begin the plowing in the morrow morning." Thus said he to him; and his younger brother did all things as his elder brother had spoken unto him to do them.

And when the morn was come, they went to the fields with their things; and their hearts were pleased exceedingly with their task in the beginning of their work. And it came to pass after this that as they were in the field they stopped for corn, and he sent his younger brother, saying, "Haste thou, bring to us corn from the farm." And the younger brother found the wife of his elder brother, as she was sitting tiring her hair. He said to her, "Get up, and give to me corn, that I may run to the field, for my elder brother hastened me, do not delay. She said to him, "Go open the bin, and thou shalt take to thyself according to thy will, that I may not drop my locks of hair while I dress them."

The youth went to the stable; he took a large measure, for he desired to take much corn; he loaded it with wheat and barley; and he went out carrying it. She said to him, "How much of the corn that is wanted, is that which is on thy shoulder?" He said to her, "Three bushels of barley, and two of wheat, in all five; these are what are upon my shoulder:" thus said he to her. And she conversed with him, saying, "There is great strength in thee, for I see thy might every day." And her heart knew him with the knowledge of youth. And she arose and came to him, and conversed with him, saying, "Come stay with me, and it shall be well for thee, and I will make for thee beautiful garments." Then the youth became like a panther of the south with fury at the evil speech which she had made to him; and she feared greatly. And he spake unto her, saying, "Behold thou art to me as a mother, thy husband is to me as a father, for he who is elder than I brought me up. What is this wickedness that thou hast said to me? Say it not to me again. For I will not tell it to any man, for I will not let it be uttered by the mouth of any man." He lifted up his burden, and he went to the field and came to his elder brother; and they took up their work, to labor at their task.

Now afterward, at eventime, his elder brother was returning to his house; and the younger brother was following after his oxen, and he loaded himself with all the things of the field; and he brought his oxen before him, to make them lie down in their stable which was in the farm. And behold the wife of the elder brother was afraid for the words which she had said. She took a parcel of fat, she became like one who is evilly beaten, desiring to say to her husband, "It is thy younger brother who has done this wrong." Her husband returned in the even as was his wont of every day: he came unto his house; he found his wife ill of violence; she did not give him water upon his hands as he used to have, she did not make a light before him, his house was in darkness, and she was lying very sick. Her husband said to her, "Who has spoken with thee?" Behold she said, "No one has spoken with me except thy younger brother. When he came to take for thee corn he found me sitting alone; he said to me, 'Come, let us stay together, tie up thy hair': thus spoke he to me. I did not listen to him, but thus spake I to him: 'Behold, am I not thy mother, is not thy elder brother to thee as a father?' And he feared, and he beat me to stop me from making report to thee, and if thou lettest him live I shall die. Now behold he is coming in the evening; and I complain of these wicked words, for he would have done this even in daylight."

And the elder brother became as a panther of the south; he sharpened his knife; he took it in his hand; he stood behind the door of the stable to slay his younger brother as he came in the evening to bring his cattle into the stable.

Now the sun went down, and he loaded himself with herbs in his daily manner. He came, and his foremost cow entered the stable, and she said to her keeper, "Behold thy elder brother standing before thee with his knife to slay thee; flee from before him." He heard what his first cow had said; and the next entering, she also said likewise. He looked beneath the door of the stable; he saw the feet of his elder brother; he was standing behind the door, and his knife was in his hand. He cast down his load to the ground, and betook himself to flee swiftly; and his elder brother pursued after him with his knife. Then the younger brother cried out unto Rā Harakhti,[10] saying, "My good lord! thou art he who divides the evil from the good." And Rā stood and heard his cry; and Rā made a wide water between him and his elder brother, and it was full of crocodiles; and the one brother was on one bank, and the other on the other bank; and the elder brother smote twice on his hands at not slaying him. Thus did he. And the younger brother called to the elder brother on the bank, saying, "Stand still until the dawn of the day; and when Rā ariseth, I shall judge with thee before him, and he discerneth between the good and the evil. For I shall not be with thee any more forever; I shall not be in the place in which thou art; I shall go to the valley of the acacia."

We need not follow the story further. Those who wish to do so are referred to Petrie's *Egyptian Tales*. From this point onward, it contains many mythological features.

This story, in the form in which we have it, was written for Seti II (1209–1205 B.C.) of the nineteenth Egyptian dynasty, while that monarch was still crown prince. Scholars of all shades of opinion have recognized in it a striking parallel to the story of Joseph in the house of Potiphar, in Genesis 39: 1–20. Joseph, like the younger brother of this tale, was trusted with everything about his master's place; Potiphar's wife, like the sister-in-law of the tale, tempted Joseph; Joseph, like the younger brother, resisted temptation; and Potiphar's wife, like the sister-in-law, charged him with the crime which he had been unwilling to commit.

Scholars of the critical school regard this as the original of the story in Genesis. While they recognize that it is a theme which is not confined to Egyptians and Hebrews (compare for other paral-

10 The sun-god.

lels Lang, *Myth, Ritual, and Religion*, II, 303, ff.), the fact that the theme of the Biblical story is laid in Egypt leads them to think it extremely probable that there is a connection between the two.

Conservative scholars on the other hand hold that in all probability there was more than one such scandal in Egypt, and account for the likeness by the similarity which would naturally present itself in such cases, holding that the Egyptian tale has no bearing on the credibility of that in Genesis.

5. Letters to a Ruler Like Joseph.—Among the letters in the Babylonian language and script found at El-Amarna in Egypt in the winter of 1887–1888,[11] many of which were written to Amenophis III and Amenophis IV, Kings of Egypt, 1411–1357 B.C., by Egyptian vassals in Palestine and Syria, there are two which were written to a Semite named Dûdu (David), which show that this Semite held at the Egyptian court a position analogous to that which Joseph, as ruler of Egypt, is said to have held (Gen. 41:39, f.; 50:26). These letters are as follows:

I [12]

1. To Dûdu, my lord, my father,
2. speaks Aziru, thy son, thy servant:
3. at the feet of my father I fall.
4. Unto my father may there be health!
5. O Dûdu, truly I have given (*i.e.*, done)
6. the wish of the king, my lord,
7. and whatever is the wish
8. of the king, my lord, let him send
9. and I will give (do) it.
10. Further: see, thou art there,
11. my father, and whatever is the wish
12. of Dûdu, my father, send it
13. and I will indeed give (do) it.
14. Behold, thou art my father and my lord
15. and I am thy son. The lands of the Amorites
16. are thy lands, and my house is thy house,
17. and whatever thy wish is,
18. send, and I
19. shall behold, and verily will give (do) it.
20. And see, thou in the presence of
21. the king, my lord, sittest.
22. ....enemies
23. words of slander
24. before my father, before
25. the king, my lord, have spoken,
26. but do thou not count them just!

11 Cf. Part I, p. 25.
12 Winckler und Abel, *Thontafelnfund von El-Amarna*, No. 40. Cf. Knudtzon, *Die El-Amarna Tafeln*, No. 158.

27. And behold thou in the presence
28. of the king, my lord, as a dignitary (?)
29. sittest........................
30. and the words of slander
31. against me do not count true.
32. Also I am a servant of the king, my lord,
33. and from the words of the king, my lord,
34. and from the words of Dûdu, my father,
35. I shall not depart forever.
36. But when the king, my lord, does not love me,
37. but hates me,
38. then I—what shall I say?

II [13]

1. To Dûdu, my lord, my father,
2. speaks Aziru, thy servant:
3. at the feet of my lord I fall.
4. Khatib has come
5. and has brought the words
6. of the king, my lord, important and good,
7. and I am very, very glad,
8. and my land and my brethren,
9. the servants of the king, my lord,
10. and the servants of Dûdu, my lord,
11. are very, very glad,
12. when there comes
13. the breath of the king, my lord,
14. unto me. From the words
15. of my lord, my god, my sun-god,
16. and from the words of Dûdu,
17. my lord, I shall not depart.
18. My lord, truly Khatib
19. stands with me.
20. I and he will come.
21. My lord, the king of the Hittites
22. has come into Nukhashshi,
23. so that I cannot come.
24. Would that the king of the Hittites would depart!
25. Then truly I would come,
26. I and Khatib.
27. May the king, my lord, my words
28. hear! My lord, I fear
29. on account of the face of the king, my lord,
30. and on account of the face of Dûdu.
31. And now by my gods
32. and my angels verily I have sworn,
33. O Dûdu and nobles
34. of the king, my lord, that truly I will come.
35. And so, Dûdu
36. and the king, my lord, and the nobles,
37. "Truly we will not conceive anything
38. against Aziru that is unfavorable,"—

[13] Winckler und Abel, *Thontafelnfund von El-Amarna*, No. 38. See also Knudtzon, *Die El-Amarna Tafeln*, No. 164.

39. even thus may ye swear
40. by my gods and the god A!
41. And truly I
42. and Khatib are faithful servants of the king.
43. O Dûdu, thou shalt truly know
44. that I will come to thee.

The Aziru of these letters was the chieftain or petty king of the Amorites, who were living at the time to the eastward of Phœnicia, between the Lebanon and Anti-Lebanon mountains. The way in which he addresses Dûdu is significant. Dûdu is classed continually with the king. Aziru fears to offend Dûdu as he fears to offend the king; the words of Dûdu are of equal importance with those of the king. Dûdu clearly occupied a position of power with the king of Egypt similar to that ascribed to Joseph in Genesis 41. Moreover, Dûdu is a Semitic name; vocalized a little differently, it becomes David.

The king to whom this letter was written was Amenophis III or Amenophis IV, in whose reigns Semitic influence was especially strong in Egypt. Amenophis III took as his favorite wife a woman named Tiy, daughter of Yuaa and Tuau, whose mummies, discovered a few years ago, show, some think, that they were Semitic. Queen Tiy was very influential during the reign of her son, Amenophis IV, and was in part the cause of the remarkable religious reform which he undertook (Part I, Chapter I, § 6 (vii)). It is not, accordingly, strange to find that the chief minister of one of these kings was a Semite. Of course, Dûdu cannot be identified with Joseph, but his career shows that such careers as that of Joseph were not impossible at this period of Egyptian history.

6. The Seven Years of Famine.—The following inscription was found cut on a rock between the island of Elephantine and the First Cataract, and was first published by Brugsch in 1891. It is written in hieroglyphic characters, and was apparently inscribed in the reign of Ptolemy X, 117–89 B.C. It relates how King Zoser, of the third dynasty, who began to reign about 2980 B.C., nearly 2,800 years before the inscription was written, appealed to Khnum, the god of Elephantine, because of a famine. The part of the text which interests us is as follows: [14]

"I am very anxious on account of those who are in the palace. My heart is in great anxiety on account of misfortune, for in my time the Nile has not overflowed for a period of seven years. There is scarcely any produce of the field; herbage fails; eatables are wanting. Every man robs his neighbor. Men-

[14] Translated from the German rendering of Ranke in Gressmann's *Altorientalische Texte und Bilder zum Alten Testament*, Tübingen, 1909, p. 223.

move (?) with nowhere to go. The children cry, the young people creep along (?). The aged heart is bowed down; their limbs are crippled; they sit (?) on the earth. Their arms are........The people of the court are at their wits' end. The store-houses (?) were built, but........and all that was in them has been consumed."

As Brugsch [15] saw, this inscription gives a graphic account of the suffering caused by seven such years of famine as are said to have occurred in the time of Joseph (Gen. 41: 30, 54, ff.). It cannot be the same seven-year famine as that referred to in Genesis, as it is placed several centuries too early to coincide with the time of Joseph. As the inscription is about 2,800 years later than the event it describes, its historical accuracy might be questioned, but it is probable that it was a renewal of an earlier inscription. But even if its historical accuracy be impugned, it witnesses to a native Egyptian tradition that such famines were possible.

7. Inscription Showing Preparation for Famine.

Inscription of Baba of El-Kab [16]

"The chief at the table of the sovereign, Baba, the risen again, speaks thus: I loved my father; I honored my mother; my brothers and sisters loved me. I went out of the door of my house with a benevolent heart; I stood there with refreshing hand; splendid were my preparations of what I collected for the festal day. Mild was (my) heart, free from violent anger. The gods bestowed upon me abundant prosperity upon earth. The city wished me health and a life of full enjoyment. I punished the evil-doers. The children who stood before me in the town during the days which I fulfilled were—great and small—60; just as many beds were provided for them, just as many chairs (?), just as many tables (?). They all consumed 120 ephahs of durra, the milk of 3 cows, 52 goats, and 9 she-asses, a hin of balsam, and 2 jars of oil.

"My words may seem a jest of the gainsayer, but I call the god Mut to witness that what I say is true. I had all this prepared in my house; in addition I put cream in the store-chamber and beer in the cellar in a more than sufficient number of hin-measures.

"I collected corn as a friend of the harvest-god. I was watchful in time of sowing. And when a famine arose, lasting many years, I distributed corn to the city each year of famine."

The Baba who wrote this inscription lived under the eighteenth Egyptian dynasty, about 1500 B.C., or a little before. Brugsch pointed out many years ago that Baba's concluding statement forms an interesting parallel to the conduct of Joseph as told in Genesis 41: 47–57. Baba claims to have done for his city, El-Kab, what Joseph is said to have done for all Egypt. His statement affords striking evidence of the historical reality of famines in Egypt, and of such economic preparation for them.

15 See his *Sieben Jahre der Hungersnot*, 1891.
16 From Brugsch's *Egypt under the Pharaohs*, London, 1881, I, 303 ff.

CHAPTER XI

PALESTINE IN THE PATRIARCHAL AGE

THE TALE OF SINUHE. COMMUNICATION BETWEEN EGYPT AND PALESTINE.
ASIATICS IN EGYPT.

1. The Tale of Sinuhe.—In the year 1970 B.C., when Amenemhet I died and was succeeded by Sesostris I, an Egyptian of high
rank, named Sinuhe, for some reason now unknown to us, fled from
Egypt to Asia. The details of his escape from Egypt are not of
interest to the Biblical student, but his description of the hardships
encountered in the desert and of his experiences in eastern Palestine
are of great value, as they afford us our earliest description of that
country outside the Bible. The following extract begins just after
Sinuhe had told how he escaped the guards in the fort which stood
at the eastern frontier of Egypt.[1]

> I went on at the time of evening,
> As the earth brightened, I arrived at Peten.
> When I had reached the lake of Kemwer,[2]
> I fell down for thirst, fast came my breath,
> My throat was hot,
> I said: "This is the taste of death."
> I upheld my heart, I drew my limbs together,
> As I heard the sound of lowing cattle,
> I beheld the Bedawin.
> That chief among them, who had been in Egypt, recognized me.
> He gave me water, he cooked for me milk.
> I went with him to his tribe,
> Good was that which they did (for me).
> One land sent me on to another,
> I loosed for Suan,
> I arrived at Kedem;[4]
> I spent a year and a half there.
> Emuienshe,[5] that sheik of Upper [Ru]tenu,[6] brought me forth

1 From Breasted's *Ancient Records, Egypt*, I, p. 237, ff.
2 An Egyptian name of the northern extension of the Gulf of Suez.
3 Some Egyptian trading-post in Asia.
4 An early name for the region east of the Jordan and the Dead Sea. It is called
Kedemah in Genesis 25: 15 and 1 Chronicles 1: 30; Kedemoth in Deuteronomy 2: 26, and
translated "East" in Judges 6: 3, 33; 7: 12; 8: 10, 11. In Genesis and Chronicles the
name is applied to a person.
5 This is an Amorite name, Ammi-anshi. It shows that the Amorites were already
in this region. Later the Hebrews found Sihon, the Amorite here; see Numbers 21: 21,
ff. and Deuteronomy 1: 4, ff.
6 The Egyptian name for the higher parts of Palestine and Syria. The Egyptians had
no *l*; they always used *r* instead. The name is identical with the Hebrew Lotan, Genesis
36: 20, of which Lot is a shorter form.

saying to me: "Happy art thou with me,
(for) thou hearest the speech of Egypt."
He said this (for) he knew my character,
He had heard my wisdom;
The Egyptians, who were there with him, bare witness of me.

The Amorite chieftain then questioned Sinuhe concerning his flight. He gave evasive answers, merging with his reply a long hymn in praise of the king. After this Emuienshe said to him:

"Behold, thou shalt now abide with me;
Good is that which I shall do for thee."
He put me at the head of his children,
He married me to his eldest daughter,
He made me select for myself of his land,
Of the choicest of that which he had,
On his boundary with another land.
It was a goodly land, named Yaa; [7]
There were figs in it and vines,
More plentiful than water was its wine,
Copious was its honey, plenteous its oil;
All fruits were upon its trees.
Barley was there and spelt,
Without end all cattle.
Moreover, great was that which came to me,
Which came for love of me,
When he appointed me sheik of the tribe,
From the choicest of his land.
I portioned the daily bread,
And wine for every day,
Cooked flesh and fowl in roast;
Besides the wild goats of the hills,
Which were trapped for me, and brought to me;
Besides that which my dogs captured for me.
There was much—made for me,
And milk in every sort of cooked dish.
I spent many years,
My children became strong,
Each the mighty man of his tribe.
The messenger going north,
Or passing southward to the court,
He turned in to me.
For I had all men turn in (to me).

The tale goes on concerning the personal prowess of Sinuhe, who, in his old age, returned to Egypt and made his peace with the king.

2. **Communication between Egypt and Palestine.**—This document from the early patriarchal age reveals a close relationship between Egypt and Palestine. There was frequent communication between Kedem and Egypt; messengers went to and fro. The Egyptian language was understood at the court of the Amorite

7 Perhaps the same name as Aiah (Ajah) of Genesis 36: 24 and 1 Chronicles 1: 40.

chieftain. These conditions throw light on the narratives of the
descent of Abraham and Jacob to Egypt. Sinuhe's description
of his life necessarily reminds one of the description of Palestine
so often met with in the Pentateuch, Joshua, and the prophets, "a
land flowing with milk and honey." (See, for example, Exod. 3:
8, 17.)

3. Asiatics in Egypt.—The entrance of Abraham and later of
Jacob and his sons into Egypt in time of famine (Gen. 12: 10 and
47: 5–12) is strikingly illuminated by the following reports of
officials stationed at fortresses on the Egyptian border.

The first of these texts was inscribed in the tomb of Harmhab,
the founder of the nineteenth dynasty, though there is reason to
believe that it was written during the reign of Amenophis IV of
the eighteenth dynasty (1375–1357 B.C.). Some of the lines are
broken. It reads as follows:

........Asiatics; others have been placed in their abodes........they have
been destroyed, and their town laid waste, and fire has been thrown.........
[they have come to entreat] the Great in Strength to send his mighty sword
before....... Their countries are starving, they live like goats of the mountain, [their] children.......saying: "A few of the Asiatics, who knew not
how they should live, have come [begg]ing [a home in the domain] of
Pharaoh......, after the manner of your fathers' fathers' since the beginning
under,.......... Now, the Pharaoh....gives them into your hand, to protect
their borders." [8]

The second text comes from the reign of Merneptah (1225–
1215 B.C.). It reads as follows:

Another matter for the satisfaction of my lord's heart [to wit]: We have
finished passing the tribes of the Shasu of Edom through the fortress of
Merneptah-Hotephirma...in Theku, to the pools of Pithom, of Merneptah-
Hotephirma in Theku, in order to sustain them and their herds in the domain
of Pharaoh..., the good sun of every land.......... I have caused them to
be brought........other names of days when the fortress of Merneptah-Hotephirma may be passed,....[9]

These texts make it evident that at different periods of Egyptian history Asiatic tribes in time of famine and stress sought and
found refuge in Egypt as the Israelites are said to have done.

8 Taken from Breasted, *Ancient Records, Egypt*, III, p. 7.
9 Taken from Breasted, *ibid.*, p. 273.

CHAPTER XII

MOSES AND THE EXODUS

The Legend of Sargon of Agade; Its Resemblance to the Story of Moses. The Pillar of Merneptah; an Appearance of the Name "Israel."

1. The Legend of Sargon of Agade.—The following legend [1] contains a story of the exposure of an infant on a river, strikingly like that told of Moses.

1. Sargon, the mighty king, king of Agade am I,
2. My mother was lowly; my father I did not know; [2]
3. The brother of my father dwelt in the mountain.
4. My city is Azupiranu, which is situated on the bank of the Euphrates.
5. My lowly mother conceived me, in secret she brought me forth.
6. She placed me in a basket of reeds, she closed my entrance with bitumen,
7. She cast me upon the river, which did not overflow me.
8. The river carried me, it brought me to Akki, the irrigator.
9. Akki, the irrigator, in the goodness of his heart lifted me out,
10. Akki, the irrigator, as his own son......brought me up;
11. Akki, the irrigator, as his gardener appointed me.
12. When I was a gardener the goddess Ishtar loved me,
13. And for four years I ruled the kingdom.
14. The black-headed [3] peoples I ruled, I governed;
15. Mighty mountains with axes of bronze I destroyed (?).
16. I ascended the upper mountains;
17. I burst through the lower mountains.
18. The country of the sea I besieged three times;
19. Dilmun [4] I captured (?).
20. Unto the great Dur-ilu I went up, I.........
21. ....I altered.........
22. Whatsoever king shall be exalted after me,
23. ....
24. Let him rule, let him govern the black-headed peoples;
25. Mighty mountains with axes of bronze let him destroy;
26. Let him ascend the upper mountains,
27. Let him break through the lower mountains;
28. The country of the sea let him besiege three times;
29. Dilmun let him capture;
30. To great Dur-ilu let him go up.

1 From *Cuneiform Texts, &c.*, in the *British Museum*, XIII, 42; cf. also King, *Chronicles of Early Babylonian Kings*, II, 87, ff.
2 Another tablet reads "a father I had not."
3 A name for the Semitic peoples of Babylonia.
4 An island in the Persian Gulf.

The rest is too broken for connected translation.

It is thought by some scholars of the critical school that the parallelism between the secret birth, the exposure, the rescue and adoption of Sargon, and the account of the secret birth, exposure, rescue, and adoption of Moses in Exodus 2: 1–10 is too close to be accidental. Conservative scholars, on the other hand, hold that, if the legend of Sargon is historical, it merely affords an example of a striking coincidence of events in two independent lives.

2. The Pillar of Merneptah.—In the fifth year of King Merneptah, who ruled from 1225–1215 B.C., and who is thought to be the Pharaoh of the exodus, he inscribed on a pillar an account of his wars and victories. The inscription concludes with the following poetic strophe.[5]

> The kings are overthrown, saying: "salaam!"
> Not one holds up his head among the nine bows.[6]
> Wasted is Tehenu,[7]
> Kheta [8] is pacified,
> Plundered is the Canaan [9] with every evil,
> Carried off is Askelon,
> Seized upon is Gezer,
> Yenoam [10] is made as a thing not existing.
> Israel is desolated, his seed is not;
> Palestine has become a widow for Egypt.
> All lands are united, they are pacified;
> Every one that is turbulent is bound by King Merneptah, who gives life
>   like Rā every day.

This inscription contains the only mention of Israel in a document of this age outside the Bible. It is, for that reason, of great importance. It should be noted that Israel is mentioned along with peoples and places in Palestine and Phœnicia. The Israel here referred to was not, accordingly, in Egypt. Israel, on the other hand, may not have been more than a nomadic people. The Egyptians used a certain "determinative" in connection with the names of settled peoples. That sign is here used with Tehenu, Kheta, Askelon, Gezer, and Yenoam, but not with Israel.

As Merneptah has been supposed by many to be the Pharaoh in whose reign the exodus occurred, the mention of Israel here has somewhat puzzled scholars, and different explanations of the fact

5 Taken from Breasted's *Ancient Records, Egypt,* III, p. 264, ff.
6 That is, the foreign nations.
7 That is, Lybia, which lay to the west of the Egyptian Delta.
8 That is, the Hittites.
9 "The Canaan" refers to the land of Canaan, probably here Phœnicia.
10 Yenoam was a town situated at the extreme north of Galilee, just at the end of the valley between the two ranges of the Lebanon mountains.

With these laws we should compare Exodus 22:18, which imposes the death penalty upon witches, and Deuteronomy 18:10, ff., which declares that there shall be no sorcerer, diviner, magician, or charmer in Israel and promises a line of prophets to render these unnecessary. Magic is banished from Israel; its presence in Babylonia is taken for granted, and only some of its exercises, which were supposed to be especially deadly, were forbidden. In § 2 the man accused of sorcery is to be tried by ordeal. He is to plunge into the river and if he can swim in its current, he is innocent. Trial by ordeal is found but once in the Hebrew laws (Num. 5: 11–28). There both the crime and the ordeal are very different from this.

Note that in these sections the false accuser suffers in just the way he has tried to bring suffering to the other. This is the law of retaliation, which appears in Deuteronomy 19:16–21, where it is applied to false witnesses in the same way as here. It will be found underlying many of the penalties of this code.

Laws Concerning False Witness

§ 3. If in a case a man has borne false witness, or accused a man without proving it, if that case is a capital case, that man shall be put to death.

§ 4. If he has borne witness in a case of grain or money, the penalty of that case he shall himself bear.

Hebrew law was similar; a false witness was to be visited with the penalty which he had purposed to bring upon his brother (Deut. 19:18, 19).

Against Reversing a Judicial Decision

§ 5. If a judge has pronounced a judgment, made a decision, caused it to sealed, and afterward has altered his judgment, that judge they shall convict on account of the case which he decided and altered; the penalty which in that case he imposed he shall pay twelvefold, and in the assembly from the seat of his judgment they shall expel him; he shall not return; with the judges in a case he shall not sit.

Hebrew law presents no parallel to this.

Against Theft

§ 6. If a man steals the goods of a god (temple) or of a palace, that man shall be put to death, and he by whose hand the stolen goods were received shall be put to death.

§ 7. If a man purchases or receives on deposit either silver, gold, man-servant, maid-servant, ox, sheep, ass, or anything whatever from the hand of a minor or a slave without witnesses or contracts, that man is a thief; he shall be put to death.

§ 8. If a man has stolen ox, or sheep, or ass, or pig, or a boat, either from a god (temple) or a palace, he shall pay thirtyfold. If he is a poor man, he shall restore tenfold. If the thief has nothing to pay, he shall be put to death.

§ 9. If a man, who has lost anything, finds that which was lost in a man's hand, (and) the man in whose hand the lost thing was found says: "A seller sold it; I bought it before witnesses"; and the owner of the lost thing says: "I will bring witnesses who know that the lost thing is mine"; if the purchaser brings the seller who sold it to him and the witnesses in whose presence it was bought, and the owner of the lost thing brings the witnesses who know that the lost thing is his, the judges shall examine their testimony. The witnesses before whom the purchaser purchased it, and the witnesses who know the lost thing, shall give their testimony in the presence of a god. The seller is a thief; he shall be put to death. The owner of the lost thing shall take that which was lost. The purchaser shall take from the house of the seller the money which he had paid.

§ 10. If the purchaser does not produce the seller who sold it to him and the witnesses before whom he bought it, and the owner of the lost thing produces the witnesses who know that the lost thing is his, the purchaser is the thief; he shall be put to death. The owner of the lost thing shall take that which he lost.

§ 11. If the owner of the lost thing does not bring the witnesses who know that the lost thing is his, he is one who has attempted fraud; he shall be put to death.

§ 12. If the seller has died, the purchaser shall recover from the house of the seller the damages of that case fivefold.

§ 13. If that man has not his witnesses near, the judges shall set an appointed time within six months; and if, within six months, his witnesses he does not produce, that man is a liar; the penalty of that case he shall himself bear.

The Hebrew laws comparable to these are found in Exodus 22: 1–4, 9, and Leviticus 6: 3–5. Exodus directs (v. 1) that, if a man steals an ox or a sheep and kills it or sells it, he shall restore five oxen for an ox and four sheep for a sheep. In case it is not sold he shall restore double (v. 9). No highly organized courts appear in the Biblical codes. The thief was brought before God and his guilt determined by some religious test. The law of Leviticus required a man guilty of theft to restore the lost property, adding to it a fifth more, and to offer a ram in sacrifice. (See Exod. 18: 13–26. Cf. 2 Chron. 19: 5–7 with 1 Chron. 23: 4 and Deut. 16: 18–20.)

The Babylonian laws presuppose a much more highly organized social community than the Hebrew.

Against Stealing Children and Slaves

§ 14. If a man steals the son of a man who is a minor, he shall be put to death.

§ 15. If a man causes a male or female slave of a palace, or the male or female slave of a workingman to escape from the city gate, he shall be put to death.

§ 16. If a man harbors in his house either a male or a female slave who has escaped from a palace or from a workingman, and does not bring him out at the summons of the officer, the owner of that house shall be put to death.

§ 17. If a man finds in a field a male or a female slave who has escaped and restores him to his owner, the owner of the slave shall pay him 2 shekels of silver.

§ 18. If that slave will not name his owner, he shall bring him unto the palace and they shall investigate his record and restore him unto his owner.

§ 19. If he shall detain that slave in his house and afterward the slave is found, that man shall be put to death.

§ 20. If the slave escapes from the hand of his captor, that man shall declare it on oath to the owner of the slave and shall be innocent.

These laws are analogous to Exodus 21 : 16 and Deuteronomy 23 : 15. The former inflicts the death penalty for stealing a man and selling him, and the latter prohibits one in whose house a fugitive slave has taken refuge from returning the slave to his master. Slavery was not in Israel such a firmly established institution as in Babylonia. (See Exod. 21 : 2–6; Deut. 15 : 12–18; Lev. 25 : 25–46.)

Housebreaking and Brigandage

§ 21. If a man breaks into a house, before that breach he shall be put to death and thrown into it.

§ 22. If a man practices brigandage and is caught, that man shall be put to death.

§ 23. If the robber is not caught, the man who is robbed shall declare his loss, whatever it is, in the presence of a god, and the city and governor in whose territory and jurisdiction the robbery was committed shall compensate him for whatever was lost.

§ 24. If it is a life, that city and governor shall pay to his relatives 1 mana of silver.[2]

Hebrew law presents an analogy to the last of these sections in Deuteronomy 21 : 1–9, though in Israel no compensation was offered to the heirs of the man who was slain, but a sacrifice was performed by the elders of the nearest city, to purge it of innocent blood.

Stealing at a Fire

§ 25. If a fire breaks out in a man's house, and a man who has come to extinguish it shall cast his eye upon the furniture of the owner of the house, and the furniture of the owner of the house shall take, that man shall be thrown into that fire.

[2] The mana consisted of sixty shekels. In English it is corrupted to *mina*.

The Duties and Privileges of Soldiers, Constables, and Tax-collectors

§ 26. If a soldier or a constable [3] who is ordered to go on a journey for the king does not go, but hires a substitute and dispatches him instead, that soldier or constable shall be put to death; his hired substitute shall appropriate his house.

§ 27. If a soldier or a constable is detained in a royal fortress and after him they give his field or garden to another and he takes it and carries it on, if the first one returns and reaches his city, they shall restore to him his field and garden, and he shall take it and carry it on.

§ 28. If a soldier or a constable who is detained in a royal fortress has a son who is able to carry on his business, they shall give to him his field and garden and he shall carry on the business of his father.

§ 29. If his son is small and not able to carry on the business of his father, they shall give one-third of his field and garden to his mother and she shall rear him.

§ 30. If a soldier or a constable from the beginning of his appointment neglects his field, garden, and house and leaves them uncared for, another after him shall take his field, garden, and house, and carry on his business for three years. If he returns and desires his field, garden, and house, they shall not give them to him. He who has taken them and carried on the business shall carry it on.

§ 31. If he leaves it uncared for but one year and returns, they shall give him his field, garden, and house, and he shall carry on his own business.

§ 32. If a merchant ransoms a soldier (?) or a constable who, on a journey of the king, was detained, and brings him back to his city, if in his house there is sufficient ransom, he shall ransom himself. If in his house there is not sufficient to ransom him, by the temple of his city he shall be ransomed. If in the temple of his city there is not a sufficient ransom, he shall be ransomed by the palace. His field, garden, and house shall not be given for ransom.

§ 33. If a governor or a magistrate harbors a deserting soldier or accepts and sends a hired substitute on an errand of the king, that governor or magistrate shall be put to death.

§ 34. If a governor or a magistrate takes the property of a soldier, plunders a soldier, or hires out a soldier, has defrauded a soldier in a suit before a sheik, or takes the present which the king has given to a soldier, that governor or magistrate shall be put to death.

§ 35. If a man buys the cattle or sheep which the king has given to a soldier, he shall forfeit his money.

§ 36. One shall not sell the field, garden, or house of a soldier, constable, or tax-collector.

§ 37. If a man has bought the field, garden, or house of a soldier, constable, or tax-collector, his tablet shall be broken, he shall forfeit his money; the field, house, or garden shall return to its owner.

§ 38. A soldier, constable, or tax-collector shall not deed to his wife or daughter the field, house, or garden, which is his perquisite, nor shall he assign them for debt.

§ 39. A field, garden, or house which he has purchased and possesses he may deed to his wife or daughter, or may assign for debt.

§ 40. A priestess, merchant, or other creditor may purchase his field, garden, or house. The purchaser shall conduct the business of the field, garden, or house which he has purchased.

---

3 The nature of these officials is in doubt. Scheil and others think the first a recruiting-officer; Delitzsch and Ungnad, a soldier. The name of the second officer is literally fish-catcher, but it is certain that here he was some kind of a fisher of men.

§ 41.   If a man has bargained for the field, garden, or house of a soldier, constable, or tax-collector and has given sureties, the soldier, constable, or tax-collector shall return to the field, house, or garden, and the sureties which were given him he shall keep.

No such officers as these are mentioned in the laws of the Old Testament, though some of them appear in earlier times in the records of Babylonia.   The tax-collectors mentioned here remind us of Solomon's tax-collectors mentioned in 1 Kings 4 : 7, ff.

Laws of Agriculture

§ 42.   If a man rents a field for cultivation and produces no grain in that field, they shall call him to account for doing no work in that field, and he shall give to the owner of the field grain similar to that of adjacent fields.

§ 43.   If he does not cultivate that field and neglects it, he shall give the owner of the field grain similar to that of adjacent fields, and the field which he neglected he shall break up with mattocks, he shall harrow, and return it to the owner of the field.

§ 44.   If a man rents an uncultivated field for three years for improvement and neglects its surface and does not develop the field, in the fourth year he shall break up the field with mattocks, he shall hoe and harrow it, and return it unto the owner of the field, and for every *Gan* of land he shall measure out 10 *Gur* of grain.

§ 45.   If a man lets his field for pay on shares to a farmer and receives his rent, and afterward the storm-god inundates the field and carries off the produce, the loss is the farmer's.

§ 46.   If the rent of his field he has not received, and he has let the field for one-half or one-third (of the crop), the farmer and the owner of the field shall divide the grain which is in the field according to agreement.

§ 47.   If the farmer, because he has not in a former year received a maintenance, entrusts the field to another farmer, the owner of the field shall not interfere.   He would cultivate it, and his field has been cultivated.   At the time of harvest he shall take grain according to his contracts.

§ 48.   If a man has a debt against him and the storm-god inundates his field and carries away the produce, or if through lack of water grain has not grown in the field, in that year he shall not make a return of grain to his creditor; his contract he shall change, and the interest of that year he shall not pay.

§ 49.   If a man borrows money from a merchant, and has given to the merchant a field planted with grain or sesame, and says to him: "Cultivate the field and harvest and take the grain or sesame which it produces"; if the tenant produces grain or sesame in the field, at the time of harvest the owner of the field shall take the grain or sesame which was produced by the field, and shall give to the merchant grain for the money which he borrowed from the merchant with its interest, and for the maintenance of the farmer.

§ 50.   If the field was already planted [with grain or] sesame, the owner of the field shall receive the grain or the sesame which is produced in the field, and the money and its interest he shall return to the merchant.

§ 51.   If there is not money to return, he shall give to the merchant [the grain or] sesame for the money and ist interest which he had received from the merchant, according to the scale of prices fixed by the king.

§ 52.   If the farmer does not produce grain or sesame in his field, he shall not alter his contract.

§ 53. If a man the side of his strong dyke has neglected and has not strengthened it, and in his dyke a break occurs, and the water destroys the farm-land, the man in whose dyke the break occurred shall restore the grain which was destroyed.

§ 54. If he is not able to restore the grain, they shall sell him and his possessions for money, and the owners of the fields whose grain was destroyed shall share it.

§ 55. If a man has opened his sluice for watering and has left it open and the water destroys the field of his neighbor, he shall measure out grain to him on the basis of that produced by neighboring fields.

§ 56. If a man opens the water and the water destroys the work[4] of a neighboring field, he shall measure out 10 *Gur* of grain for each *Bur* of land.

§ 57. If a shepherd causes his sheep to eat vegetation and has not made an agreement with the owner of the field, and without the consent of the owner of the field has pastured his sheep, the owner of the field shall harvest that field, and the shepherd who without the consent of the owner of the field caused his sheep to eat the field, shall pay the owner of the field in addition 20 *Gur* of grain for each *Bur* of land.

§ 58. If, after the sheep have come up out of the fields and are turned loose on the public common by the city gate, a shepherd turns his sheep into a field and causes the sheep to eat the field, the shepherd shall oversee the field which he caused to be eaten, and at harvest-time he shall measure to the owner of the field 60 *Gur* of grain for each *Bur* of land.

The Hebrew land laws are found in Exodus 22: 5, 6; 23: 10, 11; Leviticus 19: 9, and Deuteronomy 24: 19–22; 23: 24, 25. An examination of these passages reveals a wide difference between Babylonia and Israel. In Babylonia it seems to have often been the rule that a landlord let out the fields to tenants to work; among the Hebrews the law presupposes that each man shall work his own land. Many of the Babylonian laws are designed to secure the respective rights of landlord and tenant. Naturally, there is nothing in the Old Testament to correspond to these. Hebrew law (Exod. 22: 5), like the Babylonian, provides that one who causes a neighbor's crop to be eaten shall make restitution, but the regulations are of the most general character. In Babylonia a larger social experience had made much more specific regulations necessary.

The characters of the respective countries are reflected in the dangers from which crops might be threatened. In waterless Palestine a fire started by a careless man might burn his neighbor's crop (Exod. 22: 6); in Babylonia, where irrigation from canals was conducted to fields lower than the surface of the water, one might flood his neighbor's field and destroy his crop by carelessly leaving his sluice open.

---

[4] Such as plowing, or the young plants early in the season.

The Hebrew legislation presupposes a poorer community. It provides that the land shall lie fallow, and whatever it produces shall belong to the poor (Exod. 23:10, 11). At harvest-time, too, one must not reap the corners of his field; that was left to the poor (Lev. 19:9). If one forgot a sheaf in his field, he must not return to take it; that should be left to the poor (Deut. 24:19). Rich Babylonia made no such provision for the poor; it felt no such social sympathy.

Again, even these agricultural laws show that commerce was highly developed in Babylonia, with its necessary concomitant, the right to charge interest for money. The uncommercial Hebrews regarded interest as unlawful (Exod. 22:25), and it was Hillel, the contemporary of Herod the Great, who invented an interpretation known as the Prosbūl, which practically did away with this law and permitted Jews to take interest.

Horticultural Laws

§ 59. If a man shall cut down a tree in a man's orchard without the consent of the owner, he shall pay ½ mana of silver.

§ 60. If a man gives a field to a gardener to plant as an orchard, the gardener shall plant the orchard and cultivate it for 4 years. In the fifth year the owner of the orchard and the gardener shall share it together. The owner of the orchard shall mark off his share and take it.

§ 61. If the gardener in planting does not complete it, but leaves a part of it waste, unto his portion they shall count it.

§ 62. If the field which is given to a gardener he does not plant, if vegetation is the produce of the field for the years during which it is neglected, the gardener shall measure out to the owner of the field on the basis of the adjacent fields, and shall perform the work on the field and restore it to the owner of the field.

§ 63. If the field is [left] waste land, he shall perform the work on the field and shall restore it to its owner, and 10 *Gur* of grain for each *Bur* of land he shall measure out.

§ 64. If a man lets his orchard to a gardener to manage, as long as the gardener is in possession of the garden he shall give to the owner of the garden two-thirds of the produce; one-third he shall take himself.

§ 65. If the gardener does not manage the garden and diminishes its produce, the gardener shall measure out the produce of the orchard on the basis of adjacent orchards.[5]

§ 66. If a man has received money from a merchant, and his merchant puts him under bonds and he has nothing to give, and he gives his orchard for management unto the merchant and says: "The dates as many as are in my orchard take for thy money," that merchant shall not consent; the owner of the orchard shall take the dates that are in the orchard and the money and its interest according to the tenor of his agreement he shall bring to the merchant. The remaining dates from the orchard shall belong to the owner of the orchard.

5 At this point five columns of the pillar are erased. It is estimated that 35 sections of the laws are thus lost. § 66 is added from a fragment found at Susa.

As in Palestine, there was no system of rental; the Bible contains almost no horticultural laws. "Orchards" in Babylonia were, as the last section shows, date orchards. The corresponding fruit in Palestine was the grape. Hebrew laws deal with vineyards as with fields. If a man destroys the crop in another's vineyard, he is to give the best of his own (Exod. 22: 5). He is to leave his crop unpicked every seventh year for the poor (Exod. 23: 11). He is not, when he gathers it, to glean it carefully, but leave some for the poor (Lev. 19: 10). When one goes into his neighbor's vineyard, he may pick what he wishes to eat, but must carry nothing away. Horticulture among the Hebrews was not so highly developed as in Babylonia.

Five columns of writing have been erased after § 65 from the column on which the laws are written. This erasure was probably made by the Elamite conqueror, who carried the column as a trophy to Susa, in order to inscribe his own name on it, but unfortunately, if that was the intention, it was never carried out. We are accordingly in ignorance of his name. 'It is estimated that 35 sections of laws were thus lost. As already noted, one can be supplied from a fragment found at Susa, and from other tablets fragments of two or three other sections can be made out. One of these incomplete fragments refers to the rights of tenants of houses. It reads:

[If] a man rents a house for money, and pays the whole rent for a year to the owner of the house, and the owner of the house orders that man to vacate before the expiration of his lease, the owner of the house from the money that he received shall...........

Unfortunately, the tablet is broken and the penalty for breaking the lease is unknown. It is interesting to know that Babylonian tenants were protected from avaricious landlords, even though no parallel law exists in the Old Testament.

Two other sections of laws that once stood in this lacuna can now be supplied from a considerably defaced tablet from Nippur in the University of Pennsylvania Museum in Philadelphia, which once contained a part or all of the code of Hammurabi. These sections are as follows:

A Bankrupt Law [6]

If a man borrows grain or money from a merchant and for the payment has no grain or money, whatever is in his hand he shall in the presence of the elders give to the merchant in place of the debt; the merchant shall not refuse it; he shall receive it.

[6] Translated from Poebel, *Historical and Grammatical Texts,* Philadelphia, 1914, No. 93, col. ii.

A Partnership Law [7]

If a man gives money to a man for a partnership, the gain and profit that accrue are before the gods; together they shall do business.

The phrase "before the gods" means that the division shall be made on oath. Commercial life was not sufficiently developed among the Hebrews so that they needed such a law, consequently the Pentateuch contains no parallel to this.

After the erasure of five columns the laws have to do with agents or traveling salesmen.

Agents and Merchants

§ 100. [If an agent has received money from a merchant, he shall write down the amount and the amount of] the interest on the money, and, when the time has expired, he shall repay the merchant as much as he has received.

§ 101. If where he goes he does not meet with success, the agent shall double the amount of the money he received and return it to the merchant.

§ 102. If a merchant gives money to an agent as a favor, and where he goes he meets with misfortune, he shall restore the principal unto the merchant.

§ 103. If on the road as he travels an enemy robs him of anything he carries, the agent shall give an account of it under oath and shall be innocent.

§ 104. If a merchant has given to an agent grain, wool, or oil, or anything whatever to sell, the agent shall write down the price and shall return the money to the merchant. The agent shall take a receipt for the money which he gives to the merchant.

§ 105. If the agent is careless and does not take a receipt for the money he gave the merchant, money not receipted for shall not be placed to his account.

§ 106. If an agent receives money from a merchant and has a dispute with his merchant about it, that merchant shall put the agent on trial on oath before the elders concerning the money he received and the agent shall pay the merchant three times as much as he received.

§ 107. If a merchant lends to an agent and the agent returns to the merchant whatever the merchant had given him, if the merchant has a dispute with him about it, that agent shall put the merchant on trial on oath in the presence of the elders, and the merchant, because he had a dispute with his agent, whatever he received he shall give to the agent six times as much.

The Hebrews of the Old Testament time were not a commercial people and had no such laws. Men today are inclined to think that the drummer, or traveling salesman, is a modern invention, but these laws show that he was an old institution in Babylonia four thousand years ago.

Wine Merchants

§ 108. If a woman who keeps a wine-shop does not receive grain as the price of drink, but takes money of greater value, or makes the measure of drink smaller than the measure of grain, that mistress of a wine-shop they shall put on trial and into the water shall throw her.

7 Translated from *ibid.*, col. iii.

§ 109. If the mistress of a wine-shop collects criminals in her house, and does not seize these criminals and conduct them to the palace, that mistress of a wine-shop shall be put to death.

§ 110. If the wife of a god (*i. e.,* a consecrated temple-woman), who is not living in the house appointed, opens a wine-shop or enters a wine-shop for a drink, they shall burn that woman.

§ 111. If the mistress of a wine-shop gives 60 *Qa* of *sakani*-plant drink on credit at the time of harvest, she shall receive 50 *Qa* of grain.

The Old Testament affords no parallel. There were no wine-shops in Israel so far as we know, and such consecrated women were prohibited by Deuteronomy 23 : 17.

Deposits and Distraints

§ 112. If a man continually traveling has given silver, gold, precious stones, or property to a man and has brought them to him for transportation, and that man does not deliver that which was for transportation at the place to which it was to be transported, but has appropriated it, the owner of the transported goods shall put that man on trial concerning that which was to be transported and was not delivered, and that man shall deliver unto the owner of the transported goods five times as much as was entrusted to him.

§ 113. If a man has grain or money deposited with a man and without the consent of the owner he takes grain from the heap or the granary, they shall prosecute that man because he took grain from the heap or the granary without the consent of the owner, and the grain as much as he took he shall return, and whatever it was he shall forfeit an equal amount.

§ 114. If a man does not have against a man [a claim] for grain or money and secures a warrant against him for debt, for each warrant he shall pay ⅓ of a mana of money.

§ 115. If a man holds against a man [a claim] for grain or money and secures a warrant against him for debt and the debtor dies through his fate in the house of the creditor, that case has no penalty.

§ 116. If the debtor dies through violence or lack of care, the owner of the debtor shall prosecute the merchant; if it was the son of a man, his son shall be put to death; if the slave of a man, he shall pay ⅓ of a mana of money, and whatever [the debt] was, he shall forfeit as much.

Among the Hebrews, as among other ancient peoples, the poor at times deposited their valuables with the more powerful for safe-keeping. This was natural before the invention of banks and safe deposit vaults.

The Hebrew law in Exodus 22 : 7–11 provides that if goods are given to another man to keep and are stolen out of his house, the thief should, if found, restore double the amount taken. If the thief was not found, the owner of the house should be brought to God (so American R. V.),[8] *i.e.,* to the temple, where in some way (probably by lot) it was determined whether he was guilty. If guilty, the owner of the house had to restore twofold.

8 The translation, "be brought to the judges," has no warrant in the Hebrew.

Somewhat parallel to the Babylonia laws which permit the imprisonment of a debtor in one's house is the Hebrew law that a poor debtor might become a slave for six years (Exod. 21 : 2–6; Deut. 15 :7 –18). The Old Testament laws are not quite uniform. In reality it is only that of Deuteronomy which contemplates slavery in consequence of indebtedness; Exodus speaks as though the slave might not be bought in any way. The important point is that in Babylonia a man might be imprisoned for debt; in Israel he might become a temporary slave.

As to the deposit of valuable property with a creditor for security, the Hebrew law, while it shows that there were other kinds of pledges (Deut. 24 : 10, ff.), mentions but one kind. This was in the case of a man so poor that he had to give his outer garment as security. The law provided that this should be returned to him at night, since the poor peasants had no other blankets than these garments. A hard-hearted creditor might, by keeping the garment at night, risk the life of the debtor (Exod. 22 : 26, 27; Deut. 25 : 11–13).

Debts

§ 117. If a man is subjected to an attachment for debt and sells his wife, son, or daughter, or they are given over to service, for three years they shall work in the house of their purchaser or temporary master; in the fourth year they shall be set free.

§ 118. If he binds to service a male or a female slave, and the merchant transfers or sells him, he can establish no claim.

§ 119. If a man is subjected to an attachment for debt and sells a maid-servant who has borne him children, the owner of the maid-servant shall pay and shall release his maid-servant.

These laws are quite similar to Exodus 21 : 2–11 and Deuteronomy 15 : 12–18.

The main differences are that the Hebrew law contemplates that a man may enter slavery himself; the Babylonian only that he shall permit his wife, son, or daughter to do it. The Hebrews released such slaves at the end of six years; [9] the Babylonians at the end of three. Hebrew law recognized, too, that a man might sell his daughter into slavery (Exod. 21 : 7–11), but it stipulated that her treatment should be different from that of men. It recognizes that either her master or his son would be likely to make her a real or a secondary wife. She was not to be released at the end of seven

9 Since Deuteronomy 15: 18 says that such a slave has served "double the hire of a hireling," Dr. Johns thinks that it betrays a knowledge of the Babylonian three-year regulation. This seems, however, quite problematical.

years, but in case her master did not deal with her in certain specified ways she regained her freedom regardless of her period of
service.

Storage of Grain

§ 120. If a man has stored his grain in heaps in the building of another and
an accident happens in the granary, or the owner of the building has disturbed
the heap and taken grain, or has disputed the amount of grain that was stored
in his building, the owner of the grain shall give an account of his grain under
oath, the owner of the building shall double the amount of grain which he
took and restore it to the owner of the grain.

§ 121. If a man stores grain in a man's building, he shall pay each year
5 Qa of grain for each Gur of grain.

These laws have no Biblical parallel.

Deposits and Losses

§ 122. If a man gives to another on deposit silver or gold or anything
whatever, anything as much as he deposits he shall recount to witnesses and
shall institute contracts and make the deposit.

§ 123. If without witnesses and contracts he has placed anything on deposit
and at the place of deposit they dispute it, that case has no penalty.

§ 124. If a man gives to another on deposit silver or gold or anything whatever in the presence of witnesses and he disputes it, he shall prosecute that
man and he shall double whatever he disputed and shall repay it.

§ 125. If a man places anything on deposit and at the place of deposit either
through burglary or pillage anything of his is lost, together with anything belonging to the owner of the building, the owner of the building who was
negligent and lost what was given him on deposit shall make it good and
restore it to the owner of the goods. The owner of the house shall institute
a search for whatever was lost and take it from the thief.

§ 126. If a man has not lost anything, but says he has lost something, or
files a claim as though he had lost something, he shall give account of his
claim on oath, and whatever he brought suit for he shall double and shall
give for his claim.

There is no mention in the laws of the Old Testament of this
kind of deposit, though, as already noted, it probably was sometimes practised.

Against Slandering Women

§ 127. If a man causes the finger to be pointed at the woman of a god or
the wife of a man and cannot prove it, they shall bring him before the judges
and they shall brand his forehead.

The nearest parallel to this in the Old Testament is in Deuteronomy 22: 13–21, which is really quite a different law, for it applies
only to cases where men, when just married, slander their wives by

charging them with previous impurity. The Hebrew law provides a method of trial, a punishment for the man, if guilty, and a much severer one for the woman, if the charge is true. The two codes belong to quite a different legal development, as is shown by the fact that the Babylonian law refers to "a woman of a god," *i.e.*, one of the temple-women who, under certain religious rules, represented in a concrete way the procreative power of the god.

This code recognizes several classes of these, as will appear later, but Hebrew law forbade the existence of such women in Israel (Deut. 23:17).

Chastity, Marriage, and Divorce

§ 128. If a man takes a wife and does not execute contracts for her, that woman is no wife.

§ 129. If the wife of a man is caught lying with another man, they shall bind them and throw them into the water. If the husband of the woman would let her live, or the king would let his subject live, he may do so.

§ 130. If a man forces the betrothed wife of another who is living in her father's house and has not known a man, and lies in her loins and they catch him, that man shall be put to death and that woman shall go free.

§ 131. If the wife of a man is accused by her husband, and she has not been caught lying with another man, she shall swear her innocence and return to her house.

§ 132. If the finger has been pointed at the wife of a man because of another man and she has not been caught lying with the other man, for her husband's sake she shall plunge into the sacred river.

§ 133. If a man is taken captive and there is food in his house, his wife shall not go out from his house, her body she shall guard, into the house of another she shall not enter. If that woman does not guard her body and enters into the house of another, that woman they shall prosecute and throw her into the water.

§ 134. If a man is taken captive and in his house there is no food, and his wife enters into the house of another, that woman is not to blame.

§ 135. If a man is taken captive and there is no food in his house and his wife has openly entered into the house of another and borne children, and afterwards her husband returns and reaches his city, that woman shall return to her husband and the children shall follow their father.

§ 136. If a man deserts his city and flees and after it his wife enters into the house of another, if that man returns and would take his wife, because he deserted his city and fled, the wife of the fugitive shall not return to the house of her husband.

§ 137. If a man sets his face against a concubine who has borne him children or a wife that has presented him with children, to put her away, he shall return to that woman her marriage portion, and shall give her the income of field, garden, and house, and she shall bring up her children. From the time that her children are grown, from whatever is given to her children, a portion like that of a son shall be given to her, and the husband of her choice she may marry.

§ 138. If a man would put away his spouse who has not borne him children, he shall give her silver equal to her marriage gift, and the dowry which she brought from her father's house he shall restore to her and may put her away.

§ 139. If she had no dowry, he shall give her one mana of silver for a divorce.

§ 140. If he belongs to the laboring class, he shall give her one-third of a mana of silver.

§ 141. If the wife of a man who is living in the house of her husband sets her face to go out and act the fool, her house neglects and her husband belittles, they shall prosecute that woman. If her husband says: "I divorce her," he may divorce her. On her departure nothing shall be given her for her divorce. If her husband does not say: "I divorce her," her husband may take another wife; that woman shall dwell as a slave in the house of her husband.

§ 142. If a woman hates her husband and says: "Thou shalt not hold me," they shall make investigation concerning her into her defects. If she has been discreet and there is no fault, and her husband has gone out and greatly belittled her, that woman has no blame; she may take her marriage-portion and go to her father's house.

§ 143. If she has not been discreet, and has gone out and neglected her house and belittled her husband, they shall throw that woman into the water.

§ 144. If a man takes a priestess and that priestess gives a female slave to her husband, and she has children; if that man sets his face to take a concubine, they shall not favor that man. He may not take a concubine.

§ 145. If a man takes a priestess and she does not present him with children and he sets his face to take a concubine, that man may take a concubine and bring her into his house. That concubine shall not rank with the wife.

§ 146. If a man takes a priestess and she gives to her husband a maid-servant and she bears children, and afterward that maid-servant would take rank with her mistress; because she has borne children her mistress may not sell her for money, but she may reduce her to bondage and count her among the female slaves.

§ 147. If she has not borne children, her mistress may sell her for money.

§ 148. If a man takes a wife and she is attacked by disease, and he sets his face to take another, he may do it. His wife who was attacked by disease he may not divorce. She shall live in the house he has built and he shall support her as long as she lives.

§ 149. If that woman does not choose to live in the house of her husband, he shall make good to her the dowry which she brought from her father's house and she may go away.

§ 150. If a man presents his wife with field, garden, house, or goods, and gives to her sealed deeds, after her husband's death her children shall not press a claim against her. The mother after her death may leave it to her child whom she loves, but to a brother she may not leave it.

§ 151. If a wife who is living in the house of a husband has persuaded her husband and he has bound himself that she shall not be taken by a creditor of her husband; if that man had a debt against him before he took that woman, the creditor may not hold that woman, and if that woman had a debt against her before she entered the house of her husband, her creditor may not hold her husband.

§ 152. If they become indebted after the woman enters the man's house, both of them are liable to the merchant.

§ 153. If a woman causes the death of her husband on account of another man, that woman they shall impale.

§ 154. If a man has known his daughter, the city shall drive out that man.

§ 155. If a man has betrothed a bride to his son and his son has known her and he afterward lies in her loins and they catch him, they shall bind that man and throw him into the water.

§ 156. If a man has betrothed a bride to his son and his son has not known her and he lies in her loins, he shall pay her half a mana of silver and restore to her whatever she brought from the house of her father, and the man of her choice may marry her.

§ 157. If a man after his father's death lies in the loins of his mother, they shall burn both of them.

§ 158. If a man after his father's death is admitted to the loins of his chief wife who has borne children, that man shall be expelled from the house of his father.

§ 159. If a man who has brought a present unto the house of his father-in-law and has given a bride-price looks with longing upon another woman, and says to his father-in-law: "Thy daughter I will not take," the father of the daughter shall keep whatever was brought to him.

§ 160. If a man brings a present to the house of a father-in-law and gives a bride-price, and the father of the daughter says: "I will not give thee my daughter," whatever was brought him he shall double and restore it.

§ 161. If a man brings a present to the house of his father-in-law and gives a bride-price, and his neighbor slanders him, and the father says to the groom: "Thou shalt not take my daughter," whatever was brought he shall double and restore to him.

These Babylonian laws present numerous points of contact and of divergence, when compared with the Biblical laws on the same subject. There is no Biblical parallel to § 128. The law (§ 129) which imposes the death penalty upon a man who commits adultery with another man's wife and upon the woman, finds an exact parallel in Leviticus 20: 10 and Deuteronomy 22: 22, though the Biblical law, unlike the Babylonian, provides no way in which clemency could be extended to the offenders.

The laws in §§ 130, 156, concerning the violation of betrothed virgins, are in a general way paralleled by Leviticus 19: 20–22 and Deuteronomy 22: 23–26, though there are such differences that, while the underlying principles are the same, it is clear that there was entire independence of development. A religious element enters into Leviticus that is entirely absent from the Babylonian code. The Bible contains two laws on this subject that are without parallel in the Babylonian code. These are found in Exodus 22: 16, 17 and Deuteronomy 22: 28, 29, and impose penalties for the violation of virgins who were not betrothed. In both codes the principle is manifest that the loss of a girl's honor was to be compensated by money, though Deuteronomy 22: 28, 29 recognizes that it has a value that money cannot buy.

The laws relating to a wife whose fidelity is suspected (§§ 131, 132) find a general parallel in Numbers 5: 11–28. The provision at the end of § 132 that the wife should plunge into the sacred river is in the nature of trial by ordeal. The law in Numbers imposes on such a woman trial by ordeal, though it is of a different sort. She must drink water in which dust from the floor of the sanctuary is mingled—dust surcharged with divine potency—and if she does not swell up and die, she is counted innocent.

The laws which provide that a wife may present her husband with a slave-girl as a concubine (§§ 137, 144–147) are without parallel in the Biblical codes, but are strikingly illustrated by the patriarchal narratives. Sarah gave Hagar to Abraham (Gen. 16) ; Rachel and Leah gave Bilhah and Zilpah to Jacob (Gen. 30: 1–13). The law (§ 146) which deals with such a slave-girl who would rank with her mistress is closely parallel to the story of the treatment of Hagar in Genesis 16: 5–7 and 21: 9, 10.

The laws on divorce (§§ 138–141) are really in advance of the one Biblical law on the subject (Deut. 24:1–4). The law in Deuteronomy permits a husband to put away a wife, who in any way does not please him, without alimony, while to the wife no privilege of initiating divorce proceedings is granted at all. The Babylonian laws secure to the divorced woman a maintenance, and, while by no means according her equal rights with the man, provide (§ 142) that she may herself initiate the proceedings for divorce. The ordeal must have been an unpleasant one, but in Israel's law a woman had no such rights.[10]

The law concerning adultery with a daughter-in-law (§ 155) is identical in purpose and severity with Leviticus 20: 12. The laws in §§ 157, 158, which prohibit immorality with one's mother or the chief wife of one's father, just touch upon the great subject of incest and the prohibited degrees of marriage which are treated at considerable length in Leviticus 18:6–18; 20: 11, 19–21, and Deuteronomy 22: 30. The Babylonian laws touch but two specific cases, which may be said to be covered by Deuteronomy 22: 30, while the laws of Leviticus treat the whole subject of the prohibited degrees of marriage in a broad and comprehensive way. The main idea pervading Leviticus is holiness. Israel is to be kept free from the

---

10 In a marriage contract on a papyrus from the Jewish colony at Elephantine in Egypt, written in the fifth century B.C., it is provided that the wife may institute divorce proceedings on an equality with the husband. Some Jewish women thus secured by contract that which the law did not grant them. Christ assumed such cases among Palestinian women; see Mark 10: 12.

pollution of incest in any form. The religious motive exhibited here is foreign to the Babylonian code.

Inheritance

§ 162. If a man takes a wife and she bears him children and that woman dies, her father may not lay claim to her dowry. Her dowry belongs to her children.

§ 163. If a man takes a wife and she does not present him with children and that woman dies; if his father-in-law returns unto him the marriage-settlement, which that man brought to the house of the father-in-law, unto the dowry of that woman her husband may not lay claim. Her dowry belongs to the house of her father.

§ 164. But if his father-in-law does not return the marriage-settlement unto him, he shall deduct from her dowry the amount of the marriage-settlement, and then return the dowry to the house of her father.

§ 165. If a man has presented to his son, the first in his eyes, field, garden, or house, and written for him a sealed deed, and afterward the father dies; when the brothers divide, he shall take the present which his father gave him, and over and above they shall divide the goods of the father's house equally.

§ 166. If a man takes wives for the sons which he possesses, but has not taken a wife for his youngest son, and afterward the father dies; when the brothers divide, for their younger brother who does not have a wife they shall present over and above his portion money for a marriage-settlement, and shall enable him to take a wife.

§ 167. If a man takes a wife and she bears him children and that woman dies, and after her he takes a second and she bears him children, after the father dies, the children shall not share according to their mothers. They shall receive the dowries of their respective mothers, and the goods of their father's house they shall share equally.

§ 168. If a man has set his face to cut off his son, and says to the judges: "I will cut off my son," the judges shall make investigation concerning him; if the son has not committed a grave crime which cuts off from sonship, the father may not cut off his son from sonship.

§ 169. If he has committed against his father a grave crime which cuts off from sonship, he shall pardon him for the first offense. If he commits a grave crime the second time, the father may cut off his son from sonship.

§ 170. If a man's wife bears him children and a slave-girl bears him children, and the father during his lifetime says to the children which the slave-girl bore him: "My children," and counts them with the children of the wife, after the father dies the children of the wife and the children of the slave-girl shall divide equally the goods of their father's house. The sons that are sons of the wife shall at the sharing divide and take.

§ 171. But if the father during his lifetime has not said unto the children which the slave-girl bore him: "My children," after the father dies the children of the slave-girl shall not share with the children of the wife. The slave-girl and her children shall be given their freedom; the children of the wife may not put a claim upon the children of the slave-girl for service. The wife shall receive her dowry and a gift which her husband gave her and wrote upon a tablet and may dwell in the dwelling of her husband as long as she lives and eat. She may not sell it. After her it belongs to her children.

§ 172. If her husband has not given her a gift, they shall restore to her her dowry and she shall receive from the goods of the house of her husband the portion of one son. If the children abuse her in order to drive her from the house, the judges shall investigate concerning her and if they find the children in the wrong, that woman shall not go from the house of her husband. If that woman sets her face to go out, she shall leave with her children the gift which her husband gave her; the dowry from the house of her father she shall receive and the husband of her choice may take her.

§ 173. If that woman, where she has entered, bears children to her later husband, after that woman dies the children of her first and her later husband shall share her dowry.

§ 174. If she did not bear children to her later husband, the children of her first husband shall receive her dowry.

§ 175. If a slave of the palace or the slave of a workingman takes the daughter of a patrician and she bears children, the owner of the slave shall have no claim for service on the children of the daughter of a patrician.

§ 176. But if a slave of the palace or the slave of a workingman takes the daughter of a patrician, and when he takes her she enters together with the dowry from her father's house into the house of the slave of the palace or the slave of the workingman; if after they are united they build a house and acquire property and afterward the slave of the palace or the slave of the workingman dies, the daughter of the patrician shall receive her dowry and they shall divide into two parts whatever her husband and herself had acquired after their union. Half the owner of the slave shall take, and the daughter of the patrician shall receive half for her children. If the daughter of the patrician had no dowry, whatever her husband and herself had acquired after their union they shall divide into two parts. The owner of the slave shall take half and the daughter of the patrician shall receive half for her children.

§ 177. If a widow whose children are minors sets her face to enter the house of a second husband, she shall not do it without the consent of the judges. When she enters the house of a second husband, the judges shall inquire into the estate of her former husband, and the estate of the former husband they shall entrust to the second husband and to that woman, and shall cause them to leave a tablet (receipt). The estate they shall guard and rear the minors. The household goods they may not sell. The purchaser of household goods belonging to the children of a widow shall forfeit his money. The goods shall revert to their owners.

§ 178. If there is a wife of a god, priestess, or sacred harlot, whose father has given her a dowry and written her a record of gift, and in the record of gift he has not written, "after her she may give it to whomsoever she pleases," and has not given her full discretion; after her father dies her brothers shall take her field and garden, and according to the value of her share they shall give her grain, oil, and wool, and shall content her heart. If her brothers shall not give her grain, oil, and wool, according to the value of her share, and shall not content her heart, she may let her field and garden unto any tenant she pleases and her tenant shall maintain her. Her field, garden, or whatever her father gave her she may enjoy as long as she lives. She may not sell it for money or transfer it to another. Her heritage belongs to her brothers.

§ 179. If there is a wife of a god, priestess, or sacred harlot, whose father has given her a dowry and written a record of gift; and in the record of gift he has written, "after her she may give it to whomsoever she pleases," and has granted her full discretion; after her father dies she may give it after her to whomsoever she pleases. Her brothers have no claim upon her.

§ 180. If a father does not give a dowry to his daughter, a priestess living in the appointed house, or a sacred harlot, after the father dies she shall receive from the goods of her father's house the same share as one son, and as long as she lives she shall enjoy it. After her it belongs to her brothers.

§ 181. If the father of a priestess, sacred harlot, or temple maiden gives her to a god and does not give her a dowry, after the father dies she shall receive from the goods of her father's house a third of the portion of a son and shall enjoy it as long as she lives. After her it belongs to her brothers.

§ 182. If a father does not give a dowry to his daughter, a priestess of Marduk of Babylon, and does not write a record of gift for her; after her father dies she shall receive from the goods of her father's house one-third of the portion of a son, and shall pay no tax. A priestess of Marduk after her death may leave it to whomsoever she pleases.

§ 183. If a father presents a dowry to his daughter who is a concubine, and gives her to a husband and writes a record of gift; after the father dies she shall not share in the goods of her father's house.

§ 184. If a father does not present a dowry to his daughter who is a concubine and does not give her to a husband; after her father's death her brothers shall give her a dowry according to the value of the father's estate and shall give her to a husband.

In comparison with these Babylonian laws of inheritance those in the Old Testament are comparatively simple. We learn from Deuteronomy 21 : 15–17, that a man's firstborn son received a "double portion" of his father's estate, *i. e.,* twice as much as any other son. The inference is that the other sons shared equally. This law also provides that, when a man has two wives, the sons of the favorite wife shall have no advantage as to inheritance over the sons of the less loved wife. In Numbers 27 : 8–11 it is provided that if a man has no son, his estate (*i. e.,* real estate) may go to his daughter; if he has no daughter, it may go to his brothers; if no brothers, it goes to his father's brothers. If his father has no brothers, the estate is to go to the next of kin. In Numbers 36 : 2–12 the law that a daughter may inherit her father's estate is supplemented by the provision that such a daughter must marry within the tribe, so that the landed property may not in the next generation pass out of the tribe.

Such were the Hebrew laws of inheritance. They apply to a much less complexly organized society than the Babylonian.

§§ 168, 169 of Hammurabi's code deal with the cutting off of a son. This is parallel in Deuteronomy 21 : 18–21, though punishment inflicted by the law in Deuteronomy is quite different from the Babylonian, since the Hebrew boy, whose parents have proved him before the elders to be unworthy of sonship, was not cast out and sent away, but stoned to death. Another form of this law appears in Exodus 21 : 17.

Adoption

§ 185. If a man takes a young child in his name unto sonship and brings him up, one may not bring a claim for that adopted son.

§ 186. If a man takes a young child unto sonship, and when he has taken him he rebels against his [adopted] father and mother, that foster-child shall return to his father's house.

§ 187. One may not bring claim for the son of a temple-servant, a palace guard, or of a sacred harlot.

§ 188. If an artisan takes a son to sonship and teaches him his handicraft, one may not bring claim for him.

§ 189. If he does not teach him his handicraft, that foster-son may return to the house of his father.

§ 190. If a man does not count among his sons a young child whom he has taken to sonship and reared, that foster-child may return to his father's house.

§ 191. If a man who takes a young child to sonship and rears him and establishes a house and acquires children, afterward sets his face to cut off that foster-son, that son shall not go his way. The father who reared him shall give him from his goods one-third the share of a son and he shall go. From field, garden, or house, he shall not give him.

In the codes of the Old Testament there are no laws of adoption. The story of the adoption of Ephraim and Manasseh by Jacob in Genesis 48 shows that the idea was not unknown to the Hebrews, among whom the ceremony of adoption would seem to have consisted of the act of acknowledging the children as one's own by placing one's hands on their heads and giving them a paternal blessing.

Renunciation of Sonship

§ 192. If the son of a temple-servant or the son of a sacred harlot says to the father that brought him up or to the mother that brought him up, "Thou art not my father," or, "Thou are not my mother," they shall cut his tongue.

§ 193. If the son of a temple-servant or the son of a sacred harlot has identified his father's house and hated the father who brought him up or the mother who brought him up and goes back to his father's house, they shall pluck out his eye.

The Old Testament has no laws with which to compare these. The two classes of persons whose children are mentioned were banished from Israel by Deuteronomy 23 : 17, 18.

Wet-nurses or Foster-mothers

§ 194. If a man gives his son unto a nurse and his son dies in the hands of the nurse and the nurse substitutes another child without the consent of the father or the mother, they shall prosecute her; because she substituted another child without the consent of his father or his mother they shall cut off her breast.

This law also is without Biblical parallel.

Assault and Battery

§ 195. If a son strikes his father, they shall cut off his hand.

§ 196. If a man destroys the eye of the son of a patrician, they shall destroy his eye.

§ 197. If he breaks a man's bone, they shall break his bone.

§ 198. If one destroys the eye of a workingman or breaks the bone of a workingman, he shall pay 1 mana of silver.

§ 199. If one destroys the eye of a man's slave or breaks the bones of a man's slave, he shall pay half his value.

§ 200. If a man knocks out the tooth of a man of his own rank, they shall knock his tooth out.

§ 201. If one knocks out the tooth of a workingman, he shall pay ⅓ of a mana of silver.

§ 202. If a man shall strike the private-parts of a man who is of higher rank than he, he shall receive sixty blows with an ox-hide scourge in the assembly.

§ 203. If a patrician strikes the private-parts of a patrician of his own rank, he shall pay 1 mana of silver.

§ 204. If a workingman strikes the private-parts of a workingman, he shall pay 10 shekels of silver.

§ 205. If the slave of a patrician strikes the private-parts of the son of a patrician, they shall cut off his ear.

§ 206. If a man strikes a man in a quarrel and wounds him, he shall swear, "I did not strike with intent," and shall pay for the physician.

§ 207. If from the stroke he dies, he shall swear [as above], and if it was a patrician, he shall pay ½ mana of silver.

§ 208. If it was a workingman, he shall pay ⅓ of a mana of silver.

§ 209. If a man strikes a man's daughter and causes a miscarriage, he shall pay 10 shekels of silver for her miscarriage.

§ 210. If that woman dies, they shall put his daughter to death.

§ 211. If through a stroke one causes a miscarriage of the daughter of a workingman, he shall pay 5 shekels of silver.

§ 212. If that woman dies, he shall pay ½ mana of silver.

§ 213. If one strikes the slave-girl of a man and causes a miscarriage, he shall pay 2 shekels of silver.

§ 214. If that slave-girl dies, he shall pay ⅓ of a mana of silver.

These laws are strikingly parallel to Exodus 21 : 18–27, to which Exodus 21 : 12–14 should be prefixed. The Babylonian code, like the Hebrew, imposes the death penalty for wilful murder. Both codes provide that one who is an accidental homicide shall escape the penalty, but they do it in different ways. Hammurabi provides that the killer may take an oath that he did it without intent to kill. Exodus 21 : 13, 14 provides that the homicide may find sanctuary at the altar of God. In place of this Deuteronomy 19 : 4, ff., provides that he may flee to a city of refuge.

If a man injures another in a fight, the Bible (Exod. 21 : 18, 19) provides that he shall pay for the lost time and, as does Hammurabi, the cost of healing the injured man. Exodus 21 : 22 provides, as does Hammurabi, for the payment of a fine for causing a woman to miscarry, but Exodus does not, like the Babylonian code, fix the amount of the damage; that is left to the judges. In the laws concerning the injury of slaves the two codes differ. Exodus provides (21 : 20, 21, 26, 27) for cases in which owners injure or kill their own slaves; Hammurabi, for cases in which the injury is done by others. A mere reading of the penalties imposed by the parts of the Babylonian code translated above impresses vividly upon the mind the fact that underlying many of them is the principle so forcibly expressed in Exodus 21 : 21–25 : "life for life, eye for eye, tooth for tooth, hand for hand, foot for foot, burning for burning, wound for wound, stripe for stripe." The details of application are different, but the principle is the same. Many of the differences were caused by the more complex nature of Babylonian society, in which three classes, patricians, workingmen (or semi-serfs), and slaves, existed. Hebrew law recognizes but two classes—freemen and slaves.

Physicians

§ 215. If a physician operates upon a man for a severe wound with a bronze lancet and saves the man's life, or if he operates for cataract with a bronze lancet and saves the man's eye, he shall receive 10 shekels of silver.

§ 216. If it is a workingman, he shall receive 5 shekels of silver.

§ 217. If it is a man's slave, the owner of the slave shall give the physician 2 shekels of silver.

§ 218. If a physician operates upon a man with a bronze lancet for a severe wound, and the man dies; or operates upon a man with a bronze lancet for cataract and the man's eye is destroyed, they shall cut off his hand.

§ 219. If a physician operates with a bronze lancet upon the slave of a workingman and causes his death, he shall restore a slave of equal value.

§ 220. If he operates for cataract with a bronze lancet and destroys his eye, he shall pay ½ his price.

§ 221. If a physician sets a broken bone for a man or has cured of sickness inflamed flesh, the patient shall pay 5 shekels of silver to the physician.

§ 222. If he is a workingman, he shall give 3 shekels of silver.

§ 223. If he is the slave of a patrician, the owner of the slave shall give 3 shekels of silver to the physician.

§ 224. If an ox-doctor or an ass-doctor treats an ox or an ass for a severe wound and saves its life, the owner of the ox or the ass shall pay to the physician ⅙ of a shekel of silver as his fee.

§ 225. If he operates upon an ox or an ass for a severe wound and it dies, he shall give unto the owner of the ox or the ass ¼ of its value.

These laws about physicians have no parallel in the Old Testament, the laws of which did not take account of the existence of doctors. They are of interest, since they show the antiquity of physicians in Babylonia, not only for men, but for animals. They also reveal the fact that the practice of medicine in Babylonia was attended by some risks!

Herodotus (I, 197) declares that the Babylonians had no physicians, but brought their sick out into the streets and asked of each passer-by whether he had had a like sickness and what he had done

for it.   Possibly, as among ourselves, there were many who did not
wish to incur the expense of a doctor, and who did as Herodotus
reports, but these laws, and the existence of physicians at Nineveh
at the time of the later Assyrian kings, make it probable that
Herodotus was wrong as to their non-existence at Babylon in his
day.

Laws of Branding

§ 226.   If a brander without the consent of the owner of a slave cuts a mark
on a slave, making him unsalable, they shall cut off the hands of that brander.

§ 227.   If a man deceives a brander and he brands a slave with a mark,
making him unsalable, they shall put that man to death and cause him to perish
in the gate of his house.   The brander shall swear: "I did not brand him
knowingly" and shall go free.

These laws have no parallel in the Old Testament.   Evidently the
simpler organization of Hebrew society made them unnecessary.

Responsibility of House-buildings

§ 228.   If a builder builds a house for a man and completes it, he shall give
him as his wages 2 shekels of silver for each *Shar* of house.

§ 229.   If a builder builds a house for a man and does not make its work
strong and the house which he made falls and causes the death of the owner
of the house, that builder shall be put to death.

§ 230.   If it causes the death of the son of the owner, the son of that builder
shall be put to death.

§ 231.   If it causes the death of a slave of the owner of the house, a slave
like the slave he shall give to the owner of the house.

§ 232.   If it destroys property, he shall restore whatever was destroyed, and
because he did not build the house strong and it fell, he shall rebuild the house
that fell from his own property.

§ 233.   If a builder builds a house for a man and does not make his work
strong and a wall falls, that builder shall strengthen that wall at his own
expense.

These laws have no parallel in the Bible.   Among the agricultural population of Palestine builders were not a separate class.
The penalties inflicted by the Babylonian code were severe, and yet,
if modern legislators would put upon the house-builders of our time
a similar responsibility for good work, fewer lives would be sacrificed by falling buildings.

Responsibility of Boatmen

§ 234.   If a boatman builds a boat of 60 *Gur* for a man, he shall give him
2 shekels of silver as his wages.

§ 235.   If a boatman builds a boat for a man and does not make his work
sound and in that year the boat is sent on a voyage and meets with disaster,

that boatman shall repair that boat and from his own goods shall make it strong and shall give the boat in sound condition to the owner of the boat.

§ 236. If a man gives his boat to a boatman for hire and the boatman is careless and sink or wrecks the boat, the boatman shall restore a boat to the owner of the boat.

§ 237. If a man hires a boatman and a boat and loads it with grain, wool, oil, dates, or any other kind of freight, and that boatman is careless and sinks the boat or destroys its freight, the boatman shall replace the boat and whatever there was in it which he destroyed.

§ 238. If a boatman sinks a man's boat and re-floats it, he shall give money for ½ its value.

§ 239. If a man hires a boatman, he shall give him 6 *Gur* of grain a year.

The Hebrews were not a maritime people, and had no such laws as these or the following.

The Collision of Ships

§ 240. If a boat that is floating downstream strikes a boat that is being towed and sinks it, the owner of the boat that was sunk shall declare in the presence of a god everything that was in that boat and [the owner] of the boat floating downstream, which sunk the boat that was being towed, shall replace the boat and whatever was lost.

There is, naturally, nothing similar to this in the Old Testament.

Laws Concerning Cattle

§ 241. If a man levies a distraint upon an ox as security for debt, he shall pay ⅓ of a mana of silver.

§ 242. If a man hires for a year, the wages of a working ox is 4 *Gur* of grain.

§ 243. The hire of a milch cow, 3 *Gur* of grain for a year he shall give.

§ 244. If a man hires an ox or an ass and a lion kills it in the field, the loss falls on the owner.

§ 245. If a man hires an ox and causes its death through neglect or blows, he shall restore to the owner an ox of equal value.

§ 246. If a man hires an ox and crushes its foot or cuts the cord of its neck, he shall restore to the owner an ox of like value.

§ 247. If a man hires an ox and destroys its eye, he shall pay to the owner of the ox money to ½ its value.

§ 248. If a man hires an ox and breaks off its horn, or cuts off its tail or injures the flesh which holds the ring, money to ¼ of its value he shall pay.

§ 249. If a man hires an ox and a god strikes it and it dies, the man who hires the ox shall take an oath in the presence of a god and shall go free.

§ 250. If an ox when passing along the street gores a man and causes his death, there is no penalty in that case.

§ 251. If the ox of a man has the habit of goring and they have informed him of his fault and his horns he has not protected nor kept his ox in, and that ox gores a man and causes his death, the owner of the ox shall pay ½ mana of money.

§ 252. If it is the slave of a man, he shall pay ⅓ of a mana of money.

§ 253. If a man hires a man and puts him over his field and furnishes him with seed-grain and intrusts him with oxen and contracts with him to cultivate the field, if that man steals the seed-grain or the crop and it is found in his possession, they shall cut off his hands.

§ 254. If he takes the seed-grain, but enfeebles the cattle, from the grain which he has cultivated he shall make restoration.

§ 255. If he shall let the cattle to a man for hire, or steal the seed-grain so that there is no crop, they shall prosecute that man, and he shall pay 60 *Gur* of grain for each *Gan*.

§ 256. If he is not able to meet his obligation, they shall tear him in pieces in that field by means of the oxen.

The Biblical legislation corresponding to this is found in Exodus 21 : 28–35, but it covers only a portion of the cases of which the Babylonian law treats. It provides that, if an ox gores a man or a woman to death, the ox shall be stoned. If the ox was wont to gore and the owner had not kept it in, but it had been permitted to kill a man or a woman, the owner as well as the ox should be stoned. At the discretion of the tribunal a fine or ransom might be laid on the owner. In case the ox gored a slave, the owner of the ox was to pay 30 shekels of silver and the ox was to be stoned. If a man opened a pit and a neighbor's ox or ass fell into it, the digger of the pit must make good the loss to the owner of the animal, and the dead beast became the property of the digger of the pit. If one man's ox killed the ox of another man, the two men were to sell the live ox and divide the price. If it were known that the ox was wont to gore in the past, and its owner had not kept it in, he was to pay ox for ox, and the dead animal should be his.

It thus appears that the exigencies of Hebrew agricultural life were different from those of Babylonia, and were naturally met in different ways.

Wages of Laborers

§ 257. If a man hires a field-laborer, he shall pay him 8 *Gur* of grain per year.

§ 258. If a man hires a herdsman, he shall pay him 6 *Gur* of grain per year.

Hebrew law did not regulate wages.

On Stealing Farming-tools

§ 259. If a man steals a watering-machine from a field, he shall pay to the owner of the watering-machine 5 shekels of silver.

§ 260. If a man steals a watering-bucket or a plow, he shall pay 3 shekels of silver.

As the Hebrews did not systematically irrigate their land, the Old Testament contains no similar laws.

Laws Concerning Shepherds

§ 261. If a man hires a herdsman to tend cattle or sheep, he shall pay him 8 *Gur* of grain per year.

§ 262. If a man, oxen, or sheep.............

(The rest is broken away.)

§ 263. If he loses an ox or a sheep that is intrusted to him, he shall restore ox for ox and sheep for sheep.

§ 264. If a herdsman who has had cattle or sheep intrusted to him receives his full pay and is satisfied, and he causes the cattle or the sheep to diminish in number or lessens the birth-rate, he shall give increase and produce according to his contracts.

§ 265. If a shepherd to whom cattle or sheep have been given to tend is dishonest and alters the price or sells them, they shall prosecute him, and he shall restore to their owner 10 times the oxen or sheep which he stole.

§ 266. If in a fold there is a pestilence of a god, or a lion has slain, the shepherd shall before a god declare himself innocent, and the owner of the fold shall bear the loss of the fold.

§ 267. If the shepherd is careless and causes a loss in the fold, the shepherd shall make good in cattle or sheep the loss which he caused in the fold and shall give them to the owner.

The nearest approach in the Old Testament to laws of this character is in Exodus 22 : 10–13, which provides that, if a man deliver to his neighbor an ox, or ass, or sheep, or any beast to keep, and it dies, or is injured or is carried off when no one sees the deed, the oath of Jehovah shall be between them that the keeper has not put his hand to his neighbor's goods. The owner was to accept this, and no restitution was necessary. If the animals were stolen from the keeper, he must make restitution. If they were torn in pieces by beasts of prey, he must bring the pieces for witness, and need not make restitution.

The same general principles of the limits of responsibility underlay the two codes in these cases, though they differ in details. In Israel the shepherding of the flocks and herds of other people was not, as in Babylonia, a distinct occupation.

On Wages of Animals and Men

§ 268. If a man hires an ox for threshing, 20 *Qa* of grain is its hire.

§ 269. If he hires an ass for threshing, 10 *Qa* of grain is its hire.

§ 270. If he hires a kid for threshing, 1 *Qa* of grain is its hire.

§ 271. If he hires cattle, a wagon and a driver, he shall pay 180 *Qa* of grain per day.

§ 272. If a man hires a wagon only, he shall pay 40 *Qa* of grain per day.

§ 273. If a man hires a field-laborer from the beginning of the year until the fifth month, he shall pay him 6 *She* of silver per day; from the sixth month to the end of the year, 5 *She* of silver per day he shall pay.

§ 274. If a man hires an artisan, he shall give per day as the wages of a
.....5 *She*; as the wages of a brick-maker, 5 *She* of money; as the wages of a
tailor, 5 *She* of silver; as the wages of a stone-cutter,......*She* of silver;
............*She* of silver;...:........*She* of silver,..........of a carpenter,
4 *She* of silver; as the wages of a......4 *She* of silver; as the wages of a
.....*She* of silver; the wages of a builder,......*She* of silver.

§ 275. If a man hires a boat (?) to go upstream (?), its hire is 3 *She* of
silver per day.

§ 276. If he hires a boat to float downstream, he shall pay as its hire 2½
She of silver per day.

§ 277. If a man hires a boat of 60 *Gur* burden, he shall pay ⅙ of a shekel of
money per day.

There are no parallels to these laws in the Bible, as the Old Testament does not attempt to regulate prices. When one considers the
customs of trade all over the Orient, and the time fruitlessly consumed in making bargains, one does not wonder that the practical
sovereign of a great commercial people, such as the Babylonians
were, should regulate prices by law. As a rule, to this day, a purchaser begins by offering only a fraction of what he is willing to
give, and the seller by asking at least twice as much as he is willing to take. A long psychological battle follows, during which there
are many victories and capitulations on each side. This law was
designed to put an end to this time-consuming custom.

When the Sales of Slaves Are Void

§ 278. If a man buys a male or a female slave and before a month is past
he has an attack of rheumatism (?), he shall return to the seller, and the
purchaser shall receive back the money that was paid.

§ 279. If a man buys a male or a female slave, and another has a legal
claim upon him, the seller shall be responsible for that claim.

§ 280. If a man, while in a foreign country, purchases a male or a female
slave of a man, and, when he returns home, the former owner of the male or
the female slave recognizes his slave, if that male or female slave is a native
of the land, he shall give it its freedom without recompense.

§ 281. If they are natives of another country, the purchaser shall declare
in the presence of a god the price that he paid, and the former owner of the
male or female slave shall pay the price to the merchant, and shall receive back
his slave.

No laws similar to these are found in the Old Testament.

The Penalty for Renouncing a Master

§ 282. If a slave shall say to his owner: "Thou are not my owner," they
shall make him submit as his slave, and shall cut off his ear.

This penalty reminds one of the boring of a slave's ear (Exod.
21 : 6; Deut. 15 : 17) in token of perpetual slavery.

2. The Mosaic Code Not Borrowed from the Babylonian; Different Underlying Conceptions.—A comparison of the code of Hammurabi as a whole with the Pentateuchal laws as a whole, while it reveals certain similarities, convinces the student that the laws of the Old Testament are in no essential way dependent upon the Babylonian laws. Such resemblances as there are arose, it seems clear, from a similarity of antecedents and of general intellectual outlook; the striking differences show that there was no direct borrowing. The primitive Semitic custom of an eye for an eye and a tooth for a tooth (Exod. 21:24; Lev. 24:20; Deut. 19:21) is made the basis of many penalties in the Babylonian code. (See §§ 196, 197, 200, 229, 230, etc.) The principle underlying it is found also in many other sections. These similarities only show that Babylonia had a large Semitic element in its population. Again, Hammurabi pictured himself at the top of the pillar on which these laws are written as receiving them from the sun-god (Fig. 292). The Bible tells us that Moses received the laws of the Pentateuch from Jehovah. The whole attitude of the two documents is, however, different. Hammurabi, in spite of the picture, takes credit, both in the prologue and in the epilogue of his code, for the laws. He, not Shamash, established justice in the land. Moses, on the other hand, was only the instrument; the legislation stands as that of Jehovah himself.

This difference appears also in the contents of the two codes. The Pentateuch contains many ritual regulations and purely religious laws, while the code of Hammurabi is purely civil. As has been already pointed out, the code of Hammurabi is adapted to the land of the rivers, and to a highly civilized commercial people, while the Biblical laws are intended for a dry land like Palestine, and for an agricultural community that was at a far less advanced stage of commercial and social development.

Religion is, however, not a matter of social advancement only. In all that pertains to religious insight the Pentateuch is far in advance of Hammurabi's laws.

CHAPTER XIV

A HITTITE CODE OF LAWS [1]

Hittite Laws with Comparison of Biblical and Babylonian Laws

The following code of laws was inscribed on some tablets contained in the archive found at Boghaz Koi or Hittite-city. It comes from the time of the great Hittite dynasty which ruled there, though we do not know the name of the king under whom it was adopted and put in force. It seems probable, however, that it was either the powerful Subbiluliuma, or his son, Mursil (Mushilish). If this conjecture is correct, the code dates from about 1350 B.C.

Assault and Battery

§ 1. If anyone intentionally kills a man or a woman, that one he shall bury and give 4 persons,[2] either male or female, and (thus) discharge the penalty.

§ 2. If anyone intentionally kills a slave, or a slave girl, that one he shall bury, and give 2 persons, either male or female, and (thus) discharge the penalty.

§ 3. If anyone wounds a free man, or a free woman, and that one dies, whosoever's hand wounded him shall bury that one and give 2 persons and (thus) discharge the penalty.

§ 4. If anyone wounds a slave or a slave girl and it dies, wounding him accidentally,[3] that one he shall bury and give 1 person and (thus) discharge the penalty.

§ 5. If anyone kills a merchant of Hittite-city, he shall give 100 manas of silver and (thus) discharge the penalty; if it is in the territory of the city Luyya, or the city Balâ, he shall give 100 manas of silver and restore his possessions; if in the territory of Hittite-city, then he shall bury the merchant.

§ 6. If a person, either man or woman, dies in the city, 100 rods of cultivated land near where he dies they shall mark off and it shall take him.[4]

1 The text is published by Hrozny in *Keilschrifttexte aus Boghazkoi*, VI; it is translated by the same scholar in *Code Hittite provenant de l'Asie 'Mineur*, Paris, 1922; also *Hethitische Gesetse aus dem Staatsarchiv von Boghazkoi*, unter mitwirkung von Dr. Johannes Friedrich, übersetz von Dr. Heinrich Zimmern, Professor in Leipzig, Leipzig, 1922, (a translation of a part only); "The Hittite Code," Translated by Dr. Arnold Walther as Appendix IV in J. M. P. Smith's *Origin and History of Hebrew Law*, Chicago, 1931, pp. 246-279.

2 The "persons" so given were slaves. The Sumerian word here employed was used in that sense.

3 Literally, "by his hand."

4 Apparently for burial.

§ 7. If anyone blinds a free man, or knocks out some of his teeth, formerly he paid 1 mana of silver! now he shall pay 20 shekels of silver and discharge the penalty.

§ 8. If one blinds a slave, or a slave girl, or knocks out some teeth, he shall pay 10 shekels of silver and discharge the penalty.

§ 9. If anyone strikes a person on the head, formerly they paid 6 shekels of silver; for the blow he gave 3 shekels; to the palace he gave 3 shekels. Now the king gives up (the fine) to his palace, and he shall give 3 shekels to the one struck.

§ 10. If anyone strikes a person and makes him ill, and that one he makes unfit for work: he shall give a man instead of him: this one shall work in his house while he is convalescing; after he has recovered, then he shall give him 6 shekels of silver, and the doctor's bill he shall pay.

§ 11. If anyone breaks the hand or foot of a free man, then he shall pay 20 shekels and discharge the penalty.

§ 12. If anyone breaks the hand or foot of a slave or a slave girl, he shall give 10 shekels of silver and discharge the penalty.

§ 13. If anyone breaks the nose of a free man, he shall give 1 Mana of silver and discharge the penalty.

§ 14. If anyone breaks the nose of a slave, or a slave girl, he shall give 3 shekels of silver and discharge the penalty.

§ 15. If anyone cuts off the ear of a free man, he shall pay 12 shekels of silver and discharge the penalty.

§ 16. If anyone cuts off the ear of a slave, or of a slave girl, he shall give 3 shekels of silver and discharge the penalty.

§ 17. If anyone causes a pregnant free woman to miscarry, if it is nine months; if it is ten months, he shall give 10 shekels of silver; if it is five months, he shall give 5 shekels of silver and discharge the penalty.

§ 18. If one causes a pregnant slave girl to miscarry, if it is ten months, he shall give 5 shekels of silver.

These laws correspond in subject-matter to §§ 195–214 of the Code of Hammurabi. No corresponding laws of the Assyrians have as yet been recovered.

One interesting feature is the provision permitting a murderer to compound his crime by giving 4 to 2 persons in place of the murdered one. This shows that the Hittite had no ancient custom of blood revenge such as lay lack of both Hebrews and Babylonians. The nature of the penalties for personal injuries, such as knocking out another's tooth, shows also the absence of any law like the Semitic *lex talionis,* which is so prominent in the penalties in the Code of Hammurabi, and in the Pentateuch, by which the injured inflicted an equal injury upon the person who had harmed him.

Laws Concerning Slaves

§ 19. If any man of the city of Luyya steals a person, either man or woman, in Hittite-city, and delivers him to a master in Arzawa, and he escapes (?) he shall return to his house again. If in the town of Hattushash a man of Hittite-city steals a man of Luyya and to Luyya conducts him (to

a master)—formerly 12 slaves he gave, but now he shall give 6 slaves and for the future he is free.

§ 20. If any man of Hittite-city steals a slave of a man of Hittite-city from the territory of the city of Luyya and brings it to the territory of Hittite-city, should his master find (?) him, then he shall pay 12 shekels of silver, and discharge the obligation.

§ 21. If anyone steels a slave of a man of the city of Luyya from the territory of the city of Luyya, and brings him to the territory of Hittite-city should his master find (?) him, then he shall give him his slave; he shall pay no compensation.

§ 22. If a slave runs away and afterward anyone restores him; if a merchant catch him and if he took him near and put him in bonds, if it was on this side the river, he shall give 2 shekels of silver; if it was on the other side of the river, he shall give 3 shekels of silver.

§ 23. If a slave runs away and goes to the territory of the city of Luyya and afterward anyone restores him, then he (the slave's master) shall give him 6 shekels of silver. If he flees to an enemy's country, and anyone afterward restores him, he shall give him to that one.

§ 24. If a slave, or a slave girl runs away and is caught in the hearth of anyone, as a reward he shall pay for a man a year's (service) or........ 80(?) shekels of silver, and for a woman, a year's (service) or 40 shekels of silver.

These laws should be compared with §§ 14–20 of the Code of Hammurabi, and the Pentateuchal laws cited in that connection. It will be noted that the Hittite laws are adapted to the local political conditions, and that slaves had in Hittite-city in the fourteenth century B.C. a higher monetary value than they did in Babylon seven hundred years earlier.

A Law Against Using Another's Cooking Utensils

§ 25. If a person defiles a pot, or a jar, formerly they used to give 6 shekels of silver; to him whose it was he gave 3 shekels, and the palace used to take 3 shekels. Now the king forgives the palace's part, he shall give 3 shekels to him whose it was, and discharge the obligation.

This law is without parallel in the other codes.

Laws of Marriage

§ 26. If............a field...............that one...................
....the man shall give

§ 27. If a man takes a wife and brings her (to his house) and gives her dower rights therein; if the woman dies that man consuming the property, the goods, takes her estate, but if she dies in the house of her father, the property is for the children; that man shall not inherit of that estate.

§ 28. If a maiden is betrothed to a man and elopes with another, the bride price he escapes. Then the first man (may swear to it) in any manner whatever. The father and mother need not swear. If the father and the mother gave her to the other man; then the father and mother shall swear. If the father and mother say, "she is his" (*i. e.,* the first man's) they shall separate her from him (*i. e.,* the second man).

§ 29. If a woman is bound to a man and he has paid the bride price, and the father and mother afterward think ill of it and take her away from that man, then they shall return to him double the bride price.

§ 30. If a man does not take a woman and refuses, then the bride price which he had paid he shall lose.

§ 31. If a man likes a slave girl and lives with her and takes her for his wife and she bears children in his house, and afterward they get on badly and quarrel, they shall divide the house between them: the man shall take the children, and the woman shall take 1 child.

§ 32. If a slave take a (free) woman, their law is the same.

§ 33. If a slave takes a slave girl, their law is the same.

§ 34. If a slave pays the bride price for a woman, and takes her for his wife, and gives her (up), no one shall remit (it).

§ 35. If an administrator (?) or a shepherd takes a free woman and does not pay the bride price, then he shall serve as a slave for three years.

§ 36. If a slave pays the bride price for a free girl and as a husband lives with her, no one shall afterward take her away.

These laws should be compared with §§ 128–161 of the Code of Hammurabi, and the corresponding laws of the Pentateuch discussed in connection with them. 'It will be observed that the laws of the Hittites are much more brief, and provide for fewer contingencies than those of the Babylonian Code. They are the laws of a people who had back of them a shorter civilized experience. The underlying principles of justice are the same in both codes. They are principles approved by the universal conscience of mankind. The light which these laws shed upon the condition of slaves among the Hittites is interesting. They could apparently accumulate property for themselves, gain money with which to pay the bride price for a wife, marry a free woman, and enjoy rights guaranteed by law.

Laws Concerning Bandits

§ 37. If anyone abducts a woman and afterwards a helper comes to their hurt and two men or three men are killed, there is no penalty: "thou owest nothing to a bandit."

§ 38. If persons are on the way to a tribunal (?) and a bandit attacks them, and they defend themselves with clubs and sticks, and wound the bandit severely and he dies, there is no penalty in that case.

One gains the impression from these laws that they had grown out of recent experience and were shaped to fit the incidents of such experience. Those who framed these sections of the code had not sought out the underlying principles so as to make the legislation fit many cases. They should be compared with §§ 21–25 of the Code of Hammurabi.

Concerning Leased Land and Feudal Holdings

§ 39. If a (man) takes the fields of another, the ground rent he should pay; if he abandons the fields and takes others, he shall not cultivate (?) them.

§ 40. If a warrior disappears and a farmer comes and says: "This is my military holding and my farm," and shall appropriate the field of the soldier, and the duty of the soldier, he shall take and carry on the agricultural work. If he refuses the military duty, he shall vacate the farm and lose the holding of the soldier, and the men of the city shall cultivate it. If the king shall grant it to a prisoner of war, he shall take it and assume the military duty.

§ 41. If a peasant serf disappears and (another) peasant serf standing as a soldier says: "This is my military holding and this is my ground rent," then, as one of the peasant serfs he shall take possession of the fields, and shall assume the military duty, and render the ground rent. If he refuse (to render) the ground rent, one of the peasant serfs, taking the fields from the palace, shall render the ground rent.

These laws should be compared to §§ 26–41 of the Code of Hammurabi. Possibly the "land superintendent" of the Hittites may have performed some function kindred to those of the "tax collectors" of the Babylonians. In any event their holding of lands, like that of the soldiers, appears to have been an assignment from the public land and such assignment imposed certain obligations of service to the state.

Concerning Losses and Damages

§ 42. If anyone hires a man and he is wounded and dies, if the wages are paid, there is no penalty. If the wages are not paid, he shall give 1 slave. He shall give 12 shekels of silver as wages; the wages of a woman are 6 shekels of silver.

§ 43. If a man (is) making his bullock (variant cattle) ford a river and another joins in and he takes the tail of the bullock and crosses the river, then the owner of the bullock the river contributed, whoever he may be, shall take it.

§ 44. If with fire anyone casts a spell upon a man and he dies, he shall afterward give his son for him. If anyone purifies a man by deceit, casting upon him a spell;[5] if he casts it on the field or barn of anyone—witchcraft is a case for the king.

§ 45. If anyone takes tools, and that one shall afterward return them to the owner, he shall give him freedom; if he does not return them, he becomes a prisoner.

There is no exact parallel to these laws in the other codes. § 42 may be compared to §§ 257, 258 of the Code of Hammurabi; the only likeness is that both codes mention the wages of laborers; the laws themselves are quite different. § 44 may be compared with §§ 1, 2 of the Babylonian Code, which relate to witchcraft.

5 Read *ku-ub-tar-ra-az tu-ri-ya-aš*.

§ 45, like §§ 259–260 of the Babylonian Code, legislates concerning the stealing of tools, but the two codes treat the matter in quite different ways. § 43 is without parallel in the other codes.

Another Group of Laws Relating to Land

§ 46. If anyone in a village holds fields as an inheritance in his father's lifetime, if they are wholly given to him, he shall perform the military duty. If he holds the fields and does not perform the military duty, (they) of his father's house shall perform it. If as owner by inheritance he has come into possession of fields and divides (them), or the men of the city give him fields, he shall perform the military duty.

§ 47. If anyone received a field as a present from the king and does not perform the duty, the king may take bread from his table and give it to him. If one acquires a field from a man of arms, the duty of the field he shall perform. If he acquires only a considerable portion of the field, he shall not perform the duty. If he receives the field on condition of military service, or if the chief men give it (to him), he shall perform the duty.

§ 48. If an irrigator performs his duty to the state (i. e., works out his taxes), no one may do the irrigating for the irrigator; his son, his field, his vineyard no one may acquire. He who does the irrigating for the irrigator, shall lose by irrigating. The irrigator, since (it was) by irrigating, may take it back from him.

§ 49. If an irrigator steals there is no compensation. If (it is by) corporate act, then the corporation makes restitution. When all used to practice theft, then all were guilty;........the men became prisoners. Whoever took this one, whoever took that one used to send them to the king's prison.

It appears that Hittite land was held either by the king or by cities and was granted to individuals on condition of certain military services to the state. We have nothing in Babylonian or Hebrew law quite parallel to this; the nearest approach to it is the land granted in Babylonia to soldiers, constables, and taxgetherers, already referred to. Compare the Code of Hammurabi, §§ 26–41.

Classes Exempt from Military Service

§ 50. The......men who live in the town of Nirik, who live in Arinna, who live in Ziplanda, the priests in every village—their houses are free, and their associates shall perform the duty. If one lives in the town of Arinna eleven months, then his house, the oil house of which is enclosed, is free.

§ 51. Formerly, he who in Arinna was a weaver his house was free, and his associates and people were free; now there is freedom for his house; his associates and people shall perform the duty for him. In the town of Zippalanda [6] it is similar.

§ 52. The slaves of a stone house, the slaves of a king's son, possessors of rank, who, among armed men, have fields, shall perform the military duty.

§ 53. If an armed man and his associates are banded together and if they get on badly and break up their house, if their menage is 10 slaves, the man at arms takes 7, and his associates take three. The cattle and sheep of

6 So spelled here; but compare § 50.

their establishment they shall share in proportion. If anyone holds a grant from the king and they divide the fields they held before, the man at arms shall take two-thirds and his associates shall take one-third.

§ 54. Formerly, the Scythian soldiers, the Shala soldiers, soldiers of the city Tamalki, soldiers of the city Khatra, soldiers of the city Zalpa, soldiers of the city Tashkhima, soldiers of the city Khemuwa, archers, carpenters, workers in wood, servants and former refugees neither performed military duty nor paid ground-rent.

§ 55. If men of Hittite-city, serfs, come and prostrating themselves before the king as father, then declare: "No one pays wages, and they refuse us; we are serfs"; the king as father in the assembly shall declare: "Then you are among the stars (*i. e.,* free men?). Since you are petitioners, be such."

§ 56. Should one be under obligation to fortress-duty during a military expedition of the king and under obligation to work a vineyard (no one is exempt), the gardeners shall perform all the vineyard service.

The land of the Hittites was, as we have seen, held in common. Those to whom the privilege of occupation was granted were subject to certain military duties and were under certain obligations to produce crops. These laws define when these obligations did not hold and who were free from them. As the land systems of the Hebrews were different the codes of that people afford no exact parallels. In Israel the land was held in fee simple, though the owner, in case of war, was liable to military duty. It is, however, provided in Deuteronomy 20: 5–7 that those who had built new houses and had not lived in them, or planted vineyards of which they had not yet eaten fruit, or betrothed wives which they had not yet married, were exempt from such duty. The fact of exemption was in both countries the same, but it was enjoyed by different classes and for different reasons.

Against Stealing and Killing Domestic Animals

§ 57. If anyone steals a full-grown bull (if it is half a year old it is not a full-grown bull; if it is a yearling bull, it is not a full-grown bull; if it is a bull two years old, this is a full-grown bull), heretofore he gave 30 cattle; but now 15 cattle he may give: 5 two years old, 5 a year old, 5 half a year old he may give, and discharge the obligation.

§ 58. If anyone steals a full-grown horse (if it is half a year old, it is not a full-grown horse; if it is a yearling, it is not a full-grown horse; if it is two years old, this is a full-grown horse), heretofore he gave 30 horses; but now 15 horses he may give: 5 horses two years old, 5 horses a year old, 5 horses six months old he may give, and discharge the obligation.

§ 59. If anyone steals a ram, heretofore he gave 30 sheep, but now he may give 15 sheep: 5 wool-bearing ewes, 5 rams, 5 lambs he may give, and discharge the obligation.

On Taking Stray Cattle and Horses

§ 60. If anyone finds a ful-grown bullock and makes free with it and its owner catches him, he shall give 7 cattle: 2 two years old, 3 one year old, 2 half a year old he shall give, and discharge the obligation.

§ 61. If anyone finds a full-grown horse and makes free with it, and its owner catches him, he shall give 7 horses: 2 two years old, 3 yearlings, and 2 half a year old, and discharge the obligation.

§ 62. If anyone finds a ram and makes free with it, and its owner catches him, he shall give 7 sheep: 2 wool-bearing ewes, 3 rams, 2 lambs he shall give, and discharge the obligation.

§ 63. If anyone finds a plough-ox and steals him, formerly he gave 15 cattle; now 10 cattle he may give: 3 cattle two years old, 3 one year old, 4 half a year old he may give, and discharge the obligation.

§ 64. If anyone steals a carriage-horse, the case is similar.

§ 65. If a full-grown creature, an uncastrated male, if a......, an uncastrated male, if a mountain ram, an uncastrated male anyone steals, the compensation is as for the full-grown creature; for this it is similar.

§ 66. If a plough-ox, if a carriage-horse, if a cow, if an ass broken to the yoke wanders to the stable (of anyone); if a creature, an uncastrated male, if a wool-bearing sheep, if a ram wanders into the fold (of anyone) and its owner finds it and receives it in good condition, he shall not take (the man) a prisoner.

§ 67. If anyone steals a cow, heretofore he gave 12 cattle; but now he shall give 6 cattle, 2 cattle 2 years old, 2 cattle 1 year old, 2 cattle six months old, and discharge the obligation.

§ 68. If anyone steals a mare broken to the harness, the case is similar.

§ 69. If anyone steals a wool-bearing ewe or a ram, formerly he gave 12 sheep; but now he shall give 6 sheep: 2 wool-bearing ewes, 2 rams, 2 lambs he shall give, and discharge the obligation.

§ 70. If anyone steals an ox, if a horse, if a mule, if an ass, and the owner takes it and receives it in good condition, he shall give two-fold, and discharge the obligation.

§ 71. If anyone finds an ox, a horse, or a mule, then he should drive it into the enclosure of the king; but if he finds it in the open country and submits it to witnesses, he may harness it; if afterward the owner finds it and obtains it in good condition, he shall not take him prisoner. If he did not submit it to witnesses, then he becomes a prisoner.

§ 72. If in the field of anyone an ox dies, the owner of the field shall give 2 cattle and discharge the obligation.

§ 73. If anyone takes a living ox as a thief, then the case is similar.

§ 74. If anyone breaks the horn of an ox or the foot of an ox, he shall keep that ox and shall give a sound ox to the owner of the ox. If the owner of the ox says, "I receive my ox," he shall take his ox and shall give him [the owner] 2 shekels of silver.

§ 75. If anyone hitches up an ox, horse, mule, or ass and it dies, or a wolf devours or destroys it, and afterward gives it up entire, if he shall say: "By the act of a god it died," then he shall swear.

§ 76. If anyone hires an ox, horse, large mule, or ass and it dies under him, he shall bring it and pay its hire.

§ 77. If anyone strikes a cow with calf and it casts the calf, he shall make restitution; he shall give 2 shekels of silver. If anyone strikes a mare with foal and it casts its foal, he shall make restitution; 2 shekels of silver he shall give. If anyone destroys the eye of an ox or a horse, he shall pay 6 shekels of silver and discharge the obligation.

§ 78. If anyone hires an ox, and puts upon it harness (?) or saddle (?) and its owner find him, he shall give 1 (measure) of grain.

§ 79. If cattle break into a field and the owner of the field finds them, he may hitch them up for 1 day; as soon as the stars appear he shall return them to the owner.

§ 80. If anyone rescues a sheep from a wolf, the owner takes the meat, this one takes the sheep-skin.

§ 81. If anyone steals a grain-fed hog, he formerly paid 1 mana of silver; but now he shall pay 12 shekels of silver, and discharge the obligation.

§ 82. If anyone steals a door-yard hog, he shall give 6 shekels of silver and discharge the obligation.

§ 83. If anyone steals a pregnant sow, he shall pay 6 shekels of silver and shall account for the little pigs; for 2 little pigs he shall give 20 qas [or 1 pa] of grain and discharge the obligation.

§ 84. If anyone hurts a pregnant sow and she dies, the case is similar.

§ 85. If anyone catches little pigs running wild and steals them he shall give 20 qas [or 1 pa] of grain for 1 pair.

§ 86. If a pig enters an open field, an irrigated field, or a garden, and the owner of the open field, irrigated field, or garden wounds it and it dies, then he shall return it to its owner; if he does not give it, that one becomes a prisoner.

§ 87. If anyone wounds a shepherd's dog and it dies, he shall pay 20 shekels of silver.

§ 88. If anyone wounds a dog of a dog-raiser and it dies, he shall pay 12 shekels of silver and discharge the obligation.

§ 89. If anyone wounds a watchdog and it dies, he shall pay 1 shekel of silver.

§ 90. If a dog consumes lard and the owner of the lard catches it, kills it and takes the lard from its belly, there is no compensation.

§ 91. If anyone steals bees in a hive, formerly he paid 1 mana of silver, now he shall pay 5 shekels of silver and discharge the obligation.

§ 92. If anyone steals 2 hives, if 3 hives, formerly he was caused to be stung to death by bees, but now he shall give 6 shekels of silver. If anyone steals one hive and there were no bees in it, he shall pay 3 shekels of silver.

In the Code of Hammurabi we have no laws quite parallel to these. Perhaps the code once contained them, for they may have been in the portion which the Elamite erased. §§ 241–256 relate to cattle, but concern wages and injuries rather than theft.

In Exodus 22: 1–5 we have the Hebrew parallel. It is there ordained that, if a man steals an ox or a sheep and sells it or kills it, he shall pay five oxen for an ox and four sheep for a sheep. If the stolen property was found in his hand, he was to pay double, whether it was an ox, an ass, or a sheep. Horses play no part in either Hebrew or Babylonian laws. Swine were unclean to Semites and, although the Sumerians domesticated them and even had a swine goddess, they do not appear either in the Code of Hammurabi or in the Pentateuch, except among the unclean animals prohibited to the Hebrews in Leviticus 11 and Deuteronomy 14.

It is interesting to learn that the Hittites had domesticated the bee and that their laws protect private property in them. The other codes afford no parallel to these laws. Honey was known both to the Hebrews and Babylonians, but apparently they gathered it from wild bees.

Other Laws Against Theft

§ 93. If they catch a free man in a storehouse, he shall pay 12 shekels of silver. If they catch a slave in a storehouse and he escape to a barn, he shall pay 6 shekels of silver.

§ 94. If a free man commits theft in a house, he shall make restitution; formerly thieves paid 1 mana of silver, but now they shall pay 12 shekels of silver. If he has stolen much, much shall be exacted of him; if he has stolen little, little shall be exacted of him, and discharge his obligation.

§ 95. If a slave steals in a house, he shall make restitution; the thief shall pay 6 shekels of silver, and the nose and ears of the slave shall be cut off; afterward they shall give him to his master; if he has stolen much, much shall be exacted of him; if he has stolen little, little shall be exacted of him. If his master says: "I will make restitution," then he shall make restitution; if he refuses, then the slave shall make restitution.

§ 96. If a free man steals a storage jar of grain and the jar is found, he shall make restitution; the jar with the grain he shall refill, and 6 shekels of silver he shall pay and discharge his obligation.

§ 97. If a slave steals a storage jar of grain and the jar is found, he shall make restitution; he shall refill the jar with grain and shall pay 6 shekels of silver and discharge his obligation.

These laws against theft are based on the same principles as the laws which precede them. The king who put this code into operation modified many punishments, making them more humane. The reader will have noticed how many times occurs the phrase, "formerly the punishment was" so-and-so, "but now it shall be" so-and-so. In every such case the punishment is lightened. In § 95 the code for the first time permits mutilation. The nose and ears of a slave may be cut off. That section also throws interesting light on the limits of a master's responsibility for a slave's acts; he may or may not assume full responsibility for them as he chooses. It will be noted that slaves are presumed to have property of their own from which restitution can be made. They were not, then, mere chattels.

Laws Relating to Fires

§ 98. If a free man lights fire in a house and the house burns down and anything perishes in the house, be it human being, kine or sheep, such an one shall not make restitution.

§ 99. If a slave lights a fire in a house, his master shall make restitution for him. The nose and ears of the slave shall be cut off and he be returned to his master. If he (the master) does not make restitution for him, then he shall give him (the slave) as security.

§ 100. If anyone burns a silo (?) and consumes its grain, then for it in summer he shall raise grain (and) later give (it). If it was not in the straw, then he shall bring the grain.

These laws relating to fire are more elaborate than either those of the Hebrews or Babylonians. The one law about fire in the

Pentateuch (Exod. 22:6) refers to the accidental burning of standing grain. In dry Palestine that might easily happen, but the houses there were largely of stone and, except in time of war, destructive fires were almost unknown.

The one law about fire in the Code of Hammurabi (§ 25) refers to stealing goods that have been removed from a burning house. Babylonian houses were of brick and fires were apparently not so common as among the Hittites. Perhaps the Hittite houses were more often constructed of wood.

Horticultural Laws

§ 101. If anyone steals some vines, apple (?) trees, pear (?) trees, or onions, formerly he paid......shekel of silver for 1 vine, 1 shekel of silver for one apple (?) tree,......shekel of silver for 1 pear (?) tree,......shekel of silver for 1 measure (?) of onions, and was scourged with the rod in the palace; formerly they proceeded thus, but now, if one is a free man, he shall pay 6 shekels of silver; if he is a slave, he shall pay 3 shekels of silver.

§ 102. If anyone steals from a wood-pile, if it is 1 talent of wood, he shall pay 3 shekels of silver; if it is 2 talents of wood, he shall pay 6 shekels of silver; if it is 3 talents of wood, it is (a case) for the king's court.

§ 103. If anyone steals a standing crop—if it is *gipessar* (acre?) of standing crop, he shall replant it and shall give 1 shekel of silver. If it is 2 *gipessars* of crop, he shall replant it and pay 2 shekels of silver.

§ 104. If anyone cuts a pomegranate tree or pear (?) tree,......shekels of silver he shall pay and discharge the obligation.

§ 105. If anyone lights a fire and in (a vineyard) it catches the vines— if vines, apple (?) trees, pomegranate (?) trees, fruit trees are burned, for 1 tree he shall give 6 shekels of silver and shall replant the orchard, and discharge the obligation. If he is a slave, he shall pay 3 shekels of silver.

§ 106. If anyone lights a fire in a field and it catches the standing crop and burns the field, he who lighted it shall take the burned field and shall give a good field to the owner of the field; in place of the one he burned.

§ 107. If a person allows his sheep to enter the vineyard of a neighbor (?) and they lay it waste—if it is a cultivated vineyard, he shall give 10 shekels of silver for 1 acre; if it is a neglected vineyard, he shall give 3 shekels of silver.

§ 108. If anyone steals apple-trees from a cultivated vineyard—if he steal 100 trees, he shall pay 10 shekels of silver, and discharge the obligation; but, if in an uncultivated vineyard he steals apple-trees, he shall pay 3 shekels of silver.

§ 109. If anyone steals from an orchard of fruit trees, and it is 100 trees, he shall pay 6 shekels of silver.

§ 110. If anyone steals from a liquid [7] a butt, as much as he stole a corresponding amount he shall pay.

§ 111. If anyone is taken by............, witchcraft is a case for the king.

§ 112. If for the field of a man at arms they give grain (the work of the plantation), they shall not do, but in the fourth year........................ with the men at arms they shall take.

[7] *I. e.*, wine, cider, or olive oil.

§ 113. If anyone cuts off (a vine) and take (the vine) that is cut, he shall give (a good vine) to the owner of the vine.................................
his..he shall take.
§ 114. If...
....
§ 115. ....
....
(§§ 116 and 117 are broken away)
§ 118. ....
........owner of trees ....
..............that one...............he shall take.............
..............he shall go.................................

These horticultural laws should be compared with §§ 59–66 of the Code of Hammurabi. The two codes reveal the differences in fauna of the two countries produced by the differences in their climates. In Babylonia the orchards were planted mainly with date-palms; in the Hittite country, with vines and fruit trees. In Babylonia the laws have to do mainly with the conditions of leases; among the Hittites, mainly with theft and dangers from fire. Among the Hebrews the conditions and laws were different from those in both the other countries. Vineyards and olive orchards are the only kinds of horticulture mentioned in the codes, and the laws have to do mainly with letting them lie fallow during the seventh year and with directions to leave the gleanings for the poor. (See Exod. 23:11; Lev. 19:10; 25:3, 4.) Once (Exod. 22:5) the vineyard is mentioned in order to bring its products under the law of restitution for damages which applied to an agricultural field.

Further Laws Concerning Theft

§ 119. If a bird of a coop (?).............................a cock, anyone steals, formerly he paid........shekels of silver; but now he shall pay 12 shekels of silver and discharge the obligation.

§ 120. If anyone steals some young (?)......birds, if there are 10 birds, he shall pay 1 shekel of silver.

§ 121. If anyone steals a free peasant, they shall set him at liberty (?) ....; formerly they did thus................., but now he shall pay 6 shekels of silver and discharge the obligation. If it is a slave, he shall pay 3 shekels of silver.

§ 122. If anyone steals the contents of a chariot, formerly he paid to the storehouse 1 shekel of silver, but now........(shekels of silver he) shall pay, and discharge the penalty.

§ 123. If a.................(anyone steals).........................
........................3 shekels (of silver he shall pay and discharge the obligation).

§ 124. If a........(anyone steals..........shekels of silver) he shall pay and discharge the obligation. (If.......................................

anyone hides (?), then the field..
........then he stole.........(shekels of silver) he shall give and discharge
the obligation.

§ 125.   If anyone steals a large jar......(shekels of silver he shall pay).
If anyone steals a harness (?) or a saddle (?), he shall pay 1 shekel of silver.

§ 126.   If anyone steals an ornament (?) from the gate of the palace, he
shall pay 6 shekels of silver. If anyone steals a bronze lance from the gate
of the palace, that one shall die. If anyone steals a copper figure (?), he shall
give ½ Pa (10 Qas) of grain. If anyone steals of clothing 1 garment, he shall
give 1 woolen garment.

§ 127.   If anyone in revenge takes a door and destroys it, he shall restore
it and shall pay 1 mana of silver, and discharge the obligation.

§ 128.   If anyone steals bricks, he shall give as many as he stole. If anyone steals a foundation of stones, for 2 stones he shall give 10 stones. If anyone steals a stone figure (?) or a stone vase (?), he shall pay 2 shekels of
silver.

§ 129.   If anyone steals from a horse or from a mule the reins (?) or the
bridle......or a buckle (?) of bronze, formerly he paid 1 mana of silver, but
now he shall pay 12 shekels of silver, and discharge the obligation.

§ 130.   If from an ox or a horse anyone steals a............(..shekels of
silver he shall pay), and discharge the obligation

§ 131.   If (anyone steals) a leather helmet (?), he shall pay 6 shekels of
silver (and discharge the obligation).

§ 132.   If (anyone steals) the........of a free man (he shall pay) 6
shekels of silver (and discharge the obligation).

§ 133.   If (anyone steals the............) of a free man (he shall pay
......) shekels (of silver)...

(About 8 sections are lost at this point.)

§ 142.   (If)..
anyone goes..(and he stole)
a wooden lance (?), for 1 wooden lance (?) ½ Pa (10 Qas) of grain (he
shall give. If he is a slave) for 1 wooden lance (?)......(of grain he shall
give).

§ 143.   If anyone steals from a free man a bronze knife (?)........or
a bronze................, he shall pay 6 shekels of silver and discharge the
obligation. If he is a slave, he shall pay 3 shekels of silver.

§ 144. If (anyone steals) a bronze razor from a barber........and destroys it,.....................If a lower garment with a border (?),
...................he shall pay 10 shekels of silver. If anyone carries
away............... (shekels of silver he shall pay).

The Babylonian and Hebrew codes have nothing to compare
with these laws further than such laws against stealing as have
already been mentioned. From the greater number of laws against
theft in this code, we infer that stealing was much more common
among the Hittites than among the other peoples under consideration.

Laws Fixing the Amount of Damages

§ 145.   If anyone (rents) a cattle-stable, he shall pay 6 shekels..........
............this one in rent................

§ 146. If anyone rents a house or a village or......or............and another comes and does damage to it, and he sells it, the malefactor shall pay 1 mana of silver, and........the seller shall buy (it).

§ 147. If anyone hires an unskilled workman and another seriously injures him, the malefactor shall pay........shekels of silver.

§ 148. If anyone hires an ox, a horse, a mule or an ass and another seriously injures it, the malefactor shall pay........shekels of silver.

§ 149. If anyone sells a bull as a breeder and says: "It is dead," the owner finds it, then he shall take it and he (the malefactor) shall give for it 2 slaves, and discharge the obligation.

These laws find their nearest parallel in §§ 234–240 of the Code of Hammurabi, where the responsibility of boatmen for the collision of boats on a canal is fixed. The details of the two codes are quite different, but the principle of responsibility for damages is the same.

Laws Fixing Wages

§ 150. If a man goes for wages (for 1 month the wages are......shekels of silver). If a woman goes for wages (for 1 month the wages are........ shekels of silver).

§ 151. If anyone hires a plough-ox for 1 month (the wages are) 1 shekel of silver. If he hires.................for (1 month its wages are........ shekels of silver).

§ 152. If anyone hires a horse............(for 1 month its hire is....... shekels of silver).

(At this point about 4 sections are broken away.)

These sections should be compared with §§ 268–277 of the Code of Hammurabi, which fix the wages of animals and of people.

The Rental of Various Objects

§ 157. If it is a bronze axe of 1 mana weight, its rent for 1 month is 1 shekel of silver. If it is a bronze plate of ½ mana weight, its rental for a month is ½ shekel of silver. If it is a platter of 1 mana weight, its rental for 1 month is ½ shekel of silver.

§ 158. If a man goes for wages at harvest (?) and undertakes the management of carts, is lodged in a straw-barn, reaping a ripe field, his wages for 2 months are 30 *Pas* of barley. If a woman goes for wages in the kitchen (?), for 2 months 12 *Pas* of barley (one) shall give.

§ 159. If anyone yokes up a pair of oxen, their wages are ½ *Pa* of barley.

§ 160. If a smith makes a bronze kettle of........manas weight, his pay is 100 *Pas* of barley. If he makes a bronze axe of 2 manas weight, his pay is 1 *Pa* of sesame.

§ 161. If he makes a bronze axe of 1 mana weight, his pay is 1 *Pa* of barley.

§ 162. If anyone turns back a canal, he shall pay 1 shekel of silver; if he diverts water from above, it is a matter of bargain (?); if he diverts water from below, it is his.

While these laws have no exact equivalent in the other codes, they are in principle similar to the preceding group and should be compared to the same group of Babylonian laws.

Responsibility of a Shepherd

§ 163. If in the herd of anyone there is a motherless animal, and it wanders away, and a shepherd takes the flock and does not tell his helper, and the helper does not know, and it dies, it is compensatable.

This law should be compared with §§ 263–267 of the Code of Hammurabi, which are the same in principle.

Ritual Laws

§ 164. If anyone goes to visit a divinity and has made him angry, he should offer as a sacrifice flour and wine.

§ 165. Then he shall give 1 sheep, 10 loaves, and 1 jug of beer. Then afterward he shall offer a sacrifice for his house that the year may come around fortunately; then he may go to the front of his house.

§ 166. "If anyone sows seed upon seed, they shall put him by the side of the plough and harness a pair of oxen, and place this one over against those and them over against him, and the man [8] shall die and the oxen shall die, and he who had first sown the field shall take it." Formerly they did thus.

§ 167. Now 1 sheep shall be substituted for the man, 2 sheep shall be substituted for the oxen; he shall give 30 loaves, 3 jugs of beer; this is a purificatory sacrifice, and he who first sowed the field shall cultivate it.

This law is very interesting. Sowing one kind of seed on top of another was regarded as desecration. The feeling against it was even stronger than that which underlay the prohibition in Deuteronomy 22:11 against wearing a garment made of wool and linen mixed; it was sacrilege and in earlier time had been expiated by the killing of the offender and two oxen. In this code sheep are substituted for the man and the oxen just as in Exodus 34:20, the first-born of a man and of an ass could be redeemed with a lamb. This mingling of civil laws with ritualistic requirements has no parallel in the Babylonian Code. In this respect it stands nearer to the Pentateuch than does the Code of Hammurabi.

§ 168. If anyone will establish the boundary of a field, he shall bring an offering: the owner of the field shall mark off 1 *gipeshar* and take it. He who would establish the boundary shall give 1 sheep, 10 loaves, 1 jug of beer; then afterward the field is sacrosanct.

§ 169. If anyone acquires a field and he establishes the boundary, he shall take flour and throw it toward the sun-goddess and say: "Thou hast planted my plants in the ground!" Then he shall say: "Sun-goddess and Teshub, be not angry!"

8 The Text reads "men," but this is evidently a scribal error.

The first of these laws is similar in purpose to some of the ritual laws of Leviticus, though the details and application are different. Others are quite peculiar to the Hittites.

A Witch Law

§ 170.   If a free man kills a serpent and speaks the name of another, he shall pay 1 mana of silver; if a slave, he shall die.

Probably killing the snake as one pronounced the name of another was believed to direct the wrath of the snake toward that other so that the snake should not be satisfied until he killed the bearer of the name. It would be equivalent to casting a death-spell upon the man so named.   This law, then, should be compared with §§ 1, 2 of the Code of Hammurabi and with Exodus 22: 18 and Deuteronomy 18: 10, ff.

§ 171.   If a mother turns up the garment of her drunken (?) son, she removes him from her children.   If afterwards her son comes and seizes her door and puts away drink (?), he may return and take his bed and his pillow (?); and, as he renounces drink (?) and takes them, her son afterwards shall become her son.

This law should be compared with §§ 192, 193 of the Code of Hammurabi—the nearest approach to such a law in the other codes.

Laws Regulating Prices

§ 172.   If anyone keeps alive for a year a free man who is destitute, he shall give its equivalent; if a slave he shall give 10 shekels of silver.
§ 173.   If anyone shall resist the justice of the king, his house shall become a ruin; if anyone resist the justice of a dignitary, his head is in his power; if a slave rises against his master, he shall put him in a large pot.
§ 174.   If men are in a fight and one dies, one person he shall give.
§ 175.   If a shepherd or an ointment-maker takes a free woman and she is a slave for 2 years or 4 years, her children belong to the household; those that belong to the household no one may take.
§ 176A.   If anyone takes from the courtyard a full-grown bull, he is liable to the punishment of the king.   In the third year he genders.   The plough-ox, the ram, the billy-goat gender in the third year.
B.   If anyone hires an artisan, either a potter, a smith, a carpenter, a shoemaker, a tailor, a weaver, or a maker of lace, he shall pay 10 shekels of silver.
§ 177.   If anyone employs a skilled bird-raiser, he shall pay 25 shekels of silver; if he employs an unskilled man or woman, he shall pay 20 shekels of silver.
§ 178.   The price of a plough-ox is 15 (?) shekels of silver.   The price of a full-grown ox is 10 shekels of silver; the price of a full-grown cow is 7 shekels

of silver; the price of a plough-ox and a cow a year old is 23 (?) shekels of silver; for a six-months old bull-calf one shall give 4 shekels of silver; if it is for a pregnant cow, 8 shekels of silver; for a calf the price is 2 shekels of silver; for a stallion, a broken mare, a he-ass, a broken she-ass, the prices are similar.

§ 179. If the price of 1 sheep is 1 shekel of silver, the price of 3 goats is 2 shekels of silver; of 2 lambs, 1 shekel of silver; of 2 kids, ½ shekel of silver.

§ 180. If the price of a saddle horse is 20 shekels of silver, the price of a mule is 1 mana of silver; the price of a horse is 14 shekels of silver; the price of a stallion one year old is 10 shekels of silver; the price of a dray mare one year old is 15 shekels of silver.

§ 181. The price of a male colt and a mare six months old broken to the yoke is 4 shekels of silver. The price of 4 manas of bronze is 1 shekel of silver; of 1 *zimitan* of refined oil, is 2 shekels of silver; of 1 *zimitan* of lard, is 1 shekel of silver; of 1 *zimitan* of butter, is 1 shekel of silver; of 1 *zimitan* of honey, is 1 shekel of silver; of 2 cheeses, is (1 shekel of silver); the price of 3 (measures) of yeast is 1 shekel of silver.

§ 182. The price of a sacrificial garment is 12 shekels of silver; of a lower garment, is 30 shekels of silver; of a blue woolen garment, is 20 shekels of silver; of a ceremonial garment, is 10 shekels of silver; of an apron, (?), 3 shekels of silver; of a storm-cloak (?), is 4 shekels of silver; the price of a turban is 1 shekel of silver; of a.......is 3 shekels of silver; of a...... ....; of a web of 7 manas weight, the price is.......shekels of silver; of 1 large loin-cloth, 5 shekels of silver.

§ 183. If the price of 3 *Pas* of sesame is 1 shekel of silver, the price of 4 *Pas*........(is......shekels of silver; the price of) 1 *Pa* of wine is ½ shekel of silver; of a *Pa* (of......is......of silver); (the price of) 1 lot of land for building (?) is 3 (shekels of silver; the price) of a lot of land for a yard (?) is 2 shekels of silver (if) for a farming-field one gives 1 shekel of silver.

§ 184. This is the regulation in the city; (that for the country is) analogous.

§ 185. The price of 1 unit of a vineyard is 1 mana of silver; of the skin of a full-grown ox, is 1 shekel of silver; of 5 skins of six-months old calves is 1 shekel of silver; of 10 skins of cattle, is 1 mana (!) of silver; of the skin of a woolly sheep, is 1 shekel of silver; of 10 skins of sheared sheep, 1 shekel of silver; of 4 goat-skins is 1 shekel of silver; of 15 clipped goat-skins is 1 shekel of silver; of 20 lamb-skins is 1 shekel of silver: of 20 kid-skins is 20 shekels of silver. He who buys the flesh of two full-grown cattle shall give 1 sheep.

§ 186. Anyone who buys the flesh of 2 cattle a year old shall give 1 sheep; he who buys the flesh of 5 cattle six-months old shall give 1 sheep; the flesh of 10 calves, shall give 1 sheep; the flesh of 10 (sheep), shall give 1 sheep; the flesh of 20 lambs, shall give 1 sheep; the flesh of (20) kids, shall give 1 sheep.

These laws which fix prices are parallel to §§ 268–277 of the Code of Hammurabi, already referred to, though they differ from the Babylonian laws in detail. Like the Babylonian laws, they fix prices—a procedure from which modern economists have dissuaded most modern governments.

Against Unnatural Sins

§ 187. If a man lie with a cow, the punishment is death. They shall bring him to the gates of the king. The king may put him to death, or the king may let him live, but he shall not come near to the king.

§ 188. If with a........a man lie, the punishment is death. They shall bring him to the gates of the king. The king may put him to death, or the king may let him live, but he shall not come near to the king.

The unnatural sin here punished by death is also recognized in Exodus 22:19 and Leviticus 20:15, where the death-penalty is also imposed upon it. The Hittite law provides for a possible pardon by the king, but the Hebrew law leaves for the culprit no way of escape from death.

Against Incest

§ 189. If a man lie forcibly with his own mother, it is punishable with death; if he lie with his daughter, it is punishable with death; if he lie with his son, it is punishable with death.

§ 190. But, if they come together willingly, the man and the woman, it is not punishable. If a man lie forcibly with his step-mother it is not punishable; but, if his father is living, it is punishable.

These laws touch upon the subject treated at much greater length by the Law in Leviticus 18:6–18 and 20:10–21. The Hebrew laws were much more strict, and guarded the purity of the family circle much better than the Hittite.

Against Adultery and Fornication

§ 191. If a free man come together with the wife of a neighbor, if it is out of doors, here or there,[9] it is not punishable. If (they do it) a second time, ...it is punishable.........

The Hebrew law was much more strict in such cases; cf. Deuteronomy 22:22–29.

On Killing a Man's Wife

§ 192. If a man kill a woman, the bereaved husband may take his wife. ....it is not punishable.

A Levirate Law

§ 193. If a man takes a wife and the man dies, his brother take his wife; then his father take her; if also his father dies, the woman which he married his brother take; it is not a crime.

This law is somewhat similar to the Levirate law of Deuteronomy 25:5–10. That law, like this, provides for the marriage of a widow by a brother, only in case the brother dies without a son; it makes no provision, like the Hittite law, for the father to take her.

9 Literally, "if it is out of doors, if it is out of doors."

The Hebrew law further provides a method of renouncing the obligation to take the woman. The provision that, after one son has had the woman, the father should take her, finds a parallel in the story of Tamar in Genesis 38. The provision that, if the man's father dies, the father's brother shall take her, carries the Levirate law further than any Semitic people did.

Professor Meek has objected that the Hittites had no Levirate law, because this statute is only permissive, not obligatory. His own statement, however, "the institution with the Hittites had become quite obsolete, so obsolete and out of favor that a law had to be formulated to make it legal," [10] admits that they had the Levirate. He is probably right in thinking that it was out of favor at Hittite City, but the law is evidence that it was still practiced there, and in less civilized branches of the same stock was probably still followed.

Further Laws on Adultery and Rape

§ 194. If a free man comes together with a slave woman, either here or there, there is no penalty. If a father or brother spend the night with a free woman, there is no penalty. If a father and son spend the night with a slave girl or a prostitute, there is no penalty.

§ 195. If a man spends the night with the wife of his brother while his brother is living, it is punishable with death. If a man marries a free woman and has intercourse with her daughter, it is punishable with death. If he marries a daughter and has intercourse with her mother or sister, it is punishable with death.

These laws should be compared with Leviticus 18 and 20 and Deuteronomy 22, which treat of the same subject. Such a comparison shows that Hittite social morals and ideals were on a lower plane than those of Israel.

Against Various Kinds of Disorder

§ 196. If slave men and slave women sleep together and go to one city and another city and make a disturbance, 1 sheep for this and 1 sheep for that is the purificatory offering.

§ 197. If a man seizes a woman in the mountain and commits the human crime, he shall die. If he seizes her in a house, the woman is at fault, she shall die. If the husband finds them and they are killed, there is no penalty.

§ 198. If he brings them to the gate of the palace and says: "Let not my wife die," he may let his wife live; he may also let the ravisher live, but in that case he shall scar his head. If he shall say: "Let the two die," then they shall receive their punishment. The king may kill them; the king may let them live.

10 T. J. Meek, *Hebrew Origins*, New York, 1936, p. 58n.

The last two of these laws should be compared with Deuteronomy 22:22–27. The principles underlying the two codes are here the same, though the application is different. The Hittite code makes provision for sparing the life of the guilty man and woman, while the Hebrew law does not.

More Unnatural Sins

§ 199. If a man lies with a hog or a dog, he shall die. They shall bring him to the gate of the palace, and the king may put him to death, or the king may let him live; but he shall not come near to the king. If a bull rear upon a man, the bull shall die, but the man shall not die; 1 sheep is the purificatory offering; then they shall kill it. If a boar rear upon a man, there is no penalty.

§ 200. If a man lies with a horse or a mule there is no penalty, but he shall not come near the king and he shall not become a priest. If (a man).... sleep with a hierodoule (?).................that one....................., there is no penalty. If anyone gives a son.................(if he is) a carpenter (or a potter, or a weaver), or a shoemaker, or a tailor, or a (smith), he shall pay 6 shekels of silver. If an artisan of Teshub (?) or the sungoddess, then he shall give 1 slave.

This last section apparently refers to intercourse with religious prostitutes, though it is too broken to enable us to be sure of the details.

The code as a whole reveals the life of the Hittites as both attractive and repulsive. They were an agricultural people; the land seems to have been held by the community in common and let out on condition that it would be cultivated and certain military duties performed. Irrigation was practiced; fires were much more abundant than in Babylonia, and thefts much more frequent. Judging by the number of laws against it, the people were much given to stealing. Slaves were numerous, but seem to have been allowed a good deal of liberty. Their religious customs, as we have noted, remind one of some of the Israelitish customs and regulations, but there are such differences as to prove them independent of Israel. There is to be detected in it some influence of the Babylonian laws, but, on the whole, it is slight. The Hittite laws are so different from those of Babylon that they were clearly the product of Hittite life and experience. One interesting feature of this code is that it frequently modifies earlier customs and regulations in the interest of humanitarianism.

The final sections of the code, however, leave a painful impression. They show the Hittites as recognizing and legitimatizing a bestiality of which we would gladly think them innocent.

CHAPTER XV

PART OF AN ASSYRIAN CODE OF LAWS [1]

Assyrian Laws with Comparison of Biblical and Babylonian Laws.

During the excavation of Kalah-Sherghat, the ancient Ashur, by Andrae (see above p. 38), an archive of tablets was found which contained two tablets of considerable size and several smaller fragments on which had been written a code of Assyrian laws. It is difficult to date the writing of these documents, but, from a number of considerations, they appear to come from the period between 1450 and 1250 B.C. Perhaps they were compiled about the time the Hittite code was being put into the form in which we now have it. As the contents are only about a quarter of the length of the Code of Hammurabi and one-third the length of the Hittite code, it is fair to assume that there were originally two or three more tablets in the collection on which the whole code was inscribed.

Tablet A

Laws Concerning Women

§ 1. If a woman, the wife of a man, or the daughter of a man enters into a temple that she may steal anything from the shrine, and it is found (in her hand), they shall either examine her or establish it and shall inquire of the god; according as he commands to do to the woman, they shall do to her.

§ 2. If a woman, whether married or the daughter of a man, shall speak blasphemy or utter sedition, that woman shall bear her sin. Unto her husband, her sons, or her daughters they (the officers of the law) shall not approach.

§ 3. If a man is sick or has died and his wife steals anything from his house and gives it to a man or a woman or to any other (person), the wife of that man and the one who received (it) they shall kill. And if the wife of a man whose husband is living steals from the house of her husband, whether she gives it to a man or a woman or to anyone whatsoever, the man shall examine his wife and impose punishment (literally "fix her sin"), and the receiver who received (the goods) from the man's wife shall make restitution, and shall receive the same punishment which the man inflicts on his wife.

§ 4. If a slave or a bond-woman receives anything from a man's wife, the nose and ears of the slave or the bond-woman they shall cut off and they shall

---

1 The text is published by Otto Schroeder, *Keilschrifttexte aus Ashur Vershiedenen Inhalts*, Leipzig, 1920. It was translated by Jastrow in the *Journal of the American Oriental Society*, Vol. 41 (1921), pp. 1-59; also by V. Scheil, *Recueil de lois assyriennes*, Paris, 1921, and by G. R. Driver and John C. Miles, *The Assyrian Laws*, Oxford, 1935.

427

make restitution; the husband shall cut off the ears of his wife; but, if he spares his wife and does not cut off her ears, they shall not cut off the ears of the slave or the bond-woman and they shall not make restitution.

§ 5. If the wife of a man steals anything from the house of another man which exceeds the value of 5 manas of lead, the owner of the stolen property shall swear thus: "they were seized," and: "They were stolen from my house." If her husband wishes, he may make restitution and ransom her and cut off her ear. If her husband does not wish to ransom her, the owner of the object may take her and cut off her nose.

§ 6. If the wife of a man makes a deposit in a pawn-shop he who receives it is guilty of theft.

§ 7. If a woman stretches out her hands against a man, they shall arrest her; she shall pay 30 manas of lead and receive 20 strokes of the rod.

§ 8. If a woman in a fight crushes a man's testicle, they shall cut off one of her fingers. If a physician binds up the man and the other testicle is involved and destroyed, or becomes inflamed, or if in a fight both testicles are crushed, they shall destroy both her breasts.

§ 9. If a man lifts up his hand against the wife of a man and acts like a young wild ox (?), they shall arrest him and try him; they shall cut off one finger. If he kisses her, they shall cut off his lower lip with a poisoned bronze (knife?) whose edge is sharp.

§ 10. If a man or a woman enters (a house) and kills (a man) or a woman ....the murderers..........before him..........they shall kill..... ....they shall take..........the murderers........anything.......... a son or daughter..........in the house (?)[2]............................. ....whose........they shall destroy both.

§ 11. If a man's wife is going along the highway and a man seizes her without saying to her, "Let us embrace," she does not consent, she defends herself, he is strong, he rapes her, whether he is caught on the wife of a man or witnesses see him; they shall kill the man; the woman was not to blame.

§ 12. If the wife of a man goes from her house unto a man and goes to a place where a man lives and he has intercourse with her, and knows she is the wife of a man they shall kill both the man and the woman.

§ 13. If a man's wife and a man, either in a house of prostitution or on the highway, he knowing that she is a man's wife, has intercourse with her, as if he were the man whose wife she is (and) they agree in the deed, the man has committed adultery. If not knowing that she was a man's wife he had intercourse with her, the man is innocent of adultery. The husband shall take his wife and do with her what he pleases.

§ 14. If a man finds a man with his wife, they shall make examination and establish it and put them to death. That (putting them to death) is not his sin. If he is caught and brought before the king or the judges, they shall examine him and establish his guilt. If the husband of the woman has killed his wife, then the man they shall kill. If he has cut off his wife's nose, they shall make the man an eunuch and mutilate his whole face. If (the man) forgives his wife, the man (shall be forgiven).

§ 15. If a man's wife deceives a man, there is no blame attaching to the man; the husband of the woman shall visit punishment upon his wife as he wishes. If by force he has violated her, they shall examine him and establish it; his punishment shall be according to that of the wife of the man.

§ 16. If a man speaks to a man as follows: "They have violated thy wife," and there were no witnesses, they shall throw that man into fetters and bring him to the river.[3]

---

[2] The tablet has been broken at this point.
[3] Evidently to throw him in. It was trial by ordeal.

§ 17. If a man says to his companion either in secret or in a brawl, as follows: "They violated thy wife and I saw it" (when) it was not possible to see it and that man did not see it, they shall give him forty strokes with a scourge and he shall perform a full month of service for the king. They shall crop him and he shall pay a talent of lead.

§ 18. If anyone in secret utters a slander against his companion, as follows: "They had intercourse with thee," or in a brawl he says in the presence of men, "They had intercourse with thee and I saw thee" (when) he was not able to see, and that man did not see, they shall give him 50 lashes with a scourge, he shall perform a full month's service for the king, they shall crop him and he shall give a talent of lead.

§ 19. If a man have intercourse with his companion, they shall arrest and try him. If he had intercourse with him, they shall make him an eunuch.

§ 20. If a man strikes the daughter of a man and causes a miscarriage, they shall arrest him and try him; he shall pay 2 talents 30 manas of lead, they shall give him 50 lashes with a scourge, and he shall perform a full month's service for the king.

§ 21. If one who is neither the father, brother nor son of a man's wife, but another, seize her on the road, he shall swear that he did not know that she was a man's wife, and shall pay 2 talents of lead to her husband.

§ 22. If, when......(a man gives) shelter (to a man's wife), and if..... the man's wife is not raped (because) the man gave shelter to the man's wife, he shall go (to the river); he shall not be bound. If he returns from the river, as the woman's husband did to his wife, they shall do to him.

§ 23. If a man's wife takes another man's wife into her house and gives her to a man to have intercourse with, and he, knowing that she is the wife of a man, has intercourse with her he shall be treated as one who has had intercourse with a married woman, and the procuress shall be treated as the woman's husband has treated his adulterous wife. If the woman's husband does nothing to his adulterous wife, nothing shall be done to the adulterer and procuress; they shall release them. And, if the man's wife did not know, and the woman who received her into her house brought her because of the man's intention toward her and he had intercourse with her, if, when she goes from the house, she confesses that they had intercourse, they shall let that woman go; she is innocent. The adulterer and the procuress they shall kill. But if the woman does not confess, the husband may inflict on his wife what punishment he pleases; the adulterer and the procuress they shall kill.

§ 24. If a man's wife is, in the presence of her husband, forcibly and bodily carried away, whether within a large city or in the suburbs to a house they have appointed, and she enters the house of an Assyrian man and lives with the mistress of the house three or four times, and the master of the house does not know that it is a man's wife that is living in his house, then the owner of the house whose wife was forcibly and bodily carried away in the presence of her husband, he and his wife take the blame. The married woman with whom his wife stayed they shall seize and shall cut off her ear. As his punishment her husband shall pay 3 talents 30 manas of lead as her price and fault, and shall take his wife.

But if the owner of the house knew that it was a man's wife that was brought into his house with his wife, he shall pay thrice as much. And if he resists and says, "I did not know," they shall bring him unto the river. And if the man in whose house the man's wife was caught refuses the river, he shall pay three times as much. If the man whose wife was forcibly and bodily carried off in his presence refuses the river, he is innocent; the river settles all that, and if the man whose wife was forcibly and bodily carried off in his presence does not mutilate his wife, he shall take her as his wife; nothing further is imposed.

§ 25. If a woman is retained in her father's house and her husband dies, the brothers of her husband may not divide, though she has no son. Whatever as a free gift her husband settled upon her the brothers of her husband cannot annul; into the division it shall not go. Upon the rest that the gods have provided they may lay hands and take. To the river (ordeal) and oath they shall not be subjected.

§ 26. If a woman is detained in the house of her father and her husband dies, anything that the husband has settled on her as a free gift, if there are children of her husband, they may take; if there are no children of her husband, she may take what is left.

§ 27. If a woman is detained in the house of her father, her husband may enter, and whatever her husband has given her as a gift that he may take; to that which belongs to her father's house he may not lay claim.

§ 28. If a widow enters a man's house and brings with her her minor son from the house of her brother who had brought him up, and her husband did not write a tablet of adoption, he shall receive no share of the estate of the one who brought him up, nor can one take him as a pledge.[4] In the house of his ancestry he shall receive a portion according to his share.

§ 29. If a woman enters the house of her husband, her dowry and whatever she brings from her father's house and what her father-in-law gives her when she comes is free for her children; the sons of her father-in-law may not touch it, but if her husband divorces her, he may give it to his children as he pleases.

§ 30. If a father carries to the house of the father-in-law of his son anything that can be carried, the woman is not thereby pledged to his son. If a second son, (and) he whose wife is detained in the house of her father dies, the wife of his dead son shall be given to his other son as a possession. If the master of the daughter who received the gift is not favorable to the betrothal of his daughter, at his pleasure the father who brought the gift may take (a girl) and give as a bride to his son. At his pleasure he may take as capital as much as he brought of lead, silver and gold; but not food. Food he may not touch.

§ 31. If a man sends a betrothal gift to the house of his father-in-law and his wife dies, should his father-in-law have another daughter, at the pleasure of his father-in-law he may take the daughter of his father-in-law instead of his dead wife, or at his pleasure he may take again the silver which he had given. Grain or sheep or anything that is eatable they shall not give back to him; he receives only money.

§ 32. If a woman is retained in the house of her father and her dowry has been granted, whether she has taken it to the house of her father-in-law or has not taken it, it may be attached as interest on a debt and obligation of her husband.

§ 33. If a woman is retained in the house of her father and her husband has died and there are children,......his..................................
....
...............and......unto her father-in-law for a husband (?) it shall be given. If the husband and father-in-law have died and she has no son, she is a widow and may go wherever she pleases.

§ 34. If a man cohabits with a widow without a formal contract and she lives 2 years in his house, that woman shall not depart from his house.

§ 35. If a widow enters the house of a man, whatever she brings all belongs to her husband; and if the man enters in unto the woman, whatever he brings all belongs to the woman.

---

4 *I. e.*, as security for debt.

§ 36. If a woman is retained in the house of her father, though her husband would have her dwell in a house apart (?), and her husband has gone to the field and has not left her oil, wool, clothing, food, or anything, nor any income accruing from a field, that woman shall await her husband for 5 years and not live with (another) man. If she has children, they shall give her comfort and food; the woman shall await her husband; she shall not live with a man. If she has no children she shall await her husband five years; at the incoming of six years she may dwell with the husband of her choice. Her (first) husband on his return shall not come near to her; she is pledged to her last husband. If for five full years he is absent voluntarily and does not come near (her), either because a voice seized him and he fled, or because as a rebel he is caught and detained, he shall give a woman in place of his wife and shall take his wife. Or if the king sends him to another country and detains him for a space of five years, and his wife awaits him and does not dwell with a husband, or if before five years she does dwell with a husband and bears him children, her (first) husband on his return, because her obligation was not fulfilled,—she shall be restored to him, and he shall take the children.

§ 37. If a man divorces his wife, he may give her whatever he pleases. If he does not wish, he may give her nothing and she shall go forth empty-handed.

§ 38. If a woman is detained in the house of her father and her husband divorces her, anything which he has voluntarily settled upon her he may take. He may not touch her marriage portion which she brought; it is secured to the woman.

§ 39. If a man has given to a husband a girl not his daughter but whose father had formerly given her in pledge for a debt (and) the former debtor (?) come, he shall receive recompense for the woman from the man who gave her in marriage. If the man who gave her has nothing to give, he who pledged her may take him. But if she is living in ill-treatment, she is quit of him who ill-treats her. If the man who married the woman, either by signing a contract or executing a legal obligation, gives satisfaction, the man who gave her in marriage is quit.

§ 40. Whether wives of men.......or women.......on the street (shall veil) their heads. Men's daughters........whether out-door (?) garments ......or......garments, or......shall be veiled........their heads........ whether..........whether.. ....veiled, if she walk on the street by day she shall be veiled, the captive woman who walks on the street with a mistress shall be veiled, the hierodoule who has taken a husband shall be veiled on the street, the one who has not taken a husband her head on the street is uncovered, the foreign captive woman is veiled, the prostitute is unveiled, her head is uncovered; whoever sees a prostitute veiled shall seize her, he shall summon witnesses and take her to the portal of the palace. Her ornaments they shall not take away, but the garment in which she was seized they shall take. They shall give her 50 lashes and pour asphalt on her head. But if a man shall see a prostitute veiled and shall let her go and not bring her to the portal of the palace, they shall inflict on that man 50 stripes, his *batikan* and his garment they shall take, they shall pierce his ears, shall insert a cord in it, and bind it behind him and for one full month he shall perform work for the king. Female slaves are not veiled. Whoever sees a slave-woman veiled shall seize her and bring her to the portal of the palace; they shall cut off her ear. He who seized her shall take her garments. If a man sees a slave-woman veiled and lets her go and does not seize her, and does not take her to the portal of the palace, they shall arrest and try him; they shall give him 50 lashes, pierce his ear, insert a thread and bind it behind him, his *batikan* and garment they shall take, and for one full month he shall perform labor for the king.

§ 41. If a man veils his captive woman, brings in 5 or 6 companions, veils her in their presence and says, "She is my wife," she is his wife. That captive woman who is unveiled in the presence of men, whose man does not say, "She is my wife," is not a wife; she is a captive woman. If a man dies and his veiled wife has no children, the children of the captive woman are their children; they take their portion.

§ 42. If a man pours oil on the head of a man's daughter on the day of anointing and brings marriage-gifts (?) on a feast-day, they shall not be returned.

§ 43. If a man pours oil on the head and brings marriage-gifts(?), if the son whose wife they were betrothing either dies or flees, he may give her to whomsoever he may please among his remaining sons from the oldest to the youngest, even to one of 10 years. If the father dies and the son whose wife they were betrothing dies, should there be a son of the dead son of ten years of age, he takes her. If the grandsons are younger than ten years, the father of the girl may give the girl (in marriage) at his pleasure and make recompense in equity. If there is no son, whatever was received of precious stones, not eatables, the capital he shall return; he shall return nothing eatable.

§ 44. If an Assyrian man or an Assyrian woman is detained in a man's house as security for any sum whatever up to his full value they may flog, pluck out his hair, his ear they may mutilate and pierce.

§ 45. If a woman is married and an enemy captures her husband, and she has no father-in-law or son, she shall await her husband for two years. During these two years she may go and say that she has no food and be a dependent on the palace...
shall feed her. Its (work) she shall do, she is a.........................
....
....field...........she shall go (and say) for food...........the judges shall ask the rulers of the city that they go to the field in that city and give the field and house to her to work for her support for two years. She dwells there and they write a tablet for her. When two years have been fulfilled she may live with the husband of her choice; they write her a tablet for widowhood. If at a future time her lost husband returns to the country he may take from his wife what they had acquired together; he shall not touch the children she may have borne to her second husband; her second husband takes them. The field and house which they had given for her support at its full value is theirs together. If he does not return it to the control of the king, he shall pay the value given and then take it.[5] But if he does not return but dies in another country, he gives his field and house in place of that which the king gave.

§ 46. If a woman whose husband has died had not gone out from her house for a year, and if her husband had not assigned anything to her in the houses of her sons, she may live where it is convenient. The sons of her husband shall nourish her with food and drink; they shall bind her to themselves as a bride whom one loves. If she is a subsequent wife and had no children, she should dwell with one and together they shall support her. If she has sons, the sons of the former wife may decline to support her; in the houses of her own sons, where she pleases, she may dwell; her own sons shall support her and she shall do their work. And if among the sons of her husband the one who has taken her to support her,.........................support her.

§ 47. If either a man or a woman practises magic and is caught in the act, they shall arrest and try them; they shall kill one who practises magic. A

5 The language is obscure, but this apparently refers to the first husband.

man who witnesses the practice of magic, one who hears from the mouth of one who says "I saw sorcery," shall go and report it to the king. If a witness who should report to the king denies it, and in the presence of the divine Ox, the son of Shamash, shall say, "I never said it," he is free. The witness who reports and then denies the king shall question as much as he is able and see his inmost thoughts. When the sorcerer is brought to the king, an officer shall make him confess and say to him, "The oath which you have sworn to the king and his son he will not absolve thee; according to the tenor of the document which thou hast sworn unto the king is the oath."

§ 48. If a man has retained the daughter of a debtor as security in his house, he may ask her father and give her to a husband; if the father refuses, he may not give her. If her father has died, he shall ask one of her brothers and that one shall speak to the (other) brothers. If a brother says, "I will redeem my sister within a month"—if within a month he does not redeem her, the creditor is free to do as he pleases; he may give her to a husband.........
tenor.................give her..........she............him..............
them............them............him.

§ 49. ....with......................with the brother. But if the prostitute dies, because of this her brothers say, "her......a portion with her brothers," (then) her brothers may divide their estate (?).

§ 50. If a man strikes a woman and causes a miscarriage...............
the man's wife and.............and............he shall make, in (place of) her fruit he shall make restitution for a human life. If that woman dies, they shall kill the man. And if the husband of that woman, whose wife was struck so that she had a miscarriage, has no son, as atonement for the embryo they shall kill him who struck the blow. If what was in her womb was a developed fœtus, he shall make restitution for a human life.

§ 51. If a man strikes the wife of a man not yet advanced in pregnancy so that she has a miscarriage, for that offense he shall pay 2 talents of lead.

§ 52. If a man strikes a harlot so that she has a miscarriage, they shall inflict on him blow for blow. He shall make restitution for human life.

§ 53. If a woman by herself causes a miscarriage, they shall arrest her and put her on trial, they shall impale her on stakes and shall not bury her. If she dies in consequence of the miscarriage, they shall impale her on stakes and shall not bury her. If they curse that woman on account of her miscarriage, they shall say...
....
....

§ 54. ....
.............................there is not..............................
..................slave-girls.................................

§ 55. If a man takes a virgin from the house of her father and does not return her to her father, if she has not been deflowered or taken as a wife or held for a claim on the house of her father, any man who seizes the virgin, whether within the city or the country or by night on the highway or at a house of feasting or at a city feast, and violates her, the father of the virgin may take the wife of the seducer of the virgin and give her to be ravished. To her husband he may not return her; he takes her. The father of the ravished girl gives her to the seducer as a possession. If he has no wife, the seducer shall give to her father 3 times the price of the virgin. The seducer who seized her shall not divorce her. If the father does not wish to receive 3 times the price of the virgin, he may give his daughter to whomsoever he pleases.

§ 56. If a virgin of her own accord gives herself to a man, the man must swear (it). His wife they shall not touch. Three times the price of the virgin the adulterer shall give and the father of the girl may do with her whatever he pleases.

§ 57.   Whether one strikes or (seduces) a man's wife, a tablet is written
....
§ 58.   For all offenses............the cutting of.............and folding
(?) as a pledge (?)..........as it is written.............
§ 59.   On the correction of offenses (which are committed) which are written on (this) tablet, a man may (flog) his wife, pluck out her hair, may
bruise and destroy her ears.   There is no liability.

Here the first tablet of the Assyrian code ends, and with it the
laws relating to women.   Neither in the Code of Hammurabi nor
in the Pentateuch nor the Hittite code have we as many laws relating to women as are found in this Assyrian code.   On the whole,
Assyrian society seems to have been more barbarous and more
given to sins of lust that the Babylonian, though, in the portions
of the Assyrian code that have been recovered, we find no such
references to unnatural sins as are contained in the Hittite code.

Without going into great detail, we may note that the principles
on which adultery and rape are punished are the same as those
which underlie the Babylonian laws on chastity, marriage, and
divorce.   The same is true of the laws controlling the dower rights
of women; (see Code of Hammurabi, §§ 128–161).   These principles are some of them also found in the laws of Leviticus and
Deuteronomy.   The Biblical passages referring to them have been
cited above in Chapter XIII, p. 393 ff, and it does not seem necessary to repeat them here.   The death-penalty for adultery, for example, imposed in so many sections of the Assyrian code, is paralleled in Leviticus 20 : 10 and Deuteronomy 22 : 22.   The Assyrian
law, however, commits the wife to the mercy of her husband in a
way without parallel in the Bible.   It also provides for mutilation
of the face and hands in a way without parallel in Babylonia and
Israel.   Some slight parallel both to the power of the husband and
to mutilation is found in the Hittite code, for example, § 198, but of
all these people the Assyrians were the most primitive in their attitude toward such matters.

A number of sections of the Assyrian laws provide for the ordeal
of plunging into the river.   Sometimes the culprit was bound, as
in § 16, and sometimes unbound, as in § 22.   Hebrew law provided
an ordeal for one similar case (see Num. 5 : 11–28), though the
nature of the ordeal was different.

In § 43 of this Assyrian code we have a Levirate law which reminds us of that in Deuteronomy 25 : 5–10, though the purpose of it
is different; the Biblical law is designed to secure offspring for a

deceased man; the Assyrian, to provide a husband for a widowed woman.

In §§ 40–43 we have an interesting parallel to the Hebrew custom of piercing the ear, provided for in Exodus 21:6 and Deuteronomy 15:17, though the purpose is different in the two countries; in Palestine it was a mark of perpetual slavery voluntarily assumed; in Assyria, it was a punishment for crime.

The 47th section of the Assyrian code contains a law against the practice of witchcraft similar to that in the Code of Hammurabi, §§ 1 and 2. A similar law is found in Exodus 22:18 and another in § 170 of the Hittite code; though in each code the provisions differ in details.

The second of the tablets containing the Assyrian laws is much broken. The parts of it which can be made out are numbered with Roman numerals in order to call the reader's attention to the fact that they do not run consecutively, as do those of the first tablet.

Tablet B
Laws Concerning Real Estate

§ I. ....lands (?).................of land (the oldest son) shall lay claim to 2 portions and take them, and his brothers afterward equally shall claim and take. The youngest son may claim from cultivated land provisions and a portion (?) of whatever is cultivated. The oldest son may claim and take 1 portion, and as his second portion may demand (service) of his brothers.

§ II. If one among brothers of an undivided estate destroys human life, they shall hand him over to the master of the human life. At his pleasure the owner of the human life may kill him; but should he please, he may pardon him and take his share.

§ III. If one of the brothers of an undivided estate shall utter sedition or flee, his portion is the king's according to his pleasure.

§ IV. If brothers are on an undivided estate (and) one of the brothers sows......seed.......cultivates the field..........and goes.......the grain of his brother..........a second time.........they shall arrest him and put him on trial...................shall cultivate................shall take.

§ V. (If brothers are on) an undivided estate (and one of) them........ ....goes... ....

§ VI. (If) for silver a man would acquire (a house and field) he must bind himself not to acquire (that) house (and field) for one month. In the city of Ashur the court officer shall cause it to be cried 3 times; 3 times he shall cause to be cried in the city the house and field which he would acquire, as follows: "The house and field of So-and-So, the son of So-and-So, within the limits of this city I would acquire for (silver); whatever their demands and price may be, let them bring their tablets and deposit them with the recorder, let them state the price, let them make it free and let them take it." If within that month, adjudged as the time limit, they do not neglect to bring their tablets, the man shall establish the boundary of his field and take it. On the day that the court officer causes it to be cried in the city of Ashur, one of the officers from the king's presence, the city scribe, the court officer and a representative of the king shall sit in session. If the field and house are within (another) city, the prefect and three elders of the city shall sit in session. The court-officer shall make proclamation, they shall write their tablets and deliver (them).

But if within that month that the court officer proclaims 3 times—if in that month he does not bring his tablets and does not deposit them before the recorder, on the field and house his hand is stayed. They are free to him who had the herald make proclamation. Three tablets of the proclamation shall be written by the court officer of the judges shall be written......
....

§ VII. ....
....
as much........he may claim (?) ....for.............and the price...............(of what) they injured...............twice the price of the house........he (shall recover) for the owner of the house, unto 1 talent of lead; they shall inflict on him five (stripes) (and) he shall perform (a full month's) service for the king.

§ VIII. If a man encroaches greatly on his neighbor, they arrest him and determine his guilt; he shall give three times the area of field that he encroached. They shall cut off one of his fingers, give him 100 lashes, and for an entire month he shall perform work for the king.

§ IX. If a man violently makes a small encroachment on a lot, they shall arrest him and put him on trial; he shall pay 1 talent of lead. The area of field which he had violently taken he shall restore; they shall give him 50 lashes, and he shall perform 1 full month's service for the king.

§ X. If a man digs a well or makes a dyke in a field not his, for his well or dyke they shall give him 30 strokes; twenty days he shall (perform) work for the king. If..............the dyke..........(he shall do) work, he shall swear...........as follows: "If...........well not........and work ....owner of the field..........in..........well...................
....

§ XI. ....
....
....
and..........creditor..........to cultivate..........and whether.........
.........creditor............the tablets.............maintenance........
...........to work............the field..............for the creditor.....
...........he shall give........

§ XII. If a man shall plant an orchard in the field of (a man) or (dig) a well, or grows vegetables, or trees, if the owner of the field is willing the orchard is free to the planter. He shall give field for field unto the owner of the orchard.

§ XIII. If a man in ground not his own plants an orchard or digs a well, or he raises vegetables or trees, they arrest him and put him on trial, on the day that the owner of the field comes, he may take the orchard together with his outlay.

§ XIV. If a man in ground not his breaks up the surface and burns bricks, they arrest him and determine his guilt, he shall give three times the area of ground and they shall take his bricks. They shall give him 50 stripes and he shall perform (a full month's) service for the king.

§ XV. (If a man)........and burns bricks on ground not his, his......
........they shall take from him, they shall give him........stripes and he shall perform (a full month's service for the king).

§ XVI. ....

....

..................not...

§ XVII. (If) it is water in common (for) irrigation which they have brought (for) storage, the owners of the field share it together, each shall do his work within the bounds of his field and irrigate his field. If there is no harmony among them, one of them so minded may appeal to the judges; he may receive a tablet from the judges and may carry on the work. Those waters he may take and irrigate his field; he may irrigate nothing of another.

§ XVIII. If it is rain water they have brought to store for irrigation, the owners of the field shall share it together, each within the limits of his field shall do his work and irrigate his field. But if among them there is not harmony and one of them receives a tablet from the judges because there is not harmony (the prefect and) 5 elders.

§ XIX. ....

....

(they shall) inflict on him....(stripes and....months work he shall) perform (for the king).

§ XX. (If a man) work (the field of) his neighbor.........restrain him ....of the king (he may) work and cultivate...........and he shall go. The cultivator who has assisted (the owner) on a field............... shall be deprived of his claim. He shall pour the grain into the granary; measure for measure he shall restore the grain (according to the) yield of the field of the city....................he shall give (for) the field.

§ XXI. (If a man from) a field not his takes a little.........and fences it and places boundary stones...............say, (they shall arrest him and) put him on trial..

....

Fragments of eight other tablets were found, no one of which contains a complete line. From the parts which remain it is possible to ascertain in some cases the nature of the subjects treated. Thus tablet C contained laws concerning the sale of slaves and the sale and theft of cattle and tablet G, laws dealing with money loans. Driver and Miles have made conjectural restorations of the text of some of these,[6] but for a general work, such as ours, it does not seem wise to reproduce them.

These laws concerning real estate should be compared with the Code of Hammurabi, §§ 42–58. The Babylonian laws deal with different aspects of real estate problems, but certain underlying principles may be found in the two codes. The Pentateuch presents no real parallel to these laws. Such real estate laws as it contains are found in Exodus 22: 5–15; Deuteronomy 19: 14, but they treat mainly of other topics than those treated in the Assyrian code. The Hebrew law against removing land-marks (Deut. 19: 14) is represented in principle in the Assyrian laws by §§ VIII and IX, which clearly refer to the same subject, and by §§ X–XV, which treat of a kindred form of trespass. The Assyrian code

6 *The Assyrian Laws*, pp. 440–453.

provides penalties for the violation of its provisions. Its laws therefore had "teeth" in them, while the Biblical law had none.

Such narratives as that of Genesis 23, which tells of Abraham's purchase of the cave of Macpelah, and 1 Kings 21, which tells how Naboth refused to sell his vineyard, show that transfers of real estate were known in Israel, though we have no laws on the subject in the Pentateuch. Some of those in the Assyrian code are very interesting. That in § VI, which lays down the procedure to be followed in transferring land within a city, has a very modern sound, though perhaps the employment of a town-crier is mediæval rather than modern. Now the advertising columns of a newspaper take the place of the crier.

CHAPTER XVI

AN ALLEGED PARALLEL TO LEVITICUS—A CARTHA-GINIAN LAW CONCERNING SACRIFICES [1]

THE TEXT OF THE CARTHAGINIAN LAW. COMPARISON WITH THE LEVITICAL LAW.

1. The Text of the Carthaginian Law.

Temple of Baal[zephon]. Tar[iff of d]ues, which [the superintendents of d]ues fixed in the time [of our rulers, Khalas]baal, the judge, son of Bodtanith, son of Bod[eshmun, and of Khalasbaal], the judge, son of Bodeshmun, son of Khalasbaal, and their colleagues.

For an ox as a whole burnt-offering [2] or a prayer-offering, or a whole peace-offering,[3] the priests shall have 10 (shekels) of silver for each; and in case of a whole burnt-offering, they shall have in addition to this fee [300 shekels of fle]sh; and, in case of a prayer-offering, the trimmings, the joints; but the skin and the fat of the inwards [4] and the feet and the rest of the flesh the owner of the sacrifice shall have.

For a calf whose horns are wanting, in case of one not castrated (?), or in case of a ram as a whole burnt-offering, the priests shall have 5 shekels of silver [for each; and in case of a whole burnt-offering they shall have in addit]ion to this fee 150 shekels of flesh; and, in case of a prayer-offering, the trimmings and the joints; but the skin and the fat of the inwards and the fe[et and the rest of the flesh the owner of the sacrifice shall have].

In case of a ram or a goat as a whole burnt-offering, or a prayer-offering, or a whole peace-offering, the priests shall have 1 shekel of silver and 2 *zars* for each; and, in case of a prayer-offering, they shall [have in addition to this fee the trimmings] and the joints; but the skin and the fat of the inwards and the feet and the rest of the flesh the owner of the sacrifice shall have.

For a lamb, or a kid, or the young (?) of a hart, as a whole burnt-offering, or a prayer-offering, or a whole peace-offering, the priests shall have ¾ (of a shekel) and......*zars* of silver [for each; and, in case of a prayer-offering, they shall have in addition] to this fee the trimmings and the joints; but the skin and the fat of the inwards and the feet and the rest of the flesh the own[er of the sacrifice] shall have.

For a bird, domestic or wild, as a whole peace-offering, or a sacrifice-to-avert-calamity (?) or an oracular (?) sacrifice, the priests shall have ¾ (of a shekel) of silver and 2 *zars* for each; but the f[lesh shall belong to the owner of the sacrifice].

For a bird, or sacred first-fruits, or a sacrifice of game, or a sacrifice of oil, the priests shall have 10 g[erahs] for each; but....................

In case of every prayer-offering that is presented before the gods, the priests shall have the trimmings and the joints; and in the case of a prayer-offering..

1 From the *Corpus Inscriptionum Semiticarum*, I, No. 165.
2 It is the word so translated in Deuteronomy 33: 10.
3 So rendered in Leviticus 7: 13; 10: 14. Many scholars would render it "thank-offering."
4 Compare Exodus 29: 13, 14. The Hebrew law differed from the Carthaginian.

439

For a cake, and for milk, and for every sacrifice which a man may offer, for a meal-offering [5]...................

For every sacrifice which a man may offer who is poor in cattle, or poor in birds, the priests shall not have anything...........

Every freeman and every slave and every dependent [6] of the gods and all men who may sacrifice.........., these men [shall give] for the sacrifice at the rate prescribed in the regulations...........

Every payment which is not prescribed in this table shall be made according to the regulations which [the superintendents of the dues fixed in the time of Khalasbaal, son of Bodtani]th, and Khalasbaal, son of Bodeshmun, and their colleagues.

Every priest who shall accept payment beyond what is prescribed in this table shall be fi[ned]...........

Every person who sacrifices, who shall not give..............for the fee which...............

2. Comparison with the Levitical Law.

—This document is not earlier than the fourth or fifth century B.C. The Carthaginians, from whom it comes, were an offshoot of the Phœnicians, who were, in turn, descended from the Canaanites. They were accordingly of kindred race to the Hebrews. One can, therefore, see from this document something of how the Levitical institutions of Israel resembled and how they differed from those of their kinsmen. It will be seen that the main sacrifices bore the same names among both peoples. We find the "whole burnt-offering," the "peace-offering," and the "meal-offering." The Carthaginians had no "sin-offering," while among the Hebrews we find no "prayer-offering." The ways of rewarding the priests also differed with the two peoples. The Hebrews had no such regular tariff of priests' dues as the Carthaginians, but parts of certain offerings and all of others belonged to them. Leviticus assigns from the peace-offering the "heave-thigh" and the "wave-breast" to the priests (Lev. 7: 14, 34; Num. 5: 9, 10; 31: 29, 41). Meal- or flour-offerings belonged to the priests (Lev. 5: 13; 7: 9, 10), as did the sin- and trespass-offerings (Lev. 6: 18, 29; 7: 9, 10). Of the burnt-offerings the priests had the skin (Lev. 7: 8).

The interesting thing is that in the ritual, as in the social laws, we find that the heathen Semites had a considerable number of regulations similar to those of the Hebrews.

---

[5] This is the rendering of the Revised Version for this word. The Authorized Version rendered it less accurately "meat-offering."
[6] Each temple had a number of officials connected with it besides the priests, such as carpenters, gate-keepers, slaughterers, barbers, Sodomites, and female slaves. Another Phœnician inscription mentions these.

CHAPTER XVII

SOME LETTERS FROM PALESTINE

SOME LETTERS OF RIB-ADDA OF GEBAL. LETTERS OF EBED-HEPA OF JERU-SALEM. THEIR LIGHT UPON CONDITIONS IN THE PERIOD OF THE EGYPTIAN DOMINATION OF PALESTINE.

MANY of the El-Amarna [1] Letters were written from Palestine and Phœnicia. Some scholars think these letters come from the Patriarchal period; others hold that they are contemporary with the Hebrew conquest, and give us additional information concerning it. Some of those who hold this last view believe that the conquest of Palestine by the Hebrews was not made all at once. They think that the tribes descended from Leah entered the land before those descended from Rachel. Such scholars hold that these letters give us contemporary evidence of the wars of the Leah tribes. Whichever view one takes, the letters are most interesting, as they open to us a previously unknown chapter in the history of Jerusalem.

1. Some Letters of Rib-Adda of Gebal. [2]

I[3]

To the king, my lord, the king of the countries, speak, saying, Rib-Adda, thy servant, the footstool of thy feet; at the feet of the sun, my lord, eight times and seven times I prostrate myself. Again, there is clear to the king, my lord, the deed of Ebed-Ashera, the dog, when all the lands of the king, my lord, are made over unto him and are subservient to his land. And now behold the city of Sumur has been won over—a fold of my lord and a temple of his shrine—to him, and he has encamped in the temple of my shrine and has opened the place of the curse of my lord and won it. What is he, a man............and dog that he should judge? Again, when men say in the presence of the king, my lord: "Learn that Gebal is.............." then know that he has not taken Gebal................and it is difficult for the lands of the king, my lord. Again let the king, my lord, send his inspector who may judge.............. and may protect the city of the king, my lord. And I..............and will serve my lord, the king of the lands. And may my lord send people and let them bring whatever belongs to my..........into the presence of the king, my lord, and let not that dog take anything that belongs to thy gods. And is it clear now that he would take Gebal? See, Gebal is like Memphis, loyal to the

---

1 See Part I, Chapter I, § 7 (3).
2 From Winckler und Abel's *Thontafelnfund von El-Amarna*, No. 73. Cf. Knudtzon, *Die El-Amarna Tafeln*, No. 84.
3 The letter takes up assertions made by Rib-Adda in previous letters.

king. A second time, see Ebed-Ninib, the man whom I sent with Buhiya, is a
.... So send unto thy servant. Again see, Ummahnu is a maid-
servant of the Baal-goddess of Gebal; her husband is Ishkur............
send!.............

(The tablet is broken off at this point.)

II [4]

To the king, my lord, my sun, say: Rib-Adda, thy servant; at the feet of my
lord, my sun-god, seven times and seven times I prostrate myself. May the
king, my lord, listen to the words of his faithful servant! It is going very hard
for me! The hostility has become strong. The sons of Ebed-Ashera have
become great in Amurru; theirs is the whole land. The city of Sumur and the
city of Irkata are left to the princes. And behold in Sumur I am strong. When
it was difficult for the princes on account of the enmity, I left Gebal and......
Zimridda and..........Yapa-Addi..........with me. Behold, then wrote
the prince unto them; but they did not hearken unto him. And may the king,
my lord, hearken to the words of his faithful servant! Send aid very quickly
unto the city Sumur for its protection until the arrival of the mercenaries of
the king, the sun. And may the king, the sun, drive out the enemy from his
land. Again may the king, my lord, hearken to the word of his servant and
send men as guards to the city of Sumur and to the city of Irkata, in case that
all the guards flee from Sumur. And may it seem good to my lord, the sun of
the countries, to give to me 20 pairs of horses. And may he send help very
quickly to the city of Sumur to guard it. All the guards who remain are in
straits and few are the men in the city. If mercenaries thou dost not send,
then there will be no city remaining to thee. If there are mercenaries, we will
take all the lands for the king.

These letters mention a certain Ebed-Ashera and claim that his
sons are gaining possession of all the land of Amurru. If the
"Ebed" were dropped out of the phrase, "sons of Ebed-Ashera," [5]
there would remain "sons of Ashera," or, "sons of Asher." The
"land of Amurru," or, "land of the Amorites," lay, at the time these
letters were written, in the later home of the tribe of Asher, and a
little to the north of it, between the Lebanon and Anti-Lebanon
mountains. Some scholars hold that we have in these letters references to the coming of the "sons of Asher," or the tribe of Asher
into this region, but it is a theory which in the present state of our
knowledge we can neither prove nor disprove. If it should prove
to be true, these tablets would reflect a part of the Hebrew conquest
of this region.

2. Letters of Ebed-Hepa of Jerusalem.

I [6]

[To the king, my lord, speak, saying, E]bed-H[epa thy servant—at] the feet
[of the king, my lord,] seven times and seven times [I prostrate myself]. Behold I am not a [prefect]; a vassal am I unto [the king, my lord]. Why did

4 Winckler und Abel, *op. cit.*, No. 77, Knudtzon, *op. cit.*, No. 103.
5 These "sons of Abed-Ashera" are mentioned in many other letters.
6 Winckler und Abel, *op. cit.*, No. 174, and Knudtzon, *op. cit.*, No. 286.

not the king, [my lord], send a messenger [quickly]? In similar circumstances
sent Ienhamu.................I. [May] the king [hearken unto Ebed]-Hepa,
his servant. [Behold] there are no mercenaries. [May] the king, my lord,
[send a governor] and let him take [the prefects] with him........lands of
the king.........and people.........who are.........[and Addaya], the
governor of the king [has] their house.........So may the king care for
them and send a messenger quickly. When.........

II [7]

To the king, my lord, speak, saying, Ebed-Hepa, thy servant—at the feet of
my lord, the king, seven times and seven times I prostrate myself. What
have I done to the king, my lord? They slander and misrepresent me before
the king, my lord, [saying] : Ebed-Hepa is disloyal to the king, his lord. Behold I—neither my father nor my mother set me in this place; the arm of the
mighty king caused me to enter into the house of my father. Why should I
commit rebellion against the king, my lord? As long as the king, my lord,
lives I will say unto the governor of the king, my lord: "Why dost thou love
the Habiri and hate the prefects?" But thus he misrepresents me before the
king, my lord. Now I say, "Lost are the lands of the king, my lord." So he
misrepresents me to the king, my lord. But let the king, my lord, know (that)
after the king, my lord, set guards, Ienhamu took them all............Egypt
..........of the king, my lord; [there are no] guards there. Then may the
king care for his land! May the king care for his land! Separated are all
the lands from the king. Ilimilku has destroyed all the country of the king;
so may the king, my lord, care for his land! I say : "I will enter the presence
of the king, my lord, and I will behold the eye of the king, my lord," but the
enemy is more mighty than I, and I am not able to enter into the presence of
the king, my lord. So may it seem right to the king.........may he send
guards, and I will enter in and will behold the eyes of the king, my lord! And
so long as the king, my lord, lives, so long as the governors are withdrawn, I
will say : "Perished are the lands of the king." Thou dost not hearken to me!
All the prefects have perished; there is left no prefect to the king, my lord!
May the king turn his face toward mercenaries, so that there may come forth
mercenaries of the king, my lord. There are no lands left to the king, my lord.
The Habiri plunder all the countries of the king. If there are mercenaries in
this year, then there will be left countries of the king, my lord. If there are no
mercenaries, the countries of the king will be lost. Unto the scribe of the
king, my lord, saying: "Ebel-Hepa, thy servant. Take beautiful words to the
king, my lord! Lost are all the lands of the king, my lord."

III [8]

[To the king, my lord, [speak,] saying, Eb]ed-Hepa, thy servant. [Unto the
feet] of my lord seven [times and seven times I prostrate myself]. [I have
heard all] the words [which the king, my lord,] has sent to me..........Be-
hold the deed which..........has done.......... Copper..........word
..........He has brought [into the city Keilah]. [Cf. Josh. 15 : 44.] May
the king know that all the lands are gone and there is enmity against me. So
may the king care for his land! Behold the land of the city Gezer, the land
of the city Askelon and the city of Lakish have given them food, oil, and all
kinds of herbs. So may the king give attention to the mercenaries! May he
send mercenaries against the people who commit outrages against the king, my

7 Winckler und Abel, No. 102; Knudtzon, 286.
8 Winckler und Abel, *op. cit.,* No. 103; Knudtzon, *op. cit.,* No. 287.

lord! If there are in this year mercenaries, then there will remain lands and prefects to the king, my lord. But if there are no mercenaries, there will be no lands and prefects to the king. Behold this land of the city of Jerusalem— neither my father nor my mother gave it to me; the mighty hand, the arm of the king gave it to me. Behold this deed; it is the deed of Malkiel and the deed of the sons of Labaya, who have given the land of the king to the Habiri. Behold, O king, my lord, right is on my side as regards the Kashi-people. Let the king ask the governors whether that house is very mighty and they have committed a grievous, a great sin; they have taken their weapons and have cut off the horsemen (?)...........And may he send into that land..........who ....with..........servants. May [the king] care for them...........the lands in their hands [and] may the king provide for them much food, much oil, much clothing until Paru, the governor of the king, comes up to the country of the city of Jerusalem. Gone is Addaya, together with the guards of the vassals whom the king appointed. Let the king know that Addaya said to me: "Behold, I am going away; do not thou abandon it" (the city). This year send me men as guards and a governor, O king! Send us..........I have sent to the king, my lord.........., people, five thousand........three hundred and eighteen porters for the caravans of the king. They were indeed captured in the fields near the city Aijalon. (Cf. Josh. 10: 12.) Let the king, my lord, know that I am not able to send a caravan to the king, my lord. Indeed thou knowest it. Behold the king has set his name in the country of the city of Jerusalem forever and he ought not to abandon the lands of the city of Jerusalem.

To the scribe of the king, my lord, has Ebed-Hepa, thy servant spoken, saying: At the feet I, thy servant, prostrate myself. Take beautiful words to the king, my lord! A vassal of the king am I, exceedingly loyal (?) as regards thee. Also an evil deed has been done against me by the men of Kashi. I was all but killed by the men of Kashi in my house. May the king make investigation concerning them. Seven times and seven times, O king, justice is on my side.

IV [9]

To the king, my lord, my sun-god, speak, saying, Ebed-Hepa, thy servant. At the feet of the king, my lord, seven times and seven times I prostrate myself. Behold the king, my lord, has set his name at the rising of the sun and the setting of the sun. It is slander which they have multiplied against me. Behold I am not a prefect; a vassal of the king, my lord, am I. Behold I am a shepherd of the king and one who brings tribute to the king, am I. Neither my father nor my mother, but the arm of the mighty king set me in the house of my father.........There came unto me.........I gave 10 slaves into his hand. Shuta, the governor of the king, came unto me. Twenty-one female slaves and eighty prisoners I gave into the hand of Shuta as a present to the king, my lord. Let the king take counsel for his land! Lost is the land of the king. All of it is taken from me. Enmity is against me. As far as the lands of Seir and as far as Gath-Carmel there is peace among all the prefects, but enmity against me is practised. When I sent a man, then he said: "I do not see the eyes of the king, my lord, for hostility is against me." I set once a ship on the sea when the mighty arm of the king took Naharina and Kapasi, but, behold the Habiri take the cities of the king. There is no prefect to the king, my lord; all are lost. Behold Turbazu was killed in the city gate of Zilu and the king is inactive! Behold Zimridda of Lakish; his servants were enraged at him; he adhered to the Habiri. Yapti-Adda was killed in the city

9 Winckler und Abel, No. 104; Knudtzon, No. 288.

gate of Zilû and there is no action! Concerning it the king makes no inquiry! Let the king care for his land and let the king turn his face to mercenaries for the land of tribute! For if there are no mercenaries in this year, lost, perished are all the lands of the king, my lord. Let no one say in the presence of the king, my lord, that the land of the king, my lord, is lost and all the prefects are lost. If there are no mercenaries in this year, then let the king send a governor to bring me and my brothers unto thee and we will die with the king, our lord.

To the scribe of the king, my lord, saying, Ebed-Hepa, thy servant. At thy feet I prostrate myself. Bring beautiful words to the king. Emphatically thy servant and thy son am I.

V 10

To the king, my lord, speak, saying, Ebed-Hepa, thy servant. At the feet of my lord I prostrate myself seven times and seven times. Behold Malkiel, he has not separated himself from the sons of Labaya and from the sons of Arzaya that they may seek the hand of the king for themselves. A prefect who has done this deed—why does not the king call him to account? Behold Malkiel and Tagi—the deed which they have done is this: formerly they took Rabuda and now they seek Jerusalem. If this land belongs to the king, why is it oppressed? Gaza has sided with the king. Behold the land of Gath-Carmel belongs to Tagi and the people of Gath are on guard in Beth-shean, and verily it will happen to us when Labaya and the land of Shechem have been given to the Habiri. Malkiel has written to Tagi and his sons: "Let our two forces grant all their desire to the people of Keilah." Shall we indeed throw open Jerusalem? The guards, whom thou didst send by the hand of Haya, son of Miare, Addaya took, stationing them in his house in Gaza and twenty men has he sent to Egypt. Let the king know that there are no royal guards with me! It is so as the king lives! Verily Puru is beaten. He has gone from me and is in Gaza. May the king remember it and may the king send fifty men as guards to protect the land! All the lands of the king are in revolt. Send Yinhenhame and let him care for the land of the king. To the scribe of the king, my lord, say: Ebed-Hepa, thy servant. Beautiful words give to the king. Ever emphatically am I thy servant.

VI 11

To the king, my lord, speak, saying, Ebed-Hepa, thy servant. At the feet of the king, my lord, seven times and seven times I prostrate myself. Behold the deed which Malkiel and Shuardatu have done against the country of the king, my lord! They have won over the soldiers of Gezar, the soldiers of Gath, and the soldiers of Keilah; they have seized the country of the city of Rubute. The country of the king is fallen away to the Habiri. And now also a city of the country of Jerusalem (its name is Beth-Shemesh),[12] a city of the king, has gone over to the men of Keilah. May the king harken unto Ebed-Hepa, thy servant, and send mercenaries that the land of the king may remain unto the king. If there are no mercenaries, lost is the land of the king to the Habiri. This is the deed which Malkiel and Shuardatu have done..............May the king care for his land!

10 Winckler und Abel, No. 105 plus No. 199; Knudtzon, No. 289.
11 Winckler und Abel, No. 106; Knudtzon, No. 290.
12 The tablet reads Beth-Ninib, but scholars are agreed that it refers to Beth-Shemesh.

3. Their Light upon Conditions in the Period of the Egyptian Domination of Palestine.—These letters are among the most interesting of the many fascinating documents which have come to us from ancient times. They give us our first historical glimpse of Jerusalem, giving us a view of it 350 years before its capture by David. At this time its ruler was one Ebed-Hepa, a vassal of Amenophis IV, King of Egypt. Jerusalem was at the time the capital of a considerable territory. If the places mentioned have been rightly identified by scholars, its dominion extended to Mount Carmel on the northwest and as far as Rabbith in Issachar on the north. At the time these letters were written, Jerusalem was hard pressed by some invaders called Habiri, and Ebed-Hepa again and again appeals to the Egyptian king to send mercenaries in that year or all the territories of the king would be lost. Already the Egyptian army was composed in part of hired soldiers. We know from Egyptian sources that Amenophis was much more interested in religious reform than in statecraft. The desired troops were not sent, and apparently Ebed-Hepa was overcome, for his letters cease.

The condition of Palestine, as revealed by these letters, is the same as that of Phœnicia as revealed by the letters of Rib-Adda. Egyptian authority was breaking up; each ruler was doing his best to look after his own interests; while invaders were overrunning the country.

Who was Ebed-Hepa? All that we know of him is told in these letters. Hepa was, however, the name of a Hittite and Mitannian goddess. It has, accordingly, been inferred that Ebed-Hepa belonged to that race. Ezekiel long afterward in speaking to Jerusalem said: "The Amorite was thy father and thy mother was a Hittite" (Ezek. 16: 3, 45). If this first ruler of Jerusalem known to us was a Hittite, as seems probable, it would be a striking confirmation of Ezekiel's statement. Another interesting question is: Who were the Habiri who were invading Palestine when these letters were written? The answer to this question is not certain. Four different views have been held:

1. They have been thought to be the same as the clan Heber which was afterward a part of the tribe of Asher, and which is also mentioned in connection with Malkiel in Genesis 46: 17; Numbers 26: 45, and 1 Chronicles 7: 31. The objection to this view is that the Habiri seem far too powerful in these letters to be simply the ancestors of such a clan.

2. It has been held that the Habiri were a branch of the Hittites. This view is based upon the fact that among the tablets found by Winckler at Boghaz Koi a list of Hittite gods was headed "gods of the Habiri." This is, however, not decisive, as the gods may have been Semitic gods, whom, after the fashion of antiquity, the Hittite scribe had identified with the deities of his own country.

3. It has been held that the Habiri were Hebrews, and that we have here contemporary records of their wars of conquest.

4. Some scholars maintain that it is impossible to tell who the Habiri were.

The writer is inclined to hold that the Habiri were Hebrews, though this view is not without difficulty. The indications of the book of Exodus point to Ramses II as the Pharaoh of the oppression and to Merneptah as the Pharaoh of the Exodus. These kings belonged to the nineteenth dynasty, while Amenophis IV, to whom Ebed-Hepa wrote his letters, belonged to the eighteenth. How then could Hebrews be already in Palestine struggling to conquer it? The view has been held by a number of scholars that the Hebrew conquest took place in two parts, one of which was under the eighteenth and the other under the nineteenth dynasty. The view is not without its difficulties, but it *may* prove to be true. If the Habiri were Hebrews, it seems necessary to suppose that it is true. Perhaps further discovery will throw more light upon it.

The following letter, found in 1892 at Tell el-Hesy (Ekron?) in Palestine, belongs to the same period as the preceding letters.[13]

To the chief officer speak, saying: Pabi—at thy feet I prostrate myself. Thou shouldst know that Shiptibaal and Zimrida are conspiring together and Shiptibaal has said to Zimrida: "My father of the city Yarami has written to me: 'Give me six bows and three daggers and three swords. If I go out against the land of the king and thou wilt be the breath of life to me, then I shall surely (?) be superior to it and shall subdue it.' He who makes this plan is Pabu, so send him to me." Now I have sent thee Raphiel. He will bring to the chief officer news of this matter.

Another letter from Taanach belongs to the same general period. It is one of four found by Sellin in 1903. It is as follows:[14]

To Ishtarwashur speak, saying, Ahijah [15]—may the lord of the gods protect thy life! Thou art my brother and love is in thy bowels and in my heart. When I was detained in Gurra a workman gave to me two knives and a lance and two

13 For the text cf. Hilprecht, *Old Babylonian Inscriptions* No. 17. See also Knudtzon, *El-Amarna Tafeln*, No. 333.
14 Published by Hrozny in Sellin's *Tell-Taanek*, pp. 115 and 121.
15 In the Babylonian script, *Ahi-ya-mi.*

baskets (?) for nothing. As the lance was broken, he will repair it and send it by the hand of Buritpi. Again: is there lamentation over thy cities, or hast thou indeed put thyself in possession of them? Over my head is one who is over the cities. Now let us see whether he will do good to thee. If his countenance is favorable there will be great destruction. Further: let Ilurabi enter Rahab and either send my man to thy presence or give him protection.

This letter is chiefly interesting for the name *Ahi-ya-mi,* which is probably the Babylonian equivalent of Ahijah or Ahi-Yahweh. If this is so, and, while not certain, there is considerable collateral evidence in its favor,[16] the divine name, Yahweh (Jehovah), was already known in Palestine.

Another phrase in this letter which has recalled to some a Biblical phrase is "the lord of the gods." This has been compared with Baal-berith (*i. e.,* lord of the covenant), Judges 9:4, who is later called El-berith (god of the covenant), Judges 9:46. Such a comparison is, however, somewhat fanciful.

Another letter is believed by one scholar [17] to mention the Joshua who led the Hebrew conquest. It reads as follows: [18]

To Janhamu, my lord, speak saying: Mutbaal, thy servant (am I); at the feet of my lord I prostrate myself. Thus Mutbaal says to thee: Job has fled. He hid (?), when the king of Pihilim fled from before the elders of the king his lord who lay in wait (for him). As the king my lord lives, as the king my lord lives, my lord, Job is not in Pihilim! Indeed, 2 months ago he broke away (?). As to this, ask Biennima; ask Tadua; ask Jeshuia (Joshua) whether by the estate (?) of Di-Marduk, the city of Ashtar was helped. Now all the cities of the land of Garu (the Ghor) are hostile, viz: Dumah, Edrei, Aroer, Mishtu, Magdala, Khinabi, and Zarka. Hawini, and Jabesh are already taken. Further: behold from the time thou sentest thy letter to me, I replied to it: by the time thou returnest from thy journey, he will have arrived in Pihilim and will hear the message.

It is generally agreed that in this letter Pihilim is the later Pella, one of the cities of the Decapolis,[19] the Hebrew name for which was Pahal. The cities of Ashtar, Dumah, Edrei, Aroer, Magdala, and Jabesh are also well-known Biblical cities. The Ghor (*Garu* in the tablet) is the Jordan Valley, which is so called to the present day. Biennima is very likely the Hebrew name Benjamin, and Jeshuia, Joshua. Job is also a good Biblical name. Olmstead believes that we have here a contemporary record of a part of the Hebrew conquest of Palestine by Joshua.

16 See the writer's article, "Yahweh before Moses," in *Studies in the History of Religions Presented to C. H. Toy,* especially pp. 188–191.
17 So Professor A. T. Olmstead. See his *History of Palestine and Syria,* New York, 1931, pp. 188 and 197.
18 The text of the letter is published in Bezold and Budge's *The Tell el-Amarna Tablets in the British Museum,* London, 1892, No. 164. It was translated by H. Winckler, *Keilinschriftliche Bibliothek,* Vol. V, (Berlin, 1896), No. 237, and by J. A. Knudtzon, *Die El-Amarna Tafeln,* Berlin, 1908, No. 256.
19 See above, Part I, ch. XIV, § 6.

CHAPTER XVIII

DOCUMENTS FROM THE TIME OF ISRAEL'S JUDGES

REPORT OF WENAMON. ITS ILLUSTRATION OF CERTAIN POINTS OF BIBLICAL HISTORY ABOUT THE TIME OF DEBORAH OR GIDEON. REFERENCE TO THE PHILISTINES.

THE following vivid story of adventure dates from about 1100 B.C. and throws a vivid light on the condition of the coast-lands of Palestine and Phœnicia about the middle of the period of the Judges.

1. Report of Wenamon.[1]

Year five, third month of the third season (eleventh month), day 16, day of departure of the "eldest of the hall," of the house of Amon, the lord of the lands, Wenamon, to bring the timber for the great and august barge of Amon-Re, King of the gods, which is on the river............called: "Userhet" of Amon.

On the day of my arrival at Tanis at the palace of Nesubenebded and Tentamon, I gave to them the writings of Amon-Re, king of the gods, which they caused to be read in their presence; and they said: "I will do it, I will do it according to that which Amon-Re, king of our gods, our lord, saith." I abode until the fourth month of the third season, being in Tanis.

Nesubenebded and Tentamon sent me with the ship-captain, Mengebet, and I descended into the great Syrian sea, in the fourth month of the third season, on the first day. I arrived at Dor, a city of Thekel [a people kindred to the Philistines], and Bedel, its king, caused to be brought for me much bread, a jar of wine, and a joint of beef.

Then a man of my ship fled, having stolen:

..[vessels] of gold, [amounting to]	5 deben
4 vessels of silver, amounting to	20 deben
a sack of silver	11 deben
[Total of what] he [stole]	5 deben of gold.
	31 deben of silver.

In the morning then I rose and went to the abode of the prince, and said to him: "I have been robbed in thy harbor. Since thou art the king of this land, thou art therefore its investigator, who should search for my money. For the money belongs to Amon-Re, king of the gods, lord of the lands; it belongs to Nesubenebded, and it belongs to Hrihor, my lord, and the other magnates of Egypt; it belongs also to Weret, and to Mekmel, and to Zakar-Baal, the prince of Byblos" [Gebal]. He said to me: "To thy honor and thy excellence! but, behold, I know nothing of this complaint which thou hast lodged with me. If the thief belonged to my land, he who went on board thy ship, that he might

1 Taken from Breasted's *Ancient Records, Egypt*, IV, pp. 278, ff.

449

steal thy treasure, I would repay it to thee from my treasury till they find thy thief by name; but the thief who robbed thee belongs to thy ship. Tarry a few days here with me, and I will seek him." When I had spent nine days moored in his harbor, I went to him and said to him: "Behold, thou hast not found my money, therefore let me depart with the ship-captain, and with those who go ....the sea. He said to me: "Be silent............"...........the harbor...........[I arrived at] Tyre. I went forth from Tyre at early dawn............Zakar-Baal, the prince of Byblos [Gebal].

............the............I found 30 deben of silver therein. I seized it, saying to them: "I will take [your money, and it shall remain with me until ye find [my money. Was it not a man of Thekel] who stole it, and no thief [of ours]? I will take it............ They went away, while I............... [I] arrived........the harbor of Byblos [Gebal]. [I made a place of concealment, I hid] "Amon-the-way," and I placed his things in it. The prince of Byblos sent to me, saying: "Betake thyself from my harbor." I sent to him, saying, "................if they sail, let them take me in Egypt.".......... I spent nineteen days in his harbor and he continually sent to me daily, saying: "Betake thyself from my harbor."

Now, when he sacrificed to his gods......., the god seized one of his noble youths, making him frenzied, so that he said: "Bring [the god] hither! Bring the messenger of Amon who hath him. Send him and let him go."

Now, while the frenzied youth continued in frenzy during this night, I found a ship bound for Egypt, and I loaded all my belongings into it. I waited for the darkness, saying: "When it descends, I will embark the god also, in order that no other eye may see him."

The harbor-master came to me, saying: "Remain until morning by the prince." I said to him: "Art not thou he who continually came to me daily, saying, 'Betake thyself away from my harbor'? Dost thou not say, 'Remain in the [land'], in order to let depart the ship that I have found? thou that mayest come and say again, 'Away'? He went and told it to the prince, and the prince sent to the captain of the ship, saying: 'Remain until morning by the king.'"

When morning came he sent and had me brought up, when the divine offering occurred in the fortress where he was, on the shore of the sea. I found him sitting in his upper chamber, leaning his back against a window, while the waves of the great Syrian sea beat against the........behind him. I said to him: "Kindness of Amon!" He said to me: "How long is it until this day since thou camest away from the abode of Amon?" I said: "Five months and one day until now."

He said to me: "Behold thou art true, where is the writing of Amon, which is in thy hand? Where is the letter of the High Priest of Amon, which is in thy hand?" I said to him: "I gave them to Nesubenebded and Tentamon." Then he was very wroth, and he said to me: "Now, behold, the writing and the letter are not in thy hand! Where is the ship of cedar which Nesubenebded gave to thee? Where is its Syrian crew? He would not deliver thy business to this ship-captain........to have thee killed, that they might cast thee into the sea. From whom would they have sought the god then? And thee, from whom would they have sought thee then?" So he spake to me. I said to him: "There are indeed Egyptian ships and Egyptian crews who sail under Nesubenebded, (but) he hath no Syrian crews." He said to me: "There are surely twenty ships here in my harbor, which are in connection with Nesubenebded; and at Sidon, whither thou wouldst go, there are indeed 10,000 ships also which are in connection with Berket-el and sail to his house."

Then I was silent in this great hour. He answered and said to me: "On what business hast thou come hither?" I said to him: "I have come after the timber of the great and august barge of Amon-Re, king of gods. Thy father did it, thy grandfather did it, and thou wilt also do it." So spake I to him.

He said to me: "They did it, truly. If thou give me (something) for doing it, I will do it. Indeed my agents transacted the business; the Pharaoh,...... sent six ships, laden with the products of Egypt, and they were unloaded in their storehouses. And thou also shalt bring something for me." He had the journal of his fathers brought in, and he had them read it before me. They found 1,000 deben of every (kind of) silver, which was in his book.

He said to me: "If the ruler of Egypt were the owner of my property, and I were also his servant, he would not send silver and gold, saying: 'Do the command of Amon.' It was not the payment of tribute which they exacted of my father. As for me, I am myself neither thy servant nor am I the servant of him that sent thee. If I cry out to the Lebanon, the heavens open, and the logs lie here on the shore of the sea."

A long speech of Wenamon follows, in which he claims Egypt as the home of civilization, and claims Lebanon for Amon. He then continues:

"Let my scribe be brought to me, that I may send him to Nesubenebded and Tentamon, the rulers whom Amon hath given to the north of his land, and they will send all that of which I shall write unto them, saying: 'Let it be brought,' until I return to the south and send thee all thy trifles again." So spake I to him.

He gave my letter into the hand of his messenger. He loaded in the keel, the head of the bow and the head of the stern, with four other hewn timbers, together seven; and he had them taken to Egypt. His messenger went to Egypt, and returned to me, to Syria in the first month of the second season. Nesubenebded and Tentamon sent:

Gold: 4 *Tb*-vessels, 1 *K'k-mn*-vessel;
Silver: 5 *Tb*-vessels;
Royal linen: 10 garments, 10 *hm-ḥrd;*
Papyrus: 500 rolls;
Ox-hides: 500;
Rope: 500 (coils);
Lentils: 20 measures;
Fish: 30 measures;
She[2] sent me:
Linen 5.........., 5 *hm-ḥrd;*
Lentils: 1 measure;
Fish: 5 measures.

The prince rejoiced, and detailed 300 men and 300 oxen, placing overseers over them, to have the trees felled. They spent the second season therewith.... In the third month of the second season (seventh month) they dragged them [to] the shore of the sea. The prince came forth and stood by them.

He sent to me, saying: "Come." Now, when I had presented myself before him, the shadow of his sunshade fell upon me. Penamon, a butler, he stepped between us, saying: "The shadow of Pharaoh.........., thy lord, falls upon thee." He was angry with him, saying: "Let him alone!" I presented myself before him, and he answered and said unto me: "Behold the command which my fathers formerly executed, I have executed, although thou for thy part hast not done for me that which thy fathers did for me. Behold there has arrived the last of thy timber, and there it lies. Do according to my desire and come to load it, for they will indeed give it to thee."

2 "She" refers to Tentamon, the queen.

"Come not to contemplate the terror of the sea, (but) if thou dost contemplate the terror of the sea, thou shalt (also) contemplate mine own. Indeed I have not done to thee that which they did to the messengers of Khamwese, when they spent seventeen years in this land. They died in their place." He said to his butler; "Take him, and let him see their tomb, wherein they sleep." I said to him: "Let me not see it! As for Khamwese, (mere) people were the messengers whom he sent unto thee; but people........there was no [god among] his messengers. And yet thou sayest, 'Go and see thy companions.' Lo, art thou not glad? and dost thou not have made for thee a tablet, whereon thou sayest: 'Amon-Re, king of gods, sent to me "Amon-the-way," his [divine] messenger, and Wenamon, his human messenger, after the timber for the great and august barge of Amon-Re, king of gods? I felled it, I loaded it, I supplied him (with) my ships and my crews, I brought them to Egypt, to beseech for me 10,000 years of life from Amon, more than my ordained (life), and it came to pass.' Then in future days when a messenger comes from the land of Egypt, who is able to write, and reads thy name upon the stela, thou shalt receive water in the west, like the gods who are there." He said to me: "It is a great testimony which thou tellest me."

I said to him: "As for the many things which thou hast said to me, when I reach the place of the abode of the High Priest of Amon, and he shall see thy command in thy command, [he] will have something delivered to thee."

I went to the shore of the sea, to the place where the timbers lay; I spied eleven ships, coming from the sea, belonging to the Thekel, saying: "Arrest him! Let not a ship of his pass to Egypt!" I sat down and began to weep. The letter-scribe of the prince came out to me, and said to me: "What is the matter with thee?" I said to him: "Surely thou seest these birds which twice descend upon Egypt. Behold them! They come to the pool, and how long shall I be here, forsaken? For thou seest surely those who come to arrest me again."

He went and told it to the prince. The prince began to weep at the evil words which they spoke to him. He sent out his letter-scribe to me and brought me two jars of wine and a ram. He sent to me Tento, an Egyptian singer (feminine), who was with him, saying: "Sing for him; let not his heart feel apprehension." He sent to me, saying: "Eat, drink, and let not thy heart feel apprehension. Thou shalt hear all that I have to say unto thee in the morning."

Morning came, he had (the Thekel) called into his......., he stood in their midst and said to the Thekel: "Why have ye come?" They said to him: "We have come after the stove-up ships which thou sendest to Egypt with our...... comrades." He said to them: "I cannot arrest the messenger of Amon in my land. Let me send him away, and ye shall pursue him, to arrest him."

He loaded me on board, he sent me away.....to the harbor of the sea. The wind drove me to the land of Alasa [Cyprus]; those of the city came forth to me to slay me. I was brought among them to the abode of Heteb, the queen of the city. I found her as she was going forth from her houses and entering into her other [house]. I saluted her, I asked the people who stood about her: "There is surely one among you who understands Egyptian?" One among them said: "I understand (it)." I said to him: "Say to my mistress: 'I have heard as far as Thebes, the abode of Amon, that in every city injustice is done, but that justice is done in the land of Alasa; (but), lo, injustice is done every day here.'" She said: "Indeed! what is this that thou sayest?" I said to her: "If the sea raged and the wind drove me to land where I am, thou wilt not let them take advantage of me to slay me, I being a messenger of Amon. I am one whom they will seek unceasingly. As for the crew of the prince of Byblos whom they sought to kill, their lord will surely find ten crews of thine, and he will slay them on his part." She had the people called and stationed (before her); she said to me: "Pass the night............"

Here the papyrus, which contains this vivid personal narrative of travel, is broken off and the rest of the story is lost. We may be sure that Wenamon escaped from Cyprus and succeeded in reaching Egypt again, or the story would never have been told.

2. Its Illustration of Certain Points of Biblical History.— The story illustrates well a number of points in Biblical history. This adventure was approximately contemporary with the career of Deborah or of Gideon. It shows that the city of Dor, which was situated on the coast just south of Mount Carmel, was in the possession of a tribe kindred to the Philistines, who soon afterward appear in Biblical history. We also learn from it that Egyptian authority in Palestine and Phœnicia, which was at the time of the El-Amarna letters so rapidly decaying, had entirely disappeared. Zakar-Baal stoutly asserts his independence, while the king of the Thekel is evidently quite independent of Egypt. The way in which these petty kingdoms deal with one another is quite after the manner of the international relations reflected in the book of Judges. The expedition of Wenamon to the Lebanon for cedar wood illustrates the way Solomon obtained cedar for the temple.

Lastly, the way one of the noble youths became frenzied and prophesied, is quite parallel to the way in which Saul "stripped off his clothes and prophesied . . . and lay down naked all that day and all that night" (1 Sam. 19:24). The heed which Zakar-Baal gave to this youth shows that at Gebal, as in Israel, such ecstatic or frenzied utterances were thought to be of divine origin. Later in Israel this sort of prophecy became a kind of profession, or trade. The members of these prophetic guilds were called "sons of the prophets." The great literary prophets of Israel had nothing to do with them. Amos is careful to say that he is not a "son of a prophet" (Amos 7:14).

3. Reference to the Philistines.—Ramses III in his inscriptions makes the following statements: [3]

"The northern countries are unquiet in their limbs, even the Peleset [Philistines], the Thekel who devastate their land...................O my august father [*i. e.*, the god Amon] come to take them, being: the Peleset, the Denyen [Dardanians], and the Shekelesh [Sicilians]............
Utterance of the vanquished Peleset: "Give to us the breath for our nostrils, O king, son of Amon."

The Peleset are undoubtedly the same people who appear in the Bible as the Philistines. Ramses III, of the twentieth dynasty,

3 These statements are taken from Breasted's *Ancient Records, Egypt,* IV, §§ 44, 81, and 82.

from whose inscriptions the above quotations are taken, reigned from 1198–1167 B.C. In his reign the Philistines were coming over the sea and invading northern Egypt along with other wanderers from different parts of the Mediterranean, the Thekel, the Danaoi, and the Sicilians. Upon being repelled from Egypt by Ramses, they passed on and invaded Palestine. As the report of Wenamon shows, the Thekel were in possession of Dor by the year 1100, and no doubt the Philistines had gained a foothold also in the cities farther to the south, where we find them in the Biblical records (Judges 13–16; 1 Sam. 4–7; 13, 14; 17, 18, etc.).

Amos says the Philistines came from Caphtor (Amos 9:7). This has long been supposed to be Crete. Eduard Meyer thinks that confirmation of this has now been found. A disc inscribed in a peculiar writing, which has not yet been deciphered, was found in July, 1908, at Phæstos in Crete in strata of the third middle Minoan period, i. e., about 1600 B.C.[4] This writing is pictographic, and although not yet translated, appears to be a contract.[5] One of the frequently recurring signs represents a human head surmounted by a shock of hair (see Fig. 38), almost exactly like the hair of the Philistines as they are pictured by the artists of Ramses III on the walls of his palace at Medinet Habu (see Fig. 36). This sign was probably the determinative for man. This likeness would make the proof of the Cretan origin of the Philistines complete, were it not that some scholars think that the disc exhumed at Phætos had been brought thither from across the sea. This is possible, but does not seem very probable. The doubt will, perhaps, be resolved when we learn to read the inscription.

4 See Evans, *Scripta Minoa*, Oxford, 1909, pp. 22, ff., 273, ff.
5 See R. A. S. Macalister, *The Philistines, Their History and Civilization*, London, 1913, p. 83, ff.

CHAPTER XIX

ARCHÆOLOGICAL LIGHT ON THE BOOKS OF KINGS

GUDEA AND CEDAR-WOOD FOR HIS PALACE. THE EPONYM CANON. JEROBOAM. THE SEAL OF SHEMA. SHISHAK'S LIST OF CONQUERED ASIATIC CITIES. ASH-UR-NASIRPAL'S DESCRIPTION OF HIS EXPEDITION TO MEDITERRANEAN LANDS. SHALMANESER III'S CLAIMS REGARDING TRIBUTE FROM THE KINGS OF ISRAEL. THE MOABITE STONE. ADADNIRARI IV'S MENTION OF THE "LAND OF OMRI." INSCRIPTION DESCRIBING TIGLATH-PILESER III'S CAMPAIGN. SARGON'S CON-QUESTS. ALLEGED TRACES OF THE TEN TRIBES IN EXILE. SENNACHERIB'S WESTERN CAMPAIGNS. THE SILOAM INSCRIPTION. ESARHADDON'S LIST OF CONQUERED KINGS. ASHURBANIPAL'S SYRIAN CAMPAIGN. NECHO OF EGYPT. NEBUCHADREZZAR II. EVIL-MERODACH. DISCOVERIES IN SHEBA.

1. Gudea and Cedar-Wood for His Palace.—Gudea, a ruler of Lagash in Babylonia (the modern Telloh; see p. 36), who lived about 2450 B.C., rebuilt Eninnû, the temple of Ningirsu, at Lagash. In his account of the work he makes the following statement: [1]

> From Amanus, the mountain of cedar, cedar wood, the length of which was 60 cubits, cedar-wood, the length of which was 50 cubits, *ukarinnu*-wood, the length of which was 25 cubits, for the dwelling he made; (from) their mountain they were brought.

The Amanus mountains lay along the Mediterranean to the north of the river Orontes. They belong to the same general range as the Lebanons. Again, in the same inscription, Gudea says: [2]

> From Umanu, the mountain of Menua, from Basalla, the mountain of the Amorites, great cut stones he brought; into pillars he made them and in the court of Eninnû he erected them. From Tidanu, the mountain of the Amorites, marble in fragments (?) he brought.

This passage shows that a ruler of Babylonia came to this region for cedar-wood and stones for his temple, as Solomon is said to have done (1 Kings 5, especially vs. 6 and 17; 2 Chron. 2:8, ff.). That Egyptian rulers did the same is clearly shown by the report of Wenamon. (See p. 449, ff.)

1 See Sarzac, *Découvertes en Chaldée*, p. ix, col. v, 28, ff. See also Thureau-Dangin, *Les inscriptions de Sumer et d'Akkad*, Paris, 1905, p. 109, and his *Sumerischen und akkadischen Königsinschriften*, Leipzig, 1907, p. 68, f.
2 *Ibid.*, col. vi, 3, ff.

2. The Eponym Canon.—The Assyrians kept chronological lists called by scholars "Eponym Canons," which are of great importance in determining the chronology of Hebrew history at a number of obscure points. A translation of them has not been included in this work, since so few Biblical names occur in them that they would be of little use except to experts. Any who wish to consult them will find them translated in Rogers, *Cuneiform Parallels to the Old Testament*, pp. 219–238.

3. Jeroboam.—During Schumacher's excavation at Megiddo (see p. 118), a seal was found in the palace, it is shown in Figure 27. Its inscription reads:

Belonging to Shema, servant of Jeroboam.

We have no means of knowing whether the Jeroboam referred to was Jeroboam I (1 Kings 12:12, ff.), or Jeroboam II (2 Kings 14:23, ff.).

4. Shishak.—Sheshonk I (954–924 B.C.), the founder of the twenty-second Egyptian dynasty, the Shishak of the Bible (1 Kings 14:25–28), has left on the walls of a pylon which he erected at the temple of Karnak a relief picturing his victory. The pictures are of the conventional type, but they are accompanied by a list of conquered Asiatic cities. Of these the names of about one-hundred and twenty are legible, though it is possible to identify but a small proportion of these with known localities. As it would be of no interest to the general reader to place before him the Egyptian spelling of unidentified place names, only those are here given which have been identified or have some Biblical interest. The numbers before each name designate its distance from the beginning of Sheshonk's list. Among his conquered towns, then, are the following:[3]

11. *Gimty* = Gath. 13. *Rub'ty* = Rabbith (Josh. 19: 20). 14. *T"nqy* = Taanach (Josh. 12:21; Judges 5:19). 15. *Sh'nm'y* = Shunem (Josh. 19:18; 2 Kings 4:8). 16. *B'tysh'nry* = Beth-shean (Josh. 17:11; 1 Sam. 31:10; 1 Kings 4:12). 17. *Rwh'b'iy* = Rehob (Judges 1:31). 18. *H'pwrwmy* = Haphraim (Josh. 19:19). 22. *Myh'nm'* = Mahanaim (Gen. 32:2; Josh. 13:26; 2 Sam. 2:8; 17:24). *Q-b'-"-n'* = Gibeon (Josh. 10:1, f.). 24. *B'tyhwr'rwn* = Beth-horon(Josh. 10:10; 1 Sam. 13:18). 26. *Iywrwn* = Aijalon (Josh. 10:12; 19:42). 27. *Myqdyw* = Megiddo (Jos. 12:21; Judges 1:27). 28. *Idyrw'* = Edrei (Num. 21:33; Deut. 1:4; Josh. 12:4). 32. *"rin'* = Elon (Josh. 19:43). 38. *Sh'wka* = Soco (2 Chron. 11:7; 28:18). 39. *B'tytpwh* = Beth-tapuah (Josh. 15:53). 57. *Dymrwm* = Zemaraim (Josh. 18:22). 58.

[3] Translated from W. Max Müller's *Egyptological Researches*, Washington, D. C., 1906, Plates 75–87, with a comparison of Breasted's *Ancient Records*, IV, pp. 350–354.

[*M*]*gdrw* = Madgala (Matt. 15:39 A. V.). 71, 72. *P'hwqrw' 'b'r'm* = The field of Abram. 100. *Iwdri'* = Addar(?) (Josh. 15:3). 124. *B'ty'nt* = Bethanoth (?) (Josh. 15:59).

According to 1 Kings 14:25, ff., Sheshonk's campaign was directed against Judah, and there is no hint that the northern kingdom suffered too. This may be because the interest of the author of Kings in the house of David and in Jerusalem was greater than his interest in the north. It is clear from the list of places just quoted that Sheshonk conquered both kingdoms. He either took or received tribute from Megiddo, Taanach, Shunem, and Beth-shan, cities in the great plain of Jezreel, but crossed the Jordan and captured Mahanaim and Edrei.

5. Ashur-nasirpal.—Ashur-nasirpal, King of Assyria, 884–860 B.C., in describing his expedition to the Mediterranean lands, makes the following statement:[4]

At that time I marched along Mount Lebanon, unto the great sea of the land of the Amorites I went up. In the great sea I cleansed my weapons. I made sacrifices to the gods. The tribute of the kings by the side of the sea, from the land of the Tyrian, the land of the Sidonian, the land of the Gebalite, the land of the Mahallatite, the land of the Maisite, the land of the Kaisite, the land of the Amorite, and the city Arvad, which is in the midst of the sea; silver, gold, lead, copper, copper vessels, garments of bright colored stuffs, cloth, a great *pagutu*, a small *pagutu*, *ushu*-wood, *ukarinnu*-wood, teeth of a spermwhale porpoise, a creature of the sea, as their tribute I received; they embraced my feet. To Mount Amanus I ascended; beams of cedar, cypress, juniper, pine, I cut. Sacrifices to my gods I offered. A pillar recording my warlike deeds I set up.

This inscription records the first approach of an Assyrian king to Hebrew territory. He did not actually come into contact with the Israelites, though he took tribute from their neighbors, the Tyrians and Sidonians. The expedition of Ashur-nasirpal was, however, the precursor of many others which progressed further.

Ashur-nasirpal, like Gudea and Hrihor, secured wood from this region for his buildings, thus affording another parallel to Solomon's procedure.

6. Shalmaneser III.—Shalmaneser III, the son and successor of Ashur-nasirpal, reigned from 859 to 825 B.C. He not only approached more closely to Palestine, but claims to have taken tribute from her kings. In the case of King Jehu the claim is no doubt true. The following extracts give the accounts in Shalmaneser's own words.[5]

4 See Le Gac, *Les Inscriptions d'Assur-nasir-aplu III*, Paris, 1908, p. 111, line 84, ff.; cf. also Rogers, *Cuneiform Parallels to the Old Testament*, New York, 1912, p. 277, ff.
5 The text is published in Rawlinson's *Cuneiform Inscriptions of Western Asia*, III, 7, 8. These lines are at the bottom of p. 8. Cf. also Craig, *Hebraica*, III, 220, ff., and Rogers, *Cuneiform Parallels to the Old Testament*, 295, ff.

In the eponym year of Dan-Ashur (*i.e.*, 854 B.C.), month Aru, 14th day, I departed from the city of Nineveh; I crossed the river Tigris.........to the city of Qarqar I approached. Qarqar, his royal city, I destroyed, I devastated, I burned with fire. 1,200 chariots, 1,200 horsemen, 20,000 men of Hadadidri (Benhadad) of Damascus; 700 chariots, 700 horsemen, 10,000 men of Irhulina, the Hamathite; 2,000 chariots, 10,000 men of Ahab, the Israelite; 500 men of the Quæan (*i. e.*, Que, in Cilica) ; 1,000 men of the Musræan; 10,000 chariots, 10,000 men of the Irqantæan; 200 men of Matinu-ba'li, the Arvadite; 200 men of the Usantæan; 30 chariots, 10,000 men of Adunu-ba'li, the Shianian; 1,000 camels of Gindibu, the Arabian; 1,000 (?) men of Basa, son of Ruhubi, the Ammonite— these 12 kings he took as his helpers and they came to make battle and war against me. With the exalted power which Ashur, the lord, had given me, with powerful weapons, which Nergal, who goes before me, had presented me, I fought with them; from Qarqar to Gilzan I accomplished their defeat. 14,000 of their troops I overthrew with arms, like Adad I poured out a flood upon them; I flung afar their corpses, I filled the plain with their mighty troops. With weapons I made their blood to flow........The field was too narrow for smiting (?) them, the broad plain (?) was used (?) for burying their bodies. With their corpses I dammed the Orontes with with a dam (?). In that battle their chariots, their horsemen, their horses, harnesses, and yokes I took.

It is of especial interest that Ahab and Benhadad, two kings well known from the Bible, formed a part of the coalition that attempted to repel this first Assyrian invasion. Shalmaneser's claim of victory is probably exaggerated, for he retired without further effort to subdue the country. Had it been as sweeping a triumph as he would have us believe, he would surely have pressed forward.

Another of his inscriptions describes the battle of Qarqar as follows: [6]

In the 6th year of my reign from Nineveh I set out..........unto Qarqar I approached. Hadadidri of Damascus, Irhulina, the Hamathite, together with twelve kings of the sea-coast, trusted in their own power and came to make war and fight with me. With them I fought. 25,000 of their fighting men I destroyed with arms. Their chariots, their horses, their implements of war I took from them. They fled to save their lives. I embarked on a ship and went out to sea.

Four years later Shalmaneser records the subjugation of Carchemish, on the Euphrates (cf. Isa. 10:9; Jer. 46:2). His account of it is brief and runs thus: [7]

In the 10th year of my reign (850 B. C.), the river Euphrates I crossed for the eighth time. The cities of Sangar, the Carchemishite, I devastated, I destroyed, I burned with fire. From the cities of Carchemish I departed and approached the cities of Arame.

[6] From Layard's *Inscriptions in the Cuneiform Character from the Assyrian Monuments,* London, 1851, p. 15. Cf. Delitzsch in *Beiträge zur Assyriologie*, VI, 146.
[7] Layard, *op. cit.,* line 84, ff.

The next year Shalmaneser again tried conclusions with the kings of the west. His longer account of this runs as follows.[8]

In the 11th year of my reign (849 b. c.) I set out from Nineveh. I crossed the river Euphrates at high water for the ninth time..........At that time Hadadidri of Damascus, Irhulina the Hamathite, together with twelve kings of the sea-coast, trusted to their own power and to make war and battle with me they came. I fought with them, I accomplished their defeat. 10,000 of their fighting men I slew with arms. Their chariots, horsemen, and implements of war I took from them.

Shalmaneser's third campaign against these kings is thus described:[9]

In the 14th year of my reign I mustered the broad land without number. I crossed the Euphrates at high water with 120,000 troops. At that time Hadadidri of Damascus and Irhulina, the Hamathite, together with twelve kings of the sea-coast, upper and lower, mustered their numerous armies without number and into my presence came. I fought with them, I accomplished their defeat. I brought away their chariots and horses, their implements of war I took from them; they fled to save their lives.

A fourth campaign another inscription describes thus:[10]

In the 18th year of my reign (842 b. c.), I crossed the river Euphrates for the sixteenth time. Hazael of Damascus (cf. 1 Kings 19:15; 2 Kings 8) trusted to the great numbers of his forces and mustered his troops in large numbers. Saniru (i. e., Hermon, see Deut. 3:9), a mountain-peak at the side of Mount Lebanon, he made his fortress. I fought with him, I accomplished his defeat. 16,000 of his fighting men I slew with arms. 1,121 of his chariots, 470 of his horses with his camp I took from him. He fled to save his life. I pursued him and in Damascus, his capital city, shut him up. I cut down his parks. I marched to the mountains of Hauran. Cities innumerable I destroyed, devastated, I burned with fire; their untold spoil I took as plunder. To the mountain of Bilirasi,[11] a mountain at the head of the sea, I marched. My royal portrait in it I set up. At that time the tribute of the Tyrian, the Sidonian, and of Jehu, son of Omri, I received.

The tribute of Jehu of Israel, mentioned in the last line of this inscription, is pictured on Shalmaneser's black obelisk; (see Figs. 295, 296). Above its various panels is the following inscription:[12]

Tribute of Jehu, son of Omri; silver, gold, a bowl (?) of gold, a basin (?) of gold, cups of gold, pails (?) of gold, bars of lead, scepters (?) for the hand of the king and balsam wood I received from him.

8 Layard, op. cit., line 90, ff.
9 Ibid., line 99, ff.
10 From Rawlinson's Cuneiform Inscriptions of Western Asia, III, 5, No. 6. The text is also published in Delitzsch's Assyrische Lesestücke, 4th ed., p. 51, ff.
11 The cliff at the mouth of the Dog river, a short distance north of Beirut. This portrait, with that of Ramses II and other kings, may still be seen carved in the cliff.
12 From Abel and Winckler's Keilschrifttexte, Berlin, 1890, p. 12.

A fifth expedition is thus briefly described: [13]

In the 21st year of my reign (839 B. C.), the river Euphrates I crossed, against the cities of Hazael of Damascus I went. Four of his cities I captured. The tribute of the Tyrian, of the Sidonian, and of the Gebalite I received.

In still another inscription, which gives a summary of his wars, Shalmaneser compresses the account of his various wars in the west as follows: [14]

At that time Hadadidri of the land of Damascus, together with 12 princes, his helpers,—their defeat I accomplished. 29,000 mighty warriors I prostrated like a simoom (?). The rest of his soldiers I cast into the river Orontes. They fled to save their lives. Hadadidri forsook his land. Hazael, son of a nobody, seized the throne. He summoned his numerous soldiers and came to make war and battle with me. With him I fought, I accomplished his defeat. The wall of his camp I seized. He fled to save his life. I pursued him to Damascus, his capital city.

7. The Moabite Stone.—This stone, which bears an inscription of Mesha, King of Moab, a contemporary of King Ahab, was erected at Dibon (the modern Diban) on the north shore of the Arnon, where it was found in the last century. The upper portion of it was first seen by a Prussian clergyman, Rev. F. A. Klein, in the year 1868. Reports of its existence had previously reached the French scholar, Clermont-Ganneau, who was then in Jerusalem, and a squeeze of it was afterward taken by an Arab for this French scholar. Both the French and Prussian governments were desirous of obtaining it, and the Arabs, conceiving that they could obtain more money for it by selling it in parts, broke it up, thus greatly mutilating the inscription. Afterward the French obtained it, putting the pieces together again, and it may now be seen in the Louvre at Paris; (see Fig. 300). The inscription is as follows: [15]

I am Mesha, son of Chemoshmelek, King of Moab, the Dibonite. My father ruled over Moab thirty years, and I ruled after my father. And I made this high place to Chemosh in Qarhah (?) because of the deliverance of Mesha, because he saved me from all the kings and because he caused me to see [my desire] upon all who hated me. Omri, king of Israel—he oppressed Moab

13 Layard, *op. cit.*, p. 10, line 102, ff.
14 Messerschmidt, *Keilschrifttexte aus Assur historischen Inhalts*, Leipzig, 1911, No. 30, line 13, ff. Cf. Langdon's translation *Expository Times*, Vol. XXIII, 1911, p. 69; also Rogers, *Cuneiform Parallels*, p. 298, ff.
15 Translated from Smend and Socin's *Die Inschrift Mesa von Moab*, Freiburg I. B., 1886. Cf. also Lidzbarski, *Nordsemitische Epigraphik*, Weimar, 1898, Tafel I; G. A. Cooke, *North Semitic Inscriptions*, Oxford, 1903, p. 1, ff.; Davis, in *Hebraica*, VII (1891), 178–182; Bennett, *The Moabite Stone*, Edinburgh, 1911; and Hastings, *Dict. of the Bible*, III, 406, ff.

many days, because Chemosh was angry with his land. And his son succeeded him, and he also said I will oppress Moab. In my day he spoke according to [this] word, but I saw [my desire] upon him and upon his house, and Israel utterly perished forever. Now Omri had possessed all the land of Medeba and dwelt in it his days and half the days of his son, forty years, but Chemosh restored it in my day. And I built Baal-meon and I made in it the reservoir (?), and I built Kiryathaim. And the men of Gad had dwelt in the land of Ataroth from of old and the king of Israel had built for himself Ataroth. And I fought against the city and took it, and I slew all the people of the city, a sight [pleasing] to Chemosh and to Moab. And I brought back from there the altar-hearth of Duda and I dragged it before Chemosh in Kiryoth. And I caused to dwell in it the men of Sharon (?) and the men of Meharoth (?). And Chemosh said to me: "Go take Nebo against Israel"; and I went by night and fought against it from break of dawn till noon, and I took it and slew all, seven thousand men, boys (?), and women, and girls, for I had devoted it to Ashtar-Chemosh. And I took from there the altar-hearths of Yahweh (Jehovah), and I dragged them before Chemosh. And the king of Israel built Jabaz and dwelt in it while he fought with me and Chemosh drove him out from before me. And I took from Moab two hundred men, all its chiefs, and I led them against Jahaz and took it to add unto Dibon. And I built Qarhah (?), the wall of the forests and the wall of the hill; and I built its gates and I built its towers, and I built the king's house, and I made the sluices (?) for the reservoir of water in the midst of the city. And there was no cistern in the midst of the city, in Qarhah (?) ; and I said to all the people: "Make you each a cistern in his house;" and I cut the cuttings for Qarhah (?) with the help of the prisoners of Israel. I built Aroer and I made the highway by the Arnon. And I built Beth-bamoth, for it had been destroyed. And I built Bezer, for it was in ruins........[Chi]efs of Dibon were fifty, for all Dibon was obedient. And I ruled a hundred.........., in the cities which I had added to the land. And I built [Mede]ba and Beth-diblathan. And [as for] Beth-baal-meon, there I placed sheep-raisers....... sheep of the land. And [as for] Horonaim there dwelt in it...... and....... Chemosh said unto me: "Go down, fight against Horonaim," and I went down and...........Chemosh in my day, and from there.................. and I................

The author of this inscription is the Mesha mentioned in 2 Kings 3:4. He is there said to have been a "sheep-master" (Hebrew, *nōqēdh*). Mesha appears to say in line 30 (the word is broken) that he placed *noqĕdhim*, "sheep-raisers," or, "sheep-masters," in Bethbaal-meon. The *nōqēdh* was a raiser of a peculiar breed of sheep. Moab is excellent grazing land and raised a great many.

In general the inscription supplements the Biblical narrative. It mentions persons and places well known from the Bible, and gives us an account of a series of events of which the Bible makes no mention. The Biblical account says nothing of Mesha's revolt, while Mesha in his turn says nothing of the campaign described in 2 Kings 3. Neither document implies that the events described in the other did not occur; the two are written from two different points of view and their authors selected the events which suited the purpose of the respective writers. In spite of this consideration there are some differences of statement which are perplexing.

Mesho says in substance that Omri conquered Medeba and occupied it during his reign, half the reign of his son, a period of forty years, but Chemosh restored it to Moab in his (Mesha's) day. It is said in 2 Kings 3: 5, on the other hand, that "when Ahab was dead, the king of Moab rebelled against the king of Israel." According to 1 Kings 16: 23–29, Omri reigned twelve years and Ahab twenty-two years. All the reign of Omri, and half of that of Ahab would, accordingly, be but twenty-three years. It is possible, however, as has been suggested by several scholars, that Mesha uses the word son to denote descendant, and that he refers to the war with Israel in the reign of Jehoram, son of Ahab, described in 2 Kings 3: 6–27. Another suggestion, which seems more probable, is that the recapture of Medeba, mentioned near the beginning of Mesha's inscription, occurred about the middle of the reign of Ahab, while the capture of Ataroth may have belonged to the period of Jehoram, the whole time from Omri to Jehoram being forty years. Some scholars have supposed that the Biblical chronology is in error and that Omri and Ahab together ruled some fifty years. This supposition can hardly be correct, since the general accuracy of the chronology of this part of Kings is confirmed by the Assyrian inscriptions.

Mesha's inscription mentions a number of places which the Bible also names, the Arnon (Num. 21: 13, etc.; Deut. 2: 24; 3: 16, etc.), Aroer (Josh. 13: 16), Ataroth (Num. 32: 34), Baal-meon or Beth-baal-meon (Josh. 13: 17; Num. 32: 38), Beth-bamoth[16] (Josh. 13: 17), Bethdiblathaim (Jer. 48: 22), Bezer (Josh. 20: 8), Dibon (Num. 32: 34; Josh. 13: 17; Isa. 15: 2), Horonaim (Isa. 15: 5), Jahaz (Josh. 13: 18; Isa. 15: 4), Kerioth (Jer. 48: 24), Kirathaim (Josh. 13: 19; Jer. 48: 23), Medeba (Josh. 13: 16; Isa. 15: 2), and Nebo (Num. 32: 38; Deut. 34: 1; Isa. 15: 2).

8. **Adadnirari IV.**—Adadnirari IV of Assyria (810-782 B.C.) has left an inscription which mentions Syria and Palestine. It reads as follows:[17]

Palace of Adadnirari, the great King, the mighty king, the king of the world, the king of Assyria, who conquered from the Euphrates, the Hittite country, the Amorite land in its entirety; Tyre, Sidon, the land of Omri, Edom,

16 In Joshua the name appears as Bamoth-baal.
17 Translated from Rawlinson's *Cuneiform Inscriptions of Western Asia*, Vol. I, p. 35, No. 1. Cf. also Rogers, *Cuneiform Parallels to the Old Testament*, p. 305, ff., and the references there given to other translations.

Palastu, to the coast of the great sea, where the sun set, cast themselves at my feet; I imposed tribute and imposts upon them. To the land of Damascus I marched. Mari, King of Damascus, in Damascus his royal city I besieged. The fear of the luster of Ashur my lord overwhelmed him and he seized my feet and became subject. 2,300 talents of silver, 20 talents of gold, 3,000 talents of copper, 5,000 talents of iron, variegated garments, linen (?), an ivory bed, an ivory couch (?) with inlaid border, his goods without measure I received in the palace in his royal city Damascus.

"The land of Omri" was the kingdom of Israel. Omri had made such an impression on the East that the Assyrians still so called it. "Palastu" is Philistia. Edom is here mentioned for the first time as paying tribute to an Assyrian king, but Judah is not mentioned; she was still free. Adadnirari was a contemporary of Jehoahaz and Jehoash of Israel, and of Joash and Amaziah of Judah.

9. **Tiglath-pileser III.**—Tiglath-pileser III, one of the greatest of Assyria's kings, made several campaigns into the west and had a profound influence upon the fortunes of the Hebrew people. Unfortunately, his inscriptions have been greatly mutilated. Esarhaddon, a later king, determined to remodel Tiglath-pileser's palace for his own use. Apparently he intended to erase Tiglath-pileser's inscriptions from the wall-tablets which adorned the palace, in order to inscribe these tablets with his own. Esarhaddon died before the work had progressed very far, so that the inscriptions were not entirely ruined. The beginnings and ends of many lines are, however entirely destroyed, and at some points deplorable gaps exist in the body of an inscription. Much that is of interest to the Biblical student can still be made out, as the following translation will show: [18]

1. ....
2. [In] the progress of my expedition the tribute of ki[ngs]...........
3. ......Azariah, the Yaudæan, like............
4. ......Azariah of Yaudi in............
5. ....without number exalted to heaven.............
6. ......in the eyes, when that which from heaven...........
7. ....by the onset of infantry............
8. [the advance] of my powerful [troops] they heard and [their hearts] feared.............
9. ....I destroyed, devastated, burned with fire...........
10. ......who had joined with Azariah and had strengthened him.
11. ....like vines............
....
23. ....Azariah, the Yaudæan..........my royal palace ....
24. ....tribute like the [Assyrian I laid upon them.]
....
30. ....the city Bumame,[19] 19 districts

18 Translated from Rawlinson's *Cuneiform Inscriptions of Western Asia*, III, 9, No. 2, with a comparison of Rost, *Die Keilschrifttexte Tiglath-pilesers III.*
19 Translated from Rawlinson, *ibid.*, No. 3.

31. of the city of Hamath, together with the cities of their environs on the shore of the western sea, which sinfully and wrongfully they had seized for Azariah,
32. unto the territory of Assyria I added. I set my officers over them as governors. 30,000 men [I carried away captive]
33. ......from their cities, in the city of Ku......I settled them. 1,223 people I settled in the province of Ullubu.

....
50. ......Tribute of Kushtashpi, the Kummukhite, Rezin, the Damascene, Menahem, the Samaritan,
51. Hiram, the Tyrian, Sibitti-baal, the Gebalite, Urikke, the Queite, Pisiris of Carchemish, Eniel
52. the Hamathite, Panammu, the Samalite, Tarhulara, the Gamgumalite, Sulumal, the Melidite, Dadilu,
53. the Kaskite, Ussurmi, the Tabalite, Ushkitti, the Tunite, Urballa, the Tuhanite, Tuhammi, the Ishtundite,
54. Urimme, the Hushimnite, Zabibe, Queen of Arabia, gold, silver, lead, iron, elephant-hide, ivory.
55. variegated garments, linen cloths, purple and red wool, *ushu*-wood, *ukarinu*-wood, costly things, a royal treasure, fat sheep whose wool
56. was dyed red, winged birds of heaven whose wings were dyed purple, horses, mules, oxen and sheep, camels,
57, she-camels, together with their foals, I received.

This account relates to the campaign of 738 B.C. The Azariah referred to has been thought to be King Uzziah of Judah, who is called Azariah in 2 Kings 14:21 and 15:1–27. It is probable that he was an Azariah of Yadi, of northern Syria, mentioned in an inscription of Panammu, to whom Tiglath-pileser refers above, since the kings mentioned with him ruled in the north. Manahem of Israel (2 Kings 15:14–23) yielded to Tiglath-pileser, as did Rezin, of Damascus (2 Kings 15:37 and 16:5–9), but for some reason Azariah and Judah escaped.

This inscription, fragmentary though it is, tells us that Tiglath-pileser now practiced upon others the system of deportation from which Israel herself afterward suffered. He forcibly removed thousands from their homes to distant parts of the empire. This was an administrative measure, to prevent future rebellion. Persons who had been influential at home among their own people would be powerless to foment trouble in the midst of strange surroundings and neighbors of an unfriendly race.

The following relates to the campaigns of 733–732: [20]

1. ....his warriors I captured.............I overthrew with my weapons.
2. ....before him.
3. the charioteers and.....................their weapons I broke.

[20] Translated from Layard, *Inscriptions in the Cuneiform Character,* with a comparison of Rost. *op. cit.*

4. the[ir chariots and] horses I seized........his bowmen..........

5. ....who carried shields and spears my hands overthrew, their battle

6. ....to save his life he fled alone and

7. ....like a mouse (?) entered the gate of his city. His captains alive

8. [my hands captured and on] stakes I hung them and exhibited them to his land. 45 people (?) from his camp

9. ......I brought together before this city, and I shut him in like a bird in a cage. His parks

10. ....his orchards, which were without number, I cut down and did not leave one.

11. ....Hadara, the home of the father of Rezin of Damascus,

12. [the place where] he was born, I beslieged, I captured. 800 people, together with their possessions,

13. ......their cattle, and sheep I took as spoil. 750 prisoners of the city Kurussa,

14. ......prisoners of the city Irma, 550 prisoners of the city Mituna, I captured. 591 cities..........

15. ......of 16 districts of Damascus like a deluge heap I destroyed.

....

19. ....Hanno of Gaza[21]

20. fled before my weapons and escaped to Egypt. The city, Gaza,

21. [I captured. His goods], his possessions, his gods [I took as spoil].... my royal image

22. ....in the palace of [Hanno I set up].

....

27. The country of the house of Omri........all its people,

28. [and their possessions] I carried away unto Assyria. Pekah, their king, they had overthrown. Hoshea

29. [as king] over them I placed. 10 talents of gold......talents of silver I received as tribute from them.

57. Tribute [22] of Kushtashpi, the Kummuchite, Urikki, the Queite, Sibitti-baal, the Gebalite, Pisiris, the Carchemishite,]

58. Eni-el, the Hamathite, Panammu, the Samalite, Tarhulara, the Gurgum-ite, Sulu[mal, the Melidite, Dadilu, the Kaskite],

59. Ussurmi, the Tabalite, Urassurme, the Tabalite, Ushhitti, the Tunite, Urballa, the Turhanite, Tuhamm[e, the Ishtundite, Urimme, the Hushimnite],

60. Matanbaal, the Arvadite, Sanipu, the Beth-Ammonite, Salamanu, the Moabite,.................

61. Mitinti, the Askelonite, Jehoahaz [Ahaz], the Judæan, Kaushmalaka, the Edomite, Mus....................

62. Hanno, the Gazaite, gold, silver, lead, iron, tin, variegated garments, linen, red cloths of their lands,

63. every costly thing, products of sea and dry land produced by their countries, royal treasures, horses, mules, harnesses......[I received.]

The record of this campaign, fragmentary as it is, shows how completely Tiglath-pileser conquered the west. He accomplished the overthrow of Damascus, which his predecessors had been trying in vain to do for more than a hundred years. His invasion of

21 From Rawlinson, *op. cit.*, 10, No. 2, with a comparison of Rost, *op. cit.*
22 From Rawlinson, *op. cit.*, Vol. II, p. 67.

northern Israel led to the overthrow of Pekah, and the deportation
as captives to other parts of the empire of numerous Israelites. This
confirms 2 Kings 15:29, 30. It was this conquest of Damascus
and Israel that fulfilled Isaiah's prophecy given in 735 B.C. (Isa.
7:16). It was while Tiglath-pileser was at Damascus, receiving
the tribute, that Ahaz, whose full name was Jehoahaz, went to
Damascus to carry his tribute,—an act which prevented the invasion of Judah by Assyria at this time. While Ahaz was in
Damascus, he saw the altar of which a copy was made for the temple in Jerusalem (2 Kings 16:10, ff.). The list of kings from
whom Tiglath-pileser received tribute contains many Biblical names.
Not only Israel and Judah, but the Philistine cities, Edom, Moab,
Ammon, Damascus, Hamath, the Phœnician cities of Gebal and
Arvad, Samal in the extreme north of Syria, Que in Cilicia, and
Carchemish on the Euphrates, were all drawn into his net.

10. **Sargon, 722–705 B.C.**—Tiglath-pileser IV was succeeded
by Shalmaneser V, who ruled, as the eponym canon shows, from
727 to 722 B.C. On account of a rebellion of Hoshea, King of
Israel, Shalmaneser overran his kingdom and besieged Samaria for
three years, as recorded in 2 Kings 17:3–5. Before the city fell,
however, Shalmaneser had passed away and Sargon, the founder
of a new dynasty, was on the throne of Assyria. In Sargon's first
year Samaria fell into the hands of the Assyrian army; Sargon
counted this as his own victory and tells of it in the following
words: [23]

At the beginning of my reign, in my first year......Samaria I besieged, I
captured. 27,290 people from its midst I carried captive. 50 chariots I took
there as an addition to my royal force.........I returned and made more than
formerly to dwell. People from lands which my hands had captured I settled
in the midst. My officers over them as governors I appointed. Tribute and
taxes I imposed upon them after the Assyrian manner.

In another inscription the following summary account occurs: [24]

From the beginning of my reign to my 15th year, the defeat of Humbani-
gash, the Elamite, in the environs of Durilu I accomplished. Samaria I besieged, I captured; I carried captive 27,290 people who dwelt in it; 50 chariots
I took from them, and permitted the rest to keep their possessions (?), and
placed my governor over them and imposed on them the tribute of the former
king.

These statements confirm 2 Kings 17:6 and 24, ff. In one respect they throw an interesting light upon the captivity of Israel.

23 From Winckler's *Keilschrifttexte Sargons*, p. 1, line 10, f.
24 Translated from Winckler, *op. cit.*, p. 30, No. 64, 23, f.

Only 27,290 people were transported at this time. True, Tiglath-pileser IV had previously transported the inhabitants of several towns of Galilee. (See 2 Kings 15:29, and his inscriptions translated above.) When we put together all those who were deported, however, they were but a fraction of the population. As Sargon distinctly says, the others remained there. They intermarried with the settlers whom he brought in and became the ancestors of the sect of Samaritans. The "ten lost tribes" were not "lost," as is often popularly supposed to have been the case.

The first of the inscriptions quoted above contains also the following passage: [25]

In the second year of my reign Ilubidi, the Hamathite......collected his numerous troops at Qarqar. The oath [of Ashur he despised]. Arpad, Simirra, Damascus, Samaria, he made rebellious against me.................Sib'u, his Tartan, he summoned to his aid, and to give fight and battle came into my presence. In the name of Ashur, my lord, I accomplished his defeat. Sib'u fled like a shepherd whose sheep are stolen and escaped. Hanno I caught in my hand and took him bound unto my city Ashur. The city Raphia I devastated, destroyed, burned with fire. I took captive 9,033 people, together with their numerous possessions.

The Sib'u of this inscription is probably the same as So, King of Egypt, in 2 Kings 17:4. He cannot be identified with any known Egyptian king. He was probably a prince of a nome of the Delta. The above is Sargon's description of the battle of Raphia, which occurred in the year 720 B.C. This campaign was an aftermath of the fall of Samaria.

717 B.C.

[Sargon],[26] the exalted prince, who came upon Hummanigash, the King of Elam, in the environs of Durilu and accomplished his overthrow, who reduced to submission Yaudi, the place of which was distant, who destroyed Hamath, whose hands captured Yaubidi.

This Yaudi has been taken by some scholars for Judah, but it was probably the kingdom in northern Syria mentioned by Tiglath-pileser IV and in the inscription of Panammu, of Samal, the modern Zendjirli. We know of no Assyrian invasion of Judah at this time.

The tribute of Pharaoh, King of Egypt, of Samsi, the Queen of Arabia, Ithamara, the Sabæan, gold, the......of the mountain, horses, and camels, I received.................[27]

25 *Ibid.*, pp. 1, 2, beginning at p. 1 No. 2, line 10.
26 *Ibid.*, p. 48, line 8, ff.
27 From Winckler, *op. cit.*, p. 31, lines 27, ff. and 33, ff.

Yaubidi, the Hamathite, a soldier (?), with no right to the throne, a bad Hittite, had set his heart on the kingdom of Hamath; he caused Arpad, Simirra, Damascus, and Samaria to rebel against me, made them of one intent and collected for battle. The whole army of Ashur I mustered and in Qarqar, his favorite city, I besieged him together with his soldiers. I captured Qarqar, I burned it with fire. His skin I flayed and the partakers of his sin I killed in their cities; I established peace. 200 chariots and 200 horsemen I collected from the people of Hamath, and added to my royal force.

This passage records the overthrow of Hamath and Arpad (Isa. 10:9), and mentions the tribute of a king of Sheba, the account of the coming of whose queen to Solomon is found in 1 Kings 10:1, ff.

711 B.C.

Azuri, King of Ashdod, planned in his heart not to pay tribute, and among the kings of his neighborhood disseminated hatred of Assyria. On account of the evil he had done I cut off his lordship over the people of his land. I appointed Ahimiti, his younger (?) brother to the kingship over them. But the Hittites, planning evil, hated him and exalted over them Yamani, who had no claim to the throne, and who, like them, knew no fear of authority. In the anger of my heart the mass of my army I did not muster, I did not assemble my camp. With my usual bodyguard I marched against Ashdod. Yamani heard of the progress of my expedition from afar and fled to the borders of Egypt, which lies by the side of Melucha, and was seen no more. Ashdod, Gath, Ashdudimmu, I besieged, I conquered. I took as spoil his gods, his wife, his sons, his daughters, his possessions, the treasures of his palace, together with the people of his land. I seized those cities anew, and settled in them peoples of lands I had captured from among [the lands] of the east........With the people of Assyria I numbered them, and they bore my yoke. The king of Melucha, who among......an inaccessible place, a road......whose fathers from ancient days as far back as the moon-god, his father, had sent no messengers to my fathers to pay their respects, heard from afar of the might of Ashur, Nabu, and Marduk; the fear of the luster of my royalty covered him and fright was poured over him. He cast him [Yamani] into bonds, fetters of iron, and brought him before me into Assyria,—a long journey.[27a]

Another fragmentary account runs thus:[28]

In the 9th [error for 11th] year of my reign I marched........to the coast of the great sea......Azuri, King of Ashdod,........Ahimiti..........his younger (?) brother...........I exalted over them......tribute and taxes of my lordship......like those of......kings, I imposed upon them.....The evil in........in order not to pay tribute...........their princes......... they drove him away........Yamani, a soldier, they appointed to kingship over them. Their city.........in its environs a moat............cubits in depth they dug, they reached the water-level..........To [punish] Philistia, Judah, Edom, Moab, who inhabit the sea-coast, payers of tribute, and taxes to Ashur, my lord. Planning rebellion and untold evil against me, they bore their pledges to Pharaoh, King of Egypt, a prince who could not help them, and

27a *Ibid.*, p. 33, line 90, ff.
28 From Winckler's work previously cited, p. 44.

sought his aid. I, Sargon, the faithful prince, who honors the oath of Nabu and Marduk, who guards the name of Ashur, caused my trusty troops to cross the Tigris and Euphrates at high water. As for him, Yamani, their king, who had trusted to his own power, and had not submitted to my lordship, he heard of the advance of my army. The fear of Ashur, my lord, cast him down, and to......which is on the bank of the river......waters......his land...... far away......he fled......Ashdod......

The two passages just translated are Sargon's accounts of the events alluded to in Isaiah 20:1. These events were the occasion of the prophecy there recorded. Until the discovery of the palace of Sargon by Botta in 1845, this passage in Isaiah was the only place in extant literature where the name of Sargon had been preserved.

In the last of the passages just quoted, Sargon speaks as though he had also punished Judah on this expedition. There is no direct allusion to this in the Bible unless it be the vivid description in Isaiah 10:28–32, where an approach of an Assyrian army to Jerusalem from the north is described. It is difficult to date those verses unless they also refer to this expedition of 711 B.C.

11. Alleged Traces of the "Ten Tribes" in Exile.—In 2 Kings 15:29 it is said that Tiglath-pileser [III] captured certain cities in Galilee, and carried their inhabitants captive to Assyria. In 2 Kings 17:6 it is said that when Samaria was destroyed by the Assyrian king [Sargon, in 722 B.C.], Israelites were carried captive to Halah and Gozan, which were situated on the Kahbur River in Mesopotamia.

Two groups of cuneiform tablets, one in the museum at Berlin, the other in the British Museum, are thought to confirm these statements by the evidence they give that Hebrews who reverenced Jehovah were living in that region.[29] The evidence consists chiefly of a divine name A-u, employed as a component part of proper names just as Jo- and Jeho-, abbreviations of the name of Jehovah, are employed in Hebrew proper names in the Old Testament. Indeed, A-u is the form that Jo- or Jeho- would take, if expressed in Assyrian characters.

The names in question occur in a series of documents which record the transfer of slaves. If the men in question were Hebrews they would seem to have been interested in the business of buying

---

29 See S. Schiffer, *Keilschriftliche Spuren in der zweiten Hälfte des 8ten Johrhunderts von den Assyrern nach Mesopotamien deportierten Samarier*, Berlin, 1907.
  The text of the Berlin tablets was published by Ungnad in *Vorderasiatische Schriftdenkmäler*, I, Leipzig, 1907, Nos. 84–94, 101, 104. Those in the British Museum by Johns, in *Assyrian Deeds and Documents*, I, Cambridge, 1898, Nos. 22, 69, 73, 74, 98, 153, 154, 170, 229, 234, 245, 312.

470 ARCHÆOLOGY AND THE BIBLE

and selling slaves. The documents are much alike. It will suffice
to translate one of them:

1. Seal of Atarkhasis,
2. son of Aushezib,
3. the Kannuean,
4. owner of the slave-girl. A transfer
5. of Kabili, his slave-girl he
6. has made, and Nabushallimshunu
7. for the price of 1½ manas of silver
8. has taken her. The money in full
9. is paid. That slave
10. is purchased and delivered. Whoever in the future
11. at any time shall rise up and
12. lay claim, whether Atarkhasis
13. or his sons,—whoever against
14. Nabushallimshunu or his sons
15. legal process
16. shall begin, 10 manas of silver
17. shall pay. Against an attack of rheumatism for 100 days
18. and legal claim for all time (he is guaranteed).
19. Month Airu, 17th day,
20. eponym of Ashurrimani, rabshekeh.
21. In the presence of Padi,
22. In the presence of Khani,
23. In the presence of Ashurnadinakhi,
24. In the presence of Tubusu,
25. In the presence of Belbelshaduni,
26. In the presence of Ilumia.
27. In the presence of Ashurikhtamusur
28. In the presence of Bariku,
29. In the presence of Kennusharruni.

The significant name here is Aushezib, meaning, "Au saves."
If *Au* is a translation of *Jeho-*, the name, in its entirety, would be a
translation of one of the Hebrew forms of the name Joshua. Other
names, into which the name of the god *Au* enters, appear sometimes
in the body of a contract and sometimes among the witnesses.
They are *il A-u-salim*, "the god Au gives peace"; *A-u-iddina*, "Au
gives," equivalent to the Hebrew Jonathan; *A-u-akhiddin*, "Au has
increased the brothers"; *A-u-daninani*, "Au is our mighty-one";
A-u-eballitani, "O Au, make us live"; *il A-u-dân(?)-ilani*, "Au is
judge of the gods"; *A-u-sabi*, "Au satisfies." [30]
The tablets were written at Kannu, a place otherwise unknown,
which was near Haran in Mesopotamia. One text states that
if the seller of the slave ever brings legal action, he shall pay ten
silver manas and one gold mana "at the sanctuary of the god *A-u*,
who dwells in Kannu." If the god *A-u* be really the Hebrew

[30] From Abel und Winckler's *Keilschrifttexte*, p. 18, col. ii, 34, ff.

Jehovah, the captives from Samaria and Galilee had built for him a temple in Kannu, as the Jews at Elephantine afterward did on the island in the Nile. (See p. 486 f.)

The documents in which these names occur appear to be dated between 666 and 606 B.C. They are dated according to the Assyrian method of dating, which shows that they were written under the Assyrian monarchy, but the eponyms in which they are dated are not found in the extant portions of the Assyrian Eponymlist. They were therefore written after the 666. This fixes the dates of these documents in the seventh century—the century after Tiglath-pileser III and Sargon transported to this region parts of the ten "lost tribes," and, if *A-u* really is a form of the name Jehovah, these tablets afford us a little glimpse of some of these Hebrews in exile.

12. Sennacherib, 705–681 B.C.

Campaign of 701[30a]

In my third expedition I went to the land of the Hittites. The fear of my lordship overthrew Luli, King of Sidon, and he fled to a distance in the midst of the sea. His land I subdued. Great Sidon, little Sidon, Beth-zēt, Zareptah, Mahalliba, Ushu, Achzib, Accho, his strongholds, his fortress, the places of his food and drink, the forts in which he trusted, the might of the weapons of Ashur, my lord, overthrew them and they submitted to my feet. I caused Tubal to sit on the royal throne over them, and imposed upon him the yearly payment of tribute as the tax of my lordship. Minhimmu, the Shamsimurunian, Tubalu, the Sidonian, Abdiliti, the Arvadite, Urumilke, the Gebalite, Mitinti, the Ashdodite, Puduilu, the Beth-Ammonite, Kammusunabdi, the Moabite, Milkirammu, the Edomite, kings of the Westland, all of them, an extensive district, brought their heavy tribute together with their possessions into my presence and kissed my feet.

And Sidqa, the King of Askelon, who had not submitted to my yoke, the gods of the house of his father, himself, his wife, his sons, his daughters, his brothers, the seed of the house of his father I took away and brought him to Assyria. Sharruludari, the son of Rukibti, their former king, I placed over the people of Askelon, and imposed upon him the payment of tribute as an aid to my rule, and he bore my yoke. In the progress of my expedition Beth-Dagon, Joppa, Banabarka, Azuru, the cities of Sidqa, who had not with alacrity submitted to my feet, I besieged, I captured, I took their spoil. The governors, princes, and people of Ekron, who had cast into fetters of iron Padi, their king, my ally, bound by Ashur's oath, and had delivered him to Hezekiah, the Judæan, who as an enemy imprisoned him,—their hearts feared. The kings of Egypt, the soldiers, bows, chariots, and horses of the king of Meluhu, an unnumbered force, they summoned, and they came to their aid. In the environs of Elteke the battle array was drawn up before me; they asked for their weapons. In the might of Ashur, my lord, I fought with them and accomplished their defeat. My hands took alive in the midst of the battle the commander of the chariots and the sons of the Egyptian king, together with the commander of the chariots of the king of Meluḫu. Elteke

30a From Abel und Winckler's *Keilschrifttexte* p. 18, col. ii, 34 ff.

[and] Timnath I besieged, captured and took their spoil. I approached Ekron. The governors and princes who had committed sin I killed and on stakes round about the city I hung their bodies. The citizens who had committed wickedness and rebellion I counted as spoil. I declared the right-eousness of the rest of them, who had committed no sin and rebellion and in whom was no wickedness. I brought Padi, their king, out of the midst of Jerusalem, and on the throne of dominion over them I placed, and imposed the tribute of my over-lordship upon him.

And as to Hezekiah, the Judæan, who had not submitted to my yoke, 46 of his strongholds, fortified cities, and smaller cities of their environs without number, with the onset of battering rams and the attack of engines, mines, breaches, and axes (?) I besieged, I captured. 200,150 people, small and great, male and female, horses, mules, asses, camels, oxen, and sheep without number I brought out of their midst and counted as booty. He himself I shut up like a caged bird in Jerusalem, his capital city; I erected beleaguering works against him, and turned back by command every one who came out of his city gate. The cities which I had captured, from his country I cut off and gave them to Mitinti, King of Ashdod, Padi, King of Ekron, and Silli-baal, King of Gaza, and diminished his land. In addition to the former tribute, their yearly tax, I added a tax as the impost of my over-lordship and laid it upon them. As to Hezekiah himself, the fear of the luster of my lord-ship overcame him and the Urbi and his favorite soldiers, whom he had brought in to strengthen Jerusalem, his capital city, deserted. With 30 talents of gold, 800 talents of silver, precious stones, rouge, *dakkasi*, lapis lazuli, great *angugmi*-stones, beds of ivory, stationary ivory thrones, ele-phants' hide, ivory, *ushu*-wood, *ukarinnu*-wood, all sorts of objects, a heavy treasure; also his daughters, the women of his palace, male and female mu-sicians he sent after me to Nineveh, my capital city, and sent his messenger to present the gift and to do homage.

Inscription Under Lachish-picture, 701 B.C.

Sennacherib, king of the world, King of Assyria, sat on his throne, and the spoil of the city of Lachish passed before him;[31] (see Fig. 298).

Expedition Against Merodachbaladan, 703 B.C.

In my first expedition I accomplished the defeat of Merodachbaladan, King of Babylon, together with the forces of Elam, his ally, in the environs of the city of Kish. In the midst of that battle he left his camp and fled alone; he saved his life. The chariots, horses, wagons, and mules, which at the onset of battle he had left, my hands captured. I entered joyfully into his palace which was in Babylon. I opened his treasure-house; gold, silver, gold and silver utensils, precious stones of all kinds, his untold treasured possessions, a great booty; the women of his palace, princes, his body-guards, male and female musicians, the rest of his troops as many as there were, and the servants of his palace I brought out and counted as spoil.[32]

Campaign Against Arabia (Between 688 and 682)

Telhunu, the Queen of Arabia, in the midst of the desert—from her I took......camels. The [luster of] my [lordship] overthrew her and Hazael. They left their tents and fled to Adumatu, which is situated in the desert, ...a thirsty place, where there is neither food nor drink.[33]

31 From Winckler's *Keilschrifttextbuch*, 1892, p. 36.
32 From Abel and Winckler's *Keilschrifttexte*, p. 17, line 9, ff.
33 From *Vorderasiatische Schriftdenkmäler der königlichen Museen zu Berlin*, I, 75.

The material contained in the first two passages just quoted from Sennacherib is parallel in a general way to 2 Kings 18, 19 and Isaiah 36, 37. All Biblical students recognize that these two chapters in Isaiah are practically identical with the two in Kings. In discussing the parallelism, therefore, we shall refer to 2 Kings 18, 19 only. With reference to the bearing of this Assyrian material upon the Biblical narrative there are three different views which have been entertained by three groups of scholars.

1. One view, which was first expressed by the late Prof. Schrader,[34] of Berlin, is that the inscription of Sennacherib, while differing from the Biblical account in some particulars, really confirms it at nearly every point. Sennacherib, though he claims to have diminished Hezekiah's territory, and to have received from him a heavy tribute, does not claim to have taken Jerusalem. According to 2 Kings 18:14, ff., Hezekiah submitted to Sennacherib, sending his messenger to Lachish for the purpose, and paid him a heavy tribute; according to 2 Kings 19:35, ff., a great disaster so weakened Sennacherib's army that he was obliged to withdraw. Schrader called attention to the close correspondence between 2 Kings 18:14 and Sennacherib. Both state that Hezekiah paid 30 talents of gold, though they differ as to the amount of silver, Kings making it 300 talents, while Sennacherib makes it 800. It was supposed that the numbers in the case of the silver were really equivalent to one another, the present divergence being due to textual corruption. Assyrian kings never record their failures, but Sennacherib's admission that he did not take the city was held to be confirmation of 2 Kings 19:35, ff., which describes a great destruction of the Assyrian army and a signal deliverance of Jerusalem.

2. A second view, of which Prof. Meinhold,[35] of Bonn, may be taken as the chief exponent, starts from the fact that there seem to be two accounts in 2 Kings 18 and 19. In 18:13–16 there is a statement of how Hezekiah sent to Sennacherib, while Sennacherib was besieging Lachish, and admitted that he had done wrong and promised to bear whatever Sennacherib might choose to put upon him. Sennacherib thereupon imposed a heavy tribute upon him, which he paid. The whole transaction seems to be concluded, when at v. 17 the Tartan, or Rabsaris (Rabshakeh), appears upon the scene and taunts Hezekiah for his obstinacy and

34 *Keilinschriften und das Alte Testament*, 1872, 168, ff.
35 Meinhold, *Die Jesaiaerzählungen*, Jes. 36–39, 1898.

he submits again.   Possibly this might be considered the deta.ls of the transaction that was described in mere outline in 18: 13–16. When, however, it has all been described again, and the Rabshakeh has returned to Sennacherib at Lachish, Sennacherib again sends messengers (ch. 19:9), again demanding a surrender.   These messengers are said to have been sent when Sennacherib heard that Tirhakah, King of Ethiopia, was marching against him.   This narrative goes on to tell how Hezekiah, acting under the advice of Isaiah, delayed his surrender, and how the camp of the Assyrians was decimated by the angel of the Lord, and Jerusalem escaped.

Meinhold and his followers hold that there are here two inconsistent accounts.   According to the first, Hezekiah surrendered; according to the second, he did not.   According to the first, Hezekiah paid tribute; according to the second, Sennacherib's army was destroyed.   The first of these accounts is confirmed by Sennacherib's inscription; the second is, so Meinhold holds, shown by it to be unhistorical: first, by the fact that Sennacherib gives no hint that his army was harmed, and, secondly, by the mention of Tirhakah, who did not come to the throne until 688 B.C., and could not, therefore, have been a factor in the war of 701 B.C.

A third view was suggested by Winckler [36] and is held by Prašek,[37] Fullerton,[38] and Rogers.[39]   According to this view Sennacherib made two expeditions against Jerusalem, and 2 Kings 18: 13—19: 8 is an account of the first of these (the expedition of 701), while 2 Kings 19: 9–36 is the account of the second,—an expedition which did not occur until after the accession of Tirhakah, eight or ten years later.   The inscription of Sennacherib, already quoted, refers to the first of these expeditions only.   We have no inscription of Sennacherib referring to the later disastrous campaign, but that is not surprising, for unless the account of his expedition against the queen of Arabia, already quoted above, belongs to this period, we have no inscriptions referring to the last eight years of his reign.   It is thought by the scholars who believe that there were two expeditions, that Sennacherib would approach the queen of Arabia only from the west, so that that inscription is regarded as an incidental confirmation of this view.   Of course, an Assyrian king would not record a disaster.

36 Winckler, *Alttestamentliche Untersuchungen*, 1892, pp. 27–50.
37 Prašek, *Sanheribs Feldzüge gegen Juda*, 1903.
38 In *Bibliotheca Sacra*, LXIII (1906), 557–634.
39 *Cuneiform Parallels to the Old Testament*, 1912, 332–340.

The account in 2 Kings 19 : 9–36 receives confirmation from an interesting passage in Herodotus, the Greek "father of history." He says (Book II, 141) :

And after this the next king [of Egypt] was a priest of Hephaistos, called Sethôs. He held the warrior class of the Egyptians in contempt as though he had no need of them. He did them dishonor and deprived them of the arable lands which had been granted them by previous kings, twelve acres to each soldier. And afterward Sennacherib, King of the Arabians and Assyrians, marched a great army into Egypt. Then the soldiers of Egypt would not help him; whereupon the priest went into the inner sanctuary to the image of the god and bewailed the things which he was in danger of suffering. As he wept he fell asleep, and there appeared to him in a vision the god standing over him to encourage him, saying that, when he went forth to meet the Arabian army he would suffer no harm, for he himself would send him helpers. Trusting to this dream he collected those Egyptians who were willing to follow him and marched to Pelusium, where the entrance to his country was. None of the warriors followed him, but traders, artisans, and market men. There, as the two armies lay opposite to each other, there came in the night a multitude of field mice, which ate up all the quivers and bowstrings of the enemy, and the thongs of their shields. In consequence, on the next day they fled, and, being deprived of their arms, many of them fell. And there stands now in the temple of Hephaistos a stone statue of this king holding a mouse in his hand, bearing an inscription which says: "Let any who look on me reverence the gods."

George Adam Smith [40] pointed out several years ago that, when this passage is compared with 2 Kings 19 : 36, it points clearly to the conclusion that Sennacherib's army was attacked by bubonic plague. In modern times this plague first attacks rats and mice, which in their suffering swarm the dwellings of men and spread the disease. The Hebrews regarded the attack of such a plague as a smiting by the angel of God. This is shown by 2 Samuel 24 : 16, 17; Acts 12 : 23; 2 Kings 19 : 36. Such a pestilence would render the Assyrian army helpless, and would be regarded by the Hebrews as a divine intervention on their behalf. As it is supported by both the book of Kings and Herodotus, it probably affords us a clue to what really happened to Sennacherib's army.

We hold, then, that the last of the three views concerning the campaigns of Sennacherib to Palestine is probably correct.

The Elteke mentioned in the inscription of Sennacherib is the city referred to in Joshua 19 : 44 and 21 : 23. The Merodachbaladan referred to is mentioned in Isaiah 39 :1, where it is said that he sent to congratulate Hezekiah upon his recovery from sickness. It is clear from what the Assyrian accounts tell us that his real motive in sending to Hezekiah was to induce him to rebel against Assyria.

40 *Historical Geography of the Holy Land,* 158, ff.

13. The Siloam Inscription.—The following inscription was discovered in 1880 on the right wall of the tunnel which connects the Virgin's Well (Ain Sitti Maryam) at Jerusalem with the Pool of Siloam (Birket Silwan).

The boring through [is completed]. And this is the story of the boring through: while yet [they plied] the drill, each toward his fellow, and while yet there were three cubits to be bored through, there was heard the voice of one calling unto another, for there was a crevice in the rock on the right hand. And on the day of the boring through the stone-cutters struck, each to meet his fellow, drill upon drill; and the water flowed from the source to the pool for a thousand and two hundred cubits, and a hundred cubits was the height of the rock above the heads of the stone-cutters; [41] (see Fig. 297).

This inscription, though not dated, is believed to come from the time of Hezekiah. Hezekiah is said in 2 Kings 20:20 to have built a conduit and to have brought the water into the city. This inscription was found in a remarkable conduit which still runs under the hill at Jerusalem, cut through the solid rock. It is about 1,700 feet long. It was cleared of silt by the Parker expedition of 1909–1911, and the tunnel is about 6 feet in height throughout its entire length. When it was cut the wall of Jerusalem crossed the Tyropœon Valley just below it, so that, while the Virgin's Spring (the Biblical Gihon) lay outside the walls, this aqueduct brought the water to a pool within the walls, so that the inhabitants of the city could, in case of siege, fill their water-jars without exposing themselves to the enemy.

The inscription is now in the Imperial Ottoman Museum at Constantinople.

14. Esarhaddon, 681–668 B.C.

I overthrew the kings of the Hittite country and those beyond the sea; Baal, King of Tyre, Manassah, King of Judah, Kaushgabri, King of Edom, Musuri, King of Moab, Silbaal, King of Gaza, Mitinti, King of Askelon, Ikausu, King of Ekron, Milkiashapa, King of Gebal, Matanbaal, King of Arvad, Abibaal, King of Shamsimuruna, Puduel, King of Beth-Ammon, Ahi-milku, King of Ashdod, 12 kings of the sea-coast; Ekishtura, King of Idalion, Pilagura, King of Kiti, Kisu, King of Sillua, Ituander, King of Paphos, Erisu, King of Sillu, Damasu, King of Kuri, Atmizu, King of Tamesu, Damusi, King of Kartiha-dasti, Unasagusu, King of Lidir, Bususu, King of Nurenu; 10 kings of Cyprus in the midst of the sea—altogether 22 kings of the Hittite land, of the sea-coast and the midst of the sea—I sent to them and great cedar beams, etc.....
........[they sent].[42]

Esarhaddon, the author of the inscription from which this extract is taken, is mentioned in 2 Kings 19:37 and Isaiah 37:38 as

41 Translated from a facsimile in the Kautzsch-Gesenius, *Hebraische Grammatik*, 1902.
42 Translated from Rawlinson's *Cuneiform Inscriptions of Western Asia*, Vol. III, p. 16, col. v, line 12, ff.

Sennacherib's successor, a statement which the inscriptions abundantly confirm. The above quotation from his inscription shows that Manasseh, King of Judah, 2 Kings 20:21 and chapter 21, was a vassal of Esarhaddon. Esarhaddon is also alluded to in Ezra 4:2.

15. Ashurbanipal of Assyria, 668–626 B.C.

In my third campaign I marched against Baal, King of Tyre, who dwelt in the midst of the sea. Because he had not kept the word of my lordship nor heeded the utterance of my lips, I erected against him siege-works and cut off his exit both by land and sea; their lives I made narrow and straitened; I caused them to submit to my yoke. They brought the daughters that came forth from his loins and the daughters of his brothers into my presence to become concubines. Yahimilki, his son, who had never crossed the sea, they brought at the same time to do me service. His daughter and the daughters of his brothers with an abundant dowry I received from him. I granted him favor and returned to him the son that came forth from his loins.[43]

Yakinlu, King of Arvad, who dwells in the midst of the sea, who had not submitted to the kings, my fathers, I brought under my yoke. He brought his daughter to Nineveh with an abundant dowry and kissed my feet............

On my return I captured Ushu, which is situated on the coast of the sea. The inhabitants of Ushu, who had not been obedient to their governors, who had not paid their tribute, I killed as the tribute of their land. Among the rebellious peoples I set my staff. Their gods and their peoples I carried as booty to Assyria. The people of Accho who had not submitted I subdued. I hung their bodies on stakes around the city. The rest I took to Assyria; I preserved them and added them to the numerous army which Ashur had given unto me.[44]

These extracts from the inscriptions of Ashurbanipal show that during the reign of Manasseh he was active in reducing the rebellions of Phœnician cities, some of which, as Tyre and Accho, were at the doors of Palestine. No doubt Manasseh continued to pay him tribute and so was not molested. The name of Ashurbanipal is preserved in Ezra 4:1 in the corrupt form of Osnappar.

16. Necho of Egypt, 609–593 B.C.

Year 16, fourth month of the first season, day 16, under the majesty of Horus: Wise-hearted; king of Upper and Lower Egypt; Favorite of the two goddesses: Triumphant; Golden Horus: Beloved-of-the-gods; Uhemibre; Son of Ra, of his body, his beloved: Necho, living forever, beloved of Apis, son of Osiris.[45]

(An account of the interment of an Apis bull then follows.)

The above is the beginning of an inscription of Pharaoh Necho, whose defeat of King Josiah, of Judah, is recorded in 2 Kings 23:29, f. He became over-lord of Judah for four years and

43 *Ibid.*, Vol. V, 2, 49, f.
44 *Ibid.*, 9, 115, f.
45 From Breasted's *Ancient Records, Egypt*, IV, 498.

placed Jehoiakim on the Judæan throne (2 Kings 23 : 34). Necho was himself defeated at Carchemish on the Euphrates by Nebuchadrezzar, of Babylon, in 604 B.C., and as he retreated to Egypt Nebuchadrezzar pursued him through Palestine. The book of Jeremiah speaks of this defeat and vividly describes the pursuit which followed. (Cf. Jer. 46 : 2, f.)

17. Nebuchadrezzar II, 604–562 B.C.—Many inscriptions of Nebuchadrezzar are known, but most of them relate to buildings. The following extracts are those which best illustrate the Bible.

In exalted trust in him (Marduk) distant countries, remote mountains from the upper sea (Mediterranean) to the lower sea (Persian Gulf), steep paths, blockaded roads, where the step is impeded, [where] was no footing, difficult roads, desert paths, I traversed, and the disobedient I destroyed; I captured the enemies, established justice in the lands; the people I exalted; the bad and evil I separated from the people.[46]

Reference to the Lebanon

From the upper sea to the lower sea,.......... [which] Marduk, my lord, had entrusted to me, in [all] lands, the totality [of dwelling-places] I [exalted] the city of Babylon to the first place. I caused his name to be reverenced among the cities; the shrines of Nabu and Marduk, my lords, I made them recognize, continually............At that time the Lebanon mountain, the mountain [of cedar], the proud forest of Marduk, the odor of whose cedars is good..........of another god............no other king had...... ......my god, Marduk, the king to the palace of the princes........of heaven and earth shone as adornment..........As a foreign enemy had taken possession of (the mountain) and seized its riches, its people had fled and taken refuge at a distance. In the power of Nabu and Marduk, my lords, I drew up [my soldiers, for battle] in mount Lebanon. Its enemy I dislodged above and below and made glad the heart of the land. I collected its scattered people and returned them to their place. I did what no former king had done; I cleft high mountains, stones of the mountain I quarried, I opened passes. I made a straight road for the cedars. Mighty cedars they were, tall and strong, of wonderful beauty, whose dark appearance was remarkable,—the mighty products of mount Lebanon........I made the people of mount Lebanon to lie down in abundance; I permitted no adversary to possess it. That none might do harm I set up my royal image forever.[47]

A Building Inscription

Nebuchadrezzar, King of Babylon, the restorer of Esagila and Ezida, son of Nabopolassar am I. As a protection to Esagila, that no powerful enemy and destroyer might take Babylon, that the line of battle might not approach Imgur-Bel, the wall of Babylon, that which no former king had done [I did] ; at the enclosure of Babylon I made an enclosure of a strong wall on the east side. I dug a moat, I reached the level of the water. I then saw that the wall which

---

46 Translated from Rawlinson's *Cuneiform Inscriptions of Western Asia*, I, 33, col. ii, line 12, ff.
47 Translated from Pognon, *Les inscriptions babyloniennes du Wadi Brissa*, Pl. xiii, f., and *Recueil de traveaux relatifs a la philologie et a l'archeologie egyptiennes et assyriennes*, XXVIII, 57. See also Langdon, *Neubabylonischen Königsinchriften*, 174, ff.

my father had prepared was too small in its construction. I built with bitumen and brick a mighty wall which, like a mountain, could not be moved and connected it with the wall of my father; I laid its foundations on the breast of the under-world; its top I raised up like a mountain. Along this wall to strengthen it I constructed a third and as the base of a protecting wall I laid a foundation of bricks and built it on the breast of the under-world and laid its foundation. The fortifications of Esagila and Babylon I strengthened and established the name of my reign forever.

O Marduk, lord of the gods, my divine creator, may my deeds find favor before thee; may they endure forever! Eternal life, satisfied with posterity, a secure throne, and a long reign grant as thy gift. Thou art indeed my deliverer and my help, O Marduk, I by thy faithful word which does not change—may my weapons advance, be sharp and be stronger than the weapon of the foe![48]

Nebuchadrezzar was the king who destroyed Jerusalem and carried the most prominent of the people of Judah captive. (See 2 Kings 24 and 25.) His inscriptions give no account of these events. In the first of the quotations made above he covers all his conquests by one general reference. In the second quotation he gives a more detailed account of his conquest of the Lebanon, because that inscription was carved on the rocks at the side of one of the deep valleys of the Lebanon. The third inscription, relating to the building of Babylon, has been strikingly confirmed by Koldewey's excavation of Babylon, by which the massive walls and extensive temples were uncovered.[49] It also gives us a background for Daniel 4:29, where Nebuchadrezzar is said to have walked upon [50] the royal palace and said: "Is not this great Babylon which I have built?"

18. Evil-Merodach, 562–560 B.C.—Nebuchadrezzar was succeeded by his son, Amil-Marduk, whom the Bible (2 Kings 25:27) calls Evil-Merodach. The only inscription of his that has been found is the following, inscribed on an alabaster vase found at Susa, whither the Elamites had at some time carried it as booty: [51]

Palace of Amil-Marduk, King of Babylon, son of Nebuchadrezzar, King of Babylon.

This is the king who released Jehoiachin, King of Judah, from prison after his thirty-six years in confinement and treated him kindly.

48 Translated from the *Zeitschrift für Assyriologie*, I, 337, f.
49 See Part I, Chapter II, p. 37, f.
50 This is the reading of the margin in R. V., and correctly translates the original. He was not walking "in" the palace, but upon its flat roof, from which he could see the great city.
51 From de Morgan's *Délégation en Perse*, Vol. XIV, p. 60.

NOTE ON THE LAND OF THE QUEEN OF SHEBA.—This region, which lay in South Arabia, was explored during the nineteenth century by a number of travelers. Three of these, Thomas J. Arnaud in 1843, Joseph Halévy in 1869, and Eduard Glaser who made four expeditions between 1882 and 1894, brought back from South Arabia many inscriptions, several of which were made by rulers of Saba, the Biblical Sheba, whose queen is said to have visited Solomon (1 Kings 10:1-13). As none of these relate to that queen, it has not seemed fitting to include one of them. The inscriptions, however, show that two important kingdoms existed there, Saba and Main. Main is thought by some to be related to the Biblical Midianites. The Greek version of Job makes Job's friend, Zophar, king of Main. The kingdom of Saba lasted until 115 B.C. It established strong colonies in Africa. In 115 B.C. one colony overthrew the mother-country and established the kingdom of Saba and Raidhan, which lasted till about 300 A.D. After that Saba became apparently unimportant, but various Semitic kingdoms succeeded one another in Africa, including the present-day Abyssinian, or Ethiopian, kingdom. (The League of Nations has not yet recognized Italy's claims.) The Abyssinian king claims descent from Solomon and the Queen of Sheba. For a discussion of the relations of these lands to the Bible, James Montgomery's *Arabia and the Bible,* Philadelphia, 1934, may be consulted.

CHAPTER XX

THE END OF THE BABYLONIAN EXILE

INSCRIPTIONS OF NABUNA'ID. BEARING ON BIBLICAL STATEMENTS REGARDING BELSHAZZAR. ACCOUNT OF THE CAPTURE OF BABYLON. BEARING OF THIS ACCOUNT ON THE BOOK OF DANIEL. INSCRIPTION OF CYRUS. BEARING ON THE CAPTURE OF BABYLON. CYRUS' PERMISSION FOR THE RETURN TO JERUSALEM.

1. Inscriptions of Nabuna'id.—Several inscriptions of this king, who ruled 555–538 B.C., are known, but only a brief extract of one of them is given here, as the major part of the material has no bearing on the Bible.

> Nabuna'id, King of Babylon, the restorer of Esagila and Ezida, the worshiper of the great gods am I..........O Sin, lord of the gods of heaven and earth, god of the gods,..........as for me, Nabuna'id, King of Babylon, save me from sinning against thy great divinity. A life of many days grant as thy gift. As for Belshazzar, the firstborn son, proceeding from my loins, place in his heart fear of thy great divinity, let him not turn to sinning; let him be satisfied with fulness of life![1]

Belshazzar is here said to be the son of Nabuna'id, whereas in Daniel 5: 11, 18 Nebuchadrezzar is called his father. Nabuna'id, as the Babylonian documents show, was not a descendant of Nebuchadrezzar, but a usurper of another family. Some scholars hold that this shows the book of Daniel to be in error, while others hold that "father" in Daniel 5: 11, 18 is equivalent to "ancestor," and think Belshazzar may have been descended from Nebuchadrezzar on his mother's side.

The Nabuna'id-Cyrus Chronicle

This chronicle is known only from a tablet which is somewhat broken. The following extract will show the nature of its contents:

> In the 9th year Nabuna'id was at Tema. The son of the king, the princes, and soldiers were in Akkad. The king did not come to Babylon in Nisan, Nebo did not go to Babylon. Bel did not go out. The festival sacrifice was

1 From Rawlinson's *Cuneiform Inscriptions of Western Asia*, V, 68, No. 1.

omitted. They offered sacrifices in Esaglia and Ezida on account of Babylon and Borsippa, that the land might prosper. On the 5th of the month Nisan, the mother of the king died in Dur-karashu on the bank of the Euphrates above Sippar. The son of the king and the soldiers mourned three days. In the month Sivan there was mourning for the king's mother in Akkad.

In the month Nisan Cyrus, King of Persia, mustered his soldiers, and crossed the Tigris below Arbela and in the month Iyyar went to the land of —————, its king he killed, he took his possessions. His own governor (?) he placed in it............afterward his governor (?) and a king (?) were there.[2]

2. Bearing on Biblical Statements Regarding Belshazzar.—
Similar chronicles are given by the tablet for other years. It is stated each time what Nabuna'id was doing; where the king's son (Belshazzar) was, and what Cyrus was doing. Cyrus, who overthrew the Median king in 553 B.C., was occupied for several years in subjugating other lands before he attacked Babylon. He overthrew Crœsus, King of Lydia, in 546. It would seem that it was well known in Babylonia what he was doing each year. Those scholars who believe that Isaiah 40—55 is the work of a prophet who lived during the Babylonian Exile, claim that this chronicle explains how that prophet could refer in Isaiah 44:28; 45:1 to Cyrus as a well-known figure. They see the exercise of the prophetic gift of the prophet in the faith which he had that Cyrus would release Israel from captivity. Those who believe that the whole of the book of Isaiah is the work of the son of Amoz, see in these verses pure prediction of the rise of Cyrus as well as of the release of the Jews.

3. Account of the Capture of Babylon.—From the chronicle just quoted we have the following statement for the 17th year of the reign of Nabuna'id:

..........Nebo to go forth from Borsippa...........the king entered the temple of Edurkalama. In the month..........in the lower sea a revolt ....Bel came out; the feast of Akiti (Sept.–Oct.), according to the custom.........the gods of Marad, Zagaga, and the gods of Kish, Bêltis and the gods of Kharsagkalama entered Babylon. Unto the end of Elul (Aug.–Sept.) the gods of Borsippa, Cutha, and Sippar did not enter. In the month Tammuz (June–July) Cyrus, when he made battle in Opis, on the banks of the river Zalzallat, with the soldiers of Akkad, conquered the inhabitants of Akkad. When they assembled the people were killed. On the 14th Sippar was taken without a battle. Nabuna'id fled. In the 16th Gobryas, governor of the land of Gutium, and the soldiers of Cyrus entered Babylon without a battle. Later Nabuna'id was captured because he remained in Babylon. To the end of the month the shield-bearers of the land of Gutium assembled at the gates of Esagila. No weapon of any kind was taken into Esagila or the

2 From *Transactions of the Society of Biblical Archæology,* VII, 157, f.

temples; nor was the standard raised. On the third day of Marcheswan (Oct.-Nov.) Cyrus entered Babylon. The walls (?) were broken down before him. Cyrus proclaimed peace to all of Babylon. He appointed Gobryas his satrap, and also prefects in Babylon. From Kisleu (Nov.-Dec.) unto Adar (Feb.-March), the gods of Akkad, whom Nabuna'id had brought to Babylon, returned to their cities. In the month Marcheswan, on the night of the 11th, Gobryas unto..........the son of the king was killed. From the 27th of Adar to the 3rd of Nisan there was lamentation in Akkad. All the people bowed their heads. On the 4th day Cambyses, the son of Cyrus, went to Eshapakalama.[3]

4. Bearing of this Account on the Book of Daniel.—This interesting text here becomes too broken for connected translation. It is clear that the document means to state that Nabuna'id was king of Babylon when it was captured, and not Belshazzar, as stated in Daniel 5:30. It states, also, that Cyrus captured Babylon and not Darius the Mede, as in Daniel 5:31. It is true that Gobryas took Babylon first, and occupied it about two weeks before Cyrus arrived. He was, however, Cyrus's officer and was acting in his name. Critical scholars, who believe that Daniel was written 168–165 B.C., find in these statements a confirmation of their views. They think its author lived so far from the events that he confused their exact order. Those who defend the traditional date of Daniel think Gobryas another name for Darius the Mede, and see in the exalted position which Belshazzar held, as crown prince and commander of the army, sufficient ground for the Biblical statement that he was king. By such interpretations they harmonize this chronicle with the Bible.

Dr. Theophilus G. Pinches has published [4] some extracts from two tablets from Erech which are in the possession of an Englishman, Mr. Harding Smith, which throw some additional light on these points. It was customary for Babylonians in confirming a contract to swear by the name of the reigning king, and one of these tablets contains, a contract, dated in the 12th year of Nabuna'id, in which a man bound himself by the oath of Nabuna'id, King of Babylon, and of Belshazzar, the king's son. As Belshazzar is here associated with the king, he must have been but slightly lower in rank and power than the king himself.

Professor R. P. Dougherty [5] has shown that for several years Nabuna'id was residing at Teima in western Arabia, and that, as

---

3 From *Transactions of the Society of Biblical Archæology*, VII, 162, f., and Clay, *Light on the Old Testament from Babel*, 374, f.
4 See *Expository Times*, Vol. XXVI, 297–299 (April, 1915).
5 See his *Nabonidus and Belshazzar*, New Haven, Conn., 1929.

viceroy, Belshazzar was virtually king. This situation satisfies all that the Biblical narrative presupposes.

The other tablet quoted by Pinches shows that in the fourth year of Cambyses (*i. e.*, 524 B.C.), Gobryas was still governor of Babylon. If he is the man who in Daniel is called Darius the Mede, he exercised the powers of governor in Babylon for a considerable number of years.

5. Inscription of Cyrus.—The following is an inscription of Cyrus. The lines are much broken at the beginning, but it reads as follows: [6]

...................begat (?) him...................[the four] regions of the world..........great coward was established as ruler over the land ....a similar one he set over them; like Esagila he made........to Ur and the rest of the cities a rule not suitable for them..........he planned daily and in enmity he caused the established sacrifice to cease. He appointed ....he established within the city. The worship of Marduk, king of the gods............he wrought hostility against his city daily............his [people] all of them he destroyed through servitude, without rest. On account of their lamentation the lord of the gods was exceedingly angry and [left] their territory; the gods who dwelt among them left their dwellings. In anger because he brought [them] into Babylon, Marduk........to return to all the dwellings, their habitations, which were overthrown. The people of Sumer and Akkad, who were like corpses, he brought back and........granted them a return. Through all lands he made his way, he looked, he sought a righteous prince, a being whom he loved, whom he took by the hand. Cyrus, King of Anshan, he called by name and designated him to rule over all the lands. The land of Qutu, all the Scythian hordes, he made to submit to his feet. The black-headed people (*i. e.*, the Babylonians), whom he caused his hand to capture, in faithfulness and righteousness he sought. Marduk, the great lord, looked joyfully upon the return of his people, his kindly deeds and upright heart. To his city, Babylon, he commanded him to go; he caused him to take the road to Babylon, going as a friend and companion at his side. His numerous army, the number of which was, like the waters of a river, unknown, marched at his side girded with their weapons. He caused him to enter Babylon without war or battle. He preserved his city, Babylon, from tribulation; he filled his (Cyrus's) hand with Nabuna'id, the king who did not fear him. All the people of Babylon, all of Sumer and Akkad, the princes and governors, prostrated themselves under him and kissed his feet. They rejoiced in his sovereignty; their faces shone. The lord, who by his power makes the dead to live, who from destruction and injustice had saved them, altogether they blessed him in joy; they revered his name.

I am Cyrus, king of the world, the great king, the mighty king, king of Babylon, king of Sumer and Akkad, king of the four quarters of the world, son of Cambyses, the great king, king of Anshan, grandson of Cyrus, the great king, king of Anshan, great-grandson of Teispes, the great king, king of Anshan; an everlasting seed of royalty, whose government Bel and Nabu love, whose reign in the goodness of their hearts they desire. When I entered in peace into Babylon, with joy and rejoicing I took up my lordly dwelling in the royal palace, Marduk, the great lord, moved the understanding heart of the people of Babylon to me, while I daily sought his worship. My numerous troops dwelt peacefully in Babylon; in all Sumer and Akkad no terrorizer did

6 From Rawlinson's *Cuneiform Inscriptions of Western Asia*, V, 35.

I permit. In Babylon and all its cities in peace I looked about. The people of Babylon [I released] from an unsuitable yoke. Their dwellings—their decay I repaired; their ruins I cleared away. Marduk, the great lord, rejoiced at these deeds and graciously blessed me, Cyrus, the king who worships him, and Cambyses, my son, and all my troops, while we in peace joyfully praised before him his exalted divinity. All the kings who dwell in palaces, from all quarters of the world, from the upper sea to the lower sea, who live [in palaces], all the kings of the Westland who live in tents, brought me their heavy tribute in Babylon and kissed my feet. From..........to Ashur and Susa, Agade, Eshnunak, Zamban, Meturnu, Deri, to the border of Gutium, the cities [beyond] the Tigris, whose sites had been founded of old,—the gods who dwelt in them I returned to their places, and caused them to settle in their eternal shrines. All their people I assembled and returned them to their dwellings. And the gods of Sumer and Akkad, whom Nabuna'id, to the anger of the lord of the gods, had brought into Babylon, at the command of Marduk, the great lord, I caused in peace to dwell in their abodes, the dwellings in which their hearts delighted. May all the gods, whom I have returned to their cities, pray before Marduk and Nabu for the prolonging of my days, may they speak a kind word for me and say to Marduk, lord of the gods, "May Cyrus the king, who fears thee, and Cambyses, his son, their.......... caused all to dwell in peace".....................................

6. Bearing on the Capture of Babylon and the Return of the Jews.—This inscription confirms the statement of the chronicle already quoted that Cyrus conquered the city of Babylon without a blow. The most important feature of it for the student of the Bible is, however, its revelation of the reversal of the Assyrian policy of transportation. That policy had been inaugurated by Tiglath-pileser III more than two hundred years before. In accordance with it the kingdom of Israel had first been stripped of its more prominent inhabitants who had been carried captive to distant lands, and then the kingdom of Judah. Cyrus determined to attach his subjects to himself by gratitude instead of terror, so he permitted, as he says here, those who had been transported to return to their several countries and rebuild their temples. It was in consequence of this general policy that the Jews were permitted to return from Babylonia and rebuild the temple at Jerusalem. This is referred to in Ezra, Chapter 1. It is there implied that Cyrus made a special proclamation concerning the temple at Jerusalem. Some scholars infer from the above inscription of Cyrus, that the book of Ezra (Chapter 1) has freely interpreted the general policy of Cyrus as a special permission granted to the Jews. It may be, however, as others have held, that a special edict was issued in favor of each individual nation in order that this general policy might be carried out without opposition.

In any event, the inscription confirms the statement of Ezra that Cyrus permitted the Jews to return.

CHAPTER XXI

A JEWISH COLONY IN EGYPT DURING THE TIME OF NEHEMIAH

PAPYRI WITNESS TO THE EXISTENCE OF A COLONY AT ELEPHANTINE. TRANSLATION OF A PETITION RELATING TO THEIR TEMPLE. REPLY OF PERSIAN GOVERNOR. HISTORICAL BEARINGS OF THESE DOCUMENTS. HANANIAH'S PASSOVER LETTER. LETTER SHOWING THAT THE JEWS OF EGYPT WERE UNPOPULAR.

NUMEROUS papyri found since 1895 at Elephantine, an island at the First Cataract of the Nile, reveal the existence of a Jewish community there. The documents are dated from the year 494 B.C. to the year 400 B.C. They show that this Jewish community had at Elephantine a temple to Jehovah, that they were soldiers, and that some of them were engaged in trade. One document declares that when Cambyses conquered Egypt (525 B.C.) he then found the temple of Jehovah in existence there, and that it had been built under native Egyptian kings. How came such a community of Jews to be established there? It is thought that they were a garrison placed there by Psammetik II, King of Egypt, 593–588 B.C. This Psammetik endeavored to conquer Nubia,[1] and according to a confused statement in Josepheus (Contra, Apion, 1, 26, 27) Rhampses (perhaps a corruption of Psammetik), employed some Jews in an expedition to that country.[2] However, these Jews came to dwell at this point, and whensoever the settlement was made, the documents[3] are most interesting, and open to us a hitherto wholly unknown vista in the history of the Jews.

1. Translation of a Petition Relating to Their Temple.

Unto our lord, Bagohi, governor of Judah, thy servants Jedoniah and his associates, the priests who are in Yeb, the fortress, health! May our Lord, the God of heaven, abundantly grant unto thee at all times, and for favors may he

---

1 Herodotus, Book II, 161.

2 Josephus professes to be quoting Manetho, and puts the incident in the time of Ramses. Perhaps Aristeas in his letter refers to this colony, when he speaks of Jewish soldiers. (See Kautzsch, *Apokryphen und Pseudepigraphen*, II, 7.)

3 The documents have been published by Sayce and Cowley, *Aramaic Papyri Discovered at Assuan*, London, 1906, and Sachau, *Aramäische Papyrus und Ostraka aus Elephantine*, Leipzig, 1911. Translations of some of the important texts are found in A. Cowley's *Jewish Documents of the Time of Ezra*, London, 1919. Those translated here are Nos. 1, 4, 6, and 11 of Sachau's publication.

appoint thee before Darius, the king, and the princes of the palace more than
at present a thousand times, and long life may he grant to thee, and joy and
strength, at all times! Now thy servant, Jedoniah, and his associates thus
speak: In the month Tammuz, year 14 of Darius, the king, when Arsames
departed and went unto the king, the priests of the god Khnub, who were in
Yeb, the fortress, made an agreement with Waidrang who was acting governor
here! it was as follows: The temple of Yahu (Jehovah), the God, which is in
Yeb, the fortress they would remove from there. Afterward this Waidrang
wickedly sent a letter unto Nephayan, his son, who was commander of the
army at Syene, the fortress, saying: "The temple which is in Yeb, the fortress
they shall destroy." Afterward Nephayan, mustering Egyptians with the
other forces, came to the fortress Yeb with their quivers (?); they entered
into this temple, they destroyed it to the ground, and the pillars of stone which
were there they brake. Also it came to pass (that) five gates of stone, constructed of cut stone, which were in this temple, they destroyed, and their
swinging doors and the bronze hinges of these doors. And the roof which was
of cedar wood, all of it, together with the rest of the furnishings and the
other things which were there, the whole they burned with fire. And the
vessels of gold and silver and the things which were in this temple, the whole
was taken, and they made it their own.

Now from the days of the kings of Egypt, our fathers built this temple in
Yeb, the fortress, and when Cambyses came to Egypt, this temple was found
built, and the temples of the gods of Egypt were overthrown, but not a thing
in this temple was harmed. And after they (i. e., Waidrang and the priests
of Khnub) had done this, we and our wives and sons were clothed in sackcloth
and were fasting and praying to Yahu, God of heaven, that he would show us
this Waidrang, the cur, with the anklets torn from his feet, that all the goods
which he possesses might perish, and all the men who desired the pollution of
this temple—all might be killed, and we might see (our desire) upon them.
Also formerly, at the time this shameful deed was done to us we sent a letter
to our lord, and unto Jehohanan, the high priest, and his associates, the priests
who are in Jerusalem, and unto Ostan, the brother of Anani and the elders of
Judah, but a letter they have not sent unto us. Also from the month Tammuz of
the 14th year of Darius the king even unto this day we have worn sackcloth
and fasted, our wives have been made like widows, we have not anointed ourselves with oil, wine we have not drunk; also from then unto the 17th year
of Darius the king a meal-offering and incense and a burnt-offering they have
not offered in this temple. Now thy servants Jedoniah and his associates and
the Jews, all who are citizens of Yeb, thus speak: If unto our lord it seems
good to think on this temple to rebuild it, because they will not permit us to
rebuild it, look upon those who share thy favor and kindnesses who are here
in Egypt—let a letter be sent unto them concerning the temple of Yahu God,
to build it in Yeb, the fortress, in the way it was built formerly, and meal-
offerings and incense and burnt-offerings let them offer upon the altar of
Yahu God in thy name, and we will pray for thee at all times, we and our
wives and our sons and the Jews, all who are here. If thus they do until this
temple is built, then merit (righteousness) shall be thine before Yahu, God of
heaven, more than (that of) the man who offers to him burnt-offerings and
sacrifices of the value of a thousand pieces of silver. And concerning gold
for this we have sent information. Also the whole is told in a letter we sent
in our name to Dalajah and Shelemjah, sons of Sanballat, governor of Samaria. Also concerning this which is done to us, all of it Arsames does
not know.

On the 20th of Marcheswan, year 17 of Darius the king.

To this letter Bagohi (Bagoas) sent the following reply:

Memorandum of Bagohi and Dalajah. They spoke to me a memorandum for them: It shall be thine to say among the Egyptians before Arsames concerning the place of sacrifice of the god........of heaven, which was built in Yeb the fortress formerly before Cambyses, which this wicked Waidrang destroyed in the year fourteen of Darius the king, to build it in its place like as it was before, and meal-offerings and incense let them offer upon this altar in the manner it formerly was done.

The first of these documents is dated in the 17th year of Darius II, *i.e.*, the year 407 B.C. It states that the temple at Elephantine (Yeb) had been destroyed by Waidrang and had lain in ruins for three years. The community which worshiped in the temple had previously written to Jehohanan, high priest at Jerusalem, probably to ask that he intercede with the Persian governor Bagohi (Bagoas), but had written in vain. They now write to Bagohi himself, and also to the two sons of Sanballat, governor of Samaria (cf. Neh. 2: 10,19, etc.), with the result that the request is granted, and authority is given to rebuild the temple.

The fact that there was a temple at Elephantine at all is new and startling. Its significance is differently interpreted by different scholars. More conservative scholars claim that it is opposed to the date which the critical school assign as the date of Deuteronomy, viz.: 621 B.C., because, if the law against more altars than one had been introduced then, Jews would not have so soon violated it by building this shrine. Critics, on the other hand, hold that it fits well with their views, since they believe that Deuteronomy was accepted by Jews as a whole only gradually, and after considerable struggle.

One thing is clear: at the time the temple at Elephantine was overthrown, the Jews at Jerusalem looked upon it with disfavor.[4] They took no steps to lay the matter before the Persian governor. It was not till the aggrieved Egyptian Jews wrote to the heretical Samaritans, Dalajah and Shelemjah, sons of Sanballat, who would naturally be glad to encourage another rival to the temple at Jerusalem, that the matter was pushed and permission given to rebuild the temple.

This appeal to Sanballat's family throws interesting light on the progress of the schism between the Jews and the Samaritans.[5] (Compare Neh. 4: 1, ff.; 6: 1, ff.; and 13: 28.)

The existence of this temple has an interesting bearing upon the date of Isaiah 19. Some scholars have held that that prophecy,

---

4 Perhaps this disfavor arose in part from the fact that, as a papyrus not translated here shows, two other deities were worshiped along with Jehovah.
5 It is possible that the Elephantine colony were taken from northern Israel.

which refers to a temple of Jehovah in the land of Egypt, is late
and must refer to the temple built by Onias III, about 170 B.C.
(Cf. Josephus, *Antiquities,* xiii, 3:1,6.) It is now possible to suppose
that the reference may well have been to this hitherto unsuspected
temple at Elephantine.

2. Hananiah's Passover Letter.

To my brethren, Jedoniah and his associates, the Jewish garrison, your
brother Hananiah. The peace of my brethren may God......And now this
year, the year 5 of Darius the king, there was sent from the king unto
Arsames..........Now ye thus shall count fourteen..........and from the
15th day unto the 21st day [of Nisan].......be ye clean and guard yourselves.
Work ye shall not [do]........ye shall not drink, and all which is leavened
ye shall n[ot eat]........from the going down of the sun unto the 21st day
of Nisan........take into your rooms and seal between the days of........

This letter is from some Hananiah who seems to have stood high
in authority among Jewish communities. Several Hananiahs are
mentioned in the post-exilic literature. One of them was a military
commander in Jerusalem in the time of Nehemiah (Neh. 7:2), but
as that was at least twenty-five years before the date of our letter,
it would be precarious to assert that that Hananiah was the writer
of this letter, though it is possible that he was.

From the letter it is clear that the writer is informing the Jewish
garrison at Elephantine concerning the details of the provisions for
the observance of the Jewish Passover, as they are laid down in
Exodus 12 and Leviticus 23. It seems strange that these Jews at
Elephantine who were faithful enough to Jehovah to have a temple
in his honor, should have needed to be informed of such details, if
they had copies of the Pentateuch. Adherents of the modern school
of criticism see in this fact a confirmation of their view, that the
Levitical law had been introduced into the Jewish community at
Jerusalem only in the time of Ezra and Nehemiah, for, they urge,
this letter shows that it was unknown to the garrison at Elephantine until the reign of Darius II. To this, conservative scholars
reply that it was customary among the Jews to make yearly proclamation of the approach of the festival, and that this may be simply
such a proclamation. They also urge that ignorance of the law on
the part of some Jews is no proof that it did not exist.

3. Letter Showing that the Jews of Egypt Were Unpopular.

To my lords, Jedoniah, Uriah, and the priests of the God, Jehovah, Mattan,
son of Joshibiah and Neriah son of......thy servant Mauziyah; the peace of
my lords........and be favored before the God of heaven. And now, when
Waidrang, the chief of the garrison, came to Abydos, he imprisoned me on ac-

count of a certain precious stone which they found stolen in the hands of the traders. At last Seha and Hor, who were known to Anani, exerted themselves with Waidrang and Hornufi, under the protection of the God of heaven, until they secured my release. Now behold they are coming thither to you. Do you attend to them whatever they may desire. And whatever thing Seha and Hor may desire of you, stand ye before them so that no cause of blame may they find in you. With you is the chastisement which without cause has rested upon us, from the time Hananiah was in Egypt until now. And whatever you do for Hor you do for yourselves. Hor is known to Anani. Do you sell cheaply from our houses any goods that are at hand; whether we lose or do not lose, is one to you. This is why I am sending to you: he said to me: "Send a letter before us." Even if we should lose, credit will be established because of him in the house of Anani. What you do for him will not be hidden from Anani. To my lords, Jedoniah, Uriah, and the priests and the Jews.

This is a letter sent by a member of the Jewish colony of Elephantine to his Jewish brethren there, highly recommending to them two men. He was especially anxious to make a good impression upon these because they were acquaintances of a certain Anani. This Anani apparently was a man of influence at the Persian court. His name may be the same as Hanani, Nehemiah's brother (Neh. 7:2). It has been pointed out that the existence of two men of the same name who could have influence at the Persian court would be improbable. This letter shows that since Hananiah came to Egypt, the Jews have been in affliction, and the writer of this letter is anxious to make a good impresssion upon the friends of Anani, so that this affliction may be removed.

Scholars of the critical school see in this letter a confirmation of their view that the Levitical law had but just been introduced into the Egyptian community. The reference to the "chastisement" or "affliction" which had rested on the community is thought by them to be, probably, the friction between Jews and Egyptians caused by the less friendly relations toward foreigners, which the Levitical law imposed on its devotees. It is, of course, possible that the "chastisement" may have been due to something quite different. It should be said, too, that the papyrus is torn somewhat just where the word rendered chastisement occurs, so that the word itself is not certain.

CHAPTER XXII

A BABYLONIAN JOB

Translation of a Poem Relating to the Afflictions of a Good Man. Comparison with the Book of Job. A Fragment of Another Similar Poem.

1. **Babylonian Poem Relating to Affliction.**—The following Babylonian poem treats of a mysterious affliction which overtook a righteous man of Babylon, and has been compared with the book of Job.[1]

1. I advanced in life, I attained to the allotted span;
   Wherever I turned there was evil, evil—
   Oppression is increased, uprightness I see not.
   I cried unto god, but he showed not his face.
5. I prayed to my goddess, but she raised not her head.
   The seer by his oracle did not discern the future;
   Nor did the enchanter with a libation illuminate my case;
   I consulted the necromancer, but he opened not my understanding.
   The conjurer with his charms did not remove my ban.
10. How deeds are reversed in the world!
   I look behind, oppression encloses me
   Like one who the sacrifice to god did not bring,
   And at meal-time did not invoke the goddess,
   Did not bow down his face, his offering was not seen;
15. (Like one) in whose mouth prayers and supplications were locked,
   (For whom) god's day had ceased, a feast day become rare,
   (One who) has thrown down his fire-pan, gone away from their images,
   God's fear and veneration has not taught his people,
   Who invoked not his god, when he ate god's food;
20. (Who) abandoned his goddess, and brought not what is prescribed,
   (Who) oppresses the weak, forgets his god,
   (Who takes in vain the mighty name of his god; he says, I am like him.
   But I myself thought of prayers and supplications;
   Prayer was my wisdom, sacrifice, my dignity;
25. The day of honoring the gods was the joy of my heart,
   The day of following the goddess was my acquisition of wealth;
   The prayer of the king,—that was my delight,
   And his music,—for my pleasure was its sound.
   I gave directions to my land to revere the names of god,
30. To honor the name of the goddess I taught my people.
   Reverence for the king I greatly exalted,
   And respect for the palace I taught the people;

---

1 Translated from the *Proceedings of the Society of Biblical Archæology*, X, 478, f., and Rawlinson's *Cuneiform Inscriptions*, IV, 60*. The text has recently been translated by C. J. Ball in his *Book of Job*, Oxford, 1922, pp. 12-30, and by S. Langdon in his *Babylonian Wisdom*, 1923.

For I knew that with god these things are in favor.
What is innocent of itself, to god is evil!
35. What in one's heart is contemptible, to one's god is good!
Who can understand the thoughts of the gods in heaven?
The counsel of god is full of destruction; who can understand?
Where may human beings learn the ways of god?
He who lives at evening is dead in the morning;
40. Quickly he is troubled; all at once he is oppressed;
At one moment he sings and plays;
In the twinkling of an eye he howls like a funeral-mourner.
Like sunshine and cloud[2] their thoughts change;
They are hungry and like a corpse;
45. They are filled and rival their god!
In prosperity they speak of climbing to Heaven;
Trouble overtakes them and they speak of going down to Sheol.

(At this point the tablet is broken. We do not know how many lines are wanting before the narrative is resumed on the back of the tablet.)

Reverse

Into my prison my house is turned.
Into the bonds of my flesh are my hands thrown;
Into the fetters of myself my feet have stumbled.
....
5. With a whip he has beaten me; there is no protection;
With a staff he has transfixed me; the stench was terrible!
All day long the pursuer pursues me,
In the night watches he lets me breathe not a moment;
Through torture my points are torn asunder;
10. My limbs are destroyed, loathing covers me;
On my couch I welter like an ox,
I am covered, like a sheep, with my excrement.
My sickness baffled the conjurers,
And the seer left dark my omens.
15. The diviner has not improved the condition of my sickness;
The duration of my illness the seer could not state;
The god helped me not, my hand he took not;
The goddess pitied me not, she came not to my side;
The coffin yawned; they [the heirs] took my possessions;
20. While I was not yet dead, the death wail was ready.
My whole land cried out: "How is he destroyed!"
My enemy heard; his face gladdened;
They brought as good news the glad tidings, his heart rejoiced.
But I knew the time of all my family,
25. When among the protecting spirits their divinity is exalted.

The above is from a tablet called the "Second" of the series *Ludlul bêl nimeqi, i.e.,* "I will serve the lord of wisdom." The "Third" tablet of the series has been published by R. Campbell Thompson in the *Proceedings of the Society of Biblical Archæology,*

2 Literally, "like opening and shutting."

XXXII, p. 18, f. It is considerably broken, but the parts which are legible are as follows:

....
....
Let thy hand grasp the javelin
Tabu-utul-Bêl, who lives at Nippur,
5. Has sent me to consult thee,
Has laid his..........upon me.
In life..........has cast, he has found. [He says]:
"[I lay down] and a dream I beheld;
This is the dream which I saw by night:—
10. [He who made woman] and created man,
Marduk, has ordained (?) that he be encompassed with sickness (?)."
....
15. And..........in whatever..........
He said: "How long will he be in such great affliction and distress?
What is it that he saw in his vision of the night?"
"In the dream Ur-Bau ap[peared],
A mighty hero wearing his crown,
20. A conjurer, too, clad in strength,
Marduk indeed sent me;
Unto Shubshi-meshri-Nergal he brought abu[ndance];
In his pure hands he brought abu[ndance].
By my guardian-spirit (?) he st[opped] (?),"
25. [By] the seer he sent a message:
"A favorable omen I show to my people."
....
......he quickly finished; the......was broken
........of my lord, his heart [was satisfied];
30. ....his spirit was appeased
............my lamentation..................
.............good.... ....

Reverse

....
....
............like..................
He approached (?) and the spell which he had pronounced (?),
5. He sent a storm wind to the horizon;
To the breast of the earth it bore [a blast],
Into the depth of his ocean the disembodied spirit vanished (?);
Unnumbered spirits he sent back to the under-world.
The......of the hag-demons he sent straight to the mountain.
10. The sea-flood he spread with ice;
The roots of the disease he tore out like a plant.
The horrible slumber that settled on my rest
Like smoke filled the sky..........
With the woe he had brought, unrepulsed and bitter, he filled the earth
like a storm.
15. The unrelieved headache which had overwhelmed the heavens
He took away and sent down on me the evening dew.
My eyelids, which he had veiled with the veil of night,
He blew upon with a rushing wind and made clear their sight.
My ears, which were stopped, were deaf as a deaf man's—

20. He removed their deafness and restored their hearing.
My nose, whose nostril had been stopped from my mother's womb—
He eased its deformity so that I could breathe.
My lips, which were closed—he had taken their strength—
He removed their trembling and loosed their bond.
25. My mouth, which was closed so that I could not be understood—
He cleansed it like a dish, he healed its disease.
My eyes, which had been attacked so that they rolled together—
He loosed their bond and their balls were set right.
The tongue, which had stiffened so that it could not be raised—
30. [He relieved] its thickness, so its words could be understood.
The gullet which was compressed, stopped as with a plug—
He healed its contraction, it worked like a flute.
My spittle which was stopped so that it was not secreted—
He removed its fetter, he opened its lock.
....
....

2. Comparison with the Book of Job.—A commentary on this text, which has been preserved on a tablet, informs us that Tabu-utul-Bêl was an official of Nippur in Babylonia.[3] This story has some striking similarities to the book of Job. It presents also some striking dissimilarities.

Tabu-utul-Bêl, like Job, had been a just man. He had been also a religious man. (See lines 23 ff., p. 491.) The virtues which he claims are similar to those of Job (see Job 29 and 31) ; there is, however, this difference: Job's virtues are social; those of Tabu-utul-Bêl consist of acts of worship and loyalty. Tabu-utul-Bêl is smitten, like Job, with a sore disease. To him, as to Job, the providence is inexplicable. He, like Job, charges his god with in-scrutable injustice. The chasm which often yawns between experience and moral deserts was as keenly felt by the Babylonian as by the Hebrew.

Here the parallelism with the book of Job ends. The two works belong to widely different religious worlds. Job gains relief by a vision of God—an experience which made him able to believe that, though he could not understand the reason for the pain of life or its contradictions and tragedy, God could, and Job now knew God. (See Job 42:4-6.) Tabu-utul-Bêl, on the other hand, is said to have gained his relief through a magacian. We are apparently told by the fragmentary text that at last he found a conjurer who brought a messenger from the god Marduk, who drove away

3 Perhaps one of the antediluvian Babylonian kings. (See Part II, Chapter V.) The Sumerian form of his name was Laluralim and in Rawlinson's *Cuneiform Inscriptions of Western Asia,* Vol. V, p. 44, 17b, is glossed as Zugagib or "scorpion." Zugagib is one of the early kings of Babylonia, who is said to have ruled 840 years.

the evil spirits which caused the disease, and so Tabu-utul-Bêl was relieved. This difference sets vividly before us the greater religious value and inspiration of the book of Job. It treats the same problem that the Babylonian poet took for his theme, but between the outlook of the poet who composed Job and that of the Babylonian poet there is all the difference between a real experience of God and faith in the black art.

3. **Another Similar Lament.**—Another fragment of a lament of a somewhat similar character, written in the Sumerian language, comes to us on a tablet from Nippur, the very city with which Tabu-utul-Bêl is said to have been connected. It reads as follows: [4]

Column I

```
 1. ............................
 2. ............................
 3. ...............he carried away,
 4. ...............he destroyed,
 5. ..............spoke to..........
 6. .............was destroyed,
 7. .........completely from on high was destroyed.
 8. I, even I, am a man of destruction.
 9. With might from below he destroyed,
10. I, even I, am a man of destruction.
11. Nippur (?)—its temple verily is destroyed,
12. My city verily is destroyed.
13. O Enlil, from the height descend,
14. May Ububul destroy them!
```

Column II

```
 1. ............................
 2. ...........................
 3. ...............my food (?) is not,
 4. The ground grain is removed, with the hand he seized it;
 5. My eyes fail.
 6. The shrine of the mother which the silver-smith cast,
 7. To earth he has ground,
 8. Its contents on the earth verily he flung—
 9. I am a man of destruction!
10. Its contents on the earth verily he destroyed;
11. I am a man of destruction!
12. The man from above is wise;
13. On earth he dwells.
14. The man who went before,
15. Hides in the rear.
16. Namtar my maiden (he snatched away);
17. Who shall bring the maiden back?
```

4 Translated from S. Langdon's *Historical and Religious Texts from the Temple Library of Nippur*, Munich, 1914, No. 16.

Column III

1. Namtar verily is smitten, yea verily,
2. Who shall bring back strength?
3. The smiter has smitten,
4. Who shall strike him down?
5. The hero bearing the dagger
6. He has cast down,
7. Who shall drag him off?
8. At the gate of my palace no protector stands,
9. A man of desolation am I!
10. The land is completely overthrown, I have no defender,
11. A man of desolation am I!
12. The flood fills not the marsh land;
13. My eye thereon I lift not.
14. To man's plantations water reaches not,
15. My hand stretches not out to it.
16. To the marsh land which the flood filled
17. Truly the foot walks upon it!

From this point on the tablet is too broken for connected translation. Professor Langdon calls this the lament of a Sumerian Job, but his woes, in so far as this fragment recounts them, are due to the conquest of his land by an enemy, and to famine due to a failure of the rivers to overflow. The parallelism to Tabu-utul-Bêl and to Job might be closer, if we had the whole tablet. As this tablet is in the script of the first dynasty of Babylon, it is evident that this kind of lamentation was as early as 2000 B.C.

CHAPTER XXIII

PSALMS FROM BABYLONIA AND EGYPT

<small>CHARACTER OF THEIR PSALMS. BABYLONIAN PRAYERS TO THE GODDESS ISHTAR. COMPARISON WITH THE PSALTER. A BABYLONIAN HYMN TO THE MOON-GOD. A BABYLONIAN HYMN TO BEL. AN EGYPTIAN HYMN TO THE SUN-GOD. IS THE HYMN MONOTHEISTIC? AN EGYPTIAN HYMN IN PRAISE OF ATON. COMPARISON WITH THE PSALTER.</small>

BOTH from Babylonia and from Egypt a large number of hymns and prayers have been recovered. Some of these are beautiful on account of their form of expression, the poetical nature of their thoughts, and the sense of sin which they reveal. Most of them are clearly polytheistic, and it is rare that they rise in the expression of religious emotion to the simple sublimity of the Old Testament Psalms. Such likenesses to the Psalms as they possess only serve to set off in greater relief the rich religious heritage which we have in our Psalter.

A few examples only of the many known hymns are here given.

1. A Babylonian Prayer to the Goddess Ishtar.[1]

> O fulfiller of the commands of Bel..........
> ....
> Mother of the gods, fulfiller of the commands of Bel,
> Thou bringer-forth of verdure, thou lady of mankind,—
> 5. Begetress of all, who makest all offspring thrive,
> Mother Ishtar, whose might no god approaches,
> Majestic lady, whose commands are powerful,
> A request I will proffer, which—may it bring good to me!
> O lady, from my childhood I have been exceedingly hemmed in by
>   trouble!
> 10. Food I did not eat, I was bathed in tears!
> Water I did not quaff, tears were my drink!
> My heart is not glad, my soul is not cheerful;
> ....I do not walk like a man.
> ....

Reverse

> ....painfully I wail!
> My sighs are many, my sickness is great!

<small>1 Translated from Haupt's *Akkadische und sumerische Keilschrifttexte*, 116, ff., with comparison of Zimmern's *Babylonische Busspsalmen*, 33, f.</small>

O my lady, teach me what to do, appoint me a resting-place!
My sin forgive, lift up my countenance!

5. My god, who is lord of prayer,—may he present my prayer to thee!
My goddess, who is mistress of supplication,—may she present my prayer to thee!
God of the deluge, lord of Kharsaga,—may he present my prayer to thee,—
The god of pity, the lord of the fields,—may he present my prayer to thee!
God of heaven and earth, the lord of Eridu,—may he present my prayer to thee!

10. The mother of the great water, the dwelling of Damkina,—may she present my prayer to thee!
Marduk, lord of Babylon,—may he present my prayer to thee!
His spouse, the exalted offspring (?) of heaven and earth,—may she present my prayer to thee!
The exalted servant, the god who announces the good name,—may he present my prayer to thee!

15. The bride, the firstborn of Ninib,—may she present my prayer to thee!
The lady who checks hostile speech,—may she present my prayer to thee!
The great, exalted one, my lady Nana,—may she present my prayer to thee!

2. A Babylonian Prayer to Ishtar.[2]

...............He raises to thee a wail;
...............He raises to thee a wail;
[On account of his face which] for tears is not raised, he raises to thee a wail;
On account of his feet on which fetters are laid, he raises to thee a wail;

5. On account of his hand, which is powerless through oppression, he raises to thee a wail;
On account of his breast, which wheezes like a bellows, he raises to thee a wail;
O lady, in sadness of heart I raise to thee my piteous cry, "How long?"
O lady, to thy servant—speak pardon to him, let thy heart be appeased!
To thy servant who suffers pain—favor grant him!

10. Turn thy gaze upon him, receive his entreaty!
To thy servant with whom thou art angry—be favorable unto him!
O lady, my hands are bound, I turn to thee!
For the sake of the exalted warrior, Shamash, thy beloved husband, take away my bonds!

15. Through a long life let me walk before thee!
My god brings before thee a lamentation; let thy heart be appeased!
My goddess utters to thee a prayer, let thy anger be quieted!
The exalted warrior, Anu, thy beloved spouse,—may he present my prayer to thee!
[Shamash], god of justice,—may he present my prayer to thee!

20. ....the exalted servant,—may he present my prayer to thee!
.........the mighty one of Ebarbar,— may he present my tears to thee!
["Thine eye turn truly] to me," may he say to thee!
[Thy face turn truly to] me," may he say to thee!
["Let thy heart be at rest"], may he say to thee!

2 Translated from Haupt's *Akkadische und Sumerische Keilschrifttexte*, p. 122, f.

25. ["Let thy anger be pacified"], may he say to thee!
    [Thy heart like the heart of a mother who has brought forth], may it
        rejoice!
    [Like a father who has begotten a child], may it be glad!

3. Comparison of These Prayers with the Psalter.—The
writers of these lamentations, like the Hebrew Psalmist (see Ps.
17:1; 18:6), cried unto a deity for help. They were both in great
distress, and naturally inferred that their deity was angry, as do
Psalms 85:5; 90:7. There is, however, no great consciousness of
sin in these Babylonian complaints. They simply express distress.
Unlike the Biblical Psalms these are polytheistic and their authors
call upon other deities to intercede for them with the goddess, to
whom the prayer is addressed and whom, for the time being, they
regard as supreme. The author of this last penitential psalm asks,
"How long?" as does Psalm 6:3; 74:10; 90:13. The idea seems
to be that the suffering of the penitent will either atone for sin or
touch the heart of the deity so that the suffering shall be abated.

4. A Babylonian Hymn to Sin, the Moon-god.[3]

   O brilliant barque of the heavens, ruler in thy own right,
   Father Nannar, lord of Ur,
   Father Nannar, lord of Ekishshirgal,
   Father Nannar, lord of the brilliant rising,
5. O lord, Nannar, firstborn son of Bel,
   Thou standest, thou standest
   Before thy father Bel. Thou are ruler,
   Father Nannar; thou are ruler, thou art guide.
   O barque, when standing in the midst of heaven, thou art ruler.
10. Father Nannar, thou thyself ridest to the brilliant temple.
   Father Nannar, when, like a ship, thou goest in the midst of the deep,
   Thou goest, thou goest, thou goest,
   Thou goest, thou shinest anew, thou goest,
   Thou shinest anew, thou livest again, thou goest.
15. Father Nannar, the herd thou restorest.
   When thy father looketh on thee with joy, he commandeth thy waxing,
   Then with the glory of a king brilliantly thou risest.
   Bel a scepter for distant days for thy hands has completed.
   In Ur as the brilliant barque thou ridest,
20. As the lord, Nudimmud, thou art established;
   In Ur as the brilliant boat thou ridest.
. . . .

Reverse

. . . .
The river of Bel (?) [Nannar] fills with water.

---

3 Translated from *Cuneiform Texts from Babylonian Tablets, &c., in the British
Museum,* Part XV, pp. 16, 17. In Sumerian the god Sin was called Nannar.

The brilliant (?) river [Nannar] fills with water.
The river Tigris [Nannar] fills with water.
5. The brilliance of the Euphrates [Nannar] fills with water.
The canal with its gate Lukhe, [Nannar] fills with water.
The great marsh and the little marsh Nannar fills with water.

The preceding hymn is made up of a description of the movements and changes of the moon, together with the expression of a
superstition, which is still widely prevalent, that the moon's changes
control the rainfall. It is a fair example of a Babylonian nature-
psalm. It lacks the inspired and inspiring power of such Hebrew
nature-psalms as Psalms 8, 19, 146, 147, and 148.

5. A Babylonian Hymn to Bel.[4]

O lord of wisdom............ruler in thy own right,
O Bel, lord of wisdom...........ruler in thy own right,
O father Bel, lord of the lands,
O father Bel, lord of truthful speech,
5. O father Bel, shepherd of the black-headed ones,[5]
O father Bel, who thyself openest the eyes,
O father Bel, the warrior, prince among soldiers,
O father Bel, supreme power of the land,
Bull of the corral, warrior who leadest captive all the land.
10. O Bel, proprietor of the broad land,
Lord of creation, thou art chief of the land,
The lord whose shining oil is food for an extensive offspring,
The lord whose edicts bind together the city,
The edict of whose dwelling place strikes down the great prince
15. From the land of the rising to the land of the setting sun.
O mountain, lord of life, thou art indeed lord!
O Bel of the lands, lord of life, thou thyself are lord of life.
O mighty one, terrible one of heaven, thou are guardian indeed!
O Bel, thou art lord of the gods indeed!
20. Thou art father, Bel, who causest the plants of the gardens to grow!
O Bel, thy great glory may they fear!
The birds of heaven and the fish of the deep are filled with fear [of
thee].
O father Bel, in great strength thou goest, prince of life, shepherd of
the stars!
O lord, the secret of production thou openest, the feast of fatness estab-
lishest, to work thou callest!
25. Father Bel, faithful prince, mighty prince, thou createst the strength
of life!

A line at the end states that the hymn consisted of 25 lines.

It is a hymn to Bel of Nippur, whose Sumerian name was Enlil.
It reveals an exalted conception of Bel as supreme ruler, as a god
who gives life, as a god of justice whose rule holds society together,

---

4 Translated from *Cuneiform Texts from Babylonian Tablets, &c., in the British
Museum,* XV, 10.
5 An epithet of the inhabitants of Babylonia.

but it lacks both the poetical sublimity and the religious depth and fire of the Hebrew psalms.

6. An Egyptian Hymn to the Sun-god (about 1400 B.C.).[6]

Hail to thee, beautiful god of every day!
Rising in the morning without ceasing,
[Not] wearied in labor.
When thy rays are visible,
5. Gold is not considered,
It is not like thy brilliance.
Thou are a craftsman shaping thy own limbs;
Fashioner without being fashioned;
Unique in his qualities, traversing eternity;
10. Over ways with millions under his guidance.
Thy brilliance is like the brilliance of the sky,
Thy colors gleam more than the hues of it.
When thou sailest across the sky all men behold thee,
(Though) thy going is hidden from their sight.
15. When thou showest thyself at morning every day,
......under thy majesty, though the day be brief,
Thou traversest a journey of leagues,
Even millions and hundred-thousands of time.
Every day is under thee.
20. When thy setting comes,
The hours of the night hearken to thee likewise.
When thou hast traversed it
There comes no ending to thy labors.
All men—they see by means of thee.
25. Nor do they finish when thy majesty sets,
For thou wakest to rise in the morning,
And thy radiance, it opens the eyes (again).
When thou settest in Manu,[7]
Then they sleep like the dead.
30. Hail to thee! O disc of day,
Creator of all and giver of their sustenance
Great Falcon, brilliantly plumaged,
Brought forth to raise himself on high of himself,
Self-generator, without being born,
35. Firstborn Falcon in the midst of the sky,
To whom jubilation is made at the rising and the setting likewise.
Fashioner of the produce of the soil, .
....
Taking possession of the Two Lands (Egypt), from great to small—
40. A mother profitable to gods and men,
A craftsman of experience..........
Valiant herdsman who drives cattle,
Their refuge and the giver of their sustenance,
Who passes by, running the course of the sun-god,
45. Who determines his own birth,
Exalting his beauty in the body of Nut,
Illuminating the Two Lands (Egypt) with his disc,

6 Taken from Breasted's *Religion and Thought in Ancient Egypt*, p. 315, f.
7 A fabulous mountain beyond the western horizon, over which the sun was believed to pass at evening.

The primordial being, who himself made himself;
Who beholds that which he has made,
50. Sole lord taking captive all lands every day,
As one beholding them that walk therein;
Shining in the sky a being as the sun.
He makes the seasons by the months,
Heat when he desires,
55. Cold when he desires.
He makes the limbs to languish
When he enfolds them,
Every land is in rejoicing
At his rising every day, in order to praise him.

This hymn is, so far as its expressions go, monotheistic. One would not dream from it that there was any god but the sun-god. Nevertheless, other gods were worshiped. The monotheism here expressed was not of the intolerant kind which prevailed in Israel, and which ultimately put down the worship of all rival deities.

Such an intolerant monotheism was introduced into Egypt by Amenophis IV (see Part I, p. 19), who took an old name for the sun disc, Aton, as the name of the one god, and who tried to suppress the worship of all other gods. The movement failed, but while it lasted it produced the following beautiful hymn.

7. An Egyptian Hymn in Praise of Aton.[8]

Thy dawning is beautiful in the horizon of the sky,
O loving Aton, Beginning of life!
When thou risest in the eastern horizon,
Thou fillest every land with thy beauty.
5. Thou art beautiful, great, glittering, high above every land,
Thy rays, they encompass the lands, even all that thou hast made,
Thou art Re,[9] and thou carriest them all away captive;
Thou bindest them by thy love.
Though thou art far away, thy rays are upon the earth;
10. Though thou art on high, thy footprints are the day.

When thou settest in the western horizon of the sky,
The earth is in darkness like the dead;
They sleep in their chambers,
Their heads are wrapped up,
15. Their nostrils are stopped,
And none seeth the other,
While all their things are stolen
Which are under their heads,
And they know it not.
20. Every lion cometh forth from his den,
All serpents, they sting.
Darkness..............

8 Taken from Breasted's *Development of Religion and Thought in Ancient Egypt*, p. 324, f.
9 There is a pun on the word Re; it is the same as "all." Such puns are frequent in the Hebrew of the Old Testament prophets.

The world is in silence;
He that made them restest in his horizon.

25. Bright is the earth when thou risest in the horizon.
When thou shinest as Aton by day
Thou drivest away the darkness.
When thou sendest forth thy rays,
The Two Lands (Egypt) are in daily festivity,
30. Awake and standing upon their feet
When thou has raised them up.
Their limbs bathed, they take their clothing,
Their arms uplifted in adoration to thy dawning.
(Then) in all the world they do their work.

35. All cattle rest upon their pasturage,
The trees and the plants flourish,
The birds flutter in their marshes,
Their wings uplifted in adoration to thee.
All sheep dance upon their feet,
40. All winged things fly,
They live when thou hast shone upon them.
. . . .

The barques sail upstream and downstream alike.
Every highway is open because thou dawnest.
45. The fish in the river leap up before thee.
The rays are in the midst of the great green sea.

Creator of the germ in woman,
Maker of seed in man,
Giving life to the son in the body of his mother,
50. Soothing him in that he may not weep,
Nurse (even) in the womb,
Giver of breath to animate everyone that he maketh!
When he cometh forth from the body......on the day of his birth,
Thou openest his mouth in speech,
55. Thou suppliest his necessities.

When the fledgling in the egg chirps in the shell,
Thou gives him breath therein to preserve him alive.
When thou hast brought him together,
To (the point of) bursting it in the egg,
60. He cometh forth from the egg
To chirp with all his might.
He goeth about on his two feet
When he hath come forth therefrom.

How manifold are thy works![10]
65. They are hidden from before (us),
O sole god, whose powers no other possesseth.
Thou didst create the earth according to thy Heart
While thou wast alone:
Men, all cattle large and small,
70. All that are upon the earth,
That go about upon their feet;

10 Compare Psalm 104: 24.

[All] that are on high,
That fly with their wings.
The foreign countries, Syria and Kush,

75. The land of Egypt;
Thou settest every man into his place,
Thou suppliest their necessities.
Every one has his possessions,
And his days are reckoned.
80. The tongues are divers in speech,
Their forms likewise and their skins are distinguished.
(For) thou makest different the strangers.

Thou makest the Nile in the Nether World,
Thou bringest it as thou desirest,
85. To preserve alive the people.
For thou hast made them for thyself,
The lord of them all, resting among them;
Thou lord of every land, who risest for them,
Thou Sun of day, great in majesty.
90. All the distant countries,
Thou makest (also) their life,
Thou hast set a Nile in the sky;
When it falleth for them,
95. It maketh waves upon the mountains,
Like the great green sea,
Watering their fields in their towns.

How excellent are thy designs, O lord of eternity!
There is a Nile in the sky for the strangers
100. And for the cattle of every country that go upon their feet.
(But) the Nile, it cometh from the Nether World for Egypt.
Thy rays nourish every garden;
When thou risest they live,
They grow by thee.
105. Thou makest the seasons
In order to create all thy work:
Winter to bring them coolness,
And heat that they may taste thee.
Thou didst make the distant sky to rise therein,
110. In order to behold all that thou hast made,
Thou alone, shining in thy form as living Aton,
Dawning, glittering, going afar and returning.
Thou makest millions of forms
Through thyself alone;
115. Cities, towns, and tribes, highways and rivers.
All eyes see before them,
For thou art Aton of the day over the earth.
....
Thou art in my heart,
120. There is no other that knoweth thee
Save thy son Ikhnaton.[11]

11 Ikhnaton is the name adopted by Amenophis IV in connection with his reform. It means "Aton's man." His old name meant "Amon is gracious" and had heathen associations. On the sentiment of lines 120, 121, compare Matt. 11: 27.

Thou hast made him wise
In thy designs and in thy might.
The world is in thy hand,
125. Even as thou hast made them.
When thou has risen they live,
When thou settest they die;
For thou art length of life of thyself,
Men live through thee,
130. While (their) eyes are upon thy beauty
Until thou settest.
All labor is put away
When thou settest in the west.
....
135. Thou didst establish the world,
And raise them up for thy son,
Who came forth from thy limbs,
The king of Upper and Lower Egypt,
Living in Truth, Lord of the Two Lands,
140. Nefer-khepru-Re, Wan-Re (Ikhnaton),
Son of Re, living in Truth, lord of diadems,
Ikhnaton, whose life is long;
And for the chief royal wife, his beloved,
Mistress of the Two Lands, Nefer-nefru-Aton, Nofretete,
145. Living and flourishing for ever and ever.

8. Comparison with the Psalter.—This long hymn contains many beautiful passages, and, in addition to the line "How manifold are thy works!" often reminds one of Psalm 104, though in religious feeling it falls well below that psalm. Ikhnaton speaks of himself toward the end of his hymn as the one "whose life is long," but the poor fellow died before he was thirty years old.[12] His mummy was found a few years ago, and it is that of a young man. Vain were his hopes, unless his words refer to the immortal life.

These Egyptian hymns, like the Babylonian, exhibit a high degree of poetic and intellectual power, and much deep religious feeling, but the men who wrote them somehow lacked that deep religious insight and simple power of emotional expression that were given to the Hebrews. Their compositions but set in clearer relief the beauty, depth, and inspirational power of the Hebrew Psalms.

12 See Weigall, *The Treasury of Ancient Egypt,* London, 1911, p. 206.

CHAPTER XXIV

PARALLELS TO PROVERBS AND ECCLESIASTES

THE NATURE OF THE BOOK OF PROVERBS. SOME BABYLONIAN PROVERBS.
FROM THE LIBRARY OF ASHURBANIPAL. COMPARISON WITH THE BIBLE.
EGYPTIAN PRECEPTS OF PTAHHOTEP. COMPARISON WITH THE BIBLE. THE
WISDOM OF AMEN-EM-OPE AND ITS SUPPOSED RELATION TO PROVERBS.
PARALLEL TO ECCLESIASTES FROM THE GILGAMESH EPIC.

BOTH Egypt and Babylon furnish parallels to the book of Proverbs. The Biblical book of Proverbs contains a long connected discourse of advice (Prov. 1–9) and various collections of disconnected proverbs (Prov. 10–29). Parallels to both are found in Egypt and in Babylonia. The library of Ashurbanipal contained a collection of proverbs in two languages, arranged as reading lessons for students. A few examples are here given.

1. Some Babylonian Proverbs from the Library of Ashurbanipal.[1]

1. A hostile act thou shalt not perform, that fear of vengeance (?) shall not consume thee.
2. Thou shalt not do evil, that life (?) eternal thou mayest obtain.
3. Does a woman conceive when a virgin, or grow great without eating?
4. If I put anything down it is snatched away; if I do more than is expected, who will repay me?
5. He has dug a well where no water is; he has raised a husk without kernel.
6. Does a marsh receive the price of its reeds, or fields the price of their vegetation?
7. The strong live by their own wages; the weak by the wages of their children.
8. He is altogether good, but he is clothed with darkness.
9. The face of a toiling ox thou shalt not strike with a goad.
10. My knees go, my feet are unwearied; but a fool has cut into my course.
11. His ass I am; I am harnessed to a mule; a wagon I draw; to seek reeds and fodder I go forth.
12. The life of day before yesterday has departed today.
13. If the husk is not right, the kernel is not right; it will not produce seed.
14. The tall grain thrives, but what do we understand of it? The meager grain thrives, but what do we understand of it?

---

[1] The first twenty are culled from a tablet in the British Museum, published by Langdon in the *American Journal of Semitic Languages*, Vol. XXVIII, 217–243, under the title "Babylonian Proverbs." For convenience those quoted are numbered consecutively without reference to the parts omitted.

15. The city whose weapons are not strong—the enemy before its gates shall not be thrust through.

16. If thou goest and takest the field of an enemy, the enemy will come and take thy field.

17. Upon a glad heart oil is poured out of which no one knows.

18. Friendship is for the day of trouble; posterity for the future.

19. An ass in another city becomes its head.

The idea is similar to Matthew 13: 57: "A prophet is not without honor, save in his own country, and in his own house."

20. Writing is the mother of eloquence and the father of artists.

21. Be gentle to thy enemy as to an old oven.[2]

22. The gift of the king is the nobility of the exalted; the gift of the king is the favor of governors.

23. Friendship in days of prosperity is servitude forever.

24. There is strife where servants are; slander where anointers anoint.

25. When thou seest the gain of the fear of god, exalt god and bless the king.[3]

2. Precepts from the Library of Ashurbanipal.[4]

Thou shalt not slander, (but) speak kindly;
Thou shalt not speak evil, (but) show mercy.
Him who slanders (and) speaks evil,
With its recompense will Shamash[5] visit (?) his head.

Thou shalt not make large thy mouth, but guard thy lip;
In the time of anger thou shalt not speak at once.
If thou speakest quickly, thou wilt repent (?) afterward,
And in silence wilt thou sadden thy mind.

Daily present to thy god
Offering and prayer, appropriate to incense.
Before thy god mayest thou have a pure heart,
For that is appropriate to deity.

Prayer, petition, and prostration
Early in the morning shalt thou render him; he will judge thy burdens (?),
And with the help of god thou wilt be abundantly prosperous.

In thy wisdom learn of the tablet;
The fear (of god) begets favor,
Offering enriches life,
And prayer brings forgiveness of sins.

(The text of the rest is too broken for connected translation.)

3. Comparison with the Bible.—None of the sentiments expressed in these proverbs is identical with any in the Bible. No. 21 is on the same subject as Proverbs 24: 17; No. 22 reminds one

---

2 Translated from Delitzsch's *Assyrische Lesestücke*, 4th ed., p. 118, f.
3 Translated from Meissner's *Beiträge zum Altbabylonischen Privatrecht*, p. 108.
4 Taken from Macmillan's translation, *Beiträge zur Assyriologie*, V, 557, ff.
5 The sun-god, the god of justice.

slightly of the first clause of Proverbs 14 : 35 ; No. 23 has the same sentiment as Proverbs 18 : 24 : "He that maketh many friends doeth it to his own destruction"; while No. 6 is somewhat similar to Proverbs 24 : 21.

Among the "precepts," that on guarding the lips recalls to one's mind Proverbs 10 : 19 ; 13 : 3 ; 14 : 3 ; 17 : 28. Reference is made to the "gain of the fear of God" and it is declared to "beget favor." Job 28 : 28 declares "the fear of the Lord, that is wisdom."

4. The Precepts of Ptahhotep.—These precepts are attributed to a man who lived in the time of the fifth Egyptian dynasty, about 2650 B.C., and are at least as old as 2000 B.C. The text is very difficult. The examples given below are taken from Breasted's [6] condensation of the moral precepts which the treatise contains.

1. If thou findest a wise man in his time, a leader of understanding more excellent than thou, bend thy arms and bow thy back.

2. If thou findest, a wise man in his time, thy equal,..........be not silent when he speaks evil. Great is the approval by those who hear, and thy name will be good in the knowledge of the princes.

3. If thou findest a wise man in his time, a poor man and not thy equal, be not overbearing against him when he is unfortunate.

4. If thou art a leader (or administrator) issuing ordinances for the multitude, seek for thee very excellent matter, that thy ordinance may endure without evil therein. Great is righteousness (truth, right, justice), enduring ....; it has not been disturbed since the time of Osiris.

5. Put no fear (of thee?) among the people..........What the god commands is that which happens. Therefore live in the midst of quiet. What they (the gods?) give comes of itself.

6. If thou art a man of those who sit by the seat of a man greater than thou, take what (food) he gives......look at what is before thee, and bombard him not with many glances (don't stare at him)———.Speak not to him until he calls. One knows not what is unpleasant to (his) heart. Speak thou when he greets thee, and what thou sayest will be agreeable to (his) heart.

7. If thou art a man of those who enter, whom (one) prince sends to (another) prince,......execute for him the commission according as he saith. Beware of altering a word which (one) prince speaks to (another) prince, by displaying the truth with the like of it.

8. If thou plowest and there is growth in the field, the god gives it (as) increase in thy hand. Satisfy not thy own mouth beside thy kin.

9. If thou art insignificant, follow an able man and all thy proceedings shall be good before the god.

10. Follow thy desire as long as thou livest. Do not more than is told (thee). Shorten not the time of following desire. It is an abomination to encroach upon the time thereof. Take no care daily beyond the maintenance of thy house. When possessions come, follow desire, (for) possessions are not complete when he (the owner) is harassed.

[Compare with this precept Eccles. 11 : 9 and 7 : 15–17.]

11. If thou art an able man, (give attention to the conduct of thy son).
....

---

6 *Development of Religion and Thought in Ancient Egypt*, p. 231, f. **Breasted's** references to the sections of the original text are here omitted.

16. If thou art a leader (or administrator), hear quietly the speech of the petitioner. He who is suffering wrong desires that his heart be cheered to do that on account of which he hath come......It is an ornament of the heart to hear kindly.

17. If thou desirest to establish friendship in a house, into which thou enterest as lord, as brother, or as friend, wheresoever thou enterest in, beware of approaching the women......A thousand men are undone for the enjoyment of a brief moment like a dream. Men gain (only) death for knowing them.
[Compare Prov. 5:3, f.]

18. If thou desirest that thy procedure be good, withhold thee from all evil, beware of occasion of avarice......He who enters therein does not get on. It corrupts fathers, mothers, and mothers' brothers. It divides wife and man; it is plunder (made up) of everything evil; it is a bundle of everything base. Established is the man whose standard is righteousness, who walks in its way. He is used to make his fortune thereby, (but) the avaricious is houseless.

19. Be not avaricious in dividing......Be not avaricious towards thy kin. Greater is the fame of the gentle than (that of) the harsh.

20. If thou art successful, establish thy house. Love thy wife in husbandly embrace, fill her body, clothe her back. The recipe of her limbs is ointment. Gladden her heart as long as thou livest. She is a profitable field for her lord.
[Compare Eccles. 9:9.]

21. Satisfy those who enter to thee (come into thy office) with that which thou hast.

22. Repeat not a word of hearsay.

23. If thou art an able man who sits in the council of his lord, summon thy understanding to excellent things. Be silent.

24. If thou art a strong man, establish the respect of thee by wisdom and by quietness of speech.

25. Approach not a prince in his time. [Apparently an idiom for some particular mood.]

26. Instruct a prince (or official) in that which is profitable for him.

27. If thou art the son of a man of the council, commissioned to content the multitude,.....be not partial. Beware lest he (the man of the multitude?) say, "His plan is that of the princes. He utters the words in partiality."

....

29. If thou becomest great after thou wert little, and gettest possessions after thou wert formerly poor in the city,......be not proud-hearted because of thy wealth. It has come to thee as a gift of the god.

30. Bend thy back to thy superior, thy overseer of the king's house, and thy house shall endure because of his (or its) possessions and thy reward shall be in the place thereof. It is evil to show disobedience to a superior. One lives as long as he is gentle.

31. Do not practise corruption of children.

32. If thou searchest the character of a friend,......transact the matter with him when he is alone.

33. Let thy face be bright as long as thou livest. As for what goes out of the storehouse, it comes not in again; and as for loaves (already) distributed, he who is coscerned therefor has still an empty stomach. ["There is no use in crying over spilt milk."]

34. Know thy merchants when thy fortunes are evil.

....

37. If thou hearkenest to these things which I have said to thee, all thy plans will progress. As for the matter of the righteousness thereof, it is their worth. The memory thereof shall circulate in the mouths of men, because of the beauty of their utterances. Every word will be carried on and not perish

in this land forever........He who understands discretion is profitable in establishing that through which he succeeds on earth. A wise man is satisfied by reason of that which he knows. As for a prince of good qualities, they are in his heart and tongue. His lips are right when he speaks, his eyes see, and his ears together hear what is profitable for his son. Do right (righteousness, justice, truth), free from lying.

38. Profitable is hearkening for a son that hearkens......How good is it when a son receives that which his father says. He shall reach advanced age thereby. A hearkener is one whom the god loves. Who hearkens not is one whom the god hates. It is the heart (= understanding) which makes its possessor a hearkener or one not hearkening. The life, health, and prosperity of a man is his heart. The hearkener is one who hears and speaks. He who does what is said is one who loves to hearken. How good it is when a son hearkens to his father! How happy is he to whom these things are said! ......His memory is in the mouth of the living who are on the earth and those who shall be.

39. If the son of a man receives what his father says, none of his plans will miscarry. Instruct as thy son one who hearkens, who shall be successful in the judgment of the princes, who directs his mouth according to that which is said to him......How many mishaps befall him who hearkens not! The wise man rises early to establish himself, while the fool is scourged.

[With the first of this section compare Exod. 20:12; Deut. 5:16. With the end of it, Prov. 6:9–11; 10:26; 13:4.]

40. As for the fool who hearkens not, he accomplishes nothing. He regards wisdom as ignorance, and what is profitable as diseased........His life is death thereby,........he dies, living every day. Men pass by (avoid?) his qualities, because of the multitude of evils upon him every day.

41. A son who hearkens is a follower of Horus. He prospers after he hearkens. He reaches old age, he attains reverence. He speaks likewise to his (own) children, renewing the instruction of his father. Every man who instructs is like his sire. He speaks with his children; then they speak to their children. Attain character,........make righteousness to flourish and thy children shall live.

42. ....Let thy attention be steadfast as long as thou speakest, whither thou directest thy speech. May the princes who shall hear say, "How good is that which comes out of his mouth!"

43. So do that thy lord shall say to thee, "How good is the instruction of his father from whose limbs he came forth! He has spoken to him; it is in (his) body throughout. Greater is that which he hath done than that which was said to him." Behold, a good son, whom the god gives, renders more than his lord says to him. He does right (righteousness, etc.), his heart acts according to his way. According as thou attainest me ("what I have attained"), thy limbs shall be healthy, the king shall be satisfied with all that occurs, and thou shalt attain years of life not less than I have passed on the earth. I have attained one hundred and ten years of life [compare Gen. 50:26], while the king gave to me praise above (that of) the ancestors (in the vizierial office) because I did righteousness for the king even unto the place of reverence (the grave).

5. Comparison with the Bible.—These precepts, which were written before 1800 B.C., like most of those in the book of Proverbs, embody much worldly wisdom. They are based on experience, and while, like Proverbs, they sometimes urge a religious motive as a reason for right conduct, they frankly advocate it, as Proverbs

often does, on the ground of expediency. The points where the text is closely parallel to that of Proverbs are few, and these have been sufficiently pointed out. Some of the passages, as already noted, are closely parallel to parts of the book Ecclesiastes. The religious appeal of the precepts is to Egyptian polytheism, while that of Proverbs is to Hebrew monotheism.

6. The Wisdom of Amen-em-ope.—The work from which extracts are here presented was published by Dr. E. A. Wallis Budge in 1923.[7] These proverbs and precepts are in hieroglyphic Egyptian, but the papyrus comes from a comparatively late time. Amen-em-ope appears to have lived between 1500 and 1300 B.C. Omitting the long list of Amen-em-ope's titles, the text begins:

30. Amen-em-ope, son of Ka-nakht
....
46. Says (Chapter One)
47. Incline thy ears; listen to the words spoken!
48. Apply thy heart to understanding!
49. Profitable it is to set these in thy heart;
50. A calamity to him who passes them by!
51. Take, deposit [them] in the repositories of thy body;
52. They will effect a change in thy heart.
53. In the strife, when gales of words fly
54. They will form the support of thy tongue.
55. If thou wilt go on thy daily way with these things in thy heart,
56. Thou wilt find them [a help] in case of calamities;
57. Thou wilt find my words a treasure-house of life—
58. The health of thy body while upon the earth.

The words of this First Chapter remind one of many verses in the early chapters of the Book of Proverbs. Thus in Proverbs 2:1 ff.; 3:1 ff.; 4:20–22 we find expressions strikingly resembling those translated here.

59. Chapter Two:
60. Guard thyself from robbing the poor,
61. From treating harshly the destitute,
62. From turning away thy hand at the approach of an old man,

7 *The Teaching of Amen-em-apt, son of Kanekht,* by Sir E. A. Wallis Budge, Litt. D., etc., London, 1924. Translations and criticisms of it have also been published, by Adolf Erman, "Eine Agyptische Quelle der Srpuche Solomos," *Silzungsberichte d. preus. Ak. d. Wiss., phil-hist. Kl.,* Berlin, 1924, pp. 86–93; and H. O. Lange, *Das Weisheitsbuch des Amenemope,* Copenhagen, 1925. See also F. L. Griffith, "The Teaching of Amenophis the Son of Kanakht. Papyrus B. M. 10474" in the *Journal of Egyptian Archæology,* XII (1926), pp. 191–239; Ludwig Keimer, "The Wisdom of Amenemope and the Proverbs of Solomon," in *The American Journal of Semitic Languages,* XLIII (Oct. 1926), pp. 8–21; W. O. E. Oesterly, *The Wisdom of Egypt and of the Old Testament,* London, 1927; also his *Book of Proverbs,* New York, 1929, pp. xlvi–liv and *passim;* and R. O. Kevin, "The Wisdom of Amen-em-apt and its Possible Dependence on the book of Proverbs," in the *Journal of the Society of Oriental Research,* Vol. XIV (1930), pp. 115–157, and Breasted's *Dawn of Conscience,* New York, 1933, pp. 320–331.

63. From assuming for thyself the tone of a great man,
64. From ever thyself sending one on a dangerous mission
65. When thou carest for him who is to execute it,
66. From doing an evil deed to him who has harmed thee
67. When able to answer him in thy own behalf.
68. The worker of evil—cast him on the river-bank;
69. His own water-floods he will bring on himself.
70. Him—the north wind blowing upon him will end his day;
71. It will bring him into rough weather;
72. The storm-fiend will rise and the evil crocodiles.
73. The hot-tempered man—to thee what is he like?
74. He shrieks, he cries to heaven;
75. The moon-god stands still; he is an abomination to him.
76. Work the rudder! We must sail around this bad man!
77. Might we not have acted as he himself does?
78. Set him on his feet; give to him thy hand;
79. Commit him to the hands of the god;
80. Fill his body with bread of thy providing;
81. Satisfy him in all his desire (?);
82. Another good time is in the heart of the god;
83. Inactivity is the best of retorts!

Consideration for the poor, which is taught at the beginning of this chapter, finds expression also in such passages as Proverbs 14: 31; 28: 27. Many passages of the Book of Proverbs describe the utterances of the evil man and counsel the avoidance of contention with an angry man; see Proverbs 15: 1,18,28; 16: 32; while the treatment which the Egyptian sage recommended for the evil man strongly reminds us of Proverbs 25: 21 ff.

Omitting material not so interesting to the Biblical student, we come to line

108. Chapter Five:
109. Do not make encroachments on the dykes of the house of the god;
110. Do not act avariciously that thou mayest get gain;
111. Do not make a servant of a god stumble
112. To advance the interest of another;
113. Do not say the word "today is like tomorrow";
114. The attainment of these is like what
115. Tomorrow is to come; today is still in progress.
116. The inundation is going to be at the crest of the wave;
117. The crocodiles will appear; the hippopotomi will rise up;
118. The fishes will migrate;
119. The wolves will be sated; the birds will be at festival;
120. The protecting amulets will be left behind;
121. All the silent ones of the house of the god—
122. They will say "Great is the praise of Re."
123. O thou who art full of silence, thou shalt find life;
124. Thy body shall be healthy on the earth.

Omitting some material which has no Palestinian parallel, we find in Chapter Seven the following:

148. Do not plough the lot of another.
149. Does it befit thee to gain prosperity from their mouths?
150. Plough in the fields which thou findest allotted to thee;
151. Receive thy sustenance from thy own personal threshing-floor.
152. Better is one lot of land given thee by the god
153. Than five thousand by violence.
154. Do not practice passing the day in eating-houses.
155. Do not practice passing [it] in sipping pots of beer!
156. To those who pass their whole time in larders
157. The brightness of the world becomes [simply] eatables.
158. Better is the poor man in the hand of the god
159. Than the rich in a comfortable house.
160. Better unleavened cakes with kindliness of heart
161. Than riches with contentiousness.

The admonition not to remove land-marks (for that is what "encroaching on the dykes" and "ploughing in the fields of another" mean) reminds us of Proverbs 22:28 and 23:10 and also of the prohibitions of Deuteronomy 19:14 and 27:17. The admonitions as to eating and drinking are strikingly similar to Proverbs 23:21. Lines 160, 161 recall Proverbs 15:17.

206. Chapter Nine.
207. Do not make the hot-headed man thy intimate friend
208. Even should he come frequently to entreat thee.
209. Watch thy tongue in making answer to thy superior
210. So that thou mayest guard thyself against his revilings.
211. Do not let them throw his speech to lasso thee
212. So that thou must throw it off by thy entreaty,
213. So that thou asketh questions, entreating like a servant in thy utterance.
214. But be thou careful not to run from him.

From subsequent chapters we select the following:

254. God hates him who transgresses in talking;
255. Those are most hateful to him who cherish hatred within (?).
....
303. Better is praise with the love of men
304. Than riches in a treasure-house.
305. Better are unleavened cakes with kindliness of heart
306. Than riches with contentiousness.
....
332. Do not carry balances to falsify weights to thy profit,
333. Or to thy advantage to diminish the quantity of measures.
334. Do not wish to measure the fields,
335. To discard for thy own advantage those [measurements] of the Government-House;
336. Thoth [the god of justice] sits beside the measuring-implements;
337. These are his possessions; his heart is in the balance-pan.
338. The god, like the great Thoth, throws into the canal
339. Him who habitually devises such practices.
340. Do not make for thyself weights too small;
341. These multiply the tears of the sainted-souls with the god.

342. If thou seest another straying,
343. Thou shalt cause him to go in the right way.
....
370. Do not habitually sleep while morn is breaking,
371. What is there like dawn illumining the earth?
372. The man ignorant of the dawn—what is he like?
373. While the god is in his beneficent works
374. The man is in his affairs a failure.
375. On the one side are the words men utter;
376. On the other side are the deeds the god does.
....
409. Now truth is the great exalter of the god;
410. He gives it to the one who loves him.
411. Now one has great power who is in his likeness!
412. He removes the hurtful one who opposes his works.
....
440. Better for a man is it to speak with his own belly
441. Than that he speak in lying.
472. Cleanse thy heart of evil qualities,
473. For the hearts of men are the nose of the god.
....
525. The love of the god is more heartily to be praised
526. Than the honor of the notables of the land.
....

A comparison shows that lines 305, 306 are a repetition of lines 160, 161. This fact goes to show that The Teaching of Amen-em-ope, as is also the case with the Book of Proverbs, was compiled from different sources, in which the same saying had sometimes been included.

The many admonitions to speak the truth and to be careful in what one says find many parallels in the Book of Proverbs, as anyone may prove by looking up with the aid of a concordance the many references to "lips" and "tongue" in the Biblical book. The utterances about false weights and measures remind one of Proverbs 11 : 1 ; 16 : 11 ; 20 : 10,23. Just weights are said to belong to Jehovah, just as just measuring implements or weights belong to Thoth; Thoth's heart is with them, Jehovah takes delight in them. The words on early rising in the Egyptian work (lines 370 ff.) recall three different passages in Proverbs: Proverbs 6: 9,10; 20: 13; and 24: 33. In all of them the motive urged by the Biblical writer is prudential: early rising, coupled with industry, tends to prosperity; sluggishness and late rising, to poverty. While this motive is not absent from the Egyptian work (line 374), its author touches a higher note in the appreciation of the beauty of dawn which he expresses, and the imitation of the god which he suggests. The connection between truth and God set forth in Lines 409–412 reminds one of Proverbs 12: 17–22. Line 473 of the Egyptian document brings to mind Proverbs 20:27: "The spirit of man is the lamp of Jehovah," though the figure employed by the Egyptian is by no means as beautiful. Finally, lines 525, 526, though different, recall Job 28:28: "The fear of Jehovah is the beginning of wisdom." The Egyptian writer, like those of the Bible, commended religion. The Egyptian document, though polytheistic, rises at times to seemingly monotheistic expression.

Most scholars who have studied the Wisdom of Amen-em-ope believe that the compilers of the book of Proverbs borrowed many sayings from this Egyptian. Dr. Kevin, however, thinks he has found several passages which can be best explained by supposing that the Egyptian sage knew our book of Proverbs and borrowed from it, sometimes misunderstanding its Hebrew. If this were really so, the Egyptian work would have been composed later than the majority of scholars have thought.

Breasted, in his *Dawn of Conscience*, pp. 364–366, finds in the Wisdom of Amen-em-ope a close parallel to Jeremiah 17:5–8 and also to the First Psalm.

7. A Parallel to Ecclesiastes.—The following striking parallel to a passage in Ecclesiastes is taken from a tablet of the *Gilgamesh Epic*,[8] written in the script of the time of Hammurabi, about 2000 B.C.

> Since the gods created man,[9]
> Death they ordained for man,
> Life in their hands they hold.
> Thou, O Gilgamesh, fill indeed thy belly,
> Day and night be thou joyful,
> Daily ordain gladness,
> Day and night rage and make merry,
> Let thy garments be bright,
> Thy head purify, wash with water,
> Desire thy children which thy hand possesses,
> A wife enjoy in thy bosom,
> Peaceably thy work (?)............

This is not only in sentiment strikingly like Ecclesiastes 9:6–9, but in part closely approaches its language.

8 The Gilgamesh Epic is an early Babylonian poem in twelve tablets or cantos. It is a collection of early legends and myths. The Babylonian account of the flood, translated in Chapter VI (Part II), forms the eleventh canto of it.
9 Translated from the *Mitteilungen der vorderasiatischen Gesellschaft*, 1902, Heft 1, p. 8.

CHAPTER XXV

PARALLELS TO THE SONG OF SONGS

NATURE OF THE SONG OF SONGS. TRANSLATION OF SOME EGYPTIAN LOVE-POEMS. COMPARISON WITH BIBLICAL PASSAGES. A BABYLONIAN SONG OF SONGS.

FOR many centuries the Song of Songs has been interpreted allegorically, but even those who give it an allegorical meaning must admit that its sentiments are couched in the terms of earthly love. Love poems, which sometimes express sentiments that remind us of the Song of Songs, have been discovered on some Egyptian papyri and ostraca. The documents in which they are written range in their dates from 2000 B.C. to about 1100 B.C. Selections from these follow: [1]

I[2]

Thy love has penetrated all within me
Like [honey?] plunged into water,
Like an odor which penetrates spices,
As when one mixes juice in..........

[Nevertheless] thou runnest to seek thy sister,
Like the steed upon the battlefield,
As [the warrior rolls along] on the spokes of his wheels.

For heaven makes thy love
Like the advance of [flames in straw],
And its [longing] like the downward swoop of a hawk.

II[3]

Disturbed is the condition (?) of [my] pool.
[The mouth] of my sister is a rosebud.
Her breast is a perfume.
Her arm [is a......bough?]
[Which offers] a delusive seat.
Her forehead is a snare of *meryu*-wood.

I am a wild goose, a hunted one (?),
My gaze is at thy hair,
At a bait under the trap
That is to catch (?) me.

1 These are translated from the German rendering in W. Max Müller's *Liebpoesie der alten Ägypter*, Leipzig, 1899.
2 From Müller, p. 15.
3 *Ibid.*, p. 16.

"Brother" and "sister" are terms frequently applied to lovers in these poems. Perhaps it arose from an ancient custom of marriages between brothers and sisters, which was perpetuated in the royal families of Egypt down to Roman times.

The description of the physical attractions of the loved one reminds one of Canticles 4: 1–7.

III3a

Is my heart not softened by thy love-longing for me?
My dogfoot-(fruit) which excites thy passion,—
Not will I allow it
To depart from me.

Although cudgeled even to the "Guard of the overflow,"[4]
To Syria, with shbôd-rods and clubs,
To Ethiopia, with palm-rods,
To the highlands, with switches,
To the lowlands, with twigs,

Never will I listen to their counsel,
To abandon longing.

IV5

The voice of the wild goose cries,
(Where) she has seized their bait,
(But) thy love holds me back,
I am unable to liberate her.

I must, then, take home my net!
What shall I say to my mother,
To whom formerly I came each day
Loaded down with fowls?

I shall not set the snares today
For thy love has caught me.

This is a vivid description of the power of the tender passion.

V6

The wild goose flies up and soars,
She sinks down upon the net.

The birds cry in flocks,
But I hasten [homeward],
Since I care for thy love alone.

3a From Müller, ibid., p. 17.
4 Perhaps the name of a Nileometer station in the vicinity of Memphis.
5 Müller, ibid., p. 22.
6 Müller, ibid., p. 22.

My heart yearns for thy breast,
I cannot sunder myself from thy attractions.

This is a continuation of the preceding.

VI[7]

Thou beautiful one! My heart's desire is
To procure for thee thy food as thy husband,
My arm resting upon thy arm.[8]

Thou hast changed me by thy love.
Thus say I in my heart,
In my soul, at my prayers:
"I lack my commander tonight,
I am as one dwelling in a tomb."

Be thou but in health and strength,[9]
Then the nearness of thy countenance
Sheds delight, by reason of thy well-being,
Over a heart, which seeks thee (with longing).

This poem expresses on the part of the man a longing similar to that expressed by the woman in Canticles 8: 1–3.

VII[10]

The voice of the dove calls,
It says: "The earth is bright."
What have I to do outside?
Stop, thou birdling! Thou chidest me!

I have found my brother in his bed,
My heart is glad beyond all measure.
We each say:
"I will not tear myself away."

My hand is in his hand.
I wander together with him
To every beautiful place,
He makes me the first of maidens,
Nor does he grieve my heart.

In this poem the loved woman speaks, as in Canticles 8: 1–3.

VIII[11]

Sa'am-plants are in it,
In the presence of which one feels oneself uplifted!

7 Müller, ibid., p. 23.
8 Married couples are usually so represented in Egyptian pictures.
9 The Egyptian is here followed, rather than the German.
10 Müller, p. 24.
11 Ibid , p. 27.   It describes a walk in a garden.

I am thy darling sister,
I am to thee like a bit of land,
With each shrub of grateful fragrance.

Lovely is the water-conduit in it.
Which thy hand has dug,
While the north wind cooled us.
A beautiful place to wander,

Thy hand in my hand,
My soul inspired,
My heart in bliss,
Because we go together.

New wine it is, to hear thy voice;
I live for hearing it.
To see thee with each look,
Is better than eating and drinking.

The figure of the garden, with which this poem begins, is also used in Canticles 5:1 and 6:2,3.

IX[12]

Ta-'a-ti-plants are in it!
I take thy garlands away,
When thou comest home drunken,
And when thou art lying in thy bed
When I touch thy feet,
(And) children are (?) in thy..........
....
[I rise up] rejoicing in the morning
Thy nearness [means to me] health and strength.

In ancient as in modern times wives loved fondly, while husbands gave way to drunkenness.

The poems as a whole make it clear that in Egypt love, which lies at the basis of all home life, and is in the New Testament made a figure of the relation of Christ to the Church (see John 3:29; Rev. 21:2,9), was as warmly felt as in Israel, and was likewise poetically and passionately expressed.

A BABYLONIAN SONG OF SONGS

Among the texts from Ashur published during the year 1919 there is one which furnishes a Babylonian parallel to the book. It is part of a hymn or song employed in the worship of Tammuz. The "son" in it, originally Tammuz the son of the goddess Ishtar,

12 The garden again.

is employed as the designation of the ideal lover. In the first strophe a woman speaks; in the second, a man; in the third, a woman; in the fourth, a man. The text reads as follows:

How do I delight in joy[13]
When the lord of my right hand embraces me!
He receives me! I spread out my arms to the son!
When, O lord, wilt thou enter in hither?
I press against thy breast;
With pleasant odors is the night bewitched.
The name of the son I share;
I look on the fat of the land.
When he imparts secrets there is joy of heart!
For me, O son, brightness increases.

The bride is to me like a fragrant cedar—
A strong cedar that sustains (?) the dwelling!
Illustrious, brilliant,
It establishes our joy—our life!
The odors of cedar refine life!
At the door of the lord she is jubilant
On this evening, this night.
How luxurious she is! How brilliant!
The mighty ones of the garden shall behold thy charms.
Today my heart is joyfully tuneful.

There has gone down to the garden[14] the king who fells the cedar.
Thou, O son, lovest our breast!
Across the river is a joyful city;
Our place at the approach (?) of the month is jubilant!
Yonder one is going, O son;
When he is away, thou art my companion!
A bird, a dove passes; the light of Eros is thy gift,
Who art a god doing right; The garden is jubilant!
The day the god stands in Larsa the god
Is jubilant; he is full of passion!
Rejoice! Nana is in the garden, the abode which thou lovest!
A maiden is brought; her heart is glad!
Thus do I rejoice continually!
I rejoice in thee, O divine child!
My sealed eyes are full of sleep!
Thy love is indeed a jewel!
The enjoyment of thee, verily gold!
My love is a light which illumines the darkness!
Tonight I think upon thee!

He opened his mouth:
"After thou hast lain in the bosom of the son

13 Translated from Ebeling, work cited, No. 158, pages 273, 274. Ebeling has presented a German translation of a part of it in the *Mittheilungen der deutschen Orient-Gesellschaft*, No. 58, 1917, p. 49 f., but it is a garbled translation. He has omitted many lines apparently because they were difficult.
14 The phrase and idea are strikingly similar to Canticles 6: 2:
My beloved is gone down to his garden............
To feed in the gardens, and to gather lilies.

Thy waist (?) is a mountain of lapis-lazuli!
Joyfully I present the king!
Blessed is the darkness (?)!
In thy love is abundant life!"
Love causes embracings!

Comment seems unnecessary. While the lines have a Babylonian and a polytheistic flavor, the general theme—the praise of the charms of two lovers for one another—is identical with the theme of the Song of Songs, and the delight in love which breathes from the lines is similar to that which is expressed in Canticles. Occasionally a phrase reminds one of a phrase in Canticles and the figure of the garden comes in a similar way into both this poem and the Song of Songs.

PARALLELS TO THE SONG OF SONGS 521

Thy waist (??) is a mountain of lapis lazuli;
Joyfully I receive the king.
Blessed is the eunuch (?)
In thy love is abundance;
Love causes enjoyment . . .

CHAPTER XXVI

ILLUSTRATIONS OF PASSAGES IN THE PROPHETS

UNIQUENESS OF THE PROPHETIC BOOKS. SOME EGYPTIAN PROPHECIES. AN ASSYRIAN PROPHETIC VISION. COMPARISON WITH THE BIBLE. THE EGYPTIAN SOCIAL CONSCIENCE. TALE OF THE ELOQUENT PEASANT. COMPARISON WITH THE BIBLE. AN IDEAL KING; EXTRACT FROM THE ADMONITIONS OF IPUWER. COMPARISON WITH MESSIANIC EXPECTATIONS. SHEOL. ISHTAR'S DESCENT TO THE UNDERWORLD. COMPARISON WITH PROPHETIC PASSAGES. A LAMENTATION FOR TAMMUZ. A NORTH SYRIAN POEM ON THE "CONQUEST OF DEATH." DANIEL IN A NORTH SYRIAN POEM. THE FALL OF NINEVEH.

THERE is no other body of literature which closely corresponds to the books of the Hebrew prophets. The depth of their social passion and the power of their moral and religious insight form a unique combination. Nevertheless, texts which have come from Babylonia and Egypt do show that certain phases of prophetic thought were not without parallels elsewhere. At times they also illustrate for us thoughts and practices which the prophets abhorred. A few such texts are here translated.

In the priesthoods connected with ancient Egyptian temples there was a division or class called "prophets." Some of the predictions of these men have survived to our time. Their character may be ascertained from the following examples:

1. The Prophecy of an Egyptian Priest from the Reign of King Seneferu Before 2900 B.C.[1]

The papyrus on which the prophecy is written is torn at the beginning. The burden of the prediction is that the people of a foreign land will drink from the water of Egyptian rivers. It is to this that the first broken line refers.

To refresh themselves............
This land shall be plundered............
The......of the land is unfortunate (?), forms arise not (?);
One grasps the weapon of terror,
The land lives in uproar,
Each mouth is full of...............
All good flies away,

1 Translated from Ranke's German version in Gressmann's *Altorientalischer Texte und Bilder zum Alten Testament*, p. 204, ff.

The land is going to destruction, as (?) is appointed for it.
The..........shall be injured..........
Whatever one finds (?) shall be destroyed,
Reduced to nothing............
One plunders a man's possessions........whatever is without (?),
I give to thee, my lord...............
To bring to silence the mouth that speaks.
One replies..........
One commands (?) thereupon to kill (?) him.
....
...........his taxes
The crop is small, the corn-measure great,
It will be measured when just sprouting (?)
The sun dissolves........mankind........
It shines but for an hour;
One notes not when it is midday,
One counts not the shadows,
Faces are not illumined, if one behold a (?)....them,
One ventures not..........................
It (the sun) is as the......of heaven, as the moon,
At its time of........it does not pass over.
The......of its beams is not before it
In its rôle of predecessor.
The land is in misfortune......
One asks after the health (?)........
I make the below (?) the above for the.......
One lives in this god.
The poor will collect possessions,
And the great will be brought to nought.

A king will come from the south by the name of Ameni.
He will be born from a woman of Nubia;
He will be born in the city of Nechen;
He will seize the crown of Upper Egypt
And set the crown of Lower Egypt on his head.
He will unite the double crown
And happily join Horus and Set[2] in love.
He will hasten through............
Mighty in his time (?)............
The people will rejoice in the time of the son of man;
His name shall endure for all eternity,
For (?) they shall be far (?) from misfortune.
He who entertains hostile thoughts
Shall be confounded for fear of him.
The Asiatics shall fall before his sword,
The Lybians shall fall before his flame,
The enemies before the rage of his......
And the riotously disposed before his strength,
    While the uraeus[3] is on his brow
It quiets for him rebellious thoughts.
One shall build "the walls of the ruler,"
Which shall not permit the Asiatics to enter Egypt.
They beg for water......after the manner of......

2 Horus, the god of Lower Egypt, and Set, the god of Upper Egypt, are here symbols of the two kingdoms.
3 The uraeus was the symbolic serpent on the head-dress of a king.

To give drink to their cattle.
Truth shall again come into your state,
While falsehood shall be expelled.
He shall be glad on whom he shall look,
He who shall be in the retinue of the king.
A wise man shall sprinkle water for me
When he sees that come to pass which I predict.
One shall make the poor whole in........
One begs for bread..........
One laughs with laughter......in......
One sleeps not..............
A man's heart is directed of itself
And not directed by......today.........

This text presents certain likenesses and certain differences to Hebrew prophecy. The references to the darkness of the sun suggest that the prophecy was called forth by an eclipse, the significance of which the prophet was called upon to interpret. This he did by uttering his forebodings of disaster. He went on, however, to prophesy that a king would arise who would expel all invaders, give Egypt a government of justice, and do for that country what many Hebrew prophets expected the Messiah to do for theirs. In this connection the Egyptian prophet's use of the term "son of man" to describe the expected king is interesting. It is the term employed in Daniel 7:13 to describe the nature of the Messianic kingdom, applied later in Enoch 46:2, 48:2, to the expected Messiah, and still later appropriated by Jesus as his self-designation.

2. Prophecy of a Lamb under King Bocchoris, 718–712 B.C.[4]

Great is misfortune in Egypt. Heliopolis weeps in the east (?)........
Hermopolis (?) weeps........They make the streets of Hebit............
Thebes weeps........The lamb concludes the execrations. Psenyris says to it (the lamb): "What......?" It (the lamb) says......"At the completion of 900 years I will smite Egypt.".....He (a god?) will turn his face to Egypt. He yields before the foreign warriors...... Lies, violation of laws and statutes, as in Egypt continue (?).......They will take......the chapels of the Egyptian gods to Nineveh for themselves (?) to the territory of Amor, he......the men of Egypt go into the land of Syria, they shall smite his district, they shall find again the chapels of Egypt's gods.
Psenyris sent it (the lamb) on a new...... and delayed not to bring a barque to go to the place where the king was. One laid the roll of papyrus, concerning all the misfortune which would happen to Egypt, before the king ......The king said: "Psenyris, look to the lamb; let it be installed in a chapel (?) let it be conveyed as a god; let it be on the earth as is the custom with regard to superiors."

This interesting oracle is so different from Hebrew prophecy that comment is unnecessary. The prophesying of the lamb may

4 Translated from Ranke's German version in Gressmann's *Altorientalischer Texte und Bilder zum Alten Testament.*

be compared with the speaking of Baalam's ass in Numbers 22: 28–30.

3. A Prophetic Vision.—The following statement is taken from the annals of Ashurbanipal, king of Assyria, 668–626 B.C. It is the conclusion of a passage in which the king is relating his strenuous struggle with Tiuman, King of Elam. Ashurbanipal tells how he poured out a libation to Ishtar of Arbela and offered to her a long prayer against the Elamite king. The narrative then continues: [5]

In an hour of that night when I prayed to her, a seer lay down; he saw a prophetic dream. Ishtar caused him to see a vision of the night, and he announced it to me, saying: "Ishtar who dwells at Arbela entered, and on her right and left she was behung with quivers, she was holding a bow in her left hand, she brandished a heavy sword to make war. Thou wast sitting before her. She, like the mother who bore thee, was speaking to thee and talking to thee. Ishtar, the exalted one of the gods, was appointing thee a message: 'Thou shalt expect to accomplish that[6] at the place which is situated before thee. I am coming.' Thou wast answering her, saying: 'Where thou goest I will go with thee, O lady of ladies.' She repeated to thee, saying: 'Thou......indeed dwellest in the place of Nebo. Eat food, drink wine, appoint rejoicing, exalt my divinity until I go and accomplish this undertaking..........I will cause thee to accomplish the wish of thy heart. Thy face he shall not harm, thy feet he shall not resist; thy cry shall not come to nought.' In the midst of battle she arms thee with the desolation of her goodness. She will protect thy whole body. Before her a fire is blown to capture thy foes."

The night vision of this seer reminds one a little of Isaiah's vision of Jehovah in the temple (Isa. 6) and of Zechariah's vision of Joshua and Satan (Zech. 3:1). The Hebrew prophets as late as the time of Jeremiah often received their divine messages in dreams. (See Jer. 23:27.) Assyria had something of the same ideas as Israel as to the revelations of deity to a prophet, but she lacked Israel's ethical deity.

4. The Egyptian Social Conscience.—A remarkable appreciation of the rights of the common people is revealed in an Egyptian story called the "Tale of the Eloquent Peasant,"—a story which has come down to us in copies made before 1800 B.C. It has been claimed that this tale indicates the existence of a social conscience in Egypt analogous to that of the Hebrew prophets. The principal part of the story is, accordingly, given here.

The Eloquent Peasant [7]

There was a man, Hunanup by name, a peasant of Sechet-hemat, and he had

5 Translated from Rawlinson's *Cuneiform Inscriptions of Western Asia*, III, 32, 16, f.
6 *I.e.*, the thing thou hast prayed for.
7 Translated from the German of Vogelsang und Gardiner, *Klagen des Bauern*, Leipzig, 1908.

a wife,..........by name. Then said this peasant to his wife: "Behold, I am going down to Egypt to bring back bread for my children. Go in and measure the corn that we still have in our storehouse,........bushel." Then he measured for her 8 (?) bushels of corn. Then this peasant said to his wife: "Behold, 2 bushels of corn shall be left for bread for thee and the children. But make for me the 6 bushels into bread and beer for each of the days [that I shall be on the road]." Then this peasant went down to Egypt after he had loaded his asses with all the good products[8] of Sechet-hemat.

This peasant set out and journeyed southward to Ehnas. He came to a point opposite Per-fefi, north of Medenit, and found there a man standing on the bank, Dehuti-necht by name, who was the son of a man named Iseri, who was one of the serfs of the chief steward, Meruitensi.

Then said this Dehuti-necht, when he saw the asses of this peasant which appealed to his covetousness: "Oh that some good god would help me to rob this peasant of his goods!"

The house of Dehuti-necht stood close to the side of the path, which was narrow, not wide. It was about the width of a........-cloth, and upon one side of it was the water and upon the other side was growing grain. Then said Dehitu-necht to his servant: "Hasten and bring me a shawl from the house!" And it was brought at once. Then he spread this shawl upon the middle of the road, and it extended, one edge to the water, and the other to the corn.

The peasant came along the path which was the common highway. Then said Dehuti-necht: "Look out, peasant, do not trample on my clothes!" The peasant answered: "I will do as thou wishest; I will go in the right way!" As he was turning to the upper side, Dehuti-necht said: "Does my corn serve you as a road?" Then said the peasant: "I am going in the right way. The bank is steep and the path lies near the corn and you have stopped up the road ahead with your clothes. Will you, then, not let me go by?"

Upon that one of the asses took a mouthful of corn. Then said Dehuti-necht: "See, I will take away thy ass because it has eaten my corn.........."

Then the peasant said: "I am going in the right way. As one side was made impassable I have led my ass along the other, and will you seize it because it has taken a mouthful of corn? But I know the lord of this property; it belongs to the chief steward, Meruitensi. It is he who punishes every robber in this whole land. Shall I, then, be robbed in his domain?"

Then said Dehuti-necht: "Is it not a proverb which the people employ: 'The name of the poor is only known on account of his lord?' It is I who speak to you, but the chief steward of whom you think." [9] Then he took a rod from a green tamarisk and beat all his limbs with it, and seized his asses and drove them into his compound.

Thereupon the peasant wept loudly on account of the pain of what had been done to him. Dehuti-necht said to him: "Don't cry so loud, peasant, or thou shalt go to the city of the Silence-maker" (a name of the god of the underworld). The peasant said: "Thou beatest me and stealest my goods, and wilt thou also take the wail away from my mouth? O Silence-maker! give me my goods again! May I never cease to cry out, if thou fearest!"

The peasant consumed four days, during which he besought Dehuti-necht, but he did not grant him his rights. Then this peasant went to the south, to Ehnas, to implore the chief steward, Meruitensi. He met him as he was coming out of the canal-door of his compound to embark in his boat. Thereupon the peasant said: "Oh let me lay before thee this affair. Permit one of thy trusted servants to come to me, that I may send him to thee concerning it." Then the steward, Meruitensi, sent one of his servants to him, and he

8 The original contains a list of plants, stones, birds, etc., the modern equivalents of which are not known.

9 See Gardiner in *Proceedings of the Society of Biblical Archæology*, XXXV, 269.

sent back by him an account of the whole affair. Then the chief steward, Meruitensi, laid the case of Dehuti-necht before his attendant officials, and they said to him: "Lord, it is presumably a case of one of your peasants who has gone against another peasant near him. Behold, it is customary with peasants to so conduct themselves toward others who are near them. Shall we beat Dehuti-necht for a little natron and a little salt? Command him to restore it and he will restore it."

The chief steward, Meruitensi, remained silent; he answered neither the officials nor the peasant. The peasant then came to entreat the chief steward, Meruitensi, for the first time, and said:

"Chief steward, my lord, thou art greatest of the great, thou art guide of all that which is not and which is. When thou embarkest on the sea of truth, that thou mayest go sailing upon it, then shall not the..........strip away thy sail, then thy ship shall not remain fast, then shall no misfortune happen to thy mast, then shall thy spars (?) not be broken, then shalt thou not be stranded; if thou runnest fast aground, the waves shall not break upon thee, then thou shalt not taste the impurities of the river, then thou shalt not behold the face of fear; the shyest (?) fish shall come to thee, and thou shalt capture the fat birds. For thou art the father of the orphan, the husband of the widow, the brother of the desolate, the garment of the motherless. Let me place thy name in this land higher than all good laws: thou guide without avarice, thou great one free from meanness, who destroyest deceit, who createst truthfulness. Throw the evil to the ground. I will speak; hear me. Do justice, O thou praised one, whom the praised ones praise. Remove my oppression: behold, I have a heavy........to carry; behold, I am troubled of soul; examine me, I am in sorrow."

The reference in this address to the orphan and the widow touches a chord which runs through much of the Old Testament and is especially prominent in the prophets, as the following references will indicate: Isaiah 1:17,23; 9:17; 10:2; 47:8; Jeremiah 7:6; 15:8; 18:21; 22:3; 49:11; Ezekiel 22:7,25; Zechariah 7:10; Malachi 3:5; Deuteronomy 10:18; 14:29; Job 29:13, and Psalm 68:5.

In the Egyptian story Meruitensi was so pleased with the eloquence of the peasant that he passed him on to another officer and he to still another until he came before the king. Altogether the peasant made nine addresses. For lack of space we can reproduce but one more. For this purpose we select his eighth address.

This peasant came to implore him for the eighth time, and said:
"Chief steward, my lord, man falls on account of........Greed is absent from a good merchant. His good commerce is..........

"Thy heart is greedy; it does not become thee. Thou despoilest: this is not praiseworthy for thee........Thy daily rations are in thy house; thy body is well filled........The officers, who are set as a protection against injustice,— a curse to the shameless are these officers, who are set as a bulwark against lies.

"Fear of thee has not deterred me from supplicating thee; (if thou thinkest so), thou hast not known my heart. The silent one, who turns to report to thee his difficulties, is not afraid to present them to thee........Thy real estate is in the country; thy bread is on thy estate; thy food is in the storehouse. Thy officials give to thee and thou takest it. Art thou, then, not a robber? They drag for thee........for thee to the plots of arable land. Do the truth for the sake of the lord of truth........Thou reed of a scribe, thou roll of a book, thou palette, thou god Thoth, thou oughtest to keep thyself far removed from injustice. Thou virtuous one, thou shouldst be virtuous; thou virtuous one, thou shouldst be really virtuous. Further, truth is true to eternity. She goes with those who perform her to the region of the dead. He will be laid in the coffin and committed to the earth; his name will not perish from the earth, but men will remember him on account of his property: so runs the right interpretation of the divine word.

"Does it then happen that the scales stand aslant? Or is it thinkable that the scales incline to one side?

"Behold, if I come not, if another comes, then thou hast opportunity to speak as one who answers, as one who addresses the silent, as one who responds to him who has not spoken to thee. Thou hast not been........; thou hast not been sick. Thou hast not fled; thou hast not departed. But thou hast not yet granted me any reply to this beautiful word which comes from the mouth of the sun-god himself: 'Speak the truth; do the truth: for it is great, it is mighty, it is everlasting. It will obtain for thee merit, and will lead thee to veneration.'

"For does the scale stand aslant? It is their scale-pans that bear the objects, and in just scales there is no.........wanting."

The beauty of the sentiments about truth is obvious. The references to scales are to those that were supposed to weigh the deeds of the dead in the under-world.

After a ninth speech on the part of the peasant, the tale concludes as follows:

Then the chief steward, Meruitensi, sent two servants to bring him back. Thereupon the peasant feared that he would suffer thirst, as a punishment imposed upon him for what he had said. Then the peasant said........(The Egyptian of this address contains difficulties which have never been solved.) Then said the chief steward, Meruitensi: "Fear not, peasant! See, thou shalt remain with me." Then said the peasant: "I live because I eat of thy bread and drink thy beer forever." Then said the chief steward, Meruitensi: "Come out here........" Then he caused them to bring, written on a new roll, all the addresses of these days. The chief steward sent them to his majesty, the king of Upper and Lower Egypt, Neb-kau-re, the blessed, and they were more agreeable to the heart of his majesty than all that was in his land. His majesty said, "Pass sentence thyself, my beloved son!" Then the chief steward, Meruitensi, caused two servants to go and bring a list of the household (of Dehuti-necht) from the government office, and his possessions were six persons, with a selection from his........, from his barley, from his spelt, from his asses, from his swine, from his.............

From this point on only a few words of the tale can be made out, but it appears from these that the goods selected from the estate of Dehuti-necht were given to the peasant and he was sent home rejoicing.

5. An Ideal King.—In the wisdom literature of Egypt appear the admonitions of an Egyptian sage called Ipuwer. In these

admonitions a time of dire distress is pictured, in view of which the
sage longs for the presence of an ideal king. Some scholars have
compared the description of this ideal king with the prophetic conception of the Messiah.

It is unnecessary to quote the whole work, which is fragmentary
and difficult of translation. A few passages will answer our
purpose.

From the Admonitions of Ipuwer [10]

..........The door-keepers say: Let us go and plunder. The confectioners
..........The washerman refuses to carry his load..........The bird-catch-
ers have drawn up in line of battle..........The inhabitants of the Marshes
carry shields. The brewers........sad. A man looks upon his son as his
enemy;................

....
Noble ladies suffer like slave girls. Musicians are in the chambers within
the halls. What they sing to the goddess Mert is dirges............Forsooth,
all female slaves are free with their tongues. When the mistress speaks it is
irksome to the servants. Forsooth, princes are hungry and in distress. Servants are served............by reason of mourning. Forsooth, the hot-headed
(?) man says: "If I knew where God is, then would I make offerings unto
him." Forsooth, right is throughout the land in this its name. What men do
in appealing to it is wrong. Forsooth, all animals, their hearts weep. Cattle
moan because of the state of the land..........Forsooth, the ways are........
The roads are guarded. Men sit over the bushes until the benighted traveler
comes, in order to plunder his burden. What is upon him is taken away. He
is belaobred with blows of the stick and slain wrongfully.

Forsooth, that has perished which yesterday was seen (?). The land is left
over to its weariness (?) like the cutting of flax. Poor men are in affliction
........Would that there might be an end of men, no conception, no birth!
O that the earth would cease from noise, and tumult be no more!..........
Forsooth, grain has perished on every side. People are stripped of clothes,
spices (?) and oil. Everybody says there is none. The storehouse is ruined.
Its keeper is stretched on the ground. It is no happy thing for my heart (?)
..........Would that I had made my voice heard at that moment, that it
might save me from the pain in which I am (?)..........Behold, the power-
ful of the land, the condition of the people is not reported to them. All is ruin!
Behold, no craftsmen work. The enemies of the land have spoilt its crafts.

Similar descriptions of the disorganized state of society might be
quoted at much greater length. The passage in which Ipuwer mentions the ideal king is as follows:

..........lack of people................Re; command (?).............
the West to diminish (?)........by the [gods?]. Behold ye, wherefore does
he [seek] to fashion [mankind],..........without distinguishing the timid
man from him whose nature is violent. He bringeth coolness upon that which
is hot. It is said: he is the herdsman of mankind. No evil is in his heart.
When his herds are few, he passes the day to gather them together, their hearts
being on fire. Would that he had perceived their nature in the first generation

10 Taken from A. H. Gardiner's *Admonitions of an Egyptian Sage*, Leipzig, 1909, pp.
19 and 39, f., pp. 69 and 78.

of men; then would he have repressed evils, he would have stretched forth his arm against it, he would have destroyed their seed and their inheritance......
......Where is he today? Is he sleeping? Behold, his might is not seen.

Vogelsang held this to be a picture of a kind of ideal king, comparable in some respects to the prophetic conception of the Messiah in such passages as Isaiah 9: 1–6; 11: 1–8. To this view Gardiner has objected that the parallelism is not real, in that there seems to have been in the mind of the Egyptian sage no expectation that such a king would actually rise, but rather the belief that he once existed as the god Re and has now vanished from earth. To this Breasted and Gressmann reply that the kingly figure is a purely ideal one, and that Ipuwer feels strongly that, if he were on earth all wrongs would be set right, and that in some degree the picture is parallel to the conceptions of the Messiah.

The description of disorganized society which is here reflected is patterned on conditions which existed in Egypt before 2000 B.C., and the conception of the ideal king is equally old.

6. Sheol.—In Isaiah 14: 9–11 and Ezekiel 32: 21–31 we find descriptions of Sheol or the under-world. These descriptions are closely parallel to the following Babylonian poem.

Ishtar's Descent to the Underworld [11]

Unto the land of No-return, the land of darkness,
Ishtar, the daughter of Sin, determined to go,
The daughter of Sin determined to go,
Unto the house of darkness, the dwelling of Irkalla,
5. Unto the house whose enterer never comes out,
Along the way whose going has no return,
Unto the house whose enterer is deprived of light,
Where dust is their food, their sustenance, clay,
Light they do not see, in darkness they dwell;
10. They are clothed, like birds, with a covering of wings.
Over door and bolt the dust is spread.
Ishtar, when she arrived at the gate of the land of No-return
To the keeper of the gate addressed a word:
"Keeper of the waters, open thy gate!
15. Open thy gate! Let me enter!
If thou dost not open thy gate, that I may enter,
I will shatter the door, I will break the bolt,
I will shiver the threshold, break down the doors;
I will bring up the dead to devour the living!"
20. The keeper opened his mouth and spake,
He said to Ishtar, the great:
"Stay, my lady, do not destroy it,
Let me go, let me announce thy name to Queen Allat."
The keeper went in, he spake [to Allat]:

11 Translated from Rawlinson's *Cuneiform Inscriptions of Western Asia*, Vol. IV, p. 31.

25. "This water thy sister, Ishtar, [has crossed]
    As a servant of great powers [she comes]."
    When Allat heard this,
    Like the cutting of the tamarisk [was her laugh],
30. Like the crackling of reeds. [She cried]:
    "What has turned her mind to me?..........
    These waters I with...........
    For food I will eat clay, for drink I will drink............
    I will weep for men who have abandoned their wives,
35. I will weep for maidens torn from their husbands' bosoms,
    I will weep for children snatched away before their time.
    Go, keeper, open thy gate to her;
    Do to her according to the ancient custom."
    The keeper went and opened to her his gate:
40. "Enter, my lady; the under-world is glad,
    The palace of the land of No-return rejoices at thy coming."
    He brought her through the first gate, made it wide, he took the great
        crown from her head.
    "Why, O keeper, hast thou taken the great crown from my head?"
    "Enter, my lady, such are the commands of Allat."
45. He brought her through the second gate, he made it wide, he took the
        ornaments from her ears.
    "Why, O keeper, hast thou taken the ornaments from my ears?"
    "Enter, my lady, for such are the commands of Allat."
    He brought her through the third gate, he made it wide, he took the
        necklace from her neck.
    "Why, O keeper, hast thou taken the necklace from my neck?"
50. "Enter, O lady, for such are the commands of Allat."
    He brought her through the fourth gate, he made it wide, he took the
        ornaments from her breasts.
    "Why, O keeper, hast thou taken the ornaments from my breast?"
    "Enter, my lady, for such are the commands of Allat."
    He brought her through the fifth gate, he made it wide, he took the
        girdle with birth-stones from her waist.
55. "Why, O keeper, hast thou taken the girdle with birth-stones from my
        waist?"
    "Enter, my lady, for such are the commands of Allat."
    He brought her through the sixth gate, he made it wide, he took the
        bracelets from her hands and feet.
    "Why, O keeper, hast thou taken the bracelets from my hands and
        feet?"
    "Enter, my lady, for such are the commands of Allat."
60. He brought her through the seventh gate, he made it wide, he took the
        breech-cloth from her body.
    "Why, O keeper, hast thou taken the breech-cloth from my body?"
    "Enter, my lady, for such are the commands of Allat."
    When Ishtar had gone down to the land of No-return,
    Allat saw her and became enraged at her.
65. Ishtar took no heed; she sat down above her.
    Allat opened her mouth and spake,
    To Namtar, her messenger, she addressed a word:
    "Go, Namtar, lock [her in my palace],
    Bring out against her sixty diseases..........Ishtar,
70. Disease of the eyes against her [eyes],
    Disease of the side against her [sides],
    Disease of the feet against her [feet],

Disease of the heart against [her heart],
Disease of the head against [her head],
75. Against her altogether.........."
After Ishtar, the lady [went down to the land of No-return]
The bull with the cow did not unite, nor the ass approach the she-ass;
The man in the street no more approached the maid;
The man slept in his chamber,
80. The maid slept by her oven.
Papsukal, messenger of the great gods, was sad of countenance before [Shamash],
Clad in mourning, wearing foul garments.
Then went Shamash into the presence of Sin, his father; he wept,
Before Ea, the king, his tears flowed:
85. "Ishtar has gone down into the earth; she has not come up.
Since Ishtar went down to the land of No-return,
The bull with the cow does not unite, nor the ass approach the she-ass;
The man no more approaches the maid in the street;
The man sleeps in his chamber,
90. The maid sleeps by her oven.
Then Ea in the wisdom of his heart created a man,
He created Asushunamir, the priest.
"Go, Asushunamir, to the gate of the land without return set thy face,
The seven gates of the land without return shall be opened before thee,
95. Allat shall behold thee, and shall rejoice in thy presence.
When her heart has been appeased, and her soul revived,
Conjure her also by the name of the great gods.
Turn thy thoughts to the skin which pours forth life:
'O lady, give me the skin which pours forth life, that I may drink water from it.' "
100. When Allat heard this,
She beat upon her thigh, she bit her finger:
"Thou hast uttered a wish not to be wished.
Go, Asushunamir; I curse thee with a great curse.
The sewage of the gutters of the city shall be thy food,
105. The cesspools of the city shall be thy drink,
The shadow of the walls shall be thy dwelling,
The thresholds shall be thy habitation,
Confinement and privation shall shatter thy strength."
Allat opened her mouth and spoke,
110. To Namtar, her messenger, she addressed the word:
"Go, Namtar, knock at the palace of justice,
Tap at the thresholds of gleaming (?) stones,
Bring out the Annunaki,[12] seat them on golden thrones,
Sprinkle Ishtar with the water of life and bring her before me."
115. Namtar went, he knocked at the palace of justice,
He tapped at the thresholds of gleaming (?) stones,
He brought forth the Annunaki, he seated them on golden thrones,
He sprinkled Ishtar with the water of life, he brought her forth.
He brought her out of the first gate, he restored to her the breech-cloth of her body;
120. He brought her through the second gate, he restored to her the bracelets of her hands and feet;
He brought her through the third gate, he restored to her the girdle with birth-stones for her waist;

12 The spirits of earth.

He brought her through the fourth gate, he restored to her the ornaments of her breasts;
He brought her through the fifth gate, he restored to her the necklace of her neck;
He brought her through the sixth gate, he restored to her the ornaments of her ears;
125. He brought her through the seventh gate, he restored to her the crown of her head.
(End of legend. The priest begins:)
"If she does not grant to thee her release, turn to her again;
To Tammuz, the beloved of her youth,
Pour out water, offer good oil,
With red clothing clothe him, let him play a flute of lapis lazuli.
130. Let the joyful maidens turn..................
When Belili has established her ritual,
With precious stones her bosom is filled."
The wailing for her brother she heard; Belili interrupted the ritual of
....
With precious stones she filled the front of..............
(Voice from the dead.)
135. "My only brother, harm me not;
On the day of Tammuz, play for me the lapis lazuli flute, play the *Santu*-flute with it,
When the wailing men and women play with it,
Let the dead return, let them smell incense."

The description of the darkness of the under-world and the sad conditions of life with which this poem begins, shows that the Babylonians shared the gloomy views of Sheol which Isaiah 14 : 9–11 and Ezekiel 32 : 21–31 express.

The middle of the poem expresses the view of the ancient Semites, that the goddess of love once went down to the under-world, and that as a result all propagation of life ceased on the earth. The end of it alludes to the later belief that the goddess went down every year for her beloved Tammuz who had died, and the wailing alluded to is that spoken of by Ezekiel in Ezekiel 8 : 14, where the prophet says he saw women wailing for Tammuz. The kind of sentiment uttered in this wailing the next extract will illustrate.

7. A Lamentation for Tammuz.[13]

The lord of destiny (?) lives no more, the lord of destiny (?) lives no more.
[Tammuz the......] lives no more,......lives no more.
The bewailed one (?) lives no more, the lord of destiny (?) lives no more.
I am queen, my husband lives no more.
5. My son lives no more.
Dagalushumgalanna lives no more.
The lord of Arallu lives no more.

13 Translated from *Cuneiform Texts from Babylonian Tablets, etc., in the British Museum*, Part XV, 18.

The lord of Durgurgurru lives no more.
The shepherd, the lord Tammuz lives no more.
10. The lord, the shepherd of the folds lives no more.
The consort of the queen of heaven lives no more.
The lord of the folds lives no more.
The brother of the mother of wine lives no more.
[He who creates] the fruit of the land lives no more.
15. The powerful lord of the land lives no more.
When he slumbers the sheep and lambs slumber also.
When he slumbers the goats and kids slumber also.
As for me, to the abode of the deep will I turn my thoughts,
To the abode of the great ones I turn my thoughts.
20. "O hero, my lord, ah me," I will say,
"Food I eat not," I will say,
"Water I drink not," I will say,
"My good maiden," I will say,
"My good husbandman," I will say,
25. "Thy lord, the exalted one, to the nether world has taken his way,
Thy lord, the exalted one, to the nether world has taken his way."
On account of the exalted one of the nether world, him of the radiant
face, yea, radiant,
On account of the exalted one of the nether world, him of the dovelike
voice, yea, dovelike,
On account of the exalted one, the lord, on account of the lord,
30. Food I eat not on account of the lord,
Water I drink not, on account of the lord.
"My good maiden, because of the lord,
My good husbandman, on account of the lord,
The hero, your lord has been destroyed,
35. The god of grain, the child, your lord, has been destroyed."
His kindly look gives peace no more,
His kindly voice imparts cheer (?) no more;
..........in his place, like a dog he sleeps;
My lord in his..........slumbers iike a raven
40. Alone is he, himself,
My lord, for whom the wail is raised.

(Forty-one lines—a psalm on the flute to Tammuz.)

This poem illustrates what Ezekiel may have heard in vision,
when in spirit he was brought to the northern gate of the temple,
and heard women wailing for Tammuz (Ezek. 8:14).

8. A North Syrian Poem on the "Conquest of Death."—
Among the discoveries at Ras Shamra [14] (Ugarit) there was found,
as already noted, three liturgies. One of them is an account of
the death and resurrection of Alein. The poem is, of course,
mythological in character. It was recited during the wailing for
Alein and affords knowledge from another part of the Semitic world
as to what the wailing, which Ezekiel mentions, was involved. A
second text was discovered on a smaller tablet, which supplements

14 See above, Part I, Chapter IV, § 26.

the main poem, giving, apparently, an introduction and conclusion
to the longer text. In the following translation, therefore, the introduction and conclusion are taken from the smaller tablet.

Introduction

1. Concerning Baal [15]
2. On the mountain she lays a foundation of stone, two graven images....
3. She gashes cheeks and chin (she utters)
4. a dirge (for) her boy. She digs like a garden
5. a water-course (?) like a valley, she makes three high places.
6. "Baal is dead. Who are the people of the son of Dagan?
7. How desolate is the shrine of Baal! Let us go down
8. into the earth with him! Thou shalt go down, O Light
9. of the gods, Shephesh. Thou shalt be sated with weeping;
10. thou shalt drink like wine even tears." Also
11. she cried to the Light of the gods, Shephesh,
12. "Load, I pray, Alein Baal on me!"
13. Shephesh, the light of the gods, obeyed;
14. she lifted Aleyn Baal to the shoulder
15. of Anath. When she placed him, she (Anath) carried him up,
16. In the parched ground of Saphan she bewailed him,
17. she buried him, she sprinkled herself with ashes
18. of the barren earth. She sacrificed seventy
19. wild oxen because of the slaying of Alein
20. Baal. She sacrificed seventy oxen
21. because of the slaying of Alein Baal.
22. She sacrificed seventy sheep
23. because of the slaying of Alein Baal.
24. She sacrificed seventy stags
25. because of the slaying of Alein Baal
26. She sacrificed seventy goats
27. because of the slaying of Alein Baal.
28. She sacrificed seventy asses
29. because of the slaying of Alein Baal.

9. The Resurrection of Alein [16]

Col. i.   1. "....Alein, the lord [17]
2. ......linen on him.........
3. his........he will make tall for the gods"
4. Then indeed she set her face toward
5. El, at the source of the rivers in the midst
6. of the clefts of the two abysses, and she explored the field
7. of El, and she entered the courts
8. of the king, the father of years.[18] Before
9. El she performed a purifying rite (?) and hastened,
10. she prostrated herself and honored him.

[15] Translated from the original text published by Virolleaud in *Syria*, XV, (1934), p. 227.

[16] The text is published with transliteration and translation by Charles Virolleaud in *Syria*, Vol. XII (1931), pp. 193–224, under the title, "Un poeme phenicien de Ras Shamra."

[17] Literally, *baal*.

[18] Compare "The Ancient of Days," Dan. 7: 9, 13 and 22.

11. She lifted her voice and cried, she, Ashirat
12. and her sons rejoiced—Elat and the
13. band of her retainers: "How has Alein
14. the lord died? How has perished Zebul, lord
15. of the earth?" El also cried
16. to the lady Ashirat of the sea: "Hearken,
17. O lady Ashirat of the sea, give
18. one of thy sons (?) that I may make him king."
19. The lady Ashirat of the sea answered,
20. "No, we must make one king who knows how to rule (?)"
21. Then answered the beneficent one, El-deped,
22. "He who thrusts down created things can raise
23. them up; the lord will open (?) a resting-place (?)
24. for the son of Dagan to hide there."
25. The lady Ashirat of the sea answered,
26. "No: we will make Ashtar, the wise, king.
27. Ashtar the wise shall reign.
28. I will turn Ashtar the wise to thee;
29. he shall go up to the heights of the north;
30. he shall sit on the throne of Alein,
31. the lord; his legs shall reach the
32. footstool; his head shall reach,
33. its top." Then Ashtar, the wise, answered,
34. "Verily I will be king in the heights of the north."
35. Ashtar the wise went down, he went down
36. to the ancient abode of Alein, the lord,
37. and he ruled in the land of El, all of it;
38. ....(in) the broad places (?) and squares
39. ....in the....................

ii.   1. To.................
   2. and to..............
   3. a water-jar..............
   4. a water-jar she.................
   5. he brought the water-jar (?)............
   6. overcame her. Like the longing
   7. of a young cow for her calf, like the longing of a ewe for
   8. her lamb, so was the longing of Anath
   9. for the shrine of Baal. She seized Moth,[19]
   10. with a sandal for a weapon (?) she smote (?) him;
   11. in the utterance of a curse she raised her voice and
   12. cried, "Thou, Moth, give me my brother."
   13. And Moth, son of the gods, answered, "What
   14. dost thou wish, O virgin Anath
   15. Surely I will go and drive every
   16. mountain into the midst of the earth, every hill
   17. into the midst of the fields. Breath is restrained from
   18. the sons of women; breath has been cut off
   19. from the earth. At my pleasure the earth has become
   20. a wilderness which will continually devour the field as the lion kills
   21. prey. As to me, Alein, the lord,
   22. the blameless one, even to me is a lamb in my mouth;
   23. all of him is for the crushing of my jaws—his destruction (?); and
   24. the light of the gods, Shephesh, the burning one,

---

19 *I.e.*, death, personified as a god.

25. to injure them by the hand of the son of the gods, Moth."
26. Day followed days to days,
27. to months. The love of Anath overcame her.
28. Like the longing of the young cow for her calf, like the longing
29. of a ewe for her lamb, so was the longing of
30. Anath for the shrine of Baal. She seized
31. the son of the gods, Moth, with a sword
32. she split him open, she sifted him in the sieve,
33. in the fire she burned him,
34. in the mill she ground him, in the field
35. she sowed his flesh, that the birds
36. might eat and his fate be completed.
37. A piece of flesh cried to the flesh,

iii. (At the beginning of column iii some lines are broken away. We do not know how many. Those that remain are numbered consecutively.)

1. Like the perishing of Moth............
2. And he, (Alein the lord), lives,
3. and he, Zebul, lord (of the earth) exists,
4. In a favorable dream El-Deped (heard) :
5. "Good tidings, O my son (whom) I have begotten,
6. the heavens shall rain oil,
7. the valleys shall flow with honey,
8. and I know that Alein, the lord, lives,
9. and that Zebul, lord of the earth, exists."
10. In a favorable dream El-Deped (heard) :
11. "Good tidings, O my son (whom) I have borne,
12. the heavens shall rain oil,
13. the valleys shall flow with honey."
14. The good omen made El-Deped glad;
15. his feet he set on a footstool,
16. and put away grief and laughed.
17. He lifted up his voice and cried:
18. "I will sit down and rest
19. and my soul shall rest in my breast,
20. because Alein, the lord, lives,
21. because Zebul, lord of the earth, exists."
22. Also El cried to the virgin
23. Anath: "Hear, O virgin Anath.
24. the cry of the light of the gods Shephesh.
25. Come down, O Anath, the fields shall cause life to be!
26. Come down, O Anath, the fields El shall break up.
27. O lord, Anath is the one who ploughs.
28. Where is Alein, the lord?
29. Where is Zebul, lord of the earth?"
30. (Then) the virgin Anath strode in,
31. thither she turned her face
32. to the light of the gods, Shephesh,
33. she lifted up her voice and cried:
34. "Thou givest heat to the bull of the god, thy father;
35. thou hast been the help (?) of the villagers (?), (who say),
36. 'Come down, O Anath, the fields shall cause life to be!
37. Come down, O Anath, the fields El shall break up.
38. O lord, Anath is the one who ploughs.
39. Where is Alein, the lord?
40. Where is Zebul, lord of the earth?' "
41. Then answered the light of the gods, Shephesh,

42. "Answer, O our fields, to the vaulted dome,[20] (answer)
43. to the height with thy faithfulness,
44. and I will seek Alein, the lord."
45. Then answered the virgin Anath,
46. Where, O where, shall he cause life to be?
47. Where, O where, shall El call?
48. thou criest, O Shephesh................
49. ....shall make soft (?)...............
50. ...."
51. ....
v. 1. The lord, son of Ashirat, seized
    2. the great ones, he smote them upon the shoulder;
    3. like the sea, he smote upon the pair;
    4. the burning one (and) Moth he smote to the earth,
    5. he...............the throne of its king,
    6. ....the failure of his way,
    7. the days (?)......to the months, to the months,
    8. to the years (up to) seven
    9. years; afterward (?) the son of the gods, Moth,
   10. unto Alein, the lord, shall lift up
   11. his voice and cry, "From upon thee by..........[21]
   12. thou hast removed the curse: from upon thee my house
   13. thou has removed by the sword; from upon thee
   14. thou has removed the corruption by fire;
   15. from upon thee (thou hast removed) the..........by the mill;
   16. from upon thee thou hast removed the.......by nobility;
   17. from upon thee thou hast removed...............
   18. by the fields; from upon thee thou hast removed
   19. the coat of mail (?) by the sea....................
   20. After the concealment................
   21. shall bring thee in.................(as)
   22. one of the gods (?)...............

(The rest of the column is too broken for translation, as are the first five lines of column vi)

vi. 6. ....to the mother (?)
     7. ....the son of the gods, Moth,
     8. ....his seven coverings
     9. ....son of the gods, Moth,
    10. Released (?) are the brothers. The lord shall grant
    11. to overtake (?) the sons of my mother, my longed for ones.
    12. They shall inhabit with Baal the heights
    13. of the north. He shall lift up his voice and cry,
    14. "O brothers, I Baal have placed
    15. before me the sons of my mother, my longed for
    16. ones." They shall answer as the Gomerites (answered)
    17. Moth, "The strength of Baal is strength that will gore
    18. Moth like wild oxen; the strength of Baal
    19. is strength that will bite Moth like
    20. vipers (?); the strength of Baal is strength that will
    21. tear out (?) Moth like wild horses. The voice
    22. of Baal is the voice over us." Shephesh
    23. cried to Moth, "Hear, Moth,

20 *I.e.*, the sky.
21 There are many gaps in the text due to the crumbling of the clay.

24. O son of the gods, Moth, how wilt thou fight (?)
25. with Alein, the lord?
26. How will not hear thee the bull,
27. El, thy father? Verily he will tear out the pillar (?)
28. Of thy dwelling; verily he will overturn the throne of thy kingdom;
29. verily he will break the scepter of thy rule!"
30. The son of the gods, Moth, went down to defeat (?);
31. he loved the god Ghezer ( ). Moth bleated with
32. his voice, he...................................... .
33. "The lord will make us dwell..............................
34. his king for lord (?)
35. his restoration ....

Conclusion [22]

1. ....
2. ....she said,
3. ....mankind
4. ....at the lifting up of the voice
5. (flesh) just slaughtered also thou shalt eat
6. as bread, lamentations (?) thou shalt drink
7. as wine. The illumination (?) of Shephesh
8. shall divide the *rephaim*;[23]
9. Shephesh shall divide the *elonim*.[24]
10. Thy witnesses are the gods. Behold the dead!
11. Thy witnesses are the ritually pure—thy companions—
12. and forethought is thy knowledge
13. in the day of desire and lamentation.
14. Ritual purity and forethought [25] are power;
15. abundance are ritual purity and forethought.[26]

Colophon

16. Scribe: El-Melek, the Shibonite,
17. disciple of Ethan-Parlan, chief of
18. the priests, chief of the shepherds,
19. the Saite. Naqmad, king of Ugarit,
20. the lord, honors Baal-Sharmon.

It is clear that we have here a form of the story of Adonis centuries earlier than that given us by Lucian.[27] In later time the god was called Adon (Greek, Adonis), "Lord"; in our poem he is also called "Lord," though the word employed is the synonym Baal. That the reference is to an earlier form of the same story is further

22 Translated from *Syria*, XV, (1934), 227.
23 The *rephaim* are the "shades" of the dead. In the Old Testament the term sometimes serves as the name of the early inhabitants of Palestine (Gen. 14: 5 and 15: 20), but at other times to designate the dead, as in the Hebrew of Psalm 88: 11.
24 The word means "terebinths." The terebinth is a kind of oak. Probably it is employed here because it is the root from which the name of the god Alein comes. Alein was the terebinth-god.
25 Kasher-we-Khasis was a compound deity. The names mean "spiritual purity" and "forethought." The text makes a play on this fact, so the divine names have been translated.
26 *Ibid.*
27 Lucian, *De Syria Dea*, §§ 6–9.

made probable by the phrase *'apq thmtm,* "cleft of the two abysses" in col. i, 6, since the word for "cleft" is the word which gave the name Aphek (Josh. 13:4), the Aphaca of Lucian. "Under the towering crests of Lebanon . . . beneath a low natural bridge and a cave a great spring bursts forth in the stream bed. The road winds through pines along a terrace and comes to a second cave and a second spring with beautiful waterfalls. Facing them on a bluff, from which a third spring gushes forth through a tunnel, are the ruins of Aphek."[28] "The cleft of the two abysses" reminds one of the phrase in Psalm 42:7 descriptive of the rushing waters bursting from the springs which form the beginnings of the Jordan: *"tehom* calls to *tehom,"* i.e., "deep calleth unto deep."

The deities of the pantheon of the poem throw a flood of light on the West Semetic religion of this early time.

10. Daniel in a North Syrian Poem.—As was noted in Pt. I, ch. IV, §26 the excavation at Ras Shamra (Ugarit) brought to light a poem, of which a Daniel was the hero, and that this hero probably was the same as the Daniel referred to in Ezekiel 14:14. The poem is long and contains many mythological features, but some parts of it, which are of interest to the student of the Bible, are translated here. The text begins as follows:[29]

1. Concerning Aqahat
2. Sacrifice (?) O,..........to the midst of the waters!
3. Thou shalt call........thou shalt break (his) bow;
4. ....thou shalt break eight
5. ....to the virgin Anath.
6. She shall turn......she shall raise up a tender youth,[30]
7. ....let us take him as a prince, as a lamp,
8. And his finger (shall be) as the Desire [31]-of-the poor.[32]
9. From him thou shalt take his sandals [33]
   And he shall eat in the heavens.
10. Thou shalt drink with eagerness like that of thirsty oaks
11. The best wines (?) of his wine-vat (?), O prince.

These opening lines are evidently a prophecy of the birth of Daniel, who, in the poem, is regarded as a son of the god El. It is not clear who it is that is speaking; perhaps it is a priest, who was supposed to recite the poem at a festival. The goddess Anath was apparently Daniel's mother. Daniel is to be a prince, a lamp,

28 A. T. Olmstead, *History of Palestine and Syria*, N. Y., 1931, p. 70.
29 Translated from Charles Virolleaud's *La legende phénicienne de Danel, Paris*, 1936.
30 I take the word *tlm* to be the Arabic *tilm*, "lad," "youth."
31 *Khrs.* not "moat," as Virolleaud renders, but the Arabic *khirs*, "craving," "desire."
32 *Ebn* is not, as Virolleaud thinks, *eben*, "stone," but a defectively written *ebion*, "poor."
33 *Shnt:* cf. the Assyrian *shenu*, "sandal."

of the people. A lamp illumines. The thought is similar to that
of Isaiah 42:6, "I will give thee for a light to the Gentiles," only
here the poet is thinking not of the Gentiles, but of his own people.
The expression "Desire of the poor" is parallel to the phrase "desire
of the meek" in Psalm 10:17, and suggests the Authorized Version's rendering "Desire of the nations" in Haggai 2:7. Daniel
is here conceived as a sort of heaven-born Messiah.

The poem next introduces Aqahat, one of the two opponents of
Daniel in this legend, who in lines 12–19 utters his threats.

> Aqahat answered,
> O tender one, tender one,
> Like the serpent of El in might,
> Like the heart of his sceptre,
> I will smash it—the ornament on his bow,
> I will smash it on his shield (?).
> They are to me as brothers.
> His bow thou shalt also give to me,
> And the high place beloved (?) of Anath.
> The fruit a basket shall bring,
> The ears of grain in his jar.

The "tender one" here addressed is Daniel. Aqahat is threat-
ening to overcome him and to gain for himself the fruit and grain.
The word for ears of grain is *shibboleth,* the word the pronunciation
of which was employed in Judges 12:6 as a test of membership
in the tribe of Ephraim. In response to this challenge of Aqahat,
Daniel is said to have proceeded as follows (11. 19–24):

> Then Daniel, who cures Death,
> Who makes the Prince of Death [34] to wail,
> Raised himself up;
> He sat before the gate among the great
> Who in the threshing-floor
> Judge the cause of widows
> And secure justice for orphans.

At this point some lines of the text are broken away.

In the legend Daniel has a daughter, Paghat, who is opposed to
her father and in accord with his opponents. In lines 29–37 she
arouses suspicion against her father. In 11. 38–42, the power of
Daniel is described; in 11. 42–48, a drought.

Then (Paghat spoke):

> "In the threshing floor Daniel shall cause desolation,
> (Of corn?) he shall raise the price,
> He shall diminish the poor."
> Against the house of her father she directed the eagles.

[34] The original is paraphrased here. In it the name of one of the gods of death occurs.

He (Daniel) trapped the troop of vultures.
Paghat wept over them,
Her heart cried over them heavily.
The cunning of Daniel, who cures Death,
Who makes the Prince of Death to wail, pondered.
Then Daniel, who cures death,
Roasted the clouds with heat,
Lightning (?) darted; the clouds rained;
In that year dew distilled on the grapes.
For seven years Baal had been impotent;
The eighth, O Rider of the Clouds,
Was without dew, without showers,
Without the opening of the two deeps,[35]
Without abundance.
"Hasten, O Baal for (Paghat) has hastened,
She has outwitted Daniel, who cures Death,
Weakened is he who makes the Prince of Death to wail!"

Baal then intervenes, lines 49–54.

Then to the daughter of Daniel he cries:
"Hear, O Paghat, who hast stopped [36] the water,
Thou hast held it back.
To make the dew thou knowest,
The courses of the stars,
The covering of the wild-ass,
The saddling of the stallion,
The planting of the silver vine,
Which is the jewel of my (water)-springs" [37]

Paghat then acts; lines 54–60.

Paghat heard, she who held back
The water and stopped (it),
She who knows the courses of the stars,
And how to make the dew.
How did she cover the ass!
How did she saddle the stallion!
How did she lift up her father!
She placed him on the back of the ass,
That he might sit on the back of the stallion.

At the appearance of Daniel the god El speaks; lines 61–74:

El executed judgment; he turned his augury.
Quickly he spoke,
By omens quickly he spoke,[38]

35 That is, "The waters which were under the firmament" and "the waters which were above the firmament"; Gen. 1: 7. These two "deeps" are those which in Ps. 42:7 are said to call to one another. See above, p. 540.

36 An Egyptian loan-word. Cf. the Egyptian *skm* (Erman-Grapow, *Wörterbuch der aegyptischen Sprache*, IV, p. 317). It is not, as Virolleaud thinks, the Semitic word for shoulder.

37 From the Akkadian root *naqâbu*, from which we have *naqbu* and *me naqbi*, "water-springs." The second *n* in *nqbn* is an afformative.

38 The translation of these lines is difficult and the rendering here given is at some points uncertain. The writer can justify it philologically, though this is not the place to do so.

With eager desire quickly he embraced, he kissed,
(Saying) "I will perform my duty quickly;
It shall be effective by omens,
Quickly in carnal desire there shall be a change.[39]
The hand of Aqahat shall harvest thee, O Ghezer [40]
It shall put thee in their midst in the granary.
He [40a] shall execute judgment,
He shall restore what thou hast eaten,
He shall say:
'The ears (diminished) by eating,
The ears changed by drought,
The ears he shall embrace, he shall kiss,
(Saying), 'I will perform my duty.'
The ears thou hast taken by eating,
The ears thou hast taken by carnal appetite.
The hand of Aqahat shall harvest thee, O Ghezer,
It shall put thee with them in the granary.' "

These extracts give one an idea of the character of the poem. Daniel is its hero. His name means "judgment of El" or "El is my judge." To monotheists, like the Hebrews, it would mean "God is my judge." The poem represents Daniel as wonderfully wise, but it is a wisdom of the type that was popular in the age from which the poem comes—a time before 1500 B.C. He is skilled in magic arts, but he is just to the poor and unfortunate and has great power with El, the supreme deity. At that time the inhabitants of ancient Phœnicia thought such characteristics the acme of wisdom and righteousness. From this time onward the fame of Daniel lived in the traditions of the whole region. It was thus that Ezekiel (ch. 14:14) cited him as an ancient example of righteousness. The author of the Jewish apocryphal Book of Enoch apparently heard of Daniel through a different tradition—a tradition which emphasized his knowledge of magic arts, for he regarded Daniel as one of the fallen angels; see Enoch 6:7 and 69:2.

11. The Fall of Nineveh.—The Prophet Nahum in the second and third chapters of his book vividly predicted the siege, devastation, and overthrow of Nineveh. A text found among the tablets in the British Museum tells in detail how the prophecy approached fulfilment. A translation of it follows: [41]

In the 10th year Nabopolassar, in the month Airu (April-May), mustered the army of Akkad and marched along the bank of the Euphrates. The

39 There was a widespread belief in the ancient world that water was the spermatazoa of the gods. These amatory lines are an ancient way of expressing El's determination to send rain to revive vegetation.
40 Ghezer is a proper name. It often occurs followed by the word *moth*, "death." The two words occur thus above, where I have translated, "Prince of Death."
40a *I.E.*, Daniel.
41 Translated from the Assyrian text published by C. J. Gadd, in *The Fall of Nineveh*, London, 1923.

Sukhaites and Khindanites did not offer battle, but laid their tribute before him. In the month Ab (July-August) they reported that the Assyrian army was in the city Qablinu and Nabopolassar went up against them. On the 12th day of the month Ab the Assyrian army offered battle; the Assyrian army was put to flight before him and the humiliation of Assyria was effectually accomplished. They took much booty and captured the Mannæans who had come to their aid and also the princes of Assyria. On that day the city Qablinu was captured. During Ab the King of Akkad sent his army against Mane, Sakhiru, and Balikhu; they took plunder, collected abundant spoil, and carried off their gods. In the month Ulul (August-September) the King of Akkad and his army turned back and on his route was the city of Khindanu; its gods he took to Babylon. In the month Tashritu (September-October) the Egyptian army and the Assyrian army marched after the King of Akkad as far as the city Qablinu; they did not overtake the King of Akkad. He hastened after them. In the month Adar (February-March) the Assyrian army and the Akkadian army joined battle in the city Madana belonging to the city of Arapkhu. The Assyrian army fled before the Akkadian army; they seriously defeated them and threw them back to the river Zab. They seized their asses and horses and took much booty. His........they brought with them across the Tigris and brought into Babylon.

In the year 11 the King of Akkad mustered his army and marched along the bank of the river Euphrates and in the month Airu encamped in the heart of the country Assyria. On the........day of the month Simanu (May-June) he made an attack on the midst of a city, but did not capture the city. The King of Assyria mustered his army and the King of Akkad was expelled from the territory of Assyria and the King of Assyria and his army pursued him as far along the shore of the Tigris as the city Takritain. The King of Akkad brought his army up into the fortress of Takritain. The King of Assyria and his army encamped against the army of the King of Akkad which was shut up in Takritain and for ten days fought against them; they did not capture the city. The army of the King of Akkad, which was shut up in the fortress, defeated Assyria badly. The King of Assyria and his army.........and returned to his country. In the eighth month (November-December) the Mede came down unto Arapkhu and fought against the city.........

In the 12th year in the month Ab the Mede (went) against the city of Nineveh as.............. and hastened and captured Tabriz, a city of the district of Nineveh........He marched down the shore of the Tigris and encamped against the city of Ashur and fought against Ashur.............The city he destroyed and accomplished cruelly the destruction of the principal people; he seized their plunder and took their booty. The King of Akkad and his army, who had gone to the help of the Mede, did not arrive for the battle. The city..........The King of Akkad and Cyaxares met one another near the city and made a covenant of friendship and amity..........Cyaxares and his army returned to their country; the King of Akkad and his army returned to their country.

In the 13th year, in the month Airu, the Sukhean rebelled against the King of Akkad and committed hostilities. The King of Akkad mustered his army and marched against Sukhi. In the month Siman, on the 4th day, he made an assault upon the city of Rakhilu, a city which is in the midst of the Euphrates; on that day he captured the city. Its........he built, stones from the bank of the Euphrates he laid down before it........against the city Anati he encamped. Siege-engines from a westerly direction.............The siege-engines he brought near to the wall and made an attack upon the city, but did not capture it.............The King of Assyria and his army came down and the King of Akkad and his army turned and went back to their country
....

In the 14th year the King of Akkad mustered his army...............the men of the king of the Scythians (?) toward the King of Akkad.......... ....and they beheld one another. The King of Akkad ....and Cyaxares..........................he caused to cross and along the bank of the Tigris they marched and.......... ....against Nineveh.......................... they from the month Simanu to the month Ab three battles................ and they made a mighty assault upon the city. In the month Ab, on the...... day........(the city was captured)..................He accomplished the destruction of the (principal people) on that day. Sinsharishkun, King of Assyria.........................They took the spoil of the city, a quantity beyond computation, and turned it to a mound and a ruin. The.......... of Assyria before the king fled and the force of Akkad..................In the month Ulul, the 20th day Cyaxares and his army returned to their land and after him the King of Akkad turned.............and went to the city Nisibis; plunder and slaves (?) as booty (?)........of the land of Rapasu they brought to Nineveh to the presence of the King of Akkad................ (Ashuruballit) sat upon the throne in Harran as King of Assyria. Until the month..................(the King of Akkad remained) in Nineveh........ From the 20th day of the month...........the king...........the month Tashritu in the city.....................

In the 15th year in the month Tammuz (June-July)...........the king of Akkad..........................marched to Assyria.................... victoriously..............the army of the country Khazzu................ and of the country..............captured, they seized their plunder and took their booty.............................In the eighth month the King of Akkad turned the front of his army against the city Ruguliti.............he made an attack against it and on the 28th day of the eighth month the city was captured........not a man (escaped).......He returned to his country.

In the 16th year in the month Airu the King of Akkad mustered his army and marched against Assyria. From Airu unto the eighth month he marched victoriously in Assyria. In the eighth month the country of the Scythians (?) ....came to the help of the King of Akkad and their armies they united and marched to Harran against Ashuruballit who had occupied the throne in Assyria. Ashuruballit and the army of................which had come to his help—the fear of the enemy fell upon them, they left the city and crossed......................The King of Akkad reached Harran and the city....................was captured. The plunder of the city they took in quantity beyond computation. In the month of Adar the King of Akkad ....left their.............and returned to his country. Also the Scythians (?) who had come to his aid..............

In the month Tammuz the Assyrian king (secured) a very great Egyptian army.................He crossed the river and marched to capture Harran. The garrison which the King of Akkad had sent to its midst they cast down and killed. He encamped against Harran; until Ulul he made attacks upon Harran but (accomplished) nothing; he did not capture it. The King of Akkad came to the help of his army and joined battle.................He went up to Izalla. Many cities of their country........................their ....he burned with fire. At that time the army.............. as far as the district of the city Urashtu..........in the country.......... their..........they plundered. The garrison of the king................. they and to the city.................the King of Akkad returned to his land.

In the 18th year in the month............the King of Akkad mustered his army.

At this point this interesting text ends. Indeed the last line was written as a catch line to enable the reader to identify the next tablet. We should much like to know what happened in the 18th year, but for that we must await the discovery of the next tablet.

As we read this story of the marching and counter-marching of armies across Assyria, we can imagine what the country suffered, even as the prophet Nahum had predicted. While the actual overthrow of the Assyrian power is not told, perhaps because the tablet is broken at the end, but, more probably, because the story was continued on the next tablet, we see that kingdom tottering to its fall. A number of details are also told of which we did not before know. We learn that in the year 615 the king of Egypt, Psammetik I, was still faithful to Assyria and was fighting as her ally. We had previously supposed that he had broken with that country nearly thirty years before. We also learn that the king of Babylon destroyed the city of Ashur, the old capital of Assyria in 611 B.C., and drove in that same year the king of Assyria from Nineveh, occupying it himself. That a king of Assyria then set up his throne in Harran, an old home of Abraham, from which the Assyrian was driven and which he endeavored to capture two years later by means of an Egyptian army, is also a fact that we did not previously know. That the Medes and a people called Unnan-manda—probably Scythians from southern Russia—aided the overthrow of Assyria, had been suspected, but is now confirmed. Just how Nineveh was finally destroyed we do not yet know, but we learn from Xenophon's *Anabasis* that, when he passed its site in the year 400 B.C., it had so completely perished that he did not hear its name.

CHAPTER XXVII

A BABYLONIAN BOOK OF LAMENTATIONS[1]

THE TEXT AND ITS OCCASION. COMPARISON WITH THE LAMENTATIONS
OF JEREMIAH.

IN the year 2864 B.C. the city of Lagash, which had then been a
flourishing power for from three to four hundred years, was overthrown, sacked, and burned by Lugalzaggisi, king of the neighbor-
city of Umma. There had been war between Umma and Lagash
frequently for five hundred years and Lagash had often been triumphant. Much hatred had accumulated in the hearts of the men
of Umma and they evidently freely avenged themselves when
Lagash fell into their power. How their deeds affected one sad
heart of that far-off time this text makes clear.

The men of Umma
The Eki[2]........
With fire have destroyed;
The Antasurra[2]
With fire have destroyed.
Its silver and lapis lazuli
They have plundered.
In the Temple of Tirash
They have shed blood;
In the little sea[3]
They have shed blood;
In the sanctuary of Enlil
And the sanctuary of Utu
They have shed blood;
In the Akhush[2]
They have shed blood;
Its silver and lapis lazuli
They have plundered;
In Ebarbar[2]
They have shed blood;
Its gold and lapis lazuli
They have plundered;
In Gikana
Of the goddess Ninmakh,[4]
The sacred grove,
They have shed blood;
Its silver and lapis lazuli
They have plundered;
In Baga[2]
They have shed blood;

Its silver and lapis lazuli
They have plundered;
The storehouse
They have burned with fire;
Its silver and lapis lazuli
They have plundered;
In the ruined reservoir
They have shed blood.
The Temple of Gatumdug[4]
They have burned with fire;
Its silver and lapis lazuli
They have plundered;
Her image
They have destroyed.
The shrine of Eanna[2] of Ininni[4]
They have burned with fire;
Its silver and lapis lazuli
They have plundered;
Her image they have destroyed;
In the "House-of-the-Understanding-
Heart"[2]
They have shed blood;
Its silver and lapis lazuli
They have plundered.
In Khienda[2]
They have smashed its carved cedar.
In Kiab,[2]
The dwelling of Nindar,[4]
They have shed blood;
Its silver and lapis lazuli
They have plundered.

1 Translated from the Sumerian text published by Thureau-Dangin in Cros, *Nouvelles
Fouilles de Telloh*, 1910, p. 47.
2 The name of a temple.
3 The name of a structure corresponding to the "brazen sea" of Solomon's Temple.
4 The name of a goddess.

Kinunir,
The dwelling of Tammuz of the abyss,
They burned with fire;
Its silver and lapis lazuli
They have plundered.
The temple of Lugal-Erim
They have burned with fire;
Its silver and lapis lazuli
They have plundered.
In E-engur,[5]
Belonging to Nina,[6]
They have shed blood;
Its silver and lapis lazuli
They have plundered.
In Sag[5] . . . .
Temple of "The Mother of the Vine,"[6]
They have shed blood;
Her silver and lapis lazuli
They have plundered.
From Engurbanishub,
The field of Ningirsu,[7]
The lord of husbandmen,

They have taken the grain.

The men of Umma,
After Lagash
They had destroyed,
Mortal sin
Against Ningirsu
Committed.
The power which has come to them
Shall be cut off.
Mortal sin
On the part of Urkagina,
King of
Girsu,[8]
There was none.
Lugalzaggisi,
Priest-king
Of Umma,—
May his goddess,
Nisaba,[6]
His mortal sin
Bear on her head!

This text, like the Lamentations of Jeremiah, recites in detail the violent and sacrilegious acts of those who destroyed the city where its author lived. While it lacks the finished poetical form of the Biblical Lamentations, it must be remembered that it was written considerably more than two thousand years before that work. Its author does not, like the Biblical writer, tell how his affections have been outraged, and how he weeps for the destroyed city, and yet it is not difficult to detect the passionate personal feeling running through his catalogue. One can feel his horror, his sorrow, and his heart-breaking sadness as he tells how temple after temple has been defiled with human blood, its treasury robbed, its beautiful work defaced, and its structure burned up. His horror was the same, though his artistic power was less than that of the Biblical poets who wrote threnodies on the destruction of Jerusalem.

Running through this old Babylonian text there is a certainty that the men who committed the deeds recorded have committed a grave sin, and at the end the writer expresses the belief that they and their goddess who prompted it will pay the penalty. He has faith that justice will be exacted—yes: that vengeance will be executed, but no such sense of moral shortcoming as one finds in the Book of Lamentations, no such tender penitence, no such supplication for forgiveness.

5 The name of a temple.
6 Name of a goddess.
7 Name of a god.
8 The name of a part of Lagash, which, like greater New York, was formed by joining four cities together.

CHAPTER XXVIII

REPUTED SAYINGS OF JESUS FOUND IN EGYPT

EARLY COLLECTIONS OF THE WORDS OF JESUS. TRANSLATION OF SAYINGS
FOUND IN 1897. COMMENTS. TRANSLATION OF A LEAF FOUND IN 1904.
COMMENTS. OPINIONS AS TO THESE SAYINGS.

THE Gospel of Luke begins with the words: "Forasmuch as many
have taken in hand to draw up a narrative concerning those matters
which have been fulfilled among us,"—words which imply that there
were in the early Church many attempts at gospel writing. Some
of these attempts apparently took the form of collecting the sayings
of Jesus. At Oxyrhynchus in Egypt two different leaves of papyrus
have been found on which such sayings are written. The first of
these was found by Grenfell and Hunt in 1897; (Fig. 301). It
begins in the middle of a sentence, but it is a sentence the beginning of which can be supplied from Matthew 7:5. When complete
the sentence runs thus: [1]

[Jesus saith, Cast out first the beam from thine own eye], and
then shalt thou see clearly to cast out the mote that is in thy
brother's eye.

On this saying compare Matthew 7:5; Luke 6:42.
The second one runs:

Jesus saith, Except ye fast to the world, ye shall in no wise
find the kingdom of God; and except ye keep the sabbath, ye
shall not see the Father.

This saying does not occur in the Gospels, and has given rise to
wide discussion among scholars.
The third is as follows:

Jesus saith, I stood in the midst of the world, and in the flesh
was I seen of them, and I found all men drunken, and none'
found I athirst among them, and my soul grieveth over the

1 These sayings are translated from Grenfell and Hunt's *Sayings of Our Lord*, 1897,
with a comparison of Lock and Sanday's *Two Lectures on the Sayings of Jesus Recently
Discovered at Oxyrhynchus*, 1897.

sons of men, because they are blind in their heart [and see not], poor, and know not their poverty.

This saying also is not found in the Gospels. It is difficult to tell whether it was thought to have been spoken by Jesus before or after the resurrection.

The fourth saying is difficult of translation and interpretation, since the text is not at all clear. As amended by Harnack and Swete, it would run:

Jesus saith, Wherever there are two they are not without God, and if one is alone anywhere, I say I am with him. Raise the stone, there thou shalt find me; cleave the wood, and there I am.

This saying has given rise to much discussion and to a large literature, but reference can here be made only to Henry van Dyke's poem *Felix*. With the last part of the saying Matthew 18:20 should be compared.

The fifth saying is as follows:

Jesus saith, A prophet is not acceptable in his own country, neither doth a physician work cures upon them that know him.

The first part of this is akin to Luke 4:24; Mark 6:4; Matthew 13:57, and John 4:44. The last part of it is not in the Gospels.

The sixth one reads:

Jesus saith, A city built on the top of a high hill and firmly established can neither fall nor be hid.

In this saying the thought of Matthew 5:14 is combined with that of Matthew 7:24,25, but there is no necessary literary dependence upon Matthew.

The seventh and last saying on this leaf is:

[Jesus saith,] Thou hearest with one ear, but the other thou hast closed.

This, too, is not found in our Gospels.

In 1904 another leaf of sayings of Jesus was found at the same place. It begins with a general introduction, thus: [2]

These are the [wonderful?] [3] words which Jesus the living Lord spake [to the disciples] and to Thomas, and he said to them: Every one that hearkens to these words shall never taste of death.

These words formed the general introduction to a collection of sayings of Jesus, similar to that from which the sayings already quoted were taken. The leaf also contained a few of the sayings which stood in the collection. They are as follows:

Jesus saith, Let not him who seeks . . . cease until he finds, and when he finds he shall be astonished; astonished he shall reach the kingdom, and having reached the kingdom he shall rest.

The Gospels contain parallels to parts of this saying. (See Matthew 6:33; 7:7; 13:44; Luke 5:9.
The second of these sayings is longer:

Jesus saith, [Ye ask (?) who are those] that draw us [to the kingdom, if] the kingdom is in heaven? . . . the fowls of the air, and all the beasts that are under the earth or upon the earth, and the fishes of the sea, [these are they which draw] you, and the kingdom of heaven is within you; and whosoever shall know himself shall find it. [Strive therefore (?)] to know yourselves, and ye shall be aware that ye are the sons of the [Almighty (?)] Father; [and (?)] ye shall know that ye are in [the city of God (?)] and ye are [the city (?)].

The first part of this saying attributes to Christ a saying evidently based on the thought of Job 12:7,8. Other parts of the saying recall Luke 17:21 and Luke 20:36, though the phrases which remind us of these passages form but a small part of the saying and appear here in quite a different connection.
The third saying runs:

2 Translated from Grenfell and Hunt's *New Sayings of Jesus and Fragment of a Lost Gospel from Oxyrhynchus*, 1904.
3 Compare John 21:24, 25.

Jesus saith, A man shall not hesitate . . . to ask . . . concerning his place [in the kingdom. Ye shall know] that many that are first shall be last and the last first and [they shall have eternal life (?)].

A part of this saying follows Mark 10:31 and Matthew 19:30; cf. also Luke 13:30. The last clause is conjectural, but, if correct, is similar to John 3:16,36; 5:24.

Jesus saith, Everything that is not before thy face and that which is hidden from thee shall be revealed to thee. For there is nothing hidden which shall not be made manifest, nor buried which shall not be raised.

The last part of this saying is parallel to Matthew 10:26; Luke 12:2; see also Mark 4:22.

The fifth:

His disciples question him and say, How shall we fast and how shall we [pray (?)] . . . and what [commandment] shall we keep? . . . Jesus saith, . . . do not . . . of truth . . . blessed is he . . .

The papyrus is so broken that we cannot hope to recover this saying in its entirety, but it is clear that it differed from the others in having an introductory clause which gave the occasion when it was uttered.

Judgments have differed as to whether all these sayings are really sayings of Jesus. That there were sayings of his known in ancient times that are not recorded in our Gospels is shown by Acts 20:35. Some, at least, of these sayings are so like those of Jesus that it is not difficult to believe them his. But whether they are his or not, these papyri make clear to us what Luke meant when he said "many have taken in hand to draw up a narrative."

CHAPTER XXIX

ARCHÆOLOGICAL LIGHT ON THE ENROLMENT OF QUIRINIUS

Translation of a Papyrus Showing that in the Second Century Enrolment was made Every Fourteen Years. Comments. Translation Referring to an Enrolment in the Reign of Nero. Fragment from the Reign of Tiberius. Enrolments Probably Inaugurated by Augustus. Document Showing that People Went to their Own Towns for Enrolment. Inscription Supposed to Refer to Quirinius. Inscription from Asia Minor Referring to Quirinius. Discussion. Conclusions.

ARCHÆOLOGICAL research has recently thrown much light upon the census of Quirinius mentioned in Luke 2:1-5. The evidence has come in part from ancient records on papyri which have been dug up in Egypt, some of which are herewith translated.

The following extract from a large papyrus establishes the fact that a census or an assessment-list was made in the Roman empire every fourteen years.

1. Papyrus Showing Enrolment Every Fourteen Years.[1]

After the death of my wife Aphrodite, or, as she was called by some, Aphroditoute, having departed from the district of Herakles and Sabinos, I enrolled the other children who dwell with Mysthes who is called Ninnos, who was 33 years old, and after the others, the wife of my son Mysthes who is called Ninnos, viz.:—Zozime, freed-woman of Ptolemaios Ammoniarios, daughter of Marion Geomytha, and was 22 years old, (who was living with her mistress, in the enrolment of the 9th year; at the time of the enrolment she [Zozime] was living in the Greek quarter, but has now moved into the neighboring quarter of Apolloneios Hierax) and the children of these two, Ammonios, aged 5, and Didymos, aged 4, and Aut.........., were not otherwise enrolled in the enrolment in the first year of the Emperor Cæsar Marcus Aurelius Antoninus Augustus and the Emperor Cæsar Lucius Aurelius Verus Augustus, on the thirtieth of Payni [*i. e.*, June 24, 161 A.D.]. To Potomon, governor of the Arsinoite district of Herakles, and Asclepiades, the royal census-taker, and Agathos Daimon and Dioskoros, census-takers of the metropolis, on behalf of Mysthes who is called Ninnos, Mysthes, son of Philo, whose mother is Herais, daughter of Ammoniosone, of the citizens of the metropolis, who are enrolled from the quarter of Apolloneios Hierax: there belongs to me in the district of Ammonios 1-12 part of the place called Nekpherotios, in which I enroll myself and my household for the current enrolment of the 14th year according to the household enrolment, as aslo I enrolled myself according to the household enrolment in the 23rd year of Anton-

1 Translated from Viereck's publication of the text in *Philologus*, Vol. LII, 234, f.

554 ARCHÆOLOGY AND THE BIBLE

inus (*i.e.*, 160–161 A.D.) ; I am also Mysthes who is also called Ninnos; the one enrolled is 59 years old, and his wife, Zozime, the freed-woman of Ammoniarios, daughter of Marion, who was enrolled in the household enrolment of the 23rd year in the same quarter, is 38 years old, and the children of those two..........not enrolled in the enrolments, 11 years old, and likewise Dioskoros 10 (?) years old, and likewise........, 9 years old, and a daughter, Isidora, 8 years old: thus I make my deposition. 15th year of the Emperor Marcus Aurelius Antoninus Cæsar, the lord. Intercalary Mesore: (*i.e.*, the end of August, 175 A.D.)

This papyrus, dated in the year 175 A.D., is very important as it proves that the census came every fourteen years. The enrolment mentioned at the end of it was made in connection with the census of 174–175 A.D., since the document is dated in August of the year 175. The enrolment mentioned about the middle of the document was the enrolment of 160–161 A.D. That was dated in the summer of 161. The one mentioned near the beginning of the quotation as having been made in the 9th year must refer to the census of the year 146–147, and the 9th year of Antonius Pius, which was the year 147. The proof that the census was taken every fourteen years [2] is of the greatest importance to our subject, as will appear below.

This enrolment was made by one Mysthes Ninnos on behalf of his son, who was also called Mysthes Ninnos, the wife of the son who was a freed-woman, called Zozime, and their children, who were the grandchildren of the man making the enrolment. Mysthes Ninnos, the grandfather, had been married twice. His first wife was named Aphrodite; after her death he married Herais, the mother of the son, Mysthes Ninnos.

2. Translation Referring to an Enrolment in the Reign of Nero.[3]

Copy of an enrolment of Ammonios and........ios, the gymnasiarch and librarian of the public library in the city of Arsinoe, in the presence of Pa....xineos......Paesios, son of Myo, priest of those who are from Karanis of the district of Herakles. According to the commands through the most excellent governor, Lucius Julius Vestinus, I have enrolled today my goods which are free from debt and mortgage and lien; in the neighboring village, a third part of my father's house and courtyard, and places cleared of abodes, two lots of a half acre each, which were bought from Mesoereus, son of Nekpherōs, in the fifth year of Nero Claudius Cæsar Augustus Germanicus, Emperor, and a house in the village, which was bought from Onnophreus, son of Peteoræpeus, in the sixth year of Nero Claudius Cæsar Augustus Germanicus, Emperor. Whatever I make from these or buy in addition I will first report as it shall occur.

2 These assessments, then, occurred in the following years: 174–5; 160–1; 146–7; 132–3; 118–9; 104–5; 90–1; 76–7; 62–3; 48–9; 34–5; 20–1; 5–6; 8–7 B.C.
3 From *Hermes*, XXVIII, 1893, p. 233.

The date of this document, which is only a copy, is not given, but as it refers to two transactions in real estate, which were dated respectively in the 5th and 6th years of Nero, and as that monarch's reign began in October of the year 54 A.D., it is probable that this is a copy of an enrolment made in connection with the census of 62–63 A.D. This proves that the system of taking the census once in fourteen years was in operation as early as the reign of Nero.

3. Fragment from the Reign of Tiberius.[4]

To Eutychides and Theon, local census-takers and village census-takers, from Horion and Petosiris, priest of Isis, the most great goddess, of the temple called the Two Brothers in the city of Oxyrhynchus on the street Myrobalanos, near the Serapeum. Those who live in the house which belongs to me and my wife Tasis and to Taurius, son of Harbichis, and to Papontos, son of Nechthesorios, and to Thæchemere, in the house which is near the aforesaid temple of the Two Brothers are as follows:

The papyrus at this point becomes too mutilated for further translation.

The importance of this document is revealed by an examination of the names of the officers, Eutychides and Theon. Another papyrus from the same place, which contains a notice of a removal, is dated in the 6th year of the Emperor Tiberius.[5] As these officers were still in office when this census was taken, this must be the census of the year 20–21 A.D.

4. Enrolments Probably Inaugurated by Augustus.—An-

other papyrus contains a list of people who were exempt from poll-tax in the 41st year of the reign of Augustus.[6] As the poll-tax was intimately connected with the census, it is altogether probable that the census was inaugurated by Augustus. As he became emperor in 27 B.C. and at once proceeded to organize his empire, the census may have begun early in his reign. If there was one in 20 A.D. there would be one in 6 A.D., 9–8 B.C., and possibly in 23–22 B.C. If there was not one in 23–22, that in 9–8 B.C. would be the first. This is the one to which reference is made in Luke 2:2. If the birth of Jesus occurred at the time of this census, it must have been earlier than we usually suppose. Ramsay thinks that the taking of the census in Judah may have been delayed till 7 or 6 B.C., on account of Jewish prejudices.

---

4 Translated from Grenfell and Hunt's *Oxyrhynchus Papyri*, II, 1898, p. 214. Kenyon, *Greek Papyri in the British Museum*, II, 19, thinks that this cannot refer to a census because the term by which it is described is different, but, as Grenfell and Hunt remark, the simpler term in the papyri earlier than the year 61 A.D., indicates that we are nearer the beginning of the institution of the census.
5 *Ibid.*, p. 205; cf. p. 206.
6 *Ibid.*, p. 282.

5. Document Showing that People Went to Their Own Towns for Enrolment.

In connection with the census of Quirinius it is stated in Luke 2:3: "All went to enroll themselves, every one to his own city." This has been felt by many scholars to be an improbable statement, and has been cited as an evidence of the unhistorical character of the whole story of the census in Luke. In this connection part of a papyrus discovered in Egypt, which is dated in the 7th year of the Emperor Trajan, 103–104 A.D., is of great interest. This document contains three letters. The third of the letters is the one which relates to our subject. It is as follows: [7]

Gaius Vibius, chief prefect of Egypt. Because of the approaching census it is necessary that all those residing for any cause away from their own nomes, should at once prepare to return to their own governments, in order that they may complete the family administration of the enrolment, and that the tilled lands may retain those belonging to them. Knowing that your city has need of provisions from the country, I wish...........(At this point the papyrus becomes too fragmentary for connected translation.)

It is perfectly clear that in Egypt the enrolment was done on the basis of kinship. The word rendered "family" above [συνηθη] means "kindred" in the larger sense. The phrase rendered "belonging to" [them, i.e., the tilled lands] also means "kindred." It appears, then, that in Egypt the enrolment of each district was intended to include all the kinsmen belonging to that district, and that, lest those residing elsewhere should forget to return home for the census, proclamations were issued directing them to do so. It is well known that in many respects the customs of administration in Syria and Egypt were similar. Luke's statement, that Joseph went up from Nazareth to Bethlehem, because he was of the house and lineage of David, to enroll himself with Mary (Luke 2:4,5), turns out to be in exact accord with the governmental regulations as we now know them from the papyri.

6. Inscription Supposed to Refer to Quirinius.

A fragmentary inscription found at Rome in 1828 is thought by Mommsen and others to prove that Quirinius was governor of Syria twice, and that the governorship to which Josephus refers (*Antiquities,* XVII, i, 1), which was coincident with the deposition of Archelaus in 6 A.D., was his second appointment. The inscription as filled out by Mommsen and others reads: [8]

[7] Translated from Kenyon and Bell's *Greek Papyri in the British Museum,* Vol. III, 1907, p. 125.
[8] Translated from the *Corpus Inscriptionum Latinarum,* XIV, No. 3613.

[P. Sulpicius Quirinius, consul........; as proconsul obtained Crete and
Cyrene as a province...........; as legate of the divine Augustus, obtaining
Syria and Phœnicia he waged war with the tribe of Homonadenses who had
killed Amyntas the k]ing; when he returned into the domi[ion of the Emperor
Cæsar Augustus and the Roman people, the senate [decreed] thanksgivings
[to the immortal gods] on account of the two success[ful accomplishments]
and triumphal ornaments to him; as proconsul he ob[tained] Asia as a province; as the legate of the divine Augustus he [obtained] again Syria and
Phœnicia.

If this inscription were intact its evidence would be decisive, but
unfortunately it is only a fragment, and the name of Quirinius is
just that which has to be supplied from other inscriptions. That so
eminent a scholar as Mommsen thought that this name was the one
which once began the inscription is of weight, but it does not compensate for the loss of the name.

7. Inscription from Asia Minor Referring to Quirinius.[9]—
The following inscription, discovered by Prof. Ramsay and Mr.
J. G. C. Anderson of Oxford, is believed by Ramsay to prove that
Quirinius was governor of Syria between 10 and 7 B.C.

> To Gaius Caristanius
> (son of Gaius of the Sergian tribe) Fronto
> Caesianus Juli[us],
> Chief of engineers, pontifex,
> priest, prefect of P. Sulpicius Quirinius duumvir,
> prefect of M. Servilius.
> To him first of all men
> at public expense by decree of the decuriones,
> a statue was erected.

This inscription was found at Antioch, a fortified colony in
southeastern Phrygia or southern Galatia, in the year 1912. The
name Caristanius connects its erection with the time of the Hamo-
nadian war, 10–7 B.C. That Quirinius received the honor of an
election to the office of honorary duumvir of the colony at this time,
is held by Ramsay to prove that he had been sent to Syria as governor, and had been military commander in the war against the
Hamonades. It was the benefits which accrued to the little colony
of Antioch from his victories in this war, which led to the election
and the erection of this statue. Ramsay, accordingly, holds that
this inscription proves Quirinius to have been governor of Syria
about 11–7 B.C., and this confirms the statement of Luke 2:2, that
the census at the time when Jesus was born was the first enrolment,
when Quirinius was governor of Syria.

9 Translated after Ramsay, *Expositor*, series 8, Vol. IV, 1912, p. 401. For Ramsay's
opinions, see the article of which the inscription forms a part.

One objection to this theory is that from other sources (Josephus, *Antiquities,* XVI, x, 8; xi, 3), it appears that Sentius Saturninus was governor of Syria at this time, *i.e.,* from 9–7 B.C., just at the time when, according to the papyri, the census should occur. This is supported by a statement of Tertullian, that Jesus was born when Saturninus was governor of Syria. To meet this objection, Ramsay supposes either that the authority of Quirinius and of Saturninus overlapped, the former being military commander and the latter civil governor, or that Quirinius ruled until about July 1st of the year 8, the census year, and Saturninus then took office. These are, however, mere possibilities. We have not yet clear information concerning these points.

Later, in 6 A.D., Quirinius was sent out to Syria again (see Tacitus, *Annales,* III, 48), and took over as governor of Syria the kingdom of Judah on the deposition of Archelaus, and conducted the census there of 6–7 A.D. (See Josephus, Antiquities, XVIII, i.) Many scholars have held that Luke confused this governorship with earlier events and was accordingly in error as to his chronology by at least ten years, but the archæological facts here collected tend to corroborate Luke's accuracy on this point. It should be added that Luke knew that Quirinius had charge of the census in Palestine in 6 A.D., as Josephus states, for he says: "This was the first enrolment made when Quirinius was governor of Syria."

8. Conclusions.—It should in all candor be noted just what archæology has proved concerning this matter, and what points are still, from the archæological side, outstanding. It has proved that the census was a periodic occurrence once in fourteen years, that this system was in operation as early as 20 A.D., and that it was customary for people to go to their ancestral abodes for enrolment. It has made it probable that the census system was established by Augustus, and that Quirinius was governor of Syria twice, though these last two points are not yet fully established by archæological evidence. So far as the new material goes, however, it confirms the narrative of Luke.

CHAPTER XXX

ARCHÆOLOGICAL LIGHT ON THE ACTS AND EPISTLES

<small>THE POLITARCHS OF THESSALONICA. AN ALTAR TO UNKNOWN GODS. AN INSCRIPTION FROM DELPHI AND THE DATE OF PAUL'S CONTACT WITH GALLIO. SOME EPISTLES FROM EGYPT. KING OF ARABIA. THE SYNAGOGUE OF THE LIBERTINES. THE CHALICE OF ANTIOCH.</small>

1. The Politarchs of Thessalonica.—In Acts 17 : 6 the rulers of Thessalonica are called in the Greek "politarchs." It is a unique term, and its accuracy had been called in question by some scholars. Within the past hundred years no less than nineteen inscriptions have come to light which prove its accuracy, by referring to the rulers of Thessalonica as "politarchs." One of the most important of these is from an arch in Thessalonica. It runs in part as follows, the beginning being illegible: [1]

> In the time of the Politarchs, Sosipatros, son of Cleopatra, and Lucius Pontius Secundus Publius Flavius Sabinus, Demetrius, son of Faustus, Demetrius ot Nicopolis, Zoilos, son of Parmenio, and Meniscus Gaius Agilleius Poteitus
> . . . .

Another fragmentary inscription shows that the rulers of the city bore this title as early as the time of Augustus. It is in part: [2]

> Bosa, proconsul, made a stone-quarry for the temple of Cæsar, in the time of the priest and judge, the Emperor Cæsar, the divine son Augustus. . . . . , the politarchs remaining faithful, viz.:—Diogenes, the son of Kleon, the . . . . , etc.

It is not clear from the inscriptions whether the number of politarchs was five or six.

2. An Altar to Unknown Gods.—In Acts 17: 23 it is stated that Paul saw in Athens an altar with this inscription: TO AN UNKNOWN GOD. In the year 1909 an altar was discovered in the sacred precinct and temple of Demeter at Pergamos in Asia Minor, the home of one of the seven churches of the book of Revelation (Rev. 2: 12, f.), which bore a mutilated inscription;

<small>1 Translated from Burton's publication in the *American Journal of Theology*, II, 600.
2 Translated from *ibid.*, p. 604.</small>

(see Fig. 299). This inscription in the judgment of several impartial epigraphists should be restored as follows: [3]

To unknown gods,
Capito,
torch-bearer.

This is not only a confirmation of the statement of Acts 17:23, but of Pausanias [4] (second century A.D.) and Philostratus [5] (third century A.D.) that altars to unknown gods existed.

3. **The Date of Paul's Contact with Gallio.**—The chronology of the life of Paul cannot be fully determined from the Bible itself. Such chronological data as the New Testament affords help us only to a relative chronology. Could the year of one of the dates given by the New Testament be determined by a date of the Roman empire, it would enable scholars to fix with approximate certainty the other dates. Hitherto the endeavor to do this has centered about the recall of Felix from Palestine and the coming of Festus (Acts 24:27), but there has been so much uncertainty about the date of this recall, that systems of chronology, differing from one another by from four to five years, have been constructed. A fragmentary inscription has come to light from Delphi, which seems to give us the desired aid for our Pauline chronology in that it fixes the date of the coming of Gallio to Corinth (Acts 18:12). This inscription, as its lacunæ are supplied by Deissmann, is as follows:

Tiberius Claudius Cæsar Augustus Germanicus, Pontifex Maximus, of tribunican authority for the 12th time, imperator the 26th time, father of the country, consul for the 5th time, honorable, greets the city of the Delphians. Having long been well disposed to the city of the Delphians............I have had success. I have observed the religious ceremonies of the Pythian Apollo ....now it is said also of the citizens.....................as Lucius Junius Gallio, my friend, and the proconsul of Achaia, wrote........ on this account I accede to you still to have the first.[6].....................

At this point the inscription is too broken for translation, although the beginnings of several lines can be made out. The importance of the inscription lies (1) in the fact that it mentions Gallio as proconsul of Achaia, and (2) in the reference to the 12th tribunican year and the 26th imperatorship of Claudius. It can be deduced from these, in comparison with other inscriptions of his, that this letter was written between January and August of the year

---

3 Taken from Deissmann's *St. Paul*, p. 261, f.
4 Pausanias, i, 1:4, and v, 14:8.
5 Philostratus, *Vita Apollonii*, vi, 3.
6 Translated from Deissmann's *St. Paul*, pp. 246, 247.

52 A.D.[7] If Gallio was then in office, and had been in office long enough to give information to Claudius of material importance to the purpose of the emperor's letter to the Delphians, Gallio must have arrived in Corinth not later than the year 51. According to Dio Cassius, Claudius had decreed that new officials should start for their provinces not later than the new moon of the month of June.[8] Gallio must, therefore, have arrived in Corinth not later than July.

Paul's stay in Corinth extended over eighteen months (Acts 18: 11), and the narrative in Acts implies that a large part of it had passed before Gallio went there. Paul must, then, have arrived in Corinth not later than the end of the summer of the year 50. As the journey described in Acts 16 must have occupied some months, the council at Jerusalem, described in Acts 15, cannot have taken place later than the year 49 A.D. In Galatians 2 : 1 Paul says that this visit occurred fourteen years after the visit which followed his return from Damascus. As the Jews in counting time usually reckoned the two extremes as a part of the number, even if a part of them only should really have been included, the visit of Paul to Jerusalem, mentioned in Galatians 1 : 18, must have occurred not later than 36 A.D., nor earlier than 35 A.D. As this visit occurred "three" years after his conversion, we find, if we make similar allowance for the possibilities of Jewish reckoning, that his conversion occurred not later than 34 A.D., and possibly as early as 31 A.D.[9]

4. Some Epistles from Egypt.—The Epistles of the New Testament, especially those of Paul, are cast in the form of ancient letter-writing. This form in its more stately aspects has long been known through the letters of Aristotle, Epicurus, Cicero, Seneca, Pliny, etc., but the papyri discovered in Egypt afford us many examples of the more familiar and affectionate style of informal letter-writing, and frequently, at the beginning, afford parallels to expressions which are found in the introductions of Paul's Epistles. The following examples will illustrate this:

Isias to her brother, greeting: If you are well and other things happen as you wish, it would be in accordance with my constant prayer to the gods. I too am in good health, and so is the boy; and all at home make constant remembrance of you. When I got the letter through Horus, in which you explain that you are in sanctuary at the Serapeum in Memphis, I straightway gave thanks to the gods for your being in good health, but as for your not coming to us when the evils that threatened you there have passed away, I am

7 See Deissmann's *St. Paul*, p. 248, ff.
8 Dio Cassius, lvii, 14, 5.
9 The most reliable chronologies of the life of Christ now place his crucifixion not later than 30 A.D.

disconsolate because such a long time I have been keeping myself and the child, and am come to the lowest point on account of the price of bread, and I did think that now you were coming I should find a little relief, but you seem to have no idea of coming to us, nor to have an eye to our circumstances, as you would if you were still here. We are in need of everything, not only because such a long time and so many seasons have passed since you were here, but because you have not sent us anything. And besides that, Horus, who brought your letter, tells me further that you are released from sanctuary, and I am perfectly miserable. No, indeed! and your mother, too, takes it very hard, and you will do well to come for her sake as well as ours to the city, unless some more pressing need draws you elsewhere. Farewell, then, and have a care for your body and so as to be in health. Good-bye. Epephi 30th, of the 9th year.[10]

This letter was written in the year 172 B.C. "Brother" in it probably means husband. The husband had gone on a religious mission and had left the wife without support. He at last sent her a letter, and this is her reply. She wishes to persuade him to return, and writes with great tact. What she says about remembering her husband in her prayers, and giving thanks to the gods for his health, reminds one of the language of Paul in 1 Thessalonians 1: 2; 3: 9; 2 Thessalonians 1: 3,11; 2: 13; 1 Corinthians 1: 4; 2 Corinthians 1: 4–6; Philippians 1: 3,9; Colossians 1: 3; Philemon 4. Another letter which illustrates the same points is this:

Ammonios to his sister Tachnumi, much greeting: Before all things I pray that you may be in health, and each day I make the act of worship for you. I salute heartily my goodest little boy Leo. I am jolly and so is the horse and Melas. Don't neglect my son. I salute Senchris, and I salute your mother. I likewise salute Pachnumi and Pachnumi junior. I salute............and Amenothis. Hurry up about the boy until we go to my place. If I come to the place and see the place, I will send for you and you shall come to Pelusium, and I will come to you at Pelusium. I salute Steches, the son of Pancrates. I salute Psemmouthis and Plato. If your brothers dispute with you, come to my house and stay there until we see what to do. Don't neglect it. Write me of your own welfare and of my boy's. Hurry up over the matter of the farm. I wrote this letter in Themuis on the fifth of the month Phamenoth. We have two days more, and then we will arrive at Pelusium. Melas greets you all by name. I salute Psenchnumi, the son of Psentermout. I pray that you may be well and strong.[11]

The sentence of this letter which follows the greeting is couched in almost the same language as 3 John 2, and the number of people saluted in it and the manner of their salutation reminds one strongly of Romans 16: 3–16.

10 The original is in Berlin and the publication is not accessible to the writer. The above translation is taken from that of J. Rendel Harris in the *Expositor*, 5th series, Vol. VIII, p. 164.
11 Translated by J. Rendel Harris, *ibid.*, p. 166.

Clearly the New Testament Epistles conform in their affectionate expressions to the forms that were often employed by other letter-writers of that period of history.

5. Paul and Aretas, King of Arabia.—Paul says: "In Damascus the governor under Aretas the king guarded the city of the Damascenes in order to take me." [12] Aretas is called by Josephus king of Arabia. He was Haretat IV, King of the Nabathæan Arabs. These Nabathæans were found in Arabia by the Assyrian King Ashurbanipal (668–626 B.C.); they conquered Edom about 400 B.C., driving the Edomites over into southern Judah; they helped one of the successors of Alexander the Great at the battle of Gaza in 312 B.C., and founded a dynasty of kings that lasted until overthrown by the Roman Emperor Trajan in 106 A.D. Haretat IV belonged to this line. The following Aramaic inscription, dated in his reign, affords monumental confirmation of his existence:

This is the tomb which Halafu, son of Kosnatan, made for himself and for Shaidu, his son, and his brothers, whatever males are born from this Halifu, both their sons and descendants by right of inheritance forever. And those who may be buried in this sepulcher and in this structure are this Shaidu and Manuath, Kenushath, and Ribamath, and Umaiyath and Shalimath, daughters of this Halifu. Also no descendant of Shaidu has authority, and no man after him of their sons or descendants, to sell this sepulcher, or to inscribe an epitaph or an emblem for anyone, except for the wife of one of them, or for his daughters, or kinsman, or relative by marriage he may inscribe the tomb. If any one shall do contrary to this, then the fine of Dushara, the god, our lord, shall be imposed upon him to the extent of five hundred silver shekels of Haretat, and in accordance with this inscription shall be deposited in the temple of Kaisha. Month Nisan, year fortieth of Haretat, King of the Nabathæans, who loves his people. Rauma and Abdobodat, stone-cutters.[13]

As Haretat ruled from 9 B.C. to 40 A.D., this inscription was written in 31 A.D., just a few years before Paul escaped from the officers of Haretat at Damascus. There are many other inscriptions dated in the reign of this king.

Another reads as follows:

This is the sepulcher and two monuments over it, which Abdobodat, the general, made for Aitebel, the general, his father, and for Aitebel, the commander of the two camps which are in Luhitu and Abarta, the son of Abdobodat. This is in the district of their command, which they exercised in the two places for thirty-six years in the reign of Haretat, King of the Nabathæans, who loves his people. The above-mentioned (monument) was constructed in the forty-sixth year of his reign.[14]

12 2 Cor. 11: 32.
13 Translated from the *Corpus Inscriptionum Semiticarum,* Pars II, Tom. I, Fasc. ii, No. 209.
14 *Ibid.,* Pars II, Tom. I, Fasc. ii, No. 196.

The forty-sixth year of Haretat was the year 37 A.D. The monument here translated was found at Medeba east of the Jordan (see Num. 21:30; Josh. 13:9), and the two places mentioned in it are believed to be Nabathæan names for Medeba and Rabbah Ammon (2 Sam. 11:1, etc.). It is evidence that Haretat had held this territory for a long time. Paul's escape from Damascus (2 Cor. 11:32) occurred between the date of the preceding inscription and this one.

6. The Synagogue of the Libertines.—Captain Weill, while excavating at Jerusalem in 1913-1914, found an inscription which reads as follows: [15]

Theodotos, son of Vettenos, priest and ruler of the synagogue, son of a ruler of the synagogue, and grandson of a ruler of the synagogue, constructed the synagogue for the reading of the Law and the teaching of the commandments and also its chambers and cisterns as a hospice for the needy from abroad—which (synagogue) was founded by his fathers and the elders and Simonides.

Theodotos is a Greek translation of the name Nathaniel; he is said to have been a ruler of the synagogue and a descendant of rulers of the synagogue. His father's name is Latin and probably indicates that he had once been a bondman of the family of Vettius —a well-known Roman name. When Pompey conquered Jerusalem in 63 B.C. he carried many Jews captive to Rome, where they became slaves. Later many of them were emancipated, and became "freedmen" or, in Latin, *libertines*. We learn from Acts 6:9 that there was in Jerusalem a synagogue of the Libertines in which Stephen preached. It seems a plausible conjecture, therefore, that this inscription comes from this very synagogue. The generous builder established in connection with it a hospice for the entertainment of freedmen who made the pilgrimage to Jerusalem from Italy and who were poor.

7. The Chalice of Antioch.—Early in the year 1910 some Arabs who were digging a well on the site of the ancient city of Antioch in Syria came upon a buried treasure. They refuse to disclose the exact spot at which it was found, but state that it was in the deeply buried ruins of a cathedral. The treasure consisted of a great chalice bearing twelve figures, believed by able archæological authorities to represent Christ and the Apostles; also a plain silver chalice of early mediæval date; and two decorated silver book-covers which evidently belonged to the same volume and which were made

---

[15] Translated from the Greek text in R. Weill's *La Cité de David*, Paris, 1920, p. 186.

in the fourth century; also another book-cover and a large ornamental cross.

The Arabs divided the objects among themselves, and some of them changed hands several times and passed eastward to Mesopotamia. Salim and Constantine Kouchakji heard of the discovery and after two years or more secured and assembled the objects and sent them to their brother George of the firm of Kouchakji Fréres of Paris and New York. Of these objects by far the most important is the chalice first mentioned. When it arrived in Paris it was badly oxidized, but in time the oxidation was successfully removed by Alfred André. Soon after this the Great War broke out and, on the eve of the battle of the Marne, the chalice was forwarded by George Kouchakji to the representatives of the firm in New York—his brother Habib Kouchakji and his nephew Fahim Kouchakji, in whose care it has since been.

These gentlemen have taken the greatest interest in the object and have been most generous in permitting it to be studied. They have published two large folio volumes [16] on it, one containing descriptive text, together with critical, artistic, and archæological discussions, and the other, sixty plates on which the figures and decorations carved on the chalice are reproduced in various sizes; also, in addition, etched reproductions of the human figures. The volume was prepared by Dr. Gustavus A. Eisen, who has been aided by several artists.

It seems probable that this treasure was buried when the cathedral of Antioch was closed by order of the Emperor Julian in 362 A.D., or when it was destroyed by Chosroes II of Persia in 611 A.D. The character of some of the objects found with the chalice suggests that it was buried at the last-mentioned date. It lay hidden until accidentally found in 1910.

The chalice consists of two portions, an inner cup, hammered out of a plain sheet of silver, and an outer receptacle. On the outer receptacle the twelve figures mentioned were carved by exquisite workmanship and afterward the silver between the figures was cut away so as to let the inner cup show through the interstices. All agree that the inner cup is older than the receptacle and that it was regarded as a very sacred object—so sacred that this wonderful receptacle was made to hold it. The whole consists of an "ovoid truncated bowl or container," holding almost three

---

[16] *The Great Chalice of Antioch* by Gustavus A. Eisen, New York, Kouchakji Frères, 1923.

quarts, "supported by a low and narrow food-stand, a type in use only during the first two centuries of the Roman empire. Later, with the end of the first century, this form was superseded by others, consequent upon the introduction of blown glass as a material for vessels." The "others" referred to had a foot-stand with a broader base. This statement of Dr. Eisen as to the period when this form of base was in vogue is borne out by a wide induction from facts.

This is a type of cup-base common in the reigns of Augustus and Tiberius. It is said that only one example is known from a later date, and that is a cup pictured in a wall-painting from Pompeii; [17] but even that wall-painting may have been made as early as the reign of Tiberius, though Pompeii was not destroyed until 79 A.D. On opposite sides of the receptacle there are two figures of the same person carved in full front view; one represents him as a youth holding a roll, the other portrays him as a mature man. Around each of these two figures five other figures are grouped all looking in adoration toward one of the first-mentioned figures. The carving was evidently intended to do great honor to the person represented by the facing figures. Who was he? The way in which these figures are presented is not unlike the way the Emperor Augustus is sometimes represented, and the form of the cup and its exquisite art are in keeping with the Augustan period. If, however, these figures represented Augustus, who were the other ten, each of which is so characteristic that it seems to be the portrait of a known person? On this theory they cannot be accounted for.

Dr. Eisen, who spent nine years in the study of the cup, believed the two central figures to be figures of the Christ, one representing him as a youth, the other as the Saviour of the world. There is much in the portrayal to commend this view. The right hand of the figure, representing the Saviour of the world, touches a plate on which are five loaves and two fishes; by his side and below the plate stands a lamb; just beyond the plate is a dove. All this seems to breathe Christian symbolism derived from the Gospels— Christ the Lamb of God, on whom the Spirit descended as a dove, miraculously feeding the world. Beneath the feet of the Christ is a Roman eagle—symbol of the empire—so placed that it is beneath the feet of the figure of the Christ. Running throughout the carved decorations of the cup, artistically intertwined with

17 A cup of similar shape, but without a pedestal and base, is also pictured on the Arch of Titus, but may have been made some time before the year 70 A.D.

other forms, is the design of a vine, which could suggest Christ the true vine. (See Figs. 312, 313.)

Working on this theory Dr. Eisen, with great ingenuity, identified the other figures. The four about the youthful Christ he believes to be the four evangelists, Matthew, Mark, Luke, and John; the fifth John's brother, James, the son of Zebedee, who was added because of his kinship to John. The four about the mature Christ he believes to be Peter, Paul, James, and Jude (the last two brothers of the Lord), while Andrew, Peter's brother, is added as the fifth figure, to correspond to the addition of John's brother in the other group.

Although the figures are scarcely two inches high and the faces are about the size of a small bullet, the carving is so admirably done that each stands out with the individual characteristics of an actual portrait. Dr. Eisen, who thinks that this carved work was done in the second half of the first century not later than the year 70, believes that we possess in these figures not only actual portraits of the Apostles and evangelists, but two genuine portraits of the Christ himself. It must be said that the portraits supposed to be those of the Christ are quite unlike the imaginations of artists of later time. They are faces, strong, full of dignity and sweetness.

With reference to the artistic work, it should be added that when tested by the mathematical canons of art, which it is now known that Greek artists employed, but which were later lost, the artistic work on this cup is apparently Greek in character. It was done apparently by one of the last disciples of the Greek school —a disciple who was also a master. Dr. Eisen's view, when first propounded, strikes every scholar as preposterous, but the more he examines the archæological reasons on which it is based, the more possible it seems. If the artistic work was done in the first century, what cup, except one, would be so honored? It is immediately suggested that in the inner cup we have at last the Holy Grail—the cup actually used by Christ at the Last Supper! That view is further suggested by the fact that bits of silver have been cut from the rim of the inner cup, apparently as sacred relics. The present writer, while recognizing that possibility, is not yet fully convinced of its correctness. Scholarly criticism will still have much to say of Dr. Eisen's acute and loving work, and it is too early to pronounce a positive opinion.

If this wonderful chalice is a first century product, it will not only throw much light on such passages as 1 Corinthians 10: 14–22, but, if the four evangelists are really represented in these early figures, it will compel the revision of some current theories of the authorship of the Gospel of John and some other New Testament books. Further discussion of the subject is accordingly awaited with the greatest interest.

Mr. Fahim Kouchakji graciously permitted the writer to examine the precious chalice, and he also had the privilege of discussing some points concerning it with Dr. Eisen. The writer's knowledge of the development of early Christian literature and traditions leads him to believe that the Christian ideas represented on this cup, if it is a Christian object, as he believes it is, are appropriate to the years 120–140 A.D., rather than to the period 50–70 A.D.[18] When Dr. Eisen is asked, if it could not have been made in the second century as well as in the last half of the first, he answers with a positive negative: "It would have been impossible for any artist in the second century to do such work. They knew nothing of refined Greek art in the second century." When further questioned, however, he admits that, if he did not believe it to be a Christian work, he would date it in the reign of Augustus or Tiberius. Since, however, it is a Christian object, he feels compelled to date it later than their reigns.

With reference to this reasoning, two observations occur to the present writer. The statement that refined Greek art was unknown in the second century and that therefore it would have been quite impossible for this beautiful piece of work to have been done by a second century artist, is based on silence (*i.e.,* on a lack of examples of art of this beauty coming from that century). This sounds very like statements of a dogmatic character which one has often heard

17 The principal point to be considered is the date of the Gospel of John. The testimony of early Christian writers, as well as the verdict of modern critical scholarship, places the writing of that Gospel at about 90 to 100 A.D. On Dr. Eisen's interpretation of these figures, this chalice was carved after it was known that John was one of the Evangelists, for he is honored as such. If, therefore, this carving was done as early as 70 A.D., we should have to suppose that the Gospel of John was written at least as early as 50 A.D.—a supposition which is contrary both to tradition and critical judgment. Two eminent authorities in classical archæology, Professor Strzygowski of Vienna, and Mr. Arthur Bernard Cook of Cambridge University, England, have examined Dr. Eisen's work and have pronounced the chalice genuine. Mr. Cook says of it, "The Chalice of Antioch is certainly genuine and, as it stands, unique. There is no other like it in shape or style. The style, so far as we can tell, would suit the Greek work of the Flavian [70–96 A.D.] or, perhaps, the Trajanic period" [98–116 A.D.]. The whole matter is discussed by Professor F. J. Foakes Jackson in four articles in the *Churchman* for February 2d and 9th, and August 16th and 23d, 1924. Professor Jackson considers the opinions just quoted of great weight, and sums up the results thus: "This much seems to be established, that it is a piece of the first century, of great beauty, designed and executed by a craftsman of the first rank, a man impregnated with the best traditions of Greek art, a worthy follower of the great sculptor Scopas, who flourished some centuries earlier."

from critics, which afterward were proved to be wrong. Again, Dr. Eisen himself is compelled to date the object from thirteen to thirty years later than any portraits of similar merit that are known to him, in order to meet the necessities of his theory of its Christian significance. To the present writer it seems no more difficult to extend the possibility of the survival of this artistic knowledge and power fifty years longer. In other words, he is not convinced that our knowledge of the history of the art of this time is sufficient to enable us to rule out the possibility of a second century date.

About 120–140 A.D. Christianity attracted a number of Greeks who brought to it the Greek freedom of intellect and who devoted their talents to its interpretations. There was the author of the Epistle to Diognetus, Justin Martyr, the Athenian philosopher Aristides, who wrote an "apology" for Christianity, and others. These men were skilled in philosophy and possessed of philosophic insight. May there not have been among them a Greek artist, one of the last of his kind, who devoted his talents to the creation of this honorary receptacle for the cup from which his Lord had drunk, imitating in the form of its pedestal the form of the earlier pedestal which his displaced?

Since Dr. Eisen wrote, important contributions have been made to the discussion of the date of the Chalice of Antioch. These discussions are based on comparisons of the forms on the chalice (especially the eagle, vine, basket, lamb, and star) with the use and execution of similar motifs in the art of the Levant and in that of early Christianity. Professor Charles R. Morey, after a discussion of this nature, concludes that the chalice may be either a work of the fourth century, of a very peculiar type, or a modern forgery.[19] The Jesuit Father Guillaume de Jerphanion, Professor in the Oriental Institute at Rome, who has devoted a learned monograph to the subject, concludes that the forms and the grouping on the chalice do not appear in Christian art until after the fourth century, and that some of the features remind one of the sixth century. He would date the chalice somewhere about the year 500.[20] On the other hand, Professor B. W. Bacon,[21] of Yale, has shown that the same figures (eagle, vine, and star) are found in the art of the age of the Antonines at Baalbek, which was executed in the second century, and both he and Pro-

19 "The Chalice of Antioch" in *Art Studies, Mediaeval and Modern,* III, 1925, pp. 73–80.
20 *Le Calice d'Antioche,* Rome, 1926. See especially p. 159.
21 "Eagle and Basket on the Antioch Chalice" in the *Annual of the American Schools of Oriental Research,* 1925, pp. 1–22.

fessor R. P. Dougherty [22] have also demonstrated that these motifs
were widely employed in the Orient much earlier. The matter is
not yet determined. Professors Morey and Jerphanion are great
authorities in Christian art, but have they taken into account the
facts to which Professors Bacon and Dougherty call attention?
René Dussaud, in a brief discussion of the chalice published in
1931,[23] accepts the view of Jerphanion. To a layman it still does
not seem impossible that the chalice may be a second century product from Antioch, and that its antecedents are to be sought in the
Oriental influences which came to a focus in Syria in that century.
Meanwhile we await further light.

If this cup is a Christian chalice (and of this the writer has no
doubt), it is one of the most valuable of archæological objects.

22 Cf. the *Annual* cited in the preceding note, p. 36, N. 51.
23 See *Syria*, XII, pp. 309-313.

CHAPTER XXXI

A FEW OF THE OTHER CONTRIBUTIONS OF ARCHÆOLOGICAL RESEARCH TO THE UNDERSTANDING OF THE BIBLE AND EARLY CHRISTIAN LITERATURE

FRAGMENTS OF A HEBREW TEXT OF THE COMMANDMENTS. HEBREW TEXT OF ECCLESIASTICUS. THE BOOK OF ENOCH. OTHER APOCRYPHA. DOCUMENTS OF THE ZADOKITE SECT. THE SINAITIC MANUSCRIPT. OTHER NEW TESTAMENT MANUSCRIPTS. WASHINGTON MANUSCRIPT. THE CHESTER BEATTY PAPYRI. THE CURETONIAN AND SINAI SYRIAC. COPTIC VERSIONS. TATIAN'S DIATESSARON. THE GOSPEL AND REVELATION OF PETER. THE ODES OF SOLOMON. SUB-APOSTOLIC WRITINGS. THE APOLOGY OF ARISTIDES. THE GREEK PAPYRI. A SECOND-CENTURY FRAGMENT OF THE GOSPEL OF JOHN.

WE have now accomplished what we set out to do, and have presented the reader with the principal texts, brought to light by archæological research, which illumine certain books and passages of the Scriptures. We have, however, by no means presented a complete survey of the rich material which modern research has contributed as an aid to our understanding of the sacred text. That research has not only discovered facts which throw light on particular verses, documents, and compositions which afford parallels to whole books, but has also presented us with new copies of the text of many books—in some instances new copies of the text of the whole Bible—recovered for us many ancient writings, once closely associated with the Scriptures, and given us hundreds of documents, written in the language of the New Testament, which throw a flood of light on the New Testament Greek and help us to a new understanding of some of its difficult portions. Some of this new material has been dug from the dust-heaps where the ancients emptied their waste-baskets, some of it has been found in the receptacles into which the old books of synagogues, monasteries, and libraries were thrown. All of it belongs to what might be called literary research, but it comes from the region in which archæology and literature meet.

To treat in detail all this material would require another volume as large as this one, overgrown as this one already is. It is mani-

festly impossible to do that here. To ignore it altogether would
be to convey the impression that in the preceding pages a complete
summary of the contributions of archæology to the understanding
of the Bible and Biblical times had been given. It seems best,
therefore, in this concluding chapter, to give a brief account of
the most important of these discoveries, adding references to the
books in which more complete information may be found.

1. **Fragments of Hebrew Text.**—It is well known that the
Hebrew of the Old Testament was written in consonants only and
that for centuries the vowels were supplied by the reader. As this
led to a variety of differences in interpretation, a system of vowel
points was invented and adopted at some time between the fifth and
the ninth centuries of the Christian era. By means of this system
the meaning of the text that had become traditional among orthodox
Jews was fixed. This system is called by the Jews "Masorah," [1]
and the unknown scribes by whom it was fixed upon the text are
called "Massorets." Such was the authority of this tradition, when
once adopted, that all manuscripts which did not contain it were
destroyed or allowed to perish. It thus happens that no manuscript
of the Hebrew text of any part of the Old Testament is known
that can be dated with any certainty earlier than the tenth century
A.D.[2] A copy of the Prophetic Books is preserved at Petrograd (or
must we say Leningrad?) which was written in 916 A.D. Some
copies of other parts of the Old Testament are known, which bear
earlier dates, but these dates are, for one reason or another, believed
to be spurious.[3] All other manuscripts of the Bible are later than
this one at Petrograd.

While there are slight variations in the readings of Hebrew manuscripts, as may be seen by referring to the works of DeRossi and
Kennicott, they are of minor importance, and scholars have to
rely, for a knowledge of earlier forms of the Hebrew text, upon
the translations of it made into Greek, Latin, Syriac, and other
languages.[4] While these versions were made some centuries before
the Masorah, they are at the best but imperfect instruments with
which to work, as the translators often did not understand the
Hebrew which they were translating.

It is for this reason that four fragments of papyrus, written in
Hebrew, and forming parts of the same leaf, which were found

1 See "Masorah," in the *Jewish Encyclopedia*, VIII, 365 ff.
2 See *Encyclopædia Biblica*, IV, col. 5013.
3 See *Jewish Encyclopædia*, III, 180.
4 See A. S. Geden, *Introduction to the Hebrew Bible*, Edinburg, 1909, Ch. V.

somewhere in Egypt a few years ago, and which contain the Ten Commandments and the great commandment of Deuteronomy 6:5, is an important archæological discovery. The Commandments are given in a mixed form partly according to the version of Deuteronomy 5, and partly according to Exodus 20, though with variations in detail. The text is believed by experts in palæography to have been written not later than the second century A.D. It is not certain whether it was part of a copy of the Pentateuch or whether it was a lectionary or book of instruction, or possibly a charm. If it was part of a Bible the book of Deuteronomy was, in this copy, considerably shorter than in our Bible, for Deuteronomy 5:21 is followed by Deuteronomy 6:1a, and that by Deuteronomy 6:4,5. Some have thought it must be a part of a book, as Jews were prohibited from making excerpts for reading lessons. The composite character of the text points, however, in the opinion of the present writer, to the theory that it is not part of a Bible, but is a portion of a book of selections. The papyrus was purchased from a dealer and is (or was) owned by an English gentleman.[5] The text reads as follows:

1. I am Jehovah thy God who brought thee from the land of Egypt, from the house of bondage.
2. Thou shalt have no other gods before me. Thou shalt not make for thyself any graven image, the likeness of anything which is in the heavens above, or which is in the earth beneath, or which is in the waters under the earth: thou shalt not bow down thyself to them nor serve them, for I Jehovah, thy God, am a jealous God, visiting the iniquity of the fathers upon the children, upon the third and upon the fourth generation of them that hate me; and showing mercy unto thousands of those who love me and who keep my commandments.
3. Thou shalt not take the name of Jehovah thy God in vain, for Jehovah will not hold him guiltless who taketh his name in vain.
4. Remember the Sabbath day to keep it holy. Six days shalt thou labor and do all thy work: but on the seventh day is a Sabbath to Jehovah thy God: in it thou shalt do no work, thou and thy son, and thy daughter, and thy manservant, and thy maid-servant, thy ox and thy ass, and any of thy cattle, and thy stranger that is within thy gates: for in six days Jehovah made the heavens and the earth, and the sea, and all that is in them, and he rested on the seventh day, wherefore Jehovah blessed the seventh day and hallowed it.
5. Honor thy father and thy mother, that it may be well with thee and that thy days may be long upon the land which Jehovah thy God giveth thee.
6. Thou shalt not commit adultery.
7. Thou shalt not kill.
8. Thou shalt not steal.
9. Thou shalt not bear vain witness against thy neighbor.

5 See S. A. Cook in *Proc. of the Soc. of Bibl. Arch.*, XXV, 30–60, and Geden, *op. cit.*, 57 ff.

10. Thou shalt not covet thy neighbor's house. Thou shalt not covet thy neighbor's wife, nor his field, nor his man-servant, nor his maid-servant, nor his ox, nor his ass, nor anything which is thy neighbor's.

These are the statutes and the judgments which Moses commanded the children of Israel in the wilderness, when they went forth out of the land of Egypt.

Hear, O Israel; Jehovah, our God Jehovah, one is he: and thou shalt love Jehovah thy God with all thy heart.......................................

It is interesting to note how the text here presented differs from both Deuteronomy and Exodus. The motive given for the observance of the Sabbath Day is that of Exodus 20:11, ff. rather than that of Deuteronomy 5:15, ff. The order of the seventh and eighth Commandments is reversed, and in the great commandment of Deuteronomy 6:4, a word is added so as to make it read, "one is he." In the tenth Commandment the "house" is put before the "wife" of the neighbor. It is a most interesting text.

2. The Hebrew Text of Ecclesiasticus.—Ecclesiasticus, or the Wisdom of the Son of Sirach, is one of the Apocryphal books, still bound up in pulpit Bibles between the Old and New Testaments. It was written by one Joshua (in Greek, Jesus) the son of Sirach about 180 B.C. and translated into Greek by his grandson about 130 B.C. The Greek text of this translation formed part of the Bible of the early Christians, was translated into the various ancient languages of the people who were Christianized, and through the Latin Vulgate became a part of the Bible of the Western Church. At the Reformation the Protestants accepted for their Old Testament Canon only books that existed in Hebrew, so Ecclesiasticus was relegated to the Apocrypha, or books suited to private reading only and not authoritative in determining faith. The Hebrew text disappeared centuries ago. As the Greek version of the books of which we have the Hebrew text is a poor substitute for the Hebrew, this was a serious drawback to the understanding of the book. This lack was supplied in 1899 by the publication of the Hebrew text of "The Wisdom of Ben Sira," which had been discovered by Schechter and Taylor three years before in the Genizah of the old synagogue of Fostat near Cairo in Egypt. The word Genizah means literally "hiding-place." It is a storehouse or cemetery in which books and papers which contain the divine Name, and which cannot, therefore, be destroyed, but which have been discarded, either because they are old or are heretical, are thrown. The synagogue in which this text was found is very old. It was once a Christian Church, built in the Byzantine period, which became a

Jewish synagogue in 616 A.D., when the Persian Chosroes conquered Egypt.

Here in May, 1896, Dr. Solomon Schechter, then of Cambridge University, England, discovered a leaf of the Hebrew text of Ecclesiasticus. In December of that year he returned to Cairo and brought back to England much of the contents of this Genizah, in which were found most of the remaining parts of the Hebrew text of Sirach as well as many other treasures. The publication of this text inaugurated a new era in the study of Ecclesiasticus, and a large literature has grown up about the book during the years that have since passed.[6]

3. The Book of Enoch.—A Jewish apocalypse, which was popular among the early Christians and is quoted in verse 14 of the Epistle of Jude, is the Book of Enoch. It is made up of a series of apocalypses written between 200 B.C. and the beginning of the Christian Era, most of which were attributed to the antediluvian Patriarch Enoch.[7] After about 300 A.D. its popularity waned and after the ninth century it ceased to be quoted by Christian writers. It also ceased to be copied, so that, when the revival of learning occurred in the sixteenth century, it had been completely lost.

This important book was recovered by James Bruce (1730–1794), who endeavored between 1768 and 1773 to discover the sources of the river Nile. In this endeavor he traveled through Egypt, Nubia, and Abyssinia. In the last-mentioned country he found an Ethiopic translation of the Book of Enoch which in 1773 he brought back to Europe and thus restored this book to Christian scholarship. Twenty-nine Ethiopic manuscripts of it are now known in Europe and America.

A Greek translation of the first thirty-two chapters of Enoch were found in a Christian tomb at Akhmim in Egypt in 1886–1887 by some French archæologists. It was the custom of the ancient Egyptians to place in the hands of one who had died a roll containing those extracts from the Book of the Dead which he might need to refer to in his examination before the god Osiris. Christians kept up the same custom, only they substituted rolls containing

6 See The Wisdom of Ben Sira, by S. Schechter and C. Taylor, Cambridge, 1899; Ecclesiasticus: the Fragments Hitherto Recovered of the Hebrew Text in Facsimile, by M. Gaster, Cambridge and Oxford, 1901; The Hebrew Text of the Book of Ecclesiasticus, Leyden, 1904; also the articles "Ecclesiasticus" in Hastings' Dictionary of the Bible and the Encyclopædia Biblica, and "Sirach, the Wisdom of Jesus the Son of," in the Jewish Encyclopædia.
7 One was attributed to Noah.

extracts relating to the future life from books regarded by them as sacred or semi-sacred. It was thus that this extract from Enoch was preserved. Dr. M. R. James in 1893 discovered in the British Museum a Latin version of a part of Chapter 104. The best translations of Enoch are those by Canon R. H. Charles.[8]

Archæological reseach has thus restored to our knowledge a book of the highest importance for the understanding of the development of the Messianic idea among the Jews in the centuries just before the coming of Christ. It was originally written partly in Hebrew and partly in Aramaic. Through the researches of a Slavonic scholar, Kazok, and of two Englishmen, W. R. Morfill and R. H. Charles, another work, *The Book of the Secrets of Enoch,* was brought to light between 1892 and 1896. This is a work of no less importance for the understanding of ancient Judaism than the other. It was written originally in Egypt in the Greek language, during the first half of the first century of the Christian Era—perhaps, therefore, while Christ was still living. The manuscripts of it which have been found are written in Russian and Serbian.[9]

4. Other Apocrypha.—The recovery of the two apocalypses of Enoch mentioned above does not stand alone. By similar research a body of apocryphal literature as large or larger than that which had been preserved for us in the Greek version of the Old Testament has been recovered. Space makes it impossible to do more than make a brief mention of this literature. To treat it adequately would require a large volume.[10]

It includes the so-called *Third and Fourth Books of Maccabees,*[11] which appear to have been written before 40 A.D. and which were written in Greek; *The Book of Jubilees,*[12] written between 153 and 105 B.C., found in an Ethiopic version—a book which gives a compendium of Jewish history arranged in periods of fifty years each; *The Book of Adam and Eve,* written between the first and fourth centuries A.D. in Greek; *The Testament of Abraham*[13] and *The*

8 *The Book of Enoch,* 1893, 2d ed., 1912; also in Vol. II of *Apocrypha and Pseudepigrapha,* edited by R. H. Charles; and *The Book of Enoch* in *Translations of Early Christian Documents,* First Series, III, London, Society for Promoting Christian Knowledge. 1925. Charles has also given us the best edition of the Ethiopic text: *The Ethiopic Version of the Book of Enoch,* Oxford, 1906.

9 Translated by W. R. Morfill and R. H. Charles, *Book of the Secrets of Enoch,* Oxford, 1896.

10 The whole of this literature is translated with adequate introductions in *Apocrypha and Pseudepigrapha,* edited by R. H. Charles, 2 vols., Oxford Univ. Press, 1913.

11 In addition to the treatment in the work last cited, see *Jewish Encyclopædia,* VIII, 241–244.

12 See also R. H. Charles, *The Book of Jubilees,* London, 1902.

13 *The Testament of Abraham,* translated by S. Gaselle. London, 1927.

Apocalypse of Abraham;[14] The Assumption of Moses; and *Joseph and Aseneth;*[15] *The Martyrdom of Isaiah,* written in the first century A.D., also written in Greek; *The Testament of the Twelve Patriarchs,*[16] originally written in Hebrew before 100 B.C., later interpolated by Jews, it was translated into Greek before 50 A.D., and later again interpolated by Christians, and, in this more expanded form translated into Latin in the thirteenth century; *Sibylline Oracles,* written in Greek hexameter verse in the second century [17] B.C., to popularize Biblical history among the heathen; *The Assumption of Moses,*[18] written in Aramaic before 70 A.D.; *An Apocalypse of Baruch,*[19] written originally in Hebrew during the first century of our era by six different hands, has come down to us in a Syriac version; another, written after 50 A.D., has survived in a Greek version; while still another, called *The Rest of the Words of Baruch,* written in the second century A.D., has come to us in an Ethiopic version; *The Psalms of Solomon,*[20] written between 63 and 48 B.C., survive in Greek; and *The Story of Akhikar,*[21] a Jewish tale that has come down to us in many languages.

These books, which belong to that border-land where archæological research merges into literary study, present us with a picture of the ideas that were dominant in Judaism during the Apostolic Age—ideas which many Christians shared—and are invaluable in helping us to trace the currents of influence with which primitive Christianity was surrounded.

5. Documents of a Zadokite Sect.—Among the manuscripts brought by Dr. Schechter from the Genizah at Cairo were two that contained part of the teachings of a sect which bore the name of Zadok,[22] which seems to have regarded as their Messiah some teacher who lived about the time of the Maccabæan revolt, and the adherents of which withdrew from their brethren and went and lived in Damascus, where their founder and Messiah died. The

---

14 *The Apocalypse of Abraham,* translated by C. H. Box, London, 1918.
15 E. W. Brooks, *Joseph and Aseneth,* London, 1918.
16 See also R. H. Charles, *Greek Versions of the Testaments of the Twelve Patriarchs,* Oxford, 1908, and his *Testaments of the Twelve Patriarchs,* London, 1908; also *The Testament of the Twelve Patriarchs,* Vol. V of *Translations of early Christian Documents,* London, 1925.
17 An English translation of the *Sibylline Oracles* was made by the late Milton S. Terry and published in New York in 1890. See also H. N. Bate, *The Sibylline Oracles,* London, 1918.
18 See also Charles' *Assumption of Moses,* London, 1897.
19 See also Charles' *Apocalypse of Baruch,* London, 1896.
20 See also Ryle and James, *Psalms of Solomon,* Cambridge, 1896.
21 See also *The Story of Ahikar,* by F. C. Coneybeare, J. Rendel Harris, and Agnes Smith Lewis, London, 1898.
22 See Schechter, *Documents of the Jewish Sectaries,* I, Cambridge, 1910, and R. H. Charles, *Apocrypha and Pseudepigraphia,* II.

fragments of their writings discovered by Schechter show that they esteemed David lightly in comparison with Zadok, the priest. Their Messiah and founder was a priest who traced his descent from Zadok, and priests held an important place in the organization of the sect. They esteemed the Law highly, and were strict in their morals.

The documents make frequent reference to the *Book of Jubilees,* the calendar of which the sect had adopted. They appear to have been written, therefore, during the first century B.C. The sect appears to have continued long enough for a knowledge of it to have reached the Karaites, who split off from the main body of Jews in the eighth century A.D., whose founder makes reference to the defection of Zadok. It is not improbable, therefore, that this sect was present in Damascus when St. Paul preached there.

6. The Sinaitic Manuscript.—Through the branch of archæological research of which we are now speaking, notable additions have also been made to the documents which testify to the text of the New Testament and to those which reveal the life and spirit of the early Church. Perhaps the most famous of these contributions is the so-called "Sinaitic Manuscript," which was discovered by Constantine Tischendorf in the Convent of St. Catherine on Mount Sinai in 1859. The story has been often told [23] and need only be alluded to here. Tischendorf visited the monastery in 1844, and while there picked out of a waste-basket forty-three leaves of an old manuscript, which the monks let him take back to Europe with him. These leaves contained part of the text of the Septuagint, as the Greek translation of the Old Testament is called. Nine years later, in 1853, he visited St. Catherine's again in the hope of finding the rest of the manuscript, but secured only one leaf. He supposed that someone else had secured the rest of it during the years between his two visits. As, however, years passed and no one published the manuscript, he returned to St. Catherine's in 1859. He spent some days there, but found no trace of the treasure for which he searched. He had given up hope and was planning to leave the next day, when, on returning from a walk with the steward, that official invited Tischendorf to his cell. There, resuming a conversation which had been interrupted, the steward said: "I, too, have read a Septuagint," and taking from

---

23 See, for example, C. R. Gregory, *The Canon and Text of the New Testament,* New York, 1907, p. 329, ff., or Vincent's *History of New Testament Textual Criticism,* New York, 1899, p. 16, ff.

a corner of the room a large volume wrapped in a red cloth, he placed in Tischendorf's hands the long-looked-for treasure.

This precious volume, written during the first half of the fourth century, was afterward removed to Alexandria, and later to Petrograd. It has now been purchased by the British Museum, where it reposes among the most precious treasures of that great treasure-house in London. It has been published in facsimile. It contained the parts of the Old Testament in Greek, which Tischendorf had not previously found, the whole of the New Testament, the Epistle of Barnabas which was not previously known in Greek, and a part of the Shepherd of Hermas. The Manuscript has since been studied by many scholars and is now recognized as one of the three oldest manuscripts of the Bible known; the only others which rival it in age and importance are the "Vatican Manuscript," which was already in the Vatican Library at Rome before the first catalogue of that library was made in 1475 A.D. and the "Chester Beatty Papyri." It has been proved by Westcott and Hort that the text of the Sinaitic Manuscript is more correct than that of any other known manuscript except the one in the Vatican just mentioned.[24]

7. Other New Testament Manuscripts.—In ways somewhat similar to that by which Tischendorf discovered the famous Sinaitic Manuscript many others have been brought to light. To speak of them all is not the province of a book like this; that belongs to technical works on New Testament criticism. It is enough to say that more than a hundred uncial or large-letter manuscripts, such as were written before the tenth century, have been catalogued and studied, and more than three thousand cursive manuscripts, such as were written after the tenth century, and the number is being increased every year.[25] Through such research the text of the New Testament rests on a much more secure basis than that of any other book in the world.

8. The Washington Manuscript.—While it is impossible to speak in detail of the great mass of manuscripts, there is one that must be singled out for a word of description and comment. It is a manuscript of the Gospels, found by Copts or Arabs in Egypt and bought, near Cairo, by the late Mr. Freer, of Detroit, on December 19, 1906, together with a number of other valuable manuscripts,

24 Westcott and Hort, *New Testament in the Original Greek*, Vol. II, 1882.
25 For fuller details see C. R. Gregory's *prolegomena* to Tischendorf's *Novum Testamente Graece, editio octava critica major*, Leipzig, 1884; C. R. Gregory, *Textkritik zum Neuen Testament*, 2 vols., Leipzig, 1900–1902; Kenyon, *Handbook of New Testament Textual Criticism*, London, 1912, and H. von Soden's *Schriften des Neuen Testament*, Göttingen, 1913.

both Greek and Coptic. Internal evidence shows that this beautifully written book was made during the fourth century of our era, or, at the latest, early in the fifth. Each Gospel is preceded by a picture of the evangelist who wrote it. The manuscript contains an excellent text and takes high rank as an authority in textual criticism. It has been published in facsimile by H. A. Sanders, of Michigan University.[26] The original has been placed in Washington as the capital city of our country; hence it is called the Washington Manuscript.

9. The Chester Beatty Papyri.—In 1930 an English gentleman, Chester Beatty, Esq., acquired a group of twelve manuscripts written on papyrus. It is not known just where they were found as the statements of native Oriental dealers cannot always be relied upon. It is clear that they came from Egypt and the nature of their contents indicates that they were found in the ruins of a church or monastery. It is conjectured that the ruin was somewhere in the Fayum, but that is only conjecture. The first announcement of the nature of the contents of these documents was made in the London *Times* of November 19, 1931. About that date the University of Michigan acquired several pieces of papyrus that were evidently a part of the same book. A few fragments were also purchased by private individuals. Either the discoverer had divided the leaves so as to sell them for more money, or more than one person had participated in the discovery and the find had been divided for that reason. These papyri are parts of a Greek Bible, which contained both the Old and New Testaments.[27] They are written in beautifully clear uncial characters by a very skilful scribe. As papyrus is very brittle, when dry, the leaves of this Bible which have thus been recovered are often much broken, but those which have been found are most valuable. Few ancient Biblical manuscripts have come to us intact.

A study of these papyri has convinced scholars skilled in the reading of ancient Greek documents that this Bible was copied before the middle of the third century (*i.e.*, before 250 A.D.). The oldest manuscripts of the Bible which we had had before, the Sinaitic and Vatican manuscripts, were written about 325 A.D., so that in the Chester Beatty Papyri we have a copy of the Scriptures

26 See *Facsimile of the Washington Manuscript of the Four Gospels in the Freer Collection*, University of Michigan, 1912; also H. A. Sanders, *The New Testament Manuscripts of the Freer Collection*, New York, 1912.

27 See Sir Frederick G. Kenyon, *The Chester Beatty Biblical Papyri: Descriptions and Texts of Twelve Manuscripts on Papyrus of the Greek Bible*, London, 1933–1936. This work is still (1937) in process of publication. Some nine fasciculi have already appeared. Also Henry A. Sanders, *A Third Century Papyrus Codex of the Epistles of Paul*, Ann Arbor, Mich., 1935.

made from 75 to 100 years earlier than any that was known before. To the students of the text of the new Testament this is of thrilling interest. Such students endeavor, by comparing different manuscripts, to discover just what words the Apostolic autographs of the Bible contained, or to come as near to it as possible. In 1881–1882 Westcott and Hort, in their work, *The New Testament in Greek,* by perfecting a genealogical method of using the materials, thought they had come as near to the solution of this problem as was humanly possible, and their work has been accepted by the great majority of workers in this field, who have since attacked the problem. They found the text most nearly like the Apostolic autographs in a group of manuscripts written in Egypt, which was headed by the Vatican manuscript. The Chester Beatty Papyri have, however, thrown the whole question open again, for, though nearly a century older than the Vatican manuscript, they contain many readings belonging to a group of manuscripts which Westcott and Hort regarded with disfavor. The whole subject must be studied anew.

10. The Curetonian and Sinai Syriac.—In 1842 Canon William Cureton found among some Syriac manuscripts that had been brought a short time before to the British Museum from the Nitrian Desert, in Egypt, fragments of an old copy of the Gospels. The manuscripts containing them had been written about 450 A.D., and the translation which it contained had been made much earlier. Fifty years later, in 1892, two English women, Agnes Smith Lewis and her twin sister, Margaret Dunlop Gibson, discovered in the Convent of St. Catherine on Mount Sinai a Syriac manuscript which contained all of the four Gospels except about eight pages. This manuscript had been written in the fifth or sixth century and had been used as a Bible for about two hundred years, when it became shabby. The writing was then scratched off, and, as parchment was expensive, some lives of female saints had been written over it. A manuscript thus used a second time is called a palimpsest. In time the book became too worn for this to be read and it was cast aside. When found the leaves were so stuck together that they had to be steamed apart. The parchment, when treated chemically, revealed the original writing. By means of these two discoveries a translation of the Gospels has been recovered that was made in the second century, two hundred years before any extant Greek manuscript of the Gospels was written.[28]

28 See William Cureton, *Remains of a Very Ancient Recension of the Four Gospels in Syriac,* London, 1858; and A. S. Lewis, *The Old Syriac Gospels,* London, 1910.

11. The Old Egyptian Versions.—Christianity was carried
to Egypt earlier than to the Syriac-speaking country of Upper
Mesopotamia, and early in the second century the Bible was translated into various dialects of Coptic, as the Egyptian language of
that period is called. Remains of two of these versions, the Sahidic
of Upper Egypt and the Basmuric of the Nile Delta, have been
found and studied with some completeness, while fragments of
versions in the dialects of Middle Egypt are also known.

Some Coptic manuscripts have been known for a long time, but
in 1883 nine thousand leaves of Coptic manuscripts were discovered in the ruins of the White Monastery between Assuit and
Thebes, 250 miles south of Cairo. Among these were parts of the
oldest Coptic Bibles ever seen. Discoveries of Coptic manuscripts
have frequently been made since. Before 1885 the Borgian Museum at Rome possessed a considerable collection of Sahidic manuscripts of the Old Testament. The first Coptic manuscript of any
considerable part of the Old Testament reached the British Museum
in 1896, but by 1905 that museum contained fifty-nine fragments
of the Old Testament in Coptic and eighty-three fragments of
eighty-three different copies of the New Testament. Many more
have come to light in recent years. The Library of J. Pierpont
Morgan in New York possesses an important collection of Coptic
manuscripts which were partly edited by the distinguished Coptic
scholar, H. Hyvernat, of the Catholic University of America in
Washington. Important Coptic manuscripts were purchased by
the late Mr. Freer, of Detroit, in 1906 and now form part of the
Freer collection.

Few of these Coptic manuscripts contain the whole Bible, and
gaps in the larger manuscripts have to be filled out from scattered leaves of papyrus gathered from here and there. Editing is,
accordingly, in the case of a Coptic text, a difficult task. It has,
however, been performed for much of the Old Testament by the
Italian scholar, A. Ciasca,[29] and for most of the New Testament
by the English scholar, George Horner.[30] Others have also done
valuable work in this field.[31]

[29] A. Ciasca, *Sacrorum Bibliorum Fragmenta Copto-Sahidica Musei Borgiana*, 2 vols.,
Rome, 1885–1889.
[30] *The Coptic Version of the New Testament in the Northern Dialect*, 4 vols., London,
1898–1905; *The Coptic Version of the New Testament in the Southern Dialect*, London,
1911–1920.
[31] *E.g.*, W. H. Worrell, *The Coptic Manuscripts of the Freer Collection*, New York,
1923.

As the Egyptian versions are very old, their importance is great. The Egyptian translations of the Old Testament were made from the Greek text of the Septuagint. The importance of this translation may be illustrated by the fact that in certain books of the Old Testament, such as Job, Origen, who died about 258 A.D., marked certain passages in his great Hexapla as doubtful. These passages are usually omitted in the Sahidic version, which thus confirms Origen and bears witness to the existence of a shorter text.

Late in 1924 an Egyptian version of the Gospel of John was published.[32] The version is written on papyrus leaves which had been folded, wrapped in a rag, and thrust into an earthenware vessel, which was found in a cemetery, about eighteen inches below the surface of the ground. When found the vessel was broken and the papyrus very brittle. With much difficulty the papyrus was moistened and unwrapped. Naturally parts of it were broken away. If the book had ever borne a date it had thus been lost, but the paleography indicates that it was written in the first half of the fourth century. Only two of the known Greek manuscripts are earlier than this. The translation itself appears to have been made in the second century. The dialect in which it is written differs both from the Sahidic of Thebes and from the dialect of Akhmim, being intermediate between the two. The translation differs materially from that of the Coptic Version, and seems to have been made independently from the Greek. The text agrees in general with that of the oldest known Greek manuscripts, and belongs to the type which scholars call "Alexandrian." It omits such passages as John 5:4, and 7:53–8:11. Another valuable witness to the type of text of this Gospel that was current in Egypt in the second century is thus added.

12. The Diatessaron of Tatian.—Tatian, an Assyrian disciple of Justin Martyr, was the first to weave the four Gospels into one continuous story of the life of Christ. He called it "Diatessaron." As he died about 170 A.D., he accomplished this before that date. The work was so popular in the Syrian churches that for a time it supplanted the separate Gospels. It was finally, however, put under the ban and disappeared. As references to it were found in Christian literature, scholars regarded its recovery as impotant. Radical critics of the Gospels had claimed that it could not have

---

[32] *The Gospel of John according to the Earliest Coptic Manuscript,* edited with translation by Sir Herbert Thompson, London, 1924.

included material from the Gospel of John, as they did not believe
that that Gospel was in use so early.   In 1883 Ciasca discovered
an Arabic version of it in the Vatican Library at Rome, and it was
found that it began with the Prologue to the Gospel of John and
is compiled from our four canonical Gospels and only these.[33]

As Tatian belonged to the Syriac-speaking Church of Upper
Mesopotamia and his work was read in Syriac in the churches there,
it was long questioned whether it was originally composed in Greek
or Syriac, or whether a Greek version of it ever existed.   As noted
above (Pt. I, Ch. II, p. 52 f.) a leaf of parchment was discovered
at Dura on March 5, 1933 [34] which contains 14 lines of writing in
Greek.   These lines are part of a Greek copy of Tatian's *Diates-saron*.   They correspond to a part of Chapter LII of the Arabic
version of the *Diatessaron,* and contain excerpts from Matthew
27:56, Mark 15:40, Luke 23:49 and 54, Matthew 27:57, John
19:38, and Luke 23:51.   The leaf was found under debris which
showed that it had been buried between 254 and 257 A.D.   The
parchment was accordingly written before 250 A.D.   The year before
this parchment was discovered the ruins of a Christian Church
were uncovered—a church that had been built between 222 and
235 A.D.   It is highly probable that this parchment was part of a
book prepared for use in this church.   Its discovery proves that,
if the *Diatessaron* was not written in Greek, it was translated into
that language in less than a hundred years after its composition.

13. The Gospel and Revelation of Peter.—From the earliest
list of New Testament books that has come down to us, the so-called
Canon of Muratori, which was written about the end of the second
century, we learn that an Apocalypse or Book of Revelation was
attributed to the Apostle Peter.   Several of the Fathers make
allusion to it and quote bits of it—altogether about eight lines were
known in that way, and it was said to have contained about 300
lines of the average length of a line of Homer.

We also learn from the Church Historian, Eusebius, that the
sect of the Docetæ used a Gospel about 190–200 A.D., which was
called The Gospel of Peter.   In 1886–1887 about two-thirds of the
Apocalypse and twelve short chapters from the Gospel—chap-ters dealing with the Passion and Resurrection of Christ—were
found in the same tomb at Akhmim in Egypt in which the Greek

33 See A. Ciasca, *Tatiani Evangeliorum Harmoniæ, Arabice,* Rome, 1888, and J. H.
Hill, *The Earliest Life of Christ, being the Diatessaron of Tatian,* Edinburgh, 1904.
34 See Carl H. Kraeling, *A Greek Fragment of the Diatessaron from Dura,* being vol.
III of *Studies and Documents,* edited by Kirsopp Lake and Silva Lake, London, 1935.

extract from Enoch, mentioned above, was found. Neither of these are genuine writings of St. Peter, but they are interesting as showing some of the literature which was prized by this sect in the second century. The Gospel of Peter is clearly based on our four canonical Gospels, but changes are made here and there to make the language teach the peculiar doctrines of the Docetists. The Apocalypse describes in lurid terms the tortures of the lost, and is believed to have been one of the sources of Dante for the material for his Inferno.[35]

14. The Odes of Solomon.—About 1907 Dr. J. Rendel Harris acquired some paper manuscripts written in Syriac, which came to him from the vicinity of the Tigris river. Two years later, in examining some of them, which he had thought of little importance, he found that one contained some Christian hymns ascribed to Solomon.[36] Internal evidence indicates that they come from the first century, and that they were probably used in the Apostolic Age. Scholars are divided as to whether they were originally written by a Christian or whether a Christian expanded them from a Jewish original. In either case they reveal to us a profound type of Christian devotion and are a most welcome addition to knowledge.

15. Sub-Apostolic Writings.—To extend this catalogue of archæological contributions into the domain of Patristic literature would carry us too far. Brief mention of some of the most noteworthy additions to the literature of the second century may not, however, be out of place. Until 1859 the *Shepherd of Hermas,* a work composed probably about 140 A.D., was known to us only through translations and quotations. In that year Tischendorf found a part of the text in the Sinaitic manuscript already described. In 1888 the rest of the text was supplied from a manuscript on Mount Athos, and parts have since been found in Egyptian papyri.[37]

The same Sinaitic manuscript contained the *Epistle of Barnabas,* the Greek text of which was previously unknown.[38] This latter, attributed to the Apostle Barnabas, and written, so Lightfoot believed, in the reign of Vespasian, before 79 A.D., was in some churches regarded for a time as a part of the New Testament canon. It is now practically certain that Barnabas did not write it. A

---

35 See *The Gospel According to Peter and the Revelation of Peter,* by J. Armitage Robinson and M. R. James, London, 1892; also H. B. Swete, *The Gospel of Peter,* London, 1893.

36 See J. R. Harris, *Odes and Psalms of Solomon,* Cambridge, 1909, and J. R. Harris and A. Mingana, *Odes and Psalms of Solomon,* 2 vols., Manchester, 1916–1920.

37 See Gregory, *Canon and Text of the New Testament,* p. 330, and A. Harnack, *Geschichte der Altchristlichen Literatur bis Eusebius, Leipzig,* 1893, I, 49 ff.

38 See Gregory, *ibid.*

few years later Bishop Bryennios found another copy of it in the Library of the Church of the Holy Sepulchre in Jerusalem.

Bound up with the manuscript of Barnabas, just mentioned, Bryennios also found a most precious manual entitled, *"The Teaching of the Twelve Apostles"* [39]—a work previously unknown. Although this work consisted of less than ten short pages, its publication in 1883 caused a sensation. It is a manual of early Christian practice, believed to have been written between 110 and 125 A.D., and gives us as no other work does a cross-section of the life of the Christian Church of that time. The monarchical episcopate was not yet fully established, and Christians were largely dependent upon traveling "prophets" for their preaching. An order or class of "widows" performed the functions of district nurses. Directions are given for baptism, prayer and fasting, for the celebration of the Eucharist, and for a pure walk in life.

Another important discovery, that of the Apology of Aristides, written between 130 and 160 A.D., was made in 1889 by Dr. J. R. Harris in the Convent of St. Catherine on Mount Sinai. It is one of the important defenses of Christianity addressed by early Christians to Roman emperors, and, like every piece of Christian literature, gives welcome and inspiring glimpses into their life.[40]

Were we to permit ourselves to wander farther from the Apostolic Age, attention might be called to many other documents, but we must not deviate too far from the purpose of this book, which is to illustrate the Bible.

16. Egyptian Papyri.—Mention has been made a number of times in the preceding pages of Egyptian papyri, but in order to emphasize their importance a word more is necessary. Papyri are found in tombs from many periods of Egyptian history. Those, however, that are written in the older Egyptian scripts are only occasionally of interest to the Biblical scholar. At numerous points, however, papyri from Ptolemaic and Roman times have been found which are often of the highest interest to the Biblical student. At three points in particular papyri of this character have been found—at Tebtunis, El-Hibeh, and Oxyrhincos. At Tebtunis it was accidentally discovered that the embalmed sacred crocodiles, which were found in large numbers, were stuffed with papyri which

39 See R. D. Hitchcock, and F. Brown, *The Teaching of the Twelve Apostles,* New York, 1884; P. Schaff, *The Teaching of the Twelve Apostles,* New York, 1885; and J. R. Harris, *The Teaching of the Twelve Apostles,* Baltimore, 1887.
40 See *The Apology of Aristides,* edited and translated by J. R. Harris, with an Introduction by J. Armitage Robinson, Cambridge, 1893.

the Egyptians had thrown into their waste-baskets. At Oxyrhincos
Grenfell and Hunt found the places on the border of the desert
where, during the early centuries of the Christian Era, the inhabitants of a neighboring town had emptied their waste-baskets. Thousands of precious documents have in this way been recovered.
Many of them contain fragments of Greek literature; some contain
the text of different parts of the Bible, but many relate to all phases
of the common life. They are letters, tax receipts, depositions,
marriage certificates, lawsuits, etc. They introduce us intimately
to the life of ancient times.

How important such documents may be for some phases of
Biblical study has already been shown by the material quoted
from them in Chapters XXVIII, XXIX, and XXX. They are
equally important for the study of the language of the New Testament. The New Testament is written in a dialect which differs
much from the dialects employed in classical Greek literature, and,
until the discovery of these papyri, there were many obscure points
in the grammar and vocabulary of the New Testament. The
Egyptian papyri turn out to be written in the same dialect, and these
thousands of new documents afford numerous parallels to words
and constructions which were difficult or obscure, so that it is not
too much to say that, since their discovery, New Testament grammar
and lexicography have taken on a new phase. Archæology has thus
contributed much to a branch of Biblical study that cannot well be
illustrated in a book like this.[41]

17. A Second Century Fragment of the Gospel of John.—
The John Rylands Library, Manchester, England, obtained in 1901
a collection of Egyptian papyri that had been unearthed in Egypt
by Grenfell and Hunt in the course of those excavations in which
the Sayings of Jesus described above (Pt. II, Ch. XXVIII) were
found. The task of examining each of these fragments and of
making a catalogue of them, requiring as it does the services of

41 See A. Deissmann, *New Light on the New Testament,* Edinburgh, 1907; also his
Biblical Studies, Edinburgh, 1901; also his *Licht vom Osten,* 4te Auf. Tubingen, 1923,
translated into English from the 2d edition as *Light from the Ancient East,* London and
New York, 1910; J. H. Moulton, *Grammar of New Testament Greek,* Edinburgh, 1906–
1929; A. T. Robertson, *A Grammar of the Greek New Testament in the Light of Historical Research,* 6th ed., New York, 1935; P. M. Meyer, *Griechische Texte aus Agypt,*
Berlin, 1916; Moulton and Milligan, *Vocabulary of the Greek Testament Illustrated from
the Papyri and Other Non-Literary Sources,* London, 1914–1932; Abbott-Smith, *Manual
Lexicon of the New Testament,* 1921. For those who would read the papyri, George
Milligan's *Selections from the Greek Papyri,* Cambridge, 1912, and E. J. Goodspeed
and E. C. Colwell's *A Greek Papyrus Reader with Vocabulary,* Chicago, 1935, may
be recommended. The original texts of the papyri are scattered through many publications. The largest single series of them is the volumes of the *Egypt Exploration Fund*—
—*Græco-Roman Branch.*

a skilled papyrologist, has proceeded slowly. Mr. C. H. Roberts, who is now engaged in the task, discovered in 1934 a fragment, written in a style that attests that the copy was in all probability made before the year 150 A.D. The precious leaf contains on its front only seven lines of writing, and on its back only six, but these lines are a part of the text of St. John's Gospel. The lines on the front, when the text is filled out, give us John 18: 31-33, and those on the back, John 18: 37-38.[42]

The significance of this is great. A hundred years ago F. C. Baur was saying that the Gospel of John could not have been written till about 160 A.D., and many scholars echoed the same opinion for fifty years, but here is a fragment of a copy of the Gospel which was written before the year 150 in Egypt.

42 See C. H. Roberts, *An Unpublished Fragment of the Fourth Gospel in the John Rylands Library*, Manchester University Press, Manchester, England, 1935.

INDEX OF SCRIPTURE PASSAGES

INDEX OF SCRIPTURE PASSAGES 591

1 SAMUEL—	PAGE
7:5, ff	132
10:5	196
10:17	133
10:26	174
11:4	174
13:18	456
13:20, 21	202
17:1	151
17:4	101
17:43	180
19:24	453
22:1	132
23:1	153, 231
25:2	231
28:41	151
31:5	195
31:10	174, 456
31:10, 12	125, 257

2 SAMUEL	
1:10	197
2:8	456
2:16	195
3:27	170
5:6-8	171, 231
5:8	97, 171
5:9	107, 232
5:11	128
5:25	102
6	128
8:9, f	91
11:1	260, 564
12:27	171, 260
12:31	193
15:2	232
16:9	180
17:24	456
17:28	172
20:14	149, 151
21:9	179
21:12	125, 257
23:11	175
24	233, 235
24:16	236
24:16, 17	475
24:18, 22	176

1 KINGS—	
1:33	122
1:40	196
3:1	233
3:1, f	20, 233
4:7, ff	383
4:12	125, 257, 456
5:6, 17	455
5:13 ff	119
6:4	237
6:29, 32, 35	237
6:36	238
7:2, 6	238
7:8, 12, 23-37, 39	237, 238
7:9	193
7:27-37	238
7:48	237
7:49	237
9:15	153, 233
9:15-19	104, 130
9:16, 17	20, 165
9:24	231
10:1, ff	468

1 KINGS—	PAGE
10:1-13	480
10:5, 8-20	238
10:26, ff	130
11:14-25	158
11:27	108, 233
11:40	21
12:12, ff	456
14:25, ff	28, 116, 158, 456
14:25-28	21, 456
15:20	149, 151
15:22	115
16:22	121
16:23-29	462
16:24	120, 136, 155, 168
16:31	129
16:34	112, 169
17:10	174
19:15	459
19:19	176
21	438
21:8	196
22:39	120, 168

2 KINGS—	
2:19-22	112
3	461
3:4	461
3:5	462
3:4-12	240
3:5-27	462
4:8	151, 456
4:23	310
5:12	257
5—9	128
6:5	193
6:13	174
6:25	199
8	459
9:24	121
10:1-13	480
11:12, 13, 14, 15	324
11:12, 13	238
12:17	101
12:20	232
13:20, 21	226
14:7	217
14:8-14	104, 105
14:13	239
14:19	99
14:21	464
14:23, ff	456
15:1-27	464
15:14-23	464
15:19	67, 68
15:20	151
15:29	149, 467, 469
15:29, 30	68, 466
15:37	464
16:5-9	464
16:10, f	68, 466
16:10-16	241
16:14	237
16:23-29	462
17:3-5	466
17:4	467
17:5	68, 164
17:6, 24, ff	466
17:6	469
17:24	165

2 KINGS—	PAGE
17:24-34	121, 159
18	473
18:1-6, 9, ff	241
18:4	215
18:13	34
18:13-16	473, 474
18:13—19:8	474
18:14	99, 473
18:14, ff	472
18:17	473
18:32	180
19	473
19:9	21, 474
19:9-36	474, 475
19:35, ff	473
19:36	473, 475
19:37	35, 70, 476
20:12	69
20:20	241, 476
20:21	477
21	477
21:6	216
22:14	242
23:10	216, 242
23:29	22, 110
23:29, ff	477
23:34	22, 478
24:25	35, 71, 479
24—25	479
25:4	242
25:9, 10	242
25:22 ff	109
25:27	479
25:27-30	71

1 CHRONICLES—	
1—9	324
1:30	372
1:38, 39	148
1:40	373
2:18	156
3:18	109
4:8	156
7:29	125
7:31	446
8:12	151
11:7	117
18:9, f	91
20:4	157
21:23	176
23:4	380
29:7	204

2 CHRONICLES—	
1:5, 6	237
2:8, ff	455
3:1, ff	213
3:14	237
5:2	232
11:5-10	100
11:7	456
19:5-7	380
28:18	456
33	70

EZRA—	
1	485
2:69	204
3:12	243
4:1	477
4:2	477

INDEX

Abana, 257
Abbi-Teshub, makes treaty with Mursil, 89
Abdi-Hepa, vassal of Amenophis IV, 85
Abi-Adda, 89
Abraham, Babylonian account of farmer of this name, 147, 344
Abraham, sojourn in Egypt, 25; purchase of the cave of Machpelah, 85; home in Mesopotamia, 152; sacrifice of Isaac, 213; Testament of, 576
Abraham and Melchizedek, 230, 353
"Absalom's Pillar," 225
Abu Haba, Turkish exploration of, 37
Abu Sharain, site of Eridu, 39
Abu Shusheh (Gezer), 103
Abydos, chief town of This, 14
Acts, Archæological light on the book of, 559
Adab (Bismya), 38, 63
Adad-nirari III, King of Assyria, 58
Adad-nirari IV, 67; inscription regarding Syria and Palestine, 462, ff
Adam, Biblical account of, 343; Babylonian forms of the name, 321
Adapa and the fall of man, legend of, 311, ff
Adimê, 322
Admonitions of Ipuwer, The, 17, 528, 529
Adoni-bezek, 360
Adoni-zedek, 360
Adonis, Phœnician vegetation god, 539
Adzes, 194
Ælia Capitolina, 162, 255 (footnote)
Africanus, Julius Sextus, Chronigraphiai of, 11
Agade (Sippar), 59, 63, 374
Agricultural Implements, 175, 176; calendar, 179
Agriculture, 175
Ahab, in confederacy against Shalmaneser III, 67; palace of, 120
Ahaz, vassal to Tiglath-pileser III, 68; altar of, 241; pays tribute to Tiglath-pileser III, 466
Ahmose I, siege of Sharuhen, 151
Ai, 136
Ain Duk, 124
Ain es-Sultan (Elisha's Fountain), 112
Ain Kades, 105, 358
Ain Shems (Beth-Shemesh), 104
Ain Sitti Miriam, see Gihon
Ajjul, Tell el-, 138
Akkad, derivation of, 64
Akra, 246
Alaparos, 321
Albright, W. F., 114, 115, 116, 137, 152, 352

Alexander, Jannæus, 160, 243, 259
Alexander the Great, empire of, 23; conquests of, 72; death of, 159
Alexandra, Asmonæan Queen, 160
Alorus, 321
Alphabet, the, 129
Altar of Incense, 221,
Amanus, source of cedar, 64, 455
Amelu, 323
Amempsinos, 320
Amen-em-apt, see Amen-em-ope
Amen-em-ope, Teaching of, 511 f; comparison with book of Proverbs, 514
Amenemhet I, 372
Amenemhet III, 17
Amenophis I, 13, 151
Amenophis III, 65, 368
Amenophis III and IV, 19, 65
American Exploration Society, 96
American Palestine Exploration Society, 96
American School of Classical Studies at Athens, 264
American Schools of Oriental Research at Bagdad, 43
American School of Oriental Research in Palestine, 114
Amil-Marduk (Evil-Merodach), 71; Inscription of, 479
Amman, 260
Ammelon, 321
Ammenon, 321
Ammienshi, Amorite chieftain, 148
Ammi-Zadugga, Reign of, 58
Amorites, Conquest of the, 146
Amosis I, 18
Amraphel, King of Shinar, 347, 353
Anathoth, 120
Anderson, H. J., Explorations in Palestine, 96
Anderson, J. G. C., Inscription discovered at Antioch, 557
Andrae, W., Exploration at Kalah-Sherghat, 38; Inscription of Tukulti-Ninib, 57; on houses and temples, 208 (footnote)
Animals, Representative of Egyptian tribes, 13; domestic, 179
Anklets, 198
Antigonus, 159, 248
Antioch in Psidia, Excavation at, 273
Antioch in Syria, Excavation at, 139
Antiochus, III, 171, 205, 260
Antiochus IV, 246
Antipas, 161
Antiquities, preservation of Egyptian, 5; Babylonian, 32
Antonia, fortress, 248
Anu, 311

595

Book of Adam and Eve, 576
Book of Enoch, 575
Book of Jubilees, 576
Bor (Tyana), 92
Bork, Ferdinand, studies in the Mitanni language, 79
Bossert, H. T., 84
Botta, Paul Émil, exploration of Nineveh, 34
Bowls, 191
Box, C. H., 577
Bracelets, 197
Breasted, Henry James, accession of Mena, 13; *Ancient Records, Egypt,* 449 (footnote), 515
British Museum, trustees direct excavation at Carchemish, 76
Bruce, James, 5, 575
Brugsch, H., *History of Egypt,* 86; inscription at Elephantine, 370
Brünnow, R., studies in the Mitanni language, 77; explorations in Edom, 98
Brunton, Guy, 8
Bubastis, capital of Shishak dynasty, 29
Budge, E. A., Wallis, teaching of Amen-em-ope, 511
Bulghar-Maden, Hittite remains at, 77
Burckhardt, J. L., explorations in Palestine, 95
Burial customs, 223
Burnaburiash, 65
Burnouf Eugène, 55
Butler, H. C., explorations in Syria, 141; excavations at Sardis, 270
Buxton, Dr. L. H. Dudley, discussion of skulls, 43

Cab, 199
Cabane, Lieut., 51
Cain, list of descendants, 325
Cairo, 3, 5
Calah, made capital of Assyria, 66
Calendar, 179
Calvary, site of, 253
Cambyses, son of Cyrus, 22; extends power of Persia, 72
Canaanites, migration of the, 150
Capernaum, identification of, 111
Caphtor, home of the Philistines, 156
Captivity, Babylonian, 71
Carchemish, excavations at, 76; alliance with Syria, 91
Carthaginian law regarding sacrifices, 439
Cataracts of the Nile, 4
Carter, Howard, discovery by, 19
Cave-dwellers, 183, 229
Caves of the stone age, 143
Chaldæan Empire, 70
Chalice of Antioch, 564
Champollion, Jean François (Le Jeune), 10
Chaplin, Thomas, description of weight from Samaria, 201
Charles, B. B., explorations in Asia Minor, 76; *Travels and Studies in the Nearer East,* 79
Châteaubriand, explorations in Palestine, 95
Chedorlaomer, 349, 351
Cheops (Khufu), 15
Chester Beatty Papyri, 580

Chiera, Edward, 43, 48
Child sacrifice, 215, 242
Chisels, 193
Chosroes II, captures Jerusalem, 162
Christian Nubians, 30
Church at Dura, 52
Church of the Holy Sepulcher, 254
Churches of Asia, 264
Circumcision, prehistoric, in Assyria, 45
Cistern burial, 223
Cities, topography of Palestinian, 164; situated near springs, 228
City gates, 169
Clark, Herbert, 201
Clay, A. T., *Light on the Old Testament from Babel,* 483 (footnote)
Clermont-Ganneau, explorations in Palestine, 98, 99, 241; Moabite Stone, 460
Code of Hammurabi, 378 ff
Coins, 203 ff; Roman, 206
Colt, H. D., 140
"Columbarium," 225
Colwell, E. C., 587
Combs, 197
Conder, Lieut-Col. C. R., *The Hittites and Their Language,* 78; survey of Palestine, 96, 98
Conquest of Death, poem on, 534
Constantine, interest in holy places, 94, 95, 162
Constantinople, tablets hoarded in, 54
Contenau, G., 92
Copper mines, 119
Cor (Homer), 199
Corinth, 263
Corners, considered sacred, 169
Cossæans, see *Kassites*
Cowley, A. E., hieroglyphic Hittite, 83
Creation, epic of, 279 ff; compared with first chapter of Genesis, 295 ff; second account of, found at Babylon, 303; compared with second chapter of Genesis, 304; new Babylonian account of, 298 ff; another Sumerian account of, 306
Creation and flood, Nippur, account of, 305
Cremation, 222
Crœsus, temple of, 266; wealth of, 270; overthrown by Cyrus the Great, 203, 482
Cromlech (heap of stones), 143
Cros, Gaston, explorations of, 36
Crowfoot, J. W., 107, 121
Crucifixion, site of the, 253
Cruikshank, J., 51
Ctesiphon, 50
Cumont, F., 52
"Cuneiform" characters, origin of, 62
Curetonian Syriac, 581
Cybele, worship of, 269; temple of, 270
Cyprus, seal of Sargon found in, 63
Cyrus the Great, founder of Persian Empire, 22; conquests of, 71; overthrows Croesus, 203, 482; captures Sardis, 270; inscription, 484

Dalman, Gustaf H., explorations in Petra, 98, 185
Damascius, a neplatonic philosopher, 295
Damascus, 256, 465
Danaoi, migration of, 155

Judah, the southern kingdom, 158
Judas Maccabæas, 159
Judges, periol of, 449
Justus, house of, 264

Kadashman-turgu, 65
Kadesh, battle at, 90
Kadesh-Barnea, identification of, disputed, 105
Kadesh in the wilderness, 356, 361
Kalah-Sherghat, exploration at, 38
Kanatha, 260
Kára-Bel, Hittite remains at, 77
Karaburna, Hittite remains at, 77
Kara Dagh, Hittite remains at, 77
Karaindash, King of Babylon, 66
Karanog, exploration of, 30
Kara Su, 75
Karnak, temple of, 28
Kassites, invade Babylonia, 65; migration of the, 150
Kenan, 325
Kenyon, Sir F. G., 579
Kevin, R. O., on teaching of Amen-eni-apt and Proverbs, 511
Keys, 192
Khafaje, 49
Khafre, 15
Kharir, Tell, 51
Khartum, 4
Khattu, land, name given to Hittite settlement in Cappadocia, 84
Kheta, see Hittites
Khnum, 370
Khorsabad, site of Sargon's palace, 34, 48
Khufu (Cheops), 15
Kidron, valley of, 227
King, list of Karnak, etc., 11
King, L. W., 50, 73
Kings, books of, archæological light on, 455 ff
King's Gardens, 232
Kirkuk, 43
Kish, exploration at, 39, 43; dynasty of, 59
Kitchener, H. H., Major and Lord, survey of Palestine, 98; surveys in the Arabah, 99
Kizil Dagh, Hittite remains at, 77
Klein, F. A., 460
Knives, 193
Knudtzon, J. A., Die El-Amarna Tafeln, 368, 369
Koeppel, R., 132
Kok (shaft), 225
Koldewey, Robert, Babylonian exploration, 37, 71
Kraeling, C., 52n, 577n
Kühnel, E., 50, 51
Kudur-Mabug, 348
Kukukumal, 351
Kummukh, Hittite kingdom, 92
Kurigalzu, invasion of Elam during reign of, 65
Kyle, M. G., 115, 116

Labyrinth, 17
Lachish, excavations at, 99; walls of, 165
Lagash, kings of, 62
Lake, Kirsopp, 250

Lamatrine, A. M., explorations in Palestine, 95
Lamech, 324, 325
Lamentation for Tammuz, 533 f
Lamentations, Babylonian book of, 547 f
Lamon, Robert S., 131
Lamp-stands, 192
Langdon, Stephen, explores Kish, 42; Sumerian Epic of Paradise, the Flood, and the Fall of Man, 337 (footnote); translation of Babylonian poem, 491
Lange, H. O., 511
Laodicea, 273
Larsa, kings of, 59; divided power with Nisin, 64
Lassen, Christian, 55
Lawrence, T. E., explorations in the wilderness of Zin, 105
Layard, Austin Henry, explorations of, 34; discoveries at Nineveh, 70, 73
Lebanon, copper from, 64
Leontopolis, Jewis temple at, 29
Lepton, 206
Letters from Palestine, 441
Leviticus, alleged parallel to, 440
Lewis, Agnes S., 581
Libertines, Synagogue of, 564
Library of Ashurbanipal at Nineveh, 70
Liturgy of the time of Abraham, 353 ff
Liverpoorl, University of, directs Hittite exploration, 76
Loftus, William Kennett, explorations of, 35
Log, 199
Lotan, 148
Lowenstern, Isidore, 55
Lugaldaudu, statue of, 38; King of Adab, 63
Lugalzaggisi, 60, 63
Lydia, origin of coinage in (?), 204; kingdom of, 269
Lynch, Lieut. W. F., explorations in Palestine, 96
Lyon, D. G., excavations at Samaria, 120
Lyres, 196
Macalister, Alexander, Anatomist, 144
Macalister, R. A., Stewart, excavations at Gezer, 102; explorations in Ophel, 107; conjecture regarding walls of Gezer, 165, 229
Maccabæan period, 246
Maccabees, 159
MacIver, R., exploration at Karanog, 30
Mackay, E., 42, 53
Makenzie, Duncan, excavations at Beth-Shemesh, 104
McCown, C. C., American School of Oriental Research, 133, 136
McCown, T. D., 132
Magan, conquered by Naram-Sin, 63; quarries at, 64
Magdol, 24
Mallon, Père, 131
Mallowan, M. E. L., 51
Mana, 201
Manasseh, vassal of Esarhaddon and Ashurbanipal, 70
Manetho, Egyptian priest, 11
Manishtusu, King of Kish, 38
Manissia, Hittite sculptures and remains near, 86, 89

Marash (in Asia Minor), Hittite remains at, 77
Marash (Moresheth-Gath), 102
Marduk, central figure in Babylonian Creation Epic, 296
Marduk and Zarpanit, feast of, 309
Marduknadinakhi, King of Babylon, 57
Marquet-Krause, Mme. J., 136
Mars' Hill, 263
Marshall, Sir John, 53
Martyrdom of Isaiah, 577
Masterman, E. W. G., estimate of Parker's excavations, 122
Mattiuaza, made King of the Mitanni, 87
'Maudsley's Scarp," 100, 234
Measures, 199
Medeba, taken by Omri, 462
Meek, T. J., 60, 425
Megalaros, 321
Megiddo, battle of. 22; excavations at, 109; wall of, 130; topography of, 164; area of. 166; remains of buildings, 168, 210; gates of, 169; rock altar at, 212; seal found at, 456
Melamkish, 323
Melchizedek, time of. 229, 353, 357
Memphis, capital of Egypt, 16
Mena, accession of, 13; reign of, 14
Menahem, 68
Menant, Joachim, decipherment of Hittite inscriptions, 77
Menhir (stone columns), 143; burial in, 223
Menkaure, 15
Men-nofer, 16
Meriggi, P., 83
Merneptah, successor of Ramses II, 20; Pharaoh of the Exodus, 20; siege of Gezer, 155; pillar of, 376
Merodachbaladan, inscription at Kish, 43; takes the throne of Babylon, 69; relations with Hezekiah, 475
Meroe, 22, 30
Merrill, Selah, explorations in Palestine, 96
Meruitensi, 527
Meselim, King of Kish, 62
Mesha, King of Moab, 214, 460
Mes-kalam-dim, King of Ur, 42
Meskingashir, 323
Mesopotamian Valley, 31
Messerchmidt, L., studies in the Mitanni language, 79
Methuselah, 324, 325
Meyer, L. A., 134
Meyer, Eduard, accession of Mena, 13; origin of the Philistines, 454
Meyer, Rudolph, map of Palestine, 96
Middle Kingdom, period of (Egypt), 17
Migdol, 24
Miles, J. C., 427
Miletus, 265
Milligan, George, 587
Millo, 232
Millstones, 177
Mina, 201
Mines, Solomon's, 119
Mitanni, king of, 75; kingdom of, 62, 86
Mite, coin, 206
Mizpeh, 132
Mirsim, Tel Beit, excavations at, 116

Moabite Stone, 460
Mohammedans, prevail in Palestine, 162
Mohenjo-daro, 49
Money, 203
Monolith, at Gezer, 213
Montet, M., excavates Jebeil, 128
Montgomery, J. A., 138, 479
Mordtmann, A. D., account of Hittite inscriptions, 77
Moresheth-Gath (Marash), 102
Morey, C. E., 140
Morgan, J. de, exploration at Susa, 38, 378
Moriah, Mount, 213; site of the temple, 235
Mortars, 177
Mosaic Code, not borrowed from the Babylonians, 405
Moses, Assumption of, 577
Mosque of Omar, 213
Moth, Phœnician name of Death, 536, f.
Moulton, W. J., 114
Mount, see descriptive name
Müller, W. Max, origin of the Hittites, 75, 365
Mursil, successor of Arandas, 89; makes treaty with the Amorites, death of, 89
Mutallu, successor of Mursil, 89
Mutu-elu, 323
Mutu-sa-elu, 324
Mutu-salal-eqla, 324

Nabathæans, 217
Nabopolassar, 70
Nabuna'id, King of Babylon, 60; inscriptions of, 481
Nails, 194
Names, Sumerian, with Semitic, Babylonian, and Hebrew equivalents, 324
Napata, 18
Napoleon I, invasion of Egypt, 6
Naram-Sin, 60, 63
Nasbeh, Tell en-, excavations at, 132
Naville, E., excavation of Pithom, 27
Nebuchadrezzar I, King of Babylon, 66
Nebuchadrezzar II, defeats Necho, 22, 71; destroys Jerusalem, 242; inscription of, 478
Necho, 22, 71, 477
Necklaces, 197
Needles, 192
Nehemiah, rebuilds the walls of Jerusalem, 244
Nehushtan, 215
Neo-Babylonian period, 70
Neolithic implements, 142
Neuville, R., 132
New Testament Manuscripts, 579, 580
Nicanor's Gate, 252
Niebuhr, Carsten, inscriptions at Persepolis, 54
Nile, 3
Nineveh explored by Botta, Place and Layard, 34; Rassam, Loftus, 35; George Smith, 35, 36; by King and Thompson, 50; eclipse at, 57; Ashurbanipal's library at, 70; fall of, 543
Ninkhursag, 332, 343
Nippur, exploration of, 37; founding of, 61; account of creation and flood dis-

PLATES

FIG. 1.   SYRIAN TRADERS IN EGYPT, FROM A TOMB AT BENI HASAN.

FIG. 2.   CROWN OF   FIG. 3.   CROWN OF   FIG. 4.   CROWN OF
LOWER EGYPT.   UPPER EGYPT.   UNITED EGYPT.

FIG. 5.   SPHINX AND PYRAMID OF KHAFRE.

FIG. 6. PYRAMIDS OF KHUFU AND KHAFRE.

FIG. 7. STEP PYRAMID OF ZOSER.

FIG. 9. HEAD OF THE MUMMY OF RAMSES II.

FIG. 8. BODY FROM A PRE-DYNASTIC TOMB.

Fig. 10. A Store-Chamber at Pithom (*after Naville*).

Fig. 11. Ancient and Modern Brick-Making (*after Petrie*).

FIG. 12. PLAN OF CITY AND TEMPLE OF LEONTOPOLIS (*after Petrie*).

FIG. 13. A PASSOVER-OVEN (*after Petrie*).

FIG. 15.   THE "ISRAEL" INSCRIPTION OF MERNEPTAH.

FIG. 14.   THE ROSETTA STONE.

By permission of Thomas Nelson & Sons.

FIG. 16.   MOUNDS OF NUFFAR (*after Clay*).

FIG. 17.   EXCAVATION AT NUFFAR (*after Clay*).

FIG. 19.   PHALANX OF SOLDIERS FROM EANNATUM'S "STELE OF VULTURES."

FIG. 18.   GATE OF ISHTAR. BABYLON (after Koldeway).

FIG. 20. INSCRIBED COLUMN FROM   FIG. 21. SILVER VASE OF ENTEMENA.
             PERSEPOLIS.

FIG. 22. MOUND OF BIRS NIMRÛD (after Peters).

FIG. 23. HITTITE GATES AT BOGHAZ KOI (*after Puchstein*).

FIG. 24. HITTITE TYPES FROM EGYPTIAN MONUMENTS (*after Garstang*).

Fig. 25. A Hittite Amazon (*after Puchstein*).

Fig. 26. The Boss of Tarkondemos.

Fig. 27. The Seal of Shema, Servant of Jeroboam.

FIG. 28.   TELL EL-HESY AFTER EXCAVATION.

FIG. 29.   THE SITE OF THE OLD TESTAMENT JERICHO.

FIG. 30. EXCAVATION OF GEZER.

FIG. 31. REMAINS OF A COLONNADED STREET AT SAMARIA.

FIG. 33.   EGYPTIANS ATTACKING A PALESTINIAN CITY (after Perrot and Chipiez).

FIG. 32.   EXCAVATION AT TELL HUM.

FIG. 34. JERICHO (*after Sellin*).

FIG. 35. HOUSES AT JERICHO (*after Sellin*).

FIG. 36. PHILISTINES FROM THE PALACE OF RAMSES III.

FIG. 37. CANAANITISH FORTRESS AT JERICHO (*after Sellin*).

FIG. 38.—INSCRIBED DISC FROM PHÆSTOS (ONE-FOURTH ACTUAL SIZE).

FIG. 39.   GEBEL FUREIDIS.

FIG. 40.   BASTION FOR THE PROTECTION OF AN INSERTED TOWER (*after Macalister*).
By permission of Palestine Exploration Fund.

FIG. 41.   REMAINS OF WALLS OF MEGIDDO (*after Schumacher*).

FIG. 42. WALLS OF BUILDINGS AT SAMARIA (*after Reisner*).

FIG. 43. SPECIMENS OF STONE-WORK AT
GEZER (*after Macalister*).

By permission of Palestine Exploration Fund.

FIG. 44. BUILDING-BRICKS FROM GEZER
(*after Macalister*).

By permission of Palestine Exploration Fund.

FIG. 46. THE GREAT CITY WALL AT GEZER (after Macalister).

By permission of Palestine Exploration Fund.

FIG. 45. PLAN OF PALACE AT TAANACH (after Sellin).

FIG. 47.   ISRAELITISH HOUSES AT GEZER.
By permission of Palestine Exploration Fund.

FIG. 48.   SPECIMENS OF MOSAIC FLOORS *(after Macalister).*
By permission of Palestine Exploration Fund.

FIG. 49.   A DOORWAY AT GEZER (*after Macalister*).
By permission of Palestine Exploration Fund.

FIG. 50.   DOOR-SOCKETS FROM GEZER (*after Macalister*).
By permission of Palestine Exploration Fund.

FIG. 51. WRONGLY SUPPOSED HOUSE OF HIEL, JERICHO (*after Sellin*).

FIG. 52. FOUNDATION OF THE PALACE OF OMRI, SAMARIA (*after Reisner*).

FIG. 53. HEBREW PALACE AT MEGIDDO (*after Schumacher*).

FIG. 54.   PLAN OF THE MACCABÆAN CASTLE AT GEZER (*after Macalister*).
By permission of Palestine Exploration Fund.

FIG. 55.   STONE-WORK OF THE MACCABÆAN CASTLE (*after Macalister*).
By permission of Palestine Exploration Fund.

FIG. 56.   A FOUNDATION-DEPOSIT, GEZER (*after Macalister*).
By permission of Palestine Exploration Fund.

FIG. 57.   A CITY GATE AT MEGIDDO (*after Schumacher*).

FIG. 58.   THE SOUTH GATE AT GEZER (*after Macalister*).

By permission of Palestine Exploration Fund.

FIG. 59.   THE SOUTH GATE AT BETH-SHEMESH (*after Mackenzie*).

By permission of Palestine Exploration Fund.

FIG. 60.   ENTRANCE TO THE UNDERGROUND TUNNEL AT GEZER (*after Macalister*).
By permission of Palestine Exploration Fund.

FIG. 61.—THE NORTH GATE AT GEZER (*after Macalister*).
By permission of Palestine Exploration Fund.

FIG. 62. PLANS OF THE UNDERGROUND TUNNEL AT GEZER (after Macalister).

By permission of Palestine Exploration Fund.

FIG. 63.   PLAN OF UNDERGROUND TUNNEL AT GIBEON (*after Abel*).

FIG. 64.   ONE OF SOLOMON'S POOLS.

FIG. 65.   POST OF CITY GATE, SAMARIA (*after Reisner*).

FIG. 66.   PART OF CITY WALL AND GATE, SAMARIA (*after Reisner*).

FIG. 67. ROAD SOUTH OF GERIZIM.

FIG. 68. LINES OF ROMAN ROADS AT TELL EL-FUL.

FIG. 69. ROMAN ROAD NORTH OF AMMAN.

FIG. 70.   A GRANARY AT GEZER (*after Macalister*).
By permission of Palestine Exploration Fund.

FIG. 72.   PLAN OF A GRANARY AT GEZER (*after Macalister*).
By permission of Palestine Exploration Fund.

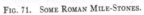

FIG. 71.   SOME ROMAN MILE-STONES.

FIG. 76. PLOWSHARES FROM MEGIDDO (after Schumacher).

FIG. 74. AN EGYPTIAN REAPING (after Wreszinski).

FIG. 73. A HOE (after Macalister). By permission of Palestine Exploration Fund.

FIG. 75. A SICKLE (after Wreszinski).

FIG. 77.   EGYPTIAN PLOWING (after Wilkinson).

FIG. 79.   EGYPTIANS THRESHING AND WINNOWING (after Wilkinson).

FIG. 80.   EGYPTIAN THRESHING-SLEDGE (after Wilkinson).

FIG. 78.   A MODERN THRESHING-FLOOR.

FIG. 81.   A SADDLE-QUERN FROM MEGIDDO (*after Schumacher*).

FIG. 82.   A ROTARY-QUERN (*after
Macalister*).

By permission of Palestine Exploration Fund.

FIG. 83.   A MORTAR AND PESTLE (*after
Macalister*).

By permission of Palestine Exploration Fund.

FIG. 84.   TWO WOMEN GRINDING AT A MILL (*after Schumacher*).

FIG. 85.   AN ANCIENT OLIVE-PRESS (*after Macalister*).
By permission of Palestine Exploration Fund.

FIG. 86.   A   MODERN OLIVE-PRESS (*after Macalister*).
By permission of Palestine Exploration Fund.

FIG. 87.   A WINE VAT (*after Macalister*).
By permission of Palestine Exploration Fund.

FIG. 88.   AN OLIVE-PRESS AT WORK (*after Macalister*).
By permission of Palestine Exploration Fund.

FIG. 89. COWS' HORNS FROM GEZER (*after Macalister*).
By permission of Palestine Exploration Fund.

FIG. 90. ANIMALS' HEADS FROM GEZER (*after Macalister*).
By permission of Palestine Exploration Fund.

FIG. 91. A HORSE'S BIT FROM GEZER
(*after Macalister*).
By permission of Palestine Exploration Fund.

FIG. 92. DRAWINGS OF HORSES FROM
GEZER (*after Macalister*).
By permission of Palestine Exploration Fund.

FIG. 93. A CLAY BIRD FROM GEZER (*after Macalister*).
By permission of Palestine Exploration Fund.

FIG. 94. A COCK FROM MARISSA (*after Peters and Thiersch*).

By permission of Palestine Exploration Fund.

FIG. 95. A BEE-HIVE FROM GEZER (*after Macalister*).

By permission of Palestine Exploration Fund.

FIG. 96.   EARLY BRONZE AGE JARS
(after Macalister).
By permission of Palestine Exploration Fund.

FIG. 97.   EARLY BRONZE AGE POTTERY
(after Macalister).
By permission of Palestine Exploration Fund.

FIG. 98.   FOUR PITCHERS FROM THE MIDDLE BRONZE STRATUM (after Macalister).
By permission of Palestine Exploration Fund.

FIG. 99.   THREE PITCHERS FROM THE
MIDDLE BRONZE STRATUM (after Macalister).
By permission of Palestine Exploration Fund.

FIG. 100.   A JAR FROM THE MIDDLE
BRONZE STRATUM (after Macalister).
By permission of Palestine Exploration Fund

FIG. 101. JUGS FROM THE LATE BRONZE STRATUM (*after Macalister*).
By permission of Palestine Exploration Fund.

FIG. 102. A JUG FROM THE LATE BRONZE STRATUM   FIG. 103. A JAR FROM THE LATE
          (*after Macalister*).   BRONZE STRATUM
                                                     (*after Macalister*).

By permission of Palestine Exploration Fund.   *By permission of Palestine Exploration Fund.*

FIG. 107. A FLAT-BOT-TOMED JUG FROM THE MIDDLE BRONZE STRATUM (after Macalister).

By permission of Palestine Exploration Fund.

FIG. 105. "EAR" AND "BUTTON" JAR-HANDLES (after Macalister).

By permission of Palestine Exploration Fund.

FIG. 106. A "PILLAR" HANDLE (after Macalister).

By permission of Palestine Exploration Fund.

FIG. 104. SOME FINE POTTERY FROM THE EARLY BRONZE STRATUM (after Macalister).

By permission of Palestine Exploration Fund.

FIG. 110. JARS FROM THE LATE BRONZE STRATUM, FROM BETH-SHEMESH (*after Mackenzie*).

By permission of Palestine Exploration Fund.

FIG. 111. HEBREW POTTERY FROM MEGIDDO (*after Schumacher*).

FIG. 108. A PAINTED PHILISTINE VASE FROM BETH-SHEMESH (*after Mackenzie*).

By permission of Palestine Exploration Fund.

FIG. 109. WAR-SCENE ON POTSHERD FROM MEGIDDO LATE BRONZE (*after Schumacher*).

FIG. 113. MIDDLE BRONZE PITCHERS AND BOWLS FROM JERICHO (*after Sellin*).

FIG. 112. MIDDLE BRONZE JARS AND PITCHERS FROM JERICHO (*after Sellin*).

FIG. 117. HEBREW POTTERY FROM GEZER (after Macalister).

By permission of Palestine Exploration Fund.

FIG. 116. AN INSCRIBED HEBREW JAR-STAMP FROM THE SHEPHELAH (after Bliss and Macalister).

By permission of Palestine Exploration Fund.

FIG. 114. A FUNNEL FROM GEZER (after Macalister).

By permission of Palestine Exploration Fund.

FIG. 115. A POTTER'S SEAL FROM GEZER (after Macalister).

By permission of Palestine Exploration Fund.

PLATE 45

FIG. 122. HELLENISTIC POTTERY FROM GEZER (after Macalister).
By permission of Palestine Exploration Fund.

FIG. 119. A JAR-HANDLE STAMPED WITH A SCARAB (after Macalister).
By permission of Palestine Exploration Fund.

FIG. 121. HELLENISTIC FILTER FROM GEZER (after Macalister).
By permission of Palestine Exploration Fund.

FIG. 118. A SCARAB USED AS A JAR-STAMP (after Macalister).
By permission of Palestine Exploration Fund.

FIG. 120. A CHALCOLITHIC JAR FROM GEZER (after Macalister).
By permission of Palestine Exploration Fund.

FIG. 123. HELLENISTIC STRAINER FROM GEZER (*after Macalister*).
By permission of Palestine Exploration Fund.

FIG. 124. ROMAN POTS FROM GEZER (*after Macalister*).
By permission of Palestine Exploration Fund.

FIG. 125. HELLENISTIC JAR FROM GEZER
(*after Macalister*).
By permission of Palestine Exploration Fund.

FIG. 126.   A LAMP OF THE MIDDLE BRONZE
PERIOD, MEGIDDO (*after Schumacher*).

FIG. 127. LAMPS FROM THE EARLY IRON AND MIDDLE BRONZE PERIODS,
GEZER (*after Macalister*).
By permission of Palestine Exploration Fund.

FIG. 128. LAMPS FROM THE MIDDLE BRONZE
TO THE PERSIAN PERIODS, GEZER (*after
Macalister*).
By permission of Palestine Exploration Fund.

FIG. 129. A BYZANTINE
LAMP FROM JERICHO (*after
Sellin*).

FIG. 130. A LAMP BEARING A CHRISTIAN LEGEND (*after Macalister*).
By permission of Palestine Exploration Fund.

FIG. 131. HELLENISTIC LAMPS FROM GEZER (*after Macalister*).
By *permission of Palestine Exploration Fund.*

FIG. 132. MIDDLE BRONZE LAMPS FROM JERICHO (*after Sellin*).

FIG. 133.   OVENS FOUND AT GEZER (*after Macalister*).

By permission of Palestine Exploration Fund.

FIG. 134.   A BAKING-TRAY FROM GEZER (*after Macalister*).

By permission of Palestine Exploration Fund.

FIG. 135.   BRONZE DISHES FROM GEZER (*after Macalister*).

By permission of Palestine Exploration Fund.

FIG. 136.   SHELL SPOONS FROM GEZER (*after Macalister*).

By permission of Palestine Exploration Fund.

FIG. 137.   SILVER DISHES FROM A PHILISTINE GRAVE AT GEZER (*after Macalister*).
By permission of Palestine Exploration Fund.

FIG. 138.   GLASS OINTMENT VESSELS FROM GEZER (*after Macalister*).
By permission of Palestine Exploration Fund.

PLATE 51

FIG. 142. BRONZE NEEDLES AND PINS FROM GEZER (after Macalister).

By permission of Palestine Exploration Fund.

FIG. 141. PHILISTINE SILVER LADLE. GEZER (after Macalister).

By permission of Palestine Exploration Fund.

FIG. 139. FEEDING-BOTTLES (?), GEZER (after Macalister).

By permission of Palestine Exploration Fund.

FIG. 140. FORKS FROM GEZER (after Macalister).

By permission of Palestine Exploration Fund.

FIG. 143.   BONE NEEDLES FROM GEZER (*after Macalister*).
By permission of Palestine Exploration Fund.

FIG. 145.   SPINDLE WHORLS FROM GEZER
(*after Macalister*).
By permission of Palestine Exploration Fund.

FIG. 144.   MODERN WOMAN SPINNING.
By permission of Mrs. Grant Williams.

FIG. 146.   A LARGE KEY FROM GEZER (*after Macalister*).
By permission of Palestine Exploration Fund.

FIG. 147.   A SMALLER
KEY FROM GEZER (*after
Macalister*).
*By permission of Palestine
Exploration Fund.*

FIG. 148.   LAMP-STANDS FROM MEGIDDO (*after Schumacher*).

FIG. 149.   FLINT KNIVES FROM JERICHO (*after Sellin*).

FIG. 151. BRONZE KNIVES FROM GEZER (after Macalister).
By permission of Palestine Exploration Fund.

FIG. 150. IRON KNIVES FROM GEZER (after Macalister).
By permission of Palestine Exploration Fund.

FIG. 152. A CHISEL FROM GEZER (after Macalister).
By permission of Palestine Exploration Fund.

FIG. 153. A FILE FROM
GEZER (after Macalister).
By permission of Palestine Exploration
Fund.

FIG. 155. A BRONZE HAMMER-
HEAD, GEZER (after Macalister).
By permission of Palestine Explora-
tion Fund.

FIG. 154. A CONE OF FLINT FOR MAKING KNIVES, GEZER
(after Macalister).
By permission of Palestine Exploration Fund.

FIG. 156. A FISH-HOOK, GEZER
(after Macalister).
By permission of Palestine Exploration Fund.

FIG. 157. A BONE AWL-HANDLE FROM GEZER (after
Macalister).
By permission of Palestine Exploration Fund.

FIG. 158. WHETSTONES FROM JERICHO (after Sellin).

FIG. 159. NAILS FROM GEZER (after
Macalister).
By permission of Palestine Explora-
tion Fund.

FIG. 161.   CARPENTERS' TOOLS FROM GEZER (after Macalister).

By permission of Palestine Exploration Fund.

FIG. 160.   AXE-HEADS FROM GEZER (after Macalister).

By permission of Palestine Exploration Fund.

FIG. 165.   BRONZE ARROW-HEADS FROM GEZER (after Macalister).

By permission of Palestine Exploration Fund.

FIG. 162.   A SCIMITAR FROM GEZER (after Macalister).

By permission of Palestine Exploration Fund.

FIG. 164.   FLINT ARROW-HEADS FROM GEZER (after Macalister).

By permission of Palestine Exploration Fund.

FIG. 163.   IMPRESSION OF A BASKET ON MUD, GEZER (after Macalister).   By permission of Palestine Exploration Fund.

Fig. 167. Bronze Spear-Heads, Gezer (after Macalister).

By permission of Palestine Exploration Fund.

Fig. 166. Bronze Swords from Gezer (after Macalister).

By permission of Palestine Exploration Fund.

FIG. 168. A PIPE FROM GEZER (*after Macalister*).   FIG. 169. AN EGYPTIAN HARP (*after Haupt*).
By permission of Palestine Exploration Fund.

FIG. 172. A BABYLONIAN HARP
(*after Haupt*).

FIG. 170. AN ASSYR-   FIG. 171. AN ASSYRIAN
IAN UPRIGHT HARP   HORIZONTAL HARP (*after
(*after Haupt*).   Haupt*).

FIG. 173. JEWISH HARPS ON COINS OF BAR COCHEBA,   FIG. 174. ASSYRIAN DULCIMER
132–135 A. D. (*after Madden*).   (*after Haupt*).

FIG. 175. SEALS FROM GEZER (*after Macalister*).
By permission of Palestine Exploration Fund.

FIG. 176. A COMB FROM GEZER (*after Macalister*).
By permission of Palestine Exploration Fund.

FIG. 176½. A MAN, WOMAN AND SERPENT, FROM A PREHISTORIC SEAL. (*Tepe Gawra.*)

FIG. 177. TOYS FROM GEZER (*after Macalister*).
By permission of Palestine Exploration Fund.

FIG. 178. STYLI FROM GEZER (*after Macalister*).
By permission of Palestine Exploration Fund.

FIG. 179. CHILDREN'S RATTLES FROM GEZER (*after Macalister*).
By permission of Palestine Exploration Fund.

FIG. 180. A PERFUME-BOX, GEZER (*after Macalister*).

By permission of Palestine Exploration Fund.

FIG. 181. A NECKLACE FROM GEZER (*after Macalister*).

By permission of Palestine Exploration Fund.

FIG. 182. BRACELETS FROM GEZER (*after Macalister*).

By permission of Palestine Exploration Fund.

FIG. 183. SPATULÆ FROM GEZER (*after Macalister*).

By permission of Palestine Exploration Fund.

FIG. 184. RINGS FROM GEZER (*after Macalister*).

By permission of Palestine Exploration Fund.

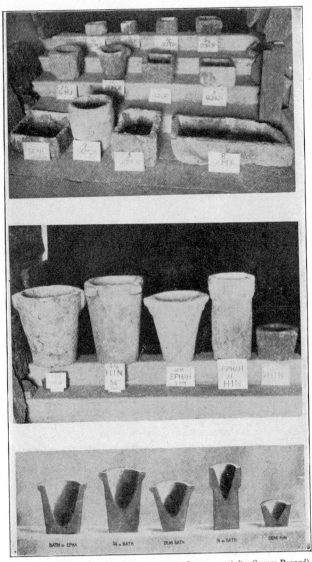

FIG. 185. SUPPOSED HEBREW MEASURES FROM JERUSALEM (*after Germer-Durand*).

FIG. 186.   A *Neseph* WEIGHT.   FIG. 187.   A *Payim* WEIGHT BELONGING
                                                  TO HAVERFORD COLLEGE.

FIG. 188.   A *Beqa* WEIGHT (*after Torrey*).   FIG. 189.   A "DARIC" OF
                                                   DARIUS (*after Benzinger*).

FIG. 190.   A TETRADRACHMA OF ALEXANDER THE GREAT (*after Benzinger*).

FIG. 191.   A COIN OF PTOLEMY LAGI (*after Benzinger*).

FIG. 192.   HALF-SHEKEL OF SIMON THE MACCABEE
(after Benzinger).

FIG. 193.   A COIN OF JOHN HYRCANUS
(after Madden).

FIG. 194.   TETRADRACHMA OF LYSIMACHUS.

FIG. 195.   A COIN OF
AUGUSTUS.

FIG. 196.   A DENARIUS OF TIBERIUS.

FIG. 197.   A COIN OF CLAUDIUS.

FIG. 198.   A COIN OF HEROD THE GREAT.

FIG. 199.   A ROMAN QUADRANS (?).

FIG. 200.   A COIN OF HEROD AGRIPPA I.

FIG. 201.   A SHEKEL OF THE REVOLT OF A. D. 70.

FIG. 202.   CAVE-DWELLERS' PLACE OF SACRIFICE, GEZER (*after Macalister*).
By permission of Palestine Exploration Fund.

FIG. 203.   PLAN OF CAVES AT SEMITIC HIGH
PLACE, GEZER (*after Macalister*).
By permission of Palestine Exploration Fund.

FIG. 204.   "PILLARS" OF THE HIGH PLACE AT
GEZER.

FIG. 205.   ROCK-ALTAR AT MEGIDDO (*after Schumacher*).

FIG. 206.   THE "BETH-EL" OF GEZER (*after Macalister*).

By permission of Palestine Exploration Fund.

FIG. 207.   THE SUPPOSED SERPENT-PEN AT GEZER (*after Macalister*).

By permission of Palestine Exploration Fund.

FIG. 208.   THE ROCK-ALTAR AT JERUSALEM (*after Dalman*).

FIG. 209.   THE LAVER AT GEZER (*after Macalister*).
By permission of Palestine Exploration Fund.

FIG. 211. A LARGE HOUSE AT TAANACH (after Sellin).

FIG. 210. THE TERRA-COTTA ALTAR FROM TAANACH (after Sellin).

FIG. 212. A LARGE HOUSE AT TELL ES-SAFI (*after Bliss and Macalister*).
By permission of Palestine Exploration Fund.

FIG. 213. LIBATION BOWL FROM TAANACH (*after Sellin*).

FIG. 214. AN ASTARTE PLAQUE FROM GEZER (*after Macalister*).
By permission of Palestine Exploration Fund.

FIG. 215.   PLAN OF THE HIGH PLACE AT PETRA (*after Brünnow*).

FIG. 216.   PLAN OF HEROD'S TEMPLE AT SAMARIA (*after Lyon*).

FIG. 217.   THE ALTAR AT PETRA (*after Brünnow*).

FIG. 218.   THE "ROUND ALTAR"
AT PETRA (*after Brünnow*).

FIG. 219.   SUPPOSED "PILLARS" AT PETRA (*after Brünnow*).

FIG. 221.   WALLS OF HEROD'S TEMPLE, SAMARIA (after Reisner).

FIG. 219a.   A BRAZEN SERPENT FROM GEZER (after Macalister).
By permission of Palestine Exploration Fund.

FIG. 220.   PLAN OF SUPPOSED SEMITIC TEMPLE AT GEZER (after Macalister).
By permission of Palestine Exploration Fund.

FIG. 222. "PILLARS" OF A LARGE HOUSE, GEZER (*after Macalister*).
By permission of Palestine Exploration Fund.

FIG. 223. A ROOM OF THE PALACE AT MEGIDDO (*after Schumacher*).

FIG. 224.   VOLUTED CAPITAL (PROBABLY PHILISTINE) FROM MEGIDDO (*after Schumacher*).

FIG. 225.   INCENSE-BURNER FROM MEGIDDO (*after Schumacher*).

FIG. 229. A CISTERN-BURIAL AT GEZER (after Macalister).

By permission of Palestine Exploration Fund.

FIG. 226. PHILISTINE GRAVES, GEZER (after Macalister).

By permission of Palestine Exploration Fund.

FIG. 228. A SHAFT-TOMB (after Bliss and Macalister).

By permission of Palestine Exploration Fund.

FIG. 227. A ROCK-HEWN TOMB AT SILOAM (after Benzinger).

FIG. 230.   A COLUMBARIUM AT PETRA (*after Dalman*).

FIG. 231.   ENTRANCE TO THE TOMB OF THE JUDGES.

FIG. 232. A SUNKEN-DOOR TOMB (*after Mitt. u. Nach. d. Deutsch. Palästina-Vereins*).

FIG. 233. *Kokim* IN THE TOMB OF THE JUDGES.

FIG. 234. PLAN OF A HELLENISTIC TOMB AT MARISSA (*after Peters and Thiersch*). *By permission of Palestine Exploration Fund.*

FIG. 235. A CROSS-SECTION OF THE TOMB OF THE JUDGES.

TOMB I—Through Chambers B and C, looking East.

TOMB I—Through E D A, looking South.

TOMB I—Through A D E, looking North.

FIG. 236.   ARCHITECTURAL DECORATION OF A HELLENISTIC TOMB AT MARISSA (*after Peters and Thiersch*).

By permission of Palestine Exploration Fund.

FIG. 237.   PLAN OF THE UPPER FLOOR OF THE TOMB OF THE JUDGES.

FIG. 238.   A TOMB WITH A ROLLING-STONE AT BEIT JIBRIN (*after Moulton*).

FIG. 239.   INTERIOR OF A HELLENISTIC TOMB AT MARISSA (*after Peters and Thiersch*). *By permission of Palestine Exploration Fund.*

Kidron Valley

Zion

Mosque of Omar

Tyropœon

Western Hill

Valley of Hinnom

FIG. 240. THE HILLS AND VALLEYS OF JERUSALEM (after Vincent).

FIG. 241. UNDERGROUND JEBUSITE TUNNEL AT GIHON, JERUSALEM (*after Vincent*).

FIG. 242. MAUDSLEY'S SCARP, JERUSALEM.

FIG. 243.   PLAN OF SOLOMON'S BUILDINGS, JERUSALEM (*after Stade*).

FIG. 244.   QUARRY-MARKS, JERUSALEM (*after Warren*).
By permission of Palestine Exploration Fund.

FIG. 245.   SHAFT AT THE SOUTHEAST CORNER OF THE TEMPLE AREA (*after Warren*).
By permission of Palestine Exploration Fund.

FIG. 246.   EXAMINING ANCIENT WALLS IN AN UNDERGROUND TUNNEL (*after Warren*).
By permission of Palestine Exploration Fund.

FIG. 247. FRONT VIEWS OF SOLOMON'S TEMPLE (*after Stade*).

FIG. 248. SIDE VIEWS OF SOLOMON'S TEMPLE (*after Stade*).

FIG. 249.   PLAN OF SOLOMON'S TEMPLE (*after Stade*).

FIG. 250.   THE SEVEN-BRANCHED LAMP-STAND FROM THE ARCH OF TITUS.

FIG. 251.   THE BRAZEN LAVER OF SOLOMON'S TEMPLE (*after Stade*).

FIG. 252.   A PORTABLE LAVER OF SOLOMON'S TEMPLE (*after Stade*).

FIG. 254. STONE-WORK IN A WALL AT JERUSALEM,
POSSIBLY NEHEMIAH'S

FIG. 253. STONE-WORK OF A WALL OF JERUSALEM
BUILT IN THE CHRISTIAN ERA

FIG. 255.   RESTORATION OF THE ASMONÆAN BRIDGE OVER THE TYROPŒON VALLEY (*after Hanauer*).

FIG. 256.   FRONT OF "DAVID'S TOWER" (HEROD'S PALACE) TODAY (*after Breen*).

FIG. 257.   RECONSTRUCTION OF HEROD'S TEMPLE (*after Caldecott*).

FIG. 258.   "SOLOMON'S STABLES."

FIG. 260. FRONT OF THE CHURCH OF THE HOLY SEPULCHER.

FIG. 259. ONE OF THE SUPPOSED POOLS OF BETHESDA (*after Hanauer*).

FIG. 261.   "GORDON'S CALVARY," LOOKING TOWARD JERUSALEM (*after Breen*).

FIG. 262.   "GORDON'S CALVARY," FROM THE CITY WALL (*after Breen*).

FIG. 263. OUTSIDE OF "GORDON'S HOLY SEPULCHER" (after Breen).

FIG. 264. INSIDE OF "GORDON'S HOLY SEPULCHER" (after Breen).

FIG. 265.   THE BARADA (ABANA), DAMASCUS.

FIG. 266.   THE STREET CALLED STRAIGHT, DAMASCUS.

FIG. 267.   PALACE AT KANATHA (*after Brünnow*).

FIG. 268.   CIRCULAR FORUM AND COLONNADED STREET, GERASA.

FIG. 269. TEMPLE OF THE SUN, GERASA.

FIG. 270. SITE OF RABBAH AMMON.

FIG. 271. THEATER AT AMMAN (PALESTINIAN PHILADELPHIA).

FIG. 272. ROMAN FORUM AT ATHENS.

FIG. 273. MARS' HILL, ATHENS.

FIG. 274. FOUNTAIN IN THE AGORA, CORINTH.

Συνα]γωγὴ Ἑβρ[αίων.

FIG. 275.   LINTEL OF JEWISH SYNAGOGUE, CORINTH (after Richardson).

FIG. 276.   LECHÆUM ROAD, CORINTH (after Richardson).

FIG. 277.   PARTHENON, ATHENS, FROM THE EAST.

FIG. 278.   MAIN STREET AT EPHESUS.

FIG. 279.   SITE OF THE TEMPLE OF DIANA, EPHESUS, IN 1902.

FIG. 280.   THE THEATER, EPHESUS.

FIG. 281.   THE AMPHITHEATER, EPHESUS.

FIG. 282.   THE STADIUM, EPHESUS.

FIG. 283.   PERGAMUM (*after Ramsay*).

FIG. 284.   THE ACROPOLIS AND PARTLY EXCAVATED TEMPLE, SARDIS (*after Butler*).

FIG. 285. EXCAVATED TEMPLE, SARDIS, LOOKING TOWARD THE HERMUS VALLEY (after Butler).

FIG. 286.   A CHRISTIAN CHURCH AT SARDIS (*after Butler*).

FIG. 287.   SMYRNA (*after Ramsay*).

FIG. 288.   A RUIN AT LAODICEA (*after Ramsay*).

FIG. 289.   A BRIDGE OVER THE JORDAN ON THE LINE OF A ROMAN ROAD.

FIG. 292. HAMMURAPI RECEIVING THE LAWS FROM THE SUN-GOD.

FIG. 293. THE SO-CALLED ADAM AND EVE SEAL.

FIG. 290. FRAGMENT OF A CREATION-TABLET.

FIG. 291. ASSYRIAN SACRED TREE CONVENTIONALIZED.

FIG. 294. A TABLET FROM NIPPUR, RE-
LATING THE BEGINNINGS OF IRRIGATION AND
AGRICULTURE (*after Langdon*).

FIG. 295. TOP OF THE BLACK OBELISK OF
SHALMANESER.

FIG. 296. JEHU OF ISRAEL DOING HOMAGE TO SHALMANESER.

FIG. 297. THE SILOAM INSCRIPTION.

FIG. 298. SENNACHERIB RECEIVING TRIBUTE AT LACHISH (*after Ball*).

FIG. 300. THE MOABITE STONE.

FIG. 299. AN ALTAR TO UNKNOWN GODS (*after Deissmann*).

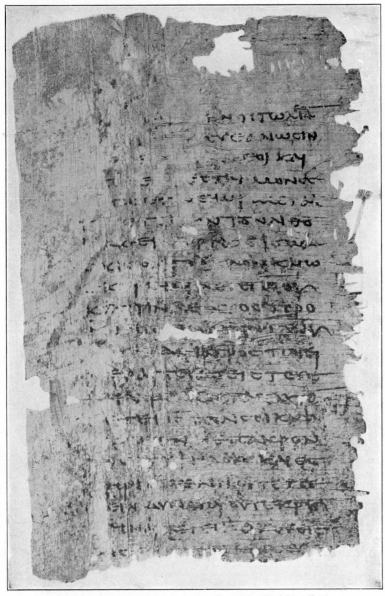

FIG. 301. PAPYRUS CONTAINING SAYINGS OF JESUS (*after Grenfell and Hunt*).

FIG. 302. PICTURE OF BABYLONIAN SEAL (*from Revue d'Assyriologie, XIII, 6*).

FIG. 303. INSCRIBED MOSAIC OF AIN DUK.

FIG. 304. STATUE OF KING TUTANKHAMEN. GUARDING INNER SEALED DOORWAY OF HIS TOMB.
By Courtesy of Howard Carter.

FIG. 305. BACK PANEL OF THE THRONE OF TUTANKHAMEN. DEPICTING KING AND QUEEN.
By Courtesy of Howard Carter.

FIG. 306. ZIGGURAT AT UR.
By Permission of University Museum.

FIG. 307.   STAIRWAY OF ZIGGURAT AT UR.
By Permission of University Museum.

FIG. 308.   THE "CANNON" OF ASHKELON; ANCIENT PILLARS IMBEDDED IN THE WALL.
By Permission of American Schools of Oriental Research.

FIG. 309.   TELL EL-FUL; PIER FROM THE THIRD FORTRESS AT GIBEAH.
By Permission of American Schools of Oriental Research.

FIG. 310. EXCAVATION ON THE HILL OPHEL, JERUSALEM, SHOWING THE WALLS OF THE MILLO
TOWER AND "THE BREACH OF DAVID."
By Courtesy of Palestine Exploration Fund.

FIG. 311. AN INSCRIPTION FOUND IN JERUSALEM THOUGHT TO REFER TO THE SYNAGOGUE OF
THE LIBERTINES. (*After Weill.*)

Fig. 312.   The Chalice of Antioch.   Showing Central Figure Believed to Represent
      Christ, with Figures Beneath Representing the Apostles Peter and Paul.
By Courtesy of Kouchakji Frères, owners of International Copyright.

FIG. 313. AN ENLARGED SECTION OF THE CHALICE OF ANTIOCH, TWICE ACTUAL SIZE. THE
FIGURE IS BELIEVED TO REPRESENT THE APOSTLE PETER. THE VINE, BASKET, AND LAMB ARE
CHRISTIAN SYMBOLS.
By Courtesy of Kouchakji Frères, owners of International Copyright.

Fig. 314. Temple of Elberith and the Holy Circle at Shechem.

Courtesy of Bishop H. M. Du Bose.

FIG. 315. CYCLOPEAN CORNER OF HOLY CIRCLE OF THE TEMPLE OF ELBERITH AT SHECHEM. *Courtesy of Bishop H. M. Du Bose.*

FIG. 316. STELE OF RAMSES II FROM BEISAN.
By courtesy of the University Museum.

FIG. 317. EXCAVATION AT ANTIOCH IN PISIDIA. LOOKING OVER BYZANTINE CHURCH IN THE FOREGROUND, UP THE STEPS OF THE PROPYLÆA TO THE ROCK SEMI-CIRCLE BACK OF THE GREAT TEMPLE.
By Courtesy of American Journal of Archæology.

FIG. 318. ANTIOCH IN PISIDIA. SQUARE OF TIBERIUS, FROM THE NORTHEAST.
By Courtesy of American Journal of Archæology.

FIG. 319.   MAP SHOWING PROBABLE COURSE OF "THIRD WALL" AT JERUSALEM.
By Courtesy of the American Schools of Oriental Research.

FIG. 320.   SECTION OF GREAT WALL AT TELL EN-NASBEH EXCAVATED BY DEAN BADÈ.
+ = ENTRANCE OF TOMB.   → = OUTER EDGE OF WALL.
By Courtesy of the American Schools of Oriental Research.